CHINESE
OF

常用动词词典

英语注释
With English Explanations

王砚农·焦庞颢 编著

平安国际出版社
HEIAN INTERNATIONAL, INC

© 1989 Federal Publications (S) Pte Ltd

First American Edition 1989

HEIAN INTERNATIONAL, INC.
P.O. Box 1013
UNION CITY, CA 94587

All rights reserved. No part of this publication may be reproduced, stored in a retrieval system, or transmitted in any form or by any means, electronic, mechanical, photocopying, recording or otherwise, without the prior permission of the publisher.

ISBN: 0-89346-313-2

Printed in Singapore

目录
Contents

前言
Preface 2-3

略语和符号
Abbreviations and symbols used
in the dictionary 4

笔画查字表
Stroke Index 5-9

词典正文
Dictionary A-Z 1-532

前言

《常用动词词典》是一部纯粹以动词搭配为主要内容的词典。在编写上，这本词典的搭配是按照汉语语法规则和语言习惯，将每个动词的前后成分搭配成多个短语和句子。

我们所以不采取先用文字解释词义，然后再举一、两个例句的编法，是因为我们发现学生在学习汉语时，不能正确的掌握动词的用法，原因不在于他们不了解词义，而是由于他们不懂得如何将它和其他字或词搭配成正确的、合乎汉语习惯的句子。所以为他们收罗各种搭配的例句作为参考是必要的。

语言现象是复杂的，千变万化的。在编写时，我们不可能把所有的语言现象都包括进去。为求实际，我们唯有从学习者的需要和接受能力出发,再根据他们的语文水平、生活环境和活动范围，采取实际语言怎么说就怎么搭配,能搭配多少就搭配多少，有用的多收没用的不收的原则编写。

为帮助使用者理解所选收的各个例句，对词典中所有生词，或较难理解的短语和句子，我们都给予正确详尽的翻译或英文注释。

《常用动词词典》共收集了1,239个常用动词。希望这部词典的出版，能同时给学生和教师带来一定的裨益和学习上的便利。

编辑部

Preface

To our knowledge, no specialised dictionary of Chinese verb usage at present exists which is sufficiently broad in scope to answer the various practical requirements of the students of Modern Chinese. It is chiefly with this view that the Dictionary has been designed.

This dictionary is mainly intended as a language tool for the use of learners of Chinese and for the Chinese language teachers. The dictionary, of course, will be beneficial for those interested in Chinese.

The present volume deals with only frequent verbs used in every day life of the Modern Chinese language. Each entry contains extensive illustrations of each verb type according to the standard grammatical patterns of the Chinese language.

This dictionary contains 1,239 verbs and their compounds, not including the verbs rarely used or those in classical Chinese.

The Editorial Board

略语和符号

Abbreviations and symbols used in the dictionary

主 = 主语	—	subject
宾 = 宾语	—	object
补 = 补语	—	complement
状 = 状语	—	adverbial clause
习用 = 习用语	—	idiomatic expressions
〈**名**〉= 名词或名词结构	—	noun or noun construction
〈**代**〉= 代词	—	pronoun
〈**动**〉= 动词或动词结构	—	verb or verb construction
〈**形**〉= 形容词	—	adjective
〈**数**〉= 数词	—	number, numbers
〈**主——谓**〉= 主谓结构	—	subject-predicate construction
〈**介**〉= 介词结构	—	preposition construction
〈**的**〉= 的字结构	—	"的" construction
〈**是……的**〉= 是……的结构	—	"是…的" construction
〈**结**〉= 结果补语	—	complement of result
〈**趋**〉= 趋向补语	—	directional complement
〈**程**〉= 程度补语	—	complement of degree
〈**可**〉= 可能补语	—	potential complement
〈**时**〉= 时量补语	—	complement of time
〈**量**〉= 动量补语	—	action-measure complement
≅ = 近义词	—	word with similar meaning
↔ = 反义词	—	antonym

笔画查字表
Stroke Index

二画					
	见 186	扔 320	闪 328	划 165	冲 53
[ㄱ]	[丿]	去 312	[ㄱ]	至 510	交 192
了(解) 242	升 339	布(置) 31	加 180	死 362	产 41
	长 489	平 295	对 115	[丨]	庆(祝) 310
三画	化 166	灭 260	[ㄴ]	当 88,89	决(定) 215
	反 126	轧 459	出 57	吐 400	充 55
[一]	气 303	[丨]	发 120	吓 430	闭 23
干 145	介(绍) 206	卡 216,303	纠(缠/正)	团 401	问 419
下 426	分 132	占 488	210	同(意) 396	闯 64
[丨]	公(布) 149	申(请) 337		吊 98	关 155
上 330	欠 305	叮 101	六画	吃 51	守 349
[丶]	[丶]	叨 98		吸 421	安 3
广(播) 156	为 413	叫 198	[一]	回 171	兴 447
[ㄱ]	斗 110	[丿]	动 108	网(罗) 411	讲 189
飞 132	计(划/较/	生 340	扛 222	[丿]	讹(诈) 119
习(惯) 424	算) 178	失(败/传/	扣 226	丢 107	设 335
	订 104	效/掉/灵)	考 222	迁(就) 304	访(问) 128
四画	认 319	342	托 405	传 62	[ㄱㄴ]
	[ㄱ]	付 137	执(行) 506	休 448	防 127
[一]	引 468	代(表/替)	扩(大/散)	延(长/期)	好 161
切 308	巴(结) 7	83	229	460	收 347
开 216	办 12	犯 127	扫 325	伤 329	欢(送/迎)
扎 479,485	劝 313	印 469	过 158	伪(造/装)	168
支 503	[ㄴ]	白(费) 9	压 457	416	买 253
不(如/止)	允(许) 477	用 472	有 474	向 441	驮 407
31		甩 356	在 481	后(悔) 164	驯 455
车 46	五画	处 60	存 70	杀 326	约 476
比 22		包 15	夸 227	企(图) 301	
止 507	[一]	[丶]	夺 117	合 162	七画
少 334	打 76	写 445	达 75	创 64	
中 512	扑 298	讨 378	列(举) 243	危(害) 412	[一]
	扒 7	让 315	迈 254	负(责) 137	弄 273
		训 455	成 49	争 499	形(成) 447
		议(论) 468	夹 182	[丶]	进 207
		记 179			戒 206

违(背/反) 414	吻 418	张 489	取 311	[、]	织 505
花 165	吹 65	改 139	枕 498	放 128	绊 14
运 477	别 29	阻(碍/止) 527	丧(失) 325	享(受) 438	经(过/受) 208
扶 135	[ノ]	忍 318	卧 420	变 25	
扼(杀) 119	针(对) 497	[乚]	刺 67	刻 225	九画
扰(乱) 317	钉 105	妨(碍) 128	画 167	怕 278	
拒(绝) 213	告(诉) 147	妒(忌) 112	卖 254	怪 154	[一]
找 493	利(用) 238		奔 21	闹 267	奏 526
批 289	吞 404	八画	殴(打) 276	卷 214	帮(助) 14
扯 46	估(计) 151		转 517,519	炖 116	珍(惜) 498
走 524	体(贴) 385	[一]	轰 163	炒 45	毒 110
抄 43	伸 338	玩 409	到 90	沾 487	挂 153
贡(献) 149	作 531	现 433	[丨]	泡 285	封 135
折 334,496,497	住 514	表 26	具(有) 213	注(意) 515	挡 88
抓 516	希(望) 423	规(定) 157	鸣 261	泼 296	拴 357
扮(演) 13	坐 529	抹 251,263,264	败(坏) 11	治 510	拾 344
抢 306	含 160	拣 184	贩(卖) 127	学 454	垫 97
抛(弃) 283	免 259	担 86	图 399	定 106	挑 387,389
投 397	删 327	押 459	[ノ]	宠 56	挣 501,503
抗 222	刨 18,283	抽 56	钓 98	审 338	指 508
抖 109	迎(接) 470	拐 154	制 510	实(现/行) 343	挤 177
扭 273	[、]	拖 405	知(道) 505	试 345	拼 294
把 8	冻 108	拍 279	垂 66	衬 47	挖 408
报 18	忘 412	顶 102	刮 152	[フ]	按 5
拟(定) 269	应(付) 471	拆 39	委(托) 417	建 187	挪 275
克(服/制) 224	怀(疑) 168	拥(抱/护) 471	供 149	肃(清) 366	带 84
连 239	怄 276		使 344	录 248	标 26
求 310	闲(聊) 431	抱 19	依 467	刷 354	相 437
束(缚) 353	闷 257	抵(抗/赖) 94	征 501	弥(补/漫) 258	查 37
还 169	判 282	拄 513	爬 277	承(担/认/受) 49	树(立) 354
来 232	没 264	拉 230	贪 371	降 191	要(求) 464,466
[丨]	沉 47	拦 235	舍(得/不得) 335	限 434	威(胁) 413
坚(持) 182	完(成) 409	拌 13	念 270	[乚]	砌 304
盯 102	证(明) 502	拧 272	刹 327	参(观/加/考) 35	砍 219
围 414	启(发) 302	招 491	采 34	贯(彻/穿) 156	耐 267
呕(吐) 276	评 295	披 290	受 350	练 240	要 354
吵 44	补 30	拨 29	胀 490	组(织) 528	牵 304
串 64	识 343	拔 7	服 136		[丨]
听 391	诉(苦) 366	抬 370	剁 118		背 20,21
呛 305,307	[フ] 尿 271 迟(到) 51		备 20		点 96

竖	354	弯	408	**十画**		钻	528	容(纳)	321	控(制)	225
省	341	度	113			称	48	宰	481	探	374
削	441	施	343	[一]		缺	314	读	110	聊	242
尝	42	恢(复)	171			笑	444	请	309	娶	312
是	346	恨	163	耗	161	牺(牲)	423	调	99,388	勒	236
盼	283	闻	418	耽(误)	87	造	484	扇	328	检(查)	184
眨	486	差	39	捞	235	租	527	谈	372	梳	351
哄	164	养	462	栽	480	透	398			救	211
显	432	送	362	振(作)	498	借	206	[ㄱ]		盛	51
冒	256	迷	259	赶	142	值	506	剥	16	袭(击)	423
趴	277	炼	240	起	302	倚	467	展(开)	488		
剐	153	炸	486	捎	334	倒	89,90	陷	435	[丨]	
咽	462	剃	385	捏	271	逛	157	陪	285	睁	502
骂	251	洒	322	埋	252,255	射	337	通	394	眯	258
响	439	浇	195	捉	523	拿	266	难(为)	267	啄	524
咯	216	测(验)	36	捆	228	舀	466	预(备/防)		啃	225
咬	465	洗	424	捐	214	爱	1		475	累	237
罚	124	活	174	损(害/坏/		皱	513	验	462	唱	42
贴	391	派	281	失)	368	饿	119			圈	313
		染	315	挺	394	留	246	[ㄥ]		崇(拜)	56
[丿]		举	211	捡	184	乘	50	绣	451		
钩	150	觉(得)	215	换	170			继(续)	180	[丿]	
卸	446	宣(布/誓)		挽	410	[丶]				铲	41
拜	11		452	捅	396	准(备)	523	**十一画**		矫(正)	197
看	219	穿	61	挨	1	病	29			符(合)	137
选	452	祝	515	恶(化)	119	疼	380	[一]		做	531
种	512	误	420	逗	110	离(开)	237	理	237	猜	33
重(复)	55	说	358	配	286	站	488	捧	288	偷	396
(视)	513			砸	479	兼	183	堵	111	售	351
复(习)	137	[ㄱ]		破	296	烤	224	描	260	停	393
顺	358	退	403	套	379	烘	164	掩(盖/护/		兜	109
修	449	费	132	较(量)	199	烧	332	饰)	460	得	91
保	16	除	59	致	512	烙	236	掉	100	盘	282
信	447	架	182			递	95	排	280	领	243
追	522	垒	237	[丨]		涉(及)	336	堆	115	脱	406
待	83			晒	327	消	442	捶	66	够	150
逃	377	[ㄥ]		晃	170	涂	399	推	401	象	441
勉(励/强)		绑	14	剔	381	浮	136	掀	430		
	259	结(合/束)		晕	477	流	245			[丶]	
怨	476		199,203	哭	226	涨	489,490	教	196	凑	68
急	176	绕	317	罢	9	烫	376	掏	376	减	186
饶	317	给	148	哼	163	涌	472	掂	95	麻(烦)	251
		绞	197			粉(碎)	134	培	285	痒	464
[丶]				[丿]		害	159	接	200	旋	453

商(量)	330	喜(欢/爱/		[丿]		摸	261	躲	117	熏	455,456
望	412	好)	425	铺	299	填	386	腾	381	算	366
惟(恐)	415	揪	210	销(毁)	443	搏(斗)	30	触	61	管	155
惦(记)	98	插	37	锁	369	塌	370	解	204		
着	492,524	搜	363	短	114	鼓(励/舞/				[丶]	
盖	141	搀	39	剩	341	掌)	151	[丶]		敲	307
粘	487	裁	33	等	92	摆	9	誊(写)	381	遮	497
断	114	搁	147	答(理/应)		搬	11	数	353	端	113
剪	185	搓	71		74,75	摇	465	煎	183	精(通)	209
清(理)	309	搂	247	集(中)	176	搞	145	塑(造)	366	熄	423
添	386	搅	197	惩(罚)	51	摊	371	煜	404	漆	300
淋	243	握	420	腌	459	斟(酌)	498	遛	247	漂	292,293
淹	459	揉	321			蒙	257	溜	244	褪	404,405
混	173	欺(负/骗)		[丶]		蒸	502	满(足)	256	滴	93
渍	524		300	装	519	献	437	滥(用)	235	演	461
淘	377	联(系)	239	善(于)	329	禁	208	滚	158	漏	247
深(入)	338	散	323,324	羡(慕)	436	想	439	塞	323	赛	323
涮	357	惹	318	尊(重)	529	聘(请)	294				
渗	339	葬	482	温	418	赖	234	[乛]		[乛]	
寄	180	敬	209	溅	189	感(动/觉/		叠	101	缩	368
		落	232,236,	滑	166	染/谢)	143,				
[乛]			249	渡	113		144	[乛]		十五画	
逮	83,86	辜(负)	151	游	473	蜇	496	嫌	431		
弹	373	逼	21	割	147	碍	3	缝	135	[一]	
堕(落)	118	裂	243	富(有)	137	碰	288	缠	40	撵	270
隐(瞒)	469	翘	308	窜(改)	69	输	351			撕	361
骑	301			雇	152			十四画		撒	322
		[丨]		谢	447	[丨]				撅	214
[乚]		菌	483			睡	358	[一]		撩	241
续	451	赏	330	[乛]		歇	444	熬	6	撑	48
维(持/护/		掌	490	强(调)	305	暗(示)	5	摘	487	撤	293,294
修)	415	量	241	属	352	照	494	摔	355	撮	72
		喷	288	隔	148	跨	228	模(仿)	262	撬	308
十二画		遇	476	登	91	跷	307	遭	482	播	30
		喊	160	骗	291	跳	390	酿	271	撞	521
[一]		晾	241			踩	118	需(要)	451	撤	47
煮	513	跌	101	[乚]		跪	157	摧(残)	70	增(加/强/	
琢(磨)	529	跑	284	缓	169	罩	496			添/长)	484
替	385	喝	161	编	24			[丨]			
揍	527	喂	417			[丿]		赚	519	飘	292
款(待)	228	喘	63	十三画		锯	213			震	498
搭	73	赌	112			签	304	[丿]		瞒	255
提	382	赎	352	[一]		愁	57	镀	113	踮	97
揭	202	赔	286			催	69				

[丨]	遵(守) 529	整(理) 502	避 23	十八画	嚼 197
暴(露) 19	憨 28	醒 448			嚷 315
瞎 426	[乛]	[丿]	十七画	翻 125	
噎 467	熨 477	赞(成) 482		戳 67	二十一画
影(响) 470	慰(问) 417	篡(夺/改) 69	[一]		
踢 382	劈 291	邀(请) 464	戴 86	十九画	霸(占) 9
踩 34	履(行) 249		擤 448		露 248
嘱(咐) 514		[丶]	擦 32	攀(登) 282	
[丿]	十六画	磨 262, 265	藏 36	蹲 116	二十二画
靠 224		辨(别/认) 25	[丨]	颤 41	
躺 375	[一]	懒(得) 235	瞪 93	爆(发/炸) 20	镶 438
[丶]	操(心/纵) 36	激(动/起) 176	[丶]		
熟(悉) 352	擅(长) 329		赢 470	二十画	
懂 108	颠 95	[乛]	糟(蹋) 483		
糊 164					

A

āi 挨(着) get close to; be next to ≃ 靠; 靠近〔**主～**〕〈名〉她们三个人的座位❶～着〔**～宾**〕〈名〉桌子～(着)墙; 加拿大❷～着美国❸; 排队的时候我姐姐～着李华; 书一本～着一本〈代〉他～着我〔**～补**〕〈结〉大家～近点儿〈趋〉～过来点儿〈程〉～得很紧; ～得太近了〔**状～**〕紧紧地～着; 肩并肩地❹～着
另见 ái 挨

1. seat **2.** Canada **3.** the United States of America **4.** shoulder to shoulder

ái 挨 ① suffer; endure ≃ 受; 遭受; 遭到〔**～宾**〕〈动〉～打; ～揍❶; ～骂; ～说❷; ～挖苦❸; ～饿; ～冻❹, ～罚〔**～补**〕〈结〉那个孩子挨打都～怕❺了〈量〉我～过他两次骂了; ～了我两拳❻; ～了她一巴掌❼〔**状～**〕莫明其妙地❽～了一顿打; 无缘无故地❾～了一顿骂; 从来没～过罚; 很少～骂; 错～了打
另见 āi 挨

1. beat (take a beating) **2.** scold (get a scolding) **3.** speak sarcastically **4.** freeze (suffer from cold) **5.** fear; dread **6.** get two punches **7.** palm; hand (get a slap) **8.** without rhyme or reason; quite unaccountably **9.** without cause or reason; for no reason at all

② delay; drag out ≃ 拖延; 熬〔**～宾**〕〈名〉～时间; ～日子〔**～补**〕〈趋〉不能再这样～下去了〈可〉他母亲的病很重❶, 恐怕❷～不过❸这个星期了〈时〉又～了一段时间; ～了三个月; ～一会儿是一会儿〔**状～**〕真难～; 好容易❹～到下班了; 艰难地❺～过了苦难❻的岁月❼; 痛苦地❽～着; 一天天地～着

1. serious **2.** I am afraid **3.** won't pull through **4.** **5.** with great difficulty **6.** suffering; misery; distress **7.** years **8.** painfully

ài 爱 ① love; be fond of ≃ 喜欢 ↔ 讨厌; 恨; 憎〔**～宾**〕〈名〉～孩子; ～花; ～鸟; ～祖国❶; ～真理❷; ～和平❸; ～名誉❹, ～地位❺; ～权势❻; ～面子❼; ～哪种颜色❽? ～那个城市交通方便❾〈代〉～我们; ～那些; ～他聪明❿; ～他伶俐⓫; ～它灵巧⓬〈动〉他特别～吃, 什么好吃, 吃什么; 他～吃鱼(～吃西餐/～吃点心⓭/～吃素⓮的/～吃荤⓯的/～吃辣⓰的/～吃甜⓱的/～吃软⓲的/～吃硬⓳的/～吃新鲜⓴的/～吃自己做的); 这个人没有别的毛病㉑, 就是～

喝(酒); ～穿西装; ～玩牌㉒; ～玩火; ～说笑话㉓; ～说废话㉔; ～说大话㉕; ～画画儿; ～照像㉖; ～下棋㉗; ～帮助人; ～听恭维话㉘; ～用香水㉙; ～迟到; ～早退㉚〈形〉～美; ～热闹㉛; ～清静; ～干净; ～整齐〔**～补**〕〈结〉他对数学㉜～到发狂㉝的程度㉞〈程〉～极了〈时〉她～了一辈子㉟金项链㊱, 结果㊲还没买上就死了〔**状～**〕总～看书; 酷㊳～文学㊴; 非常～面子

1. motherland 2. truth 3. peace 4. fame; reputation 5. position; status 6. power 7. face; reputation (be concerned about face-saving) 8. what colour? 9. have transport facilities; good transport service 10. clever; intelligent 11. clever; bright; quick-witted 12. dexterous; nimble; skilful 13. refreshments 14. vegetarian 15. meat 16. peppery; hot 17. sweet; honeyed 18. soft 19. hard 20. fresh 21. defect; fault 22. card 23. crack a joke 24. nonsense; superfluous words 25. big talk 26. take a picture 27. play chess 28. flattery 29. perfume 30. leave early 31. bustling with noise and excitement 32. mathematics 33. go mad 34. degree 35. all one's life 36. gold necklace 37. in the end; finally 38. ardently 39. literature

② be apt to; be in the habit of; easily ≃ 容易; 易于↔不易〔**～宾**〕〈动〉～哭; ～笑; ～闹❶; 纸太薄❷～破❸; 热天糖～化❹; 这东西～坏; 她身体不好, 总～病; ～吐❺; ～着急❻; ～生气; ～感冒❼; ～咳嗽❽; ～说谎❾; ～吵架; ～捣乱❿; ～挑毛病⓫; ～晕船⓬; ～晕车⓭, ～闹肚子⓮; ～褪色⓯; ～生锈⓰; 天冷, 花就～死〈形〉～弯⓱; ～冷; ～热〈主-谓〉～头疼⓲; ～脸红〔**状～**〕这孩子最～哭; 总～感冒; 那个人特别～挑毛病〔**习用**〕～理不理⓳; ～死～活, 那就随他去了

1. make a noise 2. thin 3. be torn 4. dissolve; melt 5. vomit 6. be impatient 7. catch cold 8. cough 9. tell a lie 10. make trouble 11. find fault 12. sea sick 13. car sick 14. have diarrhoea 15. fade 16. rust 17. bend 18. headache 19. look cold and indifferent; be standoffish

àihào 爱好 love; be fond of; be keen on ≃ 爱; 喜欢〔**～宾**〕〈名〉～和平❶; ～京剧❷; ～音乐❸; ～体育❹; ～文艺❺〔**状～**〕非常～; 十分～; 特别～; 从小儿❻～; 真正～

1. peace 2. Beijing (Peking) opera 3. music 4. physical culture; sports 5. literature 6. from childhood

àihù 爱护 cherish; treasure; take good care of ≃ 爱惜〔**～宾**〕〈名〉～公物❶; ～儿童; ～下一代❷; ～动物; ～图书; ～祖国〔**状～**〕; 非常～; 一点也不～

1. public property 2. future generation

àixī 爱惜 cherish; treasure; use sparingly ≅ 爱护；珍惜 〔~宾〕〈名〉~时间；~人才❶；~身体〔状~〕非常~；十分~；特别~

1. a talented person; a man of ability

ài 碍 obstruct; hinder ≅ 阻碍；妨碍〔~宾〕〈名〉你别在这儿~事❶了，快走开吧；这话有点儿~口❷，不好说；这个孩子老是~手~脚❸的；人家两个人在这里谈话，我们快走吧，别在这儿~眼❹了；东西放在这儿真~事；~着他爸爸的面子，我不好说什么〔~补〕〈可〉这事虽然~不着(zháo)我，可是我想说两句〔状~〕真~事；有点儿~口；别在这儿~手~脚的了；放在这儿不致❺~事吧

1. be in the way; be a hindrance 2. be too embarrassing to mention 3. be in the way; be a hindrance 4. be unpleasant to look at; offend the eye; be an eyesore 5. cannot go so far; be unlikely

ān 安 ① install; fix ≅ 装；安装 ↔拆〔~宾〕〈名〉~门；~窗；~玻璃；~锁❶；~电灯；~电话；~电铃❷；~扩音器❸；~天线❹；~门铃❺〔~补〕〈结〉门~好了；玻璃~上了；锁~歪了❻；窗户~反❼了；~倒❽(dào)了；螺丝❾~错了〈趋〉把大喇叭~到电线杆子❿上去了〈程〉~得真结实；电灯~得比较低⓫〈可〉锁我自己~不上〈时〉~了半天才安完；电话已经~了很长时间了〈量〉~了好几次都没安好〔状~〕赶紧⓬~；重新⓭~；往门上~；费力地⓮~；熟练地⓯~

1. lock 2. electric bell 3. megaphone 4. aerial; antenna 5. door bell 6. oblique; slant 7. inside out 8. inverted; inverse; reverse 9. screw 10. electric pole 11. lower 12. quickly 13. again 14. strenuously; with great effort; painstakingly 15. skilfully

② bring (a charge against sb.) ≅ 加〔~宾〕〈名〉~罪名❶〔~补〕〈结〉给我~上了一个莫须有❷的罪名；怎么把罪名~到我头上了〔状~〕不要随便❸~；没有根据地❹~；不能乱❺~；莫名其妙地❻~

1. charge; accusation 2. groundless; unwarranted (fabricated charge) 3. do as one pleases; wantonly; wilfully 4. groundlessly 5. at random; indiscriminately 6. be unable to make head or tail of sth.; be baffled

③ harbour (an intention) ≅ 存着；怀着〔~宾〕〈名〉~坏心❶；真不知她~的是什么心；他没~好心❷，总是想出各种办法来骗人❸〔状~〕究竟❹~着什么心？ 果然❺没~好心

1. evil intention; ill will 2. good intention 3. deceive people 4. after all; in the end 5. really; as expected; sure enough

ānchā 安插 place in a certain position; assign to a job; plant 〔**～宾**〕〈名〉～了很多他自己的人；～亲信❶；给他～一个职位；故事里～了两段对话❷〔**～补**〕〈结〉人已经～好了；还没～完呢！把他的亲戚朋友都～在重要的岗位❸上了；他把自己的人全部～上了〈趋〉能不能～进来？～到你们组里去吧！可以～到我们这儿来〈程〉～得真不少〈可〉还～得进来吗？不知道还～得了(liǎo)～不了(liǎo)？〔**状～**〕偷偷地❹～；暗中❺～；暗地里❻～；公开❼～；故意❽～；预先❾～；明目张胆地～❿；往哪儿～

1. trusted follower 2. dialogue 3. important post 4. 5. 6. secretly; in secret; on the sly 7. openly; publicly 8. intentionally; on purpose 9. beforehand; in advance 10. brazenly; flagrantly

ānpái 安排 arrange; plan 〔**～宾**〕〈名〉～生活；～时间；～人力❶；～住处❷；～人员❸；～衣、食、住、行❹；～学习；～参观访问；～工作〔**～补**〕〈结〉时间都～满❺了；生活～妥当❻了；工作～就绪了❼；会议❽～在下星期三举行❾；我的旅行计划～在明年；他们的婚期❿～在明年；～在业余时间⓫学英语；参观访问～到哪一天？〈趋〉把这项工作也一并⓬～进来吧〈程〉她把生活～得井井有条⓭；时间～得非常紧⓮；～得很紧凑⓯；～得很活泼⓰；住处～得很理想⓱；～得很满意⓲；工作～得非常合理⓳；～得乱七八糟⓴〈可〉～不了(liǎo)这么多人工作；文章太多，一版㉑可能～不下；时间太紧了，这项工作～不进来了〈时〉～了半天工作〈量〉～了几次参观都没去成；你先替我～一下儿吧！〔**状～**〕认真～；仔细～；立即～；尽力～；勉强㉒～下了；合理地㉓～；适当㉔～；任意㉕～；妥善㉖～；临时㉗～；随便㉘～；特意㉙～；必须～；重新～；难以㉚～；及时～

1. manpower 2. lodging; accommodation 3. personnel 4. clothing, food, shelter and transportation — basic necessaries of life 5. full; filled 6. appropriate; proper 7. be in order; be ready 8. conference; meeting 9. take place; hold 10. wedding day 11. spare time 12. taken as a whole; together; in the lump 13. in perfect order; methodically 14. tight; close 15. (have) a tight schedule 16. lively; vivacious; vivid 17. ideal 18. satisfied; pleased 19. rational; reasonable 20. muddled; confused 21. printing plate 22. reluctantly; grudgingly 23. rationally 24. suitably 25. wantonly; arbitrarily; wilfully 26. properly; appropriately 27. temporarily 28. as one

pleases 29. specially; for a special purpose 30. difficult to

ānwèi 安慰 comfort; console ≅ 劝〔～宾〕〈名〉～遭到不幸❶的邻居；～受慢性病❷折磨❸的病人；～破了产❹的朋友；～没被大学录取❺的同学；～死者的家属❻〔～补〕〈可〉她不听劝❼，我可～不了(liǎo)她〈时〉～了半天，她才止住❽哭〈量〉他～了我一番；好好儿～一下儿吧！〔状～〕好好儿～；多～；一再❾～；耐心地❿～；千万百计地⓫～；自我⓬～

1. meet with a misfortune 2. chronic disease 3. suffer severely from (a chronic disease) 4. go bankrupt; become insolvent 5. enroll; admit 6. family members 7. advise 8. stop 9. time and again; repeatedly 10. patiently 11. by every possible means; by hook or by crook 12. self

àn 按 ① press; push down ≅ 摁(èn)〔～宾〕〈名〉～电铃❶；～电钮❷；～键盘❸；～图钉❹；～手印❺〔～补〕〈结〉键盘～错了；电铃～响❻了；图钉～歪❼了；手都～疼了〈趋〉把半盒图钉都～上去了；把电钮～进去〈程〉手印～得很清楚；手～得真疼〈可〉这个墙～得进图钉去吗？电钮～不下去了〈时〉～了半天电铃，也没人来开门；～了一分钟〈量〉～了好几下儿；～了五、六次〔状～〕使劲儿～；轻轻地～；连续❽～

1. electric bell 2. (push) button 3. keyboard 4. drawing pin 5. an impression of the hand 6. ring 7. oblique; slant 8. successively

② keep one's hand on; keep a tight grip on; push sth. down〔～宾〕〈名〉～着帽子，别让风吹跑了；她用手～着衣襟❶，怕被风掀❷起来；售货员一手～着点心盒，一手去拿绳子❸；那个孩子～着水盆❹里的皮球，不让它浮❺上来〔～补〕〈结〉愤怒❻的群众把小偷～倒了；～在地上就打〈趋〉警察❼把那个坏蛋的头一下去；～到水里去了〈程〉～得真紧❽；～得太用力了；～得手都疼了〈可〉这个疯子❾力气太大，我～不住他；～不倒他；～不了(liǎo)〈时〉～了半天；～一会儿〈量〉帮我～一下儿〔状～〕使劲～着；往下～；用一只手～着

1. the one or two pieces making up the front of a Chinese jacket 2. lift; raise 3. string 4. wash basin 5. float 6. indignant; resentful 7. police 8. tight; taut 9. madman; lunatic

ànshì 暗示 drop a hint; hint; suggest〔～宾〕〈名〉～李华〈代〉～我；我～他快走开；～他别再说下去了〔～补〕〈结〉把我的意思～给他〈时〉～了她半天，她都没理解❶〈量〉～了他好几次；他一下儿〔状～〕用眼睛～；用手势❷～；用语言～；一再❸～

1. understand; comprehend 2.

gesture 3. time and again; repeatedly

āo 熬 cook in water; boil ≅ 煮〔~宾〕〈名〉~白菜❶；~萝卜❷；~豆腐❸；~茄子❹；~鱼〔~补〕〈结〉别把菜~烂❺了；萝卜汤~好了没有？〈程〉白菜~得太烂了；今天鱼~得不好吃；~得太多了〈可〉煤气❻快用完了，这锅豆腐可能~不熟❼了；时间短~不烂〈时〉~了半个小时；再多~一会儿〈量〉就~过一次〔状~〕多一些；旺火❽~；微火❾~；早点~

1. Chinese cabbage 2. radish 3. bean curd 4. eggplant; aubergine 5. soft 6. gas 7. half-cooked 8. a great fire 9. slow fire

áo 熬 ① boil; stew〔~宾〕〈名〉~粥❶；~药〔~补〕〈结〉药都快~干了；粥又~稀❷了；~多了；把粥~成饭了〈趋〉粥已经~出来了〈程〉~得真香；~得太稀了〈可〉水还有不少呢，~不干；药得(děi)~二十分钟；已经~了半天；刚~一会儿〔状~〕真难~；用微火❸~；分两次~

1. gruel (made of rice, millet, etc.); porridge 2. thin 3. slow fire

② endure ≅ 忍受〔主~〕〈名〉苦日子❶难~〔~宾〕〈名〉~时间；~夜❷〔~补〕〈结〉眼睛~红了；把人都~瘦了；把她~病了；真把人~死了〈趋〉苦日子无法❸~下去了；孩子大了，她现在总算~出来了〈程〉熬夜~得都瘦了；~得都快病了〈可〉这种日子她再也~不下去了；他的身体哪儿~得了(liǎo)夜啊〈时〉再~两年就好了；~了好几年〈量〉她~一次夜就病一次〔状~〕时间太难~了；苦苦地~着；再也~不了(liǎo)了；总算~出来了〔习用〕苦~岁月❹

1. bitter days (years of suffering) 2. stay up late or all night 3. unable; incapable 4. years

B

bājie 巴结 fawn on; curry favour with; make up to ≅〔～宾〕〈名〉～有钱的人；～有势力的人❶；～有地位的人❷；～名人；～对自己有用的人；～能给自己带来好处的人〔～补〕〈结〉上有钱的人了〈趋〉看见人家出名了，就～起人家来了〈可〉你想～还～不上呢〈时〉～了半天〈量〉他说他要好好～一下儿新经理❸〔～状〕决不～；从不～；专门❹～；白～了，不顾廉耻地❺～；拼命～

1. powerful man 2. a man of high position 3. new director; new manager 4. specially 5. shamelessly

bā 扒 ① hold on to; cling to ≅ 抓住〔～宾〕〈名〉小孩～（着）窗户往里看；～（着）墙头❶往外看；一只熊～着马戏❷演员❸的肩膀❹〔～补〕〈结〉～住了，别掉下来〈可〉你～得住～不住?〔～状〕别～了；两只手～着；用力～

1. the top of a wall 2. circus 3. performer 4. shoulder

② pull down ≅ 挖开；刨开〔～宾〕〈名〉～了旧房盖❶新房；～城墙❷〔～补〕〈结〉那一片旧房已经～平了；～倒❸(dǎo)了〈趋〉他们的动作❹真快，说～就～起来了〈时〉～了一天，那一排旧屋就全扒完了〔～状〕大家一起～；快点儿～；旧房子全部～完了

1. build 2. city wall 3. fall; topple 4. action

③ push aside ≅ 拨开〔～补〕〈结〉～开芦苇❶；～开荷叶❷，找青蛙；～开眼皮❸，上眼药❹〈程〉眼睛～得真疼；～得很难受❺〈时〉～了半天，一只蟋蟀❻也没捉着〔～状〕医生给病人～眼皮；轻轻地～

1. reed 2. lotus leaf 3. eyelid 4. eyedrops 5. suffer pain; feel unwell 6. cricket

bá 拔 pull out ≅ 抽出；拉出〔～宾〕〈名〉～草；～麦子❶；～牙；～刺；～剑；～钉子；从锁孔❷上～钥匙❸；～了一根头发；～萝卜❹〔～补〕〈结〉麦子～完了；～掉一颗蛀牙❺；～下一根白头发；～断❻了；钉子～弯❼了；～去了一个眼中钉❽〈趋〉～出剑来比试❾一下儿；刺已经～掉〈程〉那位牙医拔牙～得真疼；～得一点也不疼；～得真快；～得很好〈可〉钥匙怎么～不出来了；这片麦子三天～得完～不完? 钉子都锈❿了，一点也～不动了；牙医说发炎⓫的时候～不了(liǎo)

牙〈时〉这颗钉子~了半天都没拔出来；~了一个星期麦子〈量〉我只~过一次牙〔状~〕用钳子⑫~钉子；轻轻地⑬~；用力~；猛地⑭一~；一下子就~下来了；干脆⑮~掉；连根儿⑯~〔习用〕一毛儿不⑰~

1. wheat 2. the hole of a lock 3. key 4. turnip; radish 5. decayed tooth 6. broken; snapped 7. bend 8. thorn in one's flesh 9. have a competition 10. become rusty 11. inflammation 12. with a pair of pliers 13. gently 14. suddenly; vigorously 15. clear-cut; straightforward 16. pull up by the root 17. unwilling to give up even a hair — very stingy

bǎ 把 ① hold ≅ 握住〔~宾〕〈名〉~舵❶；~犁❷〔~补〕〈结〉~住了；~好了，手都~酸了❸〈程〉~得很好；~得很紧❹〈可〉你~得住~不住？我~不好犁〈时〉~了一上午犁；再~一会儿〈量〉你先替我~一下儿舵〔状~〕使劲~着；双手~着；一只手~着不行；死死地❺~着

1. rudder; helm 2. plough (plow) 3. tingle; ache 4. tight 5. fast; firmly

② guard; watch ≅ 看守; 管〔~宾〕〈名〉今天是5号队员~球门❶；有人~着大门，不能随便进去〔~补〕〈结〉~住球门，不让对方❷的球射❸进来；教外语的老师应该要~好学生发音这一关〈程〉门~得很严❹；门~得真紧

〈可〉守门员~不住球门儿〈时〉昨天轮到我值班❺，我~了一晚上校门〈量〉你替我~一下儿大门，我去一趟厕所❻〔状~〕好好儿~着；那个运动员❼全神贯注地❽~着球门儿；死死地❾~着；紧紧地~着；严格地⑩~关

1. goal 2. the other party; opponent 3. shoot 4. strict 5. to be my turn for duty 6. go to the lavatory 7. player; sportsman 8. with rapt attention 9. firmly 10. strictly

③ be close to; by ≅ 紧靠〔~宾〕〈名〉我的床~墙角❶〔~补〕〈结〉邮局就~在街角❷

1. a corner formed by two walls 2. at the street corner

④ control; monopolize ≅ 把持〔~宾〕〈名〉他不撒手地❶~着家里的钱；他一个人~着所有的工作不放；小红~着玩具不给别的孩子玩〔~补〕〈趋〉她把钱都一起来了；把权❷~过去了；~到自己手里去（来）了〈程〉~得紧；~得很厉害〈可〉~得住？~不住？〔状~〕一直~着；紧紧地~着；死死地❸~着；拼命❹~着

1. not letting go one's hold 2. power 3. firmly 4. desperately

bǎchí 把持 control; dominate; monopolize〔~宾〕〈名〉~权力❶；~钱财❷〈代〉~一切〔~补〕〈结〉一定要~住；~到自己手里〈时〉~了好几年；~了好长时间；~了一个时期〔状~〕被他

们~了；全部~过去了；紧紧地❸~着

1. power 2. money and property 3. firmly; tightly

bà 罢 stop; cease ≅ 停↔复〔~宾〕〈名〉~工；~课；~教❶〔~补〕〈趋〉又~起工来了；不答应❷这些条件就继续~下去〈时〉~了一个月课〈量〉一年之内~了好几次工〔状~〕一直~；经常~；第一次~；连续~；一连~了两次；断断续续地❸~；动不动❹就~；为增加工资❺~；为改善生活条件❻~

1. teachers' strike 2. comply with 3. off and on; intermittently 4. easily; frequently; at every turn 5. for a rise in salary 6. for improving the living conditions

bàzhàn 霸占 forcibly occupy; seize ≅ 强占〔~宾〕〈名〉~财产❶；~土地；~别国领土❷；~别人的妻子；~私人❸住宅〔~补〕〈时〉~了很多年〔状~〕非法❺~；强行❻~；被敌人~；用武力❼~；用阴谋手段❽~

1. property 2. territory 3. private; personal 4. residence; dwelling 5. illegally 6. by force 7. by arms; by force 8. by conspiratorial means

báifèi 白费 waste; in vain 〔~宾〕〈名〉~力气❶；~唇舌❷；~心思❸；~时间〔~补〕〈时〉~了三天时间〔状~〕简直❹~；不见得❺~；一点也不~；又~了；没~

1. strength 2. words; argument; explaining 3. rack one's brains in vain 4. simply; at all 5. not likely; not necessarily

bǎi 摆 ① put; place; arrange ≅ 放；陈列〔~宾〕〈名〉~花盆❶；~照片；~碗筷❷；~桌子；~家具❸；书架上~着很多书；~棋子❹；~了一桌酒席❺；~了一床脏衣服；~了一地乱七八糟的❻东西；~了一屋子旧书〔~补〕〈结〉快把碗筷~好；窗台❼上满了花盆；架子上的药瓶没~齐；棋子~错了；把会场❽的桌椅~整齐点儿；这一行椅子~斜❾了；这张画儿有时候~到这儿，有时候~到那儿〈趋〉把酒杯~上来吧；竭力❿~出一副笑脸来；把写字台~到窗户下边去好不好?〈程〉家具~得很整齐；东西~太乱⓫了；椅子~得太挤⓬了〈可〉屋子太小，家具怎么也~不好；这间屋子~得下三张床~不下？房间很大，摆两套沙发⓭也~不满；我可~不起那么多桌酒席〈时〉在橱窗里~了些日子；~了几个星期〈量〉好好~一下儿〔状~〕端端正正地⓮~了一张大照片；稀稀落落地⓯~了几盆花；按着次序⓰~；横着⓱~；竖着⓲~；往远点儿~；大~筵席；散乱地⓳~了一桌子书

1. flower-pot 2. bowls and chopsticks 3. furniture 4. piece (in a board game) 5. feast 6. messy 7.

window-sill 8. meeting place 9. oblique 10. do one's utmost 11. too messy 12. too close 13. sofa 14. straightly 15. sparsely 16. in order 17. horizontally 18. vertically 19. in disorder

② lay bare; state clearly 〔～宾〕〈名〉～矛盾❶；～问题；～事实❷；～条件❸；～理由❹〔～补〕〈结〉问题要～清楚，话必须～在明处❺〈趋〉把矛盾～出来让大家分析❻；把两个人的条件～出来，让大家看看，谁去合适❼；有理由可以～出来讨论〈程〉问题～得清清楚楚；理由～得很充分❽〈可〉你～得出几条理由来；一条也～不出来；问题怎么能～不清楚呢？〈量〉把两个人的条件～了半天，也比不出高低来❾〈量〉好好～一下儿〔状～〕好好～；心平气和地❿～；清清楚楚地～；实事求是⓫地～

1. contradiction 2. fact 3. condition 4. reason 5. If you've got anything to say, say it openly 6. analysis 7. suitable, appropriate 8. full; ample 9. hard to tell which is better 10. calmly; even-temperedly 11. seek truth from facts; be practical and realistic

③ put on; assume ≅ 显；显示；炫耀〔～宾〕〈名〉别在我面前～威风❶；因为那个人爱～架子❷，所从大家都不喜欢他；他总愿意在年青人面前～老资格❸；她～了一个看书的样子，其实❹一个字也没看下去〈形〉有些青年人挣❺的钱不多，可是总想在吃、穿上～阔气❻〔～补〕〈结〉～好了架势〈趋〉～出来一副可怜相❼；你跟我也～起老资格来了〈可〉他在这儿可～不了(liǎo)老资格〈时〉～了半天架子，没人理他〔状～〕在我面前～；故意❽～；动不动就❾～

1. power and prestige; give one's airs 2. put on airs 3. flaunt one's seniority 4. as a matter of fact 5. earn 6. parade one's wealth 7. assume a pitiful appearance 8. intentionally; wilfully 9. easily; frequently

④ sway; wave ≅ 摇动〔主～〕〈名〉柳条❶随风❷～；钟摆❸不停地❹～着〔～宾〕〈名〉她向我～～手，让我别说话；小鱼高兴地～着尾巴〔～补〕〈趋〉柳条在微风❺中～来～去〈程〉鱼的尾巴～得真灵活❻〈时〉我向他～了半天手，他都没看见〈量〉～了一下儿手〔状～〕随风～；向我～手；来回❼～；频频地❽～；在他背后～手

1. willow twig 2. bend with the wind 3. pendulum 4. ceaselessly 5. breeze 6. flexibly; nimbly 7. back and forth 8. again and again; repeatedly

bǎituō 摆脱 get rid of; extricate oneself from ; break away from 〔～宾〕〈名〉～跟踪❶的人；～纠缠❷自己的人；～经济桎梏❸；～所处的困境❹；～繁重的工作❺；～苦恼的处境❻〈动〉～他们的控制❼和干涉❽；～束缚❾；～

干扰❿；~纠缠〈形〉~贫困⓫；~烦恼⓬〔~补〕〈结〉能不能~掉?〈可〉~得了(liǎo)；~不了(liǎo)〈趋〉从困境中~出来了〔状~〕从中~；彻底⓭~；千方百计地⓮~；极力⓯~；终于~了

1. tail sb. 2. entangle 3. shackles of economy 4. plight 5. strenuous work 6. worried situation 7. control 8. interference 9. bind; tie 10. disturb; obstruct 11. poverty 12. vexation 13. thoroughly 14. by every possible means; by hook or by crook 15. do one's utmost

bàihuài 败坏 corrupt; ruin; undermine ≌ 损害〔主~〕〈名〉道德❶~了；风气❷~了〔~宾〕〈名〉不许❸~我的名誉❹；~社会风气；~朋友的声誉❺〔状~〕故意❻~；多次~；被他~了；极力❼~；竟然❽~；公然❾~

1. morals; morality 2. general mood; atmosphere; common practice 3. not allow 4. reputation 5. fame; reputation 6. intentionally; on purpose 7. do one's utmost 8. to one's surprise; unexpectedly 9. openly

bài 拜 ① do obeisance〔~宾〕〈名〉每年春节❶我都要去姑姑家~年；明天是我父亲80岁生日,我要去给他~寿❷〔~补〕〈结〉~完了年,就去看电影〈量〉每年要去他家~一次年〔状~〕给他~寿

1. the Spring Festival 2. congratulate an elderly person on his birthday

②acknowledge sb.as one's master〔~宾〕〈名〉~老师〈代〉~你为师❶〔状~〕从此❷~你为师；一定~你为师；恭恭敬敬地❸~你为师；立刻~你为师

1. master worker 2. from this time on; from now on 3. respectfully

bàifǎng 拜访 pay a visit; call on ≌ 访问〔~宾〕〈名〉~亲戚❶；~朋友；~邻居❷；~老师；~师傅❸；~名人；~老艺人❹；~著名❺作家❻；~演员❼；~书法家❽〔~补〕〈结〉已经~过了；上次去没~着(zháo)、可〉今天时间不够,~不了(liǎo)那么多人；去了几次,总~不着(zháo)她,还是约❾好了再去吧!〈量〉~过一次；咱们~一下儿他去好不好? ~过好几回〔状~〕特意❿~；专程⓫~；顺便⓬~；正式⓭~

1. relative 2. neighbour 3. master worker 4. artisan; handicraftsman 5. famous 6. writer 7. actor or actress 8. calligrapher 9. make an appointment 10. for a special purpose; specially 11. pay a special visit to sb. 12. incidentally 13. officially

bān 搬 take away; move; remove ≌ 移动；迁移〔~宾〕〈名〉~桌子；~衣柜；~花盆❶；~砖❷；~机器；~钢琴❸；~家；~宿

舍〔~补〕〈结〉他们~走了，不在这儿住了；书搬来搬去都~坏了；这个楼都~空了；教室的椅子都让人~光了；把小说~上银幕❹了〈趋〉把这把椅子先~到外边去吧；他~到楼上去了；把花~出来(~出去)晒晒太阳吧；帮我把书柜~过来吧；那个洗衣机❺他不费劲❻就能~起来〈程〉~得够慢的；~得太远了；~得离我家很近；搬东西~得我腰疼❼〈可〉不要紧，东西~不坏；东西真多，三天也~不完；你一个人~得了(liǎo)吗？~不进去；今天下雨，家又~不成了〈时〉他家东西太多，陆陆续续❽~了一个星期；~了半天儿，就搬完了；刚~一会儿，你就累了〈量〉再往这边~一下儿；~过好多次家，都搬出经验❾来了〔状~〕陆陆续续地~；一次~完；轻轻地~；慢点儿~；赶紧~；搬不动不要硬❿~；家具⓫太大，不好~；一点一点地~；限期⓬~完；提前⓭~；限日子⓮~家；跟大家一起~；往对面⓯房间~；吃力地⓰~；少~点儿〔习用〕~起石头打自己的脚⓱

1. flower-pot 2. brick 3. piano 4. screen 5. washing machine 6. effortless 7. lumbago 8. one after another; in succession 9. experience 10. force oneself to (do sth.) 11. furniture 12. within a definite time 13. ahead of time 14. by a prescribed time 15. opposite 16. strenuously 17. lift a rock only to drop it on one's own feet

bàn 办 ① do; handle official business ≅ 办理；处理；料理〔~宾〕〈名〉几点开始~公❶；还没~出院手续❷；~过一个案子❸〔~补〕〈结〉~完手续了没有？这件事情~坏了；~糟❹了；一定要事情~圆满❺；手续~晚了；几件事都没~成〈趋〉这种事~起来真费❻时间〈程〉他办事~得很认真❼；案子~得很公正❽；手续~得很完备❾；一切都~得很好；~得太糟糕了❿；~得乱七八糟⓫；~得一塌糊涂⓬；~得不太顺利⓭；~得太马虎了⓮；~得非常仔细⓯；~得十分认真；~得有条不紊⓰〈可〉这件事他~得好吗？这种事谁也~不了(liǎo)；都下班了，今天什么事也~不成了；手续两天~得完~不完？〈时〉这个案子，整整~了三年；这点事陆陆续续~了一个多星期才办完〈量〉他没~过一次漂亮事；这件事请你费心⓱给~一下儿〔状~〕快点儿~；早点儿~；对这种罪犯⓲要严⓳~；这点事情好~；积极地⓴~；赶紧㉑~；公正地~案；重新㉒~手续；马马虎虎地㉓~；脚踏实地地㉔~；实事求是地㉕~；照常㉖~公；有板有眼地㉗~；整整㉘~了一年；不妨㉙~一次试试；总是热心地㉚替别人~

1. work in an office 2. hospital discharge formalities 3. handle a case 4. fail 5. satisfactorily 6. waste 7. attentive 8. fair; just 9. perfect 10. too bad 11. at sixes and sevens; in confusion 12. in a

complete mess 13. successful 14. careless 15. very careful 16. systematic 17. take a lot of trouble 18. criminal 19. punish with severity 20. actively 21. hurriedly 22. again 23. carelessly 24. in a practical way 25. in a truthseeking way 26. as usual; usually 27. methodically 28. wholly 29. might as well 30. enthusiastically; warmly

② run ≅ 开办；经营〔～宾〕〈名〉～工厂；～学校；～工业❶；～报❷；～教育❸〔～补〕〈结〉～多了；～晚了〈趋〉退休人员❹～起业余❺教育来了；～出成绩来了；～出经验❻来了，需要继续❼～下去〈程〉～得很好；～得很糟❽；～得比较灵活❾；～得很有成绩〈可〉没有教师，学校～不了(liǎo)；没有经费❿，什么也～不起来；她很有经验，肯定⓫～得好〈时〉我们～了三年报纸；他～了一辈子⓬教育，经验很丰富〔状～〕从头儿～起；积极地⓭～；主动地⓮～；热心地⓯～；有计划地⓰～；盲目地⓱～；不要一窝蜂似地⓲都～；扎扎实实地⓳～

1. industry 2. newspaper 3. education 4. retired people 5. spare-time 6. experience 7. continue 8. too bad 9. vivid; lively 10. expenditure; fund 11. be sure to 12. all one's life 13. actively 14. initiatively 15. zealously 16. in a planned way 17. blindly; unrealistically 18. like a swarm of bees; at the same time 19. in a down-to-earth manner

③ do shopping ≅ 备置；采购〔～宾〕〈名〉～货❶；～年货❷；～酒席❸〔～补〕〈结〉货～全了没有，〈程〉酒席～得很丰盛❹；年货～得真齐全〈可〉货～不齐；酒席～得起❺～不起。〈时〉～了三天，总算办齐了〈量〉商店每年都要到外地去一次年货〈状～〕简简单单地～了几桌酒席；大❻～酒席；多～一些；少～一点；酒席由你～

1. goods; commodity 2. do Spring Festival shopping 3. feast 4. sumptuous 5. can afford 6. on a large scale

bànyǎn 扮演 play the part of; be dressed up as; disguise oneself as ≅ 演；扮；装成，化装成〔～宾〕〈名〉在那出戏❶里他～农民〔～补〕〈结〉她在戏里～一个疯子❷；～成一个小丑❸〈量〉～过两次老奶奶；～一下儿试试吧〔状～〕一直～；从来没～过

1. play 2. madman 3. clown; buffoon

bàn 拌 mix ≅ 搅〔～宾〕〈名〉给牲口❶～草料❷；～鸡丝❸〔～补〕〈结〉糖还没～匀❹呢〈趋〉这两种东西～起来好吃吗？〈程〉面～得太咸了❺〈可〉她不会拌面，总～不匀；料❻装得太多了，搅绊机❼都快～不动了〈时〉每天拌猪食❽，就要～十几分钟〈量〉好好～一下儿再吃〔状～〕用机器～混凝土❾；用筷子❿～面；给

鸡~点食；好好~一~；**多**~点儿〔**习用**〕~嘴⓫

1. draught animals 2. fodder 3. shredded chicken 4. even; well-proportioned 5. too salty 6. material; stuff 7. mixer; stirrer 8. pig feed 9. concrete 10. chopsticks 11. quarrel

bàn 绊 stumble; trip 〔**~宾**〕

〈名〉东西放在这儿真~脚❶，快挪开❷吧；~了一交❸；~了一个跟头❹(筋斗❺)〔**~补**〕〈结〉小心点，别~倒❻了〈程〉脚趾❼~得真疼〈量〉让石头~了一下儿；这个树根❽~过我三次了〔**状~**〕他故意❾~了我一下儿；看着点儿，别~倒了；被翘起来的❿砖⓫~了一下儿；差点儿~一交〔**习用**〕~脚石⓬

1. be in the way 2. move away 3. 4. 5. a fall 6. trip and fall 7. toe 8. root of a tree 9. intentionally 10. raised; protruding 11. brick 12. stumbling block; obstacle

bāngzhù 帮助 help; assist ≅ 帮 〔**~宾**〕〈名〉应该~有病的人；~受伤的人❶；~残废的人❷；~有困难的人〈代〉我想每月~他一些钱；我~你收拾❸屋子吧；他~我复习功课；~人家整理稿件❹；~他打听消息；丢在哪儿了？我~你找找〔**状~**〕〈结〉一直~到他毕业❺〈趋〉她~起人来非常热情❻〈程〉~得很及时〈可〉我可~不了 (liǎo) 你什么〈时〉在我最困难的时候，他~了

我好多年；~了我很长一段时间〈量〉~过好多次了；应该好好~他〔**状~**〕互相~；善意地❼~；耐心地❽~；诚恳地❾~；主动地❿~；尽量⓫~；千方百计地⓬~；慷慨地⓭~；无私地⓮~；竭尽全力地⓯~；勉强⓰~；心甘情愿地⓱~；在经济上⓲~；从精神上⓳~

1. the wounded 2. the disabled 3. tide up 4. sort out manuscripts 5. graduation 6. warm 7. kindly 8. patiently 9. sincerely 10. on one's own initiative 11. to the best of one's ability 12. by every possible means 13. generously 14. selflessly 15. do ones' utmost 16. reluctantly 17. of one's own free will 18. economically 19. spiritually

bǎng 绑 bind; tie ≅ 捆；系↔解 〔**~宾**〕〈名〉~扫帚❶；~刷子❷；~人〔**~补**〕〈结〉把刷子~结实❸点；敌人把他~在树上了〈趋〉把小偷~起来了〈程〉~得真紧❹；~得不结实〈可〉我的手没劲❺，绑什么也~不紧；绳子太短~不上；铁丝太细~不结实〈时〉~了一上午，才绑好；~了半天，也没绑上〈量〉好好~一下儿；~过两次了〔**状~**〕马马虎虎地❻~了；一圈一圈地~；结结实实地~；照原来的样子~；用绳子~；重新~；紧紧地~；松松地~

1. broom 2. brush 3. durably 4.

tight 5. lack of strength 6. carelessly

bāo 包 ① wrap ≌ 包装；包扎〔～宾〕<名>～饺子❶；～伤口❷；～纱布❸〔～补〕<结>刚洗完澡，把头～好了再出去；～紧❹点儿好；把这两种糖～在一起吧<趋>快把伤口～起来吧<程>～得方方正正❺的<可>这张纸太小，～不住；这种纸太容易破，我可～不好<时>我们全家一起～了半个小时饺子<量>好好～一下儿；～了好几遍〔状～〕多～几层纸，油就渗不过来了；护士给病人～伤口；一层一层地～纱布；紧紧地～；轻轻地～；用机器～糖纸

1. dumpling 2. wound 3. gauze (e.g. on wound) 4. tight 5. square and upright

② undertake the whole thing ≌ 承担〔主～〕<名>你们结婚❶买东西的事我～了〔～宾〕<名>～了一只游艇❷；～了一辆汽车〔～补〕<可>这么多工作，我一个人可～不了(liǎo)<量>～过一次游览汽车〔状～〕临时❸～一辆车〔习用〕纸里～不住火❹

1. marriage 2. yacht 3. temporarily 4. you can't wrap fire in paper — there is no concealing the truth; truth will out

bāobì 包庇 shield; harbour; conceal ≌ 袒护〔～宾〕<名>～坏人；～罪犯❶；～犯错误❷的人；不要～自己的孩子〔～补〕<趋>他企图❸把犯法❹的儿子～起来<量>过几次了〔状～〕互

相～；一再～；再三❺～；千方百计地❻～；决不～；从不～

1. criminal; offender 2. commit a mistake 3. attempt 4. violate the law 5. time and again; over and over again; repeatedly 6. by every possible means

bāohán 包含 contain; include ≌ 含有〔～宾〕<名>这句话～好几层意思❶；心理学❷～了哪些内容❸？

1. several implications 2. psychology 3. content

bāokuò 包括 include; comprise; consist of ≌ 包含〔～宾〕<名>房租❶里～水电费❷吗？～四项内容❸；～听、说、读、写四个方面；最近出版❹了一百多种新书，其中一一些古典书籍❺<代>～你在内〔～补〕<结>这几个句子不～在里面〔状～〕当然～他了

1. rent 2. charges for water and electricity 3. content 4. publish 5. classics

bāowéi 包围 surround;|encircle ≌ 围住〔～宾〕<名>～敌人；～了敌人的指挥部❶；～了总统府❷〔～补〕<结>把敌人～住了；他被人们～上了<趋>敌人从四面八方❸～过来了；从山下～上来了<程>～得很严❹，谁也出不去<可>人少～不了(liǎo) <时>～了三天三夜；～了一个星期<量>

被～过一次〔状～〕被～了；层层❺～；迅速地❻～

1. command post; headquarters 2. presidential palace 3. from all directions 4. close; tight 5. ring upon ring 6. speedily

bāo 剥 shell; peel; skin 〔～宾〕〈名〉～花生；～桔子❶；～皮〔～补〕〈结〉～完了，把皮～掉了；～干净了没有？〈趋〉把花生米❷出来，准备❸炸❹〈程〉～得真干净〈可〉里边那层皮总～不净；这么多豆子，半天也～不完〈时〉～了一个多小时了；要是人多，～一会儿就剥完了〈量〉～过一次；帮我～一下儿吧，我来不及❺了〔状～〕快点～；不好～；一层一层地～

1. orange 2. peanut kernel; shelled peanut 3. get ready 4. fry in deep fat or oil; deep-fry 5. there's not enough time (to do sth.); it's too late (to do sth.)

bǎo 保 guarantee; ensure; preserve≅保证；担保〔～宾〕〈代〉～你不迟到〈形〉～暖❶；～温❷〔～补〕〈可〉伤❸太重，腿可能～不住了；他的冠军❹不知道在这次比赛还～得住～不住了？〔状～〕一点也不～暖；非常～暖

1. 2. warm 3. wound; injure 4. champion

bǎochí 保持 keep; maintain; preserve〔～宾〕〈名〉～冷静❶的头脑❷；～优良❸传统❹；～原状❺；～原来的样子；～最高记录❻；～着一定的距离❼；～他的语言特色❽；～优良成绩❾〈动〉～中立❿；他和我们一直～着联系⓫〈形〉～安静⓬；～整洁⓭；头脑～清醒⓮〈趋〉要把好的作风～下来〈程〉优良传统～得很好〈时〉～了三年，最后还是让人家把冠军夺⓯去了〔状～〕经常～；永久～；一直～；仍然～；始终～

1. sober; calm 2. brains; mind; head 3. fine; good 4. tradition 5. original state; previous condition 6. record 7. a certain distance 8. characteristic, distinguishing feature 9. result; achievement; success 10. neutrality 11. contact; connection 12. quiet 13. clean and tidy 14. clear-headed; sober-minded 15. compete for

bǎocún 保存 preserve; conserve; keep≅存〔～宾〕〈名〉替他～东西；～蔬菜❶；～粮食❷；～文物❸；～字画❹；～文稿❺；～武器❻〔～补〕〈结〉～好文物；水果用什么办法才能～住呢；～到今天；～在什么地方？〈趋〉把古代❼文物很好地～下来了；还要继续～下去；把这些文稿好好～起来吧!〈程〉～得很完整❽；～得跟原来的一样好；蔬菜～得真新鲜〈时〉这张画～了好几百年〈量〉请你替我～一下儿〔状～〕不易～；千方百计地～❿；尽量⓫～；好不容易才～下来；用科学的方法～；完整地～着；永远～；继续～；长期～；暂时～

1. vegetable 2. grain 3. cultural relic; historical relic 4. calligraphy and painting 5. manuscript; draft 6. weapon 7. ancient times; antiquity 8. complete; intact 9. fresh 10. by hook or by crook 11. to the best of one's ability; as far as possible

bǎohù 保护 protect; safeguard
〔～宾〕〈名〉～小树苗❶；～动物～益鸟❷；～下一代❸；～身体～视力❹；～文物❺〔～补〕〈结〉把孩子～好〈趋〉把揭发❻坏人的人～起来了〈程〉文物古迹～得非常好〈可〉我连自己都～不了(liǎo)，哪儿能～别人啊！〈时〉～了她很多年〔状～〕精心地❼～；尽心地❽～；竭力❾～；暗中❿～

1. sapling 2. beneficial bird 3. future generation 4. eyesight 5. historical relic 6. expose; denounce 7. meticulously; elaborately 8. with all one's heart 9. with all one's might 10. secretly

bǎoliú 保留 retain; reserve
〔～宾〕〈名〉我要～我的意见❶；～权利❷；～看法；～着珍贵❸的礼物；这个地方还～着原来的面貌❹；～了好多套❺纪念邮票〔～补〕〈结〉～到明天中午；一直～到现在〈趋〉～下来了；还要～下去〈可〉这种特权❻再也～不住了〈时〉这个意见～了好几个月了，今天我还是要提❼〔状～〕原封不动地❽～着；至今❾仍～

着；依旧❿～着；尽量⓫～；全部～下来了；暂时～

1. opinion 2. right 3. valuable; precious 4. face; features 5. set 6. privilege 7. propose; suggest 8. with the seal unbroken; intact 9. so far; up to now 10. as before; still 11. to the best of one's ability; as far as possible

bǎomì 保密 maintain secrecy; keep sth. secret
〔主～〕〈名〉我告诉你的话要～；这件事情要～〔～补〕〈可〉那个人保不了(liǎo)密❶，什么话也不能跟他说〈时〉我替你保了半天密，你自己反而❷说出去了〈量〉这件事请你替我保一下密〔状～〕绝对❸～；暂时❹～；永久❺～；不必～；替我～；一定要～；必须～

1. secrecy 2. on the contrary; instead 3. absolutely; definitely 4. temporarily; for the time being 5. permanently; forever

bǎoquán 保全 save from damage; preserve
〔～宾〕〈名〉～性命；～面子；～名誉❶〔～补〕〈结〉不知道能不能～住性命〈可〉连面子都～不住了〔状～〕想方设法地❷～；竭力❸～；极力❹～

1. reputation 2. by every means; by hook or by crook 3. with all one's might 4. do one's utmost

bǎowèi 保卫 defend; safeguard
〔～宾〕〈名〉～祖国；～家乡❶；～国土❷；～和平❸；～人民的生

命财产❹；～已取得的权利❺；～国防❻〈形〉～大家的安全❼〔状～〕誓死❽～；竭尽全力地❾～

1. hometown 2. territory 3. peace 4. property 5. right 6. national defence 7. safe; secure 8. pledge one's life; dare to die 9. do one's utmost; do all one can

bǎozhèng 保证 pledge; guarantee; assure; ensure ≅ 担保〔～宾〕〈动〉～按时❶回来；～不迟到；～不早退❷；～完成任务；～履行诺言❸；我做的菜～合你的胃口❹；今天晚上～不会有人来打扰❺了〈形〉这里卖的鱼、肉～新鲜❻；你穿上这件衣服～好看〈主-谓〉～你能买到；～你满意〔～补〕〈可〉谁～得了(liǎo)他以后不再犯错误❼〈量〉你已经向我～过多少次了！〔状～〕必须～；无须❽～；三番五次地～

1. on time 2. leave earlier than one should; leave early 3. keep one's word; fulfill (carry out) one's promise 4. suit one's taste; be to one's taste 5. disturb; trouble 6. fresh 7. make a mistake 8. need not; not have to

bào 报 ① report; announce; declare ≅ 报告；告诉；通知〔～宾〕〈名〉从左向右～数儿❶；电台❷每隔一个小时～一次时间〔～补〕〈结〉新闻～完了吗？孩子～上名了吗？帐目❸都～清楚了吗？时间没～准❹〈趋〉把学生的名单❺～上来〈程〉账～得很清楚；时间～得很准〈可〉帐总～不清楚〈量〉天气预报❻每天早晚各～一次〔状～〕清清楚楚地～帐；重新❼～数；赶快给他～个信儿

1. number off; count off 2. broadcasting station 3. accounts 4. accurate 5. name list 6. weather forecast 7. again

② recompense; requite ≅ 回答；报答〔～宾〕〈名〉～恩❶；～德❷〔状～〕无法❸～

1. kindness; favour; grace 2. kindness; virtue, morals 3. unable; incapable

bàogào 报告 report；make known 〔～宾〕〈名〉～比赛的结果；～新闻❶；～出席❷（缺席❸）人数儿；～营业❹亏损❺的数字；～事情的经过；把孩子逃学的事情～给家长〈程〉～得不及时〔状～〕向上级❻～；立即❼～；必须～；不必～；必恭必敬地❽～；详细地❾～了事情的经过

1. news 2. number of persons present; attendance 3. number of persons absent 4. business 5. loss; deficit 6. higher level; higher authorities 7. at once; immediately 8. reverent and respectful; extremely deferential 9. in detail

bào 刨 plane〔～宾〕〈名〉～木头〔～补〕〈结〉木板全～完了吗？已经～平了〈趋〉把高出来的这块～下去吧〈程〉木工师傅

~得真快；这块板子~得很光滑❶〈可〉这个刨子❷不快❸，~不平〈时〉~了好几下儿才平〔状~〕这块木头太硬❹真不好~；太难~了；用刨子~
另见 páo 刨

1. smooth; glossy 2. plane 3. not sharp 4. too hard.

bào 抱 ① hold or carry in the arms; embrace; hug 〔~宾〕〈名〉~孩子；~着大衣；两手~着头；~着柱子❶；两手~着树；从后边~着他的腰〔~补〕〈结〉~住了，别把孩子摔❷了；~好了，别掉了〈趋〉把汽车里的东西都~出来吧；~到楼上去（来）吧；她从床上把孩子~起来了〈程〉今天出去买东西，我一直抱着孩子，~得好累啊！〈可〉这么重的东西，你~得起来吗?这么多东西，你~得了(liǎo)吗?这么多书，一趟可~不完〈时〉~了好几个小时了，累死我了〈量〉你来~一下儿，就知道重不重了！〔状~〕紧紧地❸~着；吃力地❹~着；费劲儿地❺~着；替他~着；两只手~

1. pole 2. fall 3. closely; tightly 4. 5. strenuously

② cherish; harbour ≅ 心里存着〔~宾〕〈名〉~很大希望❶；~正确❷的态度❸；不~幻想❹〔状~〕别~幻想了；到底❺~什么态度? 还~什么希望；一直~着希望；对他~很大希望；不再~什么幻想了

1. hope 2. correct; right; proper 3. attitude 4. illusion; fancy; fantasy 5. after all; in the end

③ adopt (a child) ≅ 领养〔~宾〕〈名〉她自己不能生孩子，~了一个；从邻居家~了一只猫〔~补〕〈结〉都四十岁了才抱孩子，真有点儿~晚了〈趋〉从医院里~来一个孩子〈时〉盼了好多年才~着(zháo)一个男孩〔状~〕从小~来的；从哪儿~来的?〔习用〕临时❶~佛脚❷；爱打~不平❸

1. at the time when sth. happens 2. clasp Buddha's feet — profess devotion only when in trouble 3. defend sb. against an injustice

bàoyuàn 抱怨 complain; grumble ≅ 埋怨〔~宾〕〈代〉这件事不要~别人，只能怪❶自己；自己弄坏的，你~谁呀?〔~补〕〈趋〉又~起别人来了；~来~去的〈程〉~得让人心烦〈可〉是你自己做错的，~不得别人〔状~〕总~别人；净~人家；气呼呼地❷~；互相~；没完没了(liǎo)地~

1. blame 2. in a huff; panting with rage

bàolù 暴露 expose; reveal; lay bare ≅ 显露〔主~〕〈名〉目标❶~了；敌人的破坏行动❷~了；他的身份❸~了；罪行❹~了；他的狰狞面目❺~了；缺点~了〔~宾〕〈名〉~真相〔~补〕〈结〉~在大家面前〈趋〉~出来了〈程〉~得清清楚楚〈可〉他的缺点，短时期内❻~不出来〔状~〕完全~；彻底~；在众人面前~；逐

渐❼～出来了；终于～出来了

1. objective; target 2. destructive action 3. identity 4. crime 5. ferocious features; a vile visage 6. in a short time; in a brief space of time 7. gradually; by degrees

bàofā 爆发 erupt; burst out; break out ≅ 暴发〔主～〕〈名〉火山❶～了；战争～了〔～宾〕〈名〉～了经济危机❷；～了一阵笑声（欢呼声❸／掌声）〔～补〕〈结〉人群中～出了一片欢呼声；教室里～出了一片笑声；～出了一阵热烈的掌声〈可〉战争～不了(liǎo)？〔状～〕终于～了；突然～了；在沉默❹中～

1. volcano 2. economic crisis 3. hail; cheer; acclaim 4. silent

bàozhà 爆炸 explode; blow up; detonate〔主～〕〈名〉炸弹❶～了；军火库❷～了；锅炉❸～了；煤气罐❹～了〔～宾〕〈名〉～了一个核装置❺〔状～〕突然～；一齐～；连续❻～；相继❼～；差一点～

1. bomb 2. arsenal 3. boiler 4. gas container 5. nuclear device 6. in succession; successively 7. one after another

bēi 背 carry on the back〔～宾〕〈名〉～孩子；～病人；～行李❶；～书包；～着一架照像机❷；～着一个行军壶❸；～着一支猎枪❹〔～补〕〈结〉～上书包就走了；把行李～好了〈趋〉把孩子～过来；把病人～进急诊室❺来了；那个青年人力气真大，一百斤重的东西～起来就走〈程〉今天背孩子～得太累了；～得汗流浃背〈可〉太大～不了(liǎo)；没人帮忙～不起来〈时〉～了一整天〈量〉你先～一下儿〔状～〕好～不好～；勉强❼～；难～；一口气儿❽～；再往上一一～；吃力地❾～着；不得不一〔习用〕～黑锅❿

1. luggage 2. camera 3. canteen 4. hunting gun 5. emergency ward 6. streaming with sweat (from fear or physical exertion) 7. reluctantly 8. at a stretch 9. strenuously 10. be made a scapegoat; be unjustly blamed

bèi 备 prepare; get ready ≅ 准备〔～宾〕〈名〉给牲口❶～点儿草料❷；老师要～课❸；～战❹〔～补〕〈结〉他要的东西都～齐了；明天的课～完了吗？〈趋〉又～起战来了〈程〉课～得很仔细❺；～得很充分❻；东西～得很齐全；草料～得不够多〈可〉东西一时～不齐；他没经验❼，自己还～不了(liǎo)课，需要有人帮助〈时〉只～了三天的课〔状～〕认真～；仔细～；充分～；按时❽～；提前❾～；集体❿～课；独自⓫～；反复～

1. draught animals 2. forage; fodder 3. (of a teacher) prepare lessons 4. war 5. careful; detailed 6. enough; sufficient 7. experience 8. on time 9. in advance;

ahead of time **10.** collectively **11.** alone

bèi 背 ① recite from memory; learn by heart≃记; 背诵〔**～宾**〕〈名〉～单词❶; ～课文; ～台词❷; ～电话号码; ～例句; ～了两篇文章〔**～补**〕〈结〉～完单词再看课文; 没～熟; 这几条我都～乱了; 从早～到晚〈趋〉课文都～下来了; ～出来三句忘了两句; 他～起台词来比谁都快; 他～起诗来津津有味❸〈程〉～得滚瓜烂熟❹; ～得很流畅❺; ～得结结巴巴❻的〈可〉时间短～不熟; 我总～不会; 这么长的课文, 你～得下来吗? 你真笨, 怎么也～不会; 我脑子不好, ～不了(liǎo)〈时〉～了一会儿就记住了; ～了好几天才记熟〈量〉～了四遍; ～过三次〔**状～**〕不要死❼～; 懂了以后再～; 断断续续地❽～; 从头至尾～; 认真～; 反复～; 一遍一遍地～; 结结巴巴地～

1. word **2.** actor's lines **3.** with relish; with gusto; with keen pleasure **4.** fluently; pat (have memorized sth. thoroughly); have sth. pat **5.** easy and smooth; fluent **6.** stammer; stutter **7.** mechanically **8.** off and on

② hide sth. from; do sth. behind sb's back ≃瞒; 躲避〔**～宾**〕〈名〉他做什么事都喜欢～着人; 有人说: "好事❶不～人, ～人没好事"; 她常～着我, 说我的坏话❷; 她生气了, ～着脸不看我; 他总～着父母做坏事❸〔**～补**〕〈趋〉看见我来了, 他故意❹把脸～过去〔**状～**〕立刻～过脸去; 总～着我; 常～着他

1. good deed; good turn **2.** malicious remarks; vicious talk **3.** evil deed **4.** intentionally; on purpose

bèn 奔 go straight; head for〔**～宾**〕〈名〉他们从这儿直❶～上海〔**～补**〕〈结〉～到火车站眼看着❷车开了; ～往国外去了〔**状～**〕直～; 朝前❸～〔**习用**〕各～前程❹

1. directly; straight **2.** watch helplessly **3.** ahead **4.** each pursues his own course

bī 逼 force; compel≃逼迫〔**主～**〕〈名〉寒气❶～人; 形势❷～人; 目光❸～人〔**～宾**〕〈名〉～人; ～债❹; 对犯人❺不要～口供❻〈代〉～我说出来; ～他承认错误❼〔**～补**〕〈结〉快把人～死了; ～疯❽了; 把我～糊涂❾了; 都把人～成精神病❿了; ～到不能忍受⓫的程度〈趋〉我的这点本事⓬是～出来的; 她的口供是～出来的; 他们～起人来可真利害; 天都这么晚了, 你把他～到哪儿去啊!〈程〉～得他走投无路⓭; ～得他家破人亡⓮; 你逼人～得太利害了; ～得很紧⓯; ～得真凶⓰〈时〉～了半天, 什么口供也没得着(zháo)〈量〉～了我好几次〔**状～**〕直⓱～; 一个劲儿地～; 用各种办法～; 咄咄⓲～人; 步步紧⓳～; 被～逃走⓴〔**习用**〕～上梁山㉑

1. cold air **2.** the situation **3.**

sight; vision; view 4. debt 5. prisoner; convict 6. a statement made by the accused under examination 7. admit one's mistake 8. mad 9. confused; muddled; bewildered 10. mental disease 11. unbearable 12. ability; skill; capability 13. left him no way out 14. with one's family broken up, some gone away, some dead 15. urgent; pressing 16. terrible; fearful 17. directly; straight 18. overbearing; aggressive 19. press on at every stage 20. escaped 21. be driven to revolt; be forced to do sth. desperate

bǐ 比 ① compete; match ≅ 比赛；较量〔~宾〕〈名〉~数量❶；~速度❷；~干劲❸；~耐力❹；~工作效率❺；~腕❻力；~年龄❼大小；~产量❽高低；~~高矮；~快慢；~厚薄❾；~阔气❿〈动〉跟人家~着花钱〈形〉~先进⓫〈主-谓〉~谁跑得快；~谁力气大〔~补〕〈结〉~输⓬了；~赢⓭了〈趋〉我们一定要跟他们~出个高低来；他暗中❶跟我~起来了，她的身体跟过去~起来，好多了，我跟她~起来可差⓯远了〈可〉我们大家都~不上她，我哪一点都~不过他〈时〉~了半天不分胜负⓰〈量〉咱们两个人~一下儿；我跟他~过一次〔状~〕终于~过他了；暗中~；跟谁~？和他们相~；从各方面~；逐项⓱~

1. quantity 2. speed; velocity 3. vigor; drive, enthusiasm 4. endurance; staying power, stamina 5. efficiency 6. wrist 7. age 8. output 9. thickness 10. wealth 11. advanced 12. lose; be beaten; be defeated 13. win; gain 14. secretly; in secret 15. fall short of 16. victory or defeat; success or failure 17. one item after another; item by item

② gesticulate ≅ 比画〔~宾〕〈名〉他用两个手指~了一个"八"字；他用手~了~孩子的高度〔~补〕〈结〉~大了；~薄❶了；~窄❷了〈趋〉用两只手把大小~出来了〈程〉~得不对；~得不准❸；~得太高了〈可〉我~不上来，他有多高〈时〉她用手~了半天，我也不明白她的意思〈量〉你用手~一下儿，我们就知道有多大了〔状~〕马马虎虎❹地~；随便❺~一~

1. thin 2. narrow 3. not accurate 4. careless; casual 5. casually, at random

③ copy; model〔~宾〕〈名〉~着旧衣服裁❶；~着纸样子❷裁；这双鞋是~着脚的大小买的；~着尺子画直线〔~补〕〈结〉~斜了，没~直〈趋〉~来~去也不敢剪❸〈程〉~得对不对？~得不准❹，所以没裁好〈可〉把纸样子铺❺在平一点儿的地方比，才~得好；这样比，~不准〈时〉~了半天，结果还是裁小了〈量〉~一下儿看看够不够〔状~〕好好~~；细心点❻儿~〔习用〕~上不足，~下有余❼

1. cut (paper, cloth, etc) 2. pattern 3. cut out (a garment) 4. not accurate 5. spread; extend; unfold 6. carefully; attentively 7. fall short of the best but be better than the worst; can pass muster

bǐjiào 比较 compare
〔～宾〕〈名〉～了几种方法，还是这种办法简便❶〔～补〕〈结〉～过了〈趋〉老王和老李～起来，还是老王高一点；两块布放在一起就～出好坏来了〈可〉我～不出来哪个新哪个旧〈时〉～了半天也不知道到底是哪个好哪个不好〈量〉应该把译文❷和原文❸～一下儿〔状～〕跟什么～？跟谁相～？仔细❹～；认真～；反复～

1. simple and convenient 2. translated text 3. original text 4. carefully

bǐrú 比如 for example; say; suppose ≅ 譬如
〔～宾〕〈代〉有人记生词记得非常快，～你就是这样〈动〉有些问题已经做出了决定❶，～招收❷多少学生，分几个班，开设❸哪几门课等等；我们学习一些东西必须实际❹去做，～学游泳一定要跳下水去练习才能学会

1. make a decision 2. recruit; take in 3. offer (a course in college, etc.) 4. practically; realistically

bǐsài 比赛 contest; compete; match ≅ 赛
〔主～〕〈名〉我们两个人～，好不好？〔～宾〕〈名〉～足球；～象棋❶；～射击❷〔～补〕〈结〉～输了；～赢❹了；跟他～过了〈趋〉这场球～下来，衣服都湿透❺了〈可〉主力队员❻病了，今天还～得了(liǎo)吗？〈时〉～了一下午〈量〉～过好几次了〔状～〕跟谁～？在体育馆～；经常～；第一次～；照常❼～；连续❽～

1. (Chinese) chess 2. shooting 3. be defeated; be beaten; lose 4. win; gain 5. wet through; drenched 6. top players of a team 7. as usual; usually 8. in succession; in a row; running

bì 闭 shut; close
〔～宾〕〈名〉～眼；～嘴〔～补〕〈结〉～上眼睛〈趋〉她把嘴～起来，一句话也不说〈程〉眼睛～得很紧〈可〉他的牙露❶在外边，嘴老～不上；她不停地❷说话，嘴一会儿也～不～〈时〉～了半天眼，也没睡着(zháo)；睡不着(zháo)，～一会儿眼也是休息〈量〉请你～一下儿嘴，别说了〔状～〕使劲儿～着；赶快～上；幕徐徐地❸～上了〔习用〕～门羹❹

1. reveal; show 2. ceaselessly; incessantly 3. slowly; gently 4. slam the door in sb.'s face

bì 避 avoid; evade ≅ 躲
〔～宾〕〈名〉～风；～雨；～难❶；～嫌疑❷；～～风险❸〔～补〕〈结〉～开了一场灾难❹；～过了一次风险〈程〉这场雨～得很及时❺，

衣服一点儿也没湿❻〈可〉雨越下越大，房檐❼下已经避不了(liǎo)雨了，快换个地方吧；想避嫌疑也～不开〈时〉～了一会儿，雨就不下了〈量〉在那个小亭子❽里～过一次雨；你应该～一下儿嫌疑〔**状**～〕先～～风再走；暂时❾～；赶快～一～〔**习用**〕～风港❿

1. calamity; disaster 2. suspicion 3. risk; hazard 4. calamity; disaster 5. in time 6. wet 7. eaves 8. pavilion; kiosk 9. for the moment 10. haven; harbour — place of safety or rest

bìmiǎn 避免 avoid; refrain from; avert ≅ 防止〔～**宾**〕〈名〉～了一场事故❶；～了一场灾难❷〈动〉～伤亡❸；～犯错误❹〔～**补**〕〈可〉错误是谁也～不了(liǎo)的〔**状**～〕尽量❺～；很难～；难以❻～

1. accident 2. calamity; disaster 3. injuries and deaths; casualties 4. commit a mistake 5. as far as possible; to the best of one's ability 6. difficult to

biān 编 plait; weave ≅ 编织〔～**宾**〕〈名〉～小辫儿❶；～草帽；～席子❷；～筐❸〔～**补**〕〈结〉辫子～松点儿；草帽～好了；草筐～完了；花纹❹～错了〈趋〉头发太长了，快～起小辫儿来吧；一会儿的工夫❺就～出一个小筐来〈程〉～得真快；～得非常熟练❻；～得真不错；～得挺结实❼〈可〉头发太短，还～不上

辫子；用这种草～得了(liǎo)草帽吗？三个小时～得完一张席子吗？这种图案我～不上来〈时〉再～一会儿〈量〉～一下儿看看对不对〔**状**～〕真难～；手工❽～；精心❾～；来回❿～

1. plait, pigtail 2. mat 3. basket 4. decorative pattern; figure 5. time 6. skilled; practised 7. very solid 8. by hand 9. meticulously; elaborately 10. to and fro

② organize; group; arrange ≅ 编排〔～**宾**〕〈名〉～班；～组；～号码〔～**补**〕〈结〉班～好了；小组～完了；号码～错了；把他～在我们班上；～成三个组；书太多了，应该～上号码〈趋〉把他～到初级❶班去了〈程〉班～得太大了；号码儿～得乱七八糟❷〈可〉人太少～不了(liǎo)两个班〔**状**～〕按❸年龄❹～；按特长❺～；按程度❻～；多～几个班；重新～

1. elementary; primary 2. in a mess; confused 3. according to; in accordance with; on the basis of 4. age 5. speciality; strong point 6. level; degree

③ edit; compile ≅ 编辑〔～**宾**〕〈名〉～教材❶；～字典；～杂志；～报纸〔～**补**〕〈结〉教材还没～完呢〈趋〉词典～出来了吗？这个词也应该～进去；他们开始～起报纸来了〈程〉教材～得很好；词典～得很有特色❷；课本～得太深了；～得真快；～得很乱〈可〉时间太短～不出来；～得完～不完？〈时〉还要再～一个时期❸才

能完〈量〉～过好几次教材了〔状～〕合❹～；重新～；在原来的基础❺上～；希望早点～出来；认真～

1. teaching material **2.** characteristic; distinguishing feature **3.** a period of time **4.** jointly **5.** original basis

④ write; compose ≃ 创作；写〔**～宾**〕〈名〉～剧本❶；～儿歌❷；～故事〔**～补**〕〈结〉～完了；～成童话❸〈趋〉继续～下去；把他的事迹❹都～进剧本里去了；你从什么时候开始～起电影剧本来了？〈程〉～得很有意思❺；～得不好〈可〉什么故事我也～不出来〔**状～**〕多～点儿；给孩子们～；早点～出来

1. drama; play **2.** children's song **3.** fairy tales **4.** deed; achievement **5.** interesting

biàn 变 change; become different ≃ 变化；改变〔**主～**〕〈名〉天气～了；人～了；地方～了；情况～了；样子～了；脾气❶～了；性格❷～了；颜色～了；味道❸～了；声音～了；环境❹～了；态度❺～了；方向❻～了；季节❼～了；脸色～了；看法❽～了；想法❾～了；兴趣❿～了〔**～宾**〕〈名〉他会～魔术⓫；这间屋子整理⓬以后完全～了样儿〔**～补**〕〈结〉那个孩子～好了，肯用功学习了；脾气～坏了；颜色～浅⓭了；声音～粗⓮了；这条马路～宽⓯了；她差点儿～成疯子⓰；这里已经～成一个工业城市了；两年不见他都～成大人了；他的身体～结实⓱了〈趋〉魔术师⓲从箱子⓳里～出来好几只鸽子⓴〈程〉几年不见，这个人～得太多了；他的性格～得更古怪㉑了；～得爱哭了；～得能干㉒了；～得胆小㉓了〈可〉这个失足㉔青年还～得好吗？我也会变魔术，就是～不好，经常是变出来就～不回去了〈量〉坐累了～一下姿势就好了〔**状～**〕忽然～了；逐渐㉕～；完全～了；已经～了

1. temper **2.** character **3.** taste; flavour **4.** surrounding **5.** attitude **6.** direction **7.** season **8.** view **9.** idea; opinion; what one has in mind **10.** interest **11.** magic **12.** put in order; arrange **13.** light (colour) **14.** gruff; husky **15.** wide **16.** madman **17.** strong **18.** magician **19.** chest; trunk **20.** pigeon **21.** strange; odd; queer **22.** competent; able **23.** timid; cowardly **24.** take a wrong step in life **25.** gradually

biànbié 辨别 differentiate; distinguish ; discriminate ≃ 识别〔**～宾**〕〈名〉他是色盲❶不能～颜色；他耳朵不灵❷，～音❸的能力❹很差❺；～好坏；～是非❻；～真假；～美丑；～对错〔**～补**〕〈结〉～清楚了吗？〈趋〉这两张画差不多，真假不容易～出来；这对孪生姐妹❼长得太象了，外人～起来很困难；你能～出来是什么味儿❽吗？你能～出来声音是从哪个方向来的吗？〈程〉这两个

音她～得很清楚〈可〉这个人连好坏都～不出来〈时〉我们～了半天，也没弄清这些古玩❾是原来❿的还是仿造⓫的〈量〉请专家⓬给～一下儿就知道真伪⓭了〔状～〕一下子就～出来了；用科学方法⓮～；难以～；简直⓯～不出来；仔细⓰～

1. colour blind 2. not sharp 3. sound 4. ability; capacity 5. poor 6. right and wrong 7. twin sisters 8. smell 9. antique; curio 10. original 11. imitation; replica; copy 12. expert; specialist 13. true and false 14. scientific method 15. simply; at all 16. carefully

biànrèn 辨认 identify; recognize 〔～宾〕〈名〉～字迹❶；～笔迹❷；～面貌❸；～指纹❹；～像片；～人〔～补〕〈结〉～对了；～错了〈趋〉～出来了〈可〉这是谁的字迹，你～得出来～不出来？没受❺过专门❻训练❼的人～不了(liǎo)指纹；这张照片太旧了；连人的面貌都～不清了〈时〉～了半天才看出来是谁〈量〉那张纸上的字迹，每个人都～了一次〔状～〕不容易～；难以～；一下子就～了

1. handwriting 2. a person's handwriting 3. face; features 4. loops and whorls on a finger; finger-print 5. receive 6. special; specialized 7. train, drill

biāo 标 put a mark; lay or label on ≅ 画，记〔～宾〕〈名〉这些货物❶还没～价钱❷；～个号码❸；在书上～了好几个记号❹；～了一大堆❺各式各样❻的符号❼〔～补〕〈结〉～上个记号；～明价钱，把号码～错了；把记号～在左边，记号都～乱❽了〈趋〉价钱还没～出来呢〈程〉记号～得很清楚；符号～得很明确❾〈量〉～一下儿记号，就好了〔状～〕用红笔～

1. goods 2. price 3. number 4. mark 5. a lot of 6. all sorts of 7. symbol; mark 8. in disorder; confused 9. clear and definite

biǎo 表 show; express ≅ 表示〔～宾〕〈名〉～～心意❶；他总不～态❷〈动〉～同情❸〔～补〕〈结〉～明态度❹〈量〉只是～一下儿心意〔状～〕深❺～同情；只是～～心意；向他～态

1. regard; kindly feelings 2. (make known) one's position 3. sympathy 4. attitude; position 5. deeply

biǎodá 表达 express; convey ≅ 表示〔～宾〕〈名〉～心情❶；～意思，～感情❷〔～补〕〈结〉意思没～清楚〈趋〉感情很好地～出来了〈程〉意思～得十分清楚；～得不明确❸〈可〉我的意思用简单❹几句话是～不清楚的；他学问❺不少，就是～不出来〈时〉～了半天也没表达清楚〔状～〕难以❻～；清楚地～；明确地～；不能用言语❼～

1. state of mind; mood 2. feeling; sentiment 3. clear and definite 4.

simple **5.** knowledge; learning **6.** difficult to **7.** in language

biǎojué 表决 decide by vote; vote 〔**～补**〕〈结〉～完了〈量〉一共～了三次〔**状～**〕用无记名投票❶的方式❷～；口头❸～；重新～；再一次～

1. by secret ballot; in secret voting **2.** way **3.** orally

biǎomíng 表明 make known; make clear; state clearly 〔**主～**〕〈名〉事实❶～；你的态度❷～；目前的形势❸～；种种迹象❹～；声音～；神态❺～〔**～宾**〕〈名〉～立场❻；～态度；～身份❼；～决心❽；～观点❾〔**状～**〕由他的态度～；由她的神情❿～；充分⓫～；公开⓬～；再次～

1. fact **2.** position; attitude **3.** the present situation **4.** sign; indication **5.** expression; manner **6.** position **7.** status; identity **8.** determination **9.** point of view **10.** expression; look **11.** sufficiently **12.** openly

biǎoshì 表示 show; express; indicate 〔**～宾**〕〈名〉～好感❶；～态度❷；～决心❸〈动〉～同意；～同情❹；～关怀❺；～关切❻；～支持❼；～欢迎；～祝贺❽；～慰问❾；～感谢；～赞许❿；～一定要努力工作；～愿意帮助我学习；～一定要按时⓫完成任务〈形〉～愤慨⓬；～难过⓭；～不满⓮；～满意⓯；～友好⓰〈主－谓〉～他生活很富裕⓱〔**～补**〕〈趋〉今天没～出不高兴来；从他的话里已经～出不满意来了〈程〉～得很清楚；～得很明确⓲〈量〉～过很多次了；～一下儿〔**状～**〕积极⓳～支持；坚决⓴～同意；诚恳地㉑～；衷心㉒～；点头～；用什么方式㉓～？用眼睛～；用手势㉔～；从来没～过；三番五次地～㉕

1. good opinion; favourable impression **2.** attitude **3.** determination **4.** sympathize with **5.** show loving care for **6.** be deeply concerned; show one's concern over **7.** support; back **8.** congratulate **9.** express sympathy and solicitude for; extend one's regards to; convey greetings to **10.** praise; speak favourably of **11.** on time **12.** indignation **13.** feel sorry; be grieved **14.** dissatisfied; resentful; discontented **15.** satisfied **16.** friendly **17.** rich; well-to-do; well-off **18.** clear and definite **19.** actively **20.** resolutely **21.** sincerely **22.** wholeheartedly; cordially **23.** way; fashion; style **24.** gesture **25.** over and over again

biǎoxiàn 表现 display; manifest; show 〔**～宾**〕〈名〉～了一种勇敢❶的精神❷；～了一种大无畏❸的精神；～了个人的优秀品质❹〈代〉她爱～自己〔**～补**〕〈结〉～出了她的性格；～出满不在乎❺的神态❻；～出很大方❼的样子；～出坚强的毅力❽；～出

极大的忍耐性❾〈趋〉他的聪明完全~出来了〈程〉~得很好; ~得很镇静; ~得很愚蠢❿; ~得非常积极⓫; 得很勇敢; ~得十分大方; ~得非常坚强〈可〉他的才智⓬在这里~不出来〔**状~**〕好(hào)~; 充分⓭~出来了; 故意⓮~; 极力⓯~; 较好地~出来了

1. courageous 2. spirit 3. dauntless; utterly fearless; indomitable 4. fine qualities 5. not worry at all; not care in the least 6. expression; manner 7. natural and posed; easy; unaffected 8. strong will 9. great endurance 10. stupid; foolish; silly 11. active; energetic; vigorous 12. ability and wisdom 13. fully; abundantly 14. intentionally; on purpose 15. with all one's might

biǎoyǎn 表演 perform; act; play〔**~宾**〕〈名〉~气功❶; ~舞蹈❷; ~口技❸; ~杂技❹; ~魔术❺; ~体操❻; ~节目❼; ~骑术❽〈动〉~跳伞❾; ~射击❿; ~跳水⓫〔**~补**〕〈结〉还没完呢; 这次~成功了; 上次~失败了〈趋〉~出一个精采⓬的动作⓭来〈程〉难道你~得还不够吗? ~得不成功; ~得很精采; ~得很出色⓮; ~得非常有意思; ~得不太熟练⓯〈时〉节目整整⓰~了一个晚上〈量〉~了那么多次你都没看; 不信再给你~一下儿〔**状~**〕在台上~; 为外宾⓱~; 成功地~; 一连~了三次

1. a system of deep breathing exercises 2. dancing 3. vocal mimicry; vocal imitation 4. acrobatics 5. magic 6. gymnastics 7. show; programme 8. equestrian skill; horsemanship 9. parachute jumping 10. shooting 11. diving 12. brilliant; splendid; wonderful 13. movement; motion; action 14. outstanding; remarkable 15. skilful 16. whole; full 17. for foreign guests

biǎoyáng 表扬 praise; commend〔**~宾**〕〈名〉~好人好事❶; ~优秀❷运动员❸; ~模范教师; ~工作有成绩的人; ~勤奋学习的人〔**~补**〕〈结〉~对了; ~错了〈程〉~得很及时〈量〉~了很多次; ~一下儿〔**状~**〕好好~~他; 当众❹~; 口头❺~; 再~; 经常~; 被~

1. good people and good deeds; fine people and fine deeds 2. outstanding; excellent 3. sportsman or sportswoman; athlete; player 4. before the public 5. orally

biē 憋 ① suppress; hold back〔**~宾**〕〈名〉她心里不痛快❶, ~着一口气❷出不来; ~了一肚子话❸, 没地方去说; 为那件事, 我~了一肚子火儿❹〔**~补**〕〈结〉这道难题真把我~住了〈趋〉有话就说, 不然❺会~出病来的〈程〉~得真难受❻; ~得受不了❼(liǎo)了; 这口气~得真长〈可〉她什么话也~不住❽〈时〉这句话~了好几天才说出来〔**状~**〕简直❾~不

住了；已经~了不少时候了

1. feel unhappy 2. 3. have pent-up grievances 4. be filled with pent-up anger 5. otherwise 6. feel unwell 7. unbearable 8. be unable to hold oneself back; can't contain oneself 9. simply; at all

② suffocate; feel oppressed ≌ 闷〔~补〕〈结〉这么闷热❶也不下点儿雨，都快把人~死了；在家里养了半年病，简直❷要把她~死；可把他~坏了；真把他~急❸了〈程〉~得真难受❹；气压❺太低~得透不过气来❻；心里~得慌❼〈时〉在家里~了一年多〔状~〕成天❽~在家里，整整❾~了一个月

1. hot and suffocating; sultry; muggy 2. simply; really 3. irritated 4. feel unwell 5. atmospheric pressure 6. feel suffocated 7. feel very much oppressed 8. all day long 9. whole

bié 别 fasten with a pin or clip 〔~宾〕〈名〉~校徽❶；~纪念章❷；~别针❸；~大头针❹；~胸针❺；~钢笔〔~补〕〈结〉把纪念章~上了；~住，别掉了；胸针~歪❻了；校徽~斜❼了；在衣领❽上〈趋〉~上去吧〈程〉~得不结实❾，一碰❿就掉了；~得太高了〈可〉针坏了，~不了(liǎo)了；我~不上，你帮我别吧〈时〉只~了一晚上就丢了〈量〉给我~一下儿〔状~〕别针太秃⓫了，真不好~；替我~；重

新~一下儿

1. school badge 2. souvenir badge 3. safety pin 4. pin 5. brooth 6. 7. oblique; slant 8. collar 9. not solid 10. touch; bump 11. blunt

bìng 病 fall ill 〔~补〕〈结〉他~倒❶(dǎo)了〈程〉~得很利害❷；~得起不来床了；~得吃不下东西去；~得快要死了〈可〉他身体真好，怎么折腾❸都~不了(liǎo)〈时〉~了好几个月才好；~了半年多〈量〉这个月就~了两次；~了一场〔状~〕突然~了；经常~；从来不~

1. be down with an illness; be laid up 2. serious 3. cause physical or mental suffering; get sb. down

bō 拨 ①move with hand, foot, stick; turn; stir; poke; etc.〔~宾〕〈名〉~钟；~电话号码〔补~〕〈结〉电话号码~错了；把时间~到11点〈趋〉把指针❶~过来〈程〉时间~得不对〈可〉表针怎么~不动了〈量〉表针~了两圈❷〔状~〕轻点儿~；顺着时针方向❸~；别来回❹乱❺~

1. hand (of a clock) 2. circle 3. clockwise 4. to and fro 5. at random; in confusion

② set aside; assign; allocate ≌ 调拨〔~宾〕〈名〉~款❶；~了一批货❷〔~补〕〈结〉款~多了〈趋〉~出两间屋子来就够了；把她~到我们班来了〈量〉从他手里

~过一次款〔**状~**〕多~点儿；往哪儿~？暂时❸~

1. fund; a sum of money 2. goods 3. temporarily; for the moment

bō 播 ① sow; seed ≅ 撒〔**~宾**〕〈名〉~种❶〔**~补**〕〈结〉种子全部~完了吗？〈趋〉种子已经~到地里❷去了〈程〉~得很匀❸；~得很及时❹〈可〉一上午~得完~不完？〔**状~**〕用拖拉机❺~

1. seed 2. field 3. even 4. in time 5. tractor

② broadcast; transmit ≅ 广播；播送〔**~补**〕〈结〉今天的节目❶全部~完了；天气预报❷已经~过了；电台❸最近~出了很多新歌曲❹〈趋〉新闻❺已经~过了〈程〉这个广播员❻播音~得最清楚〈可〉这篇稿子❼一个小时也~不完〈时〉那个广告整整~了十分钟〈量〉这首歌~过无数次❽了；天气预报一天~几回？〔**状~**〕按时❾~；经常；重新；偶尔❿~

1. programme 2. weather forecast 3. broadcasting station 4. new songs 5. news in brief 6. announcer; broadcaster 7. manuscript 8. innumerable; countless 9. on time 10. occasionally; once in a while

bódòu 搏斗 wrestle; fight; combat; struggle 〔**~补**〕〈趋〉那两个人在那里~起来了〈时〉两个人~了三个小时〈量〉~过一次〔**状**

~〕跟坏人~；跟生死❶~；与风浪❷~；在水里~；在悬崖❸上~；猛烈地❹~

1. life and death 2. winds and waves 3. precipice 4. fiercely; violently

bǔ 补 ① mend; patch; repair ≅ 缝〔**~宾**〕〈名〉~衣服；~鞋；~袜子❶；~车胎❷；~了一条破裤子❸；~鱼网❹〔**~补**〕〈结〉袜子~好了；衣服~完了；鞋~结实❺了吗？布又~反❻了〈趋〉把这块布~上去吧；他又自己~起车胎来了〈程〉~得真快；~得非常结实；~得太难看了；~得歪歪扭扭的❼〈可〉~得好~不好？时间这么短怎么能~得完呢？〈时〉你怎么~了那么半天还没补上啊？再~一会儿，就补好了〈量〉这件衣服~过好几次了；我帮你~一下儿吧〔**状~**〕不好~；太难~了；好容易~上了；耐心地❽~；重新~；再~一块；用布~；用皮❾~；亲手~；一针一线地~；辛辛苦苦地❿~

1. sock 2. tyre 3. ragged trousers 4. fishing net 5. solid; strong 6. in reverse; inside out 7. crooked; askew; shapeless and twisted 8. patiently 9. leather 10. take a lot of trouble; work laboriously

② fill; supply; make up for ≅ 填补〔**~宾**〕〈名〉~窟窿❶；~漏洞❷；~牙；~课；~票；~两个字〔**~补**〕〈结〉牙~好了；课都~上了吗？〈趋〉~进三个字去；把这句话~上去，意思❸就清楚

了〈程〉牙～得很好〈可〉这门课我可～不了(liǎo)〈时〉给他～了一个星期的课〈量〉张医生给我～过一次牙〔状～〕在宿舍～课；大夫给病人～牙；赶快～；及时～

1. hole; opening 2. flaw; hole; loopholes 3. meaning

③ nourish ≅ 补养〔～宾〕〈名〉～血❶；～身体；～脑❷；～肾❸〔～补〕〈可〉吃什么好东西，身体也～不上了〔状～〕用什么～？好好～一一

1. blood 2. brain 3. kidney

bùrú 不如 be not as good as 〔～宾〕〈名〉我现在的身体～十年前了〈代〉我～他〈动〉看电影～在家看电视〈主－谓〉他家～我家宽敞❶；我去～他去好；我们学校～他们学校大；我的字～她写得好〔状～〕真～；还～；简直❷～；就是～；总是～

1. spacious; commodious; roomy 2. simply; at all

bùzhǐ 不止 ① not to stop at; keep on ≅ 不停〔主～〕〈动〉大笑～；咳嗽❶～；流血❷～；腹泻❸～；疼痛❹～

1. cough 2. shed blood 3. diarrhoea 4. pain; ache; sore

②exceed ≅ 超过；↔不足；不够；不到〔～宾〕〈名〉看样子现在～4点了；每课书的生词～20个；礼堂里的座位～一千个；治❶高血压❷的药～这些〈主－谓〉我们班里～我一个人会拉小提琴❸；我们小组～我一个人戴眼镜❹〔～补〕〈时〉我进来～10分钟了〈量〉那个问题我提❺过～一次了；这个话剧我看过～两遍了〔状～〕恐怕❻～；已经～；大概～；绝对❼～；也许～

1. treat; cure 2. high blood pressure 3. play the violin 4. wear glasses 5. raise; put forward 6. perhaps; may be 7. absolutely

bùzhì 布置 fix up; arrange; decorate〔～宾〕〈名〉～会场❶；～教室；～新房❷；～橱窗❸；～展览室；～会议大厅❹；～礼堂；～阅览室〔～补〕〈结〉橱窗～晚了，明天就是春节了，今天还没～完；～早了也不行，到时候就不新鲜❺了〈趋〉～起来了〈程〉房间～得很雅致❻；～得有点儿俗气❼；大厅～得非常庄严❽〈可〉两个橱窗一个小时～得完吗?〈时〉～了好几天才布置完〈量〉好好～一下儿吧；～过两次了〔状～〕重新～；赶紧❾～；大家一起～；精心❿～

1. meeting-place; conference hall 2. bridal chamber 3. show window 4. assembly hall; conference hall 5. fresh 6. tasteful; refined 7. vulgar; in poor taste 8. solemn 9. quickly 10. meticulously

C

cā 擦 ① rub ≅ 划〔~宾〕〈名〉~了一根火柴❶〔~补〕〈结〉摔了一交，把腿~破❷了；把膝盖❸~流血了；手上~掉了一层皮〈时〉火柴~了半天也没擦着(zháo)〈量〉~了好几下儿才擦着(zháo)〔状~〕一下子就~着(zháo)了；一根接一根地~；一连❹~了三根；怪不得❺~不着(zháo)呢，原来火柴潮❻了

1. match 2. cut 3. knee 4. in succession; in a row 5. no wonder; so that's why 6. wet

② wipe ≅ 抹〔~宾〕〈名〉桌子；~地板；~黑板；~玻璃；~机器；~枪；~眼镜；~皮鞋；~汗；~眼泪；~鼻涕❶；~手；~脸；~车〔~补〕〈结〉把桌子~干净；她眼泪还没~干，又笑了；忙得他手还没~干，就跑出去了；快把脸上的水(汗)~掉吧；抹布❷不干净，把玻璃都~花了〈趋〉黑板上的字可以~掉了〈程〉汽车~得真干净〈可〉门把手❸锈❹得太利害，都~不亮了；厨房的玻璃上有油，~不干净〈时〉~了一个多小时还没擦完；还得(děi)再~多少时候？再~一会儿就行了〈量〉一天~三遍地；再用干布~一遍就可以了〔状~〕小心点儿~；快些~；轻轻地~；真难~；先别~；经常~；每天~；认真地~；一边唱歌一边~；凑凑合合地❺~；算我白~❻了

1. nasal mucus, snivel 2. rag (to wipe things with) 3. handle (of a door) 4. become rusty 5. make do 6. in vain; for nothing

③ spread on; put on ≅ 搽; 抹〔~宾〕〈名〉~粉；~头油❶；~香水❷；~肥皂❸；~口红❹；~药膏❺；~药水❻；~鞋油❼〔~补〕〈结〉~上点儿粉；手上~满了药〈趋〉这种药水刚~上去有点疼，过一会儿就好了〈程〉粉~得太多了；~得薄一点儿就好了〈可〉~不惯❽这种牌子❾的香水〈时〉一瓶头油~了半年，还没擦完〈量〉~一下儿试试〔状~〕经常~；从来不~口红；厚厚地~了一脸粉；往头上~

1. hair oil; pomade 2. perfume 3. soap 4. lipstick 5. ointment 6. liquid medicine 7. shoe polish (cream) 8. cannot get used to 9. brand

④ pass very close to; almost touching; shave ≅ 掠过〔~宾〕〈名〉~肩而过❶；燕子❷~着地面飞过；飞机~过山顶❸；海鸥❹~过江面❺〔~补〕〈趋〉海鸥从江面上~过去了；飞机从屋顶上

~过去了〔状~〕很快地~过去了；低低地~着水面；嗖地一声❻~过去了〔习用〕~胭脂抹粉儿❼

1. brush past sb. 2. swallow 3. the plane shaved the hilltops 4. sea gull 5. surface (of river) 6. whiz 7. apply powder and paint (or rouge and powder)

cāi 猜 guess; conjecture ≅ 猜测；猜想〔~宾〕<名>~谜语❶；~灯谜❷；~字谜❸ <主-谓>你~(~)我是谁？你~(~)他有多大岁数❹？你~(~)我们两个谁大；你~(~)这件衣服多少钱；你~(~)刚才谁来了；你~(~)这本字典是在哪儿买的；你~(~)他有什么心事❺〔~补〕<结>~对了；~错了；让你~着(zháo)❻了<趋>~出来了吗？<程>~得不对；~得真快；~得很准❼；~得一点也不错<可>~得着(zháo)~不着(zháo)？我怎么猜也~不对；~不出来；我~不透❽她话里的意思<时>~了半天才猜出来<量>~了三次都没猜对〔状~〕这个谜语太难了，你准~不着(zháo)；别瞎❾~了；再~一~；一下子就~出来了；怎么~也猜不着(zháo)；故意❿~错；实在⓫~不着(zháo)了

1. riddle 2. riddles written on lanterns 3. a riddle about a character or word 4. age; years 5. sth. weighing on one's mind; worry 6. (have guessed) right 7. accurate 8. not thoroughly 9. groundlessly; foolishly 10. intentionally; on purpose 11. indeed; really; honestly

cái 裁 ① cut (paper, cloth, etc) into parts ≅ 剪；剪裁〔~宾〕<名>~衣服；她不会~童装❶〔~补〕<结>~衣服~完了吗？尺寸❷~错了；裤子~长了；衣服~坏了<趋>她一会儿的工夫就~出两条短裤❸来了<程>姐姐裁衣服~得快极了<可>这块料子~不了(liǎo)（~不出来）两件连衣裙；怕~不好<时>拿到裁缝店❹去裁，得(děi)~半个月；自己要是会裁，~十分钟就完了<量>他自己~过很多次衣服〔状~〕差点儿❺~错了；万一❻~坏了，我可赔❼不起；比着❽旧衣服~；按量好的尺寸~；特殊体型❾的比较难~；机器~；手工❿~；亲手⓫~；一下子就~了三件

1. children's wear (clothing) 2. size 3. shorts 4. tailor's 5. nearly; almost 6. just in case; if by any chance 7. compensate 8. model after; copy 9. particular type of build or figure 10. by hand 11. personally

② reduce; cut down ≅ 裁减〔~宾〕<名>银行❶又~了一批❷人；~军❸〔~补〕<结>他被~掉了<程>这次裁人~得太多了〔状~〕一共~了10个人；统统❹~掉了；不得已❺~了几个人

1. bank 2. a number of 3. disarmament 4. all; completely; entirely 5. have no choice but to; cannot but; have to

cǎi 采 ① pick; pluck ≅ 摘〔~宾〕〈名〉~茶；~珍珠❶；蜜蜂~蜜；~了一筐❷草药❸〔~补〕〈时〉那位老茶农❹~了一辈子茶，经验❺可丰富了〈量〉记者❻跟药农一起在山上~过一次药〔状~〕工蜂❼终生~蜜；在山上~药，辛辛苦苦地~；飞来飞去地~蜜；在百花丛❽中~；一筐一筐地~

1. pearl 2. basket 3. medicinal herbs 4. old tea grower 5. experience 6. correspondent; journalist 7. worker (bee) 8. flowering shrubs; flowers in clusters

② extract; mine ≅ 开采〔~宾〕〈名〉~矿❶；~煤❷；~油❸〔~补〕〈结〉这个矿的煤都快~光了〈可〉煤~得完吗？〈时〉还能~多少年；~了一百多年〔状~〕一直~；不断地❹~；用先进❺的方法~

1. mine 2. coal 3. oil; petroleum 4. incessantly 5. advanced

cǎiqǔ 采取 adopt; take ≅ 采纳；采用〔~宾〕〈名〉~行动❶；~紧急措施❷；~观望态度❸；~强制手段❹；~攻势❺；~自学❻的方式❼〈形〉~主动❽〔状~〕认真❾~；主动~；一致❿~；一向⓫~；仍旧⓬~；始终⓭~；故意~；何不~？究竟⓮~什么态度？完全~

1. action 2. emergency measures 3. a wait-and-see attitude 4. compulsory means; coercive measure 5. offensive 6. study on one's own; study independently 7. form; way 8. on one's own accord 9. seriously; conscientiously 10. unanimously 11. always 12. still; yet 13. from beginning to end 14. after all

cǎiyòng 采用 adopt; use; employ ≅ 采取；采纳〔~宾〕〈名〉~新技术❶；~新式武器❷；~有效的办法❸；~简便的方法❹〔状~〕从今年开始~；仍旧❺~；逐渐❻~

1. new techniques 2. modern weapons 3. effective measures 4. a simple and convenient method 5. still; yet 6. gradually

cǎi 踩 step on; trample〔~宾〕〈名〉对不起，~了您的脚；没注意~了一脚泥❶；~了一脚水；有机会❷就~人〔~补〕〈结〉把地毯❸~脏了；那个大胖子把我的脚都~肿❹了；把火柴盒~扁❺了；~坏了；~裂❻了；~在脚底下了〈趋〉~进水里去了；~到烂泥里去了〈程〉脚~得真疼，这一下儿~得很重〈量〉为了制止❼我再继续说下去，她在桌子底下~了我一下儿〔状~〕不是故意❽~的；正好~在石子上了；偏偏❾~我那只受伤的脚〔习用〕脚~两只船❿

1. mud 2. chance; 3. carpet; rug 4. swelling; swollen 5. be crushed 6. be split; be cracked 7. prevent; stop 8. not purposely 9. as luck would have it; it so

happened that 10. straddle two boats — have a foot in either camp; sit on the fence

cānguān 参观 visit; look around〔**~宾**〕〈名〉~工厂；~学校；~医院；~幼儿园；~图书馆；~实验室❶；~名胜古迹❷〔**~补**〕〈结〉~完图书馆就走了；从上午一直~到下午〈程〉~得不仔细❸〈可〉要参观的地方太多了，两天也~不完〈时〉昨天整整~了一下午；可以多~一会儿〈量〉~过不少次；随便❹~了一下儿〔**状~**〕仔细~；认真~；多~些地方；匆匆忙忙地❺~；特地❻~；到处~；一连❼~了三天；单独❽~；集体❾~；从来没~过；走马观花地❿~

1. laboratory **2.** places of historic interest and scenic beauty; scenic spots and historical sites **3.** not carefully **4.** casually; informally **5.** hurriedly **6.** specially **7.** successively; running **8.** alone **9.** collectively **10.** look at flowers while riding on horse back — gain a superficial understanding through cursory observation

cānjiā 参加 join; attend; take part in ≃加入〔**~宾**〕〈名〉~工会❶；~舞会；~奥运会❷；~联合国大会❸；~开幕仪式❹；~结婚典礼❺；~毕业❻典礼；~竣工❼典礼；对这件事，你也~点意见吧〈动〉~讨论❽；~比赛；~谈判❾；~会谈❿；~评判⓫；~管理⓬；~运动；~试验⓭；~投票⓮；~选举⓯；~竞选⓰〔**~补**〕〈趋〉我们正在争论⓱的时候，他也~进来了；他也~起长跑⓲锻炼来了〈程〉老李参加工会~得比较晚〈时〉~了一个时期；我比她晚~了两年〈量〉他~过很多次国际⓳比赛〔**状~**〕认真~；积极~；主动⓴~；踊跃㉑~；自愿㉒~；勉强~；被迫㉓~；不得不~；准时~；特地㉔~；冒着雨~；公开~；秘密㉕~；单独㉖~；集体㉗~；大家喜气洋洋地㉘~

1. trade union **2.** the Olympic Games **3.** General Assembly of the United Nations **4.** opening ceremony **5.** marriage ceremony **6.** graduation **7.** completion **8.** discussion **9.** negotiation **10.** talks **11.** judgement (between contestants) **12.** management **13.** experiment **14.** vote **15.** election **16.** campaign for (office) **17.** dispute **18.** long-distance race **19.** international **20.** of one's own accord **21.** eagerly; enthusiastically **22.** voluntarily; of one's own free will **23.** be forced to **24.** specially **25.** secretly **26.** alone **27.** collectively **28.** radiantly

cānkǎo 参考 consult; refer to ≃参阅；参看；参见；参照〔**~宾**〕〈名〉~历史文献❶；~了很多书刊❷；~了不少有关文章；~大量的资料❸；~了大家的意见〔**状~**〕经常~；认真~；进一步~；广泛❹~；几乎~了所有的资料；无须~

1. historical documents **2.** books and periodicals **3.** a vast amount of data **4.** extensively

cáng 藏 hide; conceal≅躲藏；躲避〔～宾〕〈名〉～钱；～赃款❶；～赃物❷；～武器❸；～凶器❹；～人〔～补〕〈结〉～好了，别让人看见；你先～好了，我再去开门；～在床底下了；我刚才就～在门后边；不要把话～在肚子里〈趋〉～起来，别让他看见；快～进去，别出来；先～到壁橱❺里去吧；你把东西～到哪儿去了？〈程〉～得真快；～得谁也找不着(zháo)；～得一点儿也看不出来〈可〉柜子❻这么小，哪儿～得了(liǎo) 人啊！～得下三个人吗？狐狸尾巴❼再也～不住了；这里边儿可～不了(liǎo) 人；他～不住话〈时〉这张照片～了好几年了；你先～一会儿再出来〈量〉还是～一下儿保险❽〔状～〕分别❾～在三个地方；分散❿～；集中⓫～；不知往哪儿～；偷偷地～；一直～在皮箱里；故意⓬～起来了；幸亏⓭～起来了；究竟⓮～在哪儿？把话深深⓯地～在心里 〔习用〕捉迷～⓰；～头露尾⓱

1. money stolen **2.** stolen goods **3.** weapon; arms **4.** tool or weapon for criminal purposes **5.** a built-in wardrobe; closet **6.** cupboard **7.** fox's tail **8.** safe **9.** separately **10.** disperse; scatter; decentralize **11.** concentrate; centralize **12.** intentionally; on purpose **13.** fortunately; luckily **14.** after all; in the end **15.** deeply **16.** hide-and-seek; blindman's buff; play hide-and-seek **17.** show the tail but hide the head — tell part of the truth but not all of it

cāoxīn 操心 worry about 〔～宾〕〈名〉～自己的事；父母～孩子的事 〔～补〕〈结〉什么事都得(děi)为他～〈趋〉父母为孩子操起心来，真是没完没了❶ (liǎo)〈可〉我可操不了(liǎo) 这份心了〈时〉为孩子操了一辈子心〔状～〕请您多操点儿心；事事❷～；不必❸～；日夜～

1. without end **2.** everything **3.** there is no need; not have to

cāozòng 操纵 ①operate; control 〔～宾〕〈名〉～机器❶；～新式武器❷；～着升降机❸〔状～〕全神贯注地❹～；远距离❺～；熟练地❻～

1. machine **2.** modern weapons **3.** lift **4.** with rapt attention **5.** long-distance **6.** skilfully

② rig; manipulate≅支配；控制〔～宾〕〈名〉～市场❶；～物价❷；强国❸不应～弱国❹〔状～〕幕后❺～；暗中❻～

1. market **2.** (commodity) prices **3.** powerful nation (the strong) **4.** weak nation **5.** behind the scenes **6.** in secret, on the sly

cèyàn 测验 test 〔～宾〕〈名〉～机器的性能❶；～记忆力❷；～

技能❸；～视力❹；～耐力❺；～他有没有这种能力❻〔～补〕〈结〉～过了〈趋〉～出来了〈程〉～得真快；～得不准❼；～得不对〈可〉～得出来吗？这么多项目❽一上午也～不完〈量〉～一下儿；～过一次〔状～〕用仪器❾～；多次～；反复～；系统地❿～；定期⓫～；口头⓬～

1. function of a machine 2. the faculty of memory 3. technical ability 4. eyesight 5. endurance 6. ability 7. not accurate 8. item 9. instrument; apparatus 10. systematically 11. regularly 12. orally

chā 插 ① stick in; insert〔～宾〕〈名〉～秧❶；花瓶里～了一束紫萝兰❷；开运动会时，操场四周～了很多彩旗❸；忘了～插头❹了，所以电视显❺不出像❻来〔～补〕〈结〉秧苗全部～完了吗？花瓶里～满了花儿；笔～倒(dào)❼了；把手～在口袋里〈趋〉把笔～进笔筒❽里去了；快～进队(伍)❾里去吧；树苗～到土里去了；把桌子上的几本书都～到书架上去吧；她来晚了就把她～到第三班去了〈程〉她妹妹插秧❿～得最快；插秧～得腰酸腿疼⓫〈可〉这个花瓶儿的口儿太小，～不了(liǎo)几枝花；土太硬⓬～不进去；书架太高，这本书我～不上去；这么多秧苗一天～得完吗？〈时〉刚～一会儿，腰就直不起来⓭了〔状～〕往瓶子里～；至少⓮～两天；一齐～；一排一排地～(秧)；一片⓯一片地～；一本一本地～(书)；别乱⓰～；今年多～了一万株树苗，稀稀落落⓱地～了几株白杨⓲

1. seedling; sprout 2. a bunch of violets 3. coloured flag 4. plug 5. appear; show; reveal oneself 6. image 7. upside down; inverted 8. pen container 9. formation 10. transplant rice seedlings 11. aching back and legs 12. hard 13. can't straighten one's back 14. at least 15. a stretch 16. at random 17. few and scattered 18. white poplar

② interpose; insert〔～宾〕〈名〉书里～了一幅图；临时❶～了一个节目❷；我多～了一句话；她真爱～嘴；这件事你别～手❸〔～补〕〈结〉大家正说得热闹❹，他突然～上一句话〈趋〉小学课本里应该多～进一些图去；电视看得正有意思的时候，突然～进一个广告❺来〈可〉她说个没完，别人连半句话都～不进去；想帮忙又～不上手〔状～〕总～不上嘴；多～几张画儿；半路～了进来；大人说话，孩子别～嘴

1. temporarily 2. programme 3. have a hand in 4. lively 5. advertisement

chá 查 ① check; examine ≅ 检查；查对〔～宾〕〈名〉～卫生❶；～户口❷；～账❸；～记录本❹〔～补〕〈结〉账～清楚了〈趋〉他～起账来，认真极了；病～出来了吗？〈程〉户口～得很紧

❺；账～得很马虎❻；卫生～得很认真；～得很严❼；病～得很仔细〈可〉账上的问题～得出来～不出来？病总～不出来；账太多一天～不完〈时〉昨天夜里～了半天户口；这笔账～了一年才查出来〈量〉再～一下儿看看；再～一遍〔**状～**〕身体需要好好儿～一～；重新～；仔细～；认真～；马马虎虎地❽～；从头至尾地❾～；难～；容易～；一家一家地～；挨家挨户地❿～；一笔一笔地～；始终⓫没～出来；仍旧～不出来；一连～了半年；连续～了好多次；终于～出来了；立即～；马上～；详细地⓬～

1. hygiene; sanitation **2.** residence cards; (check) on household occupants **3.** accounts **4.** minute book **5.** strict; stringent **6.** careless **7.** strict; severe **8.** carelessly **9.** from beginning to end **10.** from door to door **11.** from beginning to end; all along; throughout **12.** in detail

② look up; consult ≃ 查找；翻阅〔**～宾**〕〈名〉～字典；～书目❶；～资料❷；～档案❸；～病历❹；～电话号码；～电话簿❺；～地图〔**～补**〕〈结〉字～着(zháo)了吗？资料～到了；～全了；号码～错了〈趋〉从档案上～出问题来了；一个字～过来～过去地查了好几遍〈程〉她查字典～得真快；资料～得不够全〈可〉这么多资料两天也～不完；这本书我～不着(zháo)；从档案里～不出什么问题来；有些小城市在地图里～不到〈时〉～了一晚上生词；这个词～了半天也没查着(zháo)；这堆资料整整～了一天〈量〉这几个字～过好几遍了，就是记不住〔**状～**〕别着急，慢慢～；一遍一遍地～；一页一页地～；仔细点儿❻～；一下子就～着(zháo)了；一连❼～了二十个生词；好容易才～着(zháo)；这个字写错了，难怪❽～不着

1. catalogue; booklist **2.** data; material **3.** archives; files **4.** medical record; case history **5.** telephone number **6.** carefully **7.** in succession; in a row **8.** no wonder

③ look into; investigate ≃ 调查〔**～宾**〕〈名〉～～失火的原因；～这件事情发生的缘由❶〈动〉～～有没有可疑❷现象❸；～～火灾❹是怎样引起❺的；～～为什么接连不断❻地发生事故❼〈主－谓〉～～煤气❽漏❾不漏气〔**～补**〕〈趋〉她自杀❿的理由⓫已经～出来了〈程〉～得很仔细；～得很认真；～得太马虎⓬〈可〉到目前为止⓭还～不出任何结果来；他到底贪污⓮了多少公款⓯，一直～不清楚〈时〉～了半年多，总算⓰～出来了；～了很长时间〈量〉出事⓱那天晚上是谁值班～⓲一下儿就知道了；～了几次都没查出来；已经～过好几遍了〔**状～**〕再～～；仔细～～；从各方面～；暗中⓳～；大家一起～；仍旧⓴～不到；始终没～出来；一连～了三个月；终于㉑～出来了；实在㉒～不出来；这种情况往往不容易～出来

1. reason; cause 2. suspicious; dubious 3. phenomenon; appearance (of things) 4. fire 5. give rise to; lead to 6. continuously 7. accident 8. gas 9. leak 10. commit suicide 11. cause; reason 12. careless 13. up to now; so far 14. corruption 15. public money 16. finally; in the end 17. have an accident 18. be on duty 19. in secret 20. still; yet 21. in the end; finally 22. really; truly

chà 差 fall short of; hove not enough of; lack ≅ 缺欠；缺少〔~宾〕<名>~两个人；~三本书；~五块钱；~一碗饭；~一张票；还~什么东西？〔~补〕<程>我跟他比~得太多了；~得太远了<可>他们两个人的生日~不了(liǎo)几天？<时>~10分钟；~两三天；~一个多月；~一年零两个星期〔状~〕只~一点儿；就~你一个人了；我的表总～3分钟；还~多少？丝毫也不~〔习用〕~劲儿❶

1. no good; disappointing

chāi 拆 ① tear open; take apart ≅ 打开〔~宾〕<名>~信；~邮包❶；~机器；~被❷〔~补〕<结>~开信一看，里边有一张照片；把机器~开，好好擦擦❸吧；这种玩具船每部分都可以~开；好好儿的一个家，被他给~散❹了；这些书是整套的❺，别~散了；<趁>把机器~下来检查❻检查<程>~得很快；~得太慢；<可>缝❼得太结实❽，~不下来

了；~不开了；一个小时~不完〔量〕~一下儿试试〔状~〕一下子就~坏了；用剪刀❾~；一点一点地～；慢慢～；赶紧～

1. postal parcel 2. quilt 3. clean 4. be broken up 5. a complete set 6. check up; examine; inspect 7. sew 8. solid 9. scissors

② pull down; dismantle ≅ 拆毁；拆除；↔搭，盖；修〔~宾〕<名>~旧房；~围墙❶；~城墙❷；~帐蓬❸；~桥❹；~障碍物❺〔~补〕<结>这一片旧房子全部~平❻了<程>帐蓬~得很快；那里的破房子~得真彻底，一间都没留<可>半天儿~得完吗？<时>再~两天就完工了〔状~〕一点一点~；大家一起~；一个人~；不好~；快点~〔习用〕~东墙补西墙❼

1. enclosure; enclosing wall 2. city wall 3. tent 4. bridge 5. obstacle; barrier 6. flat 7. tear down the east wall to repair the west wall — resort to a makeshift solution

chān 搀 ① help by the arm; support sb. with one's hand ≅ 搀扶；扶〔~宾〕<名>~着她母亲；~着老年人；~着病人；~着走路不方便❶的人；~着瞎子❷；~着瘸子❸；~着喝醉酒的人❹；~着残废的人❺〔~补〕<趋>把老人~上车来；产妇❻被~进产房❼来(去)了；把盲人❽~过马路；把病人～到楼上去吧；把受伤❾的人那位工人～到急诊室❿来吧<可>

老爷爷太胖，我~不起他〈时〉~了半天，也没把他搀起来〈量〉快~一下儿他吧，他起不来了；她~了我一把，我才起来〔状~〕吃力地⓫~着；好好儿地~；一把~住了；从楼上~下来

1. walk with difficulty 2. blind 3. a lame person; cripple 4. drunken man 5. maimed person 6. lying-in woman 7. delivery room 8. blind 9. wounded 10. emergency ward 11. strenuously

② mix ≅ 搀和；兑〔~宾〕〈名〉~水；~石灰❶；~砂子❷；一点儿白颜色〔~补〕〈结〉~上点儿水；水~多了就稀❸了；红颜色~坏了，不好看了；把水泥❹和砂子~在一起〈趋〉别把我~到你们的纠纷❺中去；我不喜欢把好米和坏米~起来吃〈程〉牛奶搀水~得太多了；这两种东西~得不匀❻〈可〉油和水~不到一起〔状~〕多~点儿；别乱❼~

1. lime 2. sand 3. watery; thin 4. cement 5. dispute 6. not even 7. at random

chán 缠 ① twine; wind ≅ 绕〔~宾〕〈名〉~线❶；~毛线❷；~电线❸；~铁丝❹；~绷带❺；~绳子❻〔~补〕〈结〉~上点儿铁丝；手上~满了绷带；绷带~松点❼儿；草绳~斜❽了；别把毛线~脏了；把毛线~成球〈趋〉线全部~到线轴上去了；用草绳把要运走的家具~起来吧〈程〉~得太密❾了；~得太多了；~真快；毛线球~得真圆；~得又

松又软❿；铁丝~得很齐；~得非常结实〈可〉绳子太细~不上；铁丝太粗⓫~不紧；圆东西没棱没角⓬~不住；这种绳子不结实~不了(liǎo)〈时〉如果你不帮助我，我一个人得(děi)~半天儿〈量〉随便⓭~一下儿就行了；多~几下儿；~了好几次都没缠好〔状~〕圆东西不好~；好容易(好不容易)才~上；一点一点地~；往线轴上~；用麻绳⓮~；给伤者~绷带；密密地~；多~一点儿

1. thread 2. knitting wool 3. electric line 4. iron wire 5. bandage 6. rope 7. loosen; slack 8. oblique; inclined 9. close; dense 10. soft 11. thick 12. without edges and corners 13. casually; at random; informally 14. rope made of hemp, flax, jute, etc.

② tangle; tie up; pester ≅ 纠缠；搅扰；绞〔~宾〕〈名〉琐事❶（病魔❷）~身；小孩子总~着妈妈〔~补〕〈结〉她刚要出门，就被事情~住了；两股线❸~在一起了；我又被那个坏蛋~上了〈趋〉再这样下去我可就不客气了〈程〉把我~得一点办法都没有了；让病~得非常苦恼❹〈时〉他~了我好几个小时不让我走；这病~她好多年〔状~〕一直~着我；天天~着我；死皮赖脸地❺~着；没完没了(liǎo)地❻~着；线紧紧地~在一起了；这个人难~❼极了

1. trifles, trivial matters 2. serious illness (be afflicted with a lingering disease) 3. thread 4. feel

vexed 5. thick-skinned and hard to shake off; brazen-faced and unreasonable 6. endlessly 7. be really hard to deal with

chǎn 产 ① give birth to;〔~宾〕〈名〉鱼~仔❶；蛔虫❷~卵❸〔状~〕一次~几万个卵；每胎❹只~二、三只；每年春季❺~仔

1. young (of domestic animals or fowls) 2. roundworm; ascarid 3. ovum 4. at a litter (at one farrow) 5. in spring

② produce ≌ 出产〔~宾〕〈名〉~石油❶；~花生；~棉花❷；~甘蔗❸；~鱼；~虾；~茶叶；~珍珠❹〔~补〕〈结〉去年棉花~少了；西瓜~少了〈程〉今年鱼虾~得都很多〈可〉一亩地~不了(liǎo)一千斤吧〔状~〕盛❺~；不~；只~；就~；专~

1. petroleum; oil 2. cotton 3. sugarcane 4. pearl 5. abundantly

chǎnshēng 产生 produce; engender〔主~〕〈名〉旧的问题解决了新的问题又~了；矛盾❶早就~了〔~宾〕〈名〉~不少困难；他们之间~了许多矛盾；对美学❷~了很大兴趣❸；对这件事~了怀疑❹；~很大影响；~副作用❺；~连锁反应❻；~了纠纷❼〔状~〕终于~了；已经~了；将要~；逐渐❽~；对他~了怀疑；矛盾是由这件事~的

1. contradiction 2. aesthetics 3. be greatly interested 4. doubt; suspect 5. side effect 6. chain reaction 7. dispute; issue 8. gradually

chǎn 铲 shovel ≌ 撮〔~宾〕〈名〉~煤；~土；~雪；~垃圾❶〔~补〕〈结〉快把这堆❷雪~走吧；把土堆❸~平了；垃圾没~干净；把煤~完了再走〈趋〉炉灰已经~到外边去了〈程〉~得又快又干净〈可〉雪都冻❹成冰了，~不动了，这一堆东西，一个小时~得完吗？〈时〉~一会儿就出汗了〈量〉我来~两下儿，你去休息休息；~过一次〔状~〕用力~；多~几下儿；一锹一锹地~；一下儿一下儿地~；一下子就~完了；一会儿就~平了；弯着腰~

1. refuse; garbage; rubbish 2. heap; pile 3. mound 4. be frozen

chàn 颤 quiver; tremble; vibrate ≌ 颤动；颤抖；振动；抖；哆嗦；打战〔主~〕〈名〉全身(发)~；手(发)~；声音(发)~；两腿(发)~；扁担❶挑❷重东西上下~；嘴唇❸激动❹得发（直）~〔~补〕〈程〉两条腿~得很利害；手~得拿不了(liǎo)东西；手~得写不了字；嘴~得说不了(liǎo)话了〔状~〕他冻❺得直~；留下❻的病根儿❼就是手总~；坐在那儿腿别~；一个劲儿地~；不住地~；不停地~；浑身乱~

1. carrying pole; shoulder pole 2. carry on the shoulder with a pole 3. lip 4. be moved to 5. freeze 6. remain 7. an incompletely cured illness

cháng 尝 taste; try the flavour of〔**～宾**〕〈名〉～～味道❶；～了一口汤；～了一点儿白酒❷；～～我家自己酿❸的酒；～了一杯酸牛奶❹；～～咸❺淡❻；～～生熟❼；～～凉热；～～我的利害❽〈主－谓〉～～这个菜好吃不好吃；～～这杯水烫❾不烫；～～熟了没有；～～鸡肉烂❿不烂〔**～补**〕〈结〉左尝一口，右尝一口，都快～饱了；～尽了人间的艰辛⓫；～到了甜头⓬；～到了挨饿⓭的滋味⓮；～够了苦头〈趋〉～出味儿来了吗？〈程〉～得太多了，也分辨不清哪个好，哪个坏了；苦头还～得不够吗？〈可〉感冒了，什么味儿也～不出来；这么多吃的，我都～不过来了〈时〉～了半天，也不知道熟了没有？〈量〉再～一下儿；～过一次了〔**状～**〕亲口～；多～儿口；少～点儿；怎么～也尝不出好坏来；让他先～；左～右～

1. taste; smell **2.** spirit usu. distilled from sorghum or maize; white spirit **3.** make (wine) **4.** yoghurt; sour milk **5.** salted **6.** tasteless (have a taste and see if it's salty enough) **7.** cooked; done **8.** (let you know) I'm not a man to be trifled with **9.** very hot; scalding; boiling hot **10.** tender; soft **11.** have experienced all the hardships of the world **12.** benefit (become aware of the benefits of) **13.** be hungry **14.** taste; flavour

chàng 唱 sing〔**～宾**〕〈名〉～歌，～国歌❶；～女高音❷；～京剧❸（京戏）；～地方戏❹；～儿歌❺；～一个歌谣❻〔**～补**〕〈结〉～完一个歌又唱一个歌；第一遍～错了；这出戏～坏了；第一次～失败了；歌词❼～熟❽了；从小儿❾就唱，都～惯了；这只歌他～走调❿了；整天唱，把人都～烦⓫了；音～高了；别把嗓子⓬～哑⓭了；每个字都应该～清楚；今天从八点一直～到现在；～够了吗？～兴奋⓮了〈趋〉歌词想了半天才～上来；他只要一～起京戏来，就什么也不顾⓯了；她～起歌来，什么烦恼都忘了〈程〉她～得多么好听啊！～得太好了；～得难听⓰极了；～得不够味；～得口干舌燥⓱；～得烦死人；～得没法睡觉；声音～得真甜⓲；～得非常柔和⓳；～得真迷人⓴〈可〉我～不好；这个曲子㉑太难，嗓子哑了，～不出来了；音那么高你～得上去吗？好久不唱这个歌了，都有点儿～不上来了；我记不住歌词，连一个完整㉒的歌都～不下来〈时〉那位演员～了一辈子民歌；她～了二十多年京剧；那个歌唱演员每天早晨都要～一个小时歌儿〈量〉～了一遍又一遍；这出戏～过无数次了〔**状～**〕大声～；高兴地～；勉强～；不由得㉓～了起来；不好意思地～；羞羞答答地㉔～；扭扭捏捏地㉕～；大大方方地～；从从容容地㉖～；到处～；随时～；难～；一口气㉗～了三支歌；一个接一个地～；天天～；边走边～；单独㉘～；情不自禁地㉙～；一边跳一边～；给孩子～；一遍又一遍

地～；无可奈何地㉚～；偶尔㉛～；反复㉜～〔**习用**〕～对台戏㉝；～高调㉞；～独角戏㉟

1. national anthem **2.** soprano **3.** Beijing (Peking) opera **4.** local opera **5.** children's song; nursery rhymes **6.** ballad; folk song; nursery rhyme **7.** words of a song **8.**familiar **9.** from childhood **10.** out of tune **11.** annoying **12.** throat; voice **13.** husky; hoarse **14.** be excited **15.** disregard **16.** unpleasant to the ear **17.** sing till one's mouth and tongue are parched **18.** sweet **19.** soft **20.** fascinating **21.** song **22.** complete; integrated **23.** can't help; cannot but **24.** bashfully **25.** be affectedly bashful **26.** calmly; unhurriedly **27.** at a stretch **28.** alone **29.** can't help (singing) **30.** have no alternative; have no way out **31.** occasionally **32.** repeatedly; time and again **33.** put on a rival show **34.** use high-flown words; affect a high moral tone **35.** put on a one-man show; go it alone

chāo 抄

① copy; transcribe ≃抄写；誊写〔**～宾**〕〈名〉～书；～文件❶；～稿子❷；～了一首诗；～了一段话；～乐谱❸；～名言❹；～语录❺；～例句；～了两张笔记❻；～了三页英语单词❼；～原文❽〔**～补**〕〈结〉稿子～完了；字～整齐点儿；～漏❾了两个字；太多了，我都～腻❿了；～满了两张纸；～在本子上；可别～乱⓫了〈趋〉他抄得真快，一会工夫⓬就全～出来了；快把这段话～下来吧；就照这样～下去吧；把这两首诗一起～下来吧〈程〉～得很好；～得真快；～得太乱⓭；～得乱七八糟⓮；～得不错；～得挺清楚〈可〉我～不了(liǎo) 五线谱⓯；这么多要抄的东西，一天可～不完；一张纸～不满⓰；那张纸太小，～不下；这么多稿件一上午都～不完 〈时〉～了一下午，才抄三篇⓱；～了三个多小时；～了一年多〈量〉～了两遍；～过三次；～一下儿看看〔**状～**〕认真⓲(地)～；仔细点儿⓳～；马马虎虎地⓴～；心不在焉地㉑～；赶紧～；要整整齐齐地～；白㉒～了；重新～；往黑板上～；用钢笔～；在纸上～；按一定格式㉓～；一笔㉔一划㉕地～；从头至尾㉖～；差不多～了五十页；照原文～

1. document **2.** manuscript **3.** music score **4.** well-known saying; famous remark **5.** quotation **6.** notes **7.** English word **8.** original text **9.** be missing; leave out **10.** be bored with; be tired of **11.** in disorder **12.** a little while **13.** be confused; disordered **14.** in a mess; in disorder **15.** staff; stave **16.** full; filled **17.** sheet **18.** conscientiously **19.** carefully **20.** carelessly **21.** absent-mindedly **22.** in vain **23.** form **24. 25.** a stroke (of a Chinese character) **26.** from beginning to end

② take a short cut ≃ 走〔**～宾**〕

〈名〉~小路; ~后路; ~近路(~近儿)〔~补〕〈趋〉从这边~过去; 从那边~过来; 他走得真快, 已经从后边~过来了; ~到我们前面去了〈可〉~得过去~不过去? 〈时〉~了半天小路, 时间也没省 ❶多少〈量〉咱们必须~一下儿近道, 才能准时 ❷赶到〔状~〕从前边~; 从哪儿~? 从什么地方~? 经常~; 偶尔 ❸~

1. save 2. in time 3. occasionally; once in a while

③ plagiarize; lift ≌ 抄袭〔~宾〕〈名〉~人家的文章; ~别人的作业〔~补〕〈结〉不好好复习, 考试时照 ❶书抄, 都~错了〈趋〉~出来的句子都不连贯 ❷〈可〉抄都~不好; ~不对; ~不全〔状~〕全部~; 整章 ❸整章地~; 成段 ❹成段地~; 从头至尾 ❺~; 一字不漏 ❻地~; 公开 ❼地~; 偷偷 ❽地~; 肆无忌惮 ❾地~; 屡次 ❿~

1. according to; in accordance with 2. not consistent 3. whole chapter 4. whole paragraph 5. from beginning to end 6. be missing; leave out 7. publicly 8. secretly 9. unscrupulously 10. time and again; repeatedly

④ search and confiscate; make a raid upon 〔~宾〕〈名〉~家; ~赌窟 ❶〔~补〕〈结〉把东西全~走了; ~光 ❷了; ~没了〈程〉家被~得乱七八糟 ❸的; ~得什么都没有了; ~得片纸不留 ❹; ~得零乱不堪 ❺〈量〉~过一次〔状~〕曾经~; 被~; 多次~

1. gambling-den 2. nothing left 3. in a mess; in disorder 4. not a single paper remains 5. in a fearful mess; in a state of utter confusion

⑤ go (walk) off with ≌ 随手拿走〔~宾〕〈代〉这些东西没人管, 谁~着, 算谁的〔~补〕〈结〉~起别人的杯子就喝; 谁把我的字典~走了〈趋〉~起棍子来就打; ~起帽子来戴上就走了〔状~〕随手 ❶~; 顺便 ❷~

1. 2. conveniently; in passing

chǎo 吵 ① quarrel; wrangle; squabble ≌ 口角; 争吵〔~宾〕〈名〉~架; ~嘴〔~补〕〈结〉原来是很好的邻居, 怎么突然~开架了; 这两个人常吵架, 可是~完了就完, 谁也不记仇 ❶; 这两家又~上了〈趋〉楼上那夫妻两个又~起来了; 为这么点儿小事就~起来了; 别吵了, 再~下去就伤感情 ❷了〈程〉他们昨天~得真利害 ❸; ~得非常激烈 ❹; ~得很凶 ❺; ~得鸡犬不宁 ❻; ~得四邻 ❼不安 ❽; ~得脸红脖子粗 ❾; ~得吃不下饭去; ~得没法在一起住下去了〈可〉为这点儿事他们~得起来~不起来? 他们两个人脾气 ❿都很好, ~不了(liǎo)架; 这两位天天吵, 真是~不完的架〈时〉~了一会儿就不吵了; ~了一上午架, 也没人劝 ⓫〈量〉~过好几次了; ~一下儿就完了, 别记仇; ~了一阵 ⓬; ~了一顿 ⓭

[**状～**]大～大闹⓮；大声(小声)～；经常～；从来也不～；从来没～过；又～了；隔两天一～；在公共汽车上～；跟邻居～；跟售货员⓯～；为孩子～；见谁跟谁～；无缘无故地⓰～；没完没了⓱(liǎo)地～；气势汹汹地⓲～；三天两头儿⓳～；哭着～；成天⓴～；没事找事地㉑～；不顾后果㉒地～；拍桌子瞪眼睛㉓地～；声嘶力竭地～㉔；哭哭啼啼地㉕～；蛮不讲理㉖地～

1. bear grudges **2.** hurt sb's feelings **3.** terrible; awful **4.** bitterly **5.** terribly; fearfully **6.** even fowls and dogs are not left in peace — general turmoil **7.** one's near neighbours **8.** intranquil; unpeaceful **9.** get red in the face from anger or excitement; flush with agitation; excitedly **10.** temper **11.** reconcile **12. 13** for a little while **14.** kick up a row; make a scene **15.** shop assistant **16.** for no reason at all **17.** endlessly **18.** furiously; fiercely **19.** every other day **20.** all day long; all the time **21.** ask for trouble **22.** regardless of the consequences **23.** gloweringly **24.** shout oneself hoarse; shout oneself blue in the face **25.** endlessly weep and wail **26.** be impervious to reason; persist in being unreasonable

② make a noise ≌扰乱；吵闹 [**～宾**]〈名〉真～人〈代〉别～他 [**～补**]〈结〉孩子被他～醒了；锯❶木头的声音把人～死了；简直❷～翻天❸了〈程〉马路上汽车的喇叭声❹～得太利害❺了；～得睡不着觉；～得无法工作；～得头昏脑胀❻；这个地方真～得慌❼；～极了〈可〉他睡得很熟❽，多大声音都～不醒；把窗户全关严❾了，外边的声音～不着(zháo)他了[**状～**]太～了；整天整夜地～；真～；非常～；从早到晚～；没完没了(liǎo)地❿～；不停地⓫～

1. saw **2.** really; truly **3.** shake the sky; overturn the heavens **4.** hoot **5.** terrible; formidable **6.** dizzy **7.** awfully; unbearably **8.** sound **9.** tight **10.** without end; endlessly **11.** incessantly

chǎo 炒 stir-fry; fry [**～宾**]〈名〉～肉丝❶；～鸡蛋；～黄瓜片；～菜；～面；～花生；～瓜子[**～补**]〈结〉菜～好了，开饭❷吧；肉～熟❸了吗？饭～咸❹一点儿；白菜～辣❺了；菜～多了；～淡❻点儿；别～过火❼了；～到什么时候才算熟啊？〈趋〉他～出来的菜特别好吃〈程〉～得真好吃；～得真香；肉～得太嫩；～得非常难吃〈可〉这种菜我～不好；小火～不熟〈时〉再～一会儿；～两三分钟就熟了；别～那么长时间〈量〉这种菜他亲手～过好几次了；明天你自己～一下儿试试[**状～**]多～～；少～一会儿；特意❽～；分两次～；随便❾～个菜就可以了；一盘一盘地～；用旺火❿～；用微火～[**习用**]～冷饭⓫

1. shredded meat 2. serve a meal 3. cooked 4. salty 5. hot 6. tasteless 7. overcook 8. specially; for a special purpose 9. do as one pleases 10. a great fire 11. heat leftover rice — say or do the same old thing; rehash

chē 车 ① lathe; turn [～宾]〈名〉一个零件❶；～螺丝钉❷[～补]〈趋〉这一筐❸料❹，上午能不能～出来?〈程〉她～得真好；～得真平❺；～得很漂亮〈可〉不知一天～得完～不完? ～得出来～不出来?〈时〉～两三个小时，就应该给机器❻上点儿油[状～]按❼要求❽～；照图纸❾～；仔细点❿儿～；差点儿⓫～坏了

1. part (of a machine) 2. screw 3. basket 4. material 5. even; flat 6. machine 7. according to; in accordance with 8. demand 9. blue-print; drawing 10. carefully 11. almost; nearly

② sew ≅ 缝制[～宾]〈名〉～衣；～衬衫❶[～补]〈结〉这几件外套❷全～好了〈趋〉这些布料❸今天～得完吗?〈程〉～得真好〈可〉这么多件，一天可～不来〈时〉～了一个星期❹还没～完〈量〉～过好几件了〔状～〕照图样❺～；小心点儿～；～错了

1. shirt 2. coat 3. cloth 4. week 5. pattern

chě 扯 ① tear ≅ 撕[～宾]〈名〉从练习本子上～了一条纸❶；她连～了三封信；～一张纸包东西；～一小块布[～补]〈结〉两个人一抢❷，把报纸一撕了；她一生气，把信全～碎❸了；这张纸又～破了；做衣服的布～多了；把纸都～成一条一条的了〈趋〉她每天都要从墙上～下一页日历❹来；从本子上～下两张纸来〈程〉～得粉碎〈可〉信封❺粘❻得太结实了，～不开了〈时〉～了半天也扯不动，只好用剪刀剪了〈量〉～一下儿试试〔状～〕先剪一个小口儿再～；用力～；慢慢～；从本子上～

1. a slip of paper 2. snatch; grab 3. be broken to pieces 4. calendar 5. envelope 6. glue; paste; stick

② chat; gossip ≅ 聊；随便谈[～宾]〈名〉～家常❶；～了很多废话❷[～补]〈结〉别把话～远了〈趋〉两个人～起来就没完；又～到出国的问题上去了；你这话～到哪儿去了?〈程〉问题～得太远了〈时〉～了一会儿闲话❸〔状～〕别乱❹～；天南海北地❺～；漫无边际地❻～；海阔天空地❼～；随便～

1. the daily life of a family; domestic trivia (engage in a small talk) 2. nonsense; superfluous words 3. gossip; digression 4. at random; recklessly; wantonly (talk nonsense) 5. start chattering away about this and that; start a bull session 6. boundlessly 7. as boundless as the sea and sky (have a rambling chat about everything under the sun)

③ pull ≅ 拉[～宾]〈名〉他～着

嗓子喊;～着我的袖子❶;孩子～着母亲的衣襟❷〈代〉别总～着我不放[～补]〈结〉没等我说完,他就把我～走了;不能把这两件事～在一起〈量〉～了我一把;～了她一下儿[状]用力～;紧紧地～;往外～〔习用〕～后腿❸;东拉西～❹

1. sleeve 2. the one or two pieces making up the front of a Chinese jacket 3. hold sb. back (from action); be a drag on sb. 4. drag in all sorts of irrelevant matters; talk at random; ramble

chè 撤 ① remove; take away ≅ 除去、拿开[～宾]〈名〉～盘子❶;～炉子❷;～碗;～职❸[～补]〈结〉把剩❹菜～走吧〈趋〉把桌布也～下来吧〈可〉这点儿小事～不了(liǎo)职;还有人没吃完呢,碗筷❺现在还～不下来[状～]快～下去吧;全～掉;统统❻～下去;一只手扶着❼,一只手～;慢慢地～

1. plate 2. stove 3. post (dismiss sb. from his post) 4. remain 5. bowls and chopsticks 6. all; completely; entirely 7. support (with the hand)

② withdraw; evacuate ≅ 退回[～宾]〈名〉～兵;～军[～补]〈结〉军队❶全部～完了〈趋〉把军队全部～回来了;～到哪儿去了?〈程〉～得真快;～得很及时❷〈时〉一个星期～得完～不完?～得回来～不回来?〈时〉～了整整一个星期;～了将近❸半个月[状～]马上～;连夜❹～;全部～一齐❺～;分批❻～;有步骤地❼～;向后～;往哪儿～?偷偷地～;赶快～;突然～;出其不意地❽～;主动❾～

1. armed forces; troops 2. in time 3. about 4. the same night; that very night 5. at the same time; simultaneously 6. in batches; in turn 7. step by step 8. unexpectedly 9. on one's own initiative

chén 沉 ① sink ↔浮〔主～〕〈名〉船～了;石头～下去了[～宾]〈名〉～了一只船[～补]〈趋〉～到水里去了〈程〉～得很快〈可〉舱❶里没进水～不了(liǎo)〔状～〕眼看着❷～下去了;一下子就要～了;快～了;地基❸下了;一点一点～下去了

1. cabin 2. watch helplessly; look on passively 3. ground; foundation

② keep down [～补]〈结〉～住了气❶,别慌❷〈趋〉脸突然～下来了〈可〉今天在会上我有点儿～不住气[状～]把脸一～;真～不住气;有点儿～不住气;别～不住气

1. keep calm; be steady 2. don't panic

chèn 衬 place sth. underneath ≅ 垫[～宾]〈名〉下边～一张纸好写;领子❶里～了一层布;机器零件❷有油,包的时候最好～一张蜡纸❸;玻璃板底下～一块绿

色❹的绒布❺〔~补〕〈结〉~上一张白纸；把布~在下边〔状~〕多(少)~一点儿；薄薄地❻~了一层；厚厚地❼~了好几层

1. collar 2. spare parts; spares 3. wax paper 4. green 5. cotton flannel 6. thinly 7. thickly

chēng 称 ① weigh ≅ 约 (yāo) 〔~宾〕〈名〉~一斤米；~一捆菜；~一~这个邮包❶有多重？〔~补〕〈结〉~完了吗？~好了吗？别~错了；~准点儿啊！~多了吧；~少了〈趋〉~出来一斤糖放在那儿，又去称别的东西了〈程〉~得真快；~得真慢；分量~得很准〈可〉这个称(chèng)❷坏了，~不准了；没有称(chèng)砣❸~不了(liǎo)；〈量〉已经~过两遍了；~一下儿看看有多少〔状~〕多~几斤；先少~点儿尝尝；再~两斤；快点儿~；一次~完；用磅称❹(chèng) ~

1. postal parcel 2. steelyard 3. the sliding weight of a steelyard 4. platform scale

② call oneself ≅ 叫；叫做〔~宾〕〈代〉~他(为)伯伯❶；~你(为)师傅❷〔~补〕〈结〉许多人把巴黎❸~为"美丽的花都"；青藏高原❹被~为"盐湖❺之家"〈可〉他~不上什么英雄❻；她~得起是全班的模范❼；你在这儿可~不了(liǎo) 专家❽〔状~〕都这么~；一直这么~；被人们~作一致❾；亲切地❿~；〔**习用**〕兄道弟⓫

1. uncle; father's elder brother 2.

master 3. Paris 4. the Qinghai-Xizang Plateau 5. salt lake 6. hero 7. model; fine example 8. expert; specialist 9. showing no difference 10. kindly; cordially 11. call each other brothers; be on intimate terms

chēng 撑 ① push or move with a pole 〔~宾〕〈名〉~船〔~补〕〈结〉谁把岸边❶的小船(给)~走了？〈趋〉把船~到对岸❷去了〈程〉船~得很好；~得不错；~得很稳❸；~得很快〈可〉船太沉❹(重zhòng)了，~不动；她胳膊❺没劲儿❻~不了(liǎo)船〔状~〕用竹竿❼~；用篙❽~

1. shore 2. opposite 3. steady 4. heavy 5. arm 6. physical strength 7. bamboo pole 8. punt-pole

② open; unfurl ≅ 张开〔~宾〕〈名〉~(着)口袋❶；~着书包〔~补〕〈结〉把帐篷❷~开；把雨伞~开；麻袋❸没~好，大米都撒❹了〈趋〉把口袋~起来〈程〉口袋口儿❺~得很大；~得不够大❻〈可〉伞坏了~不开了〔状~〕用力~；两个人一起~着；好好儿(地)~

1. bag; sack 2. tent 3. gunny-bag; gunnysack 4. spill; drop 5. mouth 6. not big enough

③ fill to the point of bursting〔~补〕〈结〉那个孩子是~病的；肚子❶都快~破了；别把胃❷~坏了；东西多得把口袋❸都快~裂❹了；枕头❺里头是用什么~满的；那只小鸡是~死的吧〈趋〉

吃那么多,容易~出毛病❻来〈程〉这孩子吃东西不知道饱❼,~得太厉害了;他~得受不了❽(liǎo)了;水喝多了,把肚子~得鼓鼓❾的〈可〉那个小伙子❿消化⓫力强⓬~不着(zháo);口袋有弹性⓭~不破〔状~〕别~着(zháo);再吃就~着(zháo)了;一下子把口袋~破了

1. belly; abdomen (be full) 2. stomach 3. bag; sack 4. split; crack 5. pillow 6. (stomach) trouble 7. have eaten one's fill 8. cannot bear; unable to endure 9. bulge; swell 10. lad; young fellow 11. digest 12. strong 13. elasticity

chéng 成 ① accomplish; succeed ≅ 成功,行;可以〔主~〕〈名〉事情~了我请客;这门婚事❶就算~了〈主-谓〉明天你不去可不~〔~补〕〈可〉这件事~得了(liǎo)~不了(liǎo)?那个人~不了(liǎo)大事❷〔状~〕已经~了;快~了;早就~了;还没~呢,这件事他去办准~❸

1. marriage; wedding 2. important matter, major event 3. certainly succeed

② become; turn into ≅ 成为,变成;是〔~宾〕〈名〉~了物理学家❶;~了废物❷;~了英雄❸;~了模范❹;~了典型❺;~了老师;~了专家❻;~了医生;~了司令❼;她再不退烧❽,明天考试就~问题了;都~了什么样子了〔~补〕〈程〉那个作家❾成名❿~得早〈可〉我永远~不了(liǎo)演员〔状~〕很早就~了;很晚才~;已经~了;一下子~了;突然~名了;一夜之间就~名了;一辈子⓫也~不了(liǎo)名;真有点儿~问题;一举⓬成名了〔习用〕他~不了什么气候⓭;~事不足,败事有余⓮;不打不~交⓯;~群结队⓰

1. physicist 2. good-for-nothing 3. hero 4. model 5. typical case 6. expert; specialist 7. commander 8. (of a person's temperature) come down 9. author 10. become famous 11. all one's life 12. with one action; at one stroke; at one fell swoop 13. will not get anywhere 14. unable to accomplish anything but liable to spoil everything 15. from an exchange of blows friendship grows 16. in crowds; in throngs

chéngshú 成熟 ripe; mature 〔主~〕〈名〉樱桃❶~了;条件~了;时机❷~了;思想~;意见❸~了〔状~〕已经~;尚未❹~;逐渐❺~;就要~了;即将❻~

1. cherry 2. opportunity 3. opinion 4. still; yet 5. gradually 6. be about to

chéngdān 承担 bear; undertake; assume ≅ 担负;担当〔~宾〕〈名〉~一切费用❶;~后果❷;~什么任务?~义务❸;~工作;~责任❹〔~补〕〈结〉费用甲方❺~多了,乙方❻~少了〈趋〉我们把这项任务~下来了;她能

～起这项工作来吗？〈程〉工作～得太多；责任～得太重❼了吧〈可〉我们～不了(liǎo)这笔费用；这些繁重❽的工作，你们～得起来吗？一切后果你们都～得了(liǎo)吗？[状～]由谁～？ 多～些；少一点儿；必须～；大胆❾～；勇敢地❿～；未加思索地⓫～下来了；独自⓬～

1. all expenses 2. consequence; aftermath 3. duty; obligation 4. responsibility 5. the first party 6. the second party 7. heavy 8. strenuous; heavy 9. boldly 10. courageously; bravely 11. without thinking; without hesitation; readily 12. alone; by oneself

chéngrèn 承认 ① recognize; admit; acknowledge ≅认可，同意 [～宾]〈名〉～错误；～了自己的缺点❶；被告❷～了这些事实❸；～犯了杀人罪❹；～有这么回事〈主-谓〉～玻璃❺是他打破的；～他是我们班最好的学生 [～补]〈程〉错误他～得很快，就是不改〈量〉你～了好几次错误了，怎么老不改呢？[状～]都～了；全部～了；一直没～；始终不～；不得不❻～；只好～；主动❼～；被迫❽～；坦率地❾～；必须～；无可奈何地❿～；彻底～了；推翻⓫了又～；大胆地⓬～；勇敢地⓭～

1. shortcoming 2. defendant; the accused 3. fact 4. commit murder 5. glass 6. be forced to; have to 7. of one's own accord; on one's own initiative 8. be forced to 9. frankly 10. have no alternative; have no way out 11. repudiate; cancel; 12. boldly 13. bravely

② give diplomatic recognition; recognize ≅认可 [～宾]〈名〉～一个新成立❶的国家 〈动〉～一个国家的独立❷

1. newly founded 2. independence

chéngshòu 承受 bear; support; endure ≅接受；禁(jīn)受 [～宾]〈名〉这座高架桥❶可以～多大重量❷？[～补]〈结〉各种考验她都～住了〈可〉这种考验，他能～得住吗？这么大的痛苦❸他～得了(liǎo)～不了(liǎo)？[状～]是否❹～得住？一次又一次地～着；一直～着；痛苦地～各种考验

1. viaduct 2. weight 3. pain; suffering 4. whether

chéng 乘 ① ride ≅坐；搭 [～宾]〈名〉～轮船❶；～游艇❷；～飞机 [～补]〈结〉现在她已经～上了飞往纽约❸的飞机；看准了车牌❹再上，别～错了车〈可〉现在还～得上八点五十的火车吗？太晚了，可能～不上了，还是坐下一趟吧〈时〉～了十几个小时的轮船，头有点儿晕❺〈量〉～过好几次飞机了[状～]你为什么不～飞机去呢？第一次～

1. steamer 2. yacht; pleasure-boat 3. New York 4. number plate (on a vehicle) 5. dizzy; giddy

② multiply ≌[~宾]〈数〉4～5等于❶20；7～8等于56；10～10是多少？[~补]〈结〉数儿～错了；～对了吗？〈趋〉应该把这个数儿～上来〈可〉这两个数儿老不对〈时〉～了半天也没乘对〈量〉～过三次了，还是不对；已经～好几遍了；再～一下儿看看[状~]多～几遍；再～一次；重新～一次；反来复去地❷～；一遍一遍地～；用笔～；在纸上～；用算盘❸～；用计算机❹～；哪个数儿跟哪个数儿～？这两个数儿相～

1. equal to 2. repeatedly; again and again 3. abacus 4. calculator

chéng 盛 ① fill; ladle ≌舀[~宾]〈名〉～了一碗饭；～了一勺汤❶；～了一盘菜；～了几勺粥；～了一碟辣酱❷；～了两碗面[~补]〈结〉～上一碗饭；～满一壶酒❸；汤～多了，菜～少了；～在盘子里，可以吗？〈趋〉饭菜已经～上来了；汤早就～出来了〈程〉别～得太满；～得太多了；～得真不少〈可〉这么多汤，一个碗～不下；没有勺子❹～不了(liǎo)饭；汤太少了，都～不上来了〈时〉～了半天才盛上一点儿汤来〈量〉今天他饿了，一共～了三次饭[状~]快点儿～；多～点儿；少～；小心点儿～；一勺一勺地～；一连～了好几勺；别～了；刚～上就吃完了；满满地～了一碗；再～一点儿；用勺子～；用汤匙❺～；往大碗里～；一下子～多了

1. ladle of soup 2. thick chilli sauce 3. wine 4. spoon; ladle 5. soup spoon

② hold; contain ≌容纳；装；放[~宾]〈名〉这个瓶子❶能～多少酒？用麻袋❷～米；用糖盒❸～糖；用竹篮❹～水果；这个礼堂能～一千人；衣柜里能～不少衣服[~补]〈结〉桶❺里～满了牛奶；小瓶儿里～满了汽油❻〈可〉屋子太小～不了(liǎo)这么多东西；那个剧场～不下两千人；抽屉❼里的东西都～不下了；房间真大，这么多家具❽都～不满；这个盒子太小了，连一斤饼干都～不下〈量〉我的这个破布包儿❾～过好几次鱼了[状~]怎么也～不下；勉强～；满满地～

1. bottle 2. gunnybag 3. box; case 4. bamboo basket 5. pail 6. gas 7. drawer 8. furniture 9. worn-out cloth bag

chéngfá 惩罚 punish; penalize ≌处罚；惩处；责罚[~宾]〈名〉～侵略者❶；～犯规❷的人[~补]〈量〉～过他三次；～他一下儿[状~]好好儿～～他；狠狠地❸～；必须～；适当地❹～；严厉地❺～

1. aggressor; invader 2. break the rules 3. vigorously 4. properly; suitably 5. severely; sternly

chī 吃 ① eat; take ≌吸；喝[~宾]〈名〉～水果；～糖；～药；～饭；～面；～饺子❶；～肉素❷；～荤❸；～零食❹；每天三顿饭；～夜宵❺；～斋❻；小孩

子已经不～奶了[**～补**]〈结〉糖都～完了；水果没洗干净，把肚子～坏了；注意点儿，别把胃❼～坏了；今天饭～多了；最近她～胖❽了；饭菜全～光了；大家都～饱了吗？吃肥肉❾～腻❿了；她吃素～惯了；那个人是吃毒药⓫～死的；这是孩子～剩下⓬的鸡蛋；这顿饭一直～到晚上八点〈趋〉为了治病⓭，药再苦也得～下去；你～出来什么味儿了吗？哎呀！把鱼刺⓮～进去了；连葡萄皮⓯儿都一起～到肚子里去了〈程〉～得太多了；～得很香；～得非常高兴；～得很难受⓰；～得不舒服；～得挺舒服⓱〈可〉已经～饱了，再也～不下了；这两天感冒了，什么东西都～不出味儿来；这么多饭菜三个人～得了(liǎo)吗？～得完吗？她怎么吃，也～不胖；羊肉我可～不来⓲；一边吃饭一边看书，结果饭也～不好，书也看不好；生⓳葱⓴生蒜㉑你都～得来吗？～得惯吗？他发烧～不下东西；穷人连一顿饱饭都～不上；这种菜太贵，我～不起；七点半以前赶到饭馆，还～得上饭〈时〉一顿饭～了两个小时；～了五分钟，菜就全光了〈量〉有时间去～一顿；你～一下儿就知道怎么样了[**状～**]好～吗？真难～；慢点儿～；不想吃别硬㉒～；勉强～；不得不～；饱饱地～了一顿；多～些有营养㉓的食物㉔；少～点带刺激性㉕的东西；不停地～糖；嘴里总～着口香糖㉖；按时～药；实在㉗～不下了；在家～；在食堂～；贪婪地㉘～；大口大口地㉙～；狼吞虎咽地㉚～；一把一把地～；细嚼烂咽地㉛～

1. jiaozi (dumpling) **2.** vegetarian meal **3.** meat or fish **4.** between-meal nibbles; snacks **5.** midnight snack; food (refreshments) taken late at night **6.** vegetarian diet adopted for religious reasons (practise abstinence from meat (as a religious exercise) **7.** stomach **8.** **9.** fat **10.** be tired of **11.** poison; toxicant **12.** remain; be left **13.** treat; cure (the sickness) **14.** fishbone **15.** grape skins **16.** feel unwell **17.** comfortable **18.** not be fond of (certain food) **19.** raw; uncooked **20.** onion **21.** garlic **22.** manage to do sth. with difficulty **23.** nourishing; nutritious **24.** food **25.** stimulant **26.** chewing gum **27.** really **28.** greedily; ravenously **29.** quickly and greedily **30.** gobble up; devour ravenously **31.** chew one's food well before swallowing it

② have one's meals; eat [**～宾**]〈名〉～食堂[**～补**]〈时〉～了一辈子❶食堂，自己从来没做过饭〈量〉那个饭馆我去～过好儿次了[**状～**]一直～；成年累月地❷～；从来没～过

1. whole life **2.** for years on end

③ suffer; incur ≃挨；受[**～宾**]〈名〉～苦头❶；～了败仗❷ [**～补**]〈结〉～尽❸了苦头〈可〉连续熬夜❹她的身体可～不消❺；这么硬❻的面包，我的胃❼可～不消；再两夜不睡，我也～得消；

chī — chōng 53

每天开夜车❽你～得消吗？她让大家批评❾得有点～不住(劲儿)了〈量〉～了一拳❿，腿上～了一枪[状～]净⓫，～败仗；又～了苦头；恐怕⓬～不消

1. suffering 2. defeat; lost battle (be defeated in battle) 3. to the utmost; to the limit 4. stay up late or all night at a stretch 5. be unable to stand 6. hard 7. stomach 8. work late into the night 9. criticize 10. get a punch 11. only; merely 12. probably; perhaps

④ annihilate; wipe out ≡ 消灭 [～宾]〈名〉～了敌人一个团❶；～了两个棋子儿；拿车❸～他的炮❹[～补]〈结〉～掉了一个坦克❺连❻；棋子都被他～光了；车、马❼都让对方❽(给)～掉了[状～]用哪个(棋)子儿～；没注意被他～了一个马；一连～了两个子儿

1. regiment 2. piece (in a board game) 3. chariot, one of the pieces in Chinese chess 4. cannon, one of the pieces in Chinese chess 5. tank 6. company 7. horse, one of the pieces in Chinese chess 8. the other side

⑤ absorb; soak up ≡ 吸收[～宾]〈名〉这种纸～墨❶；那种纸不太～水；这种菜最～油❷[～补]〈结〉把水～干了〈趋〉把墨(水/油)都～进去了〈程〉吃油～得真利害[状～]最～油；不～水；特别～墨；一下子～光了

1. Chinese ink; ink 2. oil; fat

⑥ live on（或 off）[～宾]〈名〉～利钱❶；～利息❷[～补]〈结〉这种人光吃利息就～足❸了〈时〉～了二十多年利息[状～]专❹～；光～利息〔习用〕靠山～山，靠水～水❺；～喝玩乐❻；～软不～硬❼；癞蛤蟆想～天鹅肉❽；～哑吧亏❾；～醋❿

1. 2. interest 3. sufficient; enough 4. specially 5. those living on the mountain live off (or get their living from) the mountain, those living near the water live off (or get their living from) the water — make use of local resources 6. eat, drink and be merry — idle away one's time in pleasure-seeking 7. be open to persuasion, but not to coercion 8. a toad lusting after a swan's flesh — aspiring after sth. one is not worthy of 9. be unable to speak out about one's grievances; be forced to keep one's grievances to oneself 10. be jealous (usu. of a rival in love)

chídào 迟到 be (come, arrive) late〈时〉～五分钟；～了很长时间〈量〉～过三次(迟过三次到)；～过两回(迟过两回到)[状～]从来不～；从来没无故❶～过，总～；经常❷～；每天～

1. without cause or reason 2. frequently; constantly

chōng 冲 ① pour boiling water on ≃沏；浇[**～宾**]〈名〉～鸡蛋[**～补**]〈结〉水不热，茶没～开；糖没～化❶；鸡蛋没～熟❷；咖啡～好了没有？～完了就喝〈可〉这水～不开茶；～不化糖；～不熟蛋；～不好咖啡〈时〉用温水❸～了半天也没冲开〈量〉我就～过一次鸡蛋[**状～**]多～几杯；少～一点儿；再～一碗；用开水❹～

1. melted **2.** ripe **3.** lukewarm water **4.** boiled water; boiling water

② rinse; flush ≃ 冲洗〔**～宾**〕〈名〉用水～～茶杯；～～盘子；～～地板；～厕所❶；上完厕所要～水〔**～补**〕〈结〉把茶杯里的茶叶❷用水～掉；～掉身上的污泥❸；把厕所～干净；洪水❹把房子～坍了❺；～塌了❻；～倒了❼；～垮了❽；～坏了；秧苗❾被大雨～走了；东西都被洪水～跑（～丢）了；把堤坝❿都～裂⓫了；～破了〈趋〉洪水～过来了；那片落叶被水～回来了〈程〉～得很远；厕所～得真干净；汽车～得干净极了；冲澡⓬～得挺舒服⓭；用冷水～得直哆嗦⓮；～得真凉快〈时〉每天都要～一次澡〈量〉天太热，一天要～好几次澡[**状～**]被大雨～走了；赶快～；多～～；好好～～；每天～；一遍一遍地～

1. water closet **2.** tea **3.** mud **4.** flood; innundation **5. 6. 7. 8.** collapse; fall down **9.** seedling **10.** dykes and dams **11.** split **12.** showerbath **13.** comfortable **14.** tremble; shiver

③ develop (photo) [**～宾**]〈名〉～胶卷❶；～底片❷[**～补**]〈结〉胶卷～好了吗？还没～完〈趋〉胶卷～出来了〈程〉～得真快；～得不好；～得不错〈可〉这些底片都～不了(liǎo)了；一个小时～得完吗？〈量〉我自己～过好几次胶卷了[**状～**]在照像馆❸～；一连～了好儿卷

1. roll film **2.** negative; photographic plate **3.** photo studio

④ rush; dash; charge ≃撞；冲撞[**～补**]〈结〉警察❶把游行示威❷的群众～散了；小心点，别被散场❸的人流❹～倒❺(dǎo)了〈趋〉抱着孩子，从着(zháo)火❻的屋子里～出来了；猎人❼～进树林里去了；滑雪❽运动员❾从山上～下来了；战士们从敌人的重重(chóng chóng)包围❿中～出来了；汽车开足马力⓫～上坡儿去了〈程〉～得真猛⓬；～得快极了；～得好危险⓭啊！〈可〉前边被人堵住⓮了，～不过去；5号长跑⓯运动员的力气都用尽⓰了，最后一圈⓱怎么也～不上去了〈量〉猛～了一阵⓲；～一下儿；～过两次都没冲出去〔**状～**〕猛～；向前～；从后边～；一下子～；突然～；竭尽全力地⓳～；差一点儿～散；勇敢地⓴～；出其不意地㉑～；横～直撞㉒；一窝蜂似地㉓～；急忙～了出来

1. police **2.** demonstration **3.** empty after the show (of a theatre, cinema, etc.) **4.** stream of people **5.** fall down **6.** be on fire **7.** hunter **8.** ski **9.** sportsman **10.**

surround; encircle **11.** put into high gear; go full steam ahead **12.** fierce; violent **13.** dangerous **14.** block up **15.** long-distance running **16.** use up completely; exhaust **17.** last lap **18.** for a spell **19.** do one's utmost; do all one can **20.** bravely; courageously **21.** unexpectedly **22.** push one's way by shoving or bumping; jostle and elbow one's way; dash around madly **23.** like a swarm of bees

chōng 充 ① fill; charge ≃装满；塞住〔**～宾**〕〈名〉旧电池❶～了电还可以用〈形〉饿的时候牛奶糖❷可以～饥❸〔**状～**〕暂时❹～饥〔**习用**〕～耳不闻❺

1. electric cell; battery **2.** toffee **3.** allay one's hunger **4.** temporarily; for the moment **5.** stuff one's ears and refuse to listen; turn a deaf ear to

② pretend to be; pose as; pass sth. off as ≃充当；冒充；假充〔**～宾**〕〈名〉～好人；～英雄❶；～行家❷；～内行❸；～好汉❹；～大胆儿；～数儿❺；不许拿坏的～好的〔**～补**〕〈可〉他在这儿～不了(liǎo) 内行〈量〉只能～一下儿数儿〔**状～**〕别～；总～；在大家面前～〔**习用**〕打肿脸～胖子❻

1. hero **2.** connoisseur; expert **3.** expert; adept **4.** brave man **5.** number (serve as a stopgap) **6.** slap one's face until it's swollen in an effort to look imposing — puff oneself up to one's own cost

chōngmǎn 充满 be full of; be permeated with; be full to the brim 〔**～宾**〕〈名〉～歌声；～笑声；～欢呼声；～热泪❶；～泪水❷；～香味；～火药味❸；～阳光；～信心❹；～理想❺；～矛盾❻；～感情❼；～大无畏的英雄气概❽；～生活气息❾；～青春的活力❿；～着热情⓫；～欢笑；～力量〈动〉～了对大自然的热爱⓬；～了希望；～了热切的期望⓭；～了斗争⓮；～了仇恨⓯〈形〉前途⓰～了光明⓱；～了痛苦⓲；～了欢乐⓳；～了喜悦⓴；～了对人的愤怒㉑〔**状～**〕对前途～；会场里～

1. tears **2.** tear; teardrop **3.** the smell of gunpowder **4.** confidence; faith **5.** ideal **6.** contradiction **7.** emotion; feeling; sentiment **8.** dauntless heroism **9.** flavour of life **10.** youthful vigour **11.** enthusiasm; zeal; warmth **12.** have a deep love for the nature **13.** earnest wish **14.** struggle **15.** hatred; hostility **16.** future; prospect **17.** bright **18.** pain; suffering **19.** happy; joyous **20.** happy; gay; joyous **21.** indignation; anger

chóngfù 重复 repeat; duplicate 〔**～宾**〕〈名〉～着他的话〔**～补**〕〈趋〉一句话老～来～去地❶说〈程〉话～得真烦人❷；～得让人听不下去了〈量〉这件事你已经～好儿次了；他没听明白，我又

~了一遍；请你再~一下儿〔**状~**〕别再~了；一再~又~了；一次又一次地~；三番五次地❸~；没完没了(liǎo)地❹~

1. over and over again 2. annoy 3. again and again; repeatedly 4. without end; endlessly

chóngbài 崇拜 worship; adore〔**~宾**〕〈名〉偶像❶；~英雄❷；~名人❸〔**状~**〕十分~；从来不~；一直~；非常~；狂热地❹~

1. idol; image 2. hero 3. eminent person; famous person 4. fanatically

chǒng 宠 dote on ≅ 惯；偏爱〔**~宾**〕〈名〉~孩子〔**~补**〕〈结〉孩子都让奶奶(给)~坏了〈程〉这孩子~得太利害了；~得太不象话❶了〈可〉孩子可~不得❷〔**状~**〕千万❸别~；从小儿就~；已经~坏了

1. unpresentable; unreasonable 2. must not 3. be sure

chōu 抽 ① take out (from in between); take (a part from a whole) ≅ 从中取〔**~宾**〕〈名〉~几个人去帮忙；~有经验❶的技术员❷；~时间，~空儿❸，~税❹，~签❺〔**~补**〕〈结〉有经验的工程师❻都被~走了〈趋〉从信封里~出一封信来；从书里~出一张年历❼来；从书架上~出一本书来；把那张照片从玻璃底下~出来了；张老师被~到教务处❽去工作了〈程〉这个签儿~得不好〈可〉忙得一点时间也~不出来；想去看看她，可是一直~不出身来❾〔**状~**〕把他~走；被~走了；从信封里~；一个一个地~；一连~走了好几个；几乎全~走了；一点儿也~不出时间来；一下子~走了一大批❿

1. experience 2. technician 3. time 4. tax 5. lots (draw lots) 6. engineer 7. single-page calendar 8. Dean's Office 9. unable to leave one's work 10. large numbers

② obtain by drawing, etc. ≅ 吸〔**~宾**〕〈名〉~水；~血❶；~空气❷；~骨髓❸〔**~补**〕〈结〉抽血抽得太多了，把身体都~坏了；~垮❹了；湖❺里的水快~干了；他爷爷就是抽鸦片❻~穷的〈趋〉把河里的水都~上来了；血~出来了；~起毒品❼来，就上瘾❽了；把河里的水~到田里去了〈程〉血~得太多了〈可〉水~不出来了〈时〉~了一个星期，才把湖里的水抽干〈量〉~过两次耳血；~过一次骨髓；再~一次就不抽了〔**状~**〕用抽水机往上~水；血管❾粗❿血好~；慢慢~；连续~；不停地~；永远不~了；从小河里~水；从静脉⓫里~血

1. blood 2. air 3. marrow 4. weak; bad 5. lake 6. opium 7. narcotics 8. get into the habit of 9. blood vessel 10. thick 11. vein

③ lash; whip; thrash ≅ 鞭打〔**~宾**〕〈名〉~牲口❶；~驴❷；~

马；奴隶主❸经常~奴隶❹；~陀螺❺；~~地毯❻上的尘土❼〔~补〕<把>把马~死了；把他~伤❽了；脸都被他~肿❾了；~红了；~破了❿；~流血⓫了；把驴~坏了；~瘸⓬了；~在身上<趋>这一鞭子⓭要是~上去就得(děi)疼死<可>离远点儿，就~不着(zháo)你<量>~了两下儿；~过两次；~了几鞭子〔状~〕用鞭子~；使劲儿~；猛⓮~；狠狠地⓯~；拼命⓰~；往背上~；劈头盖脸地⓱~；乱⓲~；无缘无故地⓳~；一下儿接着⓴一下儿地~

1. draught animals 2. donkey; ass 3. slave owner 4. slave 5. top 6. carpet 7. dust 8. wounded 9. swollen; swelling 10. cut 11. bleed; shed blood 12. cripple 13. whip 14. fiercely; violently 15. ruthlessly 16. with all one's might; desperately 17. right in the face 18. at random 19. without cause or reason; for no reason at all 20. follow

chóu 愁 worry; be anxious ≅忧；忧虑〔~宾〕<动>不~吃；不~穿；~找不到工作；~考不上大学；~不能完成任务❶<主-谓>~钱不够花；~病医不好〔~补〕<结>真把人~死了；~坏了；~病了；孩子刚十岁就~考大学的事了<趋>再~下去，头发就全白了；~起来连饭都吃不下<程>~得很；~得慌❷；~得要命❸；~得利害❹；~吃不下饭，睡不着(zháo)觉；~得没办法了；~

得直哭〔状~〕日夜地❺~；从早到晚地~；想起来就~；不用~；替他~；真~人；别再~了；一个劲儿地❻~；从来也不~；整天❼~〔习用〕~眉苦脸❽

1. not accomplished one's task 2. 3. 4. extremely; terribly 5. day and night 6. continuously 7. all day; the whole day 8. have a worried look

chū 出 ❶ go or come out↔入；进〔~宾〕<名>~大门以后，一直往前走；~家门；~校门；~国❶；~院❷；~海❸打鱼❹；~境❺要办手续❻；蛇❼~洞❽了；新产品什么时候~厂；火车~站了；运动员~场了；牙~血了〔~补〕<程>出院~得很快<趋>刚~去；从屋子里~来了<可>这些天忙得连家门儿都~不去；门太窄❾连大一点儿的桌子都~不去；梳子❿卡⓫在抽屉⓬里~不来，也进不去了<时>她~了四个月的差⓭<量>~过五次国〔状~〕渔民⓮一年到头⓯~海打鱼；悄悄地⓰~去了；早就~院了；前后一共~去了三次；刚~去，话很难~口

1. go abroad 2. leave hospital 3. sea 4. go fishing 5. border (leave the country) 6. go through formalities 7. snake 8. cave 9. narrow 10. comb 11. check; block 12. drawer 13. be away on official business 14. fisherman 15. year in and year out 16. quietly; silently

② exceed; go beyond ≅ 超出；离开〔~宾〕<名>火车~轨❶了；球~界❷了；字写得太大，都~格儿了；考题不能~这本书的范围❸〔~补〕<可>火车在一般情况下~不了(liǎo)轨 <时>象你这么干，不~半年就得(děi)病倒❹；不~三个月，他就能赶上❺你〔状~〕又~界了

1. (go off) the rails 2. outside 3. scope; limits; range 4. fall ill 5. catch up with

③ issue; put up ≅ 往外拿〔~宾〕<名>~主意❶；~题目❷；~考题❸；~作文题；~点子❹；~人；~力；~钱；~广告❺；~布告❻；~通知❼；~节目❽；~牌❾；~车；~专刊❿〔~补〕<结>牌~错了；考题~多了；~容易了；~难了；~重(chóng)了；题目~大了；~窄⓫了；题~偏⓬了；广告~晚了；主意帮他~对了<趋>牌一~出来，就不许往回拿了；考题都~出来了吗？<程>钱~得真不少；题~得很好；~得太难了；~得真容易<可>这点儿钱我还~得起； 他~不了(liǎo)好主意；名单⓭这星期还~不来；题还~不完<时>大家帮她~了半天主意<量>~过一次布告〔状~〕多(少)~几题；大量⓮~钱；替他~钱；给学生~题；由谁~节目？一共~了多少题？净~鬼点子⓯

1. idea; opinion 2. title 3. examination questions 4. idea; pointer 5. advertisement 6. notice; bulletin 7. notice; circular 8. programme 9. cards; dominoes 10. special issue or column 11. narrow 12. tricky (a catch question in an examination); out-of-the-way 13. name list 14. a large number; a great quantity 15. devilish advice; make a wicked suggestion

④ produce; turn out; arise; happen ≅ 出产；产生；发生〔~宾〕<名>~煤❶；~棉花❷；~花生❸；~人材❹；~成果❺；~成绩❻；~问题了；~危险；~事故❼；~事儿❽；~岔子❾；~乱子❿；~错儿⓫；~毛病⓬；~铜⓭〔~补〕<结>毛病~在什么地方？<可>放心吧，~不了(liǎo)问题<量>这里~过一次大乱子；手表~过好几次毛病了；机器~了一次故障⓮〔状~〕净~毛病；老~问题；总~故障；别~危险；又~事故了

1. coal 2. cotton 3. peanut 4. a person of ability 5. 6. result; achievement 7. accident 8. incident; accident 9. trouble; accident 10. disturbance; trouble; disorder 11. mistake 12. trouble; breakdown 13. copper 14. breakdown; trouble

⑤ put forth; vent ≅ 发出；发泄〔~宾〕<名>豆子❶~芽❷了；~汗❸；脖子❹底下~痱子❺了；别拿我~气❻；小孩子~麻疹❼了；别~声音 〔~补〕<结>气够了；麻疹~透❽了<趋>花蕾❾都~来了；气球的口儿没系好里边的气全~来了<程>汗~得太多

了；麻疹~得很轻；豆芽❿~得真大；~得真粗⓫〈可〉这口气老~不出〈时〉麻疹整整~了两天〈量〉最近鼻子⓬~了好几次血〔状~〕豆子早就~芽了；容易~血；急⓭得直~汗；一点也别~声音

1. bean 2. bud 3. sweat 4. neck 5. prickly heat 6. give vent to one's anger; vent one's spleen 7. measles 8. gone through 9. (flower) bud 10. bean sprouts 11. thick 12. nose 13. be anxious; be impatient

⑥ become visible; appear; manifest itself ≌ 显露〔~宾〕〈名〉~丑❶；~风头❷；~洋相❸；~名〔~补〕〈结〉丑~尽❹了；风头~足❺了；名~大了〈趋〉他~起洋相来真可笑；~起风头来什么也不顾❻了〈程〉她出丑~得连我都没脸见人了；风头~得十足〈可〉永远~不了(liǎo)名儿〈时〉他在那里~了半天洋相〈量〉~过一次丑〔状~〕一下子~了名儿；当面❼~丑；净~丑；别~洋相了〔习用〕一个鼻孔~气❽

1. disgraceful; scandalous (make a fool of oneself) 2. the publicity one receives (be in the limelight) 3. make an exhibition of oneself 4. to the limit 5. adequate 6. have no regard for; in spite of; regardless of 7. in sb's presence 8. breathe through the same nostrils — sing the same tune

chūxiàn 出现 appear; arise emerge〔~宾〕〈名〉天空~了一轮明月❶；他们之间~了不可调和的矛盾❷；~了解决❸不了(liǎo)的问题；~了很大的困难；~了欢乐的场面❹；国际❺上~了紧张局势❻；~了新局面❼；~了繁忙❽的景象❾；~了很多新事物❿；窗前⓫~了一个人影⓬；天空~了一架直升飞机⓭〔~补〕〈结〉~在眼前⓮；~于世界上〈程〉~得很早；~得很快〈量〉过一次〔状~〕在什么问题上~了矛盾? 曾经~过；一度⓯~；突然~；一再~；偶然⓰~；第一次~；在舞台⓱上~；在银幕⓲上~；反复⓳~；不断地~

1. a bright moon 2. uncompromising contradiction 3. resolve 4. scene 5. international 6. a tense situation 7. a new aspect 8. busy 9. scene; sight; picture 10. thing 11. in front of the window 12. shadow of a human figure 13. helicopter 14. before one's eyes 15. once; for a time 16. occasionally 17. stage 18. screen 19. repeatedly; over and over again

chú 除 ① get rid of; eliminate; remove ≌ 除掉；丢掉；消灭〔~宾〕〈名〉~了一个祸害❶；~了一个大恶霸❷；~草；~虫❸〔~补〕〈结〉~完了；~干净了；~掉杂草❹〈可〉这病~不了(liǎo)根儿❺〔状~〕彻底~；为民~害；替民~害；从榜❻上~了名；很难~净；一次全~净了

1. disaster 2. local tyrant 3. insect; worm 4. weeds 5. an

incompletely cured illness 6. a list of names posted up

② divide (math.) 〔~宾〕〈数〉2~8得4； 9被3~得3〔~补〕〈结〉数儿~错了；这次~对了吗？数儿都~尽❶了吗？〈趋〉你~出来，得多少？我~出来的数儿跟你的不一样〈程〉~得不对〈可〉这个数儿~不尽〈时〉~了半天也没除对〈量〉~了好多遍了；再~一下儿〔状~〕哪个数儿被哪个数儿~；一次~不尽；用计算机❷~；反复~；一遍一遍地~；细心点儿❸~

1. exhaustive (can be divided by) 2. calculator 3. carefully

chǔ 处 ① get along (with sb.) ≌交往〔~补〕〈结〉跟他~熟❶了才能发现❷他的优点❸；邻居❹~好了跟一家人一样 〈趋〉无法❺~下去了〈程〉他们两家~得真好；~得很熟；~得非常亲热❻；~得不错〈时〉在一起~了五年〔状~〕相~得很和睦❼；这个人好~❽；真难~；不容易~好；难怪❾~不好

1. familiar; acquainted 2. discover; find out 3. merit 4. neighbour 5. it can't be helped 6. intimate; warm-hearted 7. harmony 8. easy to get along with 9. no wonder

② be situated in; be in a certain condition 〔~补〕〈结〉~在一个伟大的时代❶； ~于热带❷〔状~〕正~在；正好~于

1. great era 2. the torrid zone

③ punish; penalize ≌处罚〔~宾〕〈名〉~徒刑❶， ~死刑❷； 绞刑❸〔~补〕〈结〉~死〈可〉~得了(liǎo)死刑~不了(liǎo)？〔状~〕因杀人~了死刑

1. imprisonment; (prison) sentence 2. death sentence 3. death by hanging

chǔlǐ 处理 handle; deal with; dispose of 〔~宾〕〈名〉~一些棘手❶的问题；~重大❷案件❸；~善后❹工作；~日常事务❺；~国家大事❻；~琐碎❼的家务〔~补〕〈结〉事情都~完了；没用的东西都~掉了；~光了；要~好婆❽媳❾关系〈趋〉把积压❿的货物⓫都~出去吧〈程〉~得很快〈可〉~得了(liǎo)吗？~得完~不完〈时〉~了好几天，才处理完；~了不少日子了〈量〉积压的东西太多，需要好好~一下儿；~过两三次了〔状~〕集中⓬~；一次~完；全部~掉；一下子都~了；及时~；成批地⓭~；尽量⓮~；随便~；不好~；公开⓯~；内部~；偷偷地~；适当(地)⓰~；合理地⓱~；尽快~；幸亏⓲~了；马上~；只好~；不得不~；不必~

1. thorny; troublesome; knotty 2. significant major; great 3. case 4. deal with problems arising from an accident, etc. 5. day-to-day work; routine duties 6. national (state) affairs 7. trifling; trivial 8. mother-in-law 9.

daughter-in-law 10. keep long in stock 11. goods 12. concentrate 13. in batches 14. as far as possible 15. publicly 16. suitably; properly; appropriately 17. rationally 18. fortunately; luckily

chù 触 touch; contact; strike ≅ 碰；遇着；接触〔～宾〕〈名〉小心❶别～了电❷；〔～补〕〈结〉那件事～动❸了他的心事❹；～到了他的痛处❺〈可〉戴着绝缘手套❻修理❼电线❽，就～不了(liǎo)电了；熟悉❾海底❿情况的老渔民⓫一般～不了(liǎo)礁⓬〈量〉小时候～过一次电〔状～〕在暴风雨之夜⓭～了礁

1. be careful; be cautious 2. get an electric shock 3. move sb.; stir up sb's feelings 4. sth. weighing on one's mind; worry; a load on one's mind 5. sore spot 6. insulating gloves 7. repair; mend 8. electric line 9. be familiar with 10. the bottom of the sea 11. old fisherman 12. run up on rocks; strike a reef 13. at a stormy night

chuān 穿 ① wear; put on; be dressed in 〔～宾〕〈名〉～衣服；～裤子❶；～鞋；～袜子❷；～裙子❸；～雨衣〔～补〕〈结〉把衣服～好；把鞋～上；雨衣都～旧了；～坏了；袜子～破了；衣服～脏❹了；鞋～错了；把衣服～整齐了再出去〈趋〉那个年轻人～起风衣❺来很神气❻；把鞋～起来吧〈程〉～得真快；～得太多；～得很少；～得很干净；～得很整齐；～得非常漂亮；～得十分讲究❼；～得最朴素❽；～得时髦❾极了；～得真难看；～得臃肿肿❿的；～得很得体⓫〈可〉孩子太小，自己～不了(liǎo)衣服；鞋太小～不进去；脚肿⓬了，连鞋都～不上了〈时〉～了半天才穿进去；太冷了，先～一会儿我这件衣服吧〈量〉你～一下儿试试〔状～〕经常～；幸亏⓭多～了两件；天不冷，不用～；不必～；一律⓮～制服；整整齐齐地～；仍旧⓯～着那件破棉衣；好容易才～上；随便⓰～；给孩子～；做饭的时候才～围裙⓱

1. trousers 2. socks 3. skirt 4. dirty 5. spring coat 6. putting on airs; cocky; overweening 7. too fastidious about 8. simple; plain 9. fashionable 10. be cumbersomely dressed 11. fit sb. beautifully 12. swelling; swollen 13. fortunately; luckily 14. all; without exception 15. still; yet 16. (do) as one pleases 17. apron

② pass through; cross ≅ 穿过；通过〔～宾〕〈名〉～过地道❶；～过树林；～过草地；～过操场；～过马路；～过大街小巷❷；～过走廊❸；～过人群；～过云层❹；灯光～过门缝❺；～过山洞；～针；～珠子；～钥匙❻〔～补〕〈结〉钥匙～在铁环❼上；用珠子～成珠帘❽；～满了；～完了；～好了；～上了〈趋〉线❾～过去了；把珠子都～起来了；我们从这条小路～过去吧；这边儿的火车从

山洞~过去了；那边的火车从山洞~过来了；小船从桥下边~过来了〈程〉她穿珠子~得真快〈可〉~得出去~不出去?〈时〉针眼❿太小，线~了半天也没穿上〈量〉用铁丝⓫~一下儿行不行?〔状~〕从这边~；一直~过去；来回~⓬；用什么线~?；老~不上；一个一个地~；珠子好不好~? 真难~; 熟练地⓭~着

1. tunnel 2. the streets and lanes 3. corridor 4. cloud layer 5. a crack between a door and its frame 6. key 7. iron hoop 8. curtain 9. thread 10. eye of a needle 11. iron wire 12. to and fro 13. skilfully

③ pierce through; penetrate ≅ 穿透〔~宾〕〈名〉墙上~了一个大洞; 皮带❶上~了几个眼儿❷; 纸上~了几个小窟窿❸; 子弹❹~过玻璃❺〔~补〕〈结〉弹片❻~破了甲板❼; 火箭❽~破了坦克❾; 钉子❿~透⓫了木板〈趋〉子弹从玻璃窗~进来了；~进去了；~出来了；~出去了〈可〉~得过去~不过去?〔状~〕好容易才~过来；正好~; 从外边儿~; 一下子~透了, 嗖地⓬一声~过了〔习用〕~小鞋⓭; ~针引线⓮

1. leather belt 2. 3. small hole 4. bullet 5. glass 6. shell fragment 7. deck 8. rocket 9. tank 10. nail 11. gone through 12. whiz 13. give sb. tight shoes to wear — make things hard for sb. by abusing one's power 14. act as a go-between

chuán 传

① pass; pass on ≅ 传递〔~宾〕〈名〉~球；给我~个话儿；~口令❶; ~命令~知识❷; ~技术❸; ~秘方❹; ~手艺❺〔~补〕〈结〉~对了吗?别~错了; 把球~给中锋❻了; ~到我手里了; 父亲把手艺~给了儿子〈趋〉快把球~过来〈程〉球~得真快; 话~得很清楚〈量〉给他两次球, 他都没接❼着(zháo)〔状~〕一个一个往下~; 赶快往后~; 立即~; 一代一代❽~下去; 悄悄地❾~着口令; 把话一五一十地❿~给他; 原原本本地⓫~

1. word of command 2. knowledge 3. technique 4. secret recipe 5. craftsmanship 6. centre forward; centre 7. catch; take hold of 8. generation after generation 9. quietly 10. (narrate) systematically and in full detail 11. from beginning to end

② spread; go round; be circulated ≅ 扩散〔~宾〕〈名〉~消息; ~捷报❶; ~佳音❷; ~喜讯❸〈数〉一~十, 十~百〔~补〕〈结〉消息~开了, 都~遍了; 消息~错了; ~到很远的地方了; 把这个文件~给大家看看〈趋〉喜讯~来, 他高兴得跳起来了; 这件事千万别~出去; 从她那里~出来的消息总是不大可靠❹; 这个消息都~到我的耳朵里来了〈程〉消息~得真快〈可〉放心吧, 这个消息决~不出去〈时〉消息都~了好几天了, 我才知道; 这个消息~了好一阵子❺〔状~〕很快~开

了；一下子~开了；一会儿的工夫❻就~开了；从他们那里~出来了；不时❼~来；从四面八方❽~来；不断❾~来；迅速❿~开了；逐渐⓫~开了

1. news of victory; report of a success 2. welcome news 3. good news 4. unreliable 5. a period of time 6. a little while 7. frequently; often 8. from all directions 9. continuously 10. rapidly 11. gradually; by degrees

③ transmit; conduct ≅ 传导 〔~宾〕〈名〉空气~热；金属❶~电；水能~声吗？〔~补〕〈趋〉声音~过去了；~过来了；从下边~上来了；从上边~下去了；声音从里边~出来了；从外边~进来了；~到这边来了；~到那去了〈程〉~得很远；~得很快〈可〉这种材料❷~得了(liǎo)热(电)吗？〔状~〕很快就~过去了；从外边~来唱歌的声音；热逐渐❸~过来了；一会儿就~来了

1. metal 2. material 3. gradually

④ summon ≅ 传唤〔~宾〕〈名〉~犯人❶；~被告❷；~证人❸出庭作证❹；~原告❺〔状~〕用传票❻~案件当事人❼；再次~；立即~

1. prisoner; convict 2. the accused 3. witness 4. appear in court as a witness 5. plaintiff 6. summons 7. party concerned

⑤ infect; be contagious ≅ 传染 〔~宾〕〈名〉疟蚊❶~疟疾❷；苍蝇❸~霍乱❹；老鼠❺~鼠疫❻〔~补〕〈结〉~上流行性感冒❼了，~上肝炎❽了〈程〉~得快极了〈可〉多注意点就~不上了〔状~〕很快地~上了；一下子~上了；千万❾别~上；莫名其妙地❿~上了〔习用〕~声筒⓫

1. anopheles mosquitos 2. malaria 3. fly 4. cholera 5. mouse; rat 6. pest 7. the flu (catch the flu) 8. hepatitis 9. be sure 10. be unable to make head or tail of sth.; be baffled 11. megaphone; one who parrots another; sb.'s mouthpiece

chuǎn 喘 breathe heavily; gasp for breath 〔~宾〕〈名〉走得太急❶，你先坐在那儿~~气再说话；等我~一口气再干；忙了半天也该~~气了；气得直~粗气❷〔~补〕〈趋〉咳嗽❸得好容易才~上一口气来〈程〉刚跑完百米❹~得很利害❺；~得上气不接下气❻；得了哮喘病❼以后，常常~得不能躺着睡觉；~得真难受；~得真可怜❽〈可〉上了五层楼，连气儿都~不上来❾了；咳嗽得不过气来了〈时〉~了好几年；~了一辈子❿〈量〉~了一大阵⓫〔状~〕好容易~上气来了；大口大口地~气；张着嘴~气；从小⓬就~；整夜整夜⓭地~；先~~气，再说话；直⓮~

1. be in a hurry 2. puff and blow 3. cough 4. run the 100-metre dash 5. terrible; awful 6. gasp for

breath; be out of breath 7. asthma 8. pitiful; pitiable; poor 9. be out of breath 10. all one's life; throughout one's life 11. a period of time 12. from childhood 13. all night long 14. incessantly

chuàn 串 ① get things mixed up 〔~宾〕〈名〉电话~线❶了；可别抄~行❸ (háng)〔~补〕〈可〉用尺子比着抄，就~不了 (liǎo) 行了〔状~〕又~行 (háng) 了；经常~线；容易~

1. line 2. copy 3. line

② go from place to place; run about 〔~宾〕〈名〉~了好几家；~亲戚❶；~门儿❷〔~补〕〈时〉昨天~了一下午门儿〔量〕到他家去了一下儿门〔状~〕经常~；从来不~；难得❸~一次门儿；整天❹~；成天❺~；偶尔❻~；东~西~❼；到处~

1. relations 2. call at sb.'s home; drop in 3. seldom; rarely 4. 5. all day long; all the time 6. occasionally; once in a while 7. here ... there

chuǎng 闯 ① rush; dash ≡ 猛冲〔~补〕〈趋〉从外边~进来一个人；他没敲门❶就~进去了〈可〉门关❷得很严❸，谁也~不进来〔状~〕突然~进一个人来；象一阵风❹似地~了进来；硬❺~进去了；大摇大摆❻地~进去了；若无其事地❼~了进去；冒冒失失地❽~了进来；不顾一切地❾~了进去；猛地❿~了进来；气冲冲地⓫~了进来

1. knock at the door 2. close; shut 3. tight 4. a blast 5. obstinately 6. strutting; swaggering 7. as if nothing had happened; calmly; casually 8. rashly; abruptly; without due consideration 9. recklessly; regardless of the consequences 10. suddenly; abruptly 11. panting with rage

② temper oneself (by battling through dffiiculties and dangers) 〔~宾〕〈名〉~路子❶；~天下❷；〔~补〕〈结〉~开一条新路子〈趋〉我们必须~出自己的路子来；他在外边待❸了那么多年也~出来了〈量〉~一下儿试试吧〔状~〕路子很难~；不好~；勇敢地❹~；在外边多~一~〔习用〕走南~北❺

1. a path 2. land under heaven (the country) 3. stay 4. bravely; courageously 5. journey north and south; travel extensively

chuàng 创 start (doing sth,); achieve (sth. for the first time) ≡ 开始做〔~宾〕〈名〉~了一项新记录❶；~一番事业❷〔~补〕〈趋〉能不能~出好的成绩❸来？〈可〉不知道这次比赛❹他~得了 (liǎo) 全国记录❺吗？〈量〉她已经~了两次世界记录❻了〔状~〕又一次~记录，首(次)❼~记录；满有把握地❽~；信心百倍地❾~；要兢兢业业地❿~一番事业

1. a new record 2. cause; undertaking 3. result; achievement; success 4. match; competition 5. national record 6. world record 7. the first time 8. with assurance 9. full of confidence 10. cautiously and conscientiously

chuī 吹 ① blow; puff〔～宾〕〈名〉～火；～蜡烛❶；～一口气❷；～～桌子上的尘土❸；理发❹要不要～风❺〔～补〕〈结〉别把火柴❻～灭❼了；把桌子上的粉笔末❽～掉❾；风把湖❿水～皱⓫了；把门～开了；把纸～跑了；嘴唇⓬都让风给～干了；～裂⓭了；把茶～凉⓮点儿再喝；春风～在脸上很舒服⓯〈趋〉从外边～进来一股冷风〈程〉风～得旗子⓰呼啦呼啦地⓱响；风～得真舒服；～得真难受⓲；头发～得很蓬松〈可〉你一口气～得灭⓳三支蜡烛吗？门窗都关严⓴了，尘土就～不进来了〈时〉洗完头发，～一会儿就干了〈量〉桌子上的土～了几次才吹干净〔状～〕一口气把火柴～灭了；用力～；轻轻地～；从门缝㉑～进来了；噗地一声㉒把蜡烛～灭了；风呼呼地㉓～；猛烈地㉔～

1. candle 2. give a puff 3. dust 4. haircut 5. dry (hair) with a blower 6. match 7. extinguished 8. powder of a chalk 9. off; away 10. lake 11. rippled 12. lip 13. split 14. make or become cool 15. comfortable 16. flag 17. be flapping in the wind 18. feel unwell 19. put out 20. close tightly 21. a crack between a door and its frame 22. puff 23. (blow) a strong current of air into 24. violently; fiercely

② play (wind, instruments)〔～宾〕〈名〉～口哨❶；～笛子❷；～口琴❸；～哨子❹；～喇叭❺；～箫❻；～歌儿；～肥皂泡❼玩〔～补〕〈结〉军号❽～响了；口琴～走调❾了；歌儿～错了；这次～对了；别把肥皂泡～破❿了；～灭⓫了〈趋〉他～出来的歌儿非常好听；～出来的曲子⓬非常优美⓭动听⓮；这个哨子～起来声音真尖⓯；请你继续～下去吧，我们都喜欢听〈程〉～得真好听；～得委婉⓰动听；～得太难听了；～得震耳朵⓱；～得太响了；～得烦死⓲人〈可〉我刚学吹箫，还～不好；喇叭坏了～不响了；这个曲子再复杂，他也～得了(liǎo)〈时〉他～了三年笛子，现在又练吹黑管⓳了〈量〉～过几次圆号⓴；～了一阵子双簧管㉑；先～一下儿试试音〔状～〕这个歌儿好～；那个舞曲㉒比较难～；容易～；大声～；小声～；有时～；偶尔㉓～；愉快地～；高兴地～；随便㉔～；熟练地㉕～；连续～了三个小时；一连～了五个；一个接着一个地～；看着乐谱㉖～；不会吹别瞎㉗～；一遍一遍地～

1. whistling sound through rounded lips; whistle 2. flute 3. harmonica 4. whistle 5. trumpet 6. a vertical bamboo flute 7. soap bubble 8. bugle 9. out of tune 10. burst 11. extinguished 12. song

13. graceful 14. interesting or pleasant to listen to 15. sharp 16. mild 17. deafen 18. extremely annoying 19. clarinet 20. French horn 21. oboe 22. dance music 23. occasionally 24. as one pleases 25. skilfully 26. music score 27. groundlessly; to no purpose

③ boast; brag ≅ 夸口〔**~宾**〕〈名〉~牛❶〈主-谓〉~自己有办法❷; ~自己能干❸; ~别人如何❹赏识❺自己; ~自己见识❻广❼; ~他多么有门路❽〔**~补**〕〈趋〉大话已经~出去了，只好努力干了〈程〉~得天花乱坠❾; ~得使人无法相信❿; ~得太利害了〈时〉~了半天，一件事都没办成〈量〉在我面前~过好几次了〔**状~**〕先别~，做出成绩⓫来再说; 到处乱~; 得机会⓬就~; 在众人面前~; 净瞎⓭~〔**习用**〕~牛拍马⓮; ~~拍拍⓯; ~鼓手⓰; ~胡子瞪眼⓱; 这事~了⓲; 他们两个人~了⓳

1. boast; brag 2. way; means; measure 3. of great ability 4. how; what 5. appreciate; recognize the worth of 6. knowledge; experience 7. wide; extensive 8. knack; way 9. boast in the most fantastic terms 10. incredible 11. success; achievement 12. opportunity; chance 13. groundlessly; foolishly 14. boast and flatter 15. boasting and toadying 16. trumpeter; bugler — eulogist 17. froth at the mouth and glare with rage; foam with rage 18. 19. break off; fall through; break up

chuí 垂 hang down; droop; let fall ≅ 滴落; 掉; 悬挂; 吊着〔**~宾**〕〈名〉~着眼皮❶; ~着手; 房檐❷上~着几根冰柱❸; 耳朵上~着一副耳环❹〔**~补**〕〈结〉困❺得~下了眼皮; 裙子❻一直~到脚面❼; 柳条❽~在水面上〈趋〉幕布❾从上边~了下来〔**状~**〕从上面~; 往下~; 低低地~着

1. eyelid 2. eaves 3. icicle 4. earrings 5. sleepy 6. skirt 7. instep 8. willow twig; osier 9. (theatre) curtain; (cinema) screen

chuí 捶 beat (with a stick or fist); thump; pound ≅ 敲; 擂〔**~宾**〕〈名〉~背❶; ~鼓❷; ~门; ~桌子; ~墙; ~胸❸〔**~补**〕〈结〉~疼了; ~累了; 把手都~红了〈趋〉~起鼓来真震❹人〈程〉鼓~得真响❺; ~得咚咚地❻响; 背~得真舒服❼〈时〉每天都得(děi)给老奶奶~一会儿背; ~了半天, 胳膊❽都酸❾了〈量〉~过一次; ~了好几下儿门, 里边才听见; ~了一阵鼓; ~了好几拳❿; ~了他一顿〔**状~**〕用力~; 猛~; 用拳头~; 用鼓槌⓫~; 轻轻地~; 一下一下地~; 一只手~; 两只手交替⓬着~; 给病人~〔**习用**〕破鼓万人~⓭

1. one's back (as in massage) 2. drum 3. chest 4. deafen 5. loud; noisy 6. rub-a-dub; rat-tat 7. comfortable 8. arm 9. ache 10. fist 11. drum stick 12. in turn 13.

everybody hits a man who is down

chuō 戳 ① jab; poke; stab ≃ 扎；刺；攮〔**～宾**〕〈名〉小心点别让棍儿❶～了眼睛；没注意笔尖❷把纸～了一个洞；～了一个小窟窿❸〔**～补**〕〈结〉别把眼睛～瞎❹了；把纸～破❺了〈量〉注意点儿，让毛衣针❻～一下儿可不得了(liǎo) ❼〔**状～**〕一下子～了；不小心～了

1. stick **2.** nib; pen point **3.** small hole **4.** blind **5.** torn **6.** knitting needle **7.** desperately serious; disastrous

② sprain; blunt〔**主～**〕〈名〉钢笔尖❶～了；手指头～了〔**～宾**〕〈名〉打排球❷的时候～了手〔**～补**〕〈结〉手～疼了；～肿❸了；笔尖～弯❹了〈程〉手～得真疼；笔～得不能用了〈量〉笔掉地下～了一下儿；～过两次手了〔**状～**〕差点儿～了；小心点儿，别～了

1. nib; pen point **2.** volleyball **3.** swelling; swollen **4.** bent

cì 刺 ① stab; prick ≃ 攮；戳；扎〔**～宾**〕〈名〉那个流氓❶用匕首❷～了一个人〔**～补**〕〈结〉这句话～疼了我的心；击剑❸时5号运动员被～伤❹了；那个售票员❺让坏蛋～死了；连那么厚❻的衣服都～透❼了；把肺❽～穿❾了；～着(zháo)你了没有？～在肩膀❿上了〈趟〉一刀就～进去了；向我～来了；向他～去了；～到肉里去了；～进了胸膛⓫〈程〉～得很深⓬；～得真疼；～得直往外冒⓭血；～得当场⓮死亡⓯〈可〉～得着(zháo)吗？～得进去～不进去？〈量〉～了一下儿没刺着(zháo)；～了两刀〔**状～**〕往身上猛⓰～；朝胸口⓱～；用剑⓲～；突然～；出其不意地⓳～；差一点儿～；一连～；连续～；恶狠狠地⓴～；故意㉑～

1. rogue **2.** dagger **3.** fencing **4.** stab and wound **5.** ticket seller; conductor **6.** thick **7.** gone through **8.** lungs **9.** pierced through **10.** shoulder **11.** chest **12.** deep **13.** emit; send out; give off **14.** on the spot **15.** die **16.** energetically; fiercely **17.** the pit of the stomach **18.** sword **19.** unexpectedly **20.** fiercely; ferociously **21.** intentionally; on purpose

② dazzle; grate on; irritate; stimulate ≃ 晃；刺激〔**～宾**〕〈名〉光～眼；声音～耳；辣味❶～鼻❷；寒风❸～骨❹；说话别～人〔**～补**〕〈结〉～到了他的痛处❺〈程〉光太强❻～得眼睛都睁不开❼〈量〉～了他一下儿〔**状～**〕真～眼；太～耳了；故意❽～人；狠狠地❾～；冷言冷语地❿～

1. hot; peppery **2.** nose (irritate the nose) **3.** cold air **4.** bone (piercing to the bones) **5.** sore spot **6.** strong **7.** cannot open one's eyes **8.** intentionally; on purpose **9.** ruthlessly; relentlessly vigorously **10.** sarcastic comments; ironical remarks

cìjī 刺激 stimulate; excite

〔～宾〕〈名〉辣椒❶ 可以～食欲❷; 强光❸～眼睛; 冷风❹～皮肤❺; 酒❻～人的神经❼〔～补〕〈程〉辣味儿❽～得她不断地❾打喷嚏❿; ～得我一个劲儿地⓫咳嗽⓬; 那件事差点儿把她～得旧病复发⓭ 了〈趋〉他神经非常健全⓮, 什么事也～不了(liǎo) 他〔状～〕强烈地⓯～; 容易～; 被～

1. hot pepper; chilli 2. appetite 3. strong light 4. cold wind 5. skin 6. wine 7. nerve 8. smelling of pepper 9. incessantly 10. sneeze 11. continuously 12. cough 13. have a recurrence of an old illness; have a relapse 14. very sound (perfect) 15. strongly; intensely; violently

còu 凑

① gather together; pool; collect ≌ 攒(cuán) 〔～宾〕〈名〉他们～钱买了一辆摩托车❶; 我不会唱, 他们硬❷把我拉来～数儿❸; ～了一套完整的教材❹; 那个立体声❺收录机, 是他们结婚时, 朋友们～钱给买的〔～补〕〈结〉出国旅行的钱～够了吗? ～齐❻了吗? ～足❼了吗? 杂志～齐了没有? 零件❽还没～全吧? 人数～够了没有? 〈趋〉钱是一点一点～起来的〈程〉～得真快, 一会儿工夫❾就～了这么多钱〈可〉不知这笔钱～得上～不上? 钱一时～不齐; 零件～得全吗? 这一大笔钱, 只靠❿我们几个人凑, 可～不上; ～不了(liǎo) ～不齐～不起来〈时〉～了一个月才凑足; ～了半年多才凑够〈量〉大家～一下儿就够了〔状～〕好容易～上了; 不好～; 不容易～; 真难～; 一点一点地～; 一时～不齐; 临时⓫～

1. motorcycle 2. obstinately 3. serve as a stopgap; make up the number or amount 4. a complete set of teaching material 5. stereo 6. even; completed 7. sufficient; enough 8. parts (of a machine) 9. time 10. depend on; rely on 11. at the time when sth. happens; for the moment

② move close to; press near 〔～补〕〈结〉大家～在一起聊天❶; 在灯下看书, ～近点儿, 看得清楚〈趋〉有两个人在公园的茶桌上下象棋❷, 很多人都～过去 (～上去)看; ～到跟前❸去(来)听; 他今天也一起热闹❹来了〈程〉～得真近; 不要～得太近〈可〉大家都很忙, 只有在节日❺家里人才～得到一起; 平时❻总～不齐❼; ～不到一起〈量〉他今天也想一下热闹〔状～〕难得❽～在一起; 很难～齐; 向前～～

1. chat 2. playing chess 3. close to; near; in front of 4. join in the fun 5. holiday; festival 6. at ordinary times; in normal times 7. not complete 8. seldom; rarely

còuhe 凑合 make do

≌ 将就; 勉强〔～宾〕〈动〉～(着)用; ～(着)穿; ～(着)看; ～(着)写; ～(着)住; ～(着)睡; ～(着)坐; 他们两个人感情不好, 只好～(着)过❶〔～补〕〈可〉这两个人脾气❷不和，总~不到一起；~不到一块儿〈时〉~了很长时间；~了好几年；再~一会儿〔**状**~〕随便❸~；一直❹~；勉强❺~；只好~；决不~

1. live; get along 2. temper 3. as one pleases 4. always 5. reluctantly; grudgingly

cuàngǎi 窜改 alter；tamper with; falsify ≅改动〔**~宾**〕〈名〉~原文❶；~记录❷；~帐目❸；~文件❹；~了我的意思❺；~原话❻〔**~补**〕〈结〉把原文都~成什么样子了！已经~过了〈程〉~得不象样子❼了；~得面目全非❽了〈量〉~过很多次了〔**状**~〕任意❾~；故意❿~；决不允许⓫随便~；明目张胆地⓬~；多次~；再三~；竟然⓭~；几乎全部~了；被他们~；毫无顾忌地⓮~

1. original text; the original 2. record; notes 3. accounts; items of an account 4. document 5. opinion; idea; meaning 6. original sentence 7. 8. (altered) beyond recognition 9. wantonly; wilfully 10. intentionally; on purpose 11. never allow 12. brazenly; flagrantly 13. unexpectedly; to one's surprise 14. free from all inhibitions

cuànduó 篡夺 usurp; seize ≅夺取〔**~宾**〕〈名〉~领导权❶；~王位❷；~皇冠❸〔**~补**〕〈结〉终于把领导权~到手了〈可〉他认为谁也~不了(liǎo)他的王位〔**状**~〕一夜之间❹就被~了；以武力❺

~；轻而易举地❻~了；易如反掌地❼~；不费吹灰之力地❽~；终于~了

1. leadership 2. throne 3. imperial crown 4. overnight 5. by force 6. without making an effort 7. as easy as turning one's hand over; as easy as falling off a log 8. as easy as blowing off dust — not needing the slightest effort

cuàngǎi 篡改 distort；tamper with; falsify〔**~宾**〕〈名〉~历史❶；~政策❷；~经典著作❸〔**~补**〕〈程〉~得面目全非❹了；~得乱七八糟❺；~得一塌糊涂❻；~得不象样子❼了〈量〉~了很多次；~了无数❽次〔**状**~〕决不许❾随便❿~；任意⓫~；明目张胆地⓬~；暗中⓭~；私自⓮~；公然⓯~；竟然⓰~；完全~；全部~；部分~；一再~；一次一次地~；屡次⓱~；已经被他们~了

1. history 2. policy 3. classical works 4. (distorted) beyond recognition 5. 6. 7. in a complete mess; in an awful state 8. innumerable 9. never allow 10. 11. wantonly; wilfully 12. brazenly; flagrantly 13. secretly 14. privately 15. publicly; openly 16. unexpectedly; to one's surprise 17. time and again; repeatedly

cuī 催 urge; hurry; press ≅催促〔**~宾**〕〈名〉你可真能~人；~小李早一点儿去〈代〉~他快说；别~我；~她快睡；~我快点儿给

他办；~他们早点交货❶；~他去理发❷；~我还钱；~我们快决定❸；~我给她做新衣服〔~补〕〈结〉把人都~烦❹了；可别把她~急❺了，催急了她就不管❻了〈趋〉他~起人来可真要命❼（可真不得了(liǎo)）〈程〉~得我都忘了锁门❽；~得人心烦，我让他~得没办法了，只好去；把我~得坐不住❾了〈可〉怎么催也~不动他；这个人可~不得❿，一催他就急〈时〉~了半天，他好象没听见一样〈量〉~过他两次了，就是不去；再~一下儿他〔状~〕一个劲儿地~；不用~；无须~；催也白⓫~；只好~；亲自⓬~；成天~；天天~；几乎每天~；三番五次地⓭~；直~；着急地⓮~

1. delivery goods 2. haircut 3. make a decision 4. bored; peeved 5. annoyed; irritated 6. not be in charge of 7. awfully; terribly 8. forget to lock the door 9. be unable to sit still 10. must not 11. in vain 12. personally 13. again and again 14. impatiently; anxiously

cuīcán 摧残 wreck；destroy；devastate〔~宾〕〈名〉~身体；~生命，~心灵❶；~健康❷；~人才❸〔~补〕〈程〉身心❹都被~得很利害❺〔状~〕任意❻~；长期❼~；一再~；用各种办法~；严重地❽~；无情地❾~

1. heart; soul; spirit 2. health 3. a talented person; a person of ability 4. body and mind 5. terrible;

awful 6. wantonly; wilfully 7. over a long period of time 8. seriously 9. mercilessly

cún 存 ① store; keep ≅ 储存；↔取〔~宾〕〈名〉仓库❶里~着足够❷的粮食；水库❸里~了很多水；他~了不少水果〔~补〕〈结〉菜~多了；~少了；水~够了；~足❹了；仓库~满了粮食；~早了；~晚了；~在仓库里；~到什么时候？〈趋〉~起来了；继续~下去；~进仓库里去了〈程〉菜~得很多；水~得太少了；~得满满的；~得不多了〈可〉~得下~不下？〈时〉~了很长时间；~了十年；~了两个星期〈量〉~过一次〔状~〕满满地~了一仓库；适当地❺~点儿；每年都~；尽量❻~

1. store; warehouse 2. enough; ample; sufficient 3. reservoir 4. enough 5. suitably 6. to the best of one's ability

② leave with ≅ 寄存〔~宾〕〈名〉~行李❶；~箱子；~手提包❷；~书包；~包裹❸；~衣物❹；~东西〔~补〕〈结〉行李~好了吗？重要文件都~进了保险柜❺〈趋〉~到行李寄存处❻去吧；手里拿这么多东西太不方便❼了，先找个地方~起来吧〈程〉东西~得太多了〈可〉这个地方只能存小件东西，~不了(liǎo)大件东西〈时〉先在这里~一会儿；~几天；多少时候？〈量〉~过一次；先在你这儿~一下儿，我过一会儿就取❽走〔状~〕暂时❾~；先~；后

~；长期❿~；早点儿~；一起~；赶快~；幸亏⓫~了；在哪儿~？人多，不好~；真难~；好容易才~上；替别人~

1. luggage 2. handbag 3. package 4. clothing and other articles of daily use 5. safe 6. check-room 7. not convenient 8. draw; take away 9. temporarily; for the moment 10. for a long time 11. fortunately; luckily

③ deposit ↔取〔~宾〕〈名〉~钱；~了一笔款❶〔~补〕〈结〉把暂时❷不用的钱先~上吧；钱都~进了银行❸；~完了钱，再去；~到明年四月才到期；这个月钱~多了；~少了；~早了；~晚了〈趋〉他把抚恤金❹都~到银行里去了；你的定期存款❺还一下去吗？她把这个月的奖金❻全~起来了；他把钱全~进来了〈程〉钱~得真多；~得不多；~得好快啊！~得太晚了〈可〉每个月~不了(liǎo)多少钱；钱都花了，一点儿也不了(liǎo)；~不住；~不起来；一年~得了一千块钱吗？~不到年底就得(děi)取出来〈时〉刚~几天；~了两年；~了很长时间了〈量〉每月都要去银行~一次钱〔状~〕一块儿~；一起~；一直~；一连~了十年；赶紧~；赶快~；暂时~；有时~；偶尔~；按时~；定期❼~；从来不~；照常❽~；最多~；至少~；总共~；每月~；分❾几次~

1. a sum of money 2. temporarily; for the moment 3. bank 4. pension for the disabled or for the family of the deceased 5. fixed deposit 6. money award; bonus 7. at regular intervals; periodically 8. as usual; usually 9. separately

④ cherish; harbour〔~宾〕〈名〉总~着戒心❶；不要再~幻想❷了，只~一线希望；不能~侥幸心理❸；不知她~的什么心〔~补〕〈可〉~不得❹侥幸心理〔状~〕一直~着；从不~；对他~着戒心；始终~；仍然~

1. vigilance; wariness 2. illusion 3. the idea of leaving things to chance; trusting to luck 4. must not

⑤ reserve; retain〔~宾〕〈名〉她~了一肚子话❶没地方去说〔~补〕〈结〉你有话可别~在肚子里〈可〉她心里~不住事儿，有一点儿小事就嘀咕❷；小李~不住话，他可做不了(liǎo)保密❸工作〈时〉这件事在心里~了好长时间，才说出来〔状~〕别~；整整~了十年；在心里~

1. be full of complaints 2. have misgivings about sth. 3. maintain secrecy; keep sth. secret

cuō 搓 rub with the hands〔~宾〕〈名〉~麻绳❶；~衣服；~手〔~补〕〈结〉孩子把饼干都~碎❷了；绳子❸~粗❹点儿结实❺；~细❻了容易断❼；棉花❽可以~成线❾；衣服洗得太多，把手都～破⑩了〈趋〉用手把裤脚⑪上的泥⑫～下去了〈程〉领子⑬、袖口⑭～得都很干净；绳子～得太松⑮了；～得太紧⑯了；～得不匀⑰；～得有松有紧；～得有粗有细〈可〉床单⑱那么大你～得干净吗？〈量〉已经～过一遍肥皂⑲了；多～几下就干净了〔**状～**〕用力～；使劲儿～；一下儿接着一下儿地～；先泡⑳一会儿再～；不要东一把西一把地㉑乱～；他冷得直～手

1. rope made of hemp, flax jute, etc. **2.** broken to pieces **3.** rope **4.** thick **5.** solid **6.** thin **7.** easy to break **8.** cotton **9.** thread **10.** broken; cut **11.** trousers leg **12.** mud **13.** collar **14.** cuff (of a sleeve) **15.** loose **16.** tight **17.** not even **18.** sheet **19.** soap **20.** steep; soak **21.**... here ... there

cuō 撮 scoop up〔二〕铲〔**～宾**〕〈名〉～土；～垃圾❶；～煤❷；～砂子❸；～白灰❹〔**～补**〕〈结〉把门口这堆❺煤～走；土～干净了吗？砂子已经～完了；簸箕❻里边～满了土〈趋〉米洒❼了一地，赶快～起来吧；把垃圾～到垃圾箱❽里去吧〈程〉～得很快；～得真干净〈可〉你估计❾一下儿这些白灰一个小时～得完～不完？没有工具❿～不出去〔**状～**〕赶快～；慢慢腾腾地⓫～；统统⓬～走；随手⓭～；用簸箕～；用铁锹⓮～

1. rubbish **2.** coal **3.** sand **4.** lime **5.** pile; heap **6.** dustpan **7.** sprinkle **8.** dustbin; ash can **9.** estimate **10.** tool; instrument **11.** slowly **12.** all; completely; entirely **13.** conveniently; without extra trouble **14.** shovel

D

dā 搭 ① put up; build ≅ 支; 架〔~宾〕〈名〉~桥; ~棚子❶; ~临时舞台❷; ~积木❸; 文章刚~架子❹, 还没正式❺写呢; ~一个凉蓬❻〔~补〕〈结〉临时舞台~好了; 桥~窄❼了, 鸟窝~在那棵大树上了〈趋〉这么快棚子就~起来了〈程〉架子~得太不结实❽了〈可〉给你一天的时间, 你~得完~不完? 材料❾不全~不起来; 孩子还太小, ~不了(liǎo)积木〈时〉~一个多小时就能搭好〈量〉~过两次; ~一下儿试试〔状~〕只要有材料什么架子都不难~; 搭完了不用, 不是白❿~了吗? 三个人一起~; 用木板~; 结结实实地~; 匆匆忙忙地⓫~; 靠墙~; 他很性急⓬说~就~; 不让他在那儿搭, 他偏⓭要在那儿~; 终于~好了; 幸亏⓮没~; 到底~不~? 辛辛苦苦地⓯~

1. shed 2. provisional stage (platform) 3. toy bricks 4. outline; framework; skeleton 5. formal; official 6. mat-awning; mat shelter 7. narrow 8. not strong 9. material 10. in vain 11. in a hurry 12. impatient; short-tempered 13. against expectation 14. fortunately; luckily 15. with much toil; industriously

② hang over; put over〔~宾〕〈名〉肩膀上❶~(着)一条毛巾; 两树之间~一根铁丝❷; 门和窗之间~一根绳子❸〔~补〕〈结〉赶快把毛巾~在绳子上; 把手~在他的肩上〈趋〉毯子❹从那边~过来〈程〉幼儿园里孩子们的毛巾~得很整齐; 衣服多, 绳子短, 所以~得很挤❺〈可〉这么重❻的东西~不了(liǎo); 个子❼矮❽, 铁丝高~不上去; 绳子短, 东西多~不开〈时〉那件衣服在绳子上~了一个星期了, 也没人收〈量〉~一下儿试试; ~了两回都没搭上〔状~〕勉强❾~; 多~几件; 哪儿有地方就在哪~; 一个挨着一个地~; 马马虎虎地❾~; 洗好了赶快~吧; 搭不了别硬❿~; 刚~上就刮风了

1. on the shoulder 2. iron wire 3. rope 4. blanket 5. pack; cram; crowd 6. heavy 7. height; stature 8. short 9. carelessly 10. unyieldingly

③ come into contact; join ≅ 接〔~宾〕〈名〉~关系❶; ~电线❷; 今天他说话有点前言不~后语❸; 我上前~了一句话; 跟谁~伴儿❹去?〔~补〕〈结〉两根电线头❺~上了; ~结实❻了没有?〈程〉电线~得很结实〈可〉他坐

在旁边~不上话; 电线烧❼断❽了, 怎么搭也~不上了〈时〉电线搭了半天也没~好〈量〉~了好几下都没搭上〔状~〕跟谁~关系; 随便❾~了一句话; 最好~伴儿去

1. establish contact with 2. electric wire 3. utter words that do not hang together; talk incoherently 4. join as partner 5. the end of electric wire 6. solid 7. burn 8. snapped 9. casually; at random

④ add ≅ 加上; 增加; 添〔~补〕〈结〉再~上这点儿, 就够一公斤了〈趋〉给别人帮忙, 他~进不少钱去了; 我们已经~进五个人去了〈程〉~得太多了; 时间~得不值得❶〈可〉时间~不起〈时〉~了一个星期的时间; ~了两个小时〔状~〕多~几个; 简直❷~不起

1. not worth 2. simply; at all

⑤ lift sth. together ≅ 抬〔~宾〕〈名〉~床; ~衣柜❶〔~补〕〈结〉我先跟他搭桌子, ~完了再去; 东西都~走了〈趋〉把书柜❷~到楼上去; 请帮我把这袋米~到车上去; ~进来〈可〉我没那么大力气, ~不动; 桌子太大, 平❸着~不出来; 这么重❹的东西, 两个人哪儿~得上去啊! 地上堆着❺这么多东西, 柜子❻~得过来吗? 〈时〉帮他~了半天家具, 胳膊❼都酸❽了〈量〉往上~一下儿; ~过两次〔状~〕跟他一起~; 从楼上~; 勉强~; 慢慢~; 横着❾~; 竖着❿~

1. wardrobe 2. bookcase 3. be on the same level 4. heavy 5. pile; heap 6. cupboard; cabinet 7. arms 8. tingle; ache 9. horizontally 10. vertically

⑥ take (a ship, plane, etc.); travel (go) by ≅ 乘; 坐〔~宾〕〈名〉~轮船❶; ~火车; ~长途巴士❷; ~飞机〔~补〕〈结〉~错车了〈可〉~不上这趟车了〈量〉~过一次他的车; ~一下儿你的车吧〔状~〕只好~下一趟了; 又~错了; 最后还是~飞机去了; 顺便❸~他的车去吧; 是否❹~轮船去

1. steamer; steamboat 2. long-distance bus 3. conveniently; in passing 4. whether; if

dāpèi 搭配 arrange in pairs or groups; go together〔~宾〕〈名〉为什么买好的~坏的呢? 不应该买瘦肉❶~肥肉❷〔~补〕〈结〉这两个词~错了, 不能~在一起〈程〉这两个词~得不合适❸〈可〉这个句子的动词和宾语❹~不上〔状~〕适当地❺~; 这个词只能跟那个词~; 硬性❻~

1. lean meat 2. fat meat 3. suitable 4. object 5. suitably; properly 6. rigidly; inflexibly

dālǐ 答理 acknowledge (sb.'s greeting, etc.); respond; answer

≅ 理睬〔~宾〕〈名〉不~人〈代〉没~我；不愿~他们〔状~〕从来不~人；不必❶~他；就不~他

1. need not; not have to

dāying 答应 ① answer; reply; respond ≅ 回答〔主~〕〈代〉你怎么不~? 我~了；我喊❶了好几声，她都不~〔~补〕〈结〉~晚了，他生气了〈时〉我~了半天，你没听见〈量〉叫了你那么多声，你都不~一下儿；~了好几声〔状~〕大声~；连声❷~；马上~；立即~

1. call (a person) 2. in succession; one after another

② agree; promise; comply with ≅ 同意〔~宾〕〈名〉~李先生了〈代〉~他们了；谁~你了?〈动〉~了我的要求❶；~写；~以后再去看他；~给我帮忙；~教我日语❷；~到我家来吃晚饭；~一起去看电影〔~补〕〈结〉这件事我~错了；~晚了〈趋〉他托❸我的事情，我已经~下来了〈程〉~得非常痛快❹；~得真干脆❺；~得很勉强❻〈量〉~过一次〔状~〕满口❼~；痛痛快快地~；已经~了；当时就~了；嘴上❽~了；必须~；不好意思❾不~；勉强~

1. demand 2. Japanese 3. ask; entrust 4. to one's heart's content; to one's great satisfaction; 5. clear-cut; straight forward 6. reluctant 7. unreservedly; profusely; glibly (readily promise)

8. orally; in words 9. feel embarrassed

dá 达 reach; attain; amount to ≅ 达到；实现〔~宾〕〈名〉不~目的❶，他是不肯罢休❷的；这些文章差不多都是长~一万多字的；这个湖❸深❹~两千多米❺；这条铁路❻长~五千里；产量❼~千斤〔~补〕〈结〉这些新产品❽已经~到了国际水平❾；只要坚持❿，一定能~到目的；~成协议⓫了吗? 你的英语已经~到什么程度⓬了?〈可〉~得到国际标准~不到?〈时〉掌声⓭~十分钟之久⓮；在国外学习~三年之久〔状~〕共~；已经~；尚未⓯~；多~；深~

1. objective; aim; purpose; goal 2. be unwilling to cease one's efforts 3. lake 4. depth 5. meter 6. railway 7. output; yield 8. new products 9. international standard 10. persist in; persevere in; insist on 11. agreement 12. level; degree 13. clapping; applause 14. of a specified duration 15. not yet

dádào 达到 achieve; attain; reach〔~宾〕〈名〉~目标❶；~完美的境地❷；~这种地步；~崇高的思想境界❸；~要求；~了最高峰❹；~看原文书❺的目的；剧情❻~了高潮❼；产品❽~了国际水平❾；~满意❿的程度⓫；~高度；~最高数目〔~补〕〈可〉达不到目的；达得到那

么高的标准达不到？〔**状～**〕尽量⓬～；好容易～了；即将⓭～；果然⓮～了；相继⓯～；从未～过；想方设法地⓰～；逐步⓱～；日益⓲～

1. goal; objective; aim; purpose **2.** perfect condition **3.** (attain) a lofty realm of thought **4.** (reach) the climax **5.** original text **6.** the story of a play or opera **7.** the climax (of the play) **8.** product **9.** international level **10.** satisfied **11.** level; degree **12.** to the best of one's ability; as far as possible **13.** soon **14.** really; as expected; sure enough **15.** one after another; in succession **16.** by every possible means; by hook or by crook **17.** gradually **18.** day by day

dǎ 打 ① strike; hit; knock; beat ≃ 敲打，击〔**～宾**〕〈名〉～锣❶；～鼓❷；～铁❸；～拍子❹；～字〔**～补**〕〈结〉拍子～错了；把鼓～响❺一点儿；眼镜❻被球～坏了；玻璃❼被～破❽了〈趋〉远处❾～起鼓来了；信已经用打字机❿～出来了〈程〉钟～得真准⓫时；她打字～得又快又好；玻璃窗⓬被子弹⓭～得粉碎⓮〈可〉～不好拍子〈时〉年轻时～过三年铁〈量〉～了一阵锣；一连～了二十多下儿钟〔**状～**〕给他们～拍子；用鼓槌⓯～鼓；准时～上课铃

1. gongs **2.** drums **3.** iron (forge iron) **4.** beat; time **5.** louder **6.** glasses **7.** glass **8.** be broken **9.** at a distance **10.** typewriter **11.** accurately **12.** glass window **13.** bullet **14.** smashed to pieces **15.** drumstick

② beat up; hit; fight; attack ≃ 殴打，攻打〔**～宾**〕〈名〉～人；～仗❶；～架❷；～我的脸〔**～补**〕〈结〉把人～晕❸了；把他～疼了；～肿❹了；把她～急❺了；把敌人～败了；把牙～流血❻了；这个仗～赢❼了；～输❽了；爸爸把孩子～重❾了；把头～破❿了；两个人打架把眼镜⓫都～掉了；～下敌人的一座城市；狗被孩子们(给)～瘸⓬了〈趋〉敌人已经～进村子里来了；谁敢进攻⓭，就把谁～回去〈程〉这一仗～得真漂亮⓮；～得真狠⓯；这两个孩子在一起玩，～不了(liǎo)架；我～不过他〈时〉这场战争整整～了十年〈量〉曾经和邻国⓰～过好几次仗；～了他一个耳光⓱；～了他一拳⓲〔**状～**〕狠狠地⓳～；劈头盖脸地⓴～；不问事实真相㉑就～；不分青红皂白㉒就～；假装㉓着～；连年㉔～仗；一气㉕之下～了他一个嘴巴㉖

1. make war; go to war **2.** fight; come to blows **3.** lose consciousness **4.** be swollen **5.** irritated; annoyed; nettled **6.** shed blood **7.** won **8.** defeated **9.** heavy **10.** be broken **11.** glasses **12.** be lame; limp **13.** attack; offensive **14.** brilliant; remarkable **15.** ruthless; ferocious **16.** neighbouring country **17.** slap sb. in the face **18.** give a punch **19.**

vigorously 20. right in the face 21. ignore the facts 22. indiscriminately 23. pretend to be 24. year in and year out 25. grow angry; get angry 26. give (him) a slap in the face

③ send; dispatch ≅ 放射；发出〔~宾〕<名>~枪❶；~炮❷；~雷❸；~信号❹；~电话；~电报❺；~针〔~补〕<结>枪~中了；五颗子弹❻都~光❼了；炮~响❽了；电话~通❾了；电报~完了；气~足❿点儿；车胎~鼓点⓫儿<趋>子弹从窗户~进来了；这个人~起电话来没完没了(liǎo)⓬；电报已经~出去了；气~进去了吗？<程>子弹~得真远；雷~得多吓人⓭啊！他打枪~得真准⓮；这一枪~得真够漂亮⓯的；气~得太足了<可>这个小邮局~不了(liǎo)电报；他的枪老~不准<时>一个电话~了半个小时；~了十分钟，才打进一点儿气去<量>电话~了三次，都没打通，再~一下儿试试〔状~〕一个电话整整(足足)~了半个小时；给谁~信号？向天~枪；对着敌人~炮

1. gun; rifle; firearm 2. cannon; big gun; artillery piece 3. thunder 4. signal 5. telegram 6. bullet 7. used up 8. start shooting; begin to exchange fire 9. get through 10. sufficient; enough 11. bulge; swell 12. endless; without end 13. frighten; 14. accurate 15. brilliant; remarkable

④ catch; hunt ≅ 捉〔~宾〕<名>~鸟；~老虎；~猎❶〔~补〕<结>~伤❷了一头大象<程>今天鱼~得真多<可>我什么也~不着(zháo)<时>老渔民~了一辈子❸鱼；~了一天猎，累得筋疲力尽❹<量>~过几次〔状~〕用鸟枪❺~鸟；用弹弓❻~麻雀❼；用鱼网❽~鱼；在树林里~；偶尔❾~

1. hunt 2. be wounded 3. all one's life 4. exhausted; tired out; played out 5. fowling piece 6. catapult; slingshot 7. sparrow 8. fishnet 9. occasionally; once in a while

⑤ draw; paint; make a mark on ≅ 画〔~宾〕<名>在练习本子上~格儿❶；~了一个大问号❷；~了两个对钩儿❸；~了三个叉子❹；地板太旧了应该~点蜡❺〔~补〕<结>格儿~歪❻了；横线❼~斜❽了；~上一个大叉子<趋>我~出来的格子不方❾<程>线~得真直❿；问号~得不清楚；地板~得真亮⓫<可>这种地板~不了(liǎo)蜡；没有尺子⓬~不好格儿<时>~了半天<量>~过两次〔状~〕用红笔~；轻轻地~；清清楚楚地~；比⓭着尺子~

1. draw squares on the exercise-book 2. question mark 3. check 4. cross 5. wax 6. slanting; oblique 7. horizontal line 8. oblique; slanting 9. not square 10. straight 11. bright 12. ruler 13. model after; copy

⑥ work out ≅ 作出、计算〔～宾〕<名>～草稿❶；～基础❷；～主意❸；～小算盘❹；先用白颜色～一层底子❺〔～补〕<结>～完草稿了；从小儿～下了牢固❻的基础；～错主意了；学外语，一定要～好发音❼基础；～错算盘了<趋>你怎么～起我的主意来了<程>算盘～得真精❽；底色❾～得太深❿了；～得太浅⓫了；他的古文⓬基础～得比较扎实⓭<可>不论⓮学什么，基础～不好是不行的<时>～了两个小时草稿；～了好几年基础<量>需要好好～一下儿基础〔状～〕薄薄⓯地～一层；扎扎实实地～好基础；认真～；净～；暗中～

1. rough draft 2. foundation; base 3. decision 4. be calculating; be petty and scheming 5. sketch (a plan, picture, etc) 6. firm; secure 7. pronunciation 8. be selfish and calculating 9. bottom 10. dark 11. light 12. prose written in the classical literary style 13. sturdy; strong 14. no matter (what; who; how, etc.) 15. thinly

⑦ raise; hoist; hold up ≅ 举〔～宾〕<名>～伞；～旗子❶；～灯笼❷〔～补〕<结>把伞～开<趋>还没下雨你就～起伞来了；～起精神来❸好好干吧<程>～得不够高<可>～得开吗？～得了(liǎo)不了(liǎo)<时>～了好几分钟了；～了一会儿<量>～一下儿；过一次〔状～〕高高地～；替他～

1. flag; banner 2. lantern 3. brace up

⑧ ladle; draw; fetch ≅ 舀取〔～宾〕<名>～开水；～饭〔～补〕<结>～完开水再去打饭；～早了，水还没开呢<趋>饭～来不吃都凉❶了；这是刚～上来的矿泉水❷<程>～得真快；～得太早了<可>人太多，打水、打饭不排队是～不上的<时>打饭～了半个多小时；～了好半天<量>一天～两次；你替我～一下儿水，可以吗？〔状～〕过一会儿再～；按时❸～；在食堂～；满满地❹～

1. get cold 2. mineral spring 3. on time 4. fully

⑨ buy ≅ 购〔～宾〕<名>我们～点儿酒喝；小孩子到商店去～酱油❶；～票；～醋❷〔～补〕<结>～满❸了；～多了<趋>～回一斤酒来<程>～得太满了；～得太少了<可>这个瓶子口儿太小～不了(liǎo)酱油；这么小的瓶子～得下一斤蜂蜜❹吗？太贵了❺，我可～不起❻<量>这个瓶子只～过一次苹果酱❼；～一下儿，看看到底能装❽多少〔状～〕满满地～；零❾～；少～点儿；一次～满

1. soy sauce 2. vinegar 3. filled; full 4. honey 5. dear; expensive 6. cannot afford 7. apple jam 8. contain 9. at retail

⑩ gather in; collect; get in ≅ 收获〔～宾〕<名>～柴❶；～麦子❷；～粮食❸；～了几千斤稻子❹〔～补〕<结>麦子已经～完了<趋>～下来的粮食晒❺干了，才能入库❻<程>今年麦子～得不

dǎ 79

少〈可〉一亩❼地～得了(liǎo)一千公斤吗?〈时〉～了半天，才打这么一点儿〔状～〕多～；少～；差不多～；大约❽～；确实❾～了不少

1. faggot; firewood 2. wheat 3. grain; food 4. rice 5. dry in the sun 6. warehouse; storehouse 7. a unit of area (= 0.0667 hectares) 8. approximately; about 9. really; truly

⑪ do; engage in ≅ 做；从事〔～宾〕〈名〉～杂儿❶；～夜班❷；～短工❸〔～补〕〈结〉今天刚～完最后一个夜班〈趋〉这星期又～起夜班来了〈程〉夜班～得很勤❹〈可〉她病刚好，暂时❺还～不了(liǎo)夜班〈时〉～过好几年短工；～了几个月杂儿；年轻时～过一阵子❻短工〈量〉一年至少❼要～五次夜班〔状～〕连续❽～；经常～；从前～过

1. odds and ends 2. night shift 3. casual labourer 4. frequent 5. temporarily; for the moment 6. a period of time 7. at least 8. in succession in a row; running

⑫ play ≅ 玩〔～宾〕〈名〉～扑克❶；～麻将❷；～桥牌❸；～秋千❹；～篮球；～太极拳❺；～雪仗❻〔～补〕〈结〉打球～累了；孩子们～完雪仗，都回教室了；打麻将～上瘾❼了〈趋〉这场篮球～出水平❽来了〈程〉这场球～得十分激烈❾；扑克～得很熟练❿；孩子们打雪仗～得多高兴

啊！打太极拳～得什么病都没有了〈可〉血压高⓫的人～不了(liǎo)秋千；打太极拳对身体有那么大好处，应该坚持～下去〈时〉～了半个小时雪仗；孩子们～了一会儿秋千，就回家了〈量〉～了一阵雪仗〔状～〕尽情地⓬～；在操场～球；偶尔⓭～

1. cards 2. mahjong 3. bridge (a card game) 4. swing 5. a kind of traditional Chinese shadow boxing 6. have a snow ball fight; throw snowballs 7. be addicted (to sth.); get into the habit of (doing sth.) 8. level 9. brilliant; splendid; wonderful 10. skilful 11. high blood pressure 12. to one's heart content; as much as one likes 13. occasionally; once in a while

⑬ indicating some actions of a man or animal〔～宾〕〈名〉～哈欠❶；～嚏喷❷；～鼾❸；～嗝儿❹；～瞌睡❺；～了一个盹儿❻；驴❼在地上～了一个滚儿❽；～冷战❾；他向我～了一个手势❿；～了一个踉跄⓫〈动〉冷得直～哆嗦⓬；醉⓭得直～晃⓮〔～补〕〈趋〉又～起冷战来了；她～起嗝来就没完，后来喝了一口水才好；坐在墙角⓯～起瞌睡来了；想打个嚏喷，一下子没～出来〈程〉鼾～得太利害了；～得真响⓰〈可〉想打嚏喷～不出来，真难受⓱；你的嗝儿也～不完了〈时〉～了一会儿瞌睡；～了半天哆嗦〈量〉我向他～了一下儿手势；～了一阵鼾，翻了一个身⓲

才不打了〔状～〕在地上～滚儿；一个接一个地～哈欠；一个劲儿地～哆嗦；直～晃；向我～手势

1. yawn 2. sneeze 3. snore 4. belch 5. doze off; nod 6. take a nap; doze off 7. ass; donkey 8. roll 9. shiver with cold 10. gesture 11. stagger 12. tremble; shiver 13. be drunk 14. stagger 15. a corner formed by two walls 16. too loud 17. feel unwell 18. turn over

⑭ come into contact with〔～宾〕〈名〉～交道❶；～官司❷；～赌❸〔～补〕〈结〉打赌～输❹了；官司～赢❺了；跟他打交道～烦❻了〈趋〉官司不能再～下去了；跟她～起交道来真麻烦❼〈程〉官司～得时间太长了；～得太不顺利❽了〈可〉不知道这场官司～得赢～不赢？〈时〉跟他～了十年交道〈量〉～过两次官司；跟他～了一下儿赌〔状～〕跟谁～？用什么～赌？为什么事～官司？经常～；一连～；一次次地～；成年❾～；不易❿～

1. come into contact with; have dealings with 2. go to court; engage in a lawsuit 3. bet; wager 4. lose; be beaten; be defeated 5. win; beat 6. be tired of 7. troublesome; inconvenient 8. not smoothly; not successfully 9. all year long 10. not easy

⑮ cut a hole; open; dig ≅ 凿〔～宾〕〈名〉村子里又～了一口井；老鼠～洞❶〔～补〕〈结〉井～浅了〈趋〉还要再～下五尺去；刚把这个洞堵❷上，该死的❸老鼠又在别处～起洞来了〈程〉这口井～得不够深❹；～得太浅❺了〈可〉这个地方～不出水来；～不出油来；水泥地❻可能就～不了了(liǎo)洞吧〈时〉～了三个月，才打出一口井来〈量〉在这儿～一下儿试试〔状～〕一连～了三口井；在什么地方～？往下～；用机器～

1. hole; cavity 2. stop up; block up 3. damned 4. deep 5. shallow 6. cemented floor

⑯ tie up; pack ≅ 捆〔～宾〕〈名〉～包裹❶；～行李❷；～了一个捆儿❸〔～补〕〈结〉赶快把行李～上吧；～紧点儿❹；～松了❺；～结实❻点儿〈趋〉行李已经～起来了吧〈程〉行李～得不大不小正合适❼〈可〉这么大的行李她一个人可能～不上；包裹我总～不紧；这一堆❽乱七八糟❾的东西～不成捆儿〈时〉行李我～了半天也没打上〈量〉你能帮我～一下儿行李吗？〔状～〕自己～；不好～

1. parcel 2. luggage 3. bundle 4. tight 5. loose 6. solid 7. suitable 8. heap; pile 9. in confusion; in a mess

⑰ knit ≅ 编织〔～宾〕〈名〉～毛衣；～草鞋❶〔～补〕〈结〉毛衣～短了〈程〉～得又快又好；～得谁也比不上〈时〉这件毛衣只～了三天就好了〈量〉这种样子的，我～

过两次〔状～〕连夜❷～；精心地～❸；赶着❹～；给别人～；一针一针地～；辛辛苦苦地❺～；一边看电视一边～；从早到晚～；整天❻～；不停地～

1. knitting work 2. the same night; that very night 3. meticulously; carefully 4. try to catch 5. painstakingly; laboriously 6. all day long

⑱ adopt; use〔～宾〕〈名〉～官腔❶；～比方❷〔～补〕〈趋〉～起官腔来真气人；她～出来的比方总是非常恰当❸；她～出来的比方有点不伦不类❹〈程〉她说话时打比方～得真多〈时〉跟我～了半天官腔〔状～〕净～官腔；经常用自然现象❺～比方〔习用〕不～不相识❻；～草惊蛇❼；三天～鱼，两天晒网❽；～退堂鼓❾；～肿脸充胖子❿；～入冷宫⓫

1. talk like a bureaucrat; stall with official jargon 2. draw analogy 3. very suitable 4. neither fish nor fowl 5. natural phenomena 6. from an exchange of blows friendship grows; no discord; no concord 7. beat the grass and startle (or frighten away) the snake — act rashly and alert the enemy; put enemy on guard by premature action; frighten away thieves by raising a scare; wake a sleeping wolf 8. spend three days fishing and two days drying nets — work in fits and starts; go fishing for three days and dry the nets for two — lack of perseverance 9. beat a retreat; back out; draw in one's horns 10. slap one's face until it's swollen in an effort to look imposing — puff oneself up to one's own cost; pose as a fat man by slapping the face until it is swollen; an impudent attempt to represent the defeat as a victory 11. relegate to limbo; consign to the back shelf

dǎbàn 打扮 dress up; make up; deck out〔～宾〕〈名〉母亲都喜欢～孩子〈代〉～自己〔～补〕〈结〉～好了没有？～成卖香烟的女人；把自己～成英雄❶；～成小丑❷〈趋〉他们已经～起来，准备参加舞会去了〈程〉节日里孩子们～得格外❸漂亮❹；那个人～得与众不同❺；～得非常怪❻；～得很大方❼；～得有点儿俗气❽；～得非常高雅❾〈可〉她不懂得美，怎么打扮，也～不出漂亮的样子来〈时〉～了那么半天才打扮好〈量〉好好～一下儿〔状～〕赶快～～；精心❿～；拼命～；成天⓫～；对着镜子⓬～；挖空心思⓭～；特意～

1. hero 2. clown 3. especially; all the more 4. beautiful; good-looking; pretty 5. out of the ordinary 6. strange; odd 7. natural and posed; easy; unaffected 8. vulgar; in poor taste 9. elegant 10. meticulously; carefully 11. all day long 12. facing the mirror;

looking in the mirror 13. rack one's brains

dǎduàn 打断 break; interrupt; cut short〔～宾〕〈名〉～狗腿❶；～了胳膊❷；～了别人的发言❸；～了你们的谈话❹；～了他的沉思❺；～了我的回忆❻；～了人家的兴致❼；～了她们的笑声；～了她的歌声〔～补〕〈量〉～了好几次，对不起，～你们一下儿〔状～〕不时❽被～；一下子～；突然～；经常～；被掌声❾～；故意❿～；从不～；被敲门声～

1. a leg of a dog 2. arm 3. speak; make a statement or speech 4. talk; conversation; chat 5. ponder; meditate 6. recollections 7. interest; mood to enjoy 8. frequently 9. clapping; applause 10. intentionally; purposely

dǎkāi 打开 open; unfold〔～宾〕〈名〉～书；～窗户；～箱子；～衣柜❶；～抽屉❷；～包袱❸；～信；～瓶盖❹；～一条路；～录音机❺；～收音机❻；～缺口❼；～眼界❽；～思路❾；～一条门缝❿〔状～〕一下子～了；慢慢地～了；替我～

1. wardrobe 2. drawer 3. cloth-wrapper; a bundle wrapped in cloth 4. cover; lid 5. tape recorder 6. radio (set) 7. breach; gap 8. field of vision; outlook 9. train of thought; thinking 10. a crack between a door and its frame

dǎliang 打量 measure with the eye; look sb. up and down; size up〔～宾〕〈名〉～这个陌生人❶；～那个孩子〈代〉～着自己〔～补〕〈结〉～上我了〈趋〉他～起我来了〈程〉～得很仔细❷；～得我很不自然❸；～得我非常难受❹；～得让人受不了❺ (liǎo)〈时〉～了我半天；～了他一会儿〈量〉只要～一下儿，就可以看出他是一个知识分子❻；～了一眼❼〔状～〕上下～；好奇地～；仔细～；互相～；偷偷地～；目光❽冷冷地❾～着我；从上到下地～；从头到脚地～

1. stranger 2. careful; attentive 3. unnatural 4. feel unwell 5. unable to endure 6. the intelligentsia; intellectual 7. a glance 8. sight; vision; view 9. coldly

dǎpò 打破 break; smash〔～宾〕〈名〉～世界记录❶；～僵局❷；～界线❸；～清规戒律❹；～铁饭碗❺；～常规❻；～框框❼〔～补〕〈可〉铁饭碗永远也～不了(liǎo)吗？〈量〉～了三次记录〔状～〕又一次～；不容易～

1. world record 2. deadlock; impasse; stalemate 3. break down barriers 4. restrictions and fetters 5. iron rice bowl — a secure job 6. break free from conventions 7. break with conventions

dǎsuàn 打算 plan; intend〔～宾〕〈动〉没～隐瞒❶你；她～

当医生；～去国外考察❷；～搬到乡下❸去住；～学一门技术❹〔～补〕〈结〉～错了〔**状**～〕没～；为别人～；仔细❺～；本来❻～；从不替自己～

1. conceal; hide; hold back 2. investigate (inspect) 3. village; country; countryside 4. technology; skill 5. carefully; attentively 6. originally; at first

dǎting 打听 ask about; inquire about ≅ 问〔**～宾**〕〈名〉～消息❶；～情况；～一件事；～一个人；～他的病情❷；～张先生的住址❸；～我的电话号码〈主-谓〉～他家发生了什么事〔～补〕〈结〉～到他的下落❹了吗？～明白以后再告诉你；这件事～来～去，到底被他打听到了〈程〉～得很详细；～得非常确切❺〈可〉一点消息也～不出来〈时〉半天也没打听对〈量〉一共～了五次；到前边去一下儿吧〔**状**～〕好好～～；仔细～～；四处～；顺便❻～；特意❼～；专门❽～；暗中～；一遍一遍地～；随便❾～；到了那里再～；千方百计地❿～；从不～；不好⓫～；不便⓬～

1. news; information 2. state of an illness 3. address 4. whereabouts 5. definite; exact; precise 6. conveniently; in passing 7. 8. specially 9. casually; at random 10. by every possible means; by hook or by crook 11. 12. not conveniently

dāi 待 stay ≅ 呆〔～补〕〈结〉在那儿别～久❶了，快点儿回来；一个人～惯❷了，不愿人多；病了很长时间，在家里都～烦❸了；～腻❹了；一个人总待着就～懒❺了；～在这儿别动；～到明年再走吧〈趋〉我不想在这儿再～下去了〈可〉我～不住；～不了(liǎo)太久〈时〉再～一会儿；在他女儿那儿～了几天〔**状**～〕多～一会儿；老～在一个地方没意思；在屋子里～着；静静地❻～在那儿；一声不响地❼～着；独自❽～

1. long 2. get used to 3. be vexed 4. be bored with; be tired of 5. lazy 6. 7. quietly 8. by oneself; alone

dǎi 逮 capture; catch ≅ 捉〔**～宾**〕〈名〉～老鼠；～小偷；～蜻蜓❶；～逃犯❷；～罪犯❸；～凶手❹〔～补〕〈结〉猫～着(zháo)一只小老鼠；把车上的扒手❺～走了〈趋〉把那个贪污犯❻～到监狱❼里去了〈程〉蝴蝶❽～得真多〈可〉～得着(zháo)～不着(zháo)？〈时〉～了一会儿；～了一夜〈量〉～过一次〔**状**～〕用网❾子～蜻蜓；带着警犬❿～；到处～；连夜⓫～；分几路～

1. dragonfly 2. escaped criminal or convict 3. criminal 4. murderer; assassin 5. pickpocket 6. grafter; embezzler 7. prison 8. butterfly 9. net 10. police dog 11. the same night; that very night

dàibiǎo 代表 represent; stand for〔**～宾**〕〈名〉～谁的利益❶？

~不同性格❷；~时代❸精神❹；~政府❺；~学校；~不同的类型❻；~大家的意见❼；~个人的看法❽〔~补〕〈可〉他~不了(liǎo)大家的意见〔状~〕只一个人；仅仅~；真正~；由他~；无法❾~；究竟❿~谁？

1. interest; benefit; profit 2. nature; temperament 3. times; age; era; epoch 4. spirit; gist; essence 5. government 6. type 7. opinion; idea; view; suggestion 8. view; a way of looking at a thing 9. unable; incapable 10. after all; in the end

dàitì 代替 replace; substitute for; take the place of 〔~宾〕〈名〉他将~我的职务❶；用奶粉❷~牛奶喂❸婴儿❹；高楼大厦❺~了老式❻建筑❼；用煤气❽~燃料❾；谁都不能~他的工作；用国货❿~进口货⓫；一架机器可以~很多人；用坏的~好的〈代〉他可以~我〔~补〕〈可〉他的工作谁也~不了(liǎo)〈量〉请你~一下儿他吧，他支持⓬不住了〔状~〕将要~；由哪个人~？暂时⓭~；无法⓮~；被机器~

1. position; post 2. milk powder substitute 3. feed; suckle; nurse 4. baby 5. building; edifice 6. old style 7. architecture 8. gas 9. fuel 10. article made one's country; 11. imported goods; imports 12. sustain; hold out; bear 13. temporarily; for a moment 14. unable; incapable

dài 带 ① take; bring; carry ≅ 携带〔~宾〕〈名〉钱包；~钥匙❶；~雨伞；~干粮❷；~水壶❸；~行李❹；~工作证❺；~驾驶执照❻；~录音机❼；~照相机❽〔~补〕〈结〉钱~少了，钥匙别~丢❾了，东西都~齐了❿了；~全了⓫；出远门要多~上点儿钱〈趋〉书我已经~上来了；我把今天的晚报~回家来了；把录音机~到教室里来(去)了；折叠伞⓬~起来很方便⓭〈程〉行李~得太多了；钱~得太少了〈可〉你一个人~得了(liǎo)那么多东西吗？〈时〉~了半天雨伞，也没下雨；这几张邮票在我钱包里~了好几个月了〔状~〕每天~着；随时⓮~着；正巧⓯~着；今天刚好⓰没~；幸亏⓱~了；从来不~

1. key 2. solid food (prepared for a journey); rations for a journey 3. kettle 4. luggage 5. employee's card 6. driving (driver's) license 7. tape recorder 8. camera 9. lost 10. 11. complete 12. folding umbrella 13. convenient 14. at all times; at any time 15. 16. happen to; chance to; as it happens 17. fortunately; luckily

② do sth. incidentally ≅ 捎带〔~宾〕〈名〉你出去时，请~上门；~个话儿❶；~点茶叶❷来；给我一张邮票来〔~补〕〈结〉请你把这把雨伞~给他；你托❸我带的东西都~到了〈趋〉把东西给他~回去吧；你下楼时，把书包给我~下来；你把这把椅子~上去吧〈可〉~不了(liǎo)那么多

dài 85

东西〈量〉我给他～过好几次邮票了〔**状～**〕顺手❹～上；顺便❺把门～上；轻轻～上；经常～东西；从家里～点儿来；给他～

1. a message 2. tea 3. ask; entrust 4. 5. conveniently; in passing

③ bear; have ≅ 有；含有〔**～宾**〕〈名〉面～笑容（怒容❶／愁容❷／病容❸）；说话～刺儿❹；这个东西～电，脸上～着幸福❺的微笑❻；～着悲哀❼的神情❽；～着机灵劲❾儿；～着惨相❿；～着得意扬扬⓫的样子；～着满脸的怒气⓬；～着憨厚⓭的表情⓮，～着凶相⓯；～着杀气⓰〔**～补**〕〈趋〉脸上～出病容来了；她说话又～起刺儿来了；两只眼睛～出凶恶的样子⓱来了〈可〉心里不高兴脸上一点儿也～不出来〔**状～**〕总～刺儿；有点～病容

1. an angry look 2. worried look; anxious expression 3. sickly look 4. harsh 5. happy 6. smile 7. sorrowful; grieved 8. expression; look 9. smart; clever; sharp intelligent 10. miserable; pitiful; tragic 11. look triumphant; be immensely proud 12. anger; rage; fury 13. straight forward and good-natured; simple and honest 14. express one's feelings; expression 15. fierce look; ferocious features 16. murderous look 17. fierce look; ferocious features

④ lead: head ≅ 引导；带领〔**～宾**〕〈名〉～队❶；～兵；～学生；

～路；～孩子出去逛逛❷〈代〉我～她去吧〔**～补**〕〈结〉别把路～错了；把学生～坏了；孩子让他舅舅❸～走了〈趋〉他把学生们～上山去（～上山来）采集❹标本❺；连长❻把队伍❼～回驻地❽去了；把队伍～到野外❾去操练❿；小学生把盲人⓫～过马路来了〈程〉他们带头儿⓬～得不错〈可〉他是当地人⓭，不会～错路；什么事他都～不起头儿来〈时〉～过一个时期⓮女兵〈量〉请你给我们～一下儿路；～过两三次〔**状～**〕把队伍往哪儿～？

1. a group; team; corps; rank 2. stroll; ramble; roam 3. mother's brother; uncle 4. gather; collect 5. specimens 6. company commander 7. troops; ranks; contingent 8. place where troops, etc. are stationed 9. open country; field 10. drill; practice 11. blind man 12. take the lead; be the first; take the initiative 13. local people 14. a period of time

⑤ have sth. attached ≅ 附带〔**～宾**〕〈名〉～把儿❶的梨❷；～盖儿❸的茶杯；～日历的表；蚌壳❹上～着很多泥沙；雨点～着泥〈动〉那个孩子放牛～割草❺；我值班❻～看(kān)门；洗衣服～做饭

1. handle; grip 2. pear 3. cover 4. shell 5. cut grass with a scythe 6. be on duty

⑥ look after; bring up; raise ≅ 养育；照顾〔**～宾**〕〈名〉～孩子

〔～补〕〈结〉她没有经验❶；把孩子～病了；她带孩子都～烦❷了；～腻❸了；孩子一直～在他自己身边〈趋〉这几个孩子都是她给～起来的〈程〉带孩子～得很有经验〈可〉她没有经验～不好孩子；这孩子太不听话❹，我～不了(liǎo)〈时〉她～了两年孩子〈量〉请她临时❺给～一下儿孩子〔状～〕这个孩子真难～；精心地❻～；从刚生❼下来就～；替她～

1. experience 2. be vexed; be annoyed 3. be bored with; be tired of 4. be disobedient 5. at the time when sth. happens; temporarily 6. carefully; meticulously 7. be born

dàibǔ 逮捕 arrest; take into custody ≅ 捉拿〔～宾〕〈名〉～了一小撮罪犯❶；～了几个走私犯❷；～了一个杀人犯❸〔～补〕〈趋〉～起来了〈量〉被～过两次了〔状～〕依法❹～；被～；秘密❺～；统统❻～起来了；立即～

1. a handful of criminals 2. smugglers 3. murderer 4. according to law 5. secretly; in secret 6. all; entirely; completely

dài 戴 put in; wear ↔ 摘；脱〔～宾〕〈名〉～帽子；～头巾❶；小姑娘头上～了一朵花儿；～耳环❷；～项链❸；～戒指❹；～口罩❺；～眼镜❻；～围巾❼；～手表；～手套❽；～手铐❾；～校徽❿〔～补〕〈结〉把头巾～好再出去；校徽～歪⓫了；刚买的围巾就～脏了；把订婚戒指～在无名指⓬上了〈趋〉你也～起老花镜⓭来了〈程〉他带眼镜～得很早〈可〉校徽总～不正；他～不惯⓮项链；手套太小，怎么戴也～不进去〈时〉～了二十年眼镜；这副手套～了半天也没戴进去〈量〉我～一下儿试试；她～过一次项链〔状～〕常常～；必须～；往头上～；从十岁就～眼镜〔习用〕张冠李～⓯

1. scarf; kerchief 2. earring 3. necklace 4. (finger) ring 5. gauze mask 6. glasses 7. scarf 8. gloves 9. handcuffs 10. school badge 11. oblique; slanting 12. ring finger 13. presbyopic glasses 14. not getting used to 15. Zhang's cap on Li's head — a misplacement; confuse one thing with another

dān 担 ① carry on a shoulder pole ≅ 挑〔～宾〕〈名〉～了两桶水；～着水果；～着秋苗❶〔～补〕〈结〉～在肩❷上；这一担(dàn)西瓜～多了〈趋〉把水到山上去了〈程〉水～得太满了〈可〉我～不动那么多菜〈时〉～了半天水，肩膀都疼了〈量〉～过一次；～一下儿试试；每天～两趟〔状～〕多～点儿；一趟一趟地往那儿～？替她～；满满地～；吃力地❸～着

1. rice shoot; rice seedling 2. shoulder 3. strenuously

② take on; undertake ≅ 承担；担负〔～宾〕〈名〉～风险❶；他怕

~责任❷；~不是❸〔~补〕〈趋〉把责任~起来〈可〉你叫我师傅❹，我可~不起❺

1. risk; hazard 2. responsibility 3. take the blame 4. master 5. cannot afford

dānrèn 担任 ≅ 担当 assume the office of; hold the post of 〔~宾〕〈名〉~主席；~班主任❶；~组长；~技师❷；~什么工作?~技术❸指导❹〔~补〕〈趋〉这个工作他~下来了；请你再继续~下去吧〈程〉他工作~得太多了〈可〉什么工作他也~不起来〈时〉她在那个中学~过三年历史课❺；我还~过一个时期❻的体育课❼〈量〉他连续~了三次主席〔状~〕只~；还~；一直~；连续~

1. a teacher in charge of a class 2. technician 3. technology; technique; skill 4. guide; direct 5. a course in history 6. a period of time 7. physical education

dānxīn 担心 ≅ 不放心 worry; feel anxious〔~宾〕〈名〉~她的身体；~我母亲的病；~明天的天气❶〈动〉~换❷了地方睡不着❸(zháo)；~一个小时作不完；~回答不上来；~会下雨；~赶不上❹最后一班车❺〈主-谓〉~他考不上大学；~她不能胜任这项工作；~我的身体坚持❻不下来；~他儿子开车出事故❼〔~补〕〈趋〉她又为孩子担起心来了〈程〉~得睡不着(zháo)觉；~极

了〈时〉担了好几天心，结果没发生什么事〔状~〕为孩子~；替别人~；一直~；非常~；不必~；实在❽~；日夜❾~；时刻~

1. weather 2. change 3. unable to sleep 4. fail to catch up with 5. last regular bus 6. persist in; insist on; persevere in 7. have an accident 8. really; truly 9. day and night

dānwù 耽误 ≅ 误 delay: hold up〔~宾〕〈名〉~时间；~事；~课；~功课；~了整个工程❶的进度❷；~青春❸；别~了孩子；怕~你的前途〈动〉~工作，~学习；~备课❹；因为出了交通事故❺，所以~了上班〈主-谓〉〔~补〕〈趋〉病再~下去，就不好治❻了〈程〉课~得太多了〈可〉时间~不起；你跟我去一趟马上就回来，~不了(liǎo)你看电影；时间可~不得❼〈时〉~了一个多月的课；他虽然病了，可是没~过一天学习；~你一会儿时间可以吗?〈量〉~了一次课〔状~〕故意❽~；一再❾~；总~；曾经~过；决不~；已经~了；几乎~；差点儿~；完全~；反而❿~了

1. engineering; project 2. rate of progress 3. youth; youthfulness 4. prepare lessons 5. traffic accident 6. cure 7. must not 8. intentionally; on purpose 9. over and over again 10. on the contrary

dāng 当 ① work as; serve as ≃ 做〔**～宾**〕〈名〉～代表❶；～老师；他留❷校～助教❸了；他都～教授❹了；给他～翻译；她的志愿❺是～一个演员；他给人家～仆人❻（佣人❼／保姆❽）；那个孩子愿意长大了～飞机驾驶员❾；弟弟想～工程师❿；他现在不～组长⓫了；他还在那个小学～校长吗？现在不～主任⓬了；～警察⓭；～律师⓮；～侦探⓯；～经理⓰；～兵；～教练⓱〔**～补**〕〈结〉那么年轻就～上爸爸了；本来想当歌唱家⓲，后来嗓子⓳坏了，结果没～成〈程〉你这个代表～得很好，真能代表大家说话〈可〉粗心⓴～不了(liǎo)好医生；他说他这辈子～不上教授了；大家对他意见太多，主任可能～不下去了〈时〉～了一辈子工人；～了一年学徒工㉑〈量〉～过一次教练；我暂时㉒～一下儿翻译；〔**状～**〕好好～代表；一直～；不曾～过；第一次～；决不～；给人家～保姆；刚刚～上讲师；组长不好～

1. deputy; delegate; representative **2.** remain **3.** assistant (of a college faculty) **4.** professor **5.** aspiration; wish; ideal **6. 7.** servant (domestic) **8.** (children's) nurse **9.** pilot **10.** engineer **11.** head of a group **12.** director; head; chairman **13.** police **14.** lawyer **15.** detective; spy **16.** manager **17.** coach; instructor; trainer **18.** singer **19.** throat **20.** careless; thoughtless **21.** apprentice **22.** temporarily; for a moment

② direct; manage; be in charge of ≃ 掌管；主持〔**～宾**〕〈名〉～家❶〔**～补**〕〈趋〉她姐姐十五岁就～起家来了〈程〉当家～得很出色❷〈可〉她太糊涂❸～不了(liǎo)家〈时〉～了一辈子❹；～了好长时间〔**状～**〕从二十岁就～家；替他～家〔**习用**〕～家作主❺；～一天和尚撞一天钟❻

1. household affairs **2.** remarkable; splendid; outstanding **3.** muddled; confused; bewildered **4.** all one's life **5.** be master in one's own house; be the master of one's own affairs **6.** muddle along; drift along aimlessly

dǎng 挡 keep off; ward off; block ≃ 遮↔躲〔**～宾**〕〈名〉墙可以～风；棚子❶可以～雨；多种树可以～风沙❷；喝点酒可以～～寒气❸；请你别～路；你躲开❹点，别～光❺；头发太长了～眼睛〔**～补**〕〈结〉用手～住了，千万❻别让球滚❼下去；没～好〈趋〉用厚厚❽的窗帘❾把窗户～起来了〈程〉窗帘把窗户～得太黑了；头发那么长～得什么也看不见了；他站在门口～得谁都出不去了；前边座位上的那个人～得我看不见了〈可〉窗帘太短～不住光；篱笆❿～不了(liǎo)风；我站在这儿～得着(zháo)你～不着(zháo)？〈时〉这个人～了半天路也不躲开，真讨厌⓫〔**状～**〕在

前边~着；用纸~光；被墙~住了〔习用〕~箭牌❷

1. shed; shack 2. sand blown by the wind 3. cold air 4. dodge; avoid 5. be in the light 6. be sure 7. roll; trundle 8. thick 9. curtain 10. bamboo or twig fence 11. disgusting; disagreeable 12. shield; excuse; pretext

dàng 当 treat as: regard as ≅ 当做

〔~宾〕〈名〉别把好心❶~恶意❷；急❸得他两步一步走；可不能把这件事~儿戏❹；把我说的话全~了耳边风❺；稿子❻被~成废纸❼扔❽了；把别人的事~自己的事去做；一个人~两个人用；别把坏人~好人；不能把亲人~仇敌❾；拿水果~饭吃不行；这孩子拿黑夜~白天了，不好好睡觉；她把白糖~盐❿了〈代〉我把他~你了〈形〉拿好~坏〔~补〕〈结〉把她~成亲妹妹看待⓫〈可〉他很尊重⓬你，你的话他~不了(liǎo)耳边风〔状~〕误⓭~；一直~；别~〔习用〕死马~做活马医⓮

1. good intention 2. evil intention; ill will 3. impatient; anxious; worry 4. trifling matter 5. a puff of wind passing the ear — unheeded advice 6. manuscript 7. waste paper 8. throw away 9. foe; enemy 10. salt 11. look upon; regard; treat 12. respect; esteem 13. by mistake 14. doctor a dead horse as if it were still alive — not give up for lost

dǎo 倒

① fall 〔主~〕〈名〉树~了；路标❶~了；积木❷~了；房子~了；墙~了〔~补〕〈结〉树~在大路上了；她~在床上哭起来了〈趋〉头一晕❸，就~下去了；受伤❹以后~下去了〈可〉这所房子非常结实❺，地震❻也~不了(liǎo)〔状~〕积木又~了；突然~了；一边~；墙咕咚一声❼~了；积木哗啦一声❽全~了

1. road sign 2. toy bricks; building blocks 3. dizzy; giddy 4. be wounded 5. solid 6. earthquake (on the Richter scale) 7. with a thud 8. with a crash

② change; exchange ≅ 换；转换〔~宾〕〈名〉拿了这么长时间了，快~~手吧；每天上下班都在这儿~车❶；右肩❷压❸疼了，~一肩吧；咱们两个人~一~座位❹可以吗？〔~补〕〈结〉我的班~到明天了；书包从左手~到了右手〈趋〉咱们两个人把座位再~回来吧；这笔钱❺~到我的帐❻上去了〈量〉一路上要~三次车〔状~〕拿不了(liǎo)快~~手吧；在下一站~车

1. change bus 2. right shoulder 3. press; push down; weigh down 4. seat 5. a sum of money 6. account

③ collapse; fail ≅ 失败，垮台〔主~〕〈名〉内阁❶~了；政权❷~了〔~宾〕〈名〉~台❸了〔状~〕突然~；终于~了；可~了；已经~了；必然❹~〔习用〕~胃口

❺; 树～猢狲散❻
另见 duò

1. cabinet 2. political power; regime 3. fall from power; downfall 4. inevitably 5. spoil one's appetite 6. when the tree falls the monkeys scatter — when an influential person falls from power, his hangers-on disperse

dào 到 ① arrive: reach ≅ 到达, 达到〔主～〕〈名〉请的人都～了; 她是昨天晚上～的; 她还没～十八岁吧〔～宾〕〈名〉汽车～站了; 我们～家了; ～八点叫我一声; 钱就要～手了; 存款❶～日子了; 假❷期～了❸; ～时间了, 该开会了; 今天开会～了多少人?〔～补〕〈结〉客人都～齐了吗?〈程〉他今天～得真早, 你今天～得比较准时❹〈可〉十二点以前～不了(liǎo)家〔时〕我也刚～一会儿; 那所房子还不～一个月就租❺出去了; ～了一个星期了〔状～〕已经～了; 他怎么还没～? 早就～了; 刚～; 因病未～

1. deposit; bank savings 2. holiday 3. expire; reach the limit 4. punctual; on time 5. rent

② go to; leave for ≅ 去, 往〔～宾〕～电影院❶去; ～朋友家去〈代〉～这儿来〔状～〕一直～; 刚巧❷～; 已经～; 常～; 总～〔习用〕～头儿来❸……

1. cinema 2. just; exactly 3. in the end; finally

dào 倒 ① pour; tip〔～宾〕〈名〉～一碗茶; ～点儿酒; ～点儿蜂蜜❶; ～一碗中药❷; 从大瓶往小瓶里～墨水❸; ～点儿香精❹; ～垃圾❺; 把剩菜❻～了〔～补〕〈结〉～满❼一杯茶; 半碗中药都给～掉了; 垃圾都～干净了吗? 茶叶～在茶叶筒❽里〈趋〉从酒壶❾里～出来了; 把这点儿蕃茄汁❿也一起～进去吧; 汤凉⓫了, 回锅⓬里去再热一热吧; 把一肚子冤屈⓭都～了出来; 把心里的话一下子都～了出来〈程〉～得太满了; 瓶子里的酒～得真干净, 连一滴⓮都没剩〈可〉茶壶嘴⓯太细⓰～不出水来; 一个人给那么多客人⓱倒酒, 有点儿～不过来了〈时〉～了半天才倒进去〈量〉～过一次了〔状～〕慢慢地～; 轻轻地～; 猛地⓲一～; 赶快～; 手哆哆嗦嗦⓳地～

1. honey 2. traditional Chinese medicine 3. China ink 4. essence 5. rubbish; refuse; garbage 6. leftovers 7. full 8. tea caddy; canister 9. wine pot; flagon 10. tomato juice 11. cool; cold 12. pot; pan 13. be wronged; suffer an injustice 14. even a drop 15. the spout 16. thin 17. guest 18. suddenly; abruptly 19. tremble; shiver

② move backward; back (a car)〔～宾〕〈名〉～车❶〔～补〕〈趋〉把车～过来〈时〉～了十分钟; ～了半天〈量〉在这儿～过一次〔状～〕好～; 难～; 别～; 没法❷～; 往后～; 慢点儿～

1. back a car 2. can do nothing about it

③ upside down: inverted; inverse; reverse ≅ 颠倒〔**主**〕〈名〉次序❶~了〔**~补**〕〈趋〉包装箱❷里装❸的是一瓶瓶的药水❹，搬运❺的时候，别~过来；这两本书放错了，赶快~过来吧；~回去吧〔**状**〕千万❻别~过来〔**习用**〕~栽葱❼；喝~采❽
另见 dǎo

1. order 2. packing box 3. contain 4. liquid medicine; lotion 5. transport 6. be sure 7. fall head over heels; fall headlong 8. make catcalls; boo and hoot

dé 得

① get; obtain; gain ≅ 得到↔失〔**~宾**〕〈名〉~病❶；~了头奖❷；~了好评❸；~分❹；~势❹；~空❺〈动〉~宠❻〔**~补**〕〈趋〉经验~来不易❼；幸福生活~来不易〈可〉我总~不着(zháo)奖；~不了(liǎo)满分❽；~不到主子❾的宠爱❿〈量〉去年她~了一场大病〔**状~**〕一直~宠；又~病了；总~奖；怎么也~不了(liǎo)；从来没~过；容易~

1. first prize 2. favourable comment; high opinion 3. score 4. be in power 5. have some spare time 6. find favour with sb. 7. not easy 8. full marks 9. master; boss 10. make a pet of sb.; dote on

② (of a calculation) result in 〔**~宾**〕〈数〉3 乘❶ 3 ~ 9〔**~补**〕〈趋〉~出来的数❷不对〈可〉这两个数相加❸~不了(liǎo)1800；~不出这个数来〔**状~**〕每次都~；总~；是否❹~？到底~多少

1. multiply 2. number 3. plus; add 4. if; whether

děi 得

need ≅ 需要；必须↔无须；不用〔**~宾**〕〈名〉这个工作~几个人才能完成？印❶这些讲义❷~用 100 张纸；修这座大桥~多少人力❸；这个工程❹~两年才能竣工❺；这架机器~三个星期才能修好；这本小说~多少天才能翻译完？她~下星期一才能出院❻〔**状~**〕总~；大概~；也许~；差不多~；是否❼~；恐怕❽~；真~

1. print 2. teaching material 3. labour force 4. engineering; project 5. (of a project) be completed 6. leave hospital 7. if; whether 8. perhaps

dēng 登

① ascend; mount; scale (a height) ≅ 上〔**~宾**〕〈名〉~山；台风❶~陆❷了；~岸❸；~台❹表演〔**~补**〕〈结〉~到了山顶❺；~上了最高峰❻〈可〉这么大年纪的人~不了(liǎo)山了；她胆子太小~不了(liǎo)梯子〈量〉别看他年纪小，已经~过好多次台了〔**状~**〕勇敢地❼~上了最高峰；经常~台演讲❽

1. typhoon 2. land; disembark 3. bank; shore; coast 4. stage; platform 5. the top of a mountain 6. the climax (peak) 7. courageously

8. give a lecture; make a speech

② publish; record; enter ≅ 记载；刊登〔~宾〕〈名〉在报纸上~一个声明❶；~报寻❷人；报上~了他的文章；~了一条新闻❸；~了什么好消息❹；他又上光荣榜❺了〔~补〕〈结〉消息~晚了；新闻~在第一版❻上了〈趋〉你的文章~出来了；照片❼也~到报纸上去了〈程〉这一版像片~得真多；消息~得太慢〈可〉我的事迹❽~不了(liǎo)报；不知为什么他写的文章还~不出来〈时〉人失踪❾了，~了一个月寻人广告，结果也没找着(zháo)〈量〉~过两三次广告了；〔状~〕一笔一笔地~；文章已经~出来了；只好~寻人广告

1. statement; declaration 2. look for; search; 3. news 4. news; information 5. honour roll 6. first edition 7. photo 8. deed; achievement 9. be missing

③ step on; tread ≅ 踩，踏〔~宾〕〈名〉~桌子；~窗台❶；~凳子❷；~着一块大石头；杂技演员❸~着另外一个演员的肩膀❹〔~补〕〈结〉~在桌子上擦❺灯罩❻〈程〉~得我肩膀真疼〈趋〉~到窗台上去了〈可〉我腿❼有毛病❽~不上去〈量〉给我扶❾着点椅子，我~一下儿〈状~〉轻点~，别把桌子踩❿坏了；小心点儿~；一使劲就~上去了；很快地~〔习用〕一步~天⓫

1. windowsill 2. stool 3. acrobat 4. shoulder 5. rub 6. lampshade 7. legs 8. have trouble 9. place a hand on sb. or sth. for support; support with the hand 10. step on; trample 11. reach the sky in a single bound — attain the highest level in one step; have a meteoric rise

děng 等 wait; await ≅ 等候；等待；等到〔~宾〕〈名〉~飞机；~人；~信；~回信❶；~电话；坐在饭馆~菜；在剧院门口~退❷票；~座位❸；~消息❹；~化验❺结果❻〈动〉~着看电影；~想好了再动笔写〈主-谓〉~问题调查❼清楚了，再研究解决的办法；~老师讲完了你再提问题；~她回来我们一起去散步；~她心情❽平静❾了，我们才继续说；~客人走了以后，我们再去；~他来；~我一起吃饭；~他们买完了我再买；~雨停了，再走〔~补〕〈结〉车还不来，我都~急❿了；要的菜还不来，他有点儿~烦⓫了；~腻⓬了；商店还没开门就有很多人在外边~上了；我等他~错了，他是最不守信用⓭的人〈趋〉~起人来可着急了；你还想在这儿~下去吗?〈程〉~得太久⓮了；~得不耐烦⓯了；~得直生气⓰〈可〉他性子⓱很急，~不了(liǎo)人；孩子~不到十点就困⓲了；他~不及⓳了，就一个人先去了；他们还不来我真有点儿~不下去了；〈时〉请你多~一会儿；~了好几年也没有消息〈量〉请~一下儿〔状~〕稍微⓴~一~；从什么时

候~起；烦燥不安地❷~；心神不定地❷~；安安静静地❷~；耐心地❷~；不耐烦地~〔习用〕~米下锅

1. write in reply; write back 2. return; give back; refund 3. seat 4. news 5. chemical examination 6. result 7. investigate; survey; inquire into 8. state of mind; mood 9. quiet 10. irritated; annoyed; nettled 11. be vexed 12. be bored with; be tired of 13. keep one's promise; be as good as one's word 14. for a long time 15. impatient 16. get angry 17. temper 18. sleepy 19. find it too late 20. for a moment 21. agitatedly 22. distractedly 23. quietly 24. patiently

děngyú 等于 egual to; equivalent to〔~宾〕〈名〉不识字❶就~睁着眼睛的瞎子❷〈数〉2加❸2~4；8乘❹9不~48〈动〉你这话说了~没说；跟你说~白费❺；你不说话就~默认❻了；~同意❼了；学了不用就~没学；这意见❽提了❾~白❿提〈主-谓〉我错了，并不~她正确⓫〔状~〕就~；不一定~，差不多~；几乎~；简直⓬~；并不~；也~

1. 2. illiterate person 3. add; plus 4. multiply 5. waste 6. give tacit consent to; tacitly approve 7. agree; consent; approve 8. idea; view; opinion 9. put forward; bring up; raise 10. in vain; for nothing 11. correct 12. simply; at all

dèng 瞪 open (one's eyes) wide; stare; glare〔~宾〕〈名〉你一眼干什么？有话好好说嘛！他~着眼喊；比赛开始了，观众一眼看着运动场❶〔~补〕〈结〉我总瞪他，有一次把他~急❷了；把那个小女孩一哭❸了〈趋〉~起眼来真利害❹；~起眼来真凶❺〈程〉眼睛~得真圆；~得真吓人❻〈时〉~了半天，她都没理会❼〈量〉~了他一下儿；~了我一眼〔状~〕恶狠狠地❽~；跟别人~眼；气呼呼地❾~；偷偷地❿~；故意⓫~；不高兴地~；直~我；老~人；从不~人；气得他干~眼⓬；一次又一次地~；惊讶地⓭~着眼睛

1. sports ground; playground 2. irritated; annoyed; nettled 3. cry 4. 5. terrible 6. terrify; frighten 7. take notice of; pay attention to 8. fierce; ferocious 9. in a huff 10. stealthily; secretly 11. intentionally; wilfully; deliberately 12. stand by anxiously; unable to help; look on in despair 13. surprisingly

dī 滴 drip〔~宾〕〈名〉房檐❶~水；往试管❷里~点儿蒸馏水❸；热得直~汗❹；往螺丝❺上~几滴油，手破❻了，直~血；你帮我~点眼药❼；~了几滴眼泪❽〔~补〕〈结〉油~多了；鼻血❿都~在衣服上了；房檐上的水都~到台阶⓫上了〈趋〉眼药都没~

进去〈程〉～得太多了；～得很快；～个没完〈可〉油～不进去了；我自己～不了(liǎo)眼药〈时〉～了半天也没滴进去； ～几天眼药就好了〈量〉一天～三次〔**状**～〕往下～； 直～❷；一个劲地❸～；多(少)～点儿；不停地～；别～了；赶快～；一点一点儿地～ ；翻着眼皮❹往里～

1. eaves 2. test tube 3. distilled water 4. sweat 5. screw 6. cut 7. shed blood 8. eye ointment or eye drops 9. tears 10. bleeding from the nose 11. stairs 12. 13. continuously 14. turn over the eyelid

dǐkàng 抵抗 resist; stand up to ≌ 反抗；抗击〔**～宾**〕〈名〉～各种❶阻力❷〈动〉～外来的❸侵略❹；～压迫❺；～敌人的反扑❻〔**～补**〕〈结〉～住了寒风❼的侵袭❽〈趋〉我们一定要坚决❾～下去〈程〉～得很坚决；～得很有力〈可〉她女儿身体太弱❿，什么细菌⓫也～不住；什么也～不了(liǎo)〈时〉～了半天，还是失败⓬了〈量〉～过多次〔**状**～〕奋力⓭～；奋起⓮～；奋勇⓯～；顽强⓰(地)～；不屈不挠地⓱～；坚决～；拼命～

1. different kind 2. obstruction; resistance 3. outside; external; foreign 4. aggression; invasion 5. oppress; repress 6. pounce on sb. again after being beaten off 7. cold wind 8. make inroads on; invade and attack 9. firm; resolute 10. poor health 11. germ; bacterium 12. be defeated 13. do all one can 14. rise with force and spirit 15. summon up all one's courage and energy 16. indomitably; staunchly 17. unyieldingly; indomitably

dǐlài 抵赖 deny; disavow ≌ 不承认〔**～宾**〕〈名〉～说过的话；～作错的事；～所犯❶的罪行❷〔**～补**〕〈结〉他企图❸把罪行～掉；你不招供❹，还想～到什么时候?〈趋〉难道❺在事实面前你还想～下去吗?〈可〉罪行抵赖是～不掉的；他再也～不下去了,只好承认❻〈时〉～了半天也没用〈量〉～过好几次了〔**状**～〕百般❼～；拼命❽～；必将❾～；不致❿～；一再⓫～；无法⓬～；当场⓭～；当面⓮～；决不～；继续～

1. commit 2. crime; guilt 3. attempt; try 4. make a confession of one's crime; confess 5. is it possible...? could it possibly be...? does it mean...? 6. admit; acknowledge 7. in a hundred and one ways; in every possible way; by every means 8. with all one's might; desperately 9. surely will 10. not likely to 11. over and over again 12. unable 13. on the spot; then and there 14. to sb.'s face; in sb.'s presence

dǐzhì 抵制 resist; boycott ≌ 阻止〔**～宾**〕〈名〉～外货❶；～歪风邪气❷；～不良的❸社会风气❹

〔~补〕〈趋〉对不好的风气要继续~下去〈程〉~得很利害〈时〉~了一个时期❺；~了一阵子；~了半天也没用〈量〉~过好多次了；非~一下儿不可❻〔状~〕认真~；一直~；坚决❼~；拼命❽~；从不~；必须~

1. foreign goods; imported goods 2. evil winds and noxious influences 3. bad; unhealthy 4. general mood 5. a period of time 6. must; have to 7. resolutely firmly 8. with all one's might

dì 递 hand over; pass; give ≅ 传送；传递〔~宾〕〈名〉请你给我~个口信儿❶；~个话儿❷；~球〔~补〕〈结〉请你把那本词典~给我；申请书❸已经~到他手里了〈趋〉报名单❹~上去了吗? 我把从后面传❺来的条子❻~到主席台❼上去了〈可〉门口堵❽满❾了人，东西~不过来〈程〉他们递球~得真快；~得真准❿〈量〉~了三次，他都没接⓫着(zháo)〔状~〕向客人~；往主席台~；及时~；一个劲儿~眼色; 没法儿~

1. oral message 2. message 3. (written) application 4. application form 5. pass 6. strip 7. rostrum; platform 8. stop up 9. full 10. accurate; exact 11. catch; take hold of

diān 掂 weigh in the hand ≅ 掂量〔~宾〕〈名〉~~多少斤；~~重量❶〔~补〕〈趋〉这两个东西，哪个重❷，~出来了吗? 〈可〉到底哪个重，我~不出来；~不准❸〈时〉~了半天也没掂出来〈量〉好好~一下儿就知道哪个轻，哪个重了〔状~〕仔细❹~~；再一~；两只手一起~

1. weight 2. heavy 3. not exact 4. carefully

diān 颠 jolt; bump ≅ 颠簸〔~补〕〈结〉车要把人~死❶了；一路可把我~坏了；把鸡蛋~碎❷了；~破❸了；路不平，车上装❹的木板都~掉了〈趋〉车走在石子路❺上，车上的苹果都~出来了〈程〉车~得太利害了〈可〉盖❻上盖儿❼，花生就~不出去了〔状~〕太~了；上下~

1. extremely; to death 2. break to pieces 3. be broken 4. loaded 5. cobbled road 6. cover 7. lid; cover

diāndǎo 颠倒 reverse; turn sth. upside down; confound (right and wrong)〔主~〕〈名〉是非❶~；主次❷~；次序~了；位置~了；上下~；神魂❸~；黑白~〔~宾〕〈名〉~是非；~历史❹；~黑白〔~补〕〈趋〉不能随便❺把历史~过来；这两个字~过来，意思就不一样了〈程〉把历史~得不成样子了❻；~得乱七八糟❼的〔状~〕故意❽~；一再❾~；任意❿~；重新~过来吧〔习用〕颠三倒四⓫

1. right and wrong 2. primary and secondary 3. state of mind; mind 4. history 5. casually; at

random 6. unpresentable; absurb 7. at sixes and sevens; in a mess; in a muddle 8. intentionally 9. repeatedly; time and again 10. wantonly; arbitrarily; wilfully 11. incoherent; disorderly; confused

diǎn 点 ① put a dot 〔~宾〕〈名〉~标点❶；~逗号❷；汉语的句号❸画圈儿❹不~点儿❺这里应该~逗号，不能~顿号❻；~三个点儿表示❼省略❽〔~补〕〈结〉句号~在句子后边，文章写好以后要检查❾一下儿标点是否❿都~上了〈趋〉这里少了一个逗号，赶快~上去吧〈程〉这个标点~得不清楚；逗号~得乱七八糟⓫〔可〕我总~不对，~不好〔状~〕在这儿~；用钢笔~；清清楚楚地~

1. punctuation 2. comma 3. full point; period 4. circle; ring 5. put a dot 6. a slight-pause mark used to set off items in a series 7. show; express 8. leave out; omit 9. examine 10. whether or not; whether; if 11. at sixes and sevens; in a mess

② drip ≅ 滴；上〔~宾〕〈名〉~眼药❶；往缝纫机❷里~点儿油❸〔~补〕〈结〉一瓶❹眼药都~完了；这瓶药是点鼻子❺的，可别~错了；每天都要点眼药，我都有点~烦❻了；~腻❼了〈趋〉我不会点眼药，常常是~进去的，还没有流❽出来的多〈程〉油~得太多了，都流出来了；药

~得不够❾〔可〕老~不进去；自己~不了(liǎo)；我~不好，一点就点到外边去了〈时〉你怎么~了那么半天，还没点进去啊〔量〕~几次就好了；再~一下儿就行了〔状~〕自己~；别人给我~；多(少)~点儿；再~点儿；按时❿~；经常~

1. eye ointment or eyedrops 2. sewing machine 3. oil 4. bottle 5. nose 6. be vexed 7. be bored with 8. flow 9. not enough 10. on time

③ check one by one ≅ 查对〔~宾〕〈名〉~钱；售货员❶正在~货❷；~~数儿❸，对不对？上课~名〔~补〕〈结〉钱~对了吗？货都~完了；数儿~错了；这一叠钞票❹没~对吧；钱要当面❺~清〈趋〉钱都~出来了吗？这点儿钱~过来~过去地点了好几遍〈程〉银行❻的工作人员点钱~得真快；她点钱~得又快又准❼；货~得很仔细❽；数儿~得一点也不错〔可〕这点儿钱我总不对〈时〉~了半天也没点清楚；刚~一会儿就乱❾了〔量〕帮我~一下儿；已经~了三次；再多~几遍〔状~〕老~错；大声❿~名；逐个⓫~名

1. shop assistant 2. goods 3. number (count) 4. bank note; paper money 5. in sb's presence; to sb.'s face 6. bank 7. accurate; exact 8. careful; meticulous 9. confused 10. in a loud voice 11. one by one

④ select; choose; order dishes

(in a restaurant) ≅ 挑选〔~宾〕〈名〉~几样❶你喜欢吃的菜❷；~几出戏❸〔~补〕〈结〉菜~好了；今天的菜~错了，一点也不好吃〈趋〉我~出来的菜，你一定喜欢〈程〉今天的菜~得不合我的口味❹；菜~得不太理想❺；~得不能让每个人都满意❻〈可〉我~不好〈量〉这个节目大家~过好几次了〔状~〕大家一起~；别净❼~广东菜，专❽~辣❾菜；随便❿~；特意⓫~

1. different kinds 2. dish 3. play; drama; show 4. not be to my taste 5. ideal 6. satisfied 7. 8. specially 9. peppery; hot 10. casually; at random 11. for a special purpose; specially

⑤ light; burn; kindle ≅ 点燃〔~宾〕〈名〉~灯笼❶；~蜡烛❷；~油灯❸；~火做饭了；~火炬❹〔~补〕〈结〉把火~上吧；灯~亮❺了〈趋〉孩子们把灯笼~起来了〈程〉灯~得真多；~得真亮；~得太早了〈时〉~了半天也没点着(zháo)〈量〉刚一~一下儿就着(zháo)了；~了好几下儿也没点着(zháo)〔状~〕春节的时候❻~灯笼；在外边~；用火柴~；用香火❼~；重新~

1. lantern 2. candle 3. oil lamp 4. torch 5. bright; light 6. in times of the Spring Festival 7. burning joss stick

⑥ nod〔~宾〕〈名〉~头儿〔~补〕〈时〉他向我~了半天头儿，我没看见〈量〉向他~了一下儿头儿〔状~〕频频❶~头；一再❷~头；向我~头

1. 2. again and again; repeatedly

⑦ hint; point out ≅ 指点〔~宾〕〈名〉这篇作文❶直到❷最后才~题❸〔~补〕〈结〉他的真实❹意图❺被我们~破了❻〈趋〉把题目❼~出来了〈程〉~得很明确❽了〔状~〕我一一~他就明白了；怎么~他也不懂〔习用〕蜻蜓~水❾

1. composition 2. until 3. bring out the theme 4. true; real 5. intention; intent 6. bring sth. out into the open 7. title; subject 8. clear and definite; clear-cut 9. like a dragonfly skimming the surface of the water — touch on sth. without going into it deeply

diǎn 踮 stand on tiptoe〔~宾〕〈名〉~脚尖❶；小孩子~着脚拿桌子上的东西〔~补〕〈趋〉~起脚来就可以看见了〈程〉~得真高〔状~〕使劲儿❷~

1. the tip of a toe; tiptoe 2. exert all one's strength

diàn 垫 ① put sth. under sth. else to raise it or make it level〔~宾〕〈名〉这个枕头❶太矮❷，再~一个枕头就舒服❸了；地不平❹，用纸垫桌腿❺~一~；椅子上~了一个很厚❻的垫子❼；抽屉❽里~一张纸，放东西比较

干净；有人喜欢写字时，纸下边~一块硬纸板❾〔~补〕〈结〉把枕头~高点儿；垫子~厚点儿；~上一个鞋垫，鞋就不大了〈趋〉粮食袋❿用木头~起来，可以防潮⓫〈程〉桌子~得不平〈时〉垫了半天才垫平〈量〉好好~一下儿；过两次了〔状~〕在桌子腿底下~；在鞋里~；高高地~；厚厚地~；随便⓬~；特意⓭~；必须~

1. pillow 2. low 3. comfortable 4. not flat 5. legs of a table 6. thick 7. mat; pad; cushion 8. drawer 9. card board; paperboard 10. sacks of grain 11. dampproof; moistureproof 12. casually; at random 13. specially

② pay for sb. and expect to be repaid later〔~宾〕〈名〉我带❶的钱不够，你给我~五块钱〔~补〕〈结〉钱不够，你先替我~上吧〈程〉~得太多了；~得不够〈可〉~不了(liǎo)多少；~不起❷；〈量〉~一下儿；~过不少次了〔状~〕先替我~；经常~

1. bring; carry 2. can't afford

diànjì 惦记 remember with concern; be concerned about ≅ 不放心〔~宾〕〈名〉他总~家里的事儿；母亲~着在外地❶上学❷的孩子；我老~着那篇没写完的文章〈代〉你不用~我，我很好〔状~〕总~着你；常常~着我；不用~

1. parts of the country other than where one is 2. go to school

diāo 叼 hold in the mouth〔~宾〕〈名〉猫~着一只老鼠；燕子❶忙碌❷地来回❸~泥❹做窝❺；狗~着一块骨头〔~补〕〈结〉猫把鱼~走了；没~住，掉了〈趋〉猫把老鼠从墙角❻~出来了；狗~起骨头来就走〈可〉小猫~得住那么大的老鼠吗？〔状~〕从床底下~；使劲儿❼~着；紧紧地~着

1. swallow 2. busy 3. come and go 4. mud; mire 5. make nest 6. a corner formed by two walls 7. exert all one's strength

diào 吊 hang; suspend ≅ 悬挂〔~宾〕〈名〉大门口~着两个灯笼❶；天花板❷上~着一盏灯；树上~着好几个毛毛虫；起重机❸上~着一车砖❹〔~补〕〈结〉有一个人~死了；~在树上了〈趋〉把这桶水泥❺从下边~上去了；敌人把老乡民❻~起来打〈可〉这桶水泥太沉❼~不起来〈时〉那个死人在树上~了三天〔状~〕用绳子❽~着；一直~着；在大门口~着；高高地~着

1. lantern 2. ceiling 3. hoist; crane; derrick 4. brick 5. cement 6. fellow-townsman; fellow-villager 7. heavy 8. rope

diào 钓 fish with a hook and line; angle〔~宾〕〈名〉~鱼；~田鸡❶；~青蛙〔~补〕〈结〉~

着(zháo)了吗？～完了鱼就回家〈趋〉～起来一看，不是鱼；～上来不少虾〈程〉～得真多；～得真快，一会就三条〈可〉你这么着急可～不了(liǎo)鱼；这个鱼钩❷不好用，～不上来〈时〉你刚～一会儿就钓了那么多，我～了半天连一条也没钓上来〈量〉我～一下儿碰碰运气❸；～过几次鱼〔状～〕经常～；每星期都～；偶尔❹；用鱼竿❺～；一边看书一边～

1. frog 2. fishhook 3. try one's luck; take a chance 4. once in a while; occasionally 5. fishing rod

diào 调 transfer; shift; move 〓调动；分派〔～宾〕〈名〉～了不少人；～了一支军队❶；～了一些粮食❷；～一批货❸；～两艘❹军舰❺；～一架飞机；～了几辆坦克〔～补〕〈结〉人～多了；上个月把他～走了〈趋〉我哥哥～到科学院去了；把我～出来协助❻他们工作；人太多，所以把他～出去了；上个月又～进三个人来；五年前调走了，现在又～回来了；把军队～过来了；我们医院想把她～来〈程〉人～得太多了；工作～得真快；～得不理想❼；～得不满意❽；～得慢极了〈可〉工作老～不成；一时❾还～不回来；想把他调出去，但是总～不走〈时〉我的工作～了十年了，还没调成〈量〉～过两次工作；请你帮忙给～一下儿〔状～〕我们两个人对❿～；暂时⓫～；经常～；一次次地～；很难～

1. armed forces; troops 2. food 3. goods 4. a measure word for ships 5. warship; naval vessel 6. help; assist 7. not ideal 8. not satisfied 9. temporarily; for the moment 10. mutual; each other; face to face 11. temporarily; for the moment

diàochá 调查 investigate; inquire into; look into; survey〔～宾〕〈名〉～失火❶的原因❷；～青少年犯罪❸的原因；～事情发生❹的经过；～产生的结果；～事情的真相❺；～罪证❻；～人口❼；～走私❽的情况〔～补〕〈结〉事情～完了；情况～清楚了〈趋〉～出什么结果来了吗？～出一点眉目❾来了；～出一些线索❿来了；还需要继续～下去吗？原因～出来了吗？这个案子⓫～起来很困难〈程〉～得很快；已经～得非常清楚了；～得差不多了〈可〉～不出什么来；他经验⓬不够，这个案子～不了(liǎo)；一时～不清楚；越来越复杂，简直⓭～不下去了；半年也～不完〈时〉～了一年多，还没有结果〈量〉再仔细⓮～一下儿；～过很多遍〔状～〕好好～～；多～～；一直容易～；认真～；耐心地⓯～；仔细地～；重新～；马马虎虎地⓰～；一时⓱～不出来；无法⓲～；无从⓳～；一次一次地～；从哪儿～？反复～；普遍⓴～；彻底～

1. catch fire; be on fire 2. cause 3. delinquency 4. happen; occur 5. truth 6. evidence of a crime 7.

population 8. smuggle 9. prospect of a solution; sign of a positive outcome 10. clue 11. case; law case 12. experience 13. simply; at all 14. carefully 15. patiently 16. carelessly 17. temporarily; for the moment 18. unable; incapable 19. have no way (of doing sth.); not be in a position (to do sth.) 20. widely; universally

diàodòng 调动 ① transfer; shift; move 〔～宾〕〈名〉～工作；～军队❶〔～补〕〈程〉工作～得太勤❷了；军队～得太频繁❸了〈可〉没有他的命令❹，谁也不了(liǎo)军队〈量〉我真想～一下儿工作；～过两次了〔状～〕一再～；经常～；一次一次地～；频繁地～；突然～；随时～

1. army; troops 2. 3. frequent 4. order

diàohuàn 调换 exchange; change ≅ 换〔～宾〕〈名〉我想～～工作；～座位❶；～一个方向❷〔～补〕〈结〉工作～成❸了；我把座位～到前边去了〈趋〉我们两个人的床～过来了；他把座位～到窗底下去了〈可〉工作～不了(liǎo)〈量〉请你跟我～一下儿座位好不好？〔状～〕我们两个人～；他跟我～；暂时❹～；别～了

1. seat; place 2. direction 3. accomplish; succeed 4. temporarily; for the moment

diào 掉 ① fall; drop; come off ≅ 落〔主～〕〈名〉牙～了；纽扣❶～了，东西～了；书皮❷儿～了，花瓣❸～了，墙上的白灰❹～了，鞋～了，钥匙❺～了〔～宾〕〈名〉～眼泪❻；～雨点儿；～头发；～牙；梳子❼～齿❽了；衣服～颜色了；～了一层❾；～了一个角儿❿；～了一点儿皮儿；～了一地⓫干树叶〔～补〕〈结〉牙都～没⓬了；衣服的颜色～浅⓭了；水桶～在井里去〈趋〉花瓣～下来了；钱包从口袋里～出去了；钱从这个缝儿⓮～进去了〈程〉颜色～得真利害；头发～得真多；牙～得太早了〈可〉缝儿那么窄⓯，硬币～不进去；我的口袋很深⓰，钱包～不出去；扶住了栏杆⓱就～不下去了；用冷水⓲洗～不了(liǎo)颜色〈时〉牙～了半年多才镶⓳上〈量〉这件衣服的颜色洗一次～一次〔状～〕快要～一把一把地～头发；一层一层地～；轻易不～眼泪；容易～色

1. button 2. book cover 3. petal 4. cement flour 5. key 6. tears 7. comb 8. tooth 9. layer 10. a corner 11. all over the floor 12. nothing left 13. light 14. crack 15. narrow 16. deep 17. place a hand on the banisters 18. cold water 19. inlay; mount

② lose, be missing ≅ 失去，遗失；遗漏〔～宾〕〈名〉～磅❶；这句话～了一个字；这一行❷～了两个标点❸；最近量❹了一下儿体重❺，又～了三斤〔～补〕〈程〉最近掉磅～得很利害；～得太多了〔状～〕哪儿～了一个字？一熬

夜❻就～磅

1. weight 2. row; line 3. punctuation 4. measure 5. weight 6. stay up late or all night

③ turn ≌ 回转〔～宾〕<名>需要～一～车头❶，把天线❷～一个方向❸，电视就清楚了；起重机❹的"长手臂"❺～了一个方向〔～补〕<趋>火车头已经～过来了；他～过脸去了 <量> 开到前边宽❻点儿的地方去～一下儿车〔状～〕在哪儿～头❼？往哪边～

1. locomotive 2. aerial; antenna 3. direction 4. hoist; crane; derrick 5. arm 6. wide; broad 7. turn round; turn about

diē 跌 ① fall; tumble ≌ 摔〔～宾〕<名>一出门就～了一交〔～补〕<结>小孩子刚学会走路容易～倒；这一交❶差点没～死；她的腿❷一伤❸了；骨头❹一断了❺；～折了(shé)了<趋>从楼梯❼上～下来了；～进泥坑❽里去了<程>这一交～得真重❾；～得不轻❿；～得太疼了〔状～〕平地⓫～了一交；下车时～了一交；扑通一声⓬～倒了

1. fall 2. leg 3. be wounded 4. bone 5. 6. snapped 7. stairs 8. mud 9. heavy 10. serious 11. flat ground 12. with a flop

② drop; fall ≌ 下降〔主～〕<名>股票❶～了〔状～〕突然～了；一下子～了；猛❷～

1. share certificate; share; stock 2. fierce; violent; energetic

dié 叠 fold ≌ 折叠〔～宾〕<名>～衣服；～被；～床；～信；～讲义❶；～纸船〔～补〕<结>衣服还没～平❷，怎么就收起来了；纸～斜❸了；把被褥❹～整齐<趋>赶快把衣服～起来吧，堆❺在那里太乱❻了<程>衣服～得很整齐<可>～不好；以前会叠，现在～不上来了；孩子老捣乱❼，妈妈连衣服都～不成了，只好带孩子出去玩<时>孩子坐在那里～了半天小飞机<量>帮我～一下儿讲义吧〔状～〕从来不～被；整整齐齐地～；马马虎虎地❽～；重新～一个；纸太小没法儿～〔习用〕～床架屋❾

1. teaching materials 2. flat 3. oblique slanting 4. bedding; bedclothes 5. pile up; heap up 6. in a mess; in disorder 7. create a disturbance; make trouble 8. carelessly 9. pile one bed upon another or build one house on top of another — needless duplication

dīng 叮 ① sting; bite〔～宾〕<名>蚊子❶～人；腿上让蚊子～了一个大包❷〔～补〕<结>～疼了；～肿了<程>～得很利害；～得不太疼；～得真痒❸<可>挂上蚊帐❹就～不着(zháo)了<时>没挂蚊帐，让蚊子～了一夜<量>让蚊子～了一下儿；～了好几口〔状～〕被蚊子～；狠狠地❺～

1. mosquito 2. swelling 3. itch 4. mosquito net 5. ruthlessly; relentlessly

② say or ask again to make sure ≅ 追问〔~宾〕〈名〉我又~了他一句,他才说出真话❶来〔~补〕〈结〉我把她~急了❷〈程〉~得很紧❸〈时〉~了半天他才说〈量〉这个问题还需要再~一下儿他〔状~〕又~;别~了

1. truth 2. irritated; annoyed 3. tight

dīng 盯 fix one's eyes on; gaze at; stare at ≅ 注视〔~宾〕〈名〉眼睛~着银幕❶;~着敌机❷;~着敌人的碉堡❸;~着靶子❹;~着墙上的照片〔~补〕〈结〉~住他,别让他跑了〈可〉他太狡猾❺了,我可~不住他〈时〉~了半天,还是让他跑掉了〔状~〕死~着一个地方;一个劲地❻~着;一动不动地❼~着;紧紧地~着;好奇地❽~着我,茫然地❾~;直拿眼睛~着我

1. (motion-picture) screen 2. an enemy plane 3. fort; stronghold 4. target 5. sly; cunning; tricky 6. 7. look with fixed eyes; watch with the utmost concentration 8. be curious; be full of curiosity 9. ignorant; in the dark; at a loss

dǐng 顶 ① carry on the head〔~宾〕〈名〉老大娘头上~着水罐❶;杂技演员❷头上~着坛子❸;他每天起得很早,~着星星去上班;~着一筐香蕉;~着一捆干草❹;他手里提❺着手提包❻,头上~着行李❼;~着一包东西〔~补〕〈结〉观众❽都替台上的杂技演员担心❾,怕头上那些碗没~好掉下来;别~歪❿了;~斜⓫了;从小就顶,都~习惯了〈趋〉那位印度⓬姑娘把一筐水果~到路边儿来了;~起来就走〈程〉~得真稳⓭;~得那么轻松⓮;~得那么吃力⓯〈可〉你~得了(liǎo)~不了(liǎo)? ~不动;~不习惯;我~不上去,你帮我一下儿〈时〉~了好几个小时,真有点儿累了;~了半天,也没人接⓰一下儿〈量〉你~一下儿就知道重⓱不重了;~了好几趟〔状~〕勉强~;来回⓲~;手不扶⓳着~;一口气⓴~了三里路

1. water pitcher 2. acrobat 3. earthern jar 4. a bundle of hay 5. carry (in one's hand with the arm down) 6. handbag 7. luggage 8. spectator; viewer; audience 9. worry 10. askew; crooked 11. oblique; slanting 12. India 13. steady 14. light; relaxed 15. entail strenuous effort 16. catch; take hold of 17. heavy 18. make a round trip; go to a place and come back 19. support with the hand 20. in one breath

② gore; butt ≅ 撞;撞击〔~宾〕〈名〉牛~人;一抬头就要~着天花板❶了〔~补〕〈结〉牛把人~死了;~伤❷了;让牛给~倒❸了〈趋〉两头牛~起头来了;黑羊把白羊从山坡上~下去了〈程〉顶人~得真利害;两头牛~得真

dǐng

猛❹；～得真凶❺；～得真狠❻〈可〉离❼它远点儿，就～不着(zháo)你〈时〉两头羊～了很久也不分胜负❽〈量〉让牛～一下儿可受不了❾(liǎo)；我小时候让羊～过一次〔状～〕两只羊互相～对❿；使劲儿～；拼命～

1. ceiling 2. be wounded; injury 3. fall; topple 4. fierce; violent; energetic 5. terrible; fearful 6. ruthless; relentless 7. leave; be away from 8. tie; draw; come out even 9. cannot bear; be unable to endure 10. face to face with each other

③ go against; set against ≅ 对面迎着〔～宾〕〈名〉今天骑车有点儿～风；～着风雪❶骑车；别～着雨走；～着困难；～着严寒❷；～着酷热❸；小船～着风浪前进〔～补〕〈程〉今天顶风～得真利害，车都骑不动了〔状～〕一直～；经常～；又～

1. face blizzards 2. severe cold; bitter cold 3. the intense heat of summer

④ retort; turn down ≅ 顶撞〔～宾〕〈名〉听了他的话很不满意❶，就～了他几句；不要跟大人～嘴❷；他一说话就～人；我想～她，又不好意思❸〔～补〕〈结〉把她～急❹了；～哭了〈趋〉两个人说着说着就～起来了；售货员❺跟顾客❻～起来了，又跟父母～起嘴来了，我几句话就把他～回去了〈程〉别人批评❼他的话，他一点儿也不服❽，～得很利害〈量〉～过他一次；我狠狠地❾～了他一下儿〔状～〕净❿～；经常～人；狠狠地～

1. not satisfied; not pleased 2. reply defiantly; answer back; talk back 3. feel embarrassed 4. irritated; annoyed; nettled 5. shop assistant; salesclerk 6. customer; shopper 7. criticise 8. refuse to obey 9. vigorously 10. only; merely

⑤ push up; push from below or behind〔～宾〕〈名〉鞋买小了，有点儿～脚〔～补〕〈结〉布鞋没穿多久就被脚趾❶～破❷了；新长出来的牙把孩子的乳牙❸给～歪❹了；树根❺把土～鼓❻了〈趋〉水蒸气❼把壶盖❽～起来了；幼芽❾从砖❿缝⓫里～出来了；脚趾从袜子⓬的破洞⓭里～出来了；旧牙还没掉新牙就～出来了；嫩叶⓮～出来了；树根～出来了；一棵嫩芽⓯把土～起来了〈程〉鞋太小，把脚～得真疼；～得真难受⓰〈可〉如果是皮鞋就～不破了吧〔状～〕实在⓱～得难受；真～得慌⓲；这双鞋还～脚吗？

1. toe 2. broken 3. milk tooth; deciduous tooth 4. askew; crooked; inclined; slanting 5. root 6. bulge; swell 7. steam; water vapour 8. cover of kettle 9. young shoot; bud 10. brick 11. crack 12. socks; stockings 13. hole 14. tender leaves 15. tender bud 16. feel unwell 17. really; truely 18. awfully; unbearably

⑥ cope with; stand up to ≅ 相当于；抵〔～宾〕<名>那个年轻人❶真有劲儿❷，做起事来一个人能～两个；两个老玉米❸能～一顿饭；一台机器能～一百个工人；一台拖拉机❹能～几十匹马力❺〔～补〕<可>一台机器～不了(liǎo)一百个工人，只能～五十个工人；只吃点心❻不行，点心～不了(liǎo)饭；象我这样的，两个也～不上他一个

1. lad; young fellow 2. physical strength 3. maize; corn 4. tractor 5. horsepower 6. light refreshments; pastry

⑦ resist; stand up to ≅ 支持〔～补〕<结>提❶什么条件❷也别同意❸，一定要～住；～到夜里三点多钟<趋>一上午连续❹作了三个手术❺，还真～下来了<可>她身体不好，走那么远路，有点儿～不住了<时>再～一会儿〔状～〕一直～；尽量～；勉强～；必须～；只好～

1. put forward; bring up; raise 2. condition 3. agree 4. in succession 5. operation

⑧ substitute; take the place of; replace ≅ 代替〔～宾〕<名>不能拿坏货❶～好货❷；～他的缺❸；～别人的名字，多要了一份儿；～她的名额❹〔～补〕<可>次货❺怎么也～不了(liǎo)好货<量>用次货～过好几次好货了〔状～〕用次品❻～；偷偷地❼～；这个缺由他～

1. goods of bad quality 2. products of quality; goods of high quality 3. vacancy 4. the number of people assigned or allowed; quota of people 5. goods of bad quality 6. substandard products; defective goods 7. stealthily; secretly; covertly; on the sly

⑨ sustain; shore up ≅ 支撑〔～宾〕<名>怕被风刮开，所以用椅子～着门〔～补〕<结>门～住了吗？～结实❶点儿<程>门～得很紧❷，推❸不开<可>门用小椅子～不住<量>用这把大椅子～过一次〔状～〕用身子～着门，不让他进来；在门后边儿～；用大桌子～〔习用〕～牛儿❹

1. solid; sturdy; durable 2. tight; close 3. push; shove 4. lock horns like bulls; clash; be at loggerheads

dìng 订 ① conclude; draw up ≅ 订立〔～宾〕<名>～约会；～工作计划❶；～开会日期；和建筑❷公司❸～修建❹合同❺；～法律❻条文❼；他们两个人已经～婚了〔～补〕<结>～完计划给我看看；～好合同了吗？<趋>把结婚❾日期～下来吧<程>条文～得很细❿；计划～得周密⓫；计划～得不实际⓬<可>计划这个星期还～不出来；日期还～不了(liǎo)<量>～一下儿学生守规⓭吧；从前～过一次〔状～〕预先～；和邻邦⓮～条约；认真～；仔细地⓯～；正式⓰～；暂时⓱

dìng 105

~；曾经~过；暗中⓲~；私下 ⓳~

1. plan 2. build; construct; erect 3. company; corporation 4. build; construct; erect 5. contract 6. law; statute 7. article; clause 8. be engaged (to be married); be betrothed 9. marry; get married 10. detailed; minute 11. careful; thorough 12. unpractical 13. rules, regulations 14. neighbouring country 15. carefully; attentively 16. formally; officially 17. temporarily 18. in secret 19. in private; in secret

② subscribe to (a newspaper etc.) book (seat, tickets, etc.) order (merchandises, etc.) 〔~宾〕〈名〉~书；~报；~杂志；~飞机票；~一台机器；~一桌酒席❶；~一批货❷〔~补〕〈结〉报纸~上了吗? 杂志~重(chóng)❸了，赶快退掉❹一份吧〈可〉过期❺就~不上了；去晚了就~不着(zháo)了；我~不起那么多杂志〈时〉又~了半年〔状~〕按月❻~；提前❼~；预先❽~；连续❾~了半年，再也不~了；从来没~过；续~❿；单~；及时~；集体⓫~

1. feast 2. goods 3. repeat; duplicate 4. return; give back; refund 5. exceed the time limit; be overdue 6. every month 7. 8. in advance; ahead of time; beforehand 9. in succession; running 10. renew one's subscription 11. collectively

③ staple together 三装订〔~宾〕〈名〉用废纸❶~一个本子；~书；~讲义❷；~报纸〔~补〕〈结〉把这些白纸~成一个本子；厚了❸；~薄❹了；书页❺~错了吧? ~倒❻(dào)了；~整齐点儿〈趋〉把这几张纸也一起~上去吧；单篇❼讲义~起来，就不容易丢~了；机器~出来的好看〈程〉这个本子~得真好；~得太厚；~得不齐❽；~得不象样❾；〈可〉这个本子太厚，我~不动；〈时〉~了半天也没订好；一个本子~了十分钟〈量〉多~几针❿；〔状~〕用钉书机⓫~；用粗线⓬~；机器~；手工⓭~；太难~了；容易~；别马马虎虎地⓮~；仔细⓯点儿~；随便⓰~

1. waste paper 2. teaching material 3. thick 4. thin; flimsy 5. page 6. upside down; reverse 7. single page 8. not neat 9. beyond recognition 10. stitch 11. stapler; stapling-machine 12. thick thread 13. by hand; manual 14. carelessly; casually 15. carefully; attentively 16. casually; informally; at random

dìng 钉

① nail 〔~宾〕〈名〉~箱子❶；~钉子❷〔~补〕〈结〉箱子~好了；钉子~歪❸了；~斜❹了；~弯❺了；把木箱~结实❻点儿；墙上~满❼了钉子，真难看❽〈趋〉钉子出来了，快把它~进去吧；钉子太大，使劲儿❾钉，才能~下去；把挂衣钩❿~到木板上去；把这些木板~起

来，就是一个很好的箱子〈程〉～得真结实；～得不错；～得真快；〈可〉木头太硬⓫～不进去；这种墙～不进钉子去；怎么钉也～不上〈时〉～了半天也没钉进去；别着急，再～一会儿就完了〈量〉让我自己～两下儿；～过一次；～了一阵〔**状～**〕多（少）～几下儿；小心点儿～；好～；难～；重新～；从这边～；往墙上～；用锤子⓬～

1. chest; box; case; trunk **2.** nail **3.** askew; crooked **4.** oblique; slanting **5.** curved; tortuous; crooked **6.** solid; sturdy **7.** full; filled **8.** ugly **9.** exert all one's strength **10.** clothes-hook **11.** hard **12.** hammer

② sew on ≃ 缝〔**宾**〕〈名〉～扣子❶；～带子❷；～帽徽❸〔**～补**〕〈结〉扣子都～上了；～齐❹了；带子～错了；～斜❺了；～反❻了；～整齐点儿；～在肩❼上；～在领子❽上〈趋〉把掉了的带子再～上去吧；把掉了的扣子都～起来吧〈程〉～得真快；～得真整齐；～得太不结实了〈可〉她笨极了，连扣子都～不好；线❾太细❿～不结实；纽扣眼⓫太小，针太粗⓬，～不了(liǎo)〈时〉～了半天还是钉歪了；～了半天也没钉上〈量〉刚～一下儿，手就扎⓭破⓮了；我给他～过好几次扣子了，多～几针〔**状～**〕太难～了；勉强～；粗针⓯～；往哪儿～？给他～；一针一针地～；密密地⓰～；稀稀地⓱～；随便～了几针；比⓲好了再～

1. button **2.** belt **3.** insignia on a cap **4.** complete **5.** oblique **6.** inside out **7.** shoulder **8.** collar **9.** thread **10.** thin; slender **11.** hole **12.** thick **13.** prick **14.** cut **15.** knitting needle **16.** closely; densely **17.** sparsely **18.** model after; copy

dìng 定 decide; fix; set ≃ 决定；规定〔**～宾**〕〈名〉～座位❶；～旅馆❷；～规矩❸；～计划❹；～价钱❺；～原则❻；～方针❼；～时间；～日子；～期限❽；～政策❾；～章程❿；～制度⓫；～条件⓬；～标准⓭；～界限⓮；～范围⓯；～地方；～了一桌菜⓰；～稿⓱；～货⓲；～婚⓳；～亲⓴；～案㉑；一盘棋㉒不能～胜负㉓；～输赢㉔；～个上下㉕；～个高低㉖；～个好坏㉗〔**～补**〕〈结〉计划～完了；价钱～高了；原则～好了；地点～错了；婚礼㉘～在下星期二举行㉙〈趋〉快把日子～下来吧；把这一条规定㉚也～进去；方针还没～出来吗？这两个人又在那儿～起条件来了〈程〉条件～得太高了；时间～得太早了；地点～得太远了；时间～得不合适㉛；价钱～得太贵㉜了；价钱～得比较合理㉝；～得偏㉞高㉟；～得偏低㊱〈可〉时间、地点都～不下来；计划还～不出来；一个人～不了(liǎo)，需要大家讨论㊲才能定〈量〉～了好几次时间，都改期㊳了；明天几点钟见面，你随便～一下儿吧〔**状～**〕由谁～稿；什么时候～婚；随便～；真难～；根

据什么~；好好儿~；别~那么多条；暂时㊴~在明天；合理地㊵~价钱；重新~

1. seat 2. hotel 3. rule; established practice 4. plan 5. price 6. principle 7. policy; guiding principle 8. term; time limit; deadline 9. policy 10. regulations 11. system; institution 12. condition 13. standard 14. limit 15. scope 16. dish 17. manuscript 18. goods 19. 20. be engaged (to be married) 21. decide on a verdict; reach a conclusion on a case 22. a game of chess 23. 24. victory or defeat; success or failure 25. 26. superiority or inferiority 27. good or bad 28. wedding 29. hold 30. rule; regulation 31. not suitable 32. dear; expensive 33. reasonable 34. inclined to one side; slanting; leaning 35. on the high side 36. on the low side 37. discuss 38. change the date 39. temporarily; for a moment 40. reasonably

diū 丢 ① lose ≌ 掉↔拾；捡〔主~〕〈名〉钥匙❶~了；钱包~了；孩子~了；月票❷~了〔~宾〕〈名〉~了很多钱；~了一只手表；~脸❸；~了不少东西；这种~人❹的事儿，谁也不干；~面子❺；这一套❻书~了一本；~了一串钥匙〔~补〕〈结〉脸~尽❼了；面子~光❽了；他丢东西都~怕了；钥匙~在哪儿了？钱包~在什么地方了？〈量〉~过好几次钱了〔状~〕你怎么总~东西

啊！想一想是在哪儿~的；屡次❾~；给家长❿~面子；从来不~东西；不小心⓫~了；经常~

1. key 2. monthly ticket 3. 4. 5. face (lose one's face) 6. a set of 7. 8. completely 9. time and again; repeatedly 10. the parent or guardian of a child 11. inattentively; through negligence

② throw; cast; toss ≌ 扔〔~宾〕〈名〉小孩子往河里~石子儿❶玩；~果皮❷；~废纸❸〔~补〕〈结〉废纸~在字纸篓里❹；把白菜❺叶~给小兔❻吃〈趋〉~到窗户外边儿去了〈程〉废纸~得哪儿都是；~得遍地都是〈可〉我手上的工作一时❼~不下〔状~〕别随便❽~；不要到处乱❾~；往垃圾箱里~

1. cobblestone; pebble 2. the skin of fruit; peel 3. waste paper 4. waste paper basket 5. Chinese cabbage 6. rabbit; hare 7. for a short while 8. casually; wantonly; wilfully 9. at random

③ put aside ≌ 放〔~补〕〈结〉把一切❶烦恼❷都~在脑后❸了〈可〉这件事我一直~不开〈时〉英语~了好多年，都忘了〔状~〕一直~不开；暂时❹~一~〔习用〕~三落(là)四❺

1. all; everything 2. vexation; worry 3. let sth. pass out of one's mind; clean forget 4. temporarily; for the moment 5. forgetful; scatterbrained

dǒng 懂 understand; know〔~宾〕〈名〉~英语; ~广东话❶; 不~西班牙语❷; ~他的意思吗? ~礼貌❸; ~道理❹; ~规矩❺; 不~政策❻; 这个孩子挺❼~事儿❽; 他年纪❾虽小, ~的东西可不少〔~补〕〈程〉~得不彻底; ~得太少了〔状~〕真~; 假~; 不太~; 彻底~; 有点儿~; 一点也不~; 似~非~❿

1. Guangdong dialect 2. Spanish 3. courtesy; politeness; manners 4. reason 5. well-behaved 6. policy 7. very 8. sensible; intelligent 9. age 10. have only a hazy notion; not quite understand

dòng 动 ① move; stir ≅ 活动 ↔静〔主~〕〈名〉心里❶一~, 想起一个主意❷来; 他嘴唇❸~了~, 想说句什么话; 小猫卧❹着不~; 孩子真老实❺坐在那里一~也不~❻; 别~人家的东西, 不许~桌子上的书〈代〉你坐着别~, 我对敌人说: "你~, 我就开枪❼"〔~宾〕〈名〉他向前~了半步〔~补〕〈结〉别把我的东西~乱❽了〈趋〉会还没散❾人们就~起来了,〈可〉把那个敌人捆❿起来了, 他一点儿也~不了(liǎo)〈时〉嘴唇~了半天, 没说话〈量〉你~一下儿, 我就开枪〔状~〕别乱~; 一动也不~; 一点也别~

1. in the heart; in (the) mind 2. idea; plan 3. lips 4. lie 5. well-behaved; good 6. not movable 7. fire with a rifle; pistol; etc.; shoot 8. in disorder; in a mess 9. be over 10. tie; bundle

② use ≅ 用〔~宾〕〈名〉~手笔, ~枪❶, ~刀, 这个人真懒❷, 光❸~嘴不~手; 有话慢慢说, 不要~武❹; ~脑筋❺; 没那笔钱〔~补〕〈趋〉他急了, ~起拳头❻来了; 构思❼好了, 一起笔来就快了〈可〉目前❽还~不了(liǎo)笔; 这笔钱可~不得❾〈量〉好好~一下儿脑筋〔状~〕多~~脑筋

1. gun 2. lazy 3. only; merely 4. use force; start a fight 5. use one's head 6. fist 7. (of writers or artists) work out the plot of a literary work or the composition of a painting 8. at present; at the moment 9. must not

③ arouse; touch (one's heart) ≅ 触动〔~宾〕〈名〉我不爱~感情❶; ~了邪念❷; ~了恻隐之心❸; 别~肝火❹; 使他~心❺了〔~补〕〈趋〉他又~起感情来了〔状~〕又~心了; 真~感情了; 别~气

1. be carried away by emotion; get worked up 2. evil thought 3. sense of pity 4. flare up 5. one's mind is perturbed; one's desire, enthusiasm or interest is aroused

dòng 冻 freeze; feel very cold; be frostbitten〔主~〕〈名〉河里的水~了; 白菜❶~了; 手脚都~了; 豆腐❷~了〔~宾〕〈名〉~手, ~脸〔~补〕〈结〉今天可把我~坏了; 鼻子都~红了; 手指~

僵❸了；脚～肿❹了；～破❺了；～烂❻了；河里的水～上冰了；把孩子～病了；房檐❼滴❽下来的水都～成冰柱了；哎呀！～死我了〈程〉他～得直哆嗦❾；冰～得真厚❿；～得真结实⓫〈可〉气温⓬还没到零下⓭，水还～不了(liǎo)冰；他出去时穿的衣服太薄⓮不知～得着(zháo)～不着(zháo)？我不穿大衣也～不坏；不病〈时〉在外边～了半天，再一会就得(děi)病了〔状～〕一下子就～上了一层冰；薄薄地～了一层；真～死了；都快～病了

1. Chinese cabbage 2. bean curd 3. numb; stiff 4. swollen 5. 6. fester 7. eaves 8. drip 9. tremble; shiver 10. thick 11. solid 12. air temperature 13. below zero 14. thin

dōu 兜 ① wrap up in a piece of cloth, etc.〔～宾〕〈名〉用衣襟❶～着花生米；～着枣子❷～了好几个鸡蛋〔补～〕〈结〉～好了；～住了〈趋〉～起来〈可〉～得了(liǎo)那么多吗？～得起来～不起来？帆～破❹了，～不住风了〈量〉～一下儿试试；～过一次〔状～〕用毛巾❺～；小孩子常用衣襟～

1. the one or two pieces making up the front of a Chinese jacket 2. jujube; date 3. sail 4. be torn 5. towel

② move round ≌ 绕〔～宾〕〈名〉他说话不直爽❶，总爱～圈子❷；在街上～了一圈儿；坐着汽车到郊外❸～风❹去了〔～补〕〈时〉～了一会儿风；他跟我～了半天圈子，我才懂〈量〉出去一下儿风吧〔状～〕最怕你跟我～圈子；驾车❺四处❻～风

1. not frank 2. go around in circles 3. suburb 4. go for a drive, ride or sail 5. harness to a cart; drive 6. all around

dǒu 抖 ① tremble; shiver; quiver ≌ 哆嗦〔主～〕〈名〉腿直❶～；全身一个劲儿地❷～；嘴唇❸在～〔～补〕〈趋〉～起来没完了〈程〉～得拿不了(liǎo)杯子了；～得太利害了；～得牙嘚嘚地响❹；～得上牙打下牙❺〈时〉～了半天也止不住❻；～一会儿就不抖了〈量〉象这样～过好多次了〔状～〕经常～；止不住地～；不停地❼～；直～；一个劲儿地～；浑身乱～

1. 2. continuously; persistently. 3. lips 4. 5. make one's teeth clatter 6. unable to stop 7. ceaselessly; incessantly

② shake; jerk ≌ 掉；甩动〔～宾〕〈名〉～一～床单❶上的土；～身上的雪；～一～衣服上的线头儿❷〔～补〕〈结〉快把身上的土～掉；身上的雪都～干净了吗？～开刚拧❸出来的衣服〈趋〉快把土～下去〈程〉衣服～得很干净〈可〉衣服上的雪都化❹了～不掉了〈时〉新衣服上的线头～了半天才抖掉；多～一会儿就下去了〈量〉再～一下儿；～了一阵〔状～〕使

劲❺～；用力～；拼命❻～；不停地❼～；一个劲儿地❽～；猛～了一阵〔习用〕～威风❾

1. sheet 2. an odd piece of thread 3. wring out 4. be melted 5. exert all one's strength 6. with all one's might 7. ceaselessly; incessantly 8. persistently; continuously 9. throw one's weight about

dòu 斗 ① make animal fight (as a game)〔～宾〕〈名〉～牛；～鸡；～蟋蟀❶〔～补〕〈结〉～赢❷了；～输❸了〈趋〉两头牛～起来了〈程〉～得真激烈❹；～得真猛❺；～得很顽强❻；～得很艰苦❼〈可〉这头黑牛～不过那头黄的〈时〉～了两个小时〈量〉那头黄牛～赢了两场；～赢过好几次〔状～〕狠❽～；两头牛勇猛地❾～

1. cricket-fight 2. win 3. lose; be beaten 4. intense; sharp 5. fierce; violent 6. indomitable; staunch; tenacious 7. arduous; difficult 8. vigorously 9. courageously; full of valour and vigour; boldly

② contest with; contend with〔～宾〕〈名〉两个人～智❶；她特别爱～心眼❷；别～气❸〔～补〕〈结〉两个人又～上气了〈程〉斗心眼～得太利害了；～得真无聊❹；～得真没意思〈可〉我～不过他；谁也～不了(liǎo)他〈时〉～了好几年心眼〈量〉～过好几次智了〔状～〕他们两个人总～；一直～；跟我～；为小事❺～

1. 2. battle of wits 3. quarrel or contend with sb. on account of a personal grudge 4. senseless; stupid; silly 5. for trifle; for minor matter

dòu 逗 ① tease; play with ≅ 引逗〔～宾〕〈名〉那条狗凶❶极了，你可别～它；他喜欢～孩子〔～补〕〈结〉把她～乐❷了；～哭了；～急❸了〈程〉～得大家哈哈大笑；逗笑～得过火❹了；～得太凶了；～得真有意思〈可〉怎么逗也～不急；～不乐〈时〉～一会儿就把他逗笑了；～了半天他也不笑〔状～〕故意❺～

1. ferocious 2. laugh; be amused 3. irritated; annoyed; nettled 4. go too far; go to extremes 5. intentionally; wilfully

② provoke (laughter, etc.); amuse ≅ 招引〔～宾〕〈名〉这个孩子真～人喜欢；～人爱〔状～〕真～；总那么～；非常～人爱

dú 毒 kill with poison〔～补〕〈结〉把人～死❶了；～死了不少老鼠〈可〉这种药～得死老鼠～不死？〔状～〕用毒药❷～

1. kill with poison 2. poison; toxicant

dú 读 ① read; read aloud ≅ 念〔～宾〕〈名〉～报；给我们～一首诗❶；他给我～了一篇好文章❷；我喜欢看小说❸，不习惯❹小说；～台词❺；我～中文，你～英文；先～课文；～文件❻；～名单❼；～～词汇❽；再～～字

母❾〔**～补**〕〈结〉他读台词总～错；读报～串行❿了；这首诗又没～对；这本英文小说你～懂了吗？把信～给他听〈趋〉请你继续～下去；她又～起诗来了〈程〉～得很流利⓫；～得太快了；～得真好听；～得非常有感情⓬；～得相当慢；～得不连贯⓭；～得抑扬顿挫⓮〈可〉一年级的孩子识字⓯不多，长篇小说还～不下来；这首诗太难，我～不懂；这篇文章真长，半个小时～不完；她看到悲哀⓰的地方，哭得～不下去了；内容⓱太枯燥⓲，我～不下去了；乐谱⓳我一点也～不出来；他没戴眼镜⓴～不了(liǎo)报〈时〉～了一个小时；～了一会儿；～了半天〈量〉～一下儿听听；再～一遍；～过很多次了〔**状～**〕大声～；小声点～；结结巴巴地㉑～；带着感情地～；断断续续地㉒～；一遍一遍地～；含着眼泪㉓～；高兴地～；难过地㉔～；在会上～；在电台上㉕～；一口气～；继续～；慢点儿～；反复～；整天～；成天～；给他～；难～；容易～；重新～；终于～到了你的文章

1. poem **2.** article; essay **3.** novel **4.** not get used to **5.** actor's lines **6.** document **7.** name list **8.** vocabularies; words and phrases **9.** letters of an alphabet **10.** miss (skip) a line **11.** fluent **12.** be full of sentiment **13.** incoherent; inconsistent **14.** modulation in tone; cadence **15.** know characters **16.** sad; sorrowful **17.** content **18.** dull and dry **19.** music score; music **20.** wear glasses **21.** stammeringly **22.** off and on; intermittently **23.** with tears in one's eyes **24.** grievously **25.** at the radio station

② attend school ≃ 上〔**～宾**〕〈名〉他哥哥正在～大学；他～中学；他弟弟～小学；～初中；～高中〔**～补**〕〈结〉她没～完大学就去工作了〈趋〉由于❶没有钱交学费❷，就没有再～下去；好容易❸才把大学～下来了〈可〉这个孩子学习不好，～不了(liǎo)大学；私立❹大学太贵❺～不起；父亲死了以后他要挣钱养家❻，怕是～不了(liǎo)了；～不下去了；～不到毕业了〈时〉只～过六年中学〈量〉先在这个系❼～一下儿试试〔**状～**〕顺利地❽～；一帆风顺地❾～；断断续续地❿～；勉强～；好不容易～；连续⓫～；一直～〔**习用**〕～死书⓬

1. owing to **2.** tuition fee; school fee **3.** with great difficulty; have a hard time (doing sth.) **4.** privately run **5.** expensive; costly; dear **6.** earn money to support one's family **7.** department (in a college) **8.** smoothly; successfully **9.** plain sailing **10.** off and on; intermittently **11.** continuously; successively **12.** study mechanically; be a bookworm

dǔ 堵 stop up; block up; feel suffocated ≃ 堵塞，闷〔**～宾**〕〈名〉罪犯❶用毛巾～她的嘴；用泥和砖～一～墙上的窟窿❷；

~树洞；你站在这儿~着门，谁也过不去；别~着路；用棉花❸~着耳朵〔~补〕〈结〉把后窗~上吧；把路都~死❹了；拿毛巾住他的嘴；汽车把路都~上❺了〈趋〉他怕吵，把两个耳朵都~起来了〈程〉心里~得慌；胸口❻~得难受❼；感冒了，鼻子❽~得出不来气❾；~得很利害；~得真难受；门口儿让东西~得连下脚的地方都没有了❿；窗户~得很严⓫〈可〉这个窟窿用砖头~不严；水管子⓬坏了，水~不住，流了一地；你一个人~得上这个墙洞~不上？没有材料⓭~不了(liǎo)〈时〉我一个人~了半天也没堵好〈量〉要好好~一下儿；~过一次〔状~〕用什么~？马上~；赶快~；严严实实地⓮~

1. criminal 2. hole 3. cotton 4. impassable; closed 5. block up 6. the pit of the stomach 7. feel unwell 8. nose 9. gasping for breath 10. not possess a speck of land 11. tight 12. waterpipe 13. material 14. tightly; closely

dǔ 赌 ① gamble ≅ 赌博〔~宾〕〈名〉~钱，~房子，~地❶；~手表，~首饰❷〔~补〕〈结〉~输❸了，~赢❹了，~穷了，~急❺了〈趋〉再~下去，前途❻就断送❼了〈程〉~得真凶❽；~得卖房子卖地；~得什么也不顾了❾；~得倾家荡产❿〈可〉他们只是随便说说⓫，实际⓬~不起来；输得~不下去了〈时〉~了一晚上，~了几年〈量〉~一下儿碰碰运气⓭；~过一次，全输了〔状~〕经常~；总~；偶尔⓮~；别~

1. land 2. (woman's personal) ornaments; jewelry 3. be defeated; be beaten 4. win 5. irritated; annoyed; nettled 6. prospect; future 7. forfeit (one's future; life, etc.); ruin 8. terrible; fearful 9. show no consideration 10. lose a family fortune 11. make some casual remarks 12. in fact 13. try one's luck 14. occasionally; once in a while

② bet ≅ 打赌〔~宾〕〈名〉咱们俩~个输❶赢❷好不好？谁输了谁请客；偏要跟他们~这口气❸〔~补〕〈结〉他~赢了，所以她很高兴；我~输了，所以我要请她吃饭〔状~〕从来不~；跟他~

1. lose 2. win 3. feel wronged and act rashly

dùjì 妒忌 be jealous (envious) of envy ≅ 忌妒〔~宾〕〈名〉~别人；不要~人家；~有钱的人；~有能力的人❶；~幸运的人❷；~受重视❸的人；~生活条件❹比自己优越❺的人；~权力❻大的人〔~补〕〈结〉~上小李了〈趋〉她们看见人家有成绩❼，就~起人家来了〈程〉~极了；~得要命；~得很利害〔状~〕别~；总~；无缘无故地❽~；莫明其妙地❾~；非常~；特别~；从来不~

1. a man of a great ability 2. lucky man 3. be taken seriously 4. living conditions 5. superior;

advantageous 6. power 7. result; achievement; success 8. without cause or reason; for no reason at all 9. without rhyme or reason; inexplicable

dù 度 spend; pass ≅ 过〔~宾〕〈名〉~过了一个幸福❶的童年❷；~日如年❸；~过了一个愉快的节日〔~补〕〈结〉假期~完了〔状~〕欢❹~；高高兴兴地~；愉快地~；虚~年华❺

1. happy 2. childhood 3. one day seems like a year 4. joyfully 5. fritter away one's time; idle away one's time

dù 渡 cross (a river, the sea, etc.) ≅ 通过；跨过；越过〔~宾〕〈名〉~过大西洋❶；~过红海❷；~过地中海❸；~过黄河❹；~过难关❺〔~补〕〈趋〉总算❻把难关~过去了〈可〉没有船~不过去〔状~〕远~重洋❼；飞~太平洋❽；横❾~大西洋；强~过去

1. the Atlantic Ocean 2. Red Sea 3. Mediterranean Sea 4. Yellow River 5. difficulty; crisis 6. at long last; finally 7. travel across the oceans 8. fly across the Pacific Ocean 9. across; transverse

dù 镀 plate〔~宾〕〈名〉~铝❶；~镍❷；~金；~银；~锌❸；~锡❹〔~补〕〈结〉~上一层❺锡；~好了吗？~完了；~满了；~薄❻点；~厚❼点〈程〉~得很好；~得很亮；~得很漂亮；

~得很厚；~得很光滑；~得真快〈可〉~得上~不上？~得好吗？~得了(liǎo)金吗？〈量〉~过一次掉了，再~一次吧〔状~〕好~；不好~；多~

1. aluminium 2. nickel 3. zinc 4. tin 5. a layer 6. thin 7. thick

duān 端 hold sth. level with both hands〔~宾〕〈名〉~盘子❶；~碗；~一碗饭；~菜；~茶；~水；~锅❷〔~补〕〈结〉把碗~平❸了；别把汤~洒❹了；盘子住，别摔❺了；把吃剩下❻的菜~走吧；把这碗饭~给他〈趋〉饭菜得了❼，都~上来吧；~上去吧；~进来吧；~进去吧；这碗莲子粥❽我给她~过去，她没吃又给我~回来了；这里没人能吃辣椒❾，请你把这盘辣豆腐❿~回去吧；他渴极了，~起啤酒⓫来就喝了；把锅~到旁边的炉子⓬上去了；她从厨房~出来一杯热气腾腾的⓭咖啡；把煤油炉子⓮~出去吧；~到门外边去吧〈可〉锅太大我~不动；~不起来；太烫⓯我~不了(liǎo)；~不过去；~不上来；~不过来；~不出来〈时〉在手里~了半天，也找不着地方放；你先~一会儿，我把桌子上的东西挪⓰一挪〔状~〕用盘子~；少~点儿；往哪儿~？给谁~？一碗一碗地~；一趟一趟地~；原封不动⓱地~了回去平着~；来回⓲~

1. plate 2. pot; pan 3. flat 4. sprinkle 5. cause to fall and break 6. remain 7. be ready 8. lotus

seed gruel 9. hot pepper; chilli 10. hot bean curd 11. beer 12. stove 13. steaming hot 14. kerosene stove 15. very hot; scalding; boiling hot 16. move 17. be left intact 18. to and fro

duǎn 短 be short of; lack ≅ 短少；少〔~宾〕〈名〉~钱花；这本书～了两页❶；别人都到了，就～他一个人〔~补〕〈程〉钱～得不多〈可〉以后～不了(liǎo)麻烦❷你；～不了(liǎo)多少钱了〔状~〕不～；至少❸～；经常；刚好～一块钱

1. two pages 2. disturb; trouble 3. at least

duàn 断 ① break; snap ≅ 折(shé)〔主~〕〈名〉绳子❶～了；铁丝❷～了；电线❸～了；表带～了；棍子～了；鞋带～了；弦❹～了；来往❺～了；关系❻～了〔~补〕〈程〉～得一截❼一截的了〈可〉绳子很结实❽，～不了(liǎo)〈时〉弦～了好多日子了〈量〉电线～过一次〔状~〕又～了；没～过；总～；一拉就～

1. rope 2. iron wire 3. electric wire 4. string 5. contact; intercourse 6. relation 7. section 8. solid

② stop; break off; cut off ≅ 停〔~宾〕〈名〉~水；～电；小孩子～奶❶了；和某国～交❷了；还没～气❸呢〔~补〕〈结〉孩子断奶～早了；～晚了〈程〉断奶～得很早〈可〉～不了(liǎo)〈时〉～了好几天电〔状~〕从不～电；连续❹～水；又～；突然～

1. weaning 2. break off diplomatic relations with a certain country 3. breathe one's last; die 4. in succession

③ judge ≅ 判断；判定〔~宾〕〈名〉~案❶〔~补〕〈结〉千万❷别～错了；能～清❸吗?〈趋〉他～起案来，脑子❹非常清楚〈程〉断案～得很公平；～得很合理❺；～得很清楚〈可〉～不清的家务事❻；～不了〔状~〕合理地～；公正地～〔习用〕~线风筝❼

1. case 2. be sure 3. settle; clear up; clean up 4. brains; mind; head 5. rational; reasonable; equitable 6. household duties 7. a kite with a broken string — a person or thing gone beyond recall

duàndìng 断定 conclude; form a judgment; decide; determine〔~宾〕〈动〉~是她写的；～是张先生的笔迹❶；～是谁的指纹❷〈主－谓〉我不敢～你是日本人，但是看样子有点儿象；～她没听懂我的话；医生～他得的是肝癌❸〔~补〕〈结〉~出那是个逃犯❹〈可〉～得出来是真是假❺吗? 我～不了(liǎo)这些文物❻是哪个朝代❼的〈量〉好好～一下儿〔状~〕很快就～出来了；无法❽～；根据❾什么～；立刻～出

1. handwriting 2. fingerprint 3.

cancer of the liver 4. escaped criminal 5. false 6. cultural relic; historical relic 7. dynasty 8. unable; incapable 9. on the basis of; according to

duī 堆 pile up; heap up; stack 〔～宾〕〈名〉～东西；～草；～了一个假山❶；桌子上～着很多书；床上～着一堆刚洗好的衣服；窗下～着很多木柴〔～补〕〈结〉～满一桌子书；～满一床衣服；别把乱七八糟的❷东西都～在桌子上；许多问题～在一起了〈趋〉把一袋袋的水泥❸都～起来了〈程〉东西～得横七竖八的❹；稻草❺～得真高〈时〉～了半天也没堆上去〔状～〕别到处乱❻～；胡乱❼～；乱七八糟地～着；满处❽～

1. rockery 2. messy 3. cement 4. in a mess; in disorder; at sixes and sevens 5. rice straw 6. 7. at random; casually 8. everywhere

duì 对 ① treat; cope with; counter ≅ 对待；对抗；针对〔～宾〕〈名〉～事不～人❶；～症下药❷〔状～〕一向❸～事不～人；总是～人不对事；必须～症下药

1. concern oneself with facts and not with people 2. suit the medicine to the illness; suit the remedy to the case 3. consistently; all along

② be directed at; be trained on ≅ 朝着；向着〔～宾〕〈名〉枪口❶～着靶心❷；办公桌❸～着房门；

窗户～着操场；我的话不是～你说的；我坐的地方正好～着镜子❹〔～补〕〈结〉准❺靶心；～准目标❻；～准方向❼〈程〉～得很准；～得正正〈可〉打枪的时候，我老～不准；～不好，～不正〈时〉～了半天也没对准；多～一会儿～了十分钟〔状～〕恰好❽～着；正好～着；正～着；必须～

1. muzzle 2. bull's-eye 3. desk; bureau 4. mirror 5. accurate; exact 6. target 7. direction 8. just right

③ set; adjust〔～宾〕〈名〉～暗号❶；～对子❷；～笔迹❸；～号码❹；～～表；～帐单❺；我们两个人～～答案❻；～像片；～距离❼；～光圈❽〔～补〕〈结〉保险柜❾的锁我没～上，所以门打不开；～好了吗？把表～准❶❶；帐都～完了；号码别～错了；这两块版❶❷没～正；～好镜头❶❸〈趋〉暗号已经～出来了〈程〉对子～得真工整❶❹；表～得很准〈可〉他也会对对子，可是～不好；题太多，答案一时❶❺～不完〈时〉～了很长时间笔迹，才找到罪犯❶❻〈量〉～一下儿号码；再把帐～一遍；已经～过两次了〔状～〕一下子就～上了；好～不好～？重点地❶❼～笔记❶❽；一点一点儿地～；机警地❶❾～暗号；准时❷⓿～表

1. secret signal (或 sign); countersign 2. antithetical couplet (written on scrolls, etc.) 3. a person's handwriting 4. number 5. bill 6. key; answer; solution 7.

distance 8. diaphragm; aperture 9. safe 10. lock 11. accurate 12. printing plate 13. lens 14. carefully and neatly done 15. temporarily; for the moment 16. criminal 17. emphatically 18. notes 19. alertly; vigilantly 20. on time

④ suit; agree; get along ≅ 适合 〔~宾〕〈名〉今天的饭菜都~我的胃口❶；她和小张有点儿不~劲儿❷，谁也不爱理谁；这种货❸很~路子❹，很快都卖出去了；他说的话很~我的心思❺〔~补〕〈可〉卖什么都~不上路子，总赔钱❻〔状~〕真~；都~；不~；不太~；正~；越说越~脾气

1. appetite 2. not get along (well) 3. goods 4. satisfy the need 5. be to one's liking 6. lose money in business transactions

⑤ mix; add ≅ 搀合〔~宾〕〈名〉牛奶里一点咖啡；~点水；~点桔汁❶；~点红颜色〔~补〕〈结〉最好多~点儿水；颜色~多了；~少了〈趋〉~进点儿水去吧〈程〉水~得太多了；桔汁~得太酸❷了；~得不够浓❸；~得太甜❹了；颜色~得太深❺了〈可〉颜色总~不好，不是深了，就是浅❻了〈时〉~了半天也没~好〈量〉~了两次水，已经不甜了〔状~〕多(少)~点儿；别~了；再~一些；稍微❼~一点儿；一下子~多了；一点一点地~；适当地❽~；按比例❾~〔习用〕驴唇不~马嘴❿；~牛弹琴⓫；~台戏⓬

1. orange juice 2. sour 3. dense; thick 4. sweet; honeyed 5. dark; deep 6. light 7. a little; a bit; slightly 8. suitable; properly 9. in proportion 10. a donkey's lips do not match a horse's jaws — incongruous; irrelevant 11. play the lute to a cow — choose the wrong audience 12. rival show

dūn 蹲 ① squat on the heels 〔~补〕〈结〉~在地上；~在树下边儿；~在墙角❶；腿都~麻❷了；~累了〈趋〉~下去；快~下来吧〈程〉~得腿都麻了；~得真累；~得眼睛冒❸金星❹〈可〉太胖了，有点~不下去了；他腿坏了~不了(liǎo)；时间太长了，我有点儿~不住了〈时〉~一会儿眼睛就发黑❺〈量〉刚~一下儿，站起来，眼睛就冒金花〔状~〕在墙角~着

1. a corner formed by two walls 2. have pins and needles in one's legs 3. emit; send out; give off 4. see stars 5. grow dim (of the eyes)

② stay ≅ 呆〔~宾〕〈名〉~监狱❶〔~补〕〈结〉你怎么总~在家里不出去啊？〈时〉~了三年监狱；在家~了半年，也没找到工作〈量〉~过两次监狱了〔状~〕别尽在家~着

1. prison

dùn 炖 stew〔~宾〕〈名〉~鸡；~肉；~了三斤；~了一锅〔~补〕〈结〉鸡已经~上了；肉~烂❶了；

~熟❷了；~好了；怎么~成这个样子了〈程〉~得很烂；~得太硬❸了；~得真香❹；~得非常好吃〈可〉一个小时~得熟不熟？~得烂不烂？~得好不好〈时〉~了一个小时了，怎么还没熟啊！再~十分钟就差不多❺了〈量〉~过一次〔状~〕多~点儿；真难~；用微火❻~；用旺火❼~；用电炉❽~；一次~了不少

1. tender 2. cooked; done 3. hard 4. savoury; appetizing 5. not far off 6. slow fire 7. a great fire 8. electric stove

duó 夺 ① take by force; seize; wrest ≅ 抢〔~宾〕〈名〉~刀子；~枪；~印❶；~权❷；~东西〔~补〕〈结〉他把钢笔从我手里~走了；从暴徒❸手里~下了刀子；权已经~到手❹了；我军❺又~下了一些城镇❻〈趋〉把钱~了过去；她一生气把像片~回去了〈可〉这个权谁也~不了(liǎo)；~得到手~不到手？我一个人~不下暴徒手里的刀子〈时〉互相~了好长时间〈量〉~了好几下儿〔状~〕拼命❼~；使劲❽~；猛❾~；从他手里~一把~了过来；一下子~走了

1. seal (seize the seal — seize power) 2. seize power; take over power 3. ruffian; thug 4. in one's hands 5. troops 6. cities and towns 7. desperately 8. exert all one's strength 9. vigorously; suddenly

② contend for; compete for; strive for ≅ 争取〔~宾〕〈名〉~冠军❶；~世界第一；~锦标❷；~第一名；~决赛权❸〔~补〕〈结〉把第一名~到手上〈趋〉今年他们又把冠军~回来了；前三名都被她们~去了，又被我们~来了〈程〉~得很艰苦❹；~得很吃力❺；~得真不容易〈可〉眼看❻就~不过来了；~不回来了；时间一到想夺也~不了(liǎo)了〈时〉~了半天也没夺过来〈量〉~过两次；好好~一下儿〔状~〕竭尽全力地❼~；吃力地~；激烈地❽~；艰苦地~；拼命❾~

1. champion 2. championship; prize 3. finals 4. arduous 5. entail strenuous effort; be a strain 6. soon; in a moment 7. spare no effort; do one's utmost 8. intensely; sharply; fiercely 9. desperately

duǒ 躲 hide (oneself) ≅ 避；藏〔代~〕〈名〉你别~，碰❶不着你；你们往旁边~一~让车过去〔~宾〕〈名〉~人；走路要注意~车；~灾❷；~债❸；~子弹❹〈代〉小红不明白最近小兰为什么要~着自己；他正在生气，你可要~着他点儿〔~补〕〈结〉请~开点儿；~在床底下了；~在家里；~过这阵雨再走吧〈趋〉他~出去了；家里太乱❺，我~出来了；~到树底下避雨去了；~到图书馆看书去了；他怕流氓❻来打他，所以~起来了；刚才你~到哪儿去了？躲来躲去这场祸❼还是没~

过去；这次难关❽总算❾~过去了〈程〉他~得很快；~得很及时；看见打架❿的，她就~得远远的〈可〉司机⓫发现⓬的太晚，已经~不及⓭了；看样子，这场灾难是~不过去了；~得了(liǎo)今天，~不了(liǎo)明天；怎么躲也~不开他〈时〉他在我那儿~了几天；先~几天再出去〈量〉在棚子⓮底下~过一次雨；在上海~过一次地震⓯；快~一下儿吧〔状~〕赶快~开；立即~开；马上~开；慢点~；老~着；在哪儿~？在房檐⓰下~；在门后边~；偷偷地⓱~；一闪身⓲~过去了；总算~过去了

1. touch 2. bad luck 3. debt 4. bullet 5. in noisy disorder 6. rogue; hooligan 7. misfortune; disaster 8. difficulty; crisis 9. after all 10. fight; come to blows 11. driver 12. discover 13. find it too late 14. shed 15. earthquake 16. eaves 17. stealthily 18. dodge

duò 剁 chop; cut 〔~宾〕〈名〉~肉馅❶；~排骨❷；~白菜❸；~甘蔗❹；~了一点儿；~了五根甘蔗〔~补〕〈结〉把肉馅~烂❺点；排骨~碎❻了；甘蔗一折(shé)❼了，把肉~成碎末❽；~成碎块❾；白菜馅~好了〈趋〉馅❿都~出来了〈程〉馅~得真细⓫；~得太粗⓬；~得很快；~得真慢；~得太多了〈可〉刀不快⓭~不下来；~不动；~不了(liǎo)；~不烂；~不折(shé)〈时〉一会就好了；~了半天也没剁下来〈量〉过一次；再~几下儿；~了几刀

〔状~〕用刀(斧子⓮)~；真难~；很容易~；别~了；快~；一点一点地~

1. meat stuffing 2. spareribs 3. Chinese cabbage 4. sugarcane 5. tender 6. break to pieces 7. broken; snapped 8. pieces 9. cubes; pieces; lumps 10. filling stuffing 11. thin; fine 12. coarse; rough; crude 13. blunt 14. axe

duòluò 堕落 degenerate; sink low 〔主~〕〈名〉思想~了；行为❶~了；道德❷~了；生活~了；那个青年~了〔~补〕〈结〉怎么~成这个样子了；想不到他竟~到这般地步❸〈趋〉你就从此~下去了吗？这个人开始~起来了〈程〉~得太快了；~得真利害〈可〉一个人可~不得啊！〔状~〕一天一天地~；慢慢地~；很快地~；一下子~；真~了；逐渐❹~了；渐渐❺~了

1. action; behaviour 2. morals; morality 3. condition; plight 4. 5. gradually

duò 跺 stamp (one's foot) 〔~宾〕〈名〉急❶得直~脚；~一脚上的雪，再进来〔~补〕〈结〉使劲❷太大，把脚都~疼了〈趋〉把鞋上的雪~下去吧！〈程〉~得楼板❸咚咚地❹响；~得脚都疼了〈时〉~了半天〈量〉~了几下儿；~了一阵〔状~〕直~脚；拼命~；一个劲儿地~；一边哭一边~

1. be impatient; be worried 2. exert all one's strength 3. floor; floorslab 4. rub-a-dub; rat-a-tat

E

ézhà 讹诈 extort under false pretences; blackmail 〔~宾〕〈名〉~钱财❶；~财物❷〔~补〕〈结〉财物都被那个坏人~走了；他企图❸讹诈，但没~成〈趋〉居然❹~到我头上来了〔状~〕被那个坏蛋~；采取❺卑鄙手段❻~；多次~；竟然❼~；到处~

1. wealth; money 2. property, 3. attempt; try; seek 4. unexpectedly; to one's surprise 5. adopt; take 6. contemptible means; dirty tricks 7. unexpectedly; to one's surprise.

èshā 扼杀 strangle; smother; throttle 〔~宾〕〈名〉~新生❶事物❷〔~补〕〈结〉~在萌芽状态中❸〔~补〕〈可〉~不了(liǎo)；~不死〔状~〕绝对❹~不了(liǎo)；被~

1. newly born 2. thing 3. in the bud 4. absolutely

èhuà 恶化 worsen; deteriorate; take a turn for the worse 〔主~〕〈名〉病情❶~了；健康状况❷~了；环境污染❸的情况~了；局势❹~了；两国关系❺~了；夫妻❻关系~了〔~补〕〈程〉~到无法挽回的程度❼〔状~〕急剧❽~；愈加❾~；日益❿~；日趋⓫~；逐渐⓬~；不断⓭~；突然⓮~

1. patient's condition 2. physical condition 3. environmental pollution 4. situation 5. the relations between two countries 6. husband and wife 7. to a irredeemable degree 8. suddenly; rapidly 9. all the more 10. day by day; increasingly 11. with each passing day; gradually 12. gradually 13. incessantly 14. suddenly

è 饿 feel hungry; starve↔饱〔~补〕〈结〉~死我了；可把他~坏了；小猪都~瘦了〈趋〉再~下去我可受不了❶(liǎo)了〈程〉~得肚子咕噜咕噜叫❷；~得走不动了；~得头发昏❸腿❹发软❺；~得一点力气❻都没有了；~得睡不着(zháo)觉；~得要命〈可〉~不死；~不着(zháo)〈时〉~了一天〈量〉~他一下儿就不挑食❼了；好好~他一顿❽就好了〔状~〕早就~了；已经~了；还没~呢

1. cannot bear 2. one's stomach keeps rumbling 3. feel giddy 4. legs 5. feel weak 6. strength 7. be too particular about food or what one eat 8. a meal

F

fā 发 ① send out; issue; deliver; distribute ≅ 送出〔~宾〕〈名〉~信；~电报❶；~信号❷；~工资❸；~球；~命令❹；~简报❺；~社论❻；~选民证❼；~榜❽；~稿❾；~奖金❿；~文件⓫；~通知⓬；~票⓭；~书；~毕业证书⓮〔~补〕〈结〉~下一份文件；稿子~晚了〈趋〉把球~过去；通知~下来了；~来一封信；~出去一份电报；~出来一股令人作呕的臭气⓯〈可〉连工资都快~不出来了；稿件这星期~不了(liǎo)；球他总~不过去；两万人的工资一上午~不完；他嗓子哑⓰了~不出声音来了〔状~〕按时⓱~工资；由12号~球；给工人~奖金；赶紧~

1. telegram 2. signal 3. wage; salary 4. order 5. brief report; bulletin 6. editorial 7. elector's certificate; voter registration card 8. a list of names posted up 9. manuscript 10. money award; bonus 11. document 12. notice; circular 13. ticket 14. diploma; graduation certificate 15. a sickening smell 16. lose one's voice 17. on time

② express; utter ≅ 表达；发表〔~宾〕~言❶；~誓❷；~议论❸；~牢骚❹〔~补〕〈结〉牢骚~完了，心里就痛快❺了〈趋〉他~起言来滔滔不绝❻；~起牢骚来就没完❼；~出来一声怪叫❽〈程〉那些人发誓~得无聊❾；她每次发言都~得比较长〈可〉没想好说什么，现在还~不了(liǎo)言〈时〉他一发言就得(děi)~半个多小时〈量〉你~过几次誓了；借着机会❿就要~一下儿牢骚〔状~〕从来不~牢骚；长篇大论⓫地~言；滔滔不绝地~言；指天⓬~誓

1. speak; make a statement or speech 2. vow; pledge; swear 3. comment; talk; discuss 4. grumble 5. very happy; delighted; joyful 6. talk on and on in a flow of eloquence 7. without end 8. (utter) in a strange voice 9. senseless; silly; stupid 10. take the opportunity of 11. a lengthy speech or article 12. By Heaven (the name of God)

③ come or bring into existence ≅ 发生；产生〔~宾〕〈名〉豆子~芽❶了；这个发电厂❷一天能~多少电？~炎❸了；吃点汤药❹~~汗❺，感冒❻就好了；月亮不能~光〔~补〕〈趋〉汗~出来，病就好了〈程〉豆芽~得

真快；天冷的时候豆芽～得比较慢〔状～〕痛痛快快地❼～点儿汗病就好了；大量❽～电

1. germinate; sprout **2.** power plant; power station **3.** inflammation **4.** a decoction of medicinal ingredients **5.** (induce) perspiration **6.** a cold **7.** simple and direct; forthright; straight forward **8.** a great quantity

④ get into a certain state; become; feel; have a feeling〔～宾〕〈名〉～脾气❶；～火儿❷；他不知怎么～了一笔大财；一个人夜里在荒野❸走路有点～毛❹〈动〉他作的事使人～笑；老虎～怒❺了；～愁❻；这个孩子又～烧❼了；吓得～抖❽；手～颤❾；头～晕❿；～问⓫〈形〉别～呆⓬；脸～白；冻⓭得嘴唇⓮～青；病刚好，脸有点～黄；身上一阵一阵地⓯～热⓰；～疯⓱；～狂⓲；～急⓳；心～慌⓴；手～麻；刚睡醒有点～懒㉑；颜色～暗㉒；蹲㉓完了站起来眼睛～黑；桔子有点儿～酸㉔；柿子㉕～涩㉖；头该洗了，直～痒㉗；吃了药以后皮肤㉘过敏㉙，浑身～痒㉚；咖啡粉放多了有点～苦；她不敢多吃东西怕～胖；这个孩子有点儿～傻；东西都～霉㉛了；～湿㉜；她的头发～干；肉不新鲜㉝，都有点～臭㉞了〔～补〕〔结〉～完酒疯㉟以后，自己也觉得不好意思㊱了〈趋〉他～起脾气来真可怕；又～起烧来了〈程〉发烧～得直乱说话；火儿～得真不小；发疯～得太凶了〈时〉～了三天烧〈量〉～了一阵㊲疯；～了一顿脾气；～过一次火儿〔状～〕大～脾气；浑身一个劲儿地㊳～抖；手直～颤；头有点～晕；动不动就～火儿；净㊴～呆

1. temperament; disposition (lose one's temper) **2.** get angry; flare up **3.** wilderness **4.** be scared; get gooseflesh **5.** flare up; get angry **6.** worry; be anxious **7.** have a fever **8.** shiver; shake; tremble **9.** quiver; shake; tremble **10.** feel dizzy **11.** ask a question **12.** be in a daze; be in a trance **13.** be frozen **14.** lips **15.** occasionally; from time to time **16.** have a fever; have a temperature **17.** **18.** mad; crazy **19.** irritated **20.** nervous; flustered **21.** lazy **22.** dull; dark; dim **23.** squat on the heels **24.** sour; tart **25.** persimmon **26.** puckery **27.** continuously itch **28.** skin **29.** allergy **30.** itch all over **31.** become mildewed; go mouldy **32.** wet **33.** not fresh **34.** bad smell; stink; offensive odour **35.** be roaring drunk **36.** feel embarrassed **37.** a fit; a peal; a burst **38.** continuously; persistently **39.** only; merely; nothing but

fābiǎo 发表 publish; issue〔主～〕〈名〉论文❶～了；文章❷～了；剧本❸～了；他写的诗～了；剪纸❹～了；木刻❺～了；录取名单❻～了；社论❼～了；考试

成绩～了〔～宾〕〈名〉～自己的看法；～声明❽；～不同的意见❾；～谈话；～了一篇精采❿的演说⓫；～评论⓬；～激烈⓭的言论⓮；～人口统计⓯数字；～国家预算⓰；～财政赤字⓱〔状～〕公开⓲～；在哪个杂志上⓳～？正式⓴～；连续㉑～；一齐㉒～；即兴㉓～，先后～；多次～；已经～；从未～过

1. thesis **2.** essay; article **3.** drama; play **4.** paper-cut **5.** woodcut **6.** admission list **7.** editorial **8.** statement; declaration **9.** different opinion **10.** brilliant; splendid; wonderful **11.** speech **12.** comment; commentary; review **13.** intense; sharp; fierce; acute **14.** speech; opinion on public affairs **15.** vital statistics **16.** budget **17.** financial deficits **18.** openly; publicly **19.** magazine **20.** officially **21.** in succession; running **22.** at the same time **23.** without preparation

fābù 发布

issue; release〔～宾〕〈名〉～上级的命令❶；～国务院❷的指示❸；～了一个爆炸性❹的新闻❺；～了大风警报❻〔～补〕〈量〉～过两次了〔状～〕由电视台～；在报纸上～；立即❼～；及时❽～；通过❾卫星❿～

1. order of the higher authorities; **2.** the State Council **3.** directives; instructions **4.** explosive **5.** news **6.** alarm; warning; alert **7.** at once; immediately **8.** in time **9.** by means of; through; by way of **10.** satellite

fāchū 发出

issue; send out; give out〔～宾〕〈名〉电铃❶～了警告❷；红灯❸～了指示❹；～警报❺；荷花❻～了一股清香❼味；～了鼾声❽；太阳～了热和光〔状～〕一阵阵地❾～；不停地～；断断续续地❿～；一到晚上就～；由机器～；一再～

1. electric bell **2.** warning; alarm **3.** red light **4.** directive; instructions **5.** alert; alarm; warning **6.** lotus **7.** delicate fragrance; faint scent **8.** sound of snoring **9.** in fits and starts; from time to time **10.** off and on; intermittently

fādòng 发动

① start; launch〔～宾〕〈名〉～战争；～攻势❶；～机器；～进攻❷；～猛攻❸〔～补〕〈趋〉又～起战争来了〈可〉天太冷，汽车发动机❹～不起来了；〈量〉～过一次进攻〔状～〕向敌人阵地❺～；竟然❻～；居然❼～；万一❽～；突然❾～

1. offensive **2.** attack; assault; offensive **3.** fiercely attack **4.** engine; motor **5.** position **6. 7.** unexpectedly; to one's surprise **8.** if by any chance; just in case **9.** suddenly; all of a sudden

② call into action; mobilize the masses〔～宾〕〈名〉～学生；～人

民〔~补〕〈结〉~晚了〈趋〉~起来了〈程〉~得很好〈可〉~得起来吗? ~得了(liǎo)~不了(liǎo)？〈时〉~了半天也没发动起来〈量〉~过好多次了; 好好~一下儿〔状~〕充分❶~; 尽量❷~; 再次❸~; 一齐❹~

1. fully; abundantly 2. to the best of one's ability; as far as possible 3. once more 4. at the same time; simultaneously

fāhuī 发挥 bring into play; give play to 〔~宾〕〈名〉~主动性❶; ~创造性❷; ~了巨大的力量❸; ~了效力❹; ~了威力❺; ~了集体❻的智慧❼; ~了他的才干❽; ~了才能❾; ~了他们的特长❿; ~专长⓫; ~作用⓬〔~补〕〈趋〉把你的聪明才智⓭全部~出来吧〈可〉~得了(liǎo)~不了(liǎo)? ~得出来~不出来? 〈量〉应该好好儿~一下儿〔状~〕充分⓮~; 尽量⓯~; 主动~; 积极~; 已经~; 全部~〔习用〕借题~⓰．

1. initiative 2. creativeness; creativity 3. tremendous force; immense strength 4. effect 5. power; might 6. collective 7. wisdom; intelligence 8. 9. ability; competence 10. 11. speciality; strong point 12. effect; role 13. intelligence and wisdom 14. fully; abundantly 15. to the best of one's ability; as far as possible 16. make use of the subject under discussion to put over one's own ideas; seize on an incident to exaggerate matters

fāshēng 发生 happen; occur; take place 〔~宾〕〈名〉这个城市~了很大的变化; ~了交通事故❶; ~意外❷; ~强烈❸地震❹; 机器❺~了故障❻; 对文学~了兴趣❼; 从未~过这种问题; ~了纠纷❽; ~口角❾; ~了奇怪❿的现象〈动〉~争吵⓫〔~补〕〈结〉事情~在1978年〈程〉事情~得很奇怪; ~得很突然⓬〈量〉过很多次〔状~〕突然~; 意外地~了; 经常~; 偶然⓭~; 连续⓮~; 屡次⓯~

1. traffic accident 2. accident; mishap 3. violent; strong; intense 4. earthquake 5. machine 6. breakdown; trouble; stoppage 7. interest 8. dispute 9. quarrel; wrangle 10. strange; surprising; odd 11. quarrel; wrangle 12. sudden 13. accidentally; by chance 14. in succession; in a row; running 15. time and again; repeatedly

fāxiàn 发现 find; discover 〔~宾〕〈名〉~了野兽❶的足迹❷; ~了重要的线索❸; ~可疑❹的迹象❺; ~了不少问题; ~了一架敌机❻; ~了新的情况; 哥伦布❼~了新大陆〈主-谓〉~这孩子说谎; ~他没来; ~他不高兴; 医生~病人的病情❾起了变化; ~他好象有什么心事❿

〔～补〕〈结〉她的病～晚了〈程〉～得太晚了；～得很及时⓫〈可〉藏⓬在这儿，谁也～不了(liǎo)〈量〉被他～过一次〔状～〕突然～；偶然⓭～；幸亏⓮～；被别人～了

1. wild animal; wild beast 2. track; footmark; footprint 3. clue 4. suspicious; dubious 5. sign; indication 6. enemy plane 7. Columbus 8. the New World — the Americas 9. patient's condition; state of an illness 10. sth. weighing on one's mind; worry 11. in time 12. hide; conceal 13. by chance; accidentally 14. luckily; fortunately

fāyáng 发扬 develop; carry on 〔～宾〕〈名〉～优点❶；～优良传统❷；～好的作风❸；～高尚❹风格❺；～互助❻友爱的精神❼〔状～〕充分❽～；大大～；必须～；认真～

1. merit; strong point 2. fine tradition 3. style; style of work 4. noble; lofty 5. style 6. mutual aid; help each other 7. spirit 8. fully; abundantly

fāzhǎn 发展 develop; expand; grow 〔主～〕〈名〉形势❶向有利❷的方面❸～了；文化教育事业❹～了；医疗卫生❺事业～了；旅游业❻～了；科学技术～了〔～宾〕〈名〉～交通运输业❼；～工业；～农业；～渔业❽；～畜牧业❾；～商业❿；～体育运动⓫；～经济⓬〔～补〕〈结〉～到今天这个样子；～成为一个现代化⓭的城市〈趋〉乒乓球运动很快～起来了〈可〉这个地方～不了(liǎo) 手工业⓮〔状～〕蓬勃⓯～；日益⓰～；大力⓱～；逐步⓲～；迅速⓳～；优先⓴～；在原有㉑的基础㉒上～

1. situation; circumstances 2. advantageous; beneficial; favourable 3. respect; aspect; side 4. cultural and educational establishments 5. medical and health 6. tourism 7. communications and transportation 8. fishery 9. animal husbandry 10. commerce 11. physical culture 12. economy 13. modernize 14. handicraft industry 15. vigorously; in the full of vitality 16. increasingly; day by day 17. energetically; vigorously 18. gradually 19. rapidly 20. give priority to; take precedence 21. original; former; primary 22. foundation; basis

fá 罚 punish; penalize 〔～宾〕〈名〉偷税漏税❶一定要～款❷；违反交通规则❸要～钱；因对方犯规❹，～了一个球❺；打赌❻输❼了，被～了两大杯酒❽〈代〉～她唱歌；～他表演❾一个节目❿〔～补〕〈程〉钱～得真多〈量〉他被～过一次〔状～〕狠狠地⓫～；重重地⓬～；必须～；只～

1. evade taxes 2. (impose) a fine or forfeit 3. violate traffic regulations 4. break the rules 5. penalty

shot; penalty kick 6. bet; wager 7. lose; be beaten; be defeated 8. be made to drink two cups of wine as a forfeit 9. perform 10. programme 11. ruthlessly; ferociously 12. heavily

fān 翻 ① turn over; reverse 〔主～〕〈名〉车～了；船～了；椅子～了〔～宾〕〈名〉～了一个身❶，又睡着(zháo)了；农民正在～地❷，准备种西瓜〔～补〕〈趋〉～过身来了〈可〉风这么大，船～得了(liǎo)～不了(liǎo)？地方太窄❸睡觉时都～不过身来❹〔状〕差一点儿～；车一下子就～了；突然❺～了

1. turn over in bed 2. turn up the soil 3. narrow 4. be unable to turn over 5. suddenly; all of a sudden

② cross; get over ≅ 爬过，越过〔～宾〕〈名〉～山；～墙；～篱笆❶；～栅栏❷；～铁栏杆❸〔～补〕〈趋〉～过去了〈量〉～过几次〔状～〕往里边～；从墙外～；一蹿❹就～过去了；登着❺石头～；猛地❻一～

1. hedge; fence 2. railings; paling 3. iron railings 4. leap up 5. step on; tread 6. suddenly; abruptly

③ reverse ≅ 推翻〔～宾〕〈名〉～案❶〔状～〕彻底❷～；公开❸～；公然❹～；多次～；只好～；不得❺～

1. (reverse) a verdict 2. thoroughly 3. 4. openly 5. have no choice but

④ rummage; search〔～宾〕〈名〉～箱子❶；～抽屉❷；～口袋❸；～书包；～报纸；～杂志；～资料❹〔～补〕〈结〉抽屉都～遍❺了，也没有找着(zháo)；所有的地方都～到了；把箱子全～乱❻了〈趋〉～出来一张十年前的旧报纸；他～过来～过去找；她～起相簿❼来兴趣❽最大〈可〉这个词我在这本小词典上～不着(zháo)，就换了一本大词典〈时〉～了半天也没找到；多～一会儿就找到了；～了一天资料〈量〉仔细❾～一下儿；～过两遍了；～了好几次了〔状～〕彻底❿～；从头到尾⓫～；一页一页地～；匆匆忙忙地～⓬；经常～；整天～

1. chest; box; trunk 2. drawer 3. pocket 4. data; material 5. all over; everywhere 6. in disorder; in a mess; in confusion 7. a photo album 8. interest 9. carefully 10. thoroughly 11. from beginning to end 12. hurriedly

⑤ translate ≅ 翻译〔～宾〕〈名〉我～了一本小说；～了一个剧本❶；～资料❷；～了一篇文章❸；～密码❹〔～补〕〈结〉把英文～成中文；这句话～错了；小说～完了没有？这次～对了吧〈趋〉这段❺话～出来了吗？他刚学两年英语，现在也～起小说来了〈程〉～得很好；～得不对；～得乱七八糟❻〈可〉这句话～不出来了；

这个剧本你～得了(liǎo)～不了(liǎo)？半年～得完～不完？我可能～不好〔**状～**〕认真❼～；仔细❽～；逐字逐句地❾～

1. drama; play **2.** data; material **3.** article; essay **4.** cipher; cipher code **5.** paragraph **6.** in a mess; in a muddle **7.** seriously; conscientiously **8.** carefully **9.** word by word

fǎn 反 oppose; combat ≅ 反对

〔**～宾**〕〈名〉～封建❶；～间谍❷；～科学❸；～潮流❹；～殖民主义❺；～军国主义❻〔**状～**〕坚决❼～；彻底❽～；一直❾～

1. feudalism **2.** spy **3.** science **4.** trend; tide **5.** colonialism **6.** militarism **7.** resolutely **8.** thoroughly **9.** continuously; always; all the time

fǎnduì 反对 oppose; be against; fight; combat ≅ 不赞成，不同意

〔**～宾**〕〈名〉～战争❶；～这门婚事❷；～官僚主义❸；～殖民主义❹；～种族歧视❺〈代〉他总～我〈动〉～滥用职权❻；～侵略❼；～贪污❽；～浪费❾〔**～补**〕〈结〉一定把歪风邪气❿～掉〈趋〉继续⓫～下去〈程〉～得十分利害⓬〈可〉～得掉吗？〈时〉～了半天也无济于事⓭〈量〉～过一次〔**状～**〕坚决⓮～；极力⓯～；一致⓰～；再三～；屡次⓱～；一向⓲～

1. war **2.** marriage; wedding **3.** bureaucracy **4.** colonialism **5.** racial discrimination **6.** abuse one's power **7.** aggression **8.** corruption **9.** waste **10.** evil winds and noxious influences **11.** go on; continue **12.** terrible; awful **13.** of no avail; to no effect **14.** resolutely; firmly **15.** do one's utmost; spare no effort **16.** unanimously **17.** over and over again; repeatedly **18.** consistently; all along

fǎnyìng 反映 reflect; mirror

〔**～宾**〕〈名〉文艺作品❶要～现实生活❷；这些意见❸～了大家的要求❹；这篇小说～了青年人的生活情况；这些建筑❺～了古代❻劳动人民的智慧和才能❼；～了人们的精神面貌❽；～了他的性格❾；～了民族特色❿；～了不同的爱好⓫(hào)；～了高尚⓬的情操⓭；～了新时代的特点⓮；～了一个人的文化程度⓯〔**～补**〕〈结〉～到小说里；～在各个方面〈趋〉～出来〈程〉～得很全面⓰；～得很真实⓱〈可〉～不出来；～不了(liǎo)〔**状～**〕完全～；向谁～？生动地⓲～；充分⓳～；明显地⓴～；主动㉑～；在一定程度上㉒～；真实地～；及时㉓～

1. works of literature and art **2.** real (actual) life **3.** opinion **4.** demand **5.** building; structure; edifice **6.** ancient times **7.** wisdom and ability **8.** mental attitude **9.** character **10.** national features **11.** love; interest; hobby **12.** noble; lofty **13.** sentiment **14.**

trait; characteristic 15. cultural level 16. comprehensive; all-round; overall 17. real; true; wholly; entirely 18. vividly 19. fully; abundantly 20. clearly; obviously; evidently 21. on one's own initiative 22. to a certain extent 23. in time

fàn 犯 violate; offend (against law, etc.); commit (a mistake) 〔～宾〕〈名〉～法❶；～罪❷；～错误❸；打篮球～规❺了；又～病了❻；心里直～疑心❼〈动〉这句话～忌讳❽〔～补〕〈结〉～下了滔天罪行❾〈趋〉～起病来了〈程〉病～得很利害❿〈可〉～不上⓫跟他生这么大的气；小小的困难～不着(zháo)发愁⓬；为这事～不着(zháo)哭〈时〉～了好几个月病；～了两次〔状～〕总～错误；又～病了；千万别～；究竟⓭～了什么法？

1. law 2. crime 3. mistake 4. play basket ball 5. break the rules 6. have an attack of one's old illness 7. suspicion 8. a taboo 9. monstrous crimes 10. terrible; awful 11. not worthwhile 12. worry 13. after all; in the end

fànmài 贩卖 traffic; peddle; sell 〔～宾〕〈名〉～毒品❶；～鸦片❷；～海洛因❸；～军火❹；～私货❺；～黑货❻；～奴隶❼〔～补〕〈结〉～到了很远的地方〈趋〉又偷偷地❽～起来了〈量〉过很多次〔状～〕大量～；竟然❾～；多次～；到处～

1. narcotic drugs; narcotics 2. opium 3. heroin 4. munitions; arms and ammunition 5. 6. smuggled goods; contraband goods 7. slave 8. secretly; stealthily 9. to one's surprise; unexpectedly

fáng 防 guard against; provide against 〔～宾〕〈名〉～旱❶；～疫❷；～灾❸；～火；～子弹❹，～盗贼❺；～毒气❻；～尘埃❼；这种表～水吗？皮衣服❽可以～寒～署；这种布～雨〈形〉～潮❾〈动〉～锈❿；～腐蚀⓫；～震⓬〈主－谓〉放点樟脑丸⓭可以～虫咬〔～补〕〈可〉～得了(liǎo)～不了(liǎo)？〔状～〕积极⓮～；及时⓯～；严⓰～

1. drought 2. epidemic 3. calamity 4. bullet 5. thief 6. poisonous gas 7. dust 8. leather clothes 9. damp; moisture 10. rust 11. corrode; etch 12. shock; shake 13. camphor ball 14. actively 15. in time 16. strictly

fángzhǐ 防止 prevent; guard against 〔～宾〕〈名〉～交通事故❶〈动〉～生锈❷；～倒塌❸；～传染❹；～发生危险❺；～出现意外❻；～感冒❼；～污染❽〈形〉～骄傲自满❾〈主－谓〉～伤口⓾感染⓫；～气管⓬发炎⓭；～患处⓮化脓⓯；～食物中毒⓰〔～

补〕〈可〉～得了(liǎo)～不了(liǎo)〔状～〕认真⓱～；尽量⓲～；竭力⓳～；必须～；不易⓴～

1. traffic accident 2. rust 3. collapse; topple down 4. infect; be contagious 5. danger 6. accident 7. common cold 8. pollution 9. swollen with pride; conceited and arrogant 10. wound 11. infect 12. trachea 13. become inflamed 14. affected part (of a patient's body) 15. fester; suppurate 16. food poisoning 17. seriously; conscientiously 18. to the best of one's ability; as far as possible 19. with all one's might; energetically 20. not easy

fáng'ài 妨碍 hinder; hamper; impede; obstruct ≅ 影响〔～宾〕〈名〉～交通❶〈动〉～儿童智力❷的发展❸；东西放在门口儿～走路〈主－谓〉你在这儿捣乱❹～我们工作；你们说话声音太大～别人休息；牙疼❺～我睡觉；路上发生了交通事故❻～车辆❼通行❽；前排❾那个人坐得太高，～后排❿的人看；咱们在这儿～他们谈话吧！〔～补〕〈可〉～得着(zháo)～不着(zháo)〔状～〕别～；真⓫～；特别⓬～；严重地⓭～

1. traffic 2. intelligence; intellect 3. development 4. make trouble; create a disturbance 5. toothache 6. traffic accident 7. vehicle; car 8. pass (go) through 9. front row 10. back row 11. really 12. especially 13. seriously; gravely

fǎngwèn 访问 visit; call on〔～宾〕〈名〉～作家；～演员❶；～导演❷；～作曲家❸；～专家❹；～英雄❺；～模范❻；～教练❼；～工会❽主席；～生物学家❾；～一个神童❿；～练气功⓫的人；～老艺人⓬；～知名人士⓭；～加拿大⓮；～欧洲各国⓯〔～补〕〈量〉他到非洲⓰去～过三次；应该去～一下儿他〔状～〕热情地⓱～；亲切地⓲～；正式⓳～；非正式⓴～；专程㉑～；再次～；顺便㉒～

1. actor; performer 2. director (of a film, play, etc) 3. composer 4. expert; specialist 5. hero 6. model; exemplary person 7. coach; instructor; trainer 8. trade union 9. biologist 10. child prodigy 11. a system of deep breathing exercises 12. old actor (or artist) 13. well-known (noted) personage; public figure; celebrity 14. Canada 15. European countries 16. Africa 17. warmly 18. cordially; kindly 19. formally; officially 20. unofficially 21. for special trip 22. conveniently; in passing

fàng 放 ① let go; set free; release〔～宾〕〈名〉～了一只蜻蜓❶；～了一个俘虏❷；～了一批人质❸〈代〉他不～我走〔～补〕〈结〉有些事可以～开手❹不管❺；

把游泳池❻的脏❼水全～掉了；谁让我的蟋蟀❽～跑了〈趋〉幼儿园❾的阿姨❿把孩子们都～到院子⓫里去玩了；把小鸟从笼子⓬里～出去了〈程〉水～得真快；～得很慢〈可〉他什么事都～不开⓭；游泳池的水三天也～不完；人质暂时⓮还～不出来〈时〉游泳池的水～了三天了才放光〈量〉～过一次〔**状**～〕偷偷地⓯～；故意⓰～；一下子全～了

1. dragonfly 2. prisoner of war; captive; captured personnel 3. hostage 4. have a free hand 5. not interfere 6. swimming pool 7. dirty 8. cricket 9. kindergarten; nursery school 10. auntie 11. courtyard 12. cage; coop 13. be kept in suspense; feel anxious 14. temporarily; for the moment 15. stealthily; secretly 16. intentionally; on purpose

② let off; give out ≅ 发出〔～宾〕〈名〉～信号弹❶；～枪❷；～炮❸；～风筝❹；～光芒❺；～气球❻；花～香味❼〔～补〕〈结〉枪～响❽了；风筝～高了就显得❾小了〈趋〉～起了三颗信号弹，没拉好线❿，结果⓫把风筝～到树上去了；茉莉花⓬～出了芬芳⓭的香味〈程〉炮～得真响；气球～得真高〈可〉风筝太大～不起来（～不上去）；他不会放，～不了(liǎo)；没有风，风筝～不起来（～不上去）〈时〉～了半天也没放起来〈量〉只～过一次炮〔**状**～〕一阵阵地⓮～香味，连续⓯～

1. signal flare 2. rifle; gun (fire with a gun) 3. artillery 4. kite (fly a kite) 5. rays of light; brilliant rays 6. balloon 7. sweet smell; flagrance; scent; perfume 8. make a sound; sound 9. look; seem; appear 10. string or wire 11. finally 12. jasmine 13. fragrant; sweet-smelling 14. from time to time; by fits and starts 15. in succession; in a row; running

③ put out to pasture ≅ 放牧〔～宾〕〈名〉～牛；～鸭子〔**～补**〕〈结〉那个孩子～丢❶了一只羊；他放牛～累了，躺❷在山坡上就睡着(zháo)了；～完了鸭子再去割草❸〈趋〉牛都～到山坡上吃草去了；孩子那么小就～起羊来了〈可〉除❹了他，谁也～不了(liǎo)那头脾气暴躁❺的水牛❻〈时〉我小时候～过三年羊〈量〉我～一下儿试试〔**状**～〕在山坡上～；曾经～过，单独❼～；到处～

1. lost 2. lie 3. cut grass (with a scythe) 4. except 5. irascible; irritable 6. (water) buffalo 7. alone; by oneself

④ let out; |expand;| make large ≅ 扩展〔～补〕〈结〉把衣服～长一点儿；领子❶再～大一点儿；把肩❷～宽❸些；把照片～大❹〈程〉～得太多了；～得太少了〈可〉～得了(liǎo)吗〈时〉～了半天也没长出多少来〈量〉～过两次了〔**状**～〕别～；再～；在照像馆❺里～照片

1. collar 2. shoulder 3. large 4. make enlargements of a photograph 5. photo studio

⑤ put in; add ≅ 加进去〔～宾〕〈名〉往锅❶里～点水；菜里～点酱油❷；汤里～点儿盐❸〔～补〕〈结〉～上点儿辣椒❹；醋❺～多了酸❻〈趋〉把可可粉❼～进牛奶里去了〈程〉胡椒粉❽～得太多了；香油❾～得太少了〈量〉～过一次了〔状～〕多～；少量❿～；大量⓫～

1. pot; pan; cauldron 2. soy sauce 3. salt 4. hot pepper 5. vinegar 6. sour 7. cocoa powder 8. pepper powder 9. sesame oil 10. a small quantity 11. a great quantity

⑥ put; place ≅ 放置〔～宾〕〈名〉靠❶门～柜子❷；箱子❸里～着很多衣服；书架❹上～着书〔～补〕〈结〉两手～在膝盖❺上；花盆❻～在窗台❼上；书架上～满❽了书；这张地图❾～高点儿；把菜～近点儿；要把精力❿～在事业⓫上；那面墙上再～上一张画就好看了〈趋〉把窗帘⓬～下来；把袖子⓭～下来；快把手里的东西～到桌子上去吧〈程〉屋子里的家具⓮～得太挤⓯了；抽屉⓰里的东西～得太多了〈可〉地方小东西多～不下了；桌子腿⓱不一般⓲长～不平；～不稳⓳〈时〉书包先在你这里～一会儿；这些东西在那儿～了好长时间了〈量〉沙发⓴靠墙～过一次；手提包㉑先在这儿～一下儿〔状～〕暂时㉒～；永久㉓～；长期～；紧挨着㉔～；按次序㉕～；多～一会儿；在窗前～

1. near; by 2. wardrobe 3. chest; trunk 4. bookshelf 5. knee 6. flowerpot 7. windowsill 8. full; filled 9. map 10. energy; vigor 11. cause; undertaking 12. curtain 13. sleeve 14. furniture 15. packed; crowded 16. drawer 17. legs of a table 18. same as; just like 19. not steady 20. sofa; settee 21. handbag 22. temporarily; for the moment 23. forever; permanently; perpetually 24. be close to 25. by order

⑦ leave alone; lay aside ≅ 搁〔～宾〕〈名〉先～一～这件事，以后再说；暂时❶～一～这个工作〔～补〕〈程〉肉～得时间太长不新鲜❷了〈可〉天气太热，吃的东西～不住〈时〉这件衣服不合适，我～了三年都没穿〈量〉把手里的工作先～一下儿〔状～〕暂时～；一直❸～着；已经～了；别再～了

1. temporarily; for the moment 2. fresh 3. all the time; continuously; always

⑧ readjust (attitude, behaviour, etc) 〔～补〕〈结〉脚步～轻点❶儿；速度❷～慢点儿❸；声音❹～～低点儿；态度～踏实点❺儿；～明白点儿❻；～稳重点儿❼；胆子～大点儿❽〈程〉脚步～得很轻；速度～得很慢〔状～〕必须～；已经～；只好～；不得不❾～

1. gently; softly 2. speed; velocity 3. slowly 4. sound; voice 5. well-behaved; good; (behave yourself) 6. be sensible 7. be steady 8. pluck up courage; stop being afraid 9. have no choice but

⑨ show; send out ≅ 放映；放送〔~宾〕〈名〉 ~电影；~电视；~幻灯❶；~录音❷；~唱片❸；~音乐〔~补〕〈趋〉那个喇叭❹~出来的声音比较柔和❺；这几部电影~过来~过去，都有点看腻❻了；隔壁❼又~起音乐来了〈程〉戏曲❽片❾~得太多了〈可〉幻灯机坏了，今天~不了(liǎo)了；没租❿着(zháo)好片子，明天可能~不成了〈时〉~了十分钟唱片〈量〉~一下儿听听好不好？~了无数⓫遍了〔状~〕每天~；经常~；偶尔⓬~；有时候~；从早到晚⓭~〔习用〕~长线，钓大鱼⓮

1. slide show 2. sound recording (play back the recording) 3. gramophone record (play a gramophone record) 4. loudspeaker 5. gentle; mild 6. be bored with; be tired of 7. next-door neighbour 8. traditional opera 9. a roll of film; film; movie 10. rent; hire 11. innumerable; countless 12. once in a while; occasionally 13. from morning till night 14. throw a long line to catch a big fish — adopt a long-term plan to secure sth. big

fàngqì 放弃 abandon; give up; renounce ≅ 丢掉〔~宾〕〈名〉~原则❶；~表决权❷；~学习的机会❸；~学医❹的打算❺；~宗教信仰❻；~自己的主张❼；~去欧洲❽旅行的计划〔状~〕全部~；不得不❾~；必须~；突然~；已经~；别~

1. principle 2. vote; right to vote 3. chance; opportunity 4. study medical science; medicine 5. plan; intention 6. religious belief 7. own view; own position; own stand 8. Europe 9. have no choice but

fàngshǒu 放手 ① let go one's hold 〔主~〕〈代〉这个工作他就是不肯❶~；我一~，风筝❷就飞起来了；她抓住❸救生圈❹不~；借到一本好的外文小说他怎么肯~呢？〔状~〕一~就跑了；别~；只好~

1. be unwilling to 2. kite 3. grab; hold; seize 4. life buoy

② have a free hand; go all out 〔~宾〕〈动〉你就~去做吧，有问题再来找我；他一气❶之下，~不管❷了；~选拔❸人材❹〔状~〕完全~；轻易❺不~；必须~

1. get angry 2. not interfere 3. select; choose 4. a talented person; a person of ability; qualified personnel 5. lightly; rashly

fàngxīn 放心 set one's mind

at rest; be at ease; make one's mind easy 〔主~〕<代>我自己能找到,你~吧<名>孩子出远门❶,父母总是不~〔~宾〕<名>我最不~她的身体<主-谓>不~孩子自己过马路〔~补〕<结>他来了电话,我们才放下了心<可>她有些~不下 〔状~〕稍微❷~了点儿;对他不~;逐渐❸~了;有些不~;完全~

1. be off to distant parts 2. a little; slightly 3. gradually

fēi 飞 ① fly; flit 〔主~〕<名>老鹰❶~;蝴蝶❷~;飞机~;雪花❸~;羽毛❹随风❺~;尘土❻满天~〔~补〕<结>麻雀❼~到树梢❽上了<趋>蜻蜓~来~去;大雁❾~过去了;飞机~起来了;从窝❿里~出来了<程>~得很高;~得快极了;~得很远<可>蜜蜂⓫的翅膀⓬断⓭了~不起来了;鸟被子弹⓮打伤⓯了~不动了;飞机坏了,~不了(liǎo)了;这种虫子~不高<时>~了一天一夜才到〔状~〕直⓰~;从房顶⓱上~;不停地⓲~;展翅⓳高~;盘旋⓴着~;到处~;满天~;轻轻地㉑~;缓缓地㉒~;在天空中~〔习用〕插翅难㉓~;笨鸟先㉔~

1. eagle 2. butterfly 3. snow flake 4. feather; plume 5. with the wind 6. dust 7. (house) sparrow 8. the tip of a tree 9. wild goose 10. nest 11. bee 12. wing 13. broken; snapped 14. bullet 15. be wounded 16. straightforward 17. roof 18. ceaselessly; incessantly 19. spread the wings; get ready for flight (soar to great heights) 20. be wheeling 21. gently; slightly 22. slowly 23. unable to escape even if given wings; even sticking on wings will not help one escape 24. clumsy birds have to start flying early — the slow need to start early

fèi 费 cost; spend; expend ≅ 花 ↔省〔~宾〕<名>自己做饭太~时间;~工夫;他叙述❶起事情来非常~劲儿❷;从楼下往上搬❸地毯❹多~力气❺啊!~了好大力气才把这件事办好;这孩子给您添❻了不少麻烦❼,让您~心❽了;一顿饭做这么多样菜多~事❾啊! 白❿~唇舌⓫〔~补〕<可>~不了(liǎo)多少〔状~〕白~;相当⓬~;特别~;比较~〔习用〕~力不讨好⓭

1. narrate; recount; relate 2. need or use great effort; be strenuous 3. remove; move 4. carpet 5. take a lot of effort 6. add; increase 7. trouble 8. give a lot of care; take a lot of trouble 9. give or take a lot of trouble 10. in vain 11. take a lot of explaining or arguing 12. quite; fairly; considerably 13. do a hard but thankless job

fēn 分 ① divide; separate; part ≅ 分开 ↔ 合〔~宾〕<名>~钱; ~

红❶；～粮食❷；两个人～一个西瓜；～了三个小组；你吃不了(liǎo)，把面包～一半给弟弟吧！他忙得一时❸无法～身❹；司机开车时千万不要～心❺；别～神❻；几个小偷正在～赃❼的时候，被警察❽抓住❾了；药❿～三次吃；工作要～两个阶段⓫进行⓬；父亲死后，儿女们把财产⓭全～了〔～补〕〈结〉把这些桔子⓮～成五份；这50个学生可以～成三个班；把花生～成两堆⓯；一间大屋子被～成了两小间；好的和坏的～开放⓰；～到一笔⓱遗产⓲〈趋〉这两个问题应该～开来谈〈程〉遗产～得很合理⓳；两边的头发～得很匀⓴；东西～得很公平〈可〉我～不好；你～得匀吗？这两个孩子好得一会儿也～不开〈时〉～了半天也没分好〈量〉～一下儿〔**状～**〕合理地～；暗中㉑～；公开地㉒～；两个人难舍难～㉓；按时㉔～；马上㉕～；头发从中间～；向左～；往右～

1. bonus (share out); dividends; profits **2.** grain **3.** for a short while; temporarily **4.** (too busy) to attend to anything else **5.** divert (distract) one's attention **6.** give some attention to **7.** the spoils; the booty (loot) **8.** police **9.** arrest **10.** medicine; drug **11.** stage; phase **12.** carry on; carry out; conduct **13.** property **14.** orange **15.** heap; pile **16.** put **17.** a sum of **18.** legacy; inheritance; heritage **19.** rational; reasonable **20.** even **21.** secretly **22.** openly; publicly **23.** loath to part from each other **24.** on time **25.** at once

② distribute; assign; allot ≃ 分配〔**～宾**〕〈名〉～房子；阿姨❶给孩子们～苹果〔**～补**〕〈结〉～给我三斤核桃❷；她毕业❸后被～到了中学去当教员；参观的票都～完了〈趋〉你们怎么私自❹～起来了；奖金❺都～下去了〈可〉东西少人多～不过来〈时〉票～了一个小时才分完〔**状～**〕公平合理地❻～；按什么标准❼～？公开地❽～；不要私自～；不能偷偷地❾～；平均❿～

1. auntie **2.** walnut **3.** graduate **4.** privately **5.** money award; bonus **6.** fair and reasonable **7.** standard; criterion **8.** openly; publicly **9.** secretly **10.** equally

③ distinguish; differentiate ≃ 辨别〔**主～**〕〈名〉这两种颜色在灯下很难～；是非❶不～〔**～宾**〕〈名〉这个人不～好坏；不～真假❷〔**～补**〕〈结〉要～清是非〈趋〉谁是谁非你能～出来吗？〈程〉～得很清楚〈可〉这一对孪生兄弟❸，外人～不出来〈时〉～了半天也没分清〔**状～**〕不好～；真难～；不容易～；很快就～出来了；一下子就～〔**习用**〕不～青红皂白❹

1. right and wrong **2.** true and false **3.** twin brothers **4.** indiscriminately; in a promiscuous manner; irrespective of right and wrong in a dispute

fēnbié 分别

① part; leave each other ≅ 离别 〔主~〕〈代〉他们两个人刚见面又~了; 她们~以前照了一张像〔~补〕〈时〉他们~不到一年又见面了; 我们已经~三年了〔状~〕暂时~; 长期~; 即将~; 已经~; 跟他~; 依依不舍地❶~; 在机场❷~

1. be reluctant to part; cannot bear to part 2. airport

② distinguish; differentiate ≅ 分辨; 区别〔主~〕〈名〉这两个词的意思不易❶~〔~宾〕〈名〉~真假❷; ~善恶❸; ~主次❹; ~轻重缓急❺〔~补〕〈趋〉差别❻虽小, 还是可以~出来的〔状~〕不易~; 很难~; 要仔细❼~

1. not easily 2. true and false 3. good and evil 4. primary and secondary 5. in order of importance and urgency 6. difference 7. carefully; meticulously

fēnpèi 分配

distribute; allot; assign ≅ 分〔~宾〕〈名〉~土地; ~宿舍❶; ~工作〔~补〕〈结〉宿舍~完了吗? 〈程〉~得很合理❷; ~得很公平 〈可〉~不出去; ~不合适〈量〉已经~三次了; 好好~一下儿〔状~〕认真~; 合情合理地❸~; 不容易~; 重新~; 按❹人口❺~; 多~; 少~

1. dormitory 2. rational 3. fair and reasonable 4. according to 5. population; number of people in a family

fēnxī 分析

analyse ≅ 〔~宾〕〈名〉~问题; ~原因; ~结果; ~思想; ~形势❶; ~文章❷; ~语法❸〔~补〕〈结〉~对了; 能把问题~清楚吗? 〈趋〉原因~出来了吗? ~起来头头是道❹; ~来~去也没有个结果〈程〉语法~得很清楚❺; 文章~得很好; 道理❻~得很透彻❼〈可〉~得出来吗? ~得好~不好? 〈时〉~了半天也没分析对〈量〉~过很多次; 再好好~一下儿〔状~〕认真❽~; 仔细❾~; 容易~; 难~; 好~; 多~~; 一层一层地❿~; 合情合理地⓫~

1. situation 2. essay; article 3. grammar 4. clear and logical; closely reasoned and well argued 5. clear 6. principle; reason; argument 7. penetrating; thorough 8. seriously; conscientiously 9. carefully 10. layer upon layer 11. fair and reasonable

fěnsuì 粉碎

smash; shatter; crush ≅ 摧毁; 打垮〔主~〕〈名〉独霸❶世界的美梦❷被~了〔~宾〕〈名〉~了他们的阴谋❸; ~了对我们的经济封锁❹〈动〉~了侵略者❺的进攻❻〔~补〕〈程〉~得很彻底❼; ~得很及时❽〔状~〕彻底~; 一举❾~; 及时~

1. dominate exclusively; monopolize 2. pipe dream; fond illusion 3. plot; scheme; conspiracy 4. economic blockade 5. invader; aggressor 6. attack; assault;

offensive **7.** thorough **8.** in time **9.** at one blow; with one action; at one stroke

fēng 封 seal; close ≅ 封闭

〔**~宾**〕〈名〉~门; ~瓶口儿❶〔**~补**〕〈结〉信已经~上了; 把瓶口儿~严❷; ~紧❸; ~结实❹; 机密文件❺已经~在保险柜❻里了〈程〉蜡❼~得真厚❽; 罐头❾~得不严; 瓶盖❿~得太结实了〈时〉门被~了一年多〔**状~**〕用蜡~瓶口; 用封条⓫~门; 厚厚地⓬~了一层⓭蜡; 严严实实地⓮~

1. the mouth of a bottle **2.** **3.**close; tight **4.** solid **5.** classified papers; confidential documents **6.** safe **7.** wax **8.** thick **9.** tin; can **10.** lid; cover **11.** a strip of paper used for sealing (doors, drawers, etc.); paper strip seal **12.** thickly **13.** layer; tier; stratum **14.** tightly; closely

féng 缝 stitch; sew 〔**~宾**〕〈名〉~被子❶; ~扣子❷; ~衣服; ~鞋〔**~补**〕〈结〉把被子~上; 伤口❸刚~好; 把扣子~结实❹点儿; 扣子~歪❺了; ~斜❻了〈趋〉把扣子~进去一点就合适❼了〈程〉~得很结实❽; ~得非常整齐❾; ~得很密❿; 针脚⓫~得太大〈可〉领子⓬拆⓭下来以后~不上了; 针⓮太小~不了 (liǎo) 鞋; 你~不好, 我帮你缝吧〈时〉~了一个晚上; ~了半天〈量〉扣子要掉⓯赶快~一下儿吧〔**状~**〕用绣花针⓰~; 用黑线~; 往衣服(帽子)上~; 仔细⓱~; 好好~; 不慌不忙地⓲~; 马马虎虎地⓳~; 一针一线地⓴~; 密密地㉑~; 稀稀地㉒~; 赶紧~; 多~几针; 用缝纫机㉓~

1. quilt **2.** button **3.** wound **4.** solid **5.** **6.** oblique; slant **7.** suitable **8.** solid **9.** very neat **10.** dense; thick **11.** stitch **12.** collar **13.** unravel **14.** needle **15.** come off **16.** embroidery needle **17.** carefully **18.** in no hurry **19.** carelessly; casually **20.** stitch by stitch **21.** densely; thickly **22.** sparsely; thinly **23.** by sewing machine

fú 扶 support with the hand; place a hand on sb. or sth. for support ≅ 搀〔**~宾**〕〈名〉~着栏杆❶; ~着梯子❷; ~着我的肩膀❸; ~着墙; 他~着老人; 护士❹~着病人; 司机❺手~方向盘❻〔**~补**〕〈结〉把病人~下床〈趋〉孩子摔倒❼了, 快把他~起来; 把病人~到这边来; 把老人~过来吧; 把病人~上床去了〈可〉他摔倒了, 我一个人~不起来; 他力气❽小~不住〈时〉你先~一会儿她, 我去找救护车❾〈量〉~他一下儿; ~了我一把〔**状~**〕一只手~着墙; 两只手~着病人; 用力~; 好好地~; 他刚要摔倒, 我一把~住了他; 小心翼翼地❿~

1. railing, banisters; balustrade **2.** ladder **3.** shoulder **4.** nurse **5.** driver **6.** steering wheel **7.** tumble over 8. physical strength; effort 9. ambulance 10. with great care; cautiously

fú 服 ① serve 〔～宾〕〈名〉那个犯人❶～刑❷已经期满❸了；我没～过兵役❹〔～补〕〈结〉～完了兵役〈时〉～了三年刑〔状～〕按期❺～

1. prisoner; convict 2. serve a sentence 3. complete a term 4. be on active service; enlist in the army 5. on schedule; on time

② be accustomed to ≅ 〔～宾〕〈名〉水土❶吗？〔～补〕〈可〉～不了(liǎo)这里的水土〔状～〕有点儿不～水土；一直❷不～；渐渐❸～了；慢慢地～了

1. natural environment and climate 2. always; all the time 3. little by little; gradually

③ be convinced; obey ≅ 服从〔主～〕〈名〉口～心不❶～〈代〉你说得有道理❷我～了；你～不～？他们两个人谁都没～〔～宾〕〈动〉他不～调动❸；那个人真不～输❹〈形〉他不～老〔状～〕彻底❺～了；真～了；总算～了；确实～了；表面上❻～

1. pretend to be convinced 2. reason 3. transfer; shift 4. lose; be beaten; be defeated 5. thoroughly 6. outwardly

④ take (medicine, poison) ≅ 吃；喝〔～宾〕〈名〉～药❶；～毒❷；～了三片阿司匹林❸；～了一瓶咳嗽药水❹就好了〔～补〕〈结〉别～错了药〈趋〉～下去〈程〉～得不多〈量〉～过一次〔状～〕按时❺～；分三次～；一次～

1. medicine; drug 2. poison 3. aspirin 4. lotion 5. on time

fúcóng 服从 obey; submit (oneself) to; be subordinated to 〔～宾〕〈名〉～指挥❶；～命令❷；～多数❸人的意见〔状～〕坚决❹～；认真～命令；严格❺～

1. command 2. order 3. majority; most 4. resolutely 5. strictly; severely

fúwù 服务 give service to; be in the service of; serve 〔～补〕〈程〉～得很周到❶；～得很好〈时〉在柜台❷上～了三十年〔状～〕热情地❸～；为顾客❹～；全心全意地❺～

1. attentive and satisfactory 2. counter 3. warmly 4. customers 5. wholeheartedly; heart and soul

fú 浮 float ↔ 沉〔～宾〕〈名〉脸上～着微笑❶〔～补〕〈结〉树叶～在水面；油～在水上〈趋〉潜水员❷～上来了；皮球按❸到水里，一撒手❹又～起来了〈可〉水太浅❺，船～不起来；～不了(liǎo)〔状～〕一直～在上面；很快地～上来了

1. smile 2. diver; frogman 3. press; push down 4. let go one's hold; let go 5. shallow

fúhé 符合 accord with; conform to; tally with 〔~宾〕<名>~青年人的要求❶；~标准❷；~实际情况❸；~录取❹条件；~人们的愿望❺；~事实〔状~〕完全~；不太~

1. demand 2. standard; criterion 3. real situation 4. enroll; recruit; admit 5. desire; wish; aspiration

fù 付 pay ≅ 交；给〔~宾〕<名>请到收款处去~款❶；~帐❷；~税❸；~息❹；~工钱〔~补〕<结>~给他一笔款；~清❺了利息❻；~出了代价❼〔状~〕如数❽钱；按期❾~息；由我~帐

1. a sum of money; fund 2. a bill 3. taxes 4. interest 5. pay off 6. interest 7. price; cost 8. exactly the number or amount (pay back in full) 9. on schedule; on time

fùzhé 负责 be responsible for; be in charge of 〔~宾〕<名>他~这项工作；李医生~三号病房❶<动> ~召集开会❷；~起草文件❸；~通知❹；~运行李❺；~执行❻这项工作；~保卫❼；~保管❽；~侦察❾动向❿；~联系⓫〔~补〕<结>~到底⓬<可>这项工作你~得了(liǎo)吗？〔状~〕积极⓭~；认真⓮~；对他~；曾经~过

1. ward 2. call (convene) a conference 3. draft (draw up) a document 4. notify 5. transport luggage 6. carry out; execute 7. defend; safeguard 8. take care of 9. reconnoitre; scout 10. trend; tendency; movement 11. contact; touch; connection 12. to the end 13. actively 14. seriously; conscientiously

fùxí 复习 review; revise 〔~宾〕<名>~功课；~生词❶；~语法❷；~了三课〔~补〕<结>~完了生词再看课文；~熟❸了，什么问题都能回答<趋>平时❹不注意听讲❺，~起来很困难；~来~去<程>生词~得很熟；语法~得不太好<可>这么多内容可能~不完了；太累了有些~不下去了；她病了，~不了(liǎo)了；明天就考试了，今天才开始复习，怎么能~得好呢？<时>~了好几天；刚~一会儿<量>~好几遍❼了；多~一下儿，就熟了〔状~〕认真~~；多~~；刚刚~；经常~；从不~；从头~；一遍一遍地~

1. new word 2. grammar 3. skilful; familiar 4. at ordinary times 5. listen to a talk; attend a lecture 6. content; substance 7. several times

fùyǒu 富有 rich in; full of ≅ 具有〔~宾〕<名>~不可战胜的❶

生命力❷；～顽强的毅力❸；～青春的活力❹；月光下的风景❺特别❻～魅力❼；～诱惑力❽；～说服力❾；～代表性❿；～一定的冒险性⓫；～正义感⓬；～诗意⓭；～浓厚的生活气息⓮；这种工艺品⓯～民族特色⓰；～地方色彩⓱；～时代的特点⓲；～经验⓳；～同情心⓴；～百折不回的精神㉑〔**状～**〕非常～；更～

1. invincible **2.** vitality; lifeforce **3.** indomitable will **4.** youthful vigour **5.** scenery (landscape) under moonlight **6.** especially **7.** glamour; charm; enchantment; fascination **8.** temptation; enticement; seducement **9.** persuasion **10.** representation **11.** adventure; risk **12.** sense of justice; righteousness; sense of what is right **13.** poetic quality or flavour **14.** rich flavour of life **15.** handicraft article **16.** national features **17.** local colour **18.** characteristic or trait of the times **19.** experience **20.** sympathy; fellow feeling **21.** indomitable spirit

G

gǎi 改 ① change; reform ≃ 改变〔**主～**〕〈名〉时间～了；地点～了；日期～了；社会风气❶～了；脾气❷～了；性格❸～了；缺点❹～了；她小时候的模样❺一点也没～；生活习惯❻～了；通讯处❼～了；电话号码～了〔**～宾**〕〈名〉上课～时间了；比赛～期了；坐累了～一个姿势❽就好了；你为什么要～姓❾；你这个人怎么一会儿一～主意❿啊！他发现自己说错了话想～口⓫，可是已经来不及⓬了〔**～补**〕〈结〉脾气～好了；坏习惯都～掉了；那个孩子现在～好了，再也不逃学⓭了；上班时间～早（～晚）了半小时；大会改在下星期二举行了；这间屋子～成仓库⓮了〈趋〉坏毛病养成⓯了～起来就困难了；坐、立、走的姿势不对，一定要尽早⓰～过来〈程〉社会风气～得比以前好多了〈可〉口吃⓱的毛病～不过来了吗？〈量〉骂人⓲的毛病真得(děi)好好儿～一下儿；～了好多次，就是改不掉〔**状～**〕随地吐痰⓳的习惯已经～了；彻底～了；完全～了；马上就～；真难～；不容易～；好容易⓴才～掉；坚决㉑～；下决心㉒～；一点一点地～；慢慢～；赶快～；痛～前非㉓

1. general mood of society **2.** temper **3.** nature; disposition; temperament **4.** defect; weakness; shortcoming **5.** appearance; look **6.** habits and customs **7.** address **8.** posture **9.** surname; family name **10.** (change) one's mind **11.** correct oneself **12.** it's too late; there's not enough time **13.** play truant; cut class **14.** warehouse; storehouse **15.** cultivate **16.** as soon as possible **17.** stammer **18.** swear (at people) **19.** spit **20.** with great difficulty **21.** resolutely **22.** make up one's mind **23.** sincerely mend one's ways; thoroughly rectify one's errors

② correct ≃ 修改〔**～宾**〕〈名〉～文章❶；～作业；～稿子❷；～卷子❸；～作文；～了几个字；～了几个标点❹；这篇文章只～了几个病句❺；～衣服〔**～补**〕〈结〉裤子～短点儿就能穿起来了；把领子❻～小点儿吧；我想把书架❼～成书柜❽；把门～宽❾一点儿出入❿就方便⓫了；大衣⓬的样子～难看了〈趋〉这个桌子原来⓭都想不要了，没想到～出来这么好；衣服～起来比重新做还麻烦⓮〈程〉衣服～得很合适⓯；家具～得比以前漂亮多了；文章～得很简练⓰；卷子～得太马虎⓱了；稿子～得真快〈可〉我的技术

⓲不高～不好这个〈时〉一条裤子拿到裁缝店⓳去改，要～两个星期才能好；自已～半天儿，就改完了〈量〉这套西装⓴～了好几次了；好好～一下儿，再穿吧〔**状～**〕稍微㉑～～就行了；马马虎虎地㉒～了一下儿；不好～；当时就～；一次一次地～；反复㉓～；仔细㉔～；细心㉕～；耐心㉖～

1. essay; article **2.** manuscript **3.** examination paper **4.** punctuation **5.** faulty sentences **6.** loose; large **7.** bookshelf **8.** bookcase **9.** wide; broad **10.** come in and go out **11.** convenient **12.** overcoat **13.** originally; formerly **14.** trouble **15.** fit; suitable **16.** terse; succinct **17.** careless; perfunctory **18.** technique **19.** tailor's **20.** a suit of Western-style clothes **21.** slightly; lightly; a little **22.** perfunctorily **23.** repeatedly, over and over again **24. 25.** carefully; attentively **26.** with patience

gǎibiàn 改变 change; alter ≅

改〔**主～**〕〈名〉主意❶～了；作风❷～了；习惯❸～了；精神面貌❹～了；国内形势❺～了；战略方针❻～了；经过长年❼海水的冲击❽这块岩石❾的形状❿逐渐～了；人和人的关系～了〔**～宾**〕〈名〉～了主意；～了想法；～了目前的状况⓫；～了原来⓬的计划；～了策略⓭；～了关系；～作风；～路线⓮；～了不利⓯的情况；～了贫穷落后⓰的面貌；～环境⓱〔**～补**〕〈结〉我们要把荒山⓲～成果园〈程〉你的主意～得真快；形势～得很突然⓳；面貌～得跟以前完全不一样了〈可〉狼的本性⓴是～不了(liǎo)的〈量〉计划～过好几次了；社会风气应该好好～一下儿〔**状～**〕经常～计划；好好～作风；坚决㉑～；逐渐～；完全～了；已经～了；突然～；骤然㉒～；无须～

1. idea; plan; decision **2.** style; style of work **3.** habit **4.** mental attitude **5.** the situation at home **6.** strategic policy **7.** over the years **8.** lash **9.** rock **10.** form **11.** condition; state; **12.** original **13.** tactics **14.** route; itinerary; line **15.** unfavourable; disadvantageous **16.** poor and backward **17.** surroundings; circumstances **18.** barren hill **19.** unexpected **20.** natural instincts (character, disposition) **21.** resolutely **22.** suddenly; abruptly

gǎigé 改革 reform 〔**主～**〕〈名〉

文字❶必须～；教育制度❷要～；教学方法❸要～〔**～宾**〕〈名〉～技术❹；～工具❺〔**～补**〕〈结〉这种选拔❻人才❼的办法很好，遗憾❽的是～晚了；～成现在这种样子〈趋〉～起来有一定的困难〈程〉～得很成功；～得不彻底❾；～得比以前好多了〈可〉～得了(liǎo)吗？总～不好〈时〉～了好几年才改革成今天的样子〈量〉～过不少次了；真需要好好～一下儿〔**状**

~〕多次~；彻底~；逐渐❿~

1. characters; writing 2. system of education 3. teaching method 4. skill 5. tool 6. select; choose 7. a person of ability 8. regret; pity 9. not thorough 10. gradually

gǎishàn 改善 improve; ameliorate 〔~宾〕〈名〉~两国的关系；~工作（生活／居住❶）条件；~目前的经济❷状况〔状~〕日益❸~；认真❹~；逐步❺~；彻底❻~；积极❼~；大大地~了

1. housing conditions 2. economy 3. increasingly; day by day 4. seriously; conscientiously 5. gradually 6. thoroughly 7. actively

gǎizào 改造 transform; reform; remould; remake 〔~宾〕〈名〉~大自然❶；~沙漠❷；~世界；~厂房❸；~人〔~补〕〈结〉把小偷、流氓❹~好了〈趋〉~起来不是很容易的〈程〉~得很好；~得不错；~得很不顺利❺〈可〉~得了(liǎo)~不了(liǎo)？~得好~不好？还~得过来吗？〈时〉~了十年；~了很长时间〈量〉~过两次；必须好好~一下儿〔状~〕彻底❻~；认真~；努力~；积极~；逐步❼~；一心~

1. nature 2. desert 3. factory building; workshop 4. rogue 5. unfavorable 6. thoroughly 7. gradually

gǎizhèng 改正 correct; amend; put right 〔~宾〕〈名〉~错误；~缺点❶〔~补〕〈趋〉所有缺点都~过来了〈程〉缺点~得真快；~得很彻底❷〈可〉~得了(liǎo)吗？~得过来~不过来？〔状~〕彻底~；诚心❸~；认真~；完全~过来了；很难~；早就~

1. weakness; defect; shortcoming 2. thorough 3. sincerely; wholeheartedly

gài 盖 ① cover 〔~宾〕〈名〉~盖儿❶；~锅盖❷；~被❸（子）；~毯子❹；~了一层土；~一个纱罩❺；~一块布；~了一张草席❻；~了一块铁板〔~补〕〈结〉把盖儿~紧❼；被没~好；把大衣~在脚底下；茶杯盖儿~错了；头发太长，都把眼睛~住了〈趋〉如果你冷，把这条毯子也~上去吧〈程〉被~得很厚❽；~得很暖和；盖儿~得不紧〈可〉怎么瓶子盖儿~不上了？~不了(liǎo)了，天热了，连毯子都~不住了〈时〉这条毛毯整整~了二十年〔状~〕轻轻地❾~；赶快~；多~点儿；给孩子~被

1. cover; lid 2. a cover for a pan 3. quilt 4. blanket 5. gauze or screen covering (over food) 6. a mat 7. close; tight 8. thick 9. slightly; gently

② affix (a seal) 〔~宾〕〈名〉~图章❶；~戳子❷；~橡皮戳❸〔~补〕〈结〉~满了图章；~错了

地方；没~清楚；~歪❹了；~在什么地方？~倒(dào)了〈趋〉怎么把图章~到这儿来了？下边垫❺点东西~出来清楚〈程〉~得模模糊糊❻的；~得端端正正❼的；~得歪歪扭扭❽的〈可〉图章太脏❾了~不清楚〔状~〕垫着一本书~；别到处乱❿~

1. 2. seal 3. rubber-stamps 4. slant; oblique 5. put sth. under sth. else to raise it or make it level 6. blurred; indistinct 7. upright 8. crooked; askew 9. dirty 10. at random

③ build ≃ 建筑↔拆〔~宾〕〈名〉~房子；~宿舍；~礼堂；~旅馆；~电影院；~剧场❶；~体育馆❷；~了一个仓库❸〔~补〕〈结〉~完了；~好了；~结实❹点儿〈趋〉刚一个多月，房子就~起来了；宿舍楼都~到大门口来了〈程〉~得真快；~得很结实；楼~得不够高〈可〉半年的时间这幢楼~得起来~不起来？~得好~不好？纪念馆❺今年~不成了〈时〉~了三个月就完工❻了；这个体育馆~了很长时间〔状~〕结结实实地~了一个小棚子❼；凑凑合合地❽~；勉强❾~；同时~

1. theatre 2. gymnasium 3. warehouse 4. solid 5. memorial hall 6. complete a project 7. shed 8. make sth. do; make do with sth. 9. reluctantly

gǎn 赶 ①catch up with; overtake; try to catch; make a dash for;

rush for ≃ 追赶〔~宾〕〈名〉~时髦❶；~前边跑的那个人；~火车，早点儿睡吧，明天还要~路❷呢；~时间；~作业；~一篇作文❸；~一篇文章❹〈动〉~织❺了一件毛衣❻〔~补〕〈结〉~上火车了吗？把作业~完了；~到车站，车已经开了；一定要~上世界先进水平❼；他的功课很快就~上大家了；没费多大力气❽就~过了他们〈趋〉她跑得真快，一下子就~到最前边去了；眼看❾他就~上来了；快~上去还有希望得第一；连她都~起时髦来了；那个孩子的成绩很快就~上来了；我今天一定要把那件毛衣~出来，明天还等着穿呢；今天晚上还有事，我一定要~回学校去；下课以后我就要~到大使馆❿去了〈程〉赶火车~得满头大汗；~得气喘吁吁⓫；~得上气不接下气⓬〈可〉天黑以前~不回来了；他已经走远了，赶也~不上了；他跑得特别快，谁也~不上他；两点以前恐怕⓭~不到集合地点⓮了吧〈时〉~了半天也没赶上他〈量〉~过两次路；今天我得(děi)~一下儿作业〔状~〕拼命⓯~，终于⓰~上了；往前~；一个劲儿地~⓱；努力~；连夜~⓲；尽量⓳~；竭尽全力地⓴~；急急忙忙地㉑~；好不容易才~上；不费吹灰之力㉒就~上了

1. fashion 2. hurry on with one's journey 3. composition 4. essay; article 5. knit 6. woolen sweater; pullover 7. advanced world levels 8. not make strenuous

gǎn — gǎndòng 143

efforts 9. soon; in a moment 10. embassy 11. pant; puff hard 12. gasp for breath; be out of breath 13. perhaps; I am afraid 14. assembly place 15. with all one's might; for all one is worth 16. at last; finally 17. persistently; continuously 18. the same night; that very night 19. to the best of one's ability 20. do one's utmost; do all one can 21. in a hurry; hastily 22. as easy as blowing off dust — not needing the slightest effort

② drive ≅ 驾御〔~宾〕〈名〉~马车❶〔~补〕〈结〉他把马车~走了；~跑了〈趋〉请把马车~过来〈程〉~得很轻松❷的样子〈量〉我小时候~过好多次牛车〔状~〕从来没~过；第一次~；往哪儿~？熟练地❸~；一边吆喝❹着一边~；用鞭子❺~

1. horse-drawn carriage 2. light; relaxed 3. skilfully 4. loudly urge on (an animal) 5. whip

③ drive away; expel ≅ 驱逐〔~宾〕〈名〉~苍蝇❶；~蚊子❷；~鸭子〔~补〕〈结〉把苍蝇~跑了；把入侵者❸~走了；他说了一个笑话，~走了我的困意❹〈趋〉把鸭子~到河里去了；把羊~到山坡上去吃草〈可〉这里的苍蝇不怕人，赶都~不动；~不出去〔状~〕往河里~；用手~

1. fly 2. mosquito 3. aggressor; invader 4. sleepy

④ happen to ≅ 遇到〔~补〕〈结〉走到那儿正~上学生放学；今天~巧❶了，他们都在家；事情都~到一块了〈程〉~得真巧❷；~得不是时候；时间~正好〈可〉十次有八、九次~不上她在家〔状~〕刚好~上；碰巧❸~上；准❹~上；从未~上过〔习用〕~早了不如~巧了，~早不~晚❺；~鸭子上架❻；~浪头❼

1. happen to; it so happened that 2. at a most opportune moment 3. by chance 4. certainly 5. It's better to hurry at the beginning than to do things in a rush at the last moment 6. drive a duck onto a perch — make sb. do sth. entirely beyond him 7. follow the trend

gǎndòng 感动 move; touch〔主~〕〈名〉生动❶的故事情节❷~了很多人；他的一席话❸~了在座❹的人；她的苦难❺经历❻~了我们每一个人〔~补〕〈程〉~极了；~得流下了眼泪❼；~得热泪盈眶❽；~得说不出话来了；~得连声道谢❾；~得赞叹不已❿〔状~〕非常~；多么~人啊! 一点也不~人；深深地⓫~了我；极为⓬~；万分⓭~；为他的精神⓮所~

1. lively; vivid 2. plot 3. what one says during a conversation 4. be present (at a meeting) 5. suffering; misery; distress 6. experience 7. shed tears 8. one's eyes filling with tears 9. hasten to

express one's thanks 10. gasp in admiration; highly praise (praise again and again) 11. deeply 12. extremely 13. very much 14. spirit

gǎnjué 感觉 feel; perceive; become aware of ≅ 觉得〔**~宾**〕〈形〉~有点发烧❶；~没有把握❷；~难办❸；~有点疼；~有点饿；~累；~渴吗?~困❹了；~恶心❺；~难受❻；~不方便；~闷❼；~别扭❽；~没意思❾；~无聊❿；~不好意思⓫；~难为情⓬；~不顺利⓭；~怎么样?〈主-谓〉~头疼⓮；~手麻⓯；~浑身⓰无力；~头重脚轻⓱；~身上不舒服⓲；~他很诚实⓳；~大祸就要临头⓴了〔**~补**〕〈结〉他们~到了问题的严重性㉑；~到地震㉒了吗?~到一股寒气㉓〈可〉~不出发烧不发烧〔**状~**〕经常~；有时候~；一阵一阵地㉔~有些冷(热)；总~累；没~疼；确实㉕~；深深地㉖~

1. have a little fever 2. assurance; certainty 3. difficult to do 4. sleepy 5. (feel) like vomiting 6. (feel) unwell 7. stuffy; close 8. awkward; uncomfortable; difficult 9. dull 10. bored 11. embarrassed; be ill at ease 12. ashamed 13. unfavorable 14. headache 15. have pins and needles; tingle 16. all over the body 17. top-heavy 18. uncomfortable 19. honest 20. disaster is imminent 21. gravity 22. earthquake 23. cold air 24. by fits and starts 25. really; indeed 26. deeply

gǎnrǎn 感染 influence; infect; affect ≅ 影响〔**主~**〕〈名〉伤口❶~了；气氛❷~人；情绪❸~人〔**~宾**〕〈名〉~了周围❹看热闹❺的群众；小说~了读者；话剧❻~了观众❼；他的悲观情绪❽~了很多人；她的动人事迹❾深深❿地~了那几个青年人；抵抗力⓫弱⓬了就容易~疾病⓭〔**~补**〕〈程〉伤口~得很利害⓮〈可〉保持⓯卫生伤口⓰就~不了(liǎo)了〈量〉伤口~过一次〔**状~**〕用美好⓱的语言~孩子们；容易~；不易⓲~

1. wound; cut 2. atmosphere 3. mood 4. around; round 5. watch the excitement; watch the fun 6. modern drama 7. spectator 8. pessimism 9. deed; achievement 10. deeply 11. resistance 12. weak 13. disease 14. terrible; awful 15. keep; maintain; preserve 16. hygiene 17. fine 18. not easy

gǎnxiè 感谢 thank; be grateful ≅ 谢谢〔**~宾**〕〈代〉~你替我找到了钥匙❶；~你来看我〈动〉~你们的帮助；~大家的关心❷；~你对我的照顾❸；~你的及时❹提醒❺〔**~补**〕〈程〉对他~得不得了❻(liǎo)〔**状~**〕衷心❼~；万分❽~；非常~；再三❾~；一再❿~；连忙⓫~

1. key 2. show solicitude for 3. give consideration to 4. in time 5. remind 6. extremely 7. wholeheartedly; cordially 8. very much 9. 10. over and over again; repeatedly 11. promptly; at once

gàn 干 do; work ≅ 做〔**～宾**〕〈名〉你是～什么工作的？～点儿正经事❶吧，别每天到处乱逛❷了；他能～这件事吗？〈代〉他正在～什么呢？〔**～补**〕〈结〉翻译❸工作她～熟❹了；～惯❺了也不觉得太累了；不能怕～错了就不干了；这个工作我都～烦❻了；快～腻❼了〈趋〉非❽～出点成绩来不可；开始不习惯，～下去就好了〈程〉小伙子❾们～得很起劲❿；工作～得很出色⓫；～得很漂亮⓬；～得很有成绩；这件事你～得太没有分寸⓭了〈可〉她什么事也～不好；这个工作你～得了(liǎo)～不了(liǎo)？～得成～不成？她～不出什么成绩来〈时〉他们～了半天也没干出什么名堂⓮来；再～一会儿就收工⓯了〈量〉不妨⓰～一下儿试试；～过两次〔**状～**〕好～；不好～；挺容易～；真难～；拼命⓱～；亲自⓲～；单独⓳～；勉强⓴～；仔细～；埋头苦～㉑；不言不语地㉒～；不声不响地㉓～；不慌不忙地㉔～；有板有眼地㉕～；充满信心地㉖～；三心二意地㉗～；慢慢腾腾地㉘～；赶紧～；不停地～；通宵达旦地㉙～；夜以继日地㉚～；连续㉛～；一连㉜～了10个小时；公开地㉝～；秘密地㉞～；偷偷摸摸地㉟～；鬼鬼祟祟地㊱～；大大方方地㊲～；大胆地㊳～；勇敢地㊴～；同心合力地㊵～

1. serious affairs 2. stroll; ramble; roam 3. translation 4. familiar 5. get used to 6. be vexed 7. be bored with; be tired of 8. must; have to 9. lad; young fellow 10. very energetically 11. outstanding; remarkable 12. brilliant; splendid 13. have no proper limits for action; have no sense of propriety 14. result; achievement 15. stop work for the day; knock off 16. there is no harm in; might as well 17. with all one's might; for all one is worth 18. personally 19. alone; by oneself 20. reluctantly; grudgingly 21. immerse oneself in; be engrossed in (quietly immerse oneself in hard work) 22. silently 23. quietly 24. unhurriedly 25. orderly 26. full of confidence 27. shilly-shally 28. slowly; unhurriedly 29. all night long 30. day and night 31. 32. in a row; running in succession 33. publicly 34. secretly 35. stealthily 36. furtively 37. generously; liberally 38. boldly 39. courageously 40. in full cooperation and with unity of purpose

gǎo 搞 do; carry on; be engaged in ≅ 干；办；弄〔**～宾**〕〈名〉～卫生❶；～一个计划；～阴谋诡计

❷；他在学校～总务❸；她是～美术❹的；我是～体育❺的；她父母都是～教育的；别～鬼❻；你能给我们～几张球赛的票吗？〈动〉～生产；～翻译❼；～运动；我～设计❽〔**～补**〕〈结〉一定要～好环境卫生❾；这句话的语法关系我没～懂；把他们两个人的名字～错了；别把这两顶帽子～混❿了；把事情全～糟⓫了；这个机器⓬是谁给～坏的？现在我才～明白是怎么回事；要～清谁是谁非；先把手续⓭～清楚；书让孩子(给)～丢了；你怎么把屋子～成这个样子了！她把身体～垮⓮了；参观券⓯～到手了吗？〈趋〉再这样～下去就危险⓰了；一定要～出点名堂来；没～出成绩来；两个人就把饭馆～起来了；这张票是他托人⓱～来的；你把我的钢笔～到哪儿去了？〈程〉试验⓲～得不理想⓳；卫生～得很彻底⓴；屋子～得乱七八糟㉑；事情～得一塌糊涂㉒；他把我～得莫明其妙㉓；～得糊里糊涂㉔的；那件事情把她～得情绪㉕很低落㉖〈可〉学的时间太短，还～不了(liǎo)翻译；这个工作太困难他有点～不下去了；连个计划都～不出来；她们两个谁是姐姐谁是妹妹我总～不清楚；他和别人的关系总～不好〈时〉～了十几年音乐了；～了半辈子㉗；～了半天也没搞出结果来〈量〉～过两次都失败㉘了；再～一下儿试试吧〔**状～**〕大～卫生；按部就班地㉙～；大胆地㉚～；暗中㉛～鬼；用非法㉜手段～；用合法㉝手段～；明着㉞～；公开地㉟～；明目张胆地㊱～；大张旗鼓地㊲～；故意地㊳～；专门～；专心～；适当地㊴～；主动㊵～；从早到晚～；无缘无故地㊶～；无拘无束地㊷～；恣意地㊸～；放肆地㊹～；出其不意地㊺～；突然～；漫不经心地㊻～；心不在焉地㊼～；有节制地㊽～；专心一意地～；踏踏实实地㊾～；毫不犹豫地㊿～；埋头51～；照样52～；直接～；间接～；决不～；任意53～

1. hygiene **2.** schemes and intrigues **3.** general affairs **4.** the fine arts **5.** physical culture **6.** play tricks **7.** translation **8.** design **9.** environmental sanitation; general sanitation **10.** mix; confuse **11.** make a mess of sth. **12.** machine **13.** procedures **14.** break down **15.** visiting ticket **16.** dangerous **17.** ask; entrust **18.** test; experiment **19.** not ideal **20.** thorough **21.** in disorder; in a mess **22.** in a complete mess; in an awful state **23.** be unable to make head or tail of sth.; be baffled **24.** muddled; confused; bewildered **25.** morale **26.** low **27.** half a lifetime **28.** fail **29.** keep to conventional ways of doing things **30.** boldly **31.** secretly; on the sly **32.** illegally **33.** legally **34.** openly; explicitly **35.** publicly **36.** flagrantly; brazenly **37.** in a big way; on a grand scale **38.** on purpose; intentionally **39.** suitably **40.** of one's own accord **41.** without cause or reason; for no reason at all **42.** unconstrainedly **43.** unscrupulously 44. wantonly 45. unexpectedly 46. carelessly; casually 47. absentmindedly 48. moderately 49. steadily 50. without the least hesitation 51. quietly immerse oneself 52. in the same old way; as before 53. wantonly; arbitrarily; wilfully

gàosu 告诉 tell; let know〔~宾〕〈代〉~你一句话；他~了我一个不好的消息❶；他把事情的经过❷全都~大家了；~他们别等我回家吃饭了，我晚上有点事；你快~我这究竟❸是怎么回事；~他们说话的声音❹小一点儿〔~补〕〈结〉开会的时间、地点可别~错了他；把这个消息~他以后，他高兴得跳起来了〈量〉有什么好消息别忘了~我一声儿〔状~〕全部~她了；一切❺都~他了；详详细细地~他；清清楚楚地~❻；一五一十地~；原原本本地~❼；偷偷地~❽；毫无隐讳地~❾；坦率地~❿；坦白地~⓫~；直截了(liǎo)当地⓬~；毫不犹豫地⓭~；偶尔⓮~；悄悄地⓯~；早已~

1. bad news 2. process; course 3. after all; in the end 4. sound 5. all; everything 6. systematically and in full detail 7. from beginning to end 8. in secret 9. without concealment 10. frankly 11. make a confession 12. straightforwardly; bluntly 13. without hesitation 14. once in a while; occasionally 15. quietly

gē 割 cut〔~宾〕〈名〉用镰刀❶~稻子❷；~点草喂❸小兔；小心点儿，别~了手；~盲肠〔~补〕〈结〉把手~破❹了；麦子还没~完呢〈程〉那个孩子割草~得真快〈可〉这把镰刀不快❺，~不动；切菜刀不快，连肉都~不下来；~不了(liǎo)〔状~〕用镰刀~；用收割机❻~麦子；一片一片地❼~肉；一把一把地❽~稻子

1. sickle 2. rice 3. feed 4. cut 5. not sharp 6. harvester; reaper 7. by slices 8. by bunches

gē 搁 put ≅ 放〔~宾〕〈名〉牛奶里多~点糖吧；窗台❶上~了一排花盆❷；这个书橱❸里~了很多书；我的钱包里没~多少钱〔~补〕〈结〉水~少了饭蒸❹得有点儿硬❺；菜里~上点味精❻好吃；糖~在水里就化❼了；怎么把孩子一个人~在家里了；抽屉❽里的东西都~满了，赶快把手里提❾的东西~下吧！〈趋〉请帮我把手提包❿~到行李架（子）⓫上去；把钱一把就~进口袋⓬里去了〈程〉酱油~得太多咸⓭死了〈可〉东西太多，一个皮包~不下吧？这间屋子~不下那么多家具⓮；地方太小，连双人床⓯都~不下〈时〉这些东西先在你这儿~一会儿；这几件衣服~了好几年我都没穿〈量〉暂时在这里~一下儿，行吗？~过一次盐⓰忘了，又~了一次〔状~〕咖啡里多~点糖；一次~得太多了；尽量⓱~；

满满地~；随便⑱~；暂时~；临时⑲~；长期~；永远~在那儿；一直~；故意⑳~在那儿了

1. windowsill 2. a row of flowerpots 3. bookcase 4. steam; warm up 5. hard 6. monosodium glutamate; gourmet powder 7. melt; dissolve 8. drawer 9. carry (in one's hand with the arm down) 10. handbag 11. luggage rack 12. pocket 13. salted 14. furniture 15. double bed 16. salt 17. to the best of one's ability; as far as possible 18. randomly; carelessly; do as one pleases 19. temporary; provisional; for a short time 20. intentionally; on purpose

② put aside 〔~宾〕〈名〉先一~这件事，等以后再说吧！〔~补〕〈结〉鸡蛋都~坏了；桔子❶都~干了；~烂❷了；天热，剩❸的饭菜都~馊❹了〈趋〉~到箱子❺里去吧；~到衣柜❻里去吧〈程〉时间~得太长了〈可〉天太热，吃的东西~不住❼〔时〕从前学过钢琴❽，~了十几年不弹❾，现在都不会弹了〔状~〕先~~；暂时~~；不能久❿~

1. orange 2. rotten 3. remain 4. spoiled 5. chest; box; case; trunk 6. wardrobe 7. won't keep 8. piano 9. play 10. long; for a long time

gé 隔 separate 〔~宾〕〈名〉~着一座山；~着一条河；~着一条马路；~着窗户向我招手❶；这间屋子不~音❷〈形〉房顶❸很厚❹既能防❺寒也能~热〔~补〕〈结〉把一间大屋~成了两小间；用帘子❻把屋子~开了〈程〉两个人~得很远说话，谁也听不清〈可〉这间屋子那么小，哪儿~得了(liǎo)两间啊！〔时〕~两个小时吃一次药；~一段时间再去看他〔状~〕相~很远；每~半小时，就响一次铃；远~重洋❼；被屏风❽~开〔习用〕~墙有耳❾

1. beckon; wave 2. sound insulation 3. roof 4. thick 5. guard against; prevent 6. curtain; screen 7. be separated by seas and oceans 8. screen 9. walls have ears; beware of eavesdroppers

gěi 给 give; grant 〔~宾〕〈代〉我~他一块糖；她~了我一张票；这件事~了我勇气❶和力量❷；~我留下很好的印象❸；我~他两份讲义❹；这件事~了我很大的打击❺；~了我很大启发❻〔~补〕〈结〉买东西的时候我把钱~多(~少)了；~错了；阅读材料❼都~全了吗？水果的分量❽~够了吗？〈趋〉~出一定的条件❾来，别人才好猜❿〈程〉~得真多；~得太少了；~得不够分量；~得不够数儿⓫〈可〉我~不起这么多钱；~不了(liǎo)学费⓬，只好停学⓭〔时〕~你五分钟好好想想；~了三天假〈量〉~了我一个耳光⓮；~了那个孩子一巴掌⓯〔状~〕多~点；主动⓰~；总共

❼~了；经常~；一次就~了那么多；大手大脚地❽~钱

1. courage 2. strength; power; force 3. impression 4. teaching materials 5. hit; strike; blow 6. enlightenment 7. reading material 8. weight 9. given conditions 10. guess 11. not enough 12. tuition 13. suspend sb. from school 14. slap sb.'s face 15. give sb. a slap 16. on one's own initiative 17. in all 18. wastefully; extravagantly

gōngbù 公布 promulgate; announce; publish; make public〔~宾〕〈名〉~名单❶；~帐目❷；~了一个新法令❸；~宪法❹；~新婚姻法❺；~罪状❻；~事情的经过；~调查❼的结果；~数字❽；~成绩❾；~名次❿〔~补〕〈结〉~完了；~早了；~于众⓫；~在布告栏⓬里〈趋〉~出来了；已经~出去了〈程〉~得太晚了；~得很及时〈可〉怎么还~不出来啊; 暂时还~不了(liǎo)〈时〉已经~好几天了；~好长时间了〔状~〕每月~；按时⓭~；计划要事先⓮~；提前⓯~；在一定范围内⓰~

1. name list 2. accounts; items of an account 3. decree; laws and decrees 4. constitution 5. new marriage law 6. facts about a crime; charges in an indictment 7. investigation 8. figure; numeral 9. result; achievement 10. position in a name list 11. the public 12. bulletin board; notice board 13. on schedule; on time 14. beforehand 15. in advance; ahead of time 16. within the certain limits

gōng 供 supply; feed ≅ 供给；供应〔~宾〕〈名〉新盖的❶那座礼堂❷可~两千人用；~三个孩子念书；~他弟弟上大学；一个人使用❸〈代〉你写吧，我~你笔和纸；我~他学费❹；这些意见❺只~你参考❻〔~补〕〈结〉把孩子~大了；~到能独立❼生活了〈趋〉他的弟弟妹妹都是他给~起来的〈可〉你这么能吃，我们可~不起❽你了〈时〉姑姑❾~了我十八年生活费❿〔状~〕仅⓫~参考；勉强⓬~；一直~到大学毕业；心甘情愿地⓭~我

1. newly built 2. assembly hall 3. use 4. tuition 5. idea; opinion 6. for your reference only 7. independent; on one's own 8. can not afford 9. aunt; father's sister 10. living expenses; cost of living 11. only 12. reluctantly; manage with an effort; do with difficulty 13. be most willing to; be perfectly happy to

gòngxiàn 贡献 contribute; dedicate; devote〔~宾〕〈名〉~一份力量❶；~全部力量❷；~了毕生❸的精力❹；~他的一生；~了宝贵❺的生命；~出了所有❻的财产❼〔~补〕〈结〉把青春❽

～给了科学事业❾〈趋〉把自己的才智❿全部～出来了〔状～〕完全～出来了；无保留地⓫～出来了；无私地⓬～出来了

1. one's bit 2. one's all to 3. all one's life 4. energy; vigour; vim 5. precious; valuable 6. all 7. wealth; property 8. youth; youthfulness 9. cause, undertaking 10. ability and wisdom 11. without reservation; unreserved-ly 12. selflessly

gōu 钩 sew with large stitches 〔**～宾**〕〈名〉～花边❶；～手套；～桌布❷；～窗帘❸〔**～补**〕〈结〉帽子～完了；花边～错了；钉子❹把衣服～住了；这么大的窗帘要～到什么时候才能钩完呢？〈趋〉她～出来的图案❺真漂亮；用拐杖❻把掉在树上的羽毛球～下来了〈程〉花边～得真快；～得很熟练❼；～得太紧❽了；～得有点松❾；～得非常好看〈可〉她什么也～不好；我～不了(liǎo)帽子，只会钩手套；今天～不完了，明天接着❿钩吧！〈时〉这个桌布整整～了一个月；需要～多长时间？每天～一会儿〈量〉这种花样⓫我～过一次；～几针试试〔**状～**〕用钩针⓬～；用粗针⓭～还是用细针⓮～？一针一针地～；耐心地⓯～；真难～；很容易～；给朋友～；亲手⓰～

1. lace 2. tablecloth 3. (window) curtain 4. nail 5. pattern; design 6. stick 7. skilful 8. tight 9. loose 10. follow 11. pattern; variety 12. crochet hook 13. thick knitting needle 14. thin knitting needle 15. patiently 16. personally; with one's own hands

gòu 够 ① be enough; be sufficient〔**主～**〕〈名〉作这项工作三个人就～了；有二千字就～了；你带的钱～不～？这个人精神不～；我们俩交情❶不～，不知他肯不肯帮忙；手边儿的资料❷不～，现在还不能动笔写❸；知识不～；时间不～；火候❹不～，炒❺出来的菜不好吃；来这么多客人，碗筷不～了；有一点儿面包就～了〔**～宾**〕〈名〉当演员❻我～不～条件❼？这包糖～不～分量❽？他长得太矮❾，不～标准❿；老孙当教练⓫还不～资格⓬；她唱的京剧⓭挺～味⓮儿；他很～朋友〈动〉钱～花吗？纸～用了；饭做得太少，不～吃；这点毛线⓯只～织⓰一件毛衣⓱；这么窄⓲的地方只～放一个沙发；他已经～为难⓳的了，别再逼⓴他了〈形〉屋子～暖和的了；她上班的地方～远的，他英语说得～好的了；这趟车真～挤㉑的；这孩子～闹人㉒的；语法～难的；这个任务㉓～困难的；事情～复杂㉔的；绳子㉕已经～长了，不用再接㉖了；电线㉗不～长；～高了；那里真～热闹的；他们的晚年㉘～幸福的了；她小时候～苦㉙的；最近～忙的吧？〔**状～**〕真～累的；完全～吃了；实在不～；只～；就～

1. friendship; friendly relations 2. material; data 3. start writing

4. duration and degree of heating, cooking, smelting etc. 5. fry 6. actor or actress 7. condition 8. weight 9. short (of stature) 10. standard 11. coach; instructor; trainer 12. qualifications 13. Beijing (Peking) opera 14. just satisfactory; just the thing 15. knitting wool 16. knit 17. woolen sweater 18. narrow 19. feel embarrassed 20. force; compel 21. crowded 22. make a noise; stir up trouble 23. task 24. complicated 25. rope 26. connect; joint 27. electric wire 28. one's remaining years 29. miserable

gūjì 估计 estimate; appraise; reckon ≌ 估量〔～宾〕〈名〉不要过高地～❶自己的力量；错误地～了形势❷ 〈主-谓〉你～～你需要多少稿纸❸；你～～这篇文章❹有多少字；你～情况将会怎么样？我～她明天不会来了；我～我们带的钱不够，我～明天下不了(liǎo)雨〔～补〕〈结〉他们把形势～错了；决不应把这次事故❺造成❻的损失❼～低❽了；不要把他的能力❾～高了；价钱～低了；要～到成功或者失败两种可能❿〈趋〉这个东西值⓫多少钱，你能～出来吗？这本书有多少字，你能～出来吗？〈程〉数字⓬～得很准⓭；价钱～得一点儿也不错；～得差不多〈可〉大家在一起～了半天也没估计对〈量〉要好好～一下儿〔状～〕大胆地⓮～；正确～；充分～；盲目地⓯～；错误地～；

过高地～；过低地～；根据⓰什么～；乐观地⓱～

1. overestimate 2. situation 3. squared or lined paper for making drafts or copying manuscripts 4. essay; article 5. accident 6. cause; create; bring about 7. loss 8. underestimate 9. ability 10. possibility 11. cost 12. figure 13. accurate; exact 14. boldly 15. blindly 16. according to; on the basis of 17. optimistically

gūfù 辜负 let down; fail to live up to; be unworthy of; disappoint〔～宾〕〈名〉别～她的一番好意❶；我～了他对我的一片好心；不要～他对你的恩情❷；没～她对我的情意〈动〉不能～大家对你的帮助；～了你们对我的期望❸；没有～他的关怀❹；～了我们对你的信任❺；～了长辈❻的教导❼；～了他老人家对我的培养❽〔状～〕决不～；永远不～；千万别～

1. good intention; kindness 2. loving-kindness 3. expectation; hope 4. solicitude 5. confidence; trust 6. elder member of a family; elder; senior 7. teaching 8. cultivation

gǔlì 鼓励 encourage; urge〔～宾〕〈代〉她(考)大学❶没考上❷有些悲观❸，你好好～～她吧；老师经常～我们；～我好好学习〔状～〕经常～；一再～；热情地❹～；多加～

1. take an examination for admission to college 2. fail in 3. pessimistic 4. warmly

gǔwǔ 鼓舞 inspire; hearten

〔~宾〕〈名〉他的报告真~人；~人心❶；~士气❷；他的讲话~了每一个人；~了大家的干劲❸和信心❹；~了我们的斗志❺〈代〉这种不屈不挠的精神~着我们；~着他们继续前进❼；~我们去攀登科学高峰❽ 〔状~〕被他的献身精神❾所~；始终❿~着我；永远~

1. public feeling 2. morale 3. vigour; enthusiasm 4. confidence; faith 5. fighting will 6. unyielding; indomitable 7. continue to make progress 8. scale new heights in science 9. devotion 10. always; from beginning to end

gǔzhǎng 鼓掌 clap one's hands; applaud

〔~补〕〈趋〉她刚唱完这首歌，观众❶就鼓起掌来了〈时〉给她鼓了半天掌〈量〉鼓了好几次掌；鼓了一阵❷掌〔状~〕热烈地❸~；疯狂地❹~；一再~；稀稀落落地❺~了几下儿

1. spectator 2. a burst of applause 3. warmly; enthusiastically 4. madly; insanely 5. sporadically

gù 雇 hire; employ

〔~宾〕〈名〉~工人；~用人❶；~了三名职员❷；~保姆❸；~保镖❹；~司机〔~补〕〈结〉保姆已经~好了〈趋〉很多人都一起保镖来了〈程〉那是个私人❺的小厂，工人~得不多〈可〉~不用人；~不到合适❻的人〈时〉~了好长时间也没雇着满意❼的；~了那么多时候才雇上〈量〉~过一次〔状~〕不好~；早点儿~；在哪儿~？为孩子~；临时❽~；需要的时候才~

1. servant 2. staff 3. (children's) nurse; baby-sitter 4. bodyguard 5. private; personal 6. suitable 7. satisfied 8. temporarily

guā 刮 ① scrape

〔~宾〕〈名〉~胡子❶；~脸；~鱼鳞❷；~铁锈❸；~污垢❹；~油漆❺〔~补〕〈结〉别把脸~破❻了；他~完了胡子才去洗脸；脸~干净了吗？~破了一点皮❼；别把锅底❽~漏❾了；铁锈全~掉了〈趋〉鱼鳞都~下去了吗？〈程〉脸~得很干净〈时〉~了半天也没刮掉❿；上午我~了一个多小时铁锈〈量〉一天要~两次脸；胡子那么长了，快~一下儿吧！〔状~〕往下~铁锈；用刀片⓫~脸；小心点儿~；轻轻地⓬~；自己对着镜子⓭~脸

1. beard 2. fish scale 3. rust 4. dirt; filth 5. paint 6. cut 7. (scrape) a bit of skin off 8. the bottom of a pot 9. leak 10. scrape off 11. razor blade 12. lightly; gently 13. facing the mirror

② blow〔～宾〕〈名〉～台风❶了；～了一阵旋风❷〔～补〕〈结〉风把树都～倒❸了；窗户没关，把墙上的地图都～掉了；帘子❹也被～开了〈趋〉挂❺在阳台❻上的东西被风～到楼下去了；从外边～进来一股冷气；又～起大风来了；尘土❼都～起来了；地上有几张纸被大风～过来～过去；我晾❽在外边的衣服不知被风～到哪儿去了？〈程〉风～得真大；～得睁不开眼❾；～得太冷了；～得他都向后退了几步；～得天昏地暗❿〈时〉大风整整～了一天一夜；再～上几天，天就更冷了〔状～〕不停地⓫～；连续不断地⓬～；天天～〔习用〕～地皮⓭

1. typhoon **2.** whirlwind **3.** be blown down **4.** curtain **5.** hang **6.** balcony **7.** dust **8.** dry in the sun; hang out the washing to dry **9.** cannot open the eyes **10.** the sky darkened and everything else obscured **11.** without interruption **12.** in succession; continuously **13.** batten on extortions

guǎ 剐 cut; slit〔～宾〕〈名〉手上～了一块肉去〔～补〕〈结〉衣服～破❶了；别～坏了〈程〉～得很利害；～得直流血❷；～得很深；～得没法缝了〈量〉椅子上这个钉子❸出来了，～过我两次了〔状～〕不知不觉地❹～破了；让树枝把尼龙丝袜子❺～了

1. be torn **2.** bleed; shed blood **3.** nail **4.** unconsciously **5.** nylon socks

guà 挂 ① hang; put up ≅悬挂↔摘〔～宾〕〈名〉墙上～着一张结婚❶照片❷；教室里～着一张世界地图；宿舍里～着几幅世界名❸画儿；礼堂❹里～着大吊灯❺；衣架❻上～着我的帽子和大衣；浴室❼里～着毛巾；身上～着一串钥匙❽；天上～着一轮明月❾；病房❿里～着温度表⓫；办公室～着日历⓬；展览室⓭里～着很多图片〔～补〕〈结〉墙上～满了画儿；天热了，把竹帘子⓮～上吧！钟～歪⓯了；把衣服～在衣架上；镜框⓰没～正〈趋〉把大衣～起来吧；把帽子～到挂钩⓱上去吧〈程〉幼儿园⓲孩子们的毛巾～得很整齐⓳；屋子里画儿别～得太多；东一张西一张～得太乱⓴了〈可〉这种墙不能钉钉子㉑，～不了(liǎo)镜框；钩子太高了，我～不上〈时〉个子㉒太矮了，～了半天也没挂上〈量〉在这边墙上～过一次地图；请你帮我往那上边～一下儿〔状～〕往墙上～；在绳子㉓上～；一直～着；刚～上就掉了

1. marriage **2.** photograph **3.** famous **4.** assembly hall; auditorium **5.** pendent lamp **6.** coat hanger **7.** bathroom **8.** a bunch of keys **9.** a bright moon **10.** ward (of a hospital) **11.** thermometer **12.** calendar **13.** exhibition room **14.** bamboo curtain **15.** inclined; crooked; askew **16.** picture frame **17.** clothes-hook **18.** kindergarten; nursery school 19. neat and tidy 20. in disorder 21. drive in a nail 22. height; stature 23. rope

② register (at a hospital; etc.) ≅ 登记〔~宾〕〈名〉~号❶；~外科❷；~耳鼻喉科❸；~妇科❹；~急诊❺；~特约❻门诊；~中医❼〔~补〕〈结〉~上号了吗？挂号~晚了〔量〕你替我~一下儿号吧〔状~〕在挂号处~；早点儿~；替你~；提前❽~；予先❾~

1. register (at a hospital; etc.) 2. surgical department 3. E.N.T. (ear-nose-throat) department; otolaryngological department 4. (department of) gynaecology 5. emergency call 6. engage by special arrangement 7. doctor of traditional Chinese medicine 8. in advance; ahead of time 9. beforehand

③ ring off〔~宾〕〈名〉你先别~电话❶，我马上去找他；等我拿起了听筒❷，对方❸已经~上电话了〔~补〕〈结〉打不通❹先上吧，过一会儿再打〔程〕电话~得真快〔状~〕老打不通，赌气地❺~上了；刚~上铃又响❻了；先别~；等一会儿再~〔习用〕~羊头卖狗肉❼

1. hold the line 2. receiver 3. the other (opposite) side; the other party 4. be unable to get through (on the telephone) 5. feel wronged and act rashly 6. ring 7. hang up a sheep's head and sell dogmeat — try to palm off sth. inferior to what it purports to be

guǎi 拐 turn〔~宾〕〈名〉~弯❶儿〔~补〕〈结〉~错了〈趋〉~进一条死胡同❷里去了；从那边~过去就是；前边路不通❸，快~回去吧〈程〉车拐弯~得太猛❹了，差一点把上边的东西甩出去❺；~得很慢；~得很稳❻〈可〉前边~得过去~不过去？〔状~〕向左~；不要猛~〔习用〕~弯抹角❼

1. turn (a corner) 2. blind alley; dead end 3. be impassable; be blocked up 4. suddenly; abruptly 5. be thrown off 6. steady 7. talk in a roundabout way; beat about the bush

guài 怪 blame ≅ 怨〔~宾〕〈代〉这件事不能~你；这件事只能~我没交代❶清楚；都~你太惯❷着他了；都~你事先不跟人商量❸；就~你太任性❹了〔~补〕〈可〉这~不着(zháo)孩子，是你没说清楚；这可~不上我，我根本❺没去；这茶杯是我打碎❻的，~不得他；考坏❼了~不得别人，只能怪自己复习得不够〔状~〕一来就~别人；总~别人；净❽~别人；从来不~别人

1. explain; make clear 2. indulge; spoil 3. talk over; consult 4. wilful; self-willed 5. simply; at all 6. break to pieces 7. fail in an examination 8. only; merely

guān 关 ① shut; close ↔ 开〔~宾〕〈名〉~门；~抽屉〔~补〕〈结〉把窗户~上；小鸟被~在笼子❶里了；别整天~在家里，天气这么好，出去玩玩吧！他被~进了监狱❷〈趋〉下雨了，快把窗户~起来吧；这些话只能~起门来说❸；把鸡都~到鸡窝❹里去了〈程〉门~得很紧❺；所有的窗户都~得紧紧的〈可〉东西太多抽屉都~不上了〈时〉夜里突然刮起了大风，我从床上起来去关窗，~了半天也没关上〈量〉把门用力一下儿，就刮不开了〔状~〕随手❻~门；成天❼~在里边；不要用那么大劲儿~门

1. cage 2. prison 3. in secret 4. chicken-coop; hen-coop 5. close 6. conveniently; without extra trouble 7. all day long; all the time

② turn off ≅ 关闭〔~宾〕〈名〉~电灯；~电视；~录音机❶；~电风扇❷；~煤气炉❸；~水龙头❹〔~补〕〈结〉把机器❺~上；看看煤气炉~好了没有？把水管子❻~紧❼；别~那么紧，关紧了容易坏；快把录音机~上吧，吵死了〈程〉水龙头~得太紧了〈可〉水管子~不紧，直滴水❽；开关❾坏了~不上了〈量〉请你帮我~一下儿吧〔状~〕随手❿~；轻轻地⓫~

1. tape recorder 2. electric fan 3. gas stove 4. (water) tap 5. machine 6. water pipe 7. tight 8. drip down 9. switch 10. conveniently; without extra trouble 11. slightly; gently

guānxì 关系 concern; affect; have a bearing on; have to do with〔~宾〕〈名〉~着大家的前途❶和命运❷〔~补〕〈结〉~到我们的事业❸；~到能不能毕业的问题；~到国民经济❹的发展〔状~〕直接❺~着；将~到

1. future prospect 2. destiny; fate 3. cause; undertaking 4. national economy 5. directly

guānxīn 关心 be concerned with; show solicitude for〔~宾〕〈名〉~学生；~孩子；~就业❶问题；他们非常~考试问题〈代〉我一直很~他〔状~〕互相~；特别~；多~~他们；从不~别人；一直~着

1. obtain employment

guǎn 管 ① manage; run; be in charge of ≅ 负责；管理〔~宾〕〈名〉我哥哥在工厂~仓库❶；她~宣传❷；我~教育；几个人~一个果园；他最爱~闲事❸；我没~过帐❹〈动〉幼儿园❺~吃、~住、不~穿〔~补〕〈结〉一定要~好这项工作；必须把帐~清楚〈趋〉开始时我只是临时❻替他管，后来就让我接着❼~下去了；你现在也~起家务❽来了〈程〉她把家务~得井井有条❾；

那个会计❿把帐~得乱七八糟⓫;~得一塌糊涂⓬;~得一团糟⓭〈可〉帐我可~不好;事情太多,一个人~得过来吗?〔状~〕专~;由谁~? 大家一起~;分工~;怎么~?

1. warehouse 2. propaganda 3. a matter that does not concern one; other people's business (like to poke one's nose into other people's business) 4. account 5. kindergarten 6. temporarily 7. follow; carry on 8. household chores 9. in perfect order 10. book keeper; accountant 11. in a mess, in a muddle 12. 13. in an awful state; in a complete mess

② subject sb. to discipline ≅ 管教〔~宾〕〈名〉~孩子;~学生;~徒弟❶〔~补〕〈结〉一定要把孩子~好;~严❷点儿,这样管就~对了〈趋〉她一起学生来很有办法❸〈程〉张先生管孩子~得很严;~得不得法❹;~得恰到好处❺〈可〉这孩子太淘气❻,除了他爸爸谁也~不了(liǎo)他;这样惯❼着,~不出好孩子来〈时〉~了好长时间,才把她的缺点管过来〈量〉这孩子可得(děi)好好~一下儿;~过好几次了,他就是不听〔状~〕放手❽~;适当地❾~;耐心地❿~;严格地⓫~;细心地⓬~;不客气地~〔习用〕不~三七二十一⓭

1. apprentice; disciple 2. strict 3. be of great ability; be competent 4. fail to grasp the main points 5. just right; appropriate; apt 6. naughty 7. indulge; spoil 8. have a free hand; go all out 9. suitably; properly 10. patiently 11. strictly 12. carefully 13. casting all caution to the winds; regardless of the consequences

guǎnlǐ 管理 manage; run; administer; supervies ≅ 管〔~宾〕〈名〉~财务❶;~家务❷;~经济❸;~图书;~宿舍❹;~旅游事业❺〔状~〕认真❻~;精心❼~;专门❽~;由谁~

1. financial affairs 2. household chores 3. economy 4. hostel 5. tourism; tourist trade 6. seriously; conscientiously 7. meticulously; carefully; elaborately 8. specially

guànchuān 贯穿 run through; penetrate〔~宾〕〈名〉~着人道主义❶精神;~着爱国主义❷思想;~着许多矛盾❸;~着悲观情绪❹〔状~〕始终~着;自始至终~着;整个~着

1. humanitarianism 2. patriotism 3. contradiction 4. pessimism

guǎngbō 广播 broadcast; be on the air〔~宾〕〈名〉电台❶~了一条重要消息;~新闻;~小说最受欢迎;~体育❷节目❸;~儿童节目;~球赛❹的实况❺;电台每天~评书❻;~歌曲〔~补〕〈结〉第一套节目全部~完了〈量〉

在电台~过三四次了吧〔状~〕每天~；按时❼~；广告❽一次一次地~；新闻要及时❾~；向全世界~

1. broadcasting station 2. physical culture 3. programme 4. ball game; match 5. what is actually happening (live telecast) 6. storytelling (by a professional storyteller) 7. on time 8. advertisement 9. in time

guàng 逛 stroll; ramble; roam 〔~宾〕〈名〉~大街；~商店〔~补〕〈结〉~够了才回来〈趋〉在大街上~过来~过去的什么也没买〈程〉今天下午~得真累〔状~〕闲~❶；随便❷~；毫无目的地❸~；独自❹~；和朋友一起~；经常~；痛痛快快地❺~；整天在外边~；到处~

1. saunter; stroll 2. casually 3. aimlessly 4. alone; by oneself 5. to one's heart's content

guīdìng 规定 stipulate; provide 〔主~〕〈名〉法律❶~；政府~；国家~；教育部❷~〔~宾〕〈名〉学校~了每周的授课❸时数❹；~了汽车行驶❺的速度❻；~假日的天数；~了上下班的时间；~了考试范围❼；~了必读❽的参考书❾；图书馆~了借书期限❿；~了必修的课程⓫〈主-谓〉工会⓬~会员每月要交纳会费⓭；医院~在探视时间⓮才许家属⓯看望病人；教育部~一般大学的学

制为三年〔~补〕〈程〉~得太死⓰；~得很好；~得不切合实际⓱；~得比较合理⓲〈可〉~得了(liǎo)吗？~不了〈时〉~了好长时间也没执行⓳；~了半年多了，我还不知道呢!〈量〉~过一次〔状~〕严格⓴~；明文㉑~；硬性㉒~；重新~

1. law 2. the ministry of education 3. give lessons 4. hours 5. (of a vehicle, ship, etc.) go 6. speed; velocity 7. scope; limits; range 8. required reading 9. reference book 10. alloted time; time limit; deadline 11. a required (obligatory) course 12. trade union 13. pay membership dues 14. visiting hours (in a hospital) 15. family members 16. fixed; rigid; inflexible; stiff 17. unpractical 18. rational; reasonable 19. carry out; execute 20. strictly; rigidly 21. in explicit terms 22. rigidly; inflexibly

guì 跪 kneel; go down on one's knees 〔主~〕〈名〉人~着；骆驼❶~着〔~补〕〈结〉马~下了；大象~在地上，等着主人骑上去；腿❷都~麻❸了；膝盖❹都~红了〈程〉~得太累了；~得腿都疼了〈可〉他的腿受伤❺以后~不下去了〈时〉~了半天，腿都疼了〔状~〕大象乖乖地❻~在那儿等着主人骑；骆驼不声不响地❼~在地上吃草；笔直地❽~着

1. camel 2. leg 3. have pins and needles 4. knee 5. be wounded 6.

gǔn 滚 roll; trundle 〔～补〕〈趋〉球从楼梯❶上～下去了；水珠❷被风吹得从荷叶❸上～下去了；铅笔从桌子上～下去了；一角钱硬币❹～到床底下去了〈程〉～得真远；～得很快〔状～〕从山坡上～；一直～；不停地～

1. stairs 2. drop of water 3. lotus leaf 4. coin

guò 过 ① cross; pass ≅ 穿过〔～宾〕〈名〉～河；～桥；～马路〔～补〕〈趋〉车～来了，上车吧；汽车刚～去；～到马路那边去〈可〉前面正在修❶路，～不去；河水很深你～得来吗? 没有船～不了(liǎo)河；来往❷的车太多，孩子自己～不去;～不了(liǎo)马路〔状～〕慢慢地～；小心点儿～；等没车的时候再～；两边都看好了再～；从我家门口～

1. build; repair 2. coming and going

② spend (time); pass (time) ≅ 度过〔～宾〕〈名〉～年❶；～着幸福的晚年❷；～了一个很悲惨❸的童年；～日子；～着舒服❹的日子〔～补〕〈结〉～完了年再走吧〈趋〉苦日子❺没法再～下去了〈程〉时间～得真快；日子～得很有意思❻；～得很愉快；～得很美满❼；～得很和谐❽；～得很和睦❾；～得很别扭❿，假期～得怎么样? 〈可〉日子～不下去了〈时〉～了好几个月才接到他的信；～了这个星期就不忙了；～了两天才来看我〔状～〕高高兴兴地～日子; 热热闹闹地⓫～年; 安静地～着; 仍旧～着; 寂寞地⓬～

1. the New Year 2. (spend) one's remaining years in happiness 3. miserable; tragic 4. comfortable 5. bitter life 6. interesting; enjoyable 7. perfectly satisfactory; happy 8. harmonious 9. concordant; harmonious 10. uncomfortable; awkward; difficult 11. joyfully 12. in solitude

③ undergo a process; go through; go over 〔～宾〕〈名〉～滤❶；～磅❷；～称❸(chèng)〔～补〕〈结〉～完了磅的放在一边〈程〉称(chèng)～得很准❹〈量〉已经～过一遍称(chèng)了〔状～〕好好～～；用磅称❺～；一遍一遍地～〔习用〕～河拆桥❻

1. filter 2. weigh 3. steelyard (weigh on the steelyard) 4. accurate 5. scale 6. remove the bridge after crossing the river — drop one's benefactor as soon as his help is not required; kick down the ladder

H

hài 害 ① do harm to; impair; cause trouble to ≅ 伤害; 坑害〔~宾〕<名>那个坏蛋~了不少好人; 你真~人不浅❶<代>这样做既~别人(人)也~自己(己); 一念之差❷~她一辈子❸没结婚❹; 那块大石头~他摔❺了一交〔~补〕<结>昨天你可~苦❻了我了, 白白❼等了你一上午, 你也没来; 老鼠真~死人, 什么好东西都被它啃❽坏了 <程>你把我的钢笔拿走, 也不说一声, ~得我找了半天; 开会的日期改了, 我忘了告诉她, ~得她白跑一趟❾; 表慢了, ~得我没赶上火车; 这个人不守信用❿, ~得我白等了他一上午; 这个人~得我无家可归⓫<时>~了他一辈子<量>~了不少次人〔状~〕真~人; 用各种办法⓬~; 用卑鄙的手段⓭~; 间接~; 直接~; 三番五次地⓮~

1. do people great harm 2. a wrong decision made in a moment of weakness (with serious consequences); a momentary slip 3. all one's life 4. marry 5. fall; tumble; lose one's balance 6. cause sb. suffering; give sb. a hard time 7. in vain 8. gnaw; nibble 9. go all the way for nothing 10. lose one's credit 11. be homeless 12. by every possible means 13. by dirty tricks; by contemptible means 14. repeatedly; over and over again

② contract (an illness); suffer from ≅ 得; 患〔~宾〕<名> ~眼病; ~了一场大病❶〔~补〕<趋>又~起病来了<时>~了一年多病<量>~过一次〔状~〕很少~病; 接连不断地❷~病; 经常~; 时常~; 年年~; 一直~; 突然❸~

1. have a serious attack of illness 2. on end; in a row; in succession 3. suddenly

③ feel (ashamed; afraid; etc.)〔~补〕<趋>他又~起羞❶来了; ~起臊❷来了; 以前走黑路不害怕, 现在怎么又~起怕来了<程>害羞~得脸都红了; 害羞~得抬不起头来了〔状~〕真~; 一点也不~; 不必~; 无缘无故地❸~; 莫明其妙地❹~; 不由得❺~; 立刻❻~

1.2. bashful; shy (feel bashful) 3. without cause or reason; for no reason at all 4. without rhyme or reason 5. can't help; involuntarily 6. at once; immediately

④ kill; murder ≅ 杀害〔主~〕<代>他昨天夜里被~了〔~宾〕<名>他~过一个人〔~补〕<结>~

死过一个人〈量〉～了一次没死，又企图❶～第二次〔状～〕突然❷被～；意外地❸～；用毒药❹～

1. attempt; try; seek 2. all of a sudden; suddenly 3. unexpectedly 4. poison; toxicant

hán 含 ① keep in the mouth 〔～宾〕〈名〉嘴里～着一块糖；～着一片药❶；～着一口水；～着一粒酸梅❷〔～补〕〈结〉嘴里～满了水；把药～在嘴里〔时〕这种糖～半天也不化❸；～了一会儿，就吐(tǔ)❹了〈量〉这种药片我～过一次〔状～〕好好～着；多～一会儿；嘴里经常～着酸梅

1. tablet 2. smoked plum 3. not melted 4. spit

② contain ≅ 包含〔～宾〕〈名〉他的话里总是～着不满❶情绪❷；～着讽刺❸的意味❹；～着羞愧❺的神态❻；脸上～着微笑❼〈动〉～怒❽而去；～笑；～恨❾终身❿〈形〉～羞〔～补〕〈结〉眼里～满了泪水⓫〔状～〕总是～着；好象⓬～着；似乎⓭～着；一直～着

1. resentful; discontented; dissatisfied 2. morale; feeling; mood; sentiments 3. satirize, mock 4. meaning; significance; implication 5. ashamed; abashed 6. expression; manner 7. smile 8. anger; rage; fury (in anger) 9. hatred (nurse one's hatred) 10. all one's life 11. tear 12. 13. it seems; as if; seemingly

hǎn 喊 shout; cry out; yell ≅ 叫〔～宾〕〈名〉楼下有人～老王接电话；京剧演员❶每天清晨都到树林里去～嗓子❷；连长❸向战士❹们～口令❺〈动〉你听，远处有人～救命；有人～"抓住❻他！"〈主-谓〉有人～"狼❼来了！"〔～补〕〈结〉口令～错了；人～醒了吗？唱歌的人就怕把嗓子～坏了；从楼上～住那个卖菜的，然后再下楼去买〈趋〉他气得大声～起来了；作梦～出声音来了；交通警察❽把那个没开汽车尾灯❾的司机～过来了；叫卖❿的声音～起来真吵⓫死人；我把他从楼下～上来了〈程〉～得声音真大；～得真吓人⓬；声音～得真宏亮⓭；口令～得乱七八糟⓮〈可〉嗓子哑了～不出声音来了；你～得了(liǎo)吗？〈时〉～了一会儿，没人回答，我就走了〈量〉～一下儿试试；～了几声〔状～〕在树林里～；大声～；凄凄惨惨地⓯～；声嘶力竭地⓰～；不停地～；哭着～；对着窗户⓱～；拼命⓲～；用喇叭⓳～；在扩音器⓴里～；扯着脖子㉑～

1. actor or actress of Beijing (Peking) opera 2. voice (cultivate the voice) 3. company commander 4. soldiers 5. word of command 6. catch; capture; arrest 7. wolf 8. traffic police 9. tail light; tail lamp 10. cry one's wares; peddle; hawk 11. make a noise 12. frighten; scare; intimidate 13. loud and clear; sonorous 14. at sixes and sevens 15. miserably;

wretchedly 16. shout oneself hoarse; shout oneself blue in the face 17. facing the window 18. with all one's might; desperately 19. loudspeaker 20. microphone 21. (shout) at the top of one's voice

hào 好 ① like; love; be fond of ≅ 喜爱↔恶〔～宾〕〈动〉他很～学；～吃；～玩；～花钱；～看书；～听恭维话❶；～表现❷；～管闲事❸；～打听❹消息；～逛❺商店；～开玩笑；～讽刺❻人；～说风凉话❼；～动脑筋❽〈形〉～热闹❾；～清静❿；～干净⓫；～安逸⓬〔状～〕一点也不～；非常～；有点儿～；特别～

1. listen to flattery (compliments) 2. show off 3. like to poke one's nose into other people's business 4. inquire about 5. stroll; ramble; roam 6. satirize; mock 7. make sarcastic comments 8. use one's brains 9. bustling with noise and excitement 10. quiet 11. clean; neat and tidy 12. easy and comfortable

② be liable to ≅ 容易 〔～宾〕〈动〉那个孩子～哭；老张～闹❶；～害臊❷；～晕车❸；～吵架❹；～骂人❺；～生气；孩子刚学会走路～摔交❻〔状～〕总～；不太～；仍旧～；比较～

1. make a noise; stir up trouble 2. be bashful 3. carsickness 4. quar-rel 5. call names; swear (at people) 6. fall; tumble

hào 耗 ① consume; cost ≅ 消耗↔省；节省〔～宾〕〈名〉～油；～电〔～补〕〈结〉～尽❶了，锅里的水都快～干了〈趋〉蜡❷～下去一大截❸〈程〉～得不多〈可〉～不了(liǎo)多少油〈时〉～了一晚上电〔状～〕最～电了；快～完了

1. exhausted; finished 2. candle 3. section; chunk; length

② waste time; dawdle ≅ 拖，拖延〔～宾〕〈名〉～时间〔～补〕〈结〉把我的时间都～光了 〈趋〉别耗了，再～下去就来不及❶了〈程〉～得真没意思❷；～得太利害了；～得心里着急❸ 〈可〉现在都很忙，时间可～不起❹〈时〉～了我两个晚上；～了半天也不走〈量〉再～一下儿，就要耽误❺大事了〔状～〕净❻～；白白地～；别～了；没事瞎❼～时间

1. there's not enough time (to do sth.); it's too late (to do sth.) 2. not interesting 3. worry; feel anxious 4. can't afford 5. hold up; delay 6. only; merely; nothing but 7. groundlessly; foolishly; to no purpose

hē 喝 drink〔～宾〕〈名〉～白开水❶；～咖啡，～药❷；～汤〔～补〕〈结〉把酒～干吧，他～醉了；汤～多了；咖啡～上瘾❸了；杯

子~空了，再倒❹点儿吧〈趋〉把药全都~下去吧；医生不让你喝酒，你怎么又一起酒来了〈程〉~得太多了；那个孩子把肚子~得鼓鼓❺的〈可〉我~不了(liǎo)这么多牛奶；~得惯❻吗？我已经~不下了〈时〉~了半天酒，然后才吃饭〈量〉这种茶我只~过一次；一连❼~了好几口〈状~〉用杯子~；咕嘟咕嘟地❽~；经常~；饭前~，还是饭后~？一口气❾~；大口大口地~；慢慢地~；从来不~；赶紧~；不好~〔习用〕~西北风❿

1. plain boiled water 2. medicine; drug 3. be addicted (to sth.); get into the habit of (doing sth.) 4. pour 5. bulge 6. be used to 7. in a row; in succession 8. bubble; gurgle 9. in one breath; without a break; at a stretch 10. drink the northwest wind — have nothing to eat

hé 合 ① close; shut ≅ 闭，合拢↔张开；打开〔~宾〕〈名〉~眼〔~补〕〈结〉困❶得眼睛都快~上了；~成一道缝❷了；应该把嘴~上，用鼻子呼吸❸；现在听写，请把书~上〈趋〉把书一起来〈程〉把眼睛~得紧紧的装❹作睡着(zháo)的样子〈可〉笑得嘴都~不拢❺了〈时〉~了半天眼也没睡着(zháo)；即使睡不着，~一会眼也是休息〈量〉连眼都来不及❻~一下儿〔状~〕轻轻地~上书；慢慢地~上了眼

1. sleepy 2. a crack 3. breathe 4. pretend; feign 5. grin from ear to ear 6. there's no time (to do sth.); it's too late (to do sth.)

② suit; agree ≅ 符合〔~宾〕〈名〉这个菜不~我的胃口❶；这样决定正~我的心意❷；这么做比较~情~理❸；不~要求；不~标准❹；不~习惯；不~潮流❺；不~理想❻；不~实际情况❼；不~情理❽；不~身分❾〔~补〕〈可〉他们两个人~得来~不来？〔状~〕非常不~；恰巧❿~；她做的菜一向⓫不~我的胃口；一直~不来；实在⓬不~理；一定~；是否⓭~；始终⓮~

1. appetite 2. intention; purpose 3. fair and reasonable; fair and sensible 4. standard; criterion 5. tide; tidal current 6. ideal 7. the actual situation; reality 8. reason; sense 9. status 10. by chance; fortunately 11. consistently; all along 12. really; truly 13. whether or not; if; whether 14. from beginning to end

③ be equal to; add up to ≅ 折合〔~宾〕〈名〉你从香港❶买的这台打字机❷，算上❸关税❹一共~多少钱？你们一天工作~多少小时？〔~补〕〈趋〉应该多少钱，~出来了吗？〈程〉~得不对；~得很清楚〈可〉我~不上来；~不对〈时〉我~了半天也没合对〈量〉~一下儿看看；~了好几遍了，错不了；~过几次了〔状~〕来回❺~；按比例❻~；按什么标准❼

~？用计算机❽~；仔细地❾~一~；替我~；一遍一遍地~

1. Hongkong 2. typewriter 3. in addition 4. customs duty; tariff 5. back and forth; to and fro 6. in proportion 7. standard; criterion 8. calculator; 9. carefully

héhū 合乎 conform with（或 to）; correspond to; accord with; tally with ≃ 符合〔**~宾**〕〈名〉~事实❶；~情理❷；~标准❸；~理想❹；你的话不~实际❺；这种想法有点不~逻辑❻；~他的想法〔**状~**〕完全~；非常~；简直❼不~；一点也不~

1. fact 2. reason 3. standard; criterion 4. ideal 5. reality 6. logic 7. simply; at all

hèn 恨 hate ≃ 憎恨↔爱〔**~宾**〕〈名〉我~欺负❶我的人；大家都~小偷；~坏人；~流氓❷；~罪犯❸〈代〉~自己不争气❹；~我太糊涂❺〔**~补**〕〈结〉我~死小偷了；~入骨髓❻〈程〉~得咬牙切齿❼；~得要命；~极了〔**状~**〕特别~；咬牙切齿地~；一直~她；最~他这一点〔**习用**〕~铁不成钢❽

1. bully 2. rogue; hooligan; gangster 3. criminal; offender 4. try to make a good showing; try to win credit for; try to bring credit to 5. muddled; confused; bewildered 6. hate sb. to the very marrow of one's bones 7. grind one's teeth with hatred 8. wish iron could turn into steel at once — set a high demand on somebody in the hope that he will improve

hēng 哼 snort; groan ≃ 呻吟〔**~补**〕〈趋〉伤❶真不轻❷，连那么硬的汉子❸都~起来了；~出声儿来了〈程〉~得真可怜❹；~得很凄惨❺；~得真难受❻；~得使我感到不安❼〈时〉病人昨天~了一夜；他牙疼❽~了一天；~了一会儿就睡着(zháo)了〈量〉疼得~了几声；那么疼他连一声都没~〔**状~**〕一个劲地❾~；不断地~；不时地❿~；断断续续地⓫~；一声接着一声地~；整夜地~；痛苦地⓬~；从来不~

1. wound 2. not slight 3. a dauntless; unyielding man; a man of iron 4. pitiful; poor; pitiable 5. wretched; miserable; tragic 6. feel unwell 7. disturbed; uneasy; restless 8. toothache 9. continuously; persistently 10. frequently; often 11. off and on; intermittently 12. in agony

hōng 轰 shoo away; drive off ≃ 赶走，驱逐〔**~宾**〕〈名〉~苍蝇❶；~麻雀❷；~鸡〔**~补**〕〈结〉把孩子~走了〈趋〉那个不知趣❸的人被主人~出来了；天黑以后把鸡都~到鸡窝❹里去了；大人们在那儿谈重要的事情，把孩子~上楼来了；把猪全~回圈

❺(juàn)里去吧；孩子们把鸭子～到水里去了；他～起人来真不客气❻；他再骂人就把他～出去〈可〉孩子们吵❼得他无法❽工作，他想让孩子到外边儿去玩一会儿，可是怎么轰也～不动〈时〉～了半天才把他们轰走〈量〉～了好几下儿〔**状**～〕用扇子❾～蚊子；为什么事～他？不客气地～；不好意思❿～；不得已只好⓫～

1. fly 2. sparrow 3. not know how to behave in a delicate situation 4. coop 5. pigsty 6. impolite; rude; blunt 7. make a noise 8. unable 9. fan 10. find it embarrassing (to do sth.); find it difficult (to do sth.) 11. have no alternative but to; have to

hōng 烘 dry or warm by the fire ≅ 烤干〔～宾〕〈名〉～面包〔～补〕〈结〉把湿衣服❶～干了再穿；面包～好了〈趋〉刚～出来的面包特别香❷〈程〉面包～得真香〈可〉～得干～不干；这种炉子～不了(liǎo) 面包〈时〉～一会就干了；～了这么长时间还没好？〈量〉再～一下儿；～过好几回了〔**状**～〕在烤箱❸里～；在炉子旁边～；多～一会儿；赶紧～

1. wet clothes 2. good-smelling 3. oven

hǒng 哄 coax; humour〔～宾〕〈名〉～孩子玩；～孩子睡觉；～孩子吃药〈代〉孩子哭了，快～一

～他吧〔～补〕〈结〉～好了；～过了〈趋〉她～起孩子来很有办法❶〈程〉～得不哭了；～得不闹❷了〈可〉～得了(liǎo) 吗？〈时〉～了半天也没用〈量〉～一下儿他；～了一阵〔**状**～〕好好～；耐心地❸～；用各种办法❹～；一再～

1. way; means; measure 2. stop making a noise 3. with patience 4. by every possible means; by hook or by crook

hòuhuǐ 后悔 regret; repent〔～宾〕〈动〉～没去参观；～看见了没买；～年轻时没好好学习；～没早去看病，～没及时❶帮助他〈主-谓〉～自己多说了一句话；～我没把孩子带去；～我没去医院看他〔～补〕〈结〉真～死了〈趋〉她为那件事又～起来了〈程〉～得连饭都吃不下去了；～得不得❷了(liǎo)；～得什么似的❸；～得要命❹〈可〉放心❺吧，保证❻你不～〈时〉事后❼我～了半天；为这件事她～了很长时间〔**状**～〕无须～；一直～；有点儿～；非常～；想起来就～；并不～

1. in time 2. 3. 4. extremely; exceedingly; awfully; terribly 5. rest assured; be at ease 6. pledge; guarantee; assure; ensure 7. after the event; afterwards

hú 糊 stick with paste; paste〔～宾〕〈名〉用纸～墙；～窗缝儿❶；～纸盒❷；～火柴盒❸；～信封；

玻璃❹破❺了，临时❻～一张报纸〔**～补**〕〈结〉为了❼防❽轰炸❾，玻璃上～满了纸条❿；把信封～成长方形⓫的好不好？把这种糊墙纸⓬～在墙上，才好看呢〈趋〉把那块破玻璃先用纸～起来吧；这种纸～到墙上去多难看⓭啊〈程〉那个工人糊纸盒～得真快；～得很熟练⓮〈可〉这种墙～不上纸；今天～得完～不完这些火柴盒？她刚学，怎么糊也～不快〈时〉～了一个多小时；～了半天〈量〉～过一次；还需要再～一下儿吗？～一下儿窗缝儿就不冷了〔**状～**〕用白纸～；用浆糊⓯～；用胶水⓰～；往墙上～；多～点儿；临时～；不必～〔**习用**〕～涂虫⓱

1. crack; crevice **2.** paper box **3.** match box **4.** glass **5.** broken **6.** temporarily **7.** in order to **8.** guard against; prevent **9.** bomb **10.** a strip of paper **11.** rectangle **12.** wall paper **13.** ugly; unsightly **14.** skilful **15.** paste **16.** glue; mucilage **17.** blunderer; bungler

huā 花 spend; expend ≃ 用 〔**～宾**〕〈名〉～钱；～时间；～工夫；～精力❶；～力气；～心血❷〔**～补**〕〈结〉钱都～光❸了；～上两年的时间准能学好；时间（工夫）都～在他身上了〈趋〉把钱都～出去了；～去了不少精力；～起钱来象流水一样❹〈程〉时间～得很多；他花钱～得很仔细❺；把钱～得一干二净❻〈可〉钱多得～不完；时间～不起〈时〉～了半年的时间写完一篇中篇小说❼；～了一个小时〔**状～**〕计划着❽～钱；随便❾～钱；净乱❿～钱；盲目地⓫～；节省着⓬～；白⓭～了；多～点精力；为他～了不少心血；零碎⓮～；至少⓯～；一共～

1. energy; vigour **2.** painstaking care (effort) **3.** nothing left **4.** without restraint; freely **5.** frugal; economical **6.** thoroughly; completely **7.** medium-length novel **8.** in a planned way **9.** at random; as one pleases **10.** extravagantly **11.** blindly **12.** frugally **13.** in vain; for nothing **14.** scrappily **15.** at least

huá 划 ① paddle; row 〔**～宾**〕〈名〉～船〔**～补**〕〈结〉把小船～走了；～远点儿，离开❶游泳❷区❸〈趋〉小船从对面❹～过来了；从桥洞❺这边～到那边去了；绕❻湖❼一圈又～回来了；他们～起龙船❽来象飞似的〈程〉～得真快；～得很轻巧❾；～得很猛❿；～得直流汗⓫；比赛⓬时～得真紧张⓭〈可〉我总～不直⓮；我～不过他；胳膊⓯没劲儿⓰～不了(liǎo) 太长时间；你～得动吗？～得过来～不过来？你手都磨⓱破了，还～得了(liǎo) 吗？〈时〉上星期日，我们～了三个多小时船；我来～一会儿〈量〉～一下儿试试桨⓲好用不好用；使劲⓳～了两桨，船就转⓴过来了〔**状～**〕用力～；慢慢地～；愉快地㉑～；两只手一起～；熟练地㉒～；往哪儿～？绕着圈～；沿湖边儿㉓～

1. leave; depart from 2. swimming 3. area; region 4. the opposite side 5. bridge opening 6. circle; move around; revolve 7. lake 8. dragon boat 9. light and handy 10. vigorous; violent; fierce 11. streaming with sweat 12. match; competition 13. tense 14. not straight 15. arm 16. no physical strength 17. rub; wear 18. oar 19. strain at the oars 20. turn 21. happily 22. skilfully 23. along the bank of a lake

② scratch; cut the surface of〔~宾〕〈名〉~火柴❶；别用刀子~桌子；新刷❷的墙上就~了很多指甲❸印儿❹〔~补〕〈结〉火柴~着(zháo)了吗？几道闪电~破了天空❺；脚~流血❻了〈趋〉那个小学生总爱拿刀子在桌上~来~去〈程〉手~得直流血；~得乱七八糟❼；~得真难看❽〈可〉火柴湿❾了~不着(zháo)了〈时〉火柴~了半天也没划着(zháo)〈量〉这种火柴不错，轻轻❿一~一下儿就着(zháo)；手~破过好几次了〔状~〕用刀子~；到处~乱⓫~；在火柴盒上~；用力~；猛⓬~；轻轻地~

1. match 2. newly painted 3. nail 4. print; mark 5. flashes of lightning streaked across the sky 6. shed blood 7. at sixes and sevens; in a mess; in a muddle 8. ugly; unsightly 9. wet 10. slightly; gently 11. at random 12. abruptly; suddenly

③ be to one's profit; pay 〔~补〕〈可〉~得来吗？〔状~〕有点儿~不来；非常~不来；还是~得来的

huá 滑 slip 〔~宾〕〈名〉~冰；~雪；在冰上~了一交❶；小孩子都喜欢~滑梯❷〔~补〕〈结〉老人~倒了，快扶起来吧；~完了冰就去吃饭〈趋〉书从腿❸上~下来掉在地上了；滑雪运动员❹从山顶❺~下去了；你从什么时候开始~起雪来了？〈程〉3号运动员~得真猛❻；姿势❼~得真优美❽；~得满头大汗❾〈可〉年纪大了，~不了(liǎo)雪了；~不快了〈时〉~了两个小时冰；~很多年了，再~一会儿〈量〉~过很多次了；~一下儿试试〔状~〕今天的冰不好~；继续❿往前⓫~；大胆地⓬~；在体育馆⓭里~冰；从高的地方往下~雪；来回⓮~；绕着⓯冰场~

1. slip and fall 2. (children's) slide 3. leg 4. sportsman; athlete 5. the top of a mountain 6. vigorous; energetic 7. posture; gesture 8. graceful 9. be sweated all over the head 10. continue; go on 11. forward 12. boldly 13. gymnasium; gym 14. back and forth; to and fro 15. circle; revolve; move round

huà 化 ① melt; dissolve ≅ 融解；融化〔主~〕〈名〉雪~了；糖

~了；盐❶~了；柏油路❷~了〔~宾〕〈名〉~雪的时候比较冷〔~补〕〈结〉积雪❸都~完了；~干净了；这块冰都~光了〈程〉天热，冰~得很快；这块冰放在那儿~得满地都是水〈可〉糖放在冷水里半天也~不开〈时〉这块水果糖放在水里~了两分钟才化完〈量〉等糖~一下儿再喝〔状~〕天热糖容易~；盐粒太大不好~；很快就~了；全部~了；慢慢地~了；逐渐❹~了；好容易❺~了

1. salt 2. asphalt road 3. piled snow 4. gradually 5. with great difficulty

② change; turn; transform ≃ 变化〔~宾〕〈名〉伤口❶~脓❷了；演员❸正在后台❹~装❺；~妆❻；~整为零❼；~险为夷❽〔~补〕〈结〉还没~完装吗？〈趋〉他~起装来真年轻❾〈程〉她化装~得真好；~得真象；化装~得非常漂亮❿〈可〉伤口周围⓫老保持⓬干净，就~不了(liǎo)脓了；〈时〉再~一会儿就完了；~了半天〈量〉自己~过一次装；请您帮我~一下儿〔状~〕千万别~脓；自己~装；给别人~；精心地⓭~

1. wound; cut 2. fester; suppurate 3. actor or actress 4. backstage 5. (of actors) make up 6. put on; make up 7. break up the whole into parts 8. turn danger into safety; head off a disaster 9. young 10. handsome; beautiful 11. around; round 12. keep; maintain 13. meticulously; carefully; elaborately

huà 画 draw; mark; delineate〔~宾〕〈名〉~画儿❶；~圈儿❷；~一张草图❸；~一张表格❹；~山水❺；~像；~叉子❻；~问号❼；~各种记号❽；~了许多符号❾〔~补〕〈结〉把~完的画儿挂在墙上❿了；别把线~歪⓫了；表格~错了；怎么把驴⓬~成马了；~在图画纸⓭上〈趋〉一会儿就~出来一张画儿；~到墙上去了〈程〉~得挺直⓮；~得非常好；~得圆极了；~得很象；~得不怎么样⓯〈可〉天快黑了，咱们还继续⓰~下去吗？照着⓱画，我都~不下来；你捣乱⓲得我都~不下去了！纸太小了，这么多内容⓳~不下；这么多插图⓴我一个人哪儿~得过来呀！我可~不了(liǎo)油画㉑〈时〉这幅㉒风景画㉓~了两个月才画完；每天都要画一会儿画儿〈量〉请你帮我把表格~一下儿；随便㉔~了几笔〔状~〕往画布㉕上~；认真地㉖~；马马虎虎地㉗~；一丝不苟地㉘~；重~；整天~；不间断地㉙~；慢慢地~；经常~；给别人~

1. drawing; picture 2. circle 3. draft 4. form; table 5. mountains and rivers; scenery with hills and waters 6. cross 7. question mark 8. different marks (signs) 9. many symbols (marks) 10. be hung on the wall 11. oblique; slanting 12. donkey; ass 13.

drawing paper 14. very straight 15. not up to much; very indifferent (not much of a painting) 16. go on; continue 17. copy; imitate 18. make trouble; create a disturbance 19. content 20. illustration; plate 21. painting 22. a measure word (e.g. for spectacles; playing cards, gloves, etc.) 23. landscape painting 24. casually; at random 25. canvas (for painting) 26. seriously; conscientiously 27. carelessly 28. not be the least bit negligent; be scrupulous about every detail 29. without interruption

huáiyí 怀疑 doubt; suspect ↔ 相信；信任〔**~宾**〕〈名〉~他的动机❶；~他说的那些话，我~那个人〈代〉~他偷❷东西；~他在后面捣鬼❸〈动〉~遇上了埋伏❹〔**~补**〕〈结〉~错了人；~到我头上了〈趋〉不要再~下去了；居然❺~起我来了〈程〉~得太过火❻了；~得大家很紧张❼〈可〉~不着(zháo)我；~不了(liǎo)你〈时〉~了半天，原来不是他；~了很长时间，对他~了一阵子❽〈量〉~过一次他〔**状~**〕被大家~；别随便❾~；千万别轻易❿~，莫明其妙地⓫~；没有根据地⓬~；不能无缘无故地⓭~；捕风捉影⓮地~；别瞎⓯~；长期~；心里~；大家都~

1. motive 2. steal 3. play tricks; do mischief 4. ambush 5. unexpectedly; to one's surprise 6. go too far; go to extremes; overdo 7. nervous 8. a period of time 9. casually; at random 10. lightly; rashly 11. without rhyme or reason; inexplicable 12. groundlessly 13. without cause or reason; for no reason at all 14. chase the wind and clutch at shadows — make groundless accusations; speak or act on hearsay evidence 15. foolishly; groundlessly

huānsòng 欢送 see off; send off ↔ 欢迎〔**~宾**〕〈名〉~代表团❶；~外宾❷；~毕业生❸；~大使❹回国；~运动员❺去参加比赛❻〔**~补**〕〈结〉~完了；~走了〈程〉~得很热烈❼；~得很热情❽〈可〉明天我有点事~不了(liǎo)你们了〈时〉~了一个多小时〈量〉好好~一下儿他；~过很多次了〔**状~**〕热烈~；热情友好地~；在机场~；亲自❾~；鼓掌❿~；一起~

1. delegation 2. foreign guest 3. graduate 4. ambassador 5. sportsman; athlete 6. match; competition 7. enthusiastic; warm; ardent 8. warm; fervent; enthusiastic 9. personally 10. with applause

huānyíng 欢迎 welcome; greet ↔ 欢送〔**~宾**〕〈名〉~贵宾❶；~外宾❷；在门口~客人；~老同

学；~参观的人❸〈代〉~大家提意见❹；~你到我家来坐坐〔~补〕〈结〉你~完了代表团❺，马上回来，这里还有事〈程〉~得很热烈❻；~得很隆重❼；~得冷冷清清❽ 〈可〉一批一批地❾来，我都~不过来了〈时〉~了一上午来宾 〈量〉在机场~过一次外宾〔状~〕热烈~；夹道❿~；真诚地⓫~；冒雨⓬~；特别~；普遍⓭~；列队⓮~

1. honoured guest; distinguished guest 2. foreign guest 3. visitor 4. make a criticism; make comments or suggestions 5. delegation 6. warm; enthusiastic 7. solemn 8. cold and cheerless; desolate 9. group by group 10. line the street 11. sincerely; earnestly; truly 12. braving the rain 13. commonly; universally; generally 14. forming a line

huán 还 give back; return; repay ≃归还↔借〔~宾〕〈名〉~钱，~东西；~债❶；~口；~手；~帐❷；讨价一价❸ 〈代〉~你钱〔~补〕〈结〉债都~清❹了，东西还没~齐❺，昨天我~完了书就回来了，把欠❻的钱都~上了吗？〈程〉他借东西~得很快；~得很准时❼〈可〉他欠的债太多了，一两年之内~不清；~得起❽再跟别人借钱，~不起就别借〔时〕~了好几年才还清 〈量〉~了三次才把钱还清；替我~一下儿〔状~〕马上~；一次~清；慢慢~；按时❾~；分期❿~；零碎⓫~；

一定~；赖着⓬不~；不用~；必须~；什么时候~？怎么还不~？〔习用〕以眼~眼，以牙~牙⓭

1. debt 2. debt; credit 3. bargain; haggle 4. completely; thoroughly (pay up what one owes) 5. complete 6. owe 7. on time; punctual 8. can afford to pay back 9. on time 10. by stages 11. scrappily 12. repudiate 13. eye for eye, tooth for tooth

huǎn 缓 delay; postpone; put off ≃ 延迟〔~宾〕〈名〉~期❶执行❷；~刑❸；~兵之计❹〔~补〕〈时〉~两天再办吧〈量〉先~一下儿再说吧〔状~〕暂❺~执行；先~一~；再~几天

1. postpone a deadline; suspend 2. execute; carry out 3. temporary suspension of the execution of a sentence; reprieve; probation 4. stratagem to gain a respite; stalling tactics 5. temporarily

huǎnhé 缓和 mitigate; alleviate; relax; ease up 〔主~〕〈名〉国际形势❶~了，局势❷~了；紧张的气氛❸~了；对立情绪❹~了；语气❺~了；口气❻~了；两个人的矛盾❼~了〔~补〕〈结〉~多了〈趋〉~下来了〈程〉气氛~得多了〈可〉短时期内~不了(liǎo)〈时〉~了一段时间，后来又紧张起来了〈量〉~一下儿〔状~〕已经~

了；有意❸~；日趋❾~；逐渐❿~；一天天地~

1. 2. situation 3. intense atmosphere 4. antagonism 5. 6. tone; manner of speaking 7. contradiction 8. deliberately 9. with each passing day; day by day 10. gradually

huàn 换 exchange; change ≅ 交换；更改 〔~宾〕〈名〉收门票的~人了；这里太晒❶，我们~个地方坐吧；我~一件新衣服再去；我们两个人~个座位❷吧；请你给我~十块钱零钱❸；孩子六、七岁就~牙❹了；眼镜度数❺不合适❻再~一个合适的吧；~一句话说❼；~煤气❽；~口胃❾，~花样❿〔~补〕〈结〉~错车了；~上一双皮鞋〈趋〉把脏衣服⓫下来洗洗吧，把零钱都~出去了〈程〉这个孩子的牙~得比较早，煤气~得真赞事⓬〈可〉在这儿~不了(liǎo)去动物园的车吧〈时〉零钱~了半天都没换开〈量〉每月~一次；请你给我~一下儿零钱吧〔状~〕少~一次车；跟他~个座位〔习用〕~汤不~药⓭

1. there's too much sun here 2. seat 3. small change 4. tooth (grow permanent teeth) 5. the strength of the lenses of glasses 6. not suitable 7. in other words 8. liquefied petroleum gas 9. taste 10. pattern; variety 11. dirty clothes 12. give or take a lot of trouble 13. the same medicine differently prepared; the same old stuff with a different label; a change in form but not in content

huǎng 晃 dazzle 〔主~〕〈名〉太阳光~眼❶；灯光~眼；湖❷水的反光❸~眼〔~宾〕〈名〉灯光~眼；不要用镜子❹~人〔~补〕〈结〉阳光太强❺把我眼睛都~花❻了〈趋〉这个孩子又用镜子~起人来了；镜子的反光都~进屋子里来了〈程〉~得睁不开眼❼了；~得什么都看不见了〈可〉把灯挡❽上一点儿，就~不着(zháo)眼睛了〈时〉雪光再~一会儿我就要吐❾了〈量〉~过好几次了；~了好几下儿〔状~〕用镜子~；被汽车灯❿~

另见huàng 晃

1. dazzle 2. lake 3. reflect light 4. mirror 5. strong 6. blurred; dim 7. unable to open one's eyes 8. block 9. vomit 10. the headlight; the head-lamp

huàng 晃 shake; sway 〔主~〕〈名〉小船在湖面❶上~；你别在我眼前~；树影❷在月光下来回❸~；人在汽车里来回~；喝醉酒的人❹走起路来直❺~〔~宾〕〈名〉~脑袋；摇头~脑❻〔~补〕〈结〉头都~晕❼了〈量〉他~了一下儿头表示❽不同意〔状~〕来回~；不停地~；一个劲儿地❿~；使劲⓫~

另见huǎng 晃

1. on the surface of a lake 2. shadow of a tree 3. back and forth; to and fro 4. drunkard 5. continuously 6. wag one's head — look pleased with oneself; assume an air of self-approbation or self-conceit 7. dizzy; giddy 8. show; express 9. not agree 10. persistently; continuously 11. with strength

huīfù 恢复 restore; recover; resume renew; regain 〔**主～**〕〈名〉两国的邦交❶已经正式❷～了；他们两个人的夫妻关系～了；健康❸～了；罢工❹破坏❺了的经济秩序❻尚未❼～；交通秩序❽～了〔**～宾**〕〈名〉希望❾你早日～健康；病人还没～知觉❿；～了元气⓫；～民主权利⓬；～了人身自由⓭；～了名誉⓮；～了原来的职务⓯；～了正常工作；～了关系；～了考试制度⓰；～了优良传统⓱；～了正常生活；～历史的本来面目⓲；这段⓳马路修⓴好以后，就可以～交通了；再也无法㉑～原状㉒了；一定要～正常㉓〈形〉过了好一会儿才～了平静㉔；血压㉕已经～了正常〔**～补**〕〈趋〉～起来了〈程〉～得很快；～得很好；～得比较慢；～得跟原来一样〈可〉～得了(liǎo)～不了(liǎo)？〈时〉～了很长时间了；～了好几年了〈量〉需要好好～一下儿〔**状～**〕刚～；完全～了；还没～呢；慢慢～；立即㉖～；迅速㉗～；逐渐㉘～；重新～；尽快㉙～；积极～；从去年起～；为他～名誉；无法～；正式～；终于～了；最近才～

1. diplomatic relations 2. formally; officially 3. health 4. strike 5. destroy; do great damage to; sabotage 6. economic order 7. not yet 8. traffic order 9. hope 10. consciousness 11. vitality; vigour 12. democratic rights 13. freedom of person 14. fame; reputation (rehabilitation of a person's reputation) 15. original post 16. examination system 17. fine tradition 18. historical truth 19. section 20. repair 21. unable; incapable 22. the former state; status quo ante 23. normal 24. calm; quiet; tranquil 25. blood pressure 26. at once 27. quickly 28. gradually 29. as quickly as possible

huí 回 ① return; go back 〔**～宾**〕〈名〉～家；～学校；～办公室❶；～乡❷；～病房❸；～原处❹〔**～补**〕〈结〉病人～到了床上，等着医生来查房❺；昨天回家～晚了〈趋〉我刚～来；你打算❻什么时候～去？你还是～到我们这儿来吧〈可〉最近工作太忙，～不了(liǎo)家；今天夜里要加班❼可能～不去了〈量〉一年～一次老家❽〔**状～**〕每天～；提前❾～；赶快～；刚～；立即❿～；

1. office 2. native place; home village 3. ward 4. original place 5. examine; inspect; check up 6.

intend; plan **7.** work overtime; work an extra shift **8.** native place; old home **9.** in advance; ahead of time **10.** at once; immediately

② answer; reply ≅ 回答〔**～宾**〕〈名〉～电话；～一封信；～电(报)❶；～个条儿❷；～个话儿❸〔**～补**〕〈结〉～过了〈程〉信～得很快；～得很及时❹〈可〉现在都下班了，所以我～不了(liǎo)电话了〔**状～**〕请速❺～；一直❻没～信；及时～；马上～；赶紧～

1. telegram **2.** receipt **3.** answer; reply **4.** in time **5.** fast; rapidly; quickly **6.** all along; all the time

③ turn round ≅ 转〔**～宾**〕〈名〉～身；～头；一～手，打碎❶了一个茶杯〔**～补**〕〈趋〉他～过头来看了看我们；她说完了话就～过头去了；上课的时候不要～过身去说话〈可〉脖子❷疼❸得连❹头儿都～不了(liǎo)了；我想看看，可是挤得❺我～不过身来〈时〉～了半天头，脖子都酸❻了〈量〉～了好几次头儿；请～一下儿身，让我过去〔**状～**〕赶快～；连忙❼～；猛～〔**习用**〕～头是岸❽

1. break to pieces **2.** neck **3.** ache; pain; sore **4.** even **5.** crowd; pack; cram **6.** tingle; ache **7.** promptly; at once **8.** repent and be saved

huídá 回答 answer; reply; response〔**～宾**〕〈名〉～问题；～他们的问话〈动〉～记者❶的提问〔**～补**〕〈结〉～对了吗？～错了吧；应该把问题～清楚〈趋〉这么难的问题他都～上来了；老师问的所有问题她都～出来了；他～起问题来很有条理❷〈程〉～得非常流利❸；～得清清楚楚；～得很简练❹；～得太罗嗦❺了；～得头头是道❻；～得有条不紊❼；～得乱七八糟❽；～得丢三落四❾；～得糊里糊涂❿；～得很好；～得不错；～得真精采⓫；～得太糟糕⓬了〈可〉～不出这个问题来；我提的问题，你～得了(liǎo)～不了(liǎo)？～得好吗？～不全；～不清楚〈时〉～了十分钟；～了好一会儿才回答完〈量〉～过一次；好好～一下儿；我没听清楚，请你再～一遍〔**状～**〕诚恳地⓭～；主动～；正面⓮～；坦率地⓯～；从从容容地⓰～；有条不紊地～；紧张地⓱～；一五一十地⓲～；从头～；圆满地⓳～；无须～；不得不⓴～；勉强～㉑；随意㉒～；马马虎虎地㉓～；仍然㉔～那几句；尽量㉕～；支支吾吾地㉖～；羞羞答答地㉗～；老老实实地㉘～；痛痛快快地㉙～；笼笼统统地㉚～；罗罗嗦嗦地～；结结巴巴地㉛～；谨慎地㉜～；客客气气地～；高高兴兴地～；毫不犹豫地㉝～；含含糊糊地㉞～；直截了当地㉟～；笑吟吟地㊱～；兴冲冲地㊲～；无可奈何地㊳～；气乎乎地㊴～；慢吞吞地㊵～；冷冰冰地㊶～；假惺惺地㊷～；娇滴滴㊸地～；恶狠狠地㊹～；胡乱地㊺～；勇敢地㊻～；漫不经心地㊼～；心不在焉地㊽～；准确地㊾～

1. reporter; correspondent; newsman; journalist 2. methodical; well-organized 3. very fluent 4. terse; succinct; pithy 5. long-winded; wordy 6. clear and logical; closely reasoned and well argued 7. in an orderly way; methodically; systematically 8. at sixes and sevens; in a mess; in confusion 9. forgetful; scatter-brained 10. muddled; confused; bewildered 11. wonderful; splendid; brilliant 12. too bad 13. sincerely 14. directly 15. frankly 16. calmly; unhurriedly; leisurely 17. nervously 18. systematically and in full detail 19. satisfactorily 20. have no choice but 21. reluctantly; grudgingly 22. at will; as one pleases 23. carelessly 24. still; yet 25. to the best of one's ability 26. evasively 27. bashfully 28. honestly 29. simply and directly 30. in very general terms 31. stammeringly 32. prudently; carefully; cautiously 33. without hesitation 34. ambiguously 35. straightforwardly 36. smilingly 37. excitedly 38. have no alternative 39. angrily 40. unhurriedly 41. coldly 42. hypocritically 43. affectedly sweet 44. ferociously 45. at random 46. courageously 47. carelessly; negligently 48. absent-mindedly 49. exactly

hùn 混 ① mix; confuse ≅ 搀杂〔主~〕〈名〉正品❶和次品❷~了〔~补〕〈结〉把白糖和盐❸~在一起了; 说话声和吵闹声❹~在一起了; 不要把我和他~为一谈❺; 把洋灰❻、砂子❼、小石子和水~在一起搅拌❽成混凝土❾〈趋〉别把好的和坏的~起来; 鱼肝油❿和牛奶可以~起来喝吗?〈程〉~得没法挑⓫出来了; ~得分不清了; ~得不匀⓬〈可〉放在两个地方были~不了(liǎo)了〈量〉~过一次, 后来又分开了〔状~〕不小心~了; 故意⓭~; 别~了; 一下子~了

1. certified products (goods); quality products (goods) 2. substandard products; defective goods 3. salt 4. confused noise; hubbub 5. lump (jumble) together; confuse sth. with sth. else 6. cement 7. sand 8. mix; stir 9. concrete 10. cod-liver oil 11. unable to select 12. not even 13. intentionally; on purpose

② pass for; pass off as ≅ 蒙混〔~宾〕〈名〉鱼目~珠❶〔~补〕〈结〉~在人群中了〈趋〉你没有工作证❷是怎么~进来的; 休想❸~过关❹去; 那个人没买车票想趁❺下车的时候~下去; 那些走私商❻想~过海关❼来是不可能的; 那个罪犯❽~到人群中来(去)了〈可〉已经布下了天罗地网❾, 这批走私犯❿想~是~不过去了〔状~〕已经~; 多次~; 差点儿⓫~; 几乎⓬~; 万一⓭~; 竟然⓮~; 好容易⓯~; 偷偷地⓰~

1. pass off fish eyes as pearls — pass off the sham as genuine 2. employee's card 3. don't imagine that it's possible 4. pass a barrier; go through an ordeal 5. take advantage of; avail oneself of 6. smuggler 7. customs 8. criminal 9. nets above and snares below; tight encirclement (spread a dragnet) 10. smuggler 11. 12. nearly; almost 13. if by any chance; just in case 14. unexpectedly; to one's surprise 15. with much difficulty 16. stealthily; secretly

③ muddle along; drift along 〔～宾〕〈名〉～日子❶；～时间；～口饭吃❷〔～补〕〈结〉你混日子还没～烦❸吗？～腻❹了；～到哪一天为止啊！〈趋〉他以前很有上进心❺，可现在却一起日子来了；你整天混，能～出什么名堂❻来？别再这样～下去了〈程〉日子～得不错；时间～得不短了；混日子～得太没有意思❼了；～得多无聊❽啊！～得一点价值都没有❾；～得一事无成❿〈可〉日子可～不得啊，一转眼⓫，人生就过去了；可能他在那里～不下去了；那个失足⓬青年说："我这辈子还～得好吗？"～不出成绩⓭来，决不回家〈时〉～了一辈子，到老一事无成；在工厂～了三年；～了一阵子〔状～〕整天～；勉强⓮～；白白地⓯～；到处～；毫无目的地⓰～；别再～了

1. drift along aimlessly 2. make a living 3. be vexed; be annoyed 4. be bored with; be tired of 5. the desire to do better; the urge for improvement 6. result; achievement 7. insipid; dull 8. bored 9. worthless 10. accomplish nothing; get nowhere 11. in the twinkling of an eye; in a flash 12. take a wrong step in life 13. result; achievement 14. reluctantly; grudgingly 15. in vain 16. aimlessly

huó 活 be alive; live ≅ 生存↔死〔主～〕〈名〉我送❶你的那条金鱼还～着吗？花儿～了；人还～着；这棵树没～〔～补〕〈结〉司机❷常常骂❸违反交通规则❹的人说："你～腻❺了！"〈趋〉由于医生的抢救❻，孩子总算❼～下来了；一定要让地震❽留下❾来的孤儿❿们好好～下去〈程〉我们要～得有意义⓫；他～得非常有意思，～得很有兴趣⓬；～得很幸福〈可〉没有氧气⓭是～不了(liǎo)的；花儿都干成这个样子了，还～得了(liǎo)吗？他很悲观⓮，有点～不下去的样子〈时〉她要是再多～几年就好了〔状～〕孤孤单单地⓯～着；孤苦伶仃地⓰～着；健康地⓱～着；幸福地～着

1. give; give as a present 2. driver 3. swear; call names 4. violate the traffic regulations 5. be bored with; be tired of 6. rescue; save 7. at last 8. earthquake 9. remain 10. orphan 11. significance; sense 12. interesting 13. oxygen 14. pessimistic 15. 16. in solitude 17. healthily

huódòng 活动 ① exercise; move about ≅ 运动〔主~〕〈名〉老年人应该经常~~；病人现在已经可以下地❶~了；上年纪❷的人总不~,腿脚❸不灵便❹了；孩子们坐了一上午，该出去~~了〔~宾〕〈名〉~~四肢❺；~~筋骨❻；~~胳膊❼；~~腿❽；你~~那个书架❾，看看腿垫平❿了没有〔~补〕〈结〉天刚亮人们就在楼下的广场⓫上~开了；~完了浑身⓬都感到舒服⓭〈趋〉学生们一到下午四点就开始~起来了〈可〉地方那么小, 人那么多，怎么能~得开呢？〈时〉每天至少⓮要~二十分钟；别总坐着不动，出去~一会儿吧!〈量〉饭后出去散散步~一下儿, 对身体有好处⓯；他一天~两次，早上一次, 晚上一次；游泳⓰时，要先在岸⓱上~一下儿筋骨；~一下儿身体〔状~〕经常~~；按时⓲~；必须~

1. leave a sickbed 2. advanced in years 3. legs and feet — ability to walk 4. have difficulty walking 5. the four limbs; arms and legs 6. bones and muscles 7. arms 8. legs 9. bookshelf 10. level up 11. public square; square 12. all over the body 13. feel well 14. at least 15. good; benefit; advantage 16. swim 17. bank; shore; coast 18. on time

② be shaky; be unsteady ≅ 摇晃；晃摇〔主~〕〈名〉门牙❶了；沙发扶手❷~了〔~补〕〈程〉桌子腿❸~得太利害了〈时〉了好长时间了〈量〉~一下儿试试结实❹不结实〔状~〕刚刚❺~；早就~了；不~了

1. front teeth 2. armrest 3. legs of a table 4. strong; solid 5. just now

③ act; operate; be in activity〔主~〕〈名〉书法❶学习小组❷今天下午~〔~补〕〈趋〉敌人在边境❸又~起来了〈程〉~得很频繁❹；~得很猖狂❺〈可〉数学❻小组这星期因故❼~不了(liǎo)了；每次人都来得不齐❽，所以歌咏小组❾总~不起来〈时〉绘画❿小组已经~了很长时间了〈量〉乐队⓫每周~两次〔状~〕一直⓬在那里~；积极⓭~；按时⓮~；暗中⓯~；到处~；长期~

1. calligraphy; penmanship 2. study group 3. border; frontier 4. frequently; often 5. furious; savage 6. mathematics 7. for some reason 8. not complete 9. singing group; chorus 10. drawing; painting 11. orchestra; band 12. continuously; always; all along 13. actively 14. on time 15. in secret; secretly

J

jīdòng 激动 excite; stir; agitate

〔~宾〕〈名〉这个故事❶非常~人心❷〔~补〕〈趋〉他听到这个消息❸以后一下子❹就~起来了〈程〉~得热泪盈眶❺;~得哭了起来;~得一夜都没睡着(zháo)觉;~得久久不能平静❻;~得说不出话来❼了;~得不得了❽ (liǎo)〈时〉~了半天才平静下来〈量〉~过一次〔状~〕有些❾~;一时❿~;太~人心了;非常~

1. story; tale 2. public feeling; the feelings of the people 3. news 4. all at once; all of a sudden 5. one's eyes brimming with tears 6. calm; quiet 7. be too excited to say anything 8. extremely; exceedingly 9. somewhat; rather 10. for a short while; temporarily; momentarily

jīqǐ 激起 arouse; evoke; stir up

≡引起〔~宾〕〈名〉~公愤❶;~了岸边❷的浪花❸;~一场风波❹〈动〉~了强烈❺的反抗❻〈形〉~了人们的不满❼〔状~〕容易~;已经~;可能~;必然❽~;竟❾~;居然❿~

1. public indignation 2. bank; shore; coast 3. spray; spindrift 4. disturbance 5. strong; intense;

violent 6. revolt; resistance 7. resentment; discontentment 8. inevitably; certainly 9. 10. unexpectedly; to one's surprise

jí 急 worry

〔~宾〕〈名〉~人〔~补〕〈结〉眼睛都~红了;孩子昨天天黑还没回来,可把她~坏了;~病了;你怎么现在才来啊,都把我~死了;丈夫病了以后她也~病了;事情发生以后他都~傻❶了〈程〉~得她连话都说不出来了;他~得要命;~得直哭;~得不知道该怎么办了;~得脸红脖子粗❷;~得吃不好睡不好的;~得到处去求人帮忙〔状~〕今天他可真~了;从来不~;你这样说他,他当然❸~了;果真❹~了;一句话不对,就~了;当时❺就~了

1. be dumbfounded; be stunned 2. get red in the face from anger or excitement 3. surely 4. really as expected 5. at that time; then

jízhōng 集中 concentrate; centralize; focus; put together ↔分散

〔~宾〕〈名〉~精力❶;~注意力❷;~火力;~力量;~大家的意见;~了大量❸财富❹;~了各方面❺的经验❻〔~补〕〈结〉很多

出口商品❼都～在这个港口❽；绝大部分❾人口❿～在沿海⓫一带⓬；～在礼堂⓭听报告；她把精力都～在学习上了；把捡⓮来的东西都～在一起交上去〈趋〉把大家提的意见都～起来了；材料⓯都～到他手里去了；～到我们这里来〈可〉那个孩子听课时精神⓰总～不了(liǎo)；意见一时还～不起来〈量〉把已经搜集⓱到的材料好好⓲～一下儿〔**状～**〕必须～；尽快⓳～；全部～；在什么地方？逐渐～；一点一点～

1. energy; vigour; vim **2.** attention **3.** a large number; a great quantity **4.** wealth; riches **5.** every aspect **6.** experience **7.** export commodities **8.** port; harbour **9.** most; the overwhelming majority **10.** population **11.** along the coast; coastal; littoral **12.** zone; area; belt **13.** assembly hall; auditorium **14.** pick up (from the ground) **15.** data; material **16.** attention; mind **17.** collect; gather **18.** in perfectly good condition **19.** as quickly as possible

jǐ 挤 ① squeeze; press〔 **～宾** 〕〈名〉～牛奶；～牙膏❶；～时间；～眼泪❷〔**～补**〕〈结〉把海绵❸里的水～干；时间被～掉了；牙膏～多了；～在牙刷上〈趋〉把柠檬汁❹都～出来了；～出时间来好好学习学习吧；眼药膏❺都～到外边去了〈程〉牙膏～得太多了；～得不够；～得满脸都是〈可〉～不出时间来；鞋油❻用完了，一点也～不出来了；～不干净〈时〉～了半天也没挤出多少❼来；～了半天手都疼❽了〈量〉～过好几次果汁；～过一遍了〔**状～**〕用力～；使劲❾～；用手～牛奶；用机器❿～；别硬⓫往外～眼泪；一点一滴地⓬～时间学习；牙膏用的时候，不要乱⓭～

1. toothpaste **2.** tears **3.** sponge **4.** lemon juice **5.** eye ointment **6.** shoe polish **7.** a small quantity **8.** ache; pain; sore **9.** exert all one's strength **10.** machine **11.** manage to do something with difficulty **12.** bit by bit **13.** in disorder

② jostle; push against〔 **～宾** 〕〈名〉每天上下班都要去～巴士❶；马路上人～人〔**～补**〕〈结〉别把孩子～坏了；把老太太～倒❷了；帽子都给～歪❸了；扣子❹都～掉❺了；把我拿的点心❻盒❼都～扁❽了；注意！别把玻璃❾～碎了❿；电影散场⓫时，把我鞋～掉了；孩子的鞋～丢⓬了；把花都～成什么样子了；小心点别把鸡蛋～破⓭了〈趋〉好容易⓮～上去了；别把我～下去；她也～上来了；扶着⓯点，别让人给～下来；你是什么时候～进来的；费了好大劲⓰才～出来；人真多，～过来～过去（～来～去）的；刚才排队⓱排得好好的，怎么忽然⓲乱⓳～起来了；把那个老头儿～到旁边去了；～到前边去看看〈程〉～得无处放脚⓴；～得满身是汗㉑〈可〉那么多人我可～不动；人多～不进来〈时〉～了半天才挤上去〈量〉再～一下儿〔**状～**〕

用力~；使劲㉒~；拼命㉓~；往上~；故意㉔~；斜着身子㉕~；侧着身子~

1. bus 2. fall 3. askew; crooked 4. button 5. drop; fall 6. light refreshments; pastry 7. box; case 8. be crushed 9. glass 10. be broken to pieces 11. empty after the show 12. lost; be missing 13. be broken 14. with much difficulty 15. support with the hand; place a hand on sb. or sth. for support 16. great effort 17. line up; queue up 18. suddenly 19. in confusion; in disorder 20. can find no place to put one's foot 21. be sweated all over 22. exert all one's strength 23. with all one's might 24. on purpose; intentionally 25. on one's side

jìhuà 计划 plan ≅ 打算〔~宾〕〈动〉~今年出一批❶新书；~今年下半年❷完工❸；~在这儿建五幢楼〔~补〕〈结〉~好了再做；~错了；~不周❹〈程〉~得很好；~得非常周密❺；~得非常详尽❻〈可〉每月的生活费❼他总~不好；这么大的事我一个人可~不了(liǎo)〈时〉钱~了半天还是不够花〈量〉先~一下儿再动手做〔状~〕事先❽~；好好~~；仔细❾~；认真❿~；周密地⓫~

1. batch; lot; group 2. the latter half of the year 3. complete a project 4. not well planned; not planned carefully enough 5. careful; thorough; well-conceived 6. detailed; exhaustive; thorough 7. living expenses; cost of living 8. in advance; beforehand 9. carefully; attentively 10. seriously; conscientiously 11. thoroughly; carefully

jìjiào 计较 haggle over; fuss about; dispute〔~宾〕〈名〉~小事〈主－谓〉~个人得失❶；从不~别人说什么〔状~〕斤斤~❷；不跟他~；一点也不~；在日常生活上❸~；决不~；何必❹~

1. personal gains and losses 2. be preoccupied with one's personal gains and losses 3. in daily life 4. there is no need; why

jìsuàn 计算 count; compute; calculate ≅ 算〔~宾〕〈名〉~日期；~人数；~分数；~工作量❶；~生产成本❷〔~补〕〈结〉仔细点❸，千万❹别~错了；没~准❺；成本❻~多了〈趋〉全部费用❼已经~出来了〈程〉~得很精确❽；~得不太准；~得不够仔细〈可〉~不出来到底❾需要多少；没经验❿~不好；~不准〈量〉~了好几遍；~过两次；好好~一下儿〔状~〕精细地⓫~；好好~~；根据⓬什么~？一遍一遍地~；反复⓭~；大概⓮~了一下儿；马马虎虎地⓯~

1. amount of work 2. cost of production 3. be careful 4. be sure (e.g. to bear it in mind) 5.

accurate; exact 6. cost 7. total expenses 8. accurate; exact; precise 9. at last; in the end; finally 10. to have no experience 11. carefully; meticulously 12. according to; on the basis of 13. repeatedly; over and over again 14. roughly 15. carelessly

jì 记

① bear (keep) in mind; remember; commit to memory ≅ 记住↔忘〔～宾〕〈名〉～生词❶；～号码❷；～门牌❸；不要～仇❹；～名字〔～补〕〈结〉电话号码～住了吗？告诉你的事都～清楚了吗？这个字我～错了；这么多内容❺我都～糊涂❻了；台词❼还没～熟❽呢；这么多生❾面孔❿哪能一下子都～住啊；把我托⓫你办的事～在心上〈程〉他的模样⓬我还～得很清楚〈可〉什么也～不住了；生词太多，一个小时可～不下来；我还记得他，可是他已经～不得我了；一天～不了(liǎo)那么多生词〈时〉这几个词真难～⓭，我～了一晚上也没记住；记仇――一辈子⓮〈量〉他非常聪明⓯，台词～两遍就会了〔状～〕死～硬背⓰；好⓱～；不太好～；真难～；一点一点地～；一下子全～住了；一一～在心上；别～仇，强～；反复⓲～；一遍一遍地～；专心⓳～

1. new word 2. number 3. house number 4. bear grudges 5. content 6. bewildered; muddled; confused 7. actor's lines 8. at one's fingertips 9. unfamiliar; unacquainted; strange 10. face 11. ask; entrust 12. look; appearance 13. hard to remember 14. all one's life 15. intelligent; clever; bright 16. mechanical memorizing 17. be easy; be convenient 18. repeatedly; again and again 19. attentively

② write down; record ≅ 记录〔～宾〕〈名〉～日记❶；～分数；～笔记；～帐❷，她专门❸能～别人讲话的要点❹；他～过一次大过❺〔～补〕〈结〉号码～错了；今天的帐都～上了吗？把通讯地址～在记事❻本上〈趋〉要点❼已经～下来了；把这笔帐也～上去吧〈程〉笔记～得很清楚；～得很整齐❽；～得很简要❾；～得非常详细❿；～得很全⓫；～得太简单⓬；～得不全；～得乱七八糟⓭〈可〉讲得太快～不下来；内容⓮没意思⓯我连笔记都～不下去了；帐目⓰太多我一个人可～不过来；他认识⓱的字太少，笔记还～不下来〔状～〕在本子上～；从小就～日记，一直～；认真～；按时⓲～；一笔一笔地～帐

1. diary 2. account 3. specially 4. the gist of a speech 5. record a serious mistake 6. keep a record of events 7. main points; essentials 8. neat; tidy; in good order 9. brief 10. detailed 11. complete 12. simple 13. disordered; at sixes and sevens 14. content 15. dull; uninteresting 16. items of an account 17. know; recognize 18. on time; on schedule

jìxù 继续 continue; go on 〔主~〕〈名〉谈判❶仍在~；大雨还在~下着；会议正在~；球赛❷仍在~〔~宾〕〈动〉明天还要~我们的试验❸；~我们的工作；~学习；~讨论；~研究；~探讨❹；~睡；~吃；雪还~下；~前进；~奋斗❺；~改进❻技术❼；~进行❽〔~补〕〈结〉~到明天早上〈趋〉这种局面❾不能再~下去了；这种情况怎么还能再~下去呢〈可〉谈判再也~不下去了〈时〉考试已经~了三个多小时了；狂风❿~了一天一夜；这种尴尬⓫的局面已经~了很长一段时间了；比赛⓬又~了半个小时〔状~〕长期~下去；仍在⓭~；正在~；还~

1. negotiation 2. ball game; match 3. experiment; test 4. inquire into; probe into 5. struggle; fight 6. improve 7. technique; technology 8. go on; be underway 9. situation; aspect 10. fierce wind 11. awkward; embarrassed 12. match; competition 13. still; yet

jì 寄 send; post; mail ≅ 邮〔~宾〕〈名〉~信；~一张明信片❶；~了一笔款❷；~书；~包裹❸；~照片❹；~稿件❺；~一点儿吃的东西；我到邮局❻去~点儿东西〔~补〕〈结〉我~完信就回来；把词典~给他了；稿子~丢❼了；航空信❽两天就能~到；已经把相片~走了；杂志❾~错了；信刚~走〈趋〉母亲给我~来一件毛衣❿；他把大衣又~回来了；把没用的东西都~回家去吧〈程〉~得真多；~得真及时⓫；~得太晚了〈可〉~得到~不到？〔状~〕往国外~；在邮局~；赶快~走；第一次~；经常~；亲自⓬~；替别人~；一共~了三封信

1. postcard 2. a sum of money 3. parcel 4. photograph; picture 5. manuscript 6. post office 7. lost; be missing 8. airmail letter 9. magazine 10. woollen sweater; sweater 11. in time; timely 12. personally; in person

jiā 加 add; increase; put in; append ≅ 增加；添↔减〔~宾〕〈名〉快跑，~油儿！油箱❶里还需要再~一点儿油；~工资❷；身上再~一件衣服；锅❸里~点儿水；汤❹里~点儿盐❺；~罪名❻；给他~一个头衔❼；这星期天我们要~班❽赶工作；~一把劲儿❾；~标点❿；~注释⓫；这篇文章应该再~上几句话；我们小组~了一个人〈形〉聪明~勤奋⓬一定能干出一番事业⓭来〈数〉2～2等于⓮4〔~补〕〈结〉应该~~快速度⓯；马路再~宽⓰一点儿就好了；把这两个数儿~在一起看看；给人~上种种罪名；水~多了；~错数了；~到一百就停止；~上他一共五个人；下雨再~上天黑，路更不好走了〈趋〉把这个数儿~进来就对了；两个班~起来有三十多个人〈程〉标点~得不对；注释~得太少；水~得不够多；盐~得太多了；给他加罪名~得太冤枉⓱了〈可〉你这个星期～得了(liǎo)班～不了(liǎo)?〈时〉这几个数儿我～了半天也没加对〈量〉锅里～过一次水了；把数儿再～一遍；多～几次；好好～一下儿〔状～〕稍⓲～分析⓳；速度大大～快了；大～赞扬⓴；在繁华㉑的街道上开车要多～小心；再～一点儿糖

1. fuel tank 2. wages; pay 3. pot; pan; boiler 4. soup 5. salt 6. charge; accusation 7. title 8. work an extra shift 9. put your back into it! 10. punctuation 11. explanatory note 12. diligence 13. cause; undertaking 14. be equal to 15. pick up speed 16. broaden; widen 17. wrong; treat unjustly 18. a little; slightly 19. analyse 20. speak highly of; praise 21. busy; flourishing; bustling

jiājǐn 加紧 step up; speed up; intensify 〔～宾〕〈名〉～脚步〈动〉～准备❶；～学习；～工作；～练习；～训练❷；～培养❸

1. prepare 2. train; drill 3. train; foster; develop

jiāqiáng 加强 strengthen; enhance; augment; reinforce〔～宾〕〈名〉～力量❶；～必胜的信心❷；～战备❸〈动〉～团结❹；～教育❺；～学习〔状～〕努力～；认真～；适当❻～；日益❼～；不断❽～；逐渐❾～；逐步❿～

1. force; strength 2. confidence 3. preparation for war 4. unity 5. teach; educate; inculcate 6. suitably; properly 7. increasingly; day by day 8. unceasingly; without cease 9. gradually; by degrees 10. step by step; progressively

jiāsù 加速 quicken; speed up; accelerate; expedite 〔～宾〕〈名〉～了前进的步伐❶〈动〉～孩子的成长；～了战争的爆发❷〔状～〕大大～；必须～；努力～

1. step; pace 2. breakout

jiāyǐ 加以 give…… to; render 〔～宾〕〈动〉～仔细研究❶；～深入讨论❷；～考虑❸；～认真总结❹；～彻底改造❺；必须～注意；～适当处理❻；～制裁❼；～修改❽；～解决；～分析❾；～推广❿；～说明⓫；～克服⓬；～区别⓭；～复习；～检查⓮〔状～〕及时⓯～制止⓰；认真⓱～研究

1. careful study 2. thoroughgoing discussion 3. consideration 4. serious summary 5. radical changes or transformation 6. properly handle or deal with 7. apply sanctions against; mete out punishment to 8. submit amendments to; make modifications 9. analyse 10. extend; popularize 11. explain 12. overcome 13.

distinguish **14.** check up **15.** timely; in time **16.** prevent; stop **17.** seriously; conscientiously

jiā 夹 press from both sides; place in between; clip〔**~宾**〕〈名〉用筷子❶~菜；~肉；手指~着一支雪茄❷；胳膊❸底下~着一本书；腋下❹~着体温表❺；敌军~着尾巴❻逃跑❼了；两座大山~着一条小河〔**~补**〕〈结〉脚让汽车门~住了；体温表~好别掉了；菜没~住掉在桌子上了；抽屉❽把手指~肿了❾；手指被~流血❿了；螃蟹⓫~住了我的手；我~给他一块鸡肉；我~在他们两个人中间坐着；把红叶~在书里〈趋〉她把鱼刺⓬从碗里~出来了；那个留学生还不会用筷子，夹了半天也没~上来；~到碗里去了〈可〉~不起来；~得上来吗？~得住~不住？~不紧；~不了(liǎo)〈时〉体温表~五分钟就可以了吧？〈量〉~了好几下儿才夹起来；让车门给~了一下儿〔**状~**〕用筷子~；往盘子⓭里~；给客人~；用夹子⓮~；用钳子⓯~；被车门~；紧紧地⓰~；特意⓱~；顺手⓲~

1. chopsticks **2.** cigar **3.** arm **4.** armpit **5.** (clinical) thermometer **6.** tails **7.** run away **8.** drawer **9.** swollen **10.** bleed; shed blood **11.** crab **12.** fishbone **13.** tray; plate **14.** clip; tongs **15.** pincers; pliers **16.** tightly; firmly **17.** specially **18.** conveniently

jià 架 put up; erect; prop up ≌ 支撑〔**~宾**〕〈名〉~桥❶；~电线❷；~梯子❸；鼻子❹上~着一副❺眼镜❻〔**~补**〕〈结〉把梯子~在墙角❼；眼镜~在鼻梁❽上〈趋〉电线已经~起来了；战士❾把机枪❿~起来了〈程〉~得很结实⓫；~得真高〔**状~**〕用木头~桥；用钢筋水泥⓬~桥；在那条小河上~

1. bridge **2.** (electric) wire **3.** ladder **4.** nose **5.** a pair of **6.** spectacles; glasses **7.** a corner formed by two walls **8.** bridge of the nose **9.** fighter **10.** machine gun **11.** strong; solid **12.** reinforced concrete

jiānchí 坚持 persist in; insist on; adhere to; uphold; stick to〔**~宾**〕〈名〉~真理❶；~原则❷；~实事求是的作风❸；~我们自己的观点❹；~自己的信仰❺；~我们原有❻的主张❼；~我们的正确立场❽；~正确的❾方向❿；~八小时工作制⓫；~错误⓬；~己见⓭；~他们的看法；~上次会上提出⓮的条件⓯〈动〉~早起跑步⓰；~学英语；~工作；每天~锻炼身体⓱；~记日记⓲；他~要走〔**~补**〕〈结〉这件事情我们一定要~到底⓳；一定要~住，千万⓴别动摇㉑；罢工㉒要~到什么时候？〈趋〉锻炼㉓对身体大㉔有好处，你应该~下去；那个人非常主观㉕，~起自己的意见㉖来，谁也说服㉗不了他〈程〉业余

㉘学习，她～得很好；～得不错〈可〉他身体不好～不了(liǎo)全天工作；我困㉙得～不住了；看样子㉚罢课㉛～不下去了〈时〉走路上班㉜，他～了半年多；早晨起来锻炼，他已经～了二十年了；还能再～一会儿吗？～了一个时期〈量〉你还能不能再～一下儿?〔状～〕始终㉝～；已经～；必须～；终于㉞～下来了；实在㉟～不了(liǎo)了；决不～；固执地㊱～；一再～

1. truth 2. principle 3. a practical and realistic style 4. point of view 5. faith 6. former; original 7. position; stand 8. a correct stand 9. correct; right 10. direction 11. eight-hour day 12. mistake; error 13. own views 14. put forward 15. condition 16. run 17. build up physical strength 18. diary 19. to the end 20. be sure to 21. shake; vacillate 22. strike 23. physical training 24. greatly 25. subjective 26. opinion 27. persuade 28. sparetime 29. sleepy 30. it seems; it looks as if 31. students strike 32. go to work 33. from beginning to end 34. at last; finally 35. really; truly 36. stubbonly; obstinately

jiān 兼 hold two or more jobs concurrently

〔～宾〕〈名〉他在外边～了很多课〈动〉副校长❶～管❷总务❸；张老师教华文❹～作班主任❺；她在学校教英语～搞❻一些翻译❼〔～补〕〈结〉职务❽～多了，忙不过来〈趋〉科学院❾的教授在大学里～起课来了〈程〉兼课❿～得太多了；兼课～得一点业余时间⓫都没有了〈可〉她身体不好～不了(liǎo)那么多职务〈时〉他～过三年副厂长⓬〈量〉～过一次物理⓭实验⓮课；主任的工作你暂时⓯先～一下儿〔状～〕长期～；临时⓰～；暂时～；由他～；是否⓱～；一直～；无法～；必须～

1. vice-principal 2. run; manage; administer 3. general affairs 4. Chinese (as a subject of study or means of communication) 5. a teacher in charge of a class 6. do; carry on; be engaged in 7. translation; interpretation 8. post; duties; job 9. academy of sciences 10. do some teaching in addition to one's main occupation 11. spare time 12. vice-director of a factory 13. physics 14. experiment; test 15. temporarily; for the time being 16. provisionally; for a short time 17. whether; if

jiān 煎 fry in shallow oil

〔～宾〕〈名〉～鸡蛋；～鱼；～饺子❶；～豆腐❷；～汤药❸〔～补〕〈结〉中药❹～好了；豆腐～碎❺了〈趋〉～出来马上吃最好〈程〉～得焦黄❻焦黄的；～得真香；～得很好吃〈可〉油太少～不了(liǎo)；～不焦❼〈时〉药～二十分钟就可以了〈量〉凉的不好吃，用油～一下儿再吃吧!〔状～〕多～一会儿；用

砂锅❽～药; 用猪油❾～饺子; 用大火(旺火❿/小火/微火⓫)～

1. dumpling (with meat and vegetable stuffing) 2. bean curd 3. a decoction of medicinal ingredients 4. herbal medicine 5. break to pieces 6. brown 7. not brown 8. clay pot 9. lard 10. a great fire; a great flaming fire 11. a slow fire

jiǎn 拣 pick up; choose; select ≅ 选、挑〔～宾〕〈名〉～了一筐❶苹果; ～重要❷的话说; ～好的买; 问题～容易的先讨论; ～便宜的买; 别～老实❸的欺负❹〔～补〕〈结〉～满了一筐, 又拣一筐; ～好了先放在一边; 把好的都～在盘子❺里吧; 把坏的～到一起; 还没～够数❻儿呢; 这些都是他们～剩下❼的〈趋〉把最好的～出来; 把烂❽的～出去〈程〉～得真快, 一会儿就是一筐; ～得太慢了; ～得真多〈可〉～不出好的来了; ～不满一筐〈时〉了半天也没拣出什么好的来; 再～一会儿〈量〉～一下儿; ～过一次了〔状～〕专❾～; 光～; 只～; 先～; 一个一个地～; 往盘子里～; 慢慢地～

1. basket 2. important; significant; major 3. honest person 4. bully; treat sb. high-handedly 5. tray; plate 6. sufficient in quantity; enough 7. be left; remain 8. rot 9. especially

jiǎn 捡 pick up; collect; gather ≅ 拾〔～宾〕〈名〉～柴❶; ～破烂儿❷; ～了一串钥匙❸; 在路上～了一个钱包; 他给我们～球; ～了一大堆❹〔～补〕〈结〉～着(zháo)一张传单❺〈趋〉他从地上～起一串钥匙; 我刚扔❻出去, 你怎么又把它～回来了〈程〉～得很多; ～得真不少; ～得很快; ～得真累〈时〉～了两个小时; ～了一上午〈量〉～过一次钱包; 替他～一下儿〔状～〕偶然❼～到的; 弯着腰❽～; 在门口～的; 往筐❾里～

1. firewood; faggot 2. search a garbage heap for odds and ends 3. a bunch of keys 4. pile; stack 5. leaflet 6. throw away 7. by chance; by accident 8. bend over 9. basket

jiǎnchá 检查 check up; inspect; examine ≅ 查〔～宾〕〈名〉～工作; ～护照❶; ～行李❷; ～信件❸; ～原因❹; ～身体; ～卫生❺; ～视力❻; ～听力❼; ～自己的言行❽; ～作业; ～机器❾; ～效果❿〔～补〕〈结〉各处都～遍⓫了; ～到什么时候为止? 〈趋〉从练习里～出不少错儿来; ～过来～过去(～来～去)的真麻烦⓬; 相隔⓭的时间太长了, 现在～起原因来确实⓮比较困难〈程〉～得很仔细⓯; ～得不彻底⓰; ～得不及时; ～得太马虎⓱了; ～得真慢; ～得真细⓲; ～得太粗⓳了〈可〉这种病～不出来; 病人这么多, 我一个人～不过来; 不化验⑳～不出是什么病来；没有这种设备㉑～不了(liǎo)〈时〉～了好几个月了，也没检查出什么毛病来；海关㉒～了半天才放他过去〈量〉在这个医院㉓～过一次眼睛；把练习～一遍再交；～一下儿，看看东西带㉔全㉕了没有〔状～〕好好～～；认真㉖～；仔细㉗～；严格㉘～；多～～；彻底㉙～；及时～；定期㉚～；按时～；按次序㉛～；挨家挨户地㉜～；一组一组地㉝～；一遍一遍地～；不负责任地㉞～；马马虎虎地㉟～；从外到里地～；从上到下地～；全面㊱～；行李要全部～；只～胃㊲；在医院～

1. passport 2. luggage 3. letters; mail 4. cause; reason 5. hygience; sanitation 6. eyesight 7. hearing 8. words and deeds 9. machine 10. effect; result 11. everywhere; all over 12. troublesome 13. at a distance from; after or at an interval of 14. really; truly 15. careful 16. thorough 17. careless 18. careful; meticulous 19. careless; negligent 20. chemical examination; laboratory test 21. equipment; installation; facilities 22. customhouse; customs 23. hospital 24. take; bring; carry 25. complete 26. conscientiously; seriously 27. carefully 28. strictly 29. thoroughly 30. regularly 31. by order 32. from door to door 33. by group 34. not responsibly 35. perfunctorily 36. overall; completely 37. stomach

jiǎn 剪 cut (with scissors); clip; trim ≅ 铰〔**～宾**〕〈名〉～头发；～辫子❶；～胡子❷；～羊毛；这种剪子❸只能～铁片❹，不能～布；～电线❺；～铁丝❻；～一块纸贴上❼；～指甲❽；上火车时在入口❾处～票❿〔**～补**〕〈结〉头发没～齐⓫；指甲～秃⓬了；把辫子～掉吧；这件衣服～坏了；裤子⓭的尺寸⓮～错了；把绳子⓯～断了；把这块布从这儿～开；铁丝让他给～成一截⓰一截的了〈趋〉一剪子就把辫子～下来了；把这个斜⓱着长⓲出来的树枝～下去吧；她～出来的衣服最合身⓳〈程〉～得太短了；头发～得不齐；剪纸⑳～得真艺术〈可〉剪子不快～不下来；普通㉑剪子～不了(liǎo)厚㉒铁片；纸太厚～不动；太硬㉓～不下来；剪子太大～不了(liǎo)胡子〈时〉～了半天；～一会儿〈量〉～过一次；～了好几下儿才剪下来；～了一剪子〔**状～**〕用剪子～；用指甲刀㉔～指甲；细心㉕点儿～

1. plait; braid 2. beard; moustache 3. shears; clippers; scissors 4. iron sheet 5. electric line 6. iron wire 7. stick; paste 8. nail 9. entrance 10. punch a ticket 11. even; neat; uniform 12. bald; bare 13. trousers 14. measurement; size 15. rope 16. section; length 17. oblique; slanting; inclined; tilted 18. grow 19. suitable 20. paper-cut 21. ordinary 22. thick 23. hard 24. nail clippers 25. carefully

jiǎn 减 reduce; decrease; subtract ↔加〔宾〕〈名〉录音机❶又价❷了；给他~了三年刑❸；汽车拐弯❹要~速❺〈数〉5~3等于❻2〔~补〕〈结〉这个数儿~错了；火车进站❼以后速度❽逐渐❾~慢了〈程〉价钱~得真不少〈可〉~不了(liǎo)多少〈时〉~了三年刑〈量〉~过一次价〔状~〕一次就~了20块钱；逐渐~慢；突然~；适当地❿~

1. tape recorder 2. price 3. penalty; punishment 4. turn a corner 5. slow down 6. be equal to 7. pull in 8. speed 9. gradually 10. appropriately; suitably

jiǎnqīng 减轻 lighten; ease; alleviate; mitigate 〔主~〕〈名〉病势❶~了；负担❷~了；工作~了；压力❸~了；责任❹~了〔~宾〕〈名〉~税收❺；~压力〈动〉~负担；~工作；~处分❻〈形〉~痛苦❼；~烦恼❽；~一点困难〔状~〕适当❾~；尽量❿~；尽可能地⓫~；千方百计地⓬~；设法⓭~；为他~

1. patient's condition 2. burden 3. pressure 4. responsibility 5. tax revenue 6. punishment 7. pain; suffering 8. vexation 9. suitably; properly 10. 11. to the best of one's ability; as far as possible 12. 13. by every possible means; by hook or by crook

jiǎnshǎo 减少 reduce; decrease; cut down ↔增加〔主~〕〈名〉人员❶~了；时间~了；工作~了；事情~了；收入❷~了；产量❸~了；疾病❹~了；文盲❺~了；犯罪现象❻~了；出口额❼~了〔~宾〕〈名〉~工作；~开支❽；~成本❾；~费用❿〔~补〕〈可〉~得了(liǎo)~不了(liǎo)〈量〉~过几次〔状~〕大大~；逐渐⓫~；突然⓬~；日益⓭~

1. personnel; staff 2. income 3. output; yield 4. disease 5. an illiterate person 6. criminal phenomenon 7. volume of export 8. expenses; expenditure 9. cost 10. spending; expenses 11. gradually 12. suddenly 13. day by day

jiàn 见 ① see; catch sight of ≅看见；见到〔~宾〕〈名〉没~过世面❶；~了一面就走了；~好的就买；~信快回信；几天没~那个孩子，他又胖❷了；只~一个人影❸从窗前闪过❹去了；这个人好象在哪儿~过面〔~补〕〈结〉~到张老师请替我问个好儿；~上几面就熟❺了；这种事情~多了，就不奇怪❻了；去了两次都没~着(zháo)我要找的人〈可〉以后恐怕❼再也~不到他了；他作过不少~不得人❽的事〈量〉我们只~过一次〔状~〕以前~过；从来没~过；也许~过；在哪儿~过；似乎❾~过；好象❿~过；仿佛⓫~过；经常~；匆匆忙忙地⓬~了一面；一定没~过；大概⓭没~过；我们是在宴会⓮上~到的

1. (have seen) the world 2. get fat 3. shadow of a person 4. flash past 5. familiar 6. strange; surprising 7. perhaps; I think 8. shameful; scandalous 9. 10. 11. as if; it seems 12. in a hurry; hastily 13. probably 14. feast; banquet

② meet with; be exposed to ≅ 接触〔~宾〕〈名〉这种药❶~光❷就失效❸了；她眼睛有病，~风就流泪❹；她一~血就晕倒❺；液化石油气❻不能~火，一见火就燃烧❼〈形〉冰❽~热就化❾；那个人~便宜❿就占⓫〔状~〕一~光就化；千万别~光

1. medicine; drug 2. light 3. lose efficacy; cease to be effective 4. shed tears 5. fall in a faint 6. liquefied petroleum gas 7. burn 8. ice 9. melt; dissolve 10. small advantages; petty gains 11. gain

③ show evidence of; appear to be ≅ 显出〔~宾〕〈名〉这种方法❶~效❷〈形〉吃了这种药❸，病有点儿~好；~轻❹；您这两年有点~老；这个孩子很~长❺(zhǎng)〔状~〕你可一点也不~老；这花老不~长(zhǎng)；这几年~；一直不~；吃了那么多剂❻汤药❼都不~效；初❽~成效❾；日❿~繁荣⓫

1. method; way 2. become effective 3. medicine; drug 4. get better 5. grow perceptibly 6. a measure word 7. a decoction of medicinal ingredients 8. first 9. produce effect 10. day by day 11. prosperous

④ meet; call on; see ≅ 会晤〔~宾〕〈名〉我要~经理❶〈代〉让他明天来~我〔~补〕〈结〉~着(zháo) 主任❷了吗？~得着(zháo) 大使❸~不着(zháo)〈量〉我想~一下儿他；我~过一次她〔状~〕我不便❹~他；立刻~；难得❺~到；偶尔❻~；偶然❼~；在什么地方~？什么时候~？设法❽~；轻易❾不~；好容易才~；在外边等着~

1. manager; director 2. head; director 3. ambassador 4. inconvenient 5. seldom; rarely 6. occasionally; once in a while 7. accidentally; by chance 8. try to 9. lightly; rashly

⑤ refer to; see ≅ 参照〔~宾〕〈名〉~生词表❶；~左图❷；~下图；~第208页〔状~〕详❸~；另❹~〔习用〕不~棺材不落泪❺；活~鬼❻；真~鬼了

1. glossary 2. chart; drawing; map 3. in detail 4. separately 5. not shed a tear until one sees the coffin — refuse to be convinced until one is faced with grim reality 6. it's sheer fantasy; you're imagining things

jiàn 建 build; construct; establish; set up ≅ 成立，建立〔~宾〕〈名〉~国；~军；~了三个体育馆❶；和别的国家~交❷〔~补〕〈结〉又~完了一座大楼；~成了

一个水库❸；高楼不能~在沙滩❹上〈趋〉不到半年的时间，这一片❺楼房都~起来了；~起了一座大桥〔~程〉现在的楼房~得比从前快多了〈可〉由于经费的关系目前还~不了(liǎo)太多；第一次用这种方法建，不知道~得好~不好；这一项工程❻很大，三年之内~不成；人力不够，一年可能~不起来〔状~〕应该有计划地❼~；刚刚~；新~；重~；重新~；马上~；跟别的国家合❽~；模仿❾外国的样式~；到处~；正在~；不要盲目地❿~；不停地~

1. gymnasium 2. diplomatic relations 3. reservoir 4. sandy beach 5. a stretch of 6. engineering; project 7. in a planned way 8. jointly 9. imitate; copy; model oneself on 10. blindly

jiànlì 建立 build; establish; set up; found 〔~宾〕〈名〉~合作❶关系；~外交关系❷；~了一个新国家；~了深厚的友谊❸；~了邦交❹；~了信心❺；~了不朽的功勋❻；~一所现代化工厂；~了一个天文台❼；~一所疗养院❽；~了新家庭〔~补〕〈可〉感情❾总~不起来〔状~〕积极❿~；是什么时候~的?即将~；重新~；相继⓫~；陆续⓬~；跟邻国⓭~；早已~

1. cooperation; collaboration 2. diplomatic relations 3. profound friendship 4. relations between two countries; diplomatic relations 5. faith 6. immortal feat 7. (astronomical) observatory 8. sanatorium; convalescent hospital 9. attachment; affection; love 10. actively 11. one after another; in succession 12. one after another 13. neighbouring country

jiànshè 建设 build; construct 〔~宾〕〈名〉~国家；~了很多工厂；~了一座大桥〔~补〕〈趋〉按❶目前❷的速度❸~下去，半年就能竣工❹了〈程〉~得真快；~得很漂亮；~得真慢〈可〉今年还~不了(liǎo)；半年之内~得完吗?~得好~不好?〔状~〕大规模❺(地)~；努力~；积极❻~；到处~；一座一座地~；一连~；必须~

1. according to 2. actual 3. speed; velocity 4. be completed 5. on a large scale 6. actively; with all one's energy

jiànyì 建议 propose; suggest; recommend 〔~宾〕〈主-谓〉~他把发音学好；~我休养❶一个时期；~你买一点儿尝尝❷；~你用我的办法试一试〔状~〕向他~；多次~；积极❸~；一再❹~

1. recuperate; convalesce 2. taste 3. actively 4. again and again; repeatedly

jiànzhù 建筑 build; construct; erect 〔~宾〕〈名〉~桥梁❶；~

铁路❷；～高楼大厦❸〔～补〕〈结〉不能把自己的幸福❹～在别人的痛苦❺上〈趋〉这座大桥是哪一年～起来的？〈程〉堡垒❻～得很结实❼；花房❽～得很别致❾；房子～得很有特色❿；宫殿⓫～得非常雄伟⓬；机场⓭大厅⓮～得非常庄严⓯〈可〉～得了(liǎo)吗？～得起来～不起来？〔状～〕按照⓰图纸⓱～；仿照⓲古代⓳的样式⓴～

1. bridge 2. railway 3. high buildings and large mansions 4. happiness 5. pain; suffering 6. fortress; stronghold 7. strong; solid 8. greenhouse 9. unique; unconventional 10. characteristic; distinguishing feature 11. palace 12. grand; magnificent 13. airport 14. hall 15. solemn; dignified 16. according to 17. blueprint; drawing 18. imitate; follow 19. ancient times; antiquity 20. style; type; form

jiàn 溅 splash; spatter 〔～宾〕〈名〉汽车从泥坑❶里开过去，～了我一裤子泥；在实验室❷解剖❸兔子的时候～了我一身血；～了一墙墨水；～了很多油点儿❹〔～补〕〈结〉泥都～在裤腿❺上了；～到鞋上了；衣服上～满了油点儿〈趋〉水都～出来了；海水冲击❻悬崖❼～起无数白色的浪花〈程〉端❽起杯子来倒❾啤酒❿，不然⓫会～得哪儿都是的；～得真利害；～得浑身上下⓬都是；～得到处都是〔状～〕向四外⓭

～；四处～；一下子～出来了

1. mud pit; mire 2. laboratory 3. dissect 4. oil stains 5. trouser legs 6. lash 7. precipice; cliff 8. hold sth. level with both hands 9. pour 10. beer 11. otherwise 12. every part of the body 13. in all directions; everywhere

jiǎng 讲 ① speak; say; tell ≅ 说〔～宾〕〈名〉～英语；～故事；～几句话；～一点意见；他爱～真话；从来不～假话；给他～个情❶；～了一套大道理❷；这个人真不～理❸；一点儿也不～信用❹；～～事情的经过❺；～～当时❻的情况；～～电影的内容❼〔～补〕〈结〉～错了；～快了我听不懂；把事情经过～仔细❽一些〈趋〉他很直爽❾～出来的话往往❿不好听；别把这件丑事⓫～出去；～过来～过去(～来～去)还是那一点事〈程〉她英语～得很流利⓬；话～得有道理⓭；～得合情合理⓮；～得不对；故事～得非常生动⓯；话～得非常有分寸⓰；～得十分鼓舞⓱人；～得很精彩⓲〈可〉他气得连话都～不出来了；我的遭遇⓳三天也～不完；她太狡辩⓴了，我可～不过她；你看了那么多小说，怎么连一个完整的㉑故事都～不上来啊？〈时〉在会上他一个人就～了半个多小时；她～了半天法语，我一句也没听懂〈量〉～过一次；～过两回；～了好几遍〔状～〕详细地㉒～；在礼堂㉓～；一遍一遍地～；反复～；大胆地㉔～；从

一开始就～；从各方面㉕～；深入地㉖～；广泛地㉗～

1. intercede; plead for sb. **2.** general principle; major principle **3.** be unreasonable **4.** trustworthiness; credit **5.** the course of the incident **6.** then; at that time **7.** content **8.** in detail **9.** frank; candid; straight forward **10.** often; frequently **11.** scandal **12.** fluent **13.** reasonable **14.** fair and reasonable **15.** vivid; lively **16.** proper limits for speech or action **17.** inspire; hearten **18.** brilliant; splendid; wonderful **19.** misfortune; hard luck **20.** quibble; indulge in sophistry **21.** complete **22.** in detail **23.** assembly hall; auditorium **24.** boldly **25.** from every respect **26.** deeply; thoroughly **27.** extensively

② explain; make clear; interpret ≅ 解释；阐述〔**～宾**〕〈名〉～课；～语法；～开会的目的❶；～～这个词的用法；～～要求❷；～～注意事项❸；到国外去～学❹〔**～补**〕〈结〉～到第几课了？课～到什么时候结束❺？一定要把课～好；语法没～清楚；用法～错了；要求没～全；讲着讲着就～乱❻了；～明自己的观点❼；～清道理〈趋〉把想法～出来就好了；懂了就别老～来～去的了〈程〉～得真清楚；～得不错；～得有声有色❽；～得有条有理❾；～得特别细致❿；～得深入浅出⓫；～得重点突出⓬；～得很有系统⓭；～得糊里糊涂⓮；～得乱七八糟⓯；～得谁都没听懂；～得头头是道⓰〈可〉这个问题我可～不清楚；我～不了(liǎo) 古文⓱；都不注意听，他有点儿～不下去了；这个词的用法我～不出来；两节课～得完这么多内容吗？〈时〉一连⓲～了四节课；开会的目的就～了十分钟；发音需要～三个星期〈量〉请你再给我～一下儿；～了好几遍他都不懂〔**状～**〕好～；不好～；真难～；反复⓳～；单独⓴～；清清楚楚地～；深入浅出地～；在教室～；给学生～；对大家～；一遍一遍地㉑～；盲目地㉒～

1. purpose; aim **2.** demand; requirement **3.** matters needing attention; points for attention **4.** give lectures; discourse on an academic subject **5.** end; finish **6.** in confusion; in a mess **7.** point of view **8.** vivid and dramatic **9.** reasonable **10.** careful; meticulous; in detail **11.** explain the profound in simple terms **12.** the focal points stand out **13.** systematic **14.** confused; muddled; bewildered **15.** in a mess; in a muddle; at sixes and sevens **16.** clear and logical **17.** prose written in the classical literary style **18.** in a row; in succession; running **19.** repeatedly; over and over again **20.** alone; by oneself; on one's own **21.** repeatedly; over and over again **22.** blindly

③ discuss; negotiate ≅ 商量〔**～宾**〕〈名〉～价钱❶；～条件❷

〔～补〕〈结〉把条件～好了再做；～清楚了再做〈可〉价钱总～不好，所以不能成交❸〈时〉～了半天条件〈量〉好好～一下儿〔状～〕从不～；先～

1. price **2.** condition **3.** strike a bargain; conclude a transaction

④ be particular about; pay attention to ≃ 讲求〔～宾〕〈名〉～科学；～卫生❶；～排场❷；～礼貌❸；～效率❹；～实际❺；～面子❻；～情理❼〈动〉～团结❽；～吃；～穿〔状～〕非常～；一向❾～吃

1. hygiene; health **2.** ostentation and extravagance **3.** courtesy; politeness; manners **4.** efficiency **5.** practice; reality **6.** face; reputation; prestige **7.** reason; sense **8.** unity **9.** consistently; all along

⑤ as to; as far as sth. is concerned ≃ 论〔～宾〕〈名〉～质量❶还是这种好；～速度❷谁也比不上他；～技术❸他不如你；～风格❹他比你高；～干劲❺；～报酬❻；～水平❼他还不算低〔状～〕只～；不～

1. quality **2.** speed **3.** technique; technology **4.** style **5.** vigour; enthusiasm; drive **6.** reward; remuneration **7.** level

jiǎngjiu 讲究

be particular about; pay attention to; stress; strive for〔～宾〕〈名〉我们要～卫生❶；～实际❷；～实际❸效果❹；～内容❺；～形式❻；～样子❼；～排场❽；～面子❾；～谈吐❿；～礼貌⓫；～服饰⓬；～风度⓭；～装潢⓮；～营养⓯〈动〉～吃喝；～打扮⓰；～享受⓱；～请客送礼；～交往⓲〔～补〕〈趋〉现在连他都～起来了〈程〉～极了；～得很〈时〉他～过一个时期，现在不讲究了；这个人～了一辈子，到老了还那么讲究〈量〉我也～一次；～一下儿〔状～〕对摆设⓳很～；十分～；一向⓴～；一直㉑～；一点儿也不～；专门㉒～；只～

1. hygiene **2.** practice; reality **3.** practical; realistic **4.** effect; result **5.** content **6.** form **7.** style; type; form **8.** ostentation and extravagance **9.** face; reputation **10.** style of conversation **11.** politeness; courtesy **12.** dress and personal adornment; dress **13.** demeanour; bearing **14.** decoration; mounting **15.** nutrition; nourishment **16.** dress; apparel **17.** enjoyment; treat **18.** association; contact **19.** furnishings; ornaments **20.** consistently; all along **21.** always; all along **22.** specially

jiàng 降

fall; drop; lower ≃ 落 ↔升〔～宾〕〈名〉天气预报❶说明天要～温❷；很多家具❸都～价❹了；因他在工作中失职❺，所以被～了一级；～旗❻；吃点药❼～血压❽；人工～水❾；人工～雨❿；气温⓫～了两度⓬；～

了三块钱〔~补〕〈结〉气温一下子~到了零下⓭三度；血压~猛⓮了，人受不了⓯(liǎo)〈趋〉体温⓰~下来了没有？血压已经~下来了；白血球⓱数儿~下来了没有？洪水⓲已经~下去了〈程〉飞机~得很快；血压~得太猛了；电梯⓳~得太快了，心脏⓴受不了(liǎo)〈可〉打了针㉑高烧㉒还~不下去〔状~〕猛~；突然㉓~；一下子~；急剧地㉔~；慢慢~；逐渐㉕~

1. weather forecast **2.** drop in temperature **3.** furniture **4.** reduce the price **5.** neglect one's duty **6.** lower a flag **7.** take medicine **8.** blood pressure **9.** artificial precipitation **10.** artificial rainfall **11.** air temperature **12.** degree **13.** below zero **14.** abruptly; suddenly **15.** cannot bear; be unable to endure **16.** (body) temperature **17.** white blood cell **18.** flood **19.** lift; elevator **20.** the heart **21.** give or have an injection **22.** high fever **23.** all at once; suddenly **24.** rapidly **25.** gradually

jiàngdī 降低 reduce; cut down; drop; lower↔升高；提高〔主~〕〈名〉价格❶~了；成本❷~了；生活费❸~了；标准❹~了；温度❺~了；血压❻~了〔~宾〕〈名〉~成本；~物价❼；~要求❽〔状~〕一再~；一点一点地~；突然~；必须~成本；一下子~；只好~

1. price **2.** cost **3.** cost of living **4.** standard; level **5.** temperature **6.** blood pressure **7.** commodity prices **8.** demand

jiāo 交 ① hand over; deliver 〔~宾〕〈名〉~练习(本)；~作业❶；~卷子❷；~稿❸；~钱；~报费❹；这幢大楼什么时候~工❺；~货❻；~帐❼；~税❽；事情办得这么糟糕❾，回去没法~差❿〔~补〕〈结〉本子都~齐⓫了吗？电费⓬~晚上；帐⓭~清⓮了；她~给我一封信；这事~给她去办⓯吧；钱~到他手里，就靠不住⓰了〈趋〉名单⓱~上去了；卷子都~上来了吧？快~出武器⓲来；这些材料⓳看完以后，请立即⓴~回来〈程〉她每次作业~得最快；~得最早〈可〉~不起那么多钱；题太多，一个小时~不了(liǎo)卷了；他催㉑我交稿子，我~不出来〈时〉报费我一气儿㉒~了半年的〈量〉每月~一次水电费〔状~〕亲手㉓~给他；当面㉔~；一手~钱，一手~货㉕；临时㉖~；按规定时间㉗~卷子；今天不~练习本；早点儿~；一次~清；分几次㉘~

1. school assignment **2.** examination paper **3.** manuscript **4.** subscription for a newspaper **5.** (hand over) a completed project **6.** delivery **7.** (hand over) the accounts **8.** pay a tax **9.** too bad **10.** report to the leadership after accomplishing a task **11.** complete **12.** charge for electricity **13.**

account 14. clear up 15. handle; do 16. unreliable 17. name list 18. weapon; arms 19. material 20. at once 21. urge; hurry; press 22. at a stretch; at one go; without a break 23. personally 24. in sb.'s presence 25. straighten things out face to face 26. temporarily 27. according to the fixed time 28. in several times

② make friends with; associate with ≃ 结交〔~宾〕〈名〉~朋友〔~补〕〈结〉~错朋友了〈趋〉这样不三不四的朋友❶别再跟他~下去了〈程〉他交朋友~得很广❷；~得不慎重❸〈可〉这种人~不了(liǎo)好朋友；~不着(zháo)理想的❹女朋友〈时〉跟她~了几个月朋友；~过一个时期，后来意见不合❺就不常来往❻了〈量〉~过一次〔状~〕有选择地❼~；慎重地❽~；不要跟不三不四的人~；诚心诚意地❾~；别乱❿朋友〔习用〕~白卷⓫

1. a friend of dubious (shady) character 2. extensive; wide-ranging; widespread 3. imprudent 4. ideal 5. divergence of opinion 6. dealings; contact; intercourse 7. by selection 8. prudently 9. earnestly and sincerely 10. indiscreetly 11. hand in a blank examination paper

jiāodài 交代 ① hand over〔~宾〕〈名〉他调❶走了，走以前需要把工作好好~~；她正在向来接班❷的人~工作〔~补〕〈结〉目前的工作进展❸情况我已经向他~清楚了；把一切该办的事都~完了〈程〉~得清清楚楚❹；~得一清二楚❺；~得干净利落❻；~得拖泥带水❼〈时〉~了一个多月；~了不少时候；~了半天〈量〉好好~一下儿；~过一次〔状~〕一一~清楚；一五一十地❽~；清清楚楚地~；整整❾~了三天；一连~了好几天；一上午就~完了；陆陆续续地❿~；一遍又一遍地⓫~；详详细细地⓬~

1. transfer 2. take one's turn on duty; take over from 3. progress; development 4. 5. clearly 6. neat; efficient 7. sloppily 8. systematically and in full detail 9. whole 10. one after another; in succession 11. again and again 12. in detail

② explain; make clear; brief; tell 〔~宾〕〈名〉~政策❶；~任务❷；~剧中人❸的去向❹；~发言❺顺序❻〔~补〕〈结〉~完了吗？~清楚了；~给我的任务，我一定按时❼完成❽〈程〉事情的来龙去脉❾~得很清楚；~得乱七八糟❿的〈可〉连这么一点小事都~不清楚；~不好〈时〉~了半天，大家还是没听懂〈量〉结果如何，你一定要来信~一下儿；这件事我必须当面⓫跟他~一下儿；~过两次了；~了好几遍〔状~〕向我们~；对大家~；一遍一遍地~；反复⓬~；再三⓭~；一再⓮~；罗罗唆唆地⓯~；在会

上～；当面～；不容易～清楚；认真⓰～；从头至尾⓱～

1. policy **2.** task **3.** characters in a play or opera **4.** the direction in which sb. has gone **5.** speak; make a statement or speech **6.** sequence; order **7.** on time; on schedule **8.** accomplish; fulfil **9.** origin and development; cause and effect **10.** at sixes and sevens; in a mess **11.** in sb.'s presence; to sb.'s face **12. 13. 14.** over and over again; time and again; repeatedly **15.** wordily **16.** seriously; conscientiously **17.** from beginning to end

③ confess 〔**～宾**〕〈名〉～问题；～罪行❶；～犯罪❷经过❸；～犯罪事实❹；～作案❺的时间和地点；～了赃物❻存放❼的地方；～了杀人的目的❽和动机❾；～了当时❿的想法⓫〈动〉～一共作过几次案；～是从哪儿偷来的东西〔**～补**〕〈结〉把罪行～清楚；没～明白；必须～彻底⓬；～完一件事，再～另一件〈趋〉已经把幕后操纵者⓭～出来了；～出来的口供⓮前后不一致⓯；还需要⓰继续～下去〈程〉犯罪的时间、地点都～得不对；～得与事实不符⓱；～得吞吞吐吐⓲；～得含含糊糊⓳；～得不合情理⓴；～得很痛快㉑；～得很干脆㉒〈可〉这样说，～得过去吗；不管怎么说，这样做是～不过去的〈时〉～了半天，也没交代清楚〈量〉他的口供～一次，推翻㉓一次；你昨天晚上到底㉔到哪儿去了？必须好好～一下儿；这个问题他前后～了几次，都不一样〔**状～**〕彻底㉕～；全部～；基本上～了；老老实实㉖地～；一五一十地㉗～；从头～；没有遗漏地㉘～出来了；主动㉙～；痛痛快快地～；只好～；被迫㉚

1. crime; guilt **2.** commit a crime **3.** the course **4.** fact **5.** commit a crime **6.** stolen goods **7.** deposit **8.** objective; purpose **9.** intention; motive **10.** at that time **11.** what one has in mind **12.** thoroughly **13.** wirepuller behind the scenes **14.** a statement made by accused under examination **15.** no consistency **16.** need **17.** be inconsistent with the facts **18.** hesitate in speech; hem and haw **19.** ambiguous; vague **20.** unreasonable; irrational **21.** simply and directly **22.** clear-cut; straightforward **23.** cancel; repudiate; reverse **24.** after all; in the end **25.** thoroughly; entirely **26.** honestly **27.** systematically and in full details **28.** without omission **29.** on one's own initiative **30.** be forced to

jiāohuàn 交换 exchange; swop

〔**主～**〕〈名〉位置❶～了；场地❷～了〔**～宾**〕〈名〉～礼物；～订婚❸戒指❹；运动员❺～了队旗❻以后，才开始比赛；～纪念品❼；～图书资料❽；～相片❾作为纪念❿；～座位⓫；～俘虏⓬；～战俘⓭；～人质⓮；～留学生；～

看法；运动员～场地；～意见⓯；～了一下儿眼光⓰〔～补〕〈量〉～过一次；～一下儿意见〔状～〕互相⓱～；定期⓲～；诚恳地⓳～意见；随时⓴～意见；多次～

1. seat; place **2.** site; place; space **3.** be engaged (to be married) **4.** (finger) ring **5.** sportsman **6.** team pennant **7.** souvenir **8.** books and reference materials **9.** photo **10.** as a souvenir **11.** seat **12.** prisoners **13.** prisoners of war **14.** hostage **15.** opinion **16.** eyesight; vision **17.** each other; mutually **18.** at regular intervals **19.** sincerely **20.** at any time

jiāoliú 交流 exchange; interflow

≃交换〔**主～**〕〈名〉文化❶～；学术❷～；思想❸～；技术❹～；经验❺～〔**～宾**〕〈名〉～思想；～经验〔**～补**〕〈量〉～过几次；需要好好～一下儿〔**状～**〕认真～；广泛❻～；定期❼～；在会上～；积极地❽～；主动❾～

1. culture **2.** learning; science **3.** thought; idea **4.** technology; skill; technique **5.** experience **6.** widely; on a large scale **7.** regularly **8.** actively **9.** on one's own initiative

jiāoshè 交涉 negotiate; make representations

〔**～宾**〕〈名〉～果园❶由谁管理❷的问题；～租用❸场地❹事宜❺；～贷款❻问题〔**～补**〕〈结〉关于派车去接❼的问题，已经～好了；关于住宿❽问题，有些～晚了；不知这件棘手❾的事还要～到什么时候；等～完了再说；事情～成了没有？〈趋〉关于交货日期❿还要继续⓫～下去；这件事～起来可不容易了〈程〉～得很顺利；～得心烦⓬〈可〉她经验⓭太少，这件事她可～不了(liǎo)；关于应由谁来赔偿损失⓮的问题，总也～不好；怎么交涉也～不成；我跟他～不下去了，换个人试试吧〈时〉～了很长时间；～了半年多；～了半天〈量〉和公司⓯方面～一下儿；～过好几次了〔**状～**〕跟有关部门⓰～；和负责人⓱～；关于这个问题已经～过了；不需要⓲再～了；正在～；口头⓳～；屡次～；再三～；一次次地～；重新～；无法～；真难～；不容易～；好容易⓴～成了；直接㉑～

1. orchard **2.** run; administer **3.** hire; rent; take on lease **4.** site **5.** arrangements; matters concerned **6.** provide (grant) a loan **7.** meet; welcome **8.** stay; put up; get accommodation **9.** knotty; troublesome; thorny **10.** date of delivery **11.** continue **12.** be vexed **13.** experience **14.** compensate for a loss **15.** company **16.** the department concerned **17.** person in charge **18.** not necessary **19.** orally **20.** with much difficulty **21.** directly

jiāo 浇 pour liquid on; sprinkle water on

〔**～宾**〕〈名〉～花；～

菜；给花～一点儿水；～地❶〔**～补**〕〈结〉雨把衣服都～湿❷了；全身都被雨水～透❸了；她让雨给～病了；再浇就把花～死了；水浇得太多，把叶子都～黄了；～上点儿汁❹，就更好吃了〈趋〉瓢泼大雨❺从头顶❻上～下来了；他把一盆水都～到花盆❼里去了〈程〉～得不够；～得很及时❽；～得太多，都流出来了；～得哪儿都是水〈可〉一下午～不完这么多地；一个人浇这么一大片地，真～不过来〈时〉每天晚饭后～一会儿花〈量〉～过两遍了；猛～了一阵❾〔**状～**〕用橡皮管❿～树；用喷壶⓫～花；多～点儿水；按时⓬～；隔一天⓭一～；不要没事就～；想起来才～；别再～了；从上往下～；被雨～；哗哗地⓮～

1. irrigate the fields **2.** wet **3.** fully; thoroughly **4.** juice **5.** heavy rain; torrential rain; downpour **6.** the crown of the head **7.** flowerpot **8.** timely; in time **9.** a period of time; a spell **10.** rubber tube **11.** watering can; sprinkling can **12.** on time; on schedule **13.** every other day **14.** pouring down

jiāo 教 teach; instruct↔学〔**～宾**〕〈名〉他父亲在中学～书；～唱歌；～英语；～绘画；～小提琴；～夜校❶；～哪本书？～第三册❷；～初中❸；～高中❹；他～学生游泳；～小孩子识字❺；师傅❻～徒弟❼裁❽衣服〈代〉他～我开汽车；我～他做饭；你～～我织毛衣❾吧〔**～补**〕〈结〉把他～会了；～好语文课不是一件容易的事儿；这几本书他都～熟❿了；这本数学还有一个月就～完了；她～给我们一套记⓫生词的方法；～到这学期结束，黄老师就不教了；直到把你们都～会为止〈趋〉总算⓬把这门课～下来了；我不想再～下去了；这班学生程度不齐⓭，～起来真费劲⓮；那位教授～出不少好学生〈程〉地理⓯老师～得真好；那个老师～得很有经验⓰；～得深入浅出⓱〈可〉我～不了(liǎo)英语；这学期～不完了；他在那儿～不下去了，想换个地方；内容⓲越来越深，她有点儿～不下来了；这门课我～不出兴趣⓳来〈时〉～过两个学期；～了一辈子⓴中学〈量〉有时间请你～一下儿我；刚～一次，他就会了〔**状～**〕认真地～；从年轻时㉑就～；在教室～；互相～；好容易㉒才～会；从下学期～；耐心地㉓～；无保留地㉔～；从头～起；用哪本教材㉕～？临时㉖～；长期～；连续㉗～；一共～了三个班；同时～

1. night school **2.** volume **3.** secondary school **4.** pre-university **5.** learn to read **6.** master **7.** apprentice **8.** cut out (cloth, paper, etc.) **9.** knit a sweater **10.** familiar **11.** remember; memorize **12.** at long last; finally **13.** not of the same level **14.** need great effort **15.** geography **16.** experience **17.** explain the profound in simple terms **18.**

jiāo — jiǎo 197

content 19. interest 20. the whole life 21. from one's young days 22. with great difficulty 23. patiently 24. without reservation 25. teaching material 26. temporarily 27. in a row; running

jiáo 嚼 chew; masticate 〔~宾〕〈名〉~馒头❶; ~花生米; ~糖; ~肉〔~补〕〈结〉~烂❷了再咽❸; ~细❹点儿; ~碎❺点儿〈可〉没牙~不了(liǎo)了; 太硬❻了不动〈时〉~了半天也没嚼烂; 多~一会儿好消化❼〈量〉~一下儿试试嚼得动嚼不动〔状~〕多~~; 吃东西要细~慢咽❽〔习用〕贪多~不烂❾

1. steamed bread 2. (of food) mashed 3. swallow 4. small 5. fragmentary; broken 6. hard 7. easy to digest 8. chew carefully and swallow slowly 9. bite off more than one can chew

jiǎo 绞 twist; entangle ≅ 绕; 扭 〔主~〕〈名〉两股❶线❷~在一起了; 两根铁丝❸~在一起了; 两件事情❹~在一起了〔~补〕〈结〉~在一起; ~到一块儿了; 为这件事~尽了脑汁; 线~成一团❻了〈量〉~过一次, 好容易❼才择开〔状~〕一下子就~; 又~; 容易~

1. strand; ply 2. thread 3. two pieces of iron wire 4. affair; matter 5. rack one's brains 6. a roundish mass; a ball 7. with much difficulty 8. disentangle

jiǎozhèng 矫正 correct; put right; rectify ≅ 改正, 纠正 〔~宾〕〈名〉~姿势❶; ~发音❷; ~牙齿; ~视力❸; ~口吃❹的毛病; ~偏差❺; ~错误〔~补〕〈结〉视力~到什么程度❻? 姿势~好了〈趋〉口吃的毛病好容易~过来了; 牙齿长得不齐❼, 岁数❽小一点儿~起来还比较容易〈可〉挤眉弄眼❾的毛病如果不注意, 时间长了就~不了(liǎo)了〈时〉~了一年, 才矫正好; ~了半天也没矫正好〈量〉~一下儿看看吧; 早~一下儿就好了〔状~〕及时~; 逐渐~; 慢慢~; 尽快❿~; 用种种方法~; 一点一点地~; 总算~; 为他~

1. posture; gesture 2. pronunciation 3. sight; vision 4. stutter; stammer 5. deviation; error 6. degree 7. irregular 8. age; years 9. make eyes; wink 10. as soon as possible

jiǎo 搅 ① stir; mix ≅ 搅拌 〔~宾〕〈名〉把牛奶里的糖~一~; 用筷子❶~鸡蛋〔~补〕〈结〉把咖啡❷里的糖~匀❸; ~碎❹; 把粥❺~凉❻了再给孩子喝; 把糖~化❼了再喝; 同时听了这么多事情, 把我脑子都~糊涂❽了; ~乱❾了〈程〉~得真匀; ~得不匀; 把我~得糊里糊涂; ~得乱七八糟❿〈可〉~得匀吗? 怎么还~不化啊? 〈时〉~了半天才把糖~化; 多~一会儿〈量〉多~几下儿; ~了一阵⓫〔状~〕用筷

子～；用勺子⓬～；多～一会儿；一个劲儿地⓭～；不停地⓮～；水泥⓯、石子放在搅拌机⓰里一阵猛～

1. chopsticks **2.** coffee **3.** even; welldivided **4.** smashed **5.** gruel (made of rice; millet, etc.); porridge **6.** cool; cold **7.** melt; dissolve **8.** confused; bewildered **9.** confused; in a turmoil **10.** in a state of disorder **11.** a period of time **12.** ladle **13.** persistently; continuously **14.** ceaselessly; incessantly **15.** cement **16.** mixer

② disturb; annoy ≌ 打扰〔**～宾**〕〈代〉她正看书，别去～她〔**～补**〕〈程〉拖拉机❶的噪音❷～得我睡不着(zháo)觉；孩子们～得我一个字也看不下去〔**状～**〕别～；总～；时常～

1. tractor **2.** noise

jiào 叫 ① cry; shout ≌ 喊〔**主～**〕〈名〉鸟～；狗～；鸡～；蟋蟀❶；青蛙～；知了❷(liǎo)～；汽笛❸～；他大～一声〔**～宾**〕〈形〉拍手～好❹；从不❺～苦❻；总～穷❼；没～过累❽；不要～屈❾〔**～补**〕〈趋〉驴❿～出来的声音真难听⓫；布谷鸟⓬又～起来了〈程〉青蛙～得真吵人；远处狗～得真吓⓭人；百灵鸟⓮～得非常好听〈时〉昨天远处的狗～了一夜，不知发生了什么事〈量〉～了几声；～了一阵〔**状～**〕大声～；不停地～；扯着脖子⓯～；声嘶力竭地⓰～；直着嗓子⓱～；乱嚷乱～⓲；怪声怪气地⓳～；一声接着一声地～；拼命地⓴～；凄凄惨惨地㉑～

1. **2.** cicada **3.** steam whistle; siren **4.** shout "bravo!" **5.** never **6.** complain of hardship or suffering **7.** complain of poverty **8.** complain of being tired **9.** complain of being wronged **10.** donkey **11.** unpleasant to hear **12.** cuckoo **13.** frighten; scare; intimidate **14.** lark **15.** shout at the top of one's voice **16.** shout oneself hoarse **17.** shout with the utmost strength **18.** in an uproar **19.** in a strange voice or affected manner **20.** with all one's might; desperately **21.** sadly

② call; greet ≌ 招呼；呼唤〔**～宾**〕〈名〉这孩子不爱～人；谁～门呢？～孩子回家〈代〉楼下有人～你；你放心❶地睡吧，到时候我～你；你在～谁呢？他每天～我起床〔**～补**〕〈结〉要不是你把我～醒❷我就迟到了；嗓子❸都快～哑❹了，你都没听见；上了四节课，喉咙❺都～干了；把大家都～到这儿来有事商量❻〈趋〉叫了那么半天才把他～出来；正在开会，他就被人～出去了；把小王～上来看电视吧；同学把她～下楼去了；外边多冷啊，快把他们～进来吧；我在外边等了有三个小时，医生才把我～进去；把孩子们都～过来吧，我们要放幻灯❼了；妈妈把孩子～回家去吃饭了；别把她～过去啊，我们这儿还有事呢〈程〉～得真响❽；声

音~得真大；他每天叫我~得真准时❾〈可〉怎么也~不应❿，里边可能没人；门怎么~不开啊? 孩子贪玩⓫怎么叫也~不回来；好多年没见了，连他的名字我都~不上来了；这种水果的名字我一时⓬~不上来了〈时〉~了半天才听见〈量〉~了好几声；~了三四次；~了好几遍〔**状~**〕在楼下~；大声~；小声~；一声接着一声地~；连声⓭~；按时⓮~；准时⓯~；孩子有礼貌地⓰~；大大方方地⓱~；勉强⓲~

1. rest assured 2. awake 3. throat 4. hoarse; husky 5. throat 6. consult; discuss 7. show slides 8. loud; resounding 9. punctual; on time 10. no answer 11. have an insatiable desire for playing 12. for a short while; temporarily 13. in succession; one after another 14. on time 15. punctually 16. politely 17. naturally 18. reluctantly; grudgingly

③ hire; order ≌ 雇；定购〔**~宾**〕〈名〉~了一桌菜；~了一碗鸡蛋汤〔**~补**〕〈可〉天晚了，~不着(zháo)车了吧；~不起❶一桌菜〔**状~**〕临时❷~了一辆车；预先❸~了一桌菜；给他~了一碗面；到哪儿去~? 用电话~

1. cannot afford 2. provisionally; at the time when sth. happens 3. in advance; beforehand

④ ask; order ≌ 使；命令〔**~宾**〕〈代〉~他明天去；~她别说话；医生~我做深呼吸❶；他~我替他寄❷一封信；他不~我去〔**状~**〕一再~；不~；只好~

1. deep breathing 2. post; mail

⑤ name; call ≌ 叫做〔**~宾**〕〈名〉~什么名字? 她~李英；冰川❶也~冰河；马铃薯❷俗名❸~土豆儿；我~她阿姨❹；天文学家❺把银河❻围绕❼成的空间❽~银河系❾〔**状~**〕以前~；现在~；原来❿~；后来~；一直⓫~〔**习用**〕~座儿⓬

1. glacier 2. potato 3. popular name 4. auntie 5. astronomer 6. the Milky Way 7. round; around 8. space 9. the Milky Way system 10. originally 11. always; all the time 12. draw a large audience; appeal to the audience

jiàoliàng 较量 measure one's strength with; have a contest〔**~补**〕〈时〉~了半天不分胜负❶〈量〉~一下儿球艺❷；~一番〔**状~**〕跟他~；好好~~；多次~；第一次~；反复❸~；再三❹~；双方❺~

1. tie; draw; come out even 2. skills in playing a ball game 3. 4. repeatedly; over and over again 5. the two parties; both sides

jiē 结 bear (fruit); form (seed)〔**~宾**〕〈名〉树上~了不少葡萄❶〔**~补**〕〈结〉树上~满了柿子❷；〈趋〉这种土壤❸~出来的苹果不好吃；这棵小树也开始~起果子

来了〔程〕今年的枣❹~得真多；~得不多；~得比较少〈可〉这块地~不出好梨❺来；~不了(liǎo)多少〔状~〕年年~；隔一年❻一~；满满地~

1. grape 2. persimmon 3. soil 4. jujube; date 5. pear 6. every other year

jiē 接 ① connect; join; put together ≌ 连接〔~宾〕〈名〉 ~电线❶；~线头❷；我~着他说；跑得我上气不~下气❸的〔~补〕〈结〉把电线~好；把摔断❹的骨头❺~上了；电话又~错了〈趋〉请把电话~到厂长❻办公室来（去）；把电线~进来；~进去；~出来；~出去；我说完以后他马上~下去说〈程〉她接线头~得又快又好；~得太慢了〈可〉电线太短~不上；电话老~不通❼；~不过来；~不过去〈量〉请给我一下儿校长办公室❽〔状~〕暗中❾~；直接❿~到

1. electric wire 2. broken threads 3. gasp for breath; be out of breath 4. broken 5. bone 6. factory director 7. the line's dead 8. principal's office 9. in secret; secretly 10. directly

② catch; take hold of〔~宾〕〈名〉~球；~过他手里的东西；~他给我的钥匙❶〔~补〕〈结〉~住；没~好；掉了；没~住〈趋〉5号运动员❷~过球来就投篮❸〈程〉接球~得很准❹；~得很好〈可〉你站在那么远扔❺，我可

不着(zháo)；你~得住吗？我可要扔了；她手破❻了~不了(liǎo)球了〈时〉~了半天也没接着(zháo)〈量〉~一次，掉一次；~了好几回❼都没接住〔状~〕双手~；一只手~；他发❽的球真难~；跳❾着~；赶快❿~

1. key 2. sportsman; athlete; player 3. shoot (a basket) 4. accurate; exact 5. throw; toss; cast 6. cut 7. several times 8. serve a ball 9. jump 10. hasten to; lose no time

③ receive ≌ 收到〔~宾〕〈名〉~了一封信；刚才我替你~了一个电话；~了一个电报；~到一个通知❶〔~补〕〈结〉录取通知❷她已经~到了；昨天~到一封信；今天又~到一封信；电话不是找我的，我~错了；你~着(zháo)我给你寄的书了吗？〈可〉这星期不知道~得着(zháo)~不着(zháo)家信❸？今天早上发❹的电报，晚上她~得到吗？〈量〉我下午要出去办点事❺，如果有我的电话，请你替我~一下儿；我替他~过好几次挂号信❻了〔状~〕替我~；给他~；高兴地~；一连❼~；好久没~；每星期都~；顺便❽~了一个电话

1. notice 2. admission notice 3. letter from home 4. send 5. handle affairs 6. registered letter 7. in a row; in succession 8. conveniently; in passing

④ meet; welcome ≌ 迎接 ↔ 送〔~宾〕〈名〉到大门口去~朋友；

去幼儿园❶~孩子；回老家❷去~母亲；去医院~病人；在机场❸~外宾❹；~外地的新生❺〈代〉~他出院❻；~我回家〔~补〕〈结〉孩子已经让他爸爸~走了；今天~早了；~晚了；~着(zháo)了吗？昨天~到你妹妹了没有？〈趋〉把朋友~到家里来住吧；孩子很早就从托儿所❼~回来了；~回去了；把他父亲从乡下❽~出来了；~出去了〈程〉~得很及时❾；~得正好❿；~得不算太早〈可〉他们又是行李⓫，又是孩子的，我一个人可~不回来；~不了(liǎo)〈时〉昨天去车站接人，~了半天也没接来〈量〉~了两次都没接着(zháo)〔状~〕在火车站~；在飞机场~；在码头⓬~；全家一起~；一个人单独⓭~；替别人~；热情地⓮~；高高兴兴地⓯~；勉强⓰~；礼节性地⓱~；一次一次地~；按约定的时间⓲~；亲自⓳~；特地⓴~

1. kindergarten 2. native place; old home 3. airport 4. foreign guest 5. new student 6. leave hospital 7. nursery; crèche 8. countryside 9. in time 10. just in time 11. luggage 12. wharf; quay; pier 13. alone; by oneself 14. warmly 15. with pleasure; happily 16. reluctantly; grudgingly 17. by courtesy 18. according to the fixed time 19. personally 20. specially; for a special purpose

⑤ take over ≅ 接替〔~宾〕〈名〉~工作；~班❶；~了一个艰巨的❷任务❸〔~补〕〈结〉今天接班~晚了；~早了；工作(任务)~多了怕完不成〈趋〉老黄调走❹了，他的工作老张都~过来了；~过去了〈程〉工作~得太多了；班~得太早了；~得比较晚；工作~得很顺利❺〈可〉他的工作我~不了(liǎo)〔状~〕按时❻~；高高兴兴地❼~；大胆地❽~；主动❾~

1. take one's turn on duty 2. arduous 3. task 4. be transferred 5. successfully; without a hitch 6. on time 7. happily 8. boldly 9. on one's own initiative

jiēchù 接触 come into contact with; get in touch with〔~宾〕〈名〉~社会❶；别~传染病人❷；~各界人士❸；没~过书本；~群众❹；到现在还没~正题❺呢；没~过这门科学〔~补〕〈结〉~多了互相就了解❻了〈趋〉他们两个人频繁地❼~起来了〈程〉~得很多；~得很频繁；~得很广❽；~得太窄❾〈可〉~不到要害❿〈时〉我们曾~过一段时间，~了不少时候〈量〉好好~一下儿；~过几次〔状~〕你平时⓫常跟谁~？广泛⓬~；普遍⓭~；初次⓮~；不容易~；无法⓯~；别~；逐渐⓰~；频繁地~；千方百计地⓱~；经常~；和……~

1. society 2. infectious; patient 3. all walks of life 4. people; masses 5. subject of a talk or essay 6. understanding 7. frequently 8.

wide; vast; extensive **9.** narrow **10.** vital part; crucial point **11.** at ordinary times; in normal times **12.** widely; extensively **13.** widely; universally **14.** the first time **15.** helplessly **16.** gradually **17.** by every possible means

jiēshòu 接受 accept〔**～宾**〕〈名〉～意见❶；～任务❷；～了这些条件❸；～某种思想❹；～礼物❺〈动〉～考验❻；～教训❼；～批评❽；～建议❾；～邀请❿；～阳光的照射⓫〔**～补**〕〈趋〉他～起意见来不够虚心⓬；把这项艰巨的⓭任务～下来了〈程〉意见～得很快；～得很痛快⓮；～得有点勉强⓯〈可〉这里被树叶挡⓰得～不着(zháo)阳光了；他送给你的礼物可～不得〈量〉～过他一次邀请〔**状～**〕虚心～；容易～；不易～；认真⓱～；诚恳地⓲～；勉强～；被他～了；好容易才～

1. opinion; view; suggestion **2.** task **3.** condition; term; requirement **4.** certain idea **5.** present; gift **6.** test **7.** lesson **8.** criticism **9.** suggestion **10.** invitation **11.** sunshine **12.** less modestly **13.** hard; difficult **14.** very happy; joyful **15.** reluctant **16.** block **17.** seriously; conscientiously **18.** sincerely

jiē 揭 take off; uncover; lift; expose〔**～宾**〕〈名〉～盖子❶；～疮疤❷；～墙纸❸〔**～补**〕〈结〉～穿❹敌人的阴谋❺；～开锅盖❻；～掉墙纸；别把那张好看的邮票❼～破了；～开事实真相❽；～开宇宙❾的秘密❿；～开序幕⓫；～开了历史的⓬新篇章⓭〈趋〉把墙上的画～下来；把布告栏⓮上的旧通知⓯～下去吧〈程〉问题～得很彻底⓰；旧广告～得不太干净〈可〉粘得⓱太结实⓲～不下来了；～不开了；～不掉了〈时〉～了好半天才揭开〔**状～**〕赶快～；往下～；一层一层地⓳～；轻轻地⓴～

1. lid; cover (take the lid off sth.; bring sth. into the open) **2.** scar (pull the scab right off his sore) **3.** wall paper **4.** expose; lay bare; show up **5.** plot; scheme; conspiracy **6.** cover for a pan **7.** stamp **8.** the truth of the matter **9.** universe **10.** secret **11.** prelude; prologue **12.** historical **13.** new page **14.** notice board **15.** notice **16.** thorough **17.** glue; stick; paste **18.** strong; solid **19.** layer after layer **20.** lightly; gently

jiēlù 揭露 expose; unmask; ferret out ≃揭穿〔**～宾**〕〈名〉～敌人❶的阴谋诡计❷；～事物❸的矛盾❹；～封建❺阶级❻的罪恶❼；～事实的真相；～他的假面具❽；～宇宙❾的秘密❿〔**～补**〕〈结〉～出了；～尽⓫了；～无遗⓬；～彻底⓭了〈趋〉他的罪行⓮我们还要继续⓯～下去；他～起自己的缺点⓰来，毫不留情⓱〈程〉～得淋漓尽致⓲；～得很彻底⓳；～得无处藏身⓴；敌人的丑恶㉑嘴脸㉒已被我们～得非常清楚了；～得不够〈可〉他的罪恶～不尽；～不完；工作中的矛盾～得出来～不出来？〈时〉～了半天也没揭露出来〈量〉非把他彻底～一下儿不可；～了他一次以后，他老实㉓多了〔状～〕彻底～；狠狠地㉔～；无情地㉕～；必须～

1. enemy **2.** schemes and intrigues **3.** thing **4.** contradiction **5.** feudal **6.** class **7.** evil **8.** false mask **9.** universe **10.** secret **11. 12. 13.** completely; utterly; nothing left **14.** crime **15.** continue; go on **16.** shortcomings; defect; weakness **17.** without showing mercy **18.** make a most telling exposure; thoroughly **19.** utterly **20.** no place to hide **21.** ugly **22.** look; features; countenance **23.** well-behaved **24.** ruthlessly **25.** mercilessly

jiéhé 结合 combine; unite; integrate; link 〔**～宾**〕〈名〉～实际情况❶；～他们的问题；～个人兴趣❷；～现有的水平❸去考虑❹；～已掌握❺的材料❻进行研究〔**～补**〕〈结〉没～上；没～紧；没～好〈趋〉～起来〈程〉两件事情～得很紧；～得不紧❼；理论❽和实际❾～得很好；～得不太好；～得不密切❿〈可〉这两件事～不紧；～不上；～不了(liǎo)；～不起来；～不上去；～不到一起〈量〉好好～一下儿；～过一次〔**状～**〕理论与实践相～；互相～；跟自己的爱好⓫～；在这个问题上～；努力～；不易～；很难～；适当地⓬～

1. real situation **2.** personal interest **3.** present level **4.** consider **5.** have in hand; control **6.** material **7.** loose **8.** theory **9.** reality; practice **10.** not close **11.** hobby; interest **12.** properly; suitably

jiéshù 结束 end; finish; conclude; wind up; close〔**主～**〕〈名〉会议～了；学期～了；宴会❶还没～；事情就这样～了；生命就要～了；水利工程❷～了；好日子已经～了；一次不愉快❸的会见❹终于～了〈动〉比赛❺～了；战争～了；考试即将❻～；测验❼～了没有？选举❽～了；评选❾～了；会谈❿～了；谈判⓫～了；讨论⓬～了；争论⓭～了；辩论⓮～了；参观～了；访问～了；旅行～了；学习～了；罢工⓯～了〔**～宾**〕〈名〉～了这场谈话；～战争状态⓰；～了自己年轻的生命；～了这次访问〔**～补**〕〈程〉事情～得很快；～得非常干脆⓱；～得太慢了；会议～得非常准时⓲〈可〉这些工作一时⓳还～不了(liǎo)〈时〉已经～一个多星期了；～多少时候了？刚～一个多小时〔**状～**〕刚～；胜利地⓴～了；在欢呼声中㉑～；在乐曲声中㉒～；已经～；就要～；即将～；尚未㉓～；终于～了；早已～了；三天前就～了；彻底㉔～了

1. banquet; feast; dinner party **2.** water conservancy project **3.** unhappy 4. interview 5. match 6. be about to 7. test 8. election 9. choose through public appraisal 10. talks 11. negotiation 12. discussion 13. dispute; controversy 14. argument 15. strike 16. state of war 17. clear cut; straightforward 18. on time 19. offhand; for the moment 20. triumphantly; successfully 21. by acclamation 22. in music 23. not yet 24. entirely; thoroughly

jiě 解 ① untie; undo ≌ 打开↔系; 扎; 绑〔～宾〕〈名〉～扣儿❶; ～衣服; ～鞋带❷; ～腰带❸; ～绳子❹〔～补〕〈结〉扣儿～开了〈趋〉把腰带～下来〈程〉～得真快; ～得很慢〈可〉孩子自己～得(liǎo)鞋带吗?〈时〉～了五分钟都没解开❺〈量〉请你帮我～一下儿〔状～〕别着急❻, 慢慢～; 耐心地❼～

1. unbutton 2. shoelace 3. waistband; belt; girdle 4. rope 5. untie; undo 6. don't worry 7. patiently

② remove; dispel; get rid of; relieve ≌ 解除〔～宾〕〈名〉饭后吃点水果可以～油腻❶; 这种药❷可以～毒❸; ～疑心❹〈动〉他被～雇❺了; 我去了以后才给他～了围❻; ～饿; ～渴; 看小说❼不是为了～闷❽〈形〉今天晚饭吃一只烤鸭❾～～馋❿; ～困⓫; 吃酸梨⓬可以～恶心⓭〔～补〕〈趋〉下午睡了一觉才～过困来〈可〉吃糖～得了(liǎo)油腻吗?〈量〉～一下儿〔状～〕非常～闷

1. greasy food; oily food 2. medicine 3. poison 4. dispel doubts 5. discharge; dismiss 6. save sb. from embarrassment 7. novel 8. divert oneself (from boredom) 9. roast duck 10. satisfy a craving for good food 11. sleepy 12. sour pear 13. remove vomiting

jiěchú 解除 remove; relieve; get rid of 〔主～〕〈名〉空袭警报❶～了; 经济危机❷～了〈形〉危险❸～了〔～宾〕〈名〉～顾虑❹; ～负担❺; ～职务❻; ～合同❼; ～禁令❽; ～武装❾; ～警报; ～婚约❿; ～灾难⓫〈形〉～痛苦⓬; ～烦恼⓭〔～补〕〈可〉～得了(liǎo)～不了(liǎo)?〔状～〕彻底⓮～; 尚未⓯～; 只好～; 不得不⓰～; 突然⓱～; 已经～了

1. air raid alarm 2. economic crisis 3. danger 4. worry; misgiving 5. burden 6. post; duties; job 7. contract 8. prohibition; ban 9. disarm 10. engagement; marriage contract 11. calamity 12. pain; suffering 13. vexation 14. thoroughly 15. not yet 16. have to 17. suddenly

jiěfàng 解放 liberate; emancipate 〔～宾〕〈名〉～思想❶; ～人类❷〔～补〕〈趋〉从封建思想的桎梏❸下～出来了〔状～〕彻底❹

~;被~;从痛苦中❺~;和平❻~;用武力❼~;是哪一年~的?

1. (emancipate) the mind; free oneself from old ideas 2. all mankind 3. the shackles of the feudal ideology 4. thoroughly; completely 5. from sufferings 6. peacefully 7. resort to force; by force

jiějué 解决 solve; resolve; settle

〔主~〕〈名〉问题~了;困难❶~了;矛盾❷~了;危机❸~了〔~宾〕〈名〉~争端❹;~纠纷❺;~问题;~困难;~疑难❻;~矛盾〔~补〕〈结〉~彻底了吗?没~好;~完了一个问题又来了一个问题〈趋〉他~起家庭纠纷来,很有办法❼〈程〉~得很好;~得很顺利❽;~得合情合理❾;~得很快;~得非常迅速❿〈可〉他什么问题也~不了(liǎo);他们之间的矛盾自己不~,谁也~不好;困难一大堆⓫,简直⓬~不完〈时〉~了半天也没解决好〈量〉矛盾要好好~一下儿;~过好几次了〔状~〕很快地~;彻底~;完全~;全部~;逐渐~;慢慢~;迟迟⓭不~;一个一个地~;逐个⓮~;用什么方法~?按照原来⓯的办法~;统统⓰~了

1. difficulty 2. contradiction 3. crisis 4. dispute; conflict 5. dispute; issue 6. difficulty; knot 7. way; means; measures 8. smooth; without a hitch 9. fair and reasonable 10. quick; fast; rapid 11. a heap of 12. simply; at all 13. tardily 14. one by one 15. original 16. all; completely

jiěsàn 解散 dismiss; dissolve; disband

〔主~〕〈名〉团体❶~了;队伍❷~了;小组~了;学校~了;公司❸~了〔~宾〕〈名〉~议会❹;~了一个非法❺的组织❻〔状~〕马上~;立即~;被迫❼~;彻底❽~;即将❾~;再次~;全部❿~;统统⓫~;必须~

1. organization; group 2. troops 3. company; firm 4. parliament 5. illegal; illicit; unlawful 6. organization 7. be forced to; reluctantly 8. thoroughly; utterly 9. soon 10. 11. all; completely

jiěshè 解释 explain; expound; interpret

〔~宾〕〈名〉~词义❶;~法律条文❷;~原因❸;~难题❹;~一种现象❺;~误会❻;~这段话的意思;~语法❼;~难词;~词的含义❽;~概念❾〔~补〕〈结〉词义~错了;误会~开了〈趋〉请不要再~下去了;他~起来总是自己有道理❿〈程〉语法~得很清楚;概念~得不对〈可〉这些问题我~不了(liǎo);雨后天空出彩虹⓫的现象你~得了(liǎo)吗?这个句子的含义我~不出来;~不清楚;这首诗他能~得好吗?〈时〉这条规定⓬~了半天也没解释清楚〈量〉这件事我跟他~过好几遍了;请你再~一下儿;~过

两次了〔**状～**〕重点⓭～；逐字逐句地⓮～；从头至尾地⓯～；我们之间的误会彻底～开了；三番五次地⓰～；再三⓱～；一再⓲～；反复⓳～；极力⓴～；不必多～；详细㉑～；一遍一遍地㉒～

1. the meaning of a word **2.** legal provisions **3.** cause **4.** difficult problem **5.** phenomena **6.** misunderstanding **7.** grammar **8.** meaning; implication **9.** concept; notion **10.** reasonable **11.** rainbow **12.** provision **13.** emphatically **14.** word by word and sentence by sentence **15.** from beginning to end **16. 17. 18. 19.** again and again; time and again; repeatedly **20.** do one's utmost **21.** in detail **22.** one after another

jièshào 介绍

introduce; present〔**～宾**〕〈名〉～朋友；～对象❶；～一本书；～一个地方；～剧情❷；～主要情节❸；～人物❹；～小说内容❺；～一个人的事迹❻；～一种烹调方法❼；～一种新产品❽；～机器❾的使用❿方法；～保养⓫方法〔**～补**〕〈结〉使用方法～清楚了吗？把我的好朋友～给小黄〈趋〉把你的好经验⓬～出来吧〈程〉～得很详细⓭；～得很好；～得不错；～得非常简要⓮〈可〉～不出什么经验来；一个小时～得完吗？〈时〉～了一个半小时；～了十分钟〈量〉～一次；给我们两个人～一下儿吧〔**状～**〕给他们～；向他～；互相～；自我⓯～；热情地⓰～；详尽地⓱～；一一～；逐个儿⓲～；一见面就～；在会上～经验；由我～；系统地⓳～；扼要地⓴～

1. a partner in marriage **2.** plot of a play **3.** essential plot **4.** person in literature; character **5.** the content of a novel **6.** deed; achievement **7.** cookery; cusine **8.** new product **9.** machine **10.** use **11.** maintain; keep in good repair **12.** experience **13.** in detail **14.** brief and to the point **15.** (introduce) oneself **16.** warmly **17.** exhaustively; thoroughly; **18.** one by one **19.** systematically **20.** briefly

jiè 戒

give up; stop〔**～宾**〕〈名〉～烟；～酒〔**～补**〕〈程〉他烟～得很快；酒～得不彻底❶〈可〉没有决心❷～不了(liǎo)烟；他抽烟喝酒的毛病老～不掉〈时〉烟～了些日子，现在又抽上了；烟酒～了一年多了〈量〉～过三次都没戒成〔**状～**〕自愿❸～；勉强❹～；主动❺～；自觉地❻～；一次一次地～

1. not thorough **2.** resolution; determination **3.** voluntarily; without being compelled **4.** reluctantly; grudgingly **5.** on one's own accord **6.** willingly; of one's own free will

jiè 借

① borrow ≃借入 ↔ 还〔**～宾**〕〈名〉我跟他～了五块钱；

我在图书馆~了一本小说；把你的铅笔~小李用一用；跟他~钳子❶用用；~地方开会〔~补〕〈结〉~到一本语法书；~给我十块钱〈趋〉东西都~来了；书从图书馆~出来了〈程〉一次不能~得太多〈可〉当月❷的杂志❸~不出来，只能到那儿去看；钱一时❹~不到，东西~不全❺；没有工作证❻~不出来〈时〉~了那么长时间还没还(huán)❼呢；~了三个多月了〈量〉~过一次；一下儿用用，行吗?〔**状**~〕跟朋友~；从图书馆~；我给(替)他~；长期~；暂时❽~；不好意思❾~；难~

1. pincers; pliers 2. that very month 3. periodical 4. for the moment 5. not complete 6. employee's card 7. return; give back 8. temporarily 9. reluctant to; embarrassed; shy; be diffident

② lend ≅ 借出↔还〔~宾〕〈名〉~钱；~书；~东西；~工具❶；~地方，~人〔~补〕〈结〉我~给他一把伞；我有好几本书都~丢❷了；我的录音机❸叫人~走了；你也借他也借都~乱❹了〈趋〉东西~来~去都借丢了；你的照相机❺~出去了吗?〈可〉他说现在~不了(liǎo)我那么多钱〈时〉他~了两个多月了才还给我〈量〉~给他好多次了〔**状**~〕他跟我~；不好意思❻不~；长期~；暂时❼~；勉强❽~；经常~；慷慨地❾~

1. tool; instrument 2. lost 3. (tape) recorder 4. in disorder 5. camera 6. reluctant to; embarrassed; shy; be diffident 7. temporarily 8. reluctantly 9. generously; liberally

③ make use of; take advantage of (an opportunity, etc.) ≅ 凭借；依靠〔~宾〕〈名〉~(着)月光看书对眼睛有害❶；~出差❷的机会❸看了看朋友；火~风力❹越烧越旺❺

1. harmful 2. be away on official business 3. occasion; opportunity 4. wind-force 5. briskly

jìn 进 ① enter; come or go into; get into ↔ 出〔~宾〕〈名〉~了屋子就把窗打开了；~厂当❶学徒❷；火车~站了；球~篮了；~监狱❸了〔~补〕〈趋〉请~来吧；门窗打开以后，新鲜空气很快就~来了；你先~去，我买点水果再去；叫孩子快~来吧，外边多冷啊；门刮❹开了，从外边~来一股冷风❺；里边正在录音❻呢，先别~去〈可〉里边没地方了，~不去了；大门那么窄❼大衣柜❽~不去吧?连门口都坐满了人，我哪儿~得去啊；〔**状**~〕赶快~；匆匆忙忙地❾~来了；突然~；蹑手蹑脚地❿~；一阵风似的⓫~来了

1. work as 2. apprentice 3. prison 4. blow 5. cold wind 6. sound recording 7. narrow 8. clothes closet; wardrobe 9. in a hurry; hastily 10. gingerly; on tiptoe 11. as a gust of wind

② advance; move forward; move ahead ↔ 退〔~宾〕〈名〉这句话的意思❶比那一句更~了一层❷；~一个(棋)子儿❸；忘了~位❹了，所以数儿不对；事情的发展❺又向前~了一步〔状~〕更~一步；向前~

1. the meaning of this sentence 2. further implications 3. chessman; piece 4. carry (a number, as in adding) 5. the development of events

③ receive 〔~宾〕〈名〉~了一批❶货❷；~款❸；这两年学校没~人〔~补〕〈结〉货~齐❹了；人多了〈程〉货~得不全❺〔状~〕多~点；每年~；最近~

1. (a measure word) batch; lot 2. goods 3. fund; a sum of money 4. complete 5. not complete

jìnxíng 进行 be in progress; be underway; go on; carry on; carry out; conduct 〔主~〕〈名〉会议正在~；讨论正在~；比赛❶正在~〔~宾〕〈动〉~建设；~教育；~争论❷；~实地考察❸；~讨论；~工作；~科学实验❹；~亲切的谈话❺；~研究；~宣传；~观察❻；~调查❼；~锻炼❽；~比赛；~访问〔~补〕〈结〉~到最后；刚~到这一步〈趋〉讨论还要~下去〈程〉工作~得很快；~得非常顺利；工作~得怎么样了？~得很好〈可〉试验~不下去了；第一册书这学期~得完~不完？这学期恐怕连第十四课

都~不到〈时〉比赛~了两个多小时；~了一个多星期〔状~〕正在~；顺利地❾~；如何~？对这种病~研究；照样❿~；千方百计~

1. match 2. dispute; debate 3. on-the-spot investigation 4. scientific experiment 5. cordial conversation 6. observation 7. investigation 8. have physical training; take exercise 9. smoothly; successfully 10. as before

jìnzhǐ 禁止 prohibit; ban; forbid 〔~宾〕〈名〉~车辆❶通行❷〈动〉~吸烟；~大声喧哗❸；~随地吐痰❹；~乱扔❺果皮；~乱扔废纸❻；~在此停车❼；~堆放❽东西；~张贴布告❾；~随处倒(dào)垃圾；~赌博❿；〔~补〕〈可〉~得了(liǎo)~不了(liǎo)？~得住~不住？〔状~〕严格⓫~；一律⓬~；绝对⓭~；一直~

1. vehicle; car 2. pass through (traffic) 3. confused noise; hubbub; uproar 4. spit; expectorate 5. throw about 6. waste paper 7. no parking here 8. pile up; stack 9. put up a notice 10. gambling 11. strictly 12. all; without exception 13. absolutely

jīngguò 经过 pass; go through; undergo ≅ 通过〔~宾〕〈名〉你为什么~家门口都不进来坐坐啊！这块岩石❶~了漫长的岁月❷，

已经风化❸了；要~好几道手续❹吗？〈动〉~实践❺才证明❻这个理论是正确的；~这个打击❼，他的精神大不如前❽了；~这次挫折❾，他对人生更明白了；~详细❿调查⓫才弄清了是非⓬；~仔细讨论，我们才理解了这个词的含义⓭和用法；~充分⓮准备，所以课讲得不错；~不断地学习，他进步很快；~这么一解释，我才明白，不~研究怎么能作决定呢？~讨论，得出了一致⓯的结论⓰〈主-谓〉~老师辅导⓱，他有了很大的进步；这些条文⓲都是~政府批准⓳的；~大家分析⓴，才找到了发生火灾㉑的真正原因〔~补〕〈时〉~了一年零㉒四个月的考察㉓；~了很多年〈量〉我每天~你家两次〔状~〕从这里~；迅速地~；来回㉔都~；不断地~

1. rock 2. during the long years; over the years 3. weather away 4. procedures (several steps in the process) 5. practice 6. prove; testify 7. blow; strike; attack 8. not as good as before 9. setback; reverse 10. detailed 11. investigation 12. thrash out the rights and wrongs; distinguish right from wrong 13. meaning; implication 14. full; ample 15. identical; unanimous 16. conclusion 17. coach 18. article; clause 19. ratify; approve 20. analyse 21. fire (as a disaster) 22. odd 23. inspection; investigation 24. back and forth

jīngshòu 经受 undergo; experience; withstand; stand; weather
〔~宾〕〈动〉~考验❶；~磨练❷~了各种严刑拷打❸；~锻炼❹〔~补〕〈结〉什么恶劣的坏境❺他都能~住〈可〉小树苗~不住暴风雨的摧残❻；~不住精神上❼的打击❽；~不住寒风❾的袭击❿；~不住严峻的考验⓫；再也~不起刺激⓬了；~不了(liǎo)折磨⓭〈时〉~过很长一段时间的考验〈量〉~了一次锻炼〔状~〕在困难的坏境中~；一直~着；痛苦地~⓮

1. test; trial 2. temper onself; steel oneself 3. subject sb. to severe torture 4. have physical training 5. adverse circumstances 6. wreck; destroy; devastate 7. on one's mind 8. hit; blow; strike 9. cold wind 10. be hit 11. severe (rigorous) test 12. provocation; upset 13. torment; physical or mental suffering 14. bitterly

jīngtōng 精通 | be proficient in; have a good command of; master
〔~宾〕〈名〉~木工手艺❶；~英语；~两门外语；~业务❷〔~补〕〈程〉~得很；~极了〔状~〕特别~；非常~；十分~

1. carpentry 2. vocational work; professional work

jìng 敬 offer politely
〔~宾〕〈名〉~客人一杯酒；~一杯茶〔~补〕〈结〉~上一杯酒〔状~〕诚心

诚意地❶~；给他~；双手~你一杯茶

1. earnestly and sincerely

jiūchán 纠缠 get entangled; be in a tangle 〔~宾〕〈名〉~人；孩子总~着母亲〔~补〕〈结〉被事情~住了；他又~上我了；不要把这两件事~在一起〈趋〉~起人来，可烦了；你再~下去，我就不客气了〈程〉~得真利害；被他~得烦死了〈可〉问题总~不清❶〈时〉他~了半天才走；~了好长时间〈量〉~过我好几次了〔状~〕别跟他~；被他~；死死地❷~着我；一直❸~着我

1. too tangled up to unravel 2. stubbornly 3. always; all the time

jiūzhèng 纠正 correct; put right; redress ≅ 矫正；改正〔~宾〕〈名〉~错误；~发音；~不正之风❶；~恶习❷；~骄傲自满❸的情绪❹〔~补〕〈结〉~晚了，坏习惯已经养成❺了；~到改正来为止〈趋〉终于把随地吐痰❻的习惯❼~过来了；学外语开始不注意发音，以后~起来就困难了；这种不正之风还需要继续~下去〈程〉~得很及时❽；~得不彻底；~得比较晚了〈可〉口吃❾的毛病怎么也~不过来了；~不了(liǎo)了，还~得动吗？〈时〉~了好长时间才把那个孩子的坏毛病改过来〈量〉一天~好几次，就是改不过来〔状~〕及时；严格❿~；

反复⓫~；一次一次地~；不容易~；很难~；完全~过来了；已经~过来了；不断~；彻底⓬~；认真⓭~；必须~；马上~

1. unhealthy tendency 2. bad habit 3. conceited and arrogant 4. morale; feeling; mood 5. cultivate 6. spit 7. habit 8. in time 9. stammer 10. strictly 11. repeatedly 12. thoroughly; entirely 13. seriously; conscientiously

jiū 揪 ① hold tight; seize ≅ 抓住〔~宾〕〈名〉~头发；~辫子❶；~(着)衣服；~耳朵；~(着)衣领❷；~(着)绳子❸的一头儿别撒手❹〔~补〕〈结〉~住小偷别让他跑了；把头发都~掉了〈趋〉以前学生在课堂上捣乱❺，老师就把他~出去；把流氓❻从地上~起来拉走了〈程〉~得很紧❼；~得真疼❽〈可〉马跑得太快了，我可~不住〈量〉~了一下儿我的辫子；~了一下儿我的衣服〔状~〕一把~住；紧紧地~着；使劲❾~着；用力~着；不松劲地❿~着；被他~住了，死死地~着；两只手~着

1. plait; braid; pigtail 2. collar 3. rope 4. let go one's hold 5. create a disturbance; make trouble 6. rogue; hooligan 7. tight 8. ache; pain; sore 9. with all one's effort 10. without relaxing one's efforts

② pull; draw ≅ 拉〔~宾〕〈名〉~着绳子❶；从针眼❷里往外~线头❸〔~补〕〈结〉绳子被他~断了

❹〈趋〉我把他~来了，大家罚他请客吧；我看不见，你帮我把线头从针眼里~出来吧；~过来了吗？〈程〉耳朵让他~得真疼❺；绳子~得太紧❻了〈可〉这种线真结实❼用手都~不断〈时〉线头~了半天也没揪过来〈量〉用力~一下儿〔状~〕怎么也~不出来；狠狠地❽~着他的耳朵；从楼下把他~上来了

1. rope 2. the eye of the needle 3. the end of a thread 4. snapped 5. ache; pain; sore 6. tight 7. solid 8. firmly; resolutely

jiù 救

① rescue; save ↔ 害 〔~宾〕〈名〉~人啊！ ~~孩子吧；~了一条命❶；~国〔~补〕〈结〉把受伤的人~活❷了〈趋〉掉在水里的孩子被~上来了；被~起来了；把她从火坑❸里~出来了；经过多方面努力，总算❹把那个失足❺青年~过来了；他从火海❻里~出几个人来；5号运动员❼~起来一个险❽球〈程〉~得很及时〈可〉伤❾太重❿~不活了；我~不了(liǎo)你；这个球怎么救也~不起来了；溺水⓫的时间太长了，恐怕~不过来了〈时〉~了半天才救活〈量〉~一下儿我吧；~过他一次〔状~〕主动~；想方设法⓬~；赶紧~；无法~；已经~；急着⓭~；勇敢地⓮~；奋不顾身地⓯~

1. life 2. bring sb. back to life 3. pit of hell; abyss of suffering 4. at long last; finally 5. take a wrong step in life 6. a sea of fire 7. sportsman; athlete; player 8. danger; peril; risk; indefensible 9. wound; injury 10. severe; serious 11. drown 12. by every possible means; by hook or by crook 13. impatiently 14. courageously; bravely 15. completely disregarding one's own safety

② relieve; help 〔~宾〕〈名〉~火； ~灾❶ 〈形〉~急❷〔~补〕〈结〉火~晚了，东西都烧光〈时〉~了两个多小时的火；~了半天火〈量〉消防队❸来我们这儿~过两次火了〔状~〕赶快❹~；奋不顾身地❺~；一起~；勇敢地❻~

1. calamity; disaster 2. an emergency; an urgent need (help meet an urgent need) 3. fire brigade 4. as soon as possible; quickly 5. completely disregarding one's own safety 6. bravely; courageously

jǔ 举

① raise; lift; hold up 〔~宾〕〈名〉~着火把； ~着白旗❶投降❷； ~手发言❸； ~杯畅饮❹〔~补〕〈结〉把杯子~到他面前〈趋〉把手~起来；芭蕾舞男演员❺把女演员❻~起来了〈程〉~得很高；~得真费劲❼〈可〉~不动吧？ ~得了(liǎo)这么重的东西吗？你~得上去~不上去？我可~不起来〈时〉~了半天也举不动〈量〉我~过两次手，老师都没叫我回答问题；你~一下儿试试〔状

jǔ

〜)使劲❽〜；往上〜；双手〜；一只手〜；高高兴兴地〜着；勉强❾〜；简直❿〜不动；很吃力地⓫〜

1. white flag 2. surrender 3. speak; make a statement or speech 4. drink one's fill 5. ballet dancer 6. ballerina 7. make strenuous efforts 8. with all one's strength 9. reluctantly; grudgingly 10. simply; at all 11. entail strenuous effort; be a strain

② cite; enumerate ≌ 提出〔〜宾〕〈名〉〜一个例子❶；〜两件事情〔〜补〕〈结〉例子〜少了不行，得(děi)多举几个才能说清楚〈趋〉他立刻〜出一个实例❷来；她〜出来的例子都比较恰当❸；你〜起例子来总是那么生动有趣❹；老是那个例子〜过来（来）〜过去（去）的，我都听腻❺了；一个例子就够了，用不着再一下去了〈程〉例子〜得非常不合适❻；〜得很好；〜得太多了；〜得不够；〜得通俗易懂❼；例子〜得深入浅出❽〈可〉一时〜不出例子来；〜不好；你〜得出有力的证据❾吗？〈时〉〜了半天例子来说明，我才懂〈量〉那个人没〜过一次恰当的例子〔状〜〕经常〜；一时〜不出；一再〜；多〜几个

1. example 2. living example 3. proper; suitable; appropriate 4. vivid and interesting 5. be tired of listening 6. unsuitable 7. easy to understand 8. explain the profound in simple terms 9. strong evidence; convincing proof

jǔbàn 举办

conduct; hold; run〔〜宾〕〈名〉〜展览会❶；〜音乐会❷；〜舞会；〜酒会；〜文艺晚会❸；〜书法展览❹；〜学术讲座❺；〜训练班❻〔〜补〕〈量〉〜过两次〔状〕定期❼〜；为专家❽〜；热心❾〜；多次〜

1. exhibition 2. concert 3. an evening of entertainment 4. painting and calligraphy show 5. scientific course of lectures 6. training class 7. regularly 8. for experts 9. warmly; enthusiastically

jǔxíng 举行

hold (a meeting, ceremony, etc.)〔〜宾〕〈名〉〜庆祝大会❶；〜舞会；〜开幕仪式❷；〜毕业典礼❸；〜开学典礼❹；〜结婚典礼❺；〜授奖仪式❻；〜追悼会❼〈动〉〜会谈；〜谈判❽；〜乒乓球比赛；〜游行示威❾；〜罢工❿〔〜补〕〈结〉〜完了；〜过了〈程〉典礼〜得很隆重⓫；婚礼⓬〜得非常热闹⓭〈可〉没有合适的地方⓮，晚会⓯〜不了(liǎo)了〈时〉〜了三个多小时〈量〉〜过三次〔状〜〕公开⓰〜；秘密⓱〜；连续⓲〜；一连⓳〜；一共〜；经常〜；在什么地方〜？哪一天〜？再次〜

1. celebration meeting 2. opening ceremony 3. graduation (ceremony); commencement 4. the opening ceremony (of school) 5. the nuptial ceremony 6. prize-giving ceremony 7. memorial

meeting 8. negotiation 9. demonstration 10. strike 11. solemn; grand; ceremonious 12. wedding ceremony 13. lively; bustling with noise and excitement 14. suitable place 15. evening party 16. openly; publicly 17. in secret 18. 19. in succession; in a row; running

jùjué 拒绝 refuse 〔~宾〕〈代〉她~了他〈动〉~回答；~邀请❶；~了金钱的诱惑❷；~别人善意的批评❸；~了他的不合理要求❹；~参加；~讨论这个问题；在报纸上发表❺；~做那件事〔补〕〈量〉~过我一次〔状~〕坚决❻~；毅然❼~；再次~；无理❽~；斩钉截铁地~；干脆❿~；婉言⓫

1. invitation 2. temptation; seduction 3. well-meaning criticism 4. irrational demands 5. publish in a newspaper 6. resolutely 7. firmly; resolutely 8. unreasonably 9. categorically 10. straightforwardly 11. graciously; politely

jùyǒu 具有 possess; have; be provided with ≅ 有〔~宾〕〈名〉~现实意义❶；~历史意义；~深远的意义❷；~勇往直前的精神❸；~舍己为人的精神❹；~优良传统❺；~必胜的信心❻；~极强的说服力❼；~吸水❽的性能❾；~爆炸能力❿；~感人的⓫力量；~风化⓬作用；~法律效力⓭；~破坏力⓮〔状~〕必须~；一定~

1. practical significance 2. profound significance 3. the spirit of going forward courageously and fearlessly 4. the spirit of self-sacrifice 5. fine tradition 6. full confidence of victory 7. be very convincing 8. absorbtion of water 9. function 10. explosive force 11. moving 12. weathering 13. legal effect 14. destructive power

jù 锯 saw 〔~宾〕〈名〉~树；~木头；~板子❶〔~补〕〈结〉~歪❷了；~斜❸了；~长了；~短了；~薄❹了；~厚❺了；把那棵树~掉吧；~多了，不够长了；把板子~成木条；~少了，还要再锯下一点去；把板子~开〈趋〉把枯❻树枝都~下来了〈程〉~得真快；~得长短不齐❼；~得一般❽长；~得一般厚；~得很好；~得真吵❾〈可〉这把锯不快❿，木头~不下来；我手没劲⓫~不动；你~得了(liǎo)吗？他技术⓬太差，~不直⓭；我~不好〈时〉这块木头真硬⓮，~了十分钟才锯下来；~了半天，胳膊⓯都酸⓰了〔量〕~过一次；你来一下儿〔状~〕用电锯⓱~；用手锯⓲~；把锯拿直了再~；真难~；好容易⓳才~下来

1. board 2. askew; crooked; inclined 3. oblique; inclined 4. thin

5. thick 6. withered 7. not the same length 8. same as; just like 9. make a noise; disturb 10. not sharp 11. strength; energy 12. technique; skill 13. not straight 14. hard 15. arm 16. tingle; ache 17. electric saw 18. handsaw 19. with great difficulty

juān 捐 contribute; present; donate ≌ 捐献〔～宾〕〈名〉～款❶；～了不少钱；～了很多东西〔～补〕〈结〉～给国家了〈趋〉为了救济灾区居民❷，从各地～来很多东西；把稿费❸都～出去了；刚～一个星期，就这么多钱了〈量〉～过一次款〔状～〕多一点儿；为孤儿❹～；一次～了，一共～了

1. contribute money 2. provide relief to the people in a disaster area 3. author's remuneration; contribution fee 4. orphan

juǎn 卷 ① roll up〔～宾〕〈名〉～席了❶；～帘子❷；～画儿❸；～袖子❹；～头发〔～补〕〈结〉别把画～坏了; 把画～松❺点儿; 把那本杂志～紧❻点儿再寄❼走；竹帘子❽～高点儿；～低点儿; 裤子太长，～上点儿就好了; 画儿～斜❾了〈趋〉把袖子～起来吧; 把帘子～上去了〈程〉～得很松；～得很紧；～得很高；～得太低了；～得很整齐❿，～得很快〈可〉头发太短～不上；～不了(liǎo)；～不起来；～不紧〈时〉～了半天还是没卷好；～了半个小时〈量〉请你帮我把袖子～一下儿，我手上有油〔状～〕往里～；往外～；往上～；松松地⓫～；紧紧地⓬～；高高地～；再～一道

1. mat 2. screen; curtain 3. drawing 4. sleeve 5. loose; slack 6. tight 7. post; mail 8. a bamboo curtain 9. oblique; inclined 10. in good order; neat and tidy 11. loosely 12. tightly

② sweep off; carry along〔～宾〕〈名〉风～着雨点；汽车～着尘土❶〔～补〕〈结〉大风～走了我的帽子；一个大浪把小船～走了〈趋〉汽车飞驰❷而过，～起来一股尘土；一阵旋风❸把墙角❹的干树叶～起来了〔状～〕突然～；猛地❺～；一下子～；被风～

1. dust 2. speed along 3. whirlwind 4. a corner formed by two walls 5. abruptly; suddenly; violently

juē 撅 ① stick up; pout (one's lips)〔～宾〕〈名〉～着尾巴；他～着嘴坐在那里生气〔～补〕〈趋〉他一生气就把嘴～起来；老虎尾巴～起来了〈程〉嘴～得高高的〈时〉一个人坐在那儿～了半天嘴〔状～〕向上～；气得直～嘴

② break (sth. long and narrow) ≌ 折断〔～宾〕〈名〉～竹竿❶；～树枝，～粉笔❷；～甘蔗❸〔～补〕〈结〉～断❹了；把干枝❺都～掉吧；～成两截❻了；～成一段❼一段的了〈趋〉把干树枝都～下去了〈程〉～得不一般长；～得

一个长一个短〈可〉你～得动～不动？太粗❽我～不动；～不下来〈时〉～了半天还是撅不断〈量〉请你帮我～一下儿；我来～一下儿试试〔状～〕一下子～；用力～；不好～；好容易❾～断了

1. bamboo pole 2. chalk 3. sugarcane 4. snapped 5. dried branch 6. cleave sth. in two 7. section; segment; part 8. too thick 9. with great difficulty

juédìng 决定 decide; resolve; make up one's mind; determine〔～宾〕〈动〉～下星期二动身❶；～哪天出发❷？～考文科❸；～大学毕业以后考研究生❹；～回国来探亲❺；～坐飞机去；中学生运动会❻～在下月中旬❼举行❽；那位老教授～死后把自己的尸体❾献给❿医院做科研⓫用；～收他作徒弟⓬〔～补〕〈结〉这件事你～晚了；～错了〈趋〉人选⓭问题就这样～下来了〈程〉～得很快；～得很好；～得太匆忙⓮了；～得太草率⓯了；～得不够慎重⓰〈可〉买还是不买，他一时～不了(liǎo)；你一个人～得了(liǎo)～不了(liǎo)？〔状～〕赶快～；真难～；不好～；一时无法～；暂时这样～；早已～了；仍未⓱～；多想想再～；大胆⓲～；单独⓳～；盲目⓴～；突然～；只好这么～；别匆忙㉑～；草率㉒～

1. set out (on a journey) 2. set out; start off 3. liberal arts 4. postgraduate 5. visit one's family or go to visit one's relatives 6. sports meet 7. the second ten days 8. hold; take place 9. corpse; dead body 10. offer; dedicate; donate 11. scientific research 12. apprentice 13. choice of persons; person selected 14. hurried; hasty 15. careless; perfunctory; rash 16. cautious; prudent 17. not yet 18. boldly 19. alone; by oneself 20. blindly 21. in a hurry; hastily 22. carelessly; perfunctorily

juéde 觉得 ① feel〔～宾〕〈形〉～热；～累；～冷；～难受❶；一点也不～疲倦❷；～不舒服❸；～不好意思❹；～恶心❺〈主－谓〉～头晕❻；～两腿发麻❼；～浑身❽无力〔状～〕一点也不～；没～；还没～；总～；确实～；一阵阵地❾～冷

1. unwell; pain; ill 2. tired; weary 3. not comfortable 4. feel embarrassed; be ill at ease 5. feel nauseated; feel like vomiting 6. dizzy; giddy 7. have pins and needles in two legs 8. all over (the body) 9. from time to time; not regularly; by fits

② think; feel〔～宾〕〈动〉我～应该先跟他商量❶商量；～应该告诉他一声〈主－谓〉我～这个方法不错；你～这个房子怎么样？我～他情绪❷不好；～他神色不对❸〔状～〕总～；倒～；不～；真～

1. consult; discuss 2. mood; feeling; sentiments 3. look queer

K

kǎ 卡 block; check 〔~宾〕〈名〉那个坏蛋用双手~她的脖子❶〔~补〕〈结〉来往的车辆都把路~住了〈程〉他把我~得透不出气❷了〈可〉用什么办法也~不住;~不死他们〈时〉~了我们好几年〈量〉从财政❸上一下儿他们〔状~〕用手~;使劲❹~;拼命❺~;狠狠地❻~;一再~;在钱财上~;故意❼~;一下子~住了

1. neck 2. be out of breath 3. financially 4. exert all one's strength 5. with all one's might; desperately 6. firmly; resolutely 7. intentionally; on purpose

kǎ 咯 cough up ≅ 吐 〔~宾〕〈名〉~血❶;~痰❷〔~补〕〈趋〉~出血来了;鱼刺❸~出来了吗? 把痰~出来〈时〉~了一年多的血〈量〉~过一次血〔状~〕使劲❹~;用力❺~;拼命❻~;猛地❼~一~

1. blood 2. phlegm; sputum 3. fishbone 4. 5. exert all one's strength; put forth one's strength 6. with all one's might 7. vigorously; energetically; suddenly

kāi 开 ① open; open up 〔主~〕〈名〉门~了;锁❶怎么~了?〔~宾〕〈名〉~锁;~窗户;~箱子❷;~柜子❸;~抽屉❹;~幕❺了;从这儿~一条路;~矿❻;~了一条河;~山;~荒❼〔~补〕〈结〉把窗~开;领子❽~大了;门~窄❾了;路~通❿了〈趋〉稻田全部~出来了〈程〉门~得不够大〈可〉抽屉~不开了〈时〉这把锁锈⓫得很厉害,~了足足十分钟才开;门~一会儿再关〈量〉今天来的客人真多,一会儿的功夫我就~了五次门〔状~〕抽屉太紧⓬不好~;用这把钥匙⓭~;她老不~口;再~大点儿;从这儿往那儿~一条路

1. lock 2. chest; trunk 3. wardrobe 4. drawer 5. curtain (open; inaugurate) 6. mine 7. wasteland 8. collar 9. narrow 10. remove obstacles from; dredge; clear 11. rust 12. tight; close 13. key

② start; operate ≅ 发动 〔主~〕〈名〉汽车~了;轮船❶~了〔~宾〕〈名〉~飞机;~汽船;~机器;~灯;~收音机;~枪❷;~炮❸〔~补〕〈结〉轮船~走了;机器~动了;~错电钮❹了〈趋〉火车~进站了;把汽车~进来;把汽船~到对岸❺去了〈程〉飞机~得很稳❻;收音机的声音~得太

大了〈可〉机器有点儿～不动了,是不是该上油了〈量〉请～一下儿灯〔状～〕快～；慢点儿～；准时～；同时～；一齐～

1. steamer; steamship 2. gun 3. artillery 4. push button 5. the opposite bank; the other side of a river 6. steady

③ set up; run ≅ 开办〔**～宾**〕〈名〉～工厂；～了一门课；～商店；～旅馆；～银行❶；～医院；～诊疗所❷；～训练班❸；～药房❹；～照像馆❺；～个户口❻存钱❼〔**补～**〕〈结〉～在大街上～在僻静的地方❽〈趋〉净赔钱❾不想继续❿～下去了〈程〉～得太多了〈可〉经费⓫太少～不了(liǎo)；人手不够～不成；没经验⓬～不好〈时〉～了一学期汉语课；～了一段时间小吃店〈量〉～过一次〔**状～**〕在什么地方～？多～几个；同时～；两门课一起～

1. bank 2. clinic 3. training class; training course 4. drugstore; chemist's shop 5. photo studio 6. (open) an account 7. deposit money 8. secluded place 9. lose money in business transactions 10. continue 11. funds 12. experience

④ begin; start ≅ 开始〔**～宾**〕〈名〉儿号～学；～工；那个商店明天～业❶；～饭❷了！你们什么时候～课？你先～个头儿〔**～补**〕〈程〉今年开学比往年～得晚；饭～得太晚了〈可〉到时候～不了(liǎo)工怎么办？一个小时之内还～不了(liǎo)饭吧〈量〉一天～三次饭〔状～〕准时❸～；按时❹～；什么时候～？已经～了；还没～呢

1. start business 2. serve a meal 3. 4. on time; on schedule

⑤ hold (a meeting, exhibition, etc.) ≅ 举行〔**～宾**〕〈名〉～运动会❶；～联欢会❷；～舞会❸〔**～补**〕〈结〉～完会，请组长❹留❺一下；运动会～到下午五点〈趋〉下雨了，运动会还～下去吗？现在到处都～起舞会来了〈程〉会～得很成功❻；～得很有意思❼；～得很隆重❽〈可〉人来得这么少，会还～得成吗？讨论会两个小时～得完吗？雨下大了，运动会～不下去了〈时〉欢送会❾～了一下午〈量〉一年～两次运动会〔**状～**〕常～舞会；准时～大会；连续❿～；通宵达旦地⓫～

1. sports meet 2. get-together 3. dance; ball 4. group leader 5. remain 6. successful 7. interesting 8. grand; solemn 9. farewell meeting 10. successively; in succession 11. all night long

⑥ write out; make a list of ≅ 写出〔**～宾**〕〈名〉不用～收据❶了；～了一张一万元的支票❷；～药方❸〔**～补**〕〈趋〉介绍信❹早就～出来了〈程〉药方～得很清楚；发票❺～得太慢了〈可〉他不是医生，～不了(liǎo)药方〔**状～**〕马上～；给病人～；一起～

1. receipt 2. cheque; check 3. prescription 4. letter of introduction 5. invoice

⑦ open out; come loose〔主~〕〈名〉花儿~了；衣服扣儿❶~了〔~补〕〈程〉这种花儿~得最早〈时〉昙花❷~几个小时就谢了〔状~〕花儿已经~了；接连❸不断地❹~〔习用〕~快车❺；~夜车❻；~倒车❼

1. button 2. broad-leaved epiphyllum 3. on end; in a row; in succession 4. ceaselessly; incessantly 5. step on the gas; open the throttle; speed up; hurry through one's work 6. work late into the night; put in extra time at night 7. turn the clock back; turn back the wheel of history

kāifā 开发 develop; open up; exploit〔~宾〕〈名〉~煤矿❶；~油田❷；~山区❸；~自然资源❹；~水利资源❺〔~补〕〈趋〉~出来一片荒山❻〈可〉~得了(liǎo)~不了(liǎo)?〈时〉~了好多年〔状~〕大力❼~；积极❽~；努力~

1. coal mine 2. oil field 3. mountain area 4. natural resources (wealth) 5. water resources 6. barren hill 7. vigorously; energetically 8. actively, positively

kāifàng 开放 be open (to the public)〔主~〕〈名〉港口❶~了；城市❷~了；游泳池❸~了〔~宾〕〈名〉~了几个风景区❹〔~补〕〈程〉~得很早，~得比较晚〈可〉博物馆❺没修缮❻好，现在还~不了(liǎo)〈时〉~好多年了〔状~〕即将~；按时~；照常~；免费~；对外~；暂不~

1. harbour; port 2. town; city 3. swimming pool 4. scenic spot 5. museum 6. repair

kāipì 开辟 open up; start〔~宾〕〈名〉~了历史的新纪元❶；~航线❷；报纸~专栏❸；~了新时代，~了大片农场❹；~牧场❺；~通商港口❻；~了一条公路〔~补〕〈结〉~成一个市场〈趋〉新航线已经~出来了〔状~〕正式❼~；重新~；首次~；广泛❽~；努力~

1. new era 2. air or shipping line 3. special column 4. farm 5. grazing land; pasture 6. trading port 7. officially; formally 8. widely

kāishǐ 开始 begin; start↔结束〔主~〕〈名〉新学年❶~了；比赛下午四点~〔~宾〕〈名〉~了一项科学实验❷；~了新的生活〈动〉~练太极拳❸；他刚~学习写作；~报名；合同❹~生效❺；我去年才~学英语〔状~〕什么时候~？重新~；早已~；尚未❻~

1. academic year; school year 2. scientific experiment 3. a kind of

traditional Chinese shadow boxing **4.** contract **5.** become effective; go into effect **6.** not yet

kān 看 look after; take care of; tend ≅ 照顾；看管〔~宾〕〈名〉~门；~家；~仓库❶；~行李❷；~牛；~机器；~孩子；~病人；~小偷❸〔~补〕〈结〉怎么把坏蛋~跑了；警察❹暗中❺~上他了；别把牛~丢了；没把孩子~好〈程〉她看孩子~得真好；~得很有经验❻；~得很累❼〈可〉我一个人~不了(liǎo)十台机器〈时〉请你给我~一会儿家，我出去一下就回来〈量〉你给我~一下儿书包〔状~〕好好~；认真负责地❽~；日夜❾~；轮流❿~；精心地⓫~；整天~

1. warehouse **2.** luggage **3.** petty thief; pilferer **4.** police **5.** secretly **6.** experience **7.** tired **8.** seriously; conscientiously **9.** day and night **10.** by turns **11.** meticulously; with the best of care

kǎn 砍 ① cut; chop; hack 〔~宾〕〈名〉上山去~柴❶；那个罪犯❷用斧子❸~了一个人〔~补〕〈结〉把树都~倒了；把人~伤❹以后，凶手❺逃跑了；文章❻太长得(děi)~去一半儿〈趋〉把树枝~下来〈可〉斧子不快❼~不下来；木头太硬❽~不动〈时〉~了半天也没砍下来〈量〉~了好几下儿都没砍动；被坏人~了一刀〔状~〕使劲儿❾~；多~点儿柴；别在这儿~树；猛❿~

1. firewood **2.** criminal; offender **3.** axe **4.** hurt; injure **5.** murderer; assassin **6.** article; essay **7.** not sharp **8.** hard **9.** exert all one's strength; exert oneself physically **10.** fiercely; violently; vigorously

kàn 看 ① see; watch; look at ≅ 瞧〔~宾〕〈名〉~电影；~电视；~球赛；~京剧❶；~展览❷；~杂技❸；~人〔~补〕〈结〉~完电影再去买东西；你~清她长(zhǎng)得什么样儿了吗？对不起，我~错人了；人已经死了，自己~开些❹吧；~在眼里，记在心上；我~透❺他了；他的诡计❻被我~穿❼了；昨天在汽车上~见他了；你把我~成什么人了？别把人~扁❽了；不要~轻❾自己；体育老师喊："向右~齐！"〈趋〉我~出来他今天有点儿不高兴；这个电视剧没意思，我不想继续❿~下去了；她一上台我就~出她有点紧张；你功课刚作了一半，怎么就~起电视来了；他一起球赛来连饭都顾不上吃了；她以前一点也不喜欢京剧，现在也~起京剧来了〈程〉他看什么问题都~得很开；别把个人的利益⓫~得高于一切；把什么都~得那么重要〈可〉~不出来，他还会弹钢琴⓬；那个人太骄傲⓭了，总~不起别人；那种无聊⓮的电影我们都~不下去；他把那个孩子打得太利害了，我~不过去⓯又把孩子拉到我家来〈时〉昨天~了一下午展览〈量〉那个片子我~过三遍了；

一个月~了两次球赛；他偷偷地❶~了她一眼〔状~〕偷偷地~；聚精会神地❶~；左~右~也没看见一个熟人❶；翻来复去地❶~；一遍一遍地❷~；连续❹~了两场电影

1. Beijing opera 2. exhibition 3. acrobatics 4. look at the bright side of things 5. understand thoroughly; see through 6. crafty plot; cunning scheme; trick; ruse 7. see through 8. flat (don't underestimate people) 9. underestimate; look down upon 10. continue 11. personal interest 12. play the piano 13. arrogant; conceited 14. bored; senseless; silly 15. hate to see; cannot bear the sight 16. secretly; stealthily 17. with rapt attention 18. acquaintance; friend 9. over and over again; repeatedly 20. one after another 21. in succession; in a row

② read ≅ 阅读〔~宾〕〈名〉~书；~报，~小说；~文件❶；~图纸❷，~指纹❸〔~补〕〈结〉这封英文信你~懂了吗？图纸~明白了吗？指纹~清楚了没有？〈趋〉一本法文小说硬❹让我~下来了；内容虽然没意思，我还是要~下去，这两个指纹不一样，你~出来了没有？一张晚报~过来~过去，连广告❺都看完了；我~起小说来连觉都不睡了〈程〉他看书~得非常仔细❻；看小说~得废寝忘食❼〈可〉这本英文小说你~得懂~不懂？杂志❽订❾得太多

了，都~不过来了；精神❿不集中⓫，什么书也~不进去〈时〉先借我~几天，可以吗？每天~一个小时的报纸；再~一会儿就看完了〈量〉我已经~过两遍了；先~一下儿再说；把题目⓬先好好儿~一遍；多~几次⓭〔状~〕认真地~；仔细点儿⓮~？再~~；多~~；一字一句地~；一行一行地~；一篇一篇地~；一口气~完

1. documents; papers 2. blueprint 3. fingerprint 4. manage to do sth. with difficulty 5. advertisement 6. very attentive (careful) 7. (so absorbed or occupied as to) forget food and sleep 8. magazine 9. subscribe 10. spirit; mind 11. (be) absent-minded 12. subject 13. several times 14. carefully; attentively

③ call on; visit ≅ 看望〔~宾〕〈名〉我想明天去~老李；今天医院不能~病人；到宿舍去~学生〈代〉有空我来~你〔~补〕〈结〉~完了小张再去吃饭〈趋〉我先去看看，~回来再商量❶怎么办〈时〉她正在住院❷，每星期我都去~她一次；你先在这儿看看书，我去~一下儿学生，马上❸就回来〔状~〕顺便~；特意❹~；专程❺~；匆匆忙忙地❻~；经常~；偶尔❼~；隔一天❽一~

1. consult; discuss 2. be in hospital; be hospitalized 3. at once; immediately 4. specially; for a special purpose 5. special trip 6.

in a hurry 7. once in a while; occasionally 8. every other day

④ treat (a patient, or an illness) ≅ 诊治〔~**宾**〕〈名〉~病；~急诊❶；~外科❷；~眼睛；~中医❸〔~**补**〕〈结〉大夫把病给他~好了；我的病反而❹叫他~坏了〈趋〉护士❺也给人~起病来了〈程〉这个大夫~得很仔细❻；~得太马虎❼〈可〉癌❽~不好；中医~得了(liǎo)这种病吗?〈时〉~了好几年都没看好；~了两个月就全好了〈量〉张医生给我~过一次病；~一下儿试试吧〔**状**~〕认真负责地❾~；马马虎虎地❿~；在门诊⓫~；彻底⓬~一~

1. emergency call; emergency treatment 2. surgical department 3. traditional Chinese medical science 4. on the contrary 5. nurse 6. careful; attentive 7. careless 8. cancer 9. seriously; conscientiously 10. carelessly; casually 11. clinic; outpatient service 12. thoroughly

⑤ observe ≅ 观察〔~**宾**〕〈名〉~问题要全面❶；~人要~本质❷〈主-谓〉~~事情怎么发展再说❸；~~情况如何变化再作决定❹〔~**补**〕〈结〉~清形势❺；~错了方向；~准❻问题〈趋〉~出里边的问题来了没有?〈程〉形势~得很清楚；问题~得比较深刻❼〈可〉~不出问题来；~不清形势〈时〉~了半天也没看出来；~了好一会儿〈量〉好好~一下儿；~了一遍又一遍❽；~过多次〔**状**~〕仔细❾~~；从种种迹象❿~；别从表面~

1. comprehensive; overall; all-sidedly 2. essence; innate character; intrinsic quality 3. put off until some time later 4. make a decision 5. make a correct appraisal of the situation 6. accurate 7. deep; profound 8. time and again 9. carefully; attentively 10. sign; indication

⑥ think; consider ≅ 认为〔~**宾**〕〈主-谓〉我~今天不会下雨；我~他说的是真话❶；我~明天她来不了(liǎo)；你~这个办法行不行?我~他说得很有道理❷，我们可以按照❸他说的去试一试〔~**补**〕〈结〉你~错了；你没~准❹〈程〉别把什么事情都~得那么简单❺；~得那么严重❻〈可〉~得出来~不出来?~得准~不准?〔**状**~〕怎么~；大概~错了；也许~对了

1. true; real; genuine 2. reasonable 3. according to 4. accurate 5. simple 6. serious

⑦ depend on ≅ 决定〔~**宾**〕〈名〉整个比赛就~这一局了；一切都准备好了，能不能去，就~天气了〈代〉这件事能否❶成功全~了〈主-谓〉我们能不能看上这场电影，全~他买得着(zháo)买不着(zháo)票了；她学习成绩❷的好坏，完全~她用功不用功了；是否动手术❸，要~你退不退烧❹〔**状**~〕完全~；就~；只~；都~；全~

1. whether or not 2. result; achievement; success 3. perform an operation 4. bring down (allay) a fever; (of a person's temperature) come down

káng 扛 carry on the shoulder; shoulder 〔～宾〕〈名〉～(着)行李❶；～(着)一个皮箱❷；～(着)一袋粮食❸；～(着)枪❹〔～补〕〈结〉他帮我把行李～走了〈趋〉请帮我把行李～到楼上来吧；一个人就把桌子～上来了；他又把多余❺的东西～回去（回来）了；～得很吃力❻；～得特别费力❼〔可〕太重❽，他～不动；你～得了(liǎo)这包东西吗?〈时〉～了半天，肩膀❾都疼❿了〈量〉～过一次；帮他～一下吧；你～一下儿试试〔状～〕你用左肩⓫～还是用右肩～？往上～；多～一点儿；吃力地⓬～着

1. luggage 2. leather trunk; leather suitcase 3. a sack of grain 4. rifle; gun 5. superfluous; unnecessary; surplus 6. 7. entail strenuous effort; be a strain 8. too heavy 9. shoulder 10. ache; pain; sore 11. shoulder 12. strenuously

kàng 抗 ① resist; combat; fight ≅ 抵抗〔～宾〕〈名〉～灾❶；～洪❷〈动〉～冻❸〈形〉～旱❹〔～补〕〈量〉～过一次旱〔状～〕积极❺～；坚持不懈地❻～；全力以赴地❼～

1. calamity 2. flood 3. frost 4. drought 5. actively 6. unremittingly 7. go all out, spare no effort

② refuse; defy ≅ 拒绝；抗拒〔～宾〕〈名〉～税❶；～租❷〔～补〕〈量〉～过一次租〔状～〕团结一致地❸～；坚决❹～

1. taxes 2. rent 3. unite as one 4. resolutely; firmly

kǎo 考 give or take an examination, test or quiz 〔～宾〕〈名〉～大学；～文科；～理科；～外语❶；～医学院❷；～专科学校❸；～博士学位❹〈代〉～～你〔～补〕〈结〉～上大学了没有？失败了；～完了吗？～到九点半〈趋〉～出水平❺来了；你是哪一年～进大学来的？再～下去可真受不了❻(liǎo)了；他终于～进了理想❼的大学〈程〉～得很好；～得真糟糕；～得不怎么样〈可〉～得上吗？～不上怎么办？今天我准❽～不好〈时〉～了一个星期〈量〉～过两次大学；他～了我三次〔状～〕第一次～；非常难～；一次一次地～；决不～；容易～

1. foreign language 2. medical college 3. college for professional training; training school 4. doctor's degree; doctorate 5. level; standard 6. be unable to endure; cannot bear 7. ideal 8. certainly; surely

kǎochá 考查 examine; check ≅ 检查

〔~宾〕〈名〉~学生成绩❶;~教学❷进度❸;~计划❹完成的情况〔~补〕〈结〉~完了吗? ~到什么时候?〈趋〉~出一些问题;~起来很困难;无法~下去〈程〉~得很仔细❺;~得非常认真❻〈可〉~得出来吗?〈时〉~了三个多月;~了一个学期❼〈量〉需要好好一下儿;~过好多遍了;多~几次吧〔状~〕认真~;仔细~;反复❽~;全面❾~;定期❿~

1. result; achievement (students' work) 2. teaching 3. rate of progress (advance) 4. plan; project; programme 5. careful 6. very serious 7. school term 8. repeatedly; again and again 9. overall 10. regularly

kǎochá 考察 inspect; make an on-the-spot investigation

〔~宾〕〈名〉~矿藏资源❶;~水利工程❷;~沙漠❸地区❹的降雨量❺〔~补〕〈结〉~完了;~过了〈趋〉他刚从北极❻~回来〈程〉~得很仔细❼〈时〉~了一年多〈量〉一年~两次〔状~〕认真❽~;重新❾~;曾经~过;多次~;从未❿~过;实地⓫~;细心⓬~;在实践中⓭~;反复⓮~

1. mineral resources 2. irrigation works; water conservancy project (works) 3. desert 4. area; district; region 5. rainfall 6. the North Pole; the Arctic Pole 7. careful 8. seriously; conscientiously 9. again 10. never 11. on the spot 12. carefully; attentively 13. in practice 14. repeatedly; time and again; over and over again

kǎolǜ 考虑 think over; consider

〔~宾〕〈名〉~情况;~问题;~前途❶;~工作;~个人利益❷;~个人得失❸;~时间;~钱;不~名誉❹、地位❺〈动〉~去不去?~要不要〈主-谓〉~谁担任❻这个工作合适❼;~我应该采取❽什么态度❾〔~补〕〈结〉~好了告诉我一声;~不周❿〈程〉~得很仔细;~得很周到⓫;~得太马虎⓬了;~得不够〈时〉~了很长时间;让我再~一会儿;又~了好几天〈量〉~了好几遍;~过不少次了;再~一下儿吧〔状~〕正在~;仔细~;从各方面~;必须~;再三⓭~;反复⓮~;无从⓯~;多加~

1. future; prospect 2. personal interests 3. gain or loss; success and failure 4. fame; reputation 5. position; standing; place; status 6. assume the office of; hold the post of 7. suitable; appropriate; right 8. adopt; take 9. attitude 10. not thoughtful; not attentive and satisfactory 11. thoughtful 12. careless 13. 14. time and again; over and over again; repeatedly 15. having no way (of doing sth.)

kǎo 烤 bake; roast; toast〔~宾〕

〈名〉~面包；~鸭；~肉；~火❶〔~补〕〈结〉鸭子~黄❷了；衣服~干了〈趋〉~得很好吃；~得真香；~得不脆❸〈程〉~得真热；~得挺难受〈可〉~不熟❹；~不好〈时〉衣服~了半天才干；~一会儿就行了〔状~〕大火（小火／慢火／快火）~；用烤炉❺~面包；大家围着炉子❻~火；在火上~

1. fire (warm oneself by a fire) 2. become yellow 3. not crisp 4. not well-cooked 5. oven 6. around the stove

kào 靠 ① lean against; lean on ≅挨〔~宾〕〈名〉~（着）墙；~（着）树；~（着）椅子；~（着）床；孩子~（着）妈妈，我们两个人背~（着）背〔~补〕〈结〉~近点儿；把梯子~在墙上；~在枕头上；~在一起〈趋〉~过来点儿；~到他那边去〈程〉~得很紧；~得太近了〈可〉这个墙可~不得，一靠就弄一身白〈时〉~了半天；~了一会儿〈量〉往后~一下儿；~了好几次〔状~〕别~；紧紧地~；半躺半坐地~；往后~；一根大木头斜❶~在墙上；并排❷~；互相~着

1. obliquely 2. side by side

② keep to; get near; come up to〔~宾〕〈名〉船~岸❶了；~码头❷了；房子前边~山，后边~海；~马路边儿❸〔状~〕向左~；往后~；小船慢慢~岸了

1. bank 2. wharf 3. the side of the street

③ depend on; rely on〔~宾〕〈名〉不能只~一时的热情❶；~大家的智慧❷和力量；~他的工资❸维持生活❹〈代〉~他养活❺；~他帮助；学习主要~自己〈动〉~平时❻的努力〔~补〕〈结〉你可~错人了，他不行〈可〉谁也~不上，只能靠自己；这个人~得住~不住?这个消息~得住吗?〔状~〕全~；就~；必须~；主要~〔习用〕~山吃山，~水吃水❼

1. enthusiasm; zeal; warmth 2. intelligence; wisdom 3. pay; wage 4. support oneself or one's family 5. support; feed 6. at ordinary times 7. those living on a mountain live off the mountain; those living near the water live off the water

kèfú 克服 surmount overcome; conquer〔~宾〕〈名〉~学习上的困难；~张口骂人的习惯❶〔~补〕〈趋〉~起来是很不容易的〈程〉~得不错〈可〉~得了(liǎo)吗?~得了(liǎo)~不了(liǎo)〔状~〕认真❷~；努力~；逐渐❸~；完全~；彻底❹~；已经~；必须~；立即❺~

1. habit 2. seriously; conscientiously 3. gradually 4. thoroughly 5. at once; immediately

kèzhì 克制 restrain ≅ 抑制〔**～宾**〕〈名〉～着自己激动❶的感情❷〔**～补**〕〈结〉～住〈程〉～得很利害〈可〉～不住内心❸的喜悦❹；～不了(liǎo)自己的感情；～不住欢乐的眼泪❺〈时〉～了半天也没克制住〈量〉好好～一下儿自己〔**状～**〕拼命❻～；竭力❼～；尽量❽～；极力❾～；尽力❿～；无法⓫；一再⓬～

1. excite; stir; agitate **2.** emotion; feeling; sentiment **3.** heart; innermost being **4.** happiness; joy **5.** tear **6. 7.** with all one's might; for all one is worth **8.** as far as possible; to the best of one's ability **9.** do one's utmost; spare no effort **10.** do all one can; try one's best **11.** unable; incapable **12.** time and again; again and again

kè 刻 carve; engrave; cut〔**～宾**〕〈名〉～图章❶；～字；～标记；❷～剪纸❸〔**～补**〕〈结〉图章还没～好；～清楚点儿；～坏了；～错了；～完了吗？把这块象牙❹～成一条大船〈趋〉他现在给人～起图章来了〈程〉～得很好；字～得真漂亮〈可〉这块石头上～得了(liǎo)这么多字吗？我～不好；～不清楚〈量〉刚～一下儿就刻坏了；～过一次〔**状～**〕不容易～；仔细❺～；用象牙～；在核桃❻里～山水画❼

1. seal; stamp **2.** sign; mark; symbol **3.** paper-cut; scissor-cut **4.** ivory; elephant's tusk **5.** carefully **6.** walnut **7.** landscape painting

kěn 啃 gnaw; nibble ≅ 咬〔**～宾**〕〈名〉～骨头❶；～书本〔**～补**〕〈结〉老鼠把抽屉❷～坏了〈趋〉～下一块来〈可〉书的内容❸太难，～不下来〈时〉～上半年，就能初步❹掌握❺〈量〉不管怎样我要～一下儿试试〔**状～**〕使劲❻～；用力❼～；拼命❽～；不停地❾～；一点一点地～〔**习用**〕蚂蚁～骨头❿

1. bone **2.** drawer **3.** content **4.** initial; preliminary; tentative **5.** grasp; master; know well **6. 7.** exert all one's strength; exert oneself physically **8.** with all one's might; for all one is worth **9.** without cease; ceaselessly; incessantly **10.** ants gnawing at a bone — plod away at a big job bit by bit

kòngzhì 控制 control; dominate; command〔**～宾**〕〈名〉～局面❶；～形势❷；～险要❸之地❹；～感情❺；～温度❻；～人口增长❼率❽；～体重❾；～市场❿；～物价⓫〈动〉～传染病⓬的蔓延⓭；～飞机的起飞和降落〔**～补**〕〈结〉～住局势⓮〈程〉～得很好〈可〉～不住内心⓯的激动⓰；～不住满腔⓱的仇恨⓲〈量〉必须～一下儿〔**状～**〕由电子计算机⓳～；用雷达⓴～；森林㉑发

生火灾❷后，火势❷很难~；不容易~；极力❷~自己的紧张❷心情❷; 已经~; 尚未❷~; 严密❷~; 严格❷~; 牢牢❸~

1. aspect; phase; situation 2. situation 3. strategically located and difficult of access 4. place; locality 5. emotion; feeling; sentiment 6. temperature 7. population growth (increase) 8. rate 9. (body) weight 10. market 11. (commodity) prices 12. infectious disease; contagious disease 13. spread; extend 14. situation 15. heart 16. excitement 17. have one's bosom filled with 18. hatred; enmity; hostility 19. electronic calculator 20. radar 21. forest 22. fire (as a disaster; conflagration) 23. burning 24. do one's utmost; spare no effort 25. tense; intense; strained 26. state of mind; mood 27. not yet 28. tightly; closely 29. strictly; rigorously 30. firmly; safely

kòu 扣 ① button up; buckle〔~宾〕〈名〉~扣子❶; ~门〔~补〕〈结〉把扣子~上了; 把衣服~好再出去; 把门~严❷; 把扣子都~齐❸了; 扣子~错了〈趋〉把扣子都~起来了〈程〉~得很整齐❹; ~得很严〈可〉扣子坏了，~不上了; ~不紧❺了〔状~〕好~; 不好~; 真难~; 用力~

1. button 2. close; tight 3. complete 4. in good order; neat; tidy 5. not tight; not close

② deduct ≅ 扣除〔~宾〕〈名〉~工资❶; ~奖金❷; ~水电费❸; ~医药费❹; ~房租❺; ~钱〔~补〕〈结〉上个月的托儿❻费~错了; 买电视的钱怎么还没~完呢? 这个月的房租、水电费~多了吧? 〈趋〉上个月的钱~得太多了; 家具❼费~得不对了; 钱~得不算多〈程〉每月房租~不了(liǎo) 多少钱〔状~〕按月❽~钱; 多~了五毛; 少~点儿吧; 分期❾~; 一次~清

1. wages; pay 2. money award; bonus 3. charges for water and electricity 4. medical expenses (costs) 5. rent 6. child-care 7. furniture 8. by the month 9. by stages

③ detain; take into custody; arrest ≅ 扣压; 拘留〔~宾〕〈名〉~了他的驾驶执照❶; ~了一个走私犯❷〔~补〕〈结〉交通警察❸把那个违反交通规则❹的人~住了〈趋〉把小偷❺~起来了〈时〉~了很长时间; ~了不少时候〈量〉~过一次〔状~〕被警察~住了; 毫不客气地❻~了; 差一点儿~; 几乎~

1. driving license 2. smuggler 3. traffic police 4. violate traffic regulations 5. petty thief; pilferer 6. showing no mercy; giving no quarter

kū 哭 cry ↔ 笑〔~补〕〈结〉眼泪❶都快~干了; 眼睛~肿❷了; 别把眼睛~瞎❸了; 嗓子❹~哑❺

了〈趋〉~出来吧,憋❻在心里要生病的;说着说着~起来了〈程〉~得很伤心❼;~得很利害❽;~得真可怜❾;~得真烦人❿〈可〉人死,哭也~不活了〈时〉~了半天,~一会儿就不哭了;整整~了一个月〈量〉那个孩子一天~好几次;大~了一阵⓫,~了几回;~了一场〔状~〕动不动⓬就~;经常~;从来也不~;非常委屈地⓭;想起来就~;一说就~;放声大~;呜呜咽咽地⓮~;抽抽噎噎地⓯~;大声痛~⓰;边说边~;捶胸顿足地⓱~;呼天抢地地⓲~;一阵阵地⓳~;嚎啕大⓴~

1. tear 2. swelling; swollen 3. blind 4. throat 5. hoarse; husky 6. feel oppressed; suffocate 7. sad; grieved; broken-hearted 8. terrible; awful 9. pitiful; pitiable; poor 10. annoying 11. a period of time 12. easily; frequently; at every turn 13. feel wronged; nurse a grievance 14. 15. with a sob 16. be choked with tears 17. beat one's breast and stamp one's feet (in deep sorrow, etc.) 18. lament to heaven and knock one's head on earth — utter cries of anguish 19. from time to time; by fits and starts; not regularly 20. loudly

kuā 夸 praise ≅ 夸奖〔~宾〕〈名〉

~自己的孩子;~这个班的学生〈代〉这里没有人不~他好的;~他聪明❶;~他能干❷;~他有学问❸;~他老实❹;~他待人和气❺;~她懂事❻〔~补〕〈结〉把孩子~骄傲❼了〈趋〉又在人面前~起自己的孩子来了〈程〉~得过分❽了;~得过头❾了;~得比什么都好〈可〉这个孩子可~不得〔状~〕适当地❿~;当面⓫~;背地⓬~;自⓭~;互相~;故意⓮~;成天⓯~

1. intelligent; bright; clever 2. competent; able; capable 3. knowledge; learning 4. honest; frank 5. be kind with people 6. sensible; intelligent 7. arrogant; conceited 8. excessive 9. overdo; go beyond the limit 10. suitably; properly; appropriately 11. in sb.'s presence; to sb.'s face 12. behind sb.'s back; privately 13. self; oneself; one's own 14. intentionally; purposely 15. all day long

kuādà 夸大 exaggerate; overstate magnify ↔ 缩小〔~宾〕〈名〉~事实❶;~成绩❷;~自己的优点❸〔补~〕〈趋〉又~起来了〈程〉~得太利害了;~得不得了〈可〉成绩~不得〔状~〕过分❹~;故意❺~;决不❻~

1. fact 2. result; achievement 3. merit 4. excessively 5. intentionally; purposely 6. never

kuāyào 夸耀 brag about; show off; flaunt ≅ 显示〔~宾〕〈名〉~

自己的见识❶； ~能力❷； ~成绩❸； ~自己的孩子〔~补〕〈趋〉一~起自己来就没完〈程〉~得使人烦❹； ~得过火❺了〈量〉~过无数次了〔状~〕到处~； 一再~； 从不~； 在别人面前❻~

1. experience; knowledge 2. ability 3. result; achievement 4. be vexed; be irritated; be annoyed 5. go too far 6. before other people

kuà 跨

① step; stride ≅ 迈步〔~宾〕〈名〉~着大步❶〔~补〕〈结〉一步~上了三级台阶❷〈趋〉~进门来了；你能~过这条沟❸去(~过这条沟来)吗？〈程〉步子~得真大〈可〉沟太宽❹，你~得过来~不过来?〈量〉~过一次小河沟〔状~〕向前~；一步~了过去

1. stride 2. stair 3. ditch 4. too wide

② bestride; straddle ≅ 骑〔~补〕〈结〉~上战马❶; 这座大桥~过了一条宽宽的大河〈趋〉一下就~到马背❷上去了〈程〉~得真利落❸; ~得挺快〈可〉脚踏车❹太高，我~不上去〔状~〕一步就~上去了；从后边~；猛地❺一~

1. battle steed; war-horse 2. horseback 3. dexterous; nimble; agile 4. bicycle 5. all of a sudden; abruptly

③ cut across, go beyond ≅ 超过〔~宾〕〈名〉~年度❶，~行业❷，~地区❸；亚洲❹地~寒❺、温❻、热❼三带〔~补〕〈结〉~入❽新的一年〔状~〕横❾~大西洋❿

1. year 2. trade; profession 3. area; region; district 4. Asia 5. frigid zone 6. temperate zone 7. torrid zone 8. stride into 9. stretch over or across 10. the Atlantic Ocean

kuǎndài 款待 treat cordially; entertain 〔~宾〕〈名〉~客人；~朋友；~贵宾❶〔状~〕热情地❷~; 殷切地❸~; 盛情❹~; 诚恳地❺~

1. honoured guest; distinguished guest 2. warmly; enthusiastically 3. eagerly; ardently 4. with great kindness; with boundless hospitality 5. sincerely; honestly

kǔn 捆 tie; bind; bundle up 〔~宾〕〈名〉~行李❶, ~东西；~麦子❷, ~柴火❸, ~了一捆书; ~了一捆旧报纸〔~补〕〈结〉把行李~好；把东西~紧点儿❹; 把那个小偷~上了; 把这两个东西~在一起吧〈趋〉把小偷~起来了〈程〉~得很好; ~得真快; ~得不象样子❺〈可〉我力气小，~不紧, 这绳子❻~不结实〈时〉~了半天也捆不上〈量〉帮我~一下儿〔状~〕使劲儿❼~; 用麻绳❽~; 太难~了, 稍微❾~一~就行了; 赶快~吧! 你替我~; 在床上~行李; 紧紧地❿~

1. luggage 2. wheat 3. faggot; firewood 4. closely; tightly 5. in no shape to be seen; unpresentable 6. rope 7. exert all one's strength; exert oneself physically 8. rope made of hemp, flax, jute, etc. 9. a little; a bit; slightly 10. closely; tightly; firmly

kuòdà 扩大 enlarge; expand; extend ≌增加↔缩小〔主～〕〈名〉房屋面积❶～了；工厂～了；学校～了；场地❷～了；招生❸范围❹～了；知识面❺～了；眼界❻～了〔～宾〕〈名〉～旅游业❼；～势力范围❽；～地盘❾；～种植面积❿；～建筑面积⓫；～订户⓬；～眼界〔**状～**〕逐渐⓭～；日益⓮～；一点一点地～；逐年⓯～；在原有基础上⓰～

1. area 2. space; place; site 3. enrol new students; recruit students 4. scope; limits 5. range of knowledge 6. field of vision 7. tourism; tourist trade 8. sphere of influence 9. territory under one's control; domain 10. growing areas; areas sown 11. building areas 12. subscriber 13. gradually 14. increasingly; day by day 15. year after year; year by year 16. on what has already been achieved

kuòsàn 扩散 spread; diffuse 〔主～〕〈名〉防止消息❶～；病菌❷～了；癌❸～了；毒液❹～了〔～宾〕〈名〉别～谣言❺；～病菌〔～补〕〈结〉～开了〈趋〉已经～出去了；别～到外边去〈程〉～得真快；～得很远〔状～〕已经～了；别～；慢慢地～；逐渐❻～

1. news 2. germs; pathogenic bacteria 3. cancer 4. venom 5. rumour 6. gradually

L

lā 拉 ① pull; draw; tug; drag↔推〔**～宾**〕〈名〉牛～车；爱斯基摩人❶用狗来～雪撬❷；～抽屉❸；～锯❹；主人❺～开门请客人进来；～弓❻〈代〉孩子哭闹❼不走，大人只好～着他走〔**～补**〕〈结〉车让谁给～走了？把抽屉～开；两个孩子打起来了，快把他们～开；他把妹妹～到一边对着耳朵说了几句话〈趋〉把那个落水的人从水里～上来了；他不想进来是我硬❽把他～进来的；两个人一起锯木头，一个～过来，一个～过去；把马～过来〈程〉这匹马拉车～得真慢；抽屉～得太猛❾了，差点儿掉出来〈可〉年纪大❿了～不动车了；门怎么～不开啊！东西卡住⓫了，抽屉～不出来了；东西重，绳子⓬细～不上来；他手一点儿劲⓭都没有，这张弓根本⓮～不开〈时〉抽屉～了半天也没拉开〈量〉～了我一把〔**状～**〕使劲～；轻轻地～；往外(里)～；一把就～过来了；来回⓯～锯；用马～；直着⓰～

1. Eskimo **2.** sled; sledge; sleigh **3.** drawer **4.** saw **5.** master; host **6.** bow **7.** make a tearful scene **8.** manage to do sth. with difficulty **9.** too violent **10.** advanced in years **11.** block; check **12.** rope **13.** physical strength **14.** simply; at all **15.** to and fro **16.** straight

② play (certain musical instruments) ≅弹，奏〔**～宾**〕〈名〉～小提琴❶；～大提琴❷；～手风琴❸；～个曲子❹；～个歌儿〔**～补**〕〈结〉曲子～错了；把A调～成C调了；弦❺～断了❻；别把琴～坏了；～走调❼了；这次～对了吧〈趋〉我刚学，～出来不好听；你是从什么时候开始～起提琴来的？〈程〉～得不行❽；～得很熟练❾；～得很轻快❿；～得很在行⓫；～得多动听⓬啊！拉小夜曲⓭把自己都～得陶醉⓮了〈可〉这个曲子太难，我～不了(liǎo)；我不看乐谱⓯～不下来；怎么老～不对啊！～不出节奏⓰来〈时〉～了一辈子小提琴；每天都～一两个小时；这个孩子没有毅力⓱，～一会儿就放下⓲了〈量〉每个曲子都得～好多遍；～一次不行再～一次；这个琴好不好，你～一下儿试试〔**状～**〕这支曲子不好～；随便⓳～；反复～；一遍一遍地～；全神贯注地⓴～；无精打彩地㉑～；整天～

1. violin **2.** cello **3.** accordion **4.** tune; melody; song **5.** the string of a musical instrument **6.** snapped; broken **7.** out of tune **8.** be no good; not work **9.** skilful **10.**

lively; light-hearted 11. be expert at sth.; be good at 12. interesting or pleasant to listen to; beautifully; pretty good 13. serenade 14. be intoxicated (with success, etc.) 15. music score; music 16. rhythm 17. willpower; will 18. lay down; put down 19. (do) as one please 20. with rapt attention 21. in low spirits; out of sorts

③ draw sb. over to one's side; rope in; canvass; draw in ≅ 拉拢〔~宾〕〈名〉~关系❶；~交情❷；~选票❸；~主顾❹〔~补〕〈结〉~上关系了；主顾都被对面的饭馆~走了〈趋〉跟我~起关系来了〈可〉这家商店❺的服务态度❻很坏❼，难怪❽~不上主顾；~不上任何关系；~不着(zháo)选票〈量〉~过两次关系都没拉上〔状~〕拼命❾~；一个劲儿地❿~；有意地⓫~；千方百计地⓬~；不择手段地⓭~

1. relationship 2. friendly relations; friendship (try to form tie; with; cotton up to) 3. vote; ballot 4. customer; client 5. store; shop 6. attitude in attending to or waiting on guests, customers, etc. 7. too bad 8. no wonder 9. with all one's might for all one is worth 10. continuously; persistently 11. purposely; intentionally; deliberately 12. by every possible means; by hook or by crook 13. by fair means or foul; unscrupulously

④ empty the bowels ≅ 排泄〔~宾〕〈名〉~屎❶；~肚子❷；~痢疾❸；~虫子❹〔~补〕〈结〉把人都~坏了；~瘦❺了〈趋〉~出来两条虫子〈程〉~得人都瘦了；~得面黄肌瘦❻；~得浑身❼无力❽；~得腿都软❾了；~得太虚弱❿了〈时〉~了三天肚子〈量〉~过好几次肚子〔状~〕突然~；经常~

1. excrement; faeces; dung; droppings (empty the bowels; shit) 2. have loose bowels; suffer from diarrhoea 3. dysentery 4. worm (e.g. roundworm, tapeworm, etc.) 5. thin; emaciated 6. sallow and emaciated; lean and haggard 7. from head to foot; all over 8. feel weak 9. one's legs feel like jelly 10. in poor health; weak; debilitated

⑤ give a helping hand；help ≅ 帮助〔~补〕〈结〉是我把他~大❶的〈趋〉是我把他~起来的〈量〉~他一下儿；他犯了错误，要~他一把❷〔状~〕他遇到了困难，我立即❸~了他一把；一手❹~大的，亲手❺~；辛辛苦苦地❻~；好不容易~；及时❼~；从小❽~

1. bring up (a child) 2. give some help 3. at once; immediately 4. all by oneself; all alone 5. personally; oneself; with one's own hands 6. take a lot of trouble; take great pains; work laboriously 7. in time 8. from childhood; as a child

⑥ space out; increase the distance between ≅ 拖长〔**~补**〕〈结〉~长声音；~开嗓门唱❶；~开距离❷，把比分❸~平❹了〈程〉队形❺~得很长；比分~得很远〈可〉距离~得开~不开？〔**状~**〕一下子~开了；逐渐~大了；一向❻~长声音说话；~下脸来

1. sing 2. distance (space out) 3. score 4. even up 5. formation 6. consistently; all along

là 落 ① leave out; be missing ≅ 遗漏；丢下〔**~宾**〕〈名〉~了两个字；~了三行❶；~了一大段❷；~好几个标点❸；~了三个符号❹；~了一个注释❺；~了两个号码❻；~了一个小标题❼；~了一张图；~了一张表格❽〔**~补**〕〈结〉字~多了；要开车了，检查❾一下儿~下人了没有？钥匙❿在家里了〈程〉~得太多了；落⓫字~得都看不懂了〈可〉一个人看稿子⓬一个人念，好好对一对⓭就~不了(liǎo)了；多检查几遍就~不了(liǎo)了〈量〉~了好几次引号⓮了〔**状~**〕又~了；千万⓯别~；不小心~

1. line; row 2. paragraph 3. punctuation 4. symbol; mark 5. explanatory note; annotation 6. number 7. title; heading 8. form; table 9. check up; examine; inspect 10. key 11. be missing 12. draft; sketch; manuscript 13. check 14. quotation marks 15. be sure

② lag behind ≅ 掉在后边〔**~宾**〕〈名〉~了一个半月的课；~了两节数学❶课；~了一段❷路〔**~补**〕〈结〉他走得太慢，~在别人后边了；生了一场大病，好几门课都~下了；那个孩子非常聪明❸，虽然开学时晚来了不少日子，可是一点功课也没~下；课~多了，补❹都不好补了〈程〉课~得太多了；路~得太远了〈可〉你们走多快都~不下我〈时〉整整~了一个月；~了半个学期〈量〉~过一次课〔**状~**〕一下子~了；整整~了；千万别~；被别人~下了

另见 luò 落

1. mathematics 2. section; segments; part 3. intelligent; clever 4. make up

lái 来 ① come; arrive ↔ 去〔**主~**〕〈名〉老师~了；信~了；客人~了；警察❶~了；您要的车~了；菜~了，快吃吧；今天的报纸怎么到现在还没~〈代〉大家都~了〔**~宾**〕〈名〉远处~了一条小船；前天~了两个人；最近家里~信了吗？昨天家里~了一封电报；商店❷里~货了〔**~补**〕〈结〉~早了，可以先看看书；人都~齐❸了吗？报纸又~晚了；屋子太小，人~多了连坐的地方都没有了〈程〉车子~得很快；你~得很准时；你们~得真巧❹；她每天都比我~得早；他的信~得真勤❺〈可〉我有事儿明天~不了(liǎo)〈时〉我~了一会儿了；~了半天了〈量〉请你~一下儿；

~了好几次都没遇到❻；你〔状~〕等了好几天，信终于❼了；你是单独❽~的吗？我们是一起~的；特意❾~看看你；陆续❿~；她怎么还不~啊！快~吧！幸亏⓫~了；高高兴兴地⓬~了；朝⓭这个方向⓮~了；果然⓯~了；突然⓰~了；恰巧⓱他~了

1. police; policeman 2. shop 3. complete 4. at a most opportune moment 5. frequent 6. meet 7. at last; in the end; finally 8. alone; by oneself 9. for a special purpose; specially 10. successively 11. luckily; fortunately 12. cheerfully; happily 13. facing; towards 14. this direction 15. really; as expected; sure enough 16. suddenly; all of a sudden 17. by chance; fortunately; as chance would have it

② crop up; take place ≅ 发生 到来〔主~〕〈名〉事情~了，要沉着❶；问题~了，先别着急❷；雷阵雨❸马上就要~了；暴风雪❹~了；寒潮❺~了；台风❻了〔~补〕〈程〉病~得很快；~得很急❼〈可〉暴风雪今天夜里~得了(liǎo)~不了(liǎo)？〔状~〕已经~了；即将~；马上~

1. cool-headed; composed; steady 2. don't worry 3. thunder shower 4. snowstorm; blizzard 5. cold wave 6. typhoon 7. fast; rapid; violent

③〔主~〕〈代〉别客气❶，我自己~吧；你歇歇❷，让我~吧；下棋你~不~？〔~宾〕〈名〉~一瓶汽水❸；~两杯啤酒❹；~一盘棋；喝得太多了，少~两杯吧！唱得真好，再~一个；~一个竞赛❺；~一个总动员❻；~了一个180度的大转变❼〔~补〕〈结〉~上一壶酒❽喝好不好？〈程〉他这句话~得真厉害；这一招儿~得好；~得真快〈可〉象棋❾我可~不过你；扑克❿你大概~不过我〈量〉再~一遍；~两次了〔状~〕多~一碗；好好~一盘棋；照这样再~一份〔习用〕~劲儿⓫

1. please don't bother 2. take a rest 3. aerated water; soda water 4. beer 5. contest; competition; emulation 6. general (total) mobilization 7. do an about-face; make a 180-degree turn 8. a pot of wine 9. (Chinese) chess 10. playing cards 11. full of enthusiasm; in high spirits

láibují 来不及 there's not enough time (to do sth.); it's too late (to do sth.) ↔来得及〔主~〕〈代〉你现在才复习可能~了；他将来后悔❶可就~了；你去晚了就~了；你们写信已经~了，还是给他打个电报❷吧〔~宾〕〈动〉今天你~回去了，就在我们这里住一夜吧；时间不够了，~去看她了；我~告诉他了，请你替我说一声吧；时间太紧❸，看都~看，就又还给他了；想都~想就说出来了；水都~喝就走了；话都~说；这篇文章要得太急❹，~再好好修改❺了〔状~〕已经~

了；恐怕❻~了；到那时可就~了；差点儿~

1. regret; repent 2. telegram 3. pressing 4. urgent 5. revise; amend; modify 6. I think; perhaps

láidejí 来得及
there's still time; be able to do sth. in time ↔ 来不及〔主~〕〈动〉八点上班，现在都七点了，还~吗？现在出发❶完全~；乘这趟火车还~；现在时间还早，走着去都~；商店还没关门，走快两步❷还~；离出国考试还有一段时间，现在准备还~〔~宾〕〈动〉~去；~买；~看；~通知❸他；~回家；~告诉家里一声；~想；~说；~研究❹；~讨论❺；~吃；~处理❻；~写信；~打电话；~准备〔状~〕还~；完全~；肯定❼~；也许❽~；大概~；当然~

1. set out; start off 2. quicken one's steps (pace) 3. notify 4. discuss; study 5. discuss 6. handle; deal with; dispose of 7. certainly; surely 8. probably; perhaps; maybe

lài 赖
① hang on in a place; drag out one's stay in a place〔主~〕〈名〉那个人占❶了别人的房子还~着不走；孩子在转椅❷上~着不下来〔~补〕〈结〉~在那儿不走；不知somehow~到哪一天？不能~在别人家里不走〈可〉~不了(liǎo)了，只好走；他知道再也~不下去了〈时〉~了好几年；他想~一会儿是一会儿〈量〉孩子走到儿童商店❸门口一次就~一次，每次都要买玩具〔状~〕拼命❹~着；厚颜无耻❺地~在别国；一直~

1. occupy; seize; take 2. swivel chair; revolving chair 3. children's store 4. desperately; for all one is worth; with all one's might 5. shamelessly; impudently

② deny one's error or responsibility ≅ 抵赖；不承认〔主~〕〈名〉那个人做错了事还想~〈代〉他偷❶了东西还想~；明明❷是他打破❸的茶杯，他还想~；我看见是你弄坏❹的，你想~是不行的〔~宾〕〈名〉这个人爱~帐〔~补〕〈结〉说过的话想赖是没法~掉的〈趋〉他又~起来了〔程〕~得真厉害；~得真气人〈可〉想赖是~不掉的〈时〉~了半天也没赖掉〈量〉这个人~过无数次❺了〔状~〕经常~；千方百计地❻~；决不~；当面❼~；硬着头皮❽~

1. steal 2. obviously; plainly; undoubtedly 3. break 4. ruin; put out of order; make a mess of 5. innumerable; countless 6. by every possible means; by hook or crook 7. to sb.'s face; in sb.'s presence 8. toughen one's scalp — brace oneself; force oneself to do sth. against one's will

③ blame sb. wrongly; put the blame on sb. else ≅ 诬赖；责怪

〔～宾〕〈名〉这件事大家都有责任❶，不能～哪一个人〈代〉自己做错了，不要～别人；别总～我〔～补〕〈结〉这事怎么～上我了；自己做错了，就应该承认❷，不能～在别人身上；又～到我头上了〈趋〉明明是你说的，怎么～起我来了；她～起人来真叫人受不了❸〈可〉这事我一点也不知道，可～不上我；考不好，谁也～不了(liǎo)，只能怪❹自己没复习好〈时〉～了半天别人，结果证明❺还是他自己做的〈量〉他～过我好几次了〔状～〕互相～；居然❻～；故意❼～；动不动❽就～；总～人；别～人〔习用〕～皮～脸❾

1. responsible for 2. acknowledge; admit 3. unbearable; terrible 4. blame 5. prove 6. unexpectedly; to one's surprise 7. intentionally; purposely 8. easily; frequently 9. act shamelessly

lán 拦 bar; block; hold back ≅ 阻挡

〔～宾〕〈名〉～着孩子，别让他们过去；～着铁丝网❶；～着绳子❷〈代〉我要买一辆摩托车❸，他～着我不让买；你别～人家说话〔～补〕〈结〉汽车拐弯❹时没开指示灯❺，被交通警察❻给～住了；马路上的交通灯❼把车辆和行人都～住了〈趋〉我刚要说话，被她～回去了〈可〉他非要去，我怎么拦也～不住他；谁也～不了(liǎo)他〈时〉～了半天也没拦回去；铁栏杆已经～了好几年了〈量〉～过他不少次了，他就是不听〔状～〕一再～；三番五次地～；被她～；决不～；从这儿到那儿～一根绳子；用手一～〔习用〕～路虎❽

1. wire entanglement 2. rope 3. motorbike; motorcycle 4. turn a corner 5. pilot lamp (light); indicator lamp 6. traffic police 7. traffic lights 8. obstacle; stumbling block

lǎnde 懒得 not feel like (doing sth.); not be in the mood to

〔～宾〕〈动〉～去；～看这种人的脸色❶；～写信；～动笔❷；～问人；～出去；～看病；～求人；～管❸；～说话；～尝❹；～洗；～买〔状～〕真～去；总是～看病

1. facial expression 2. take up the pen 3. manage; run; be in charge of 4. taste

lànyòng 滥用 abuse; misuse; use indiscrminately

〔～宾〕〈名〉～职权❶；～经费❷；～典故❸〔状～〕多次～

1. powers or authority of office 2. funds; outlay 3. allusion; literary quotation

lāo 捞 ① dredge up; drag for; scoop up (from water)

〔～宾〕〈名〉下河去～鱼；～了一筐❶小虾❷；～了不少蝌蚪❸；～饺子❹；～面条〔～补〕〈结〉～满了一小桶〈趋〉～上来很多螃蟹❺；那群孩子跳进水里就～起鱼来了；

从小河里~上来很多虾〈程〉~得真不少〈可〉~不着(zháo)什么东西；~得上来吗？〈时〉~了一上午也没捞着(zháo)一条鱼；~了半天，再~一会儿〈量〉~过两次〔状~〕从金鱼缸❻里~出两条金鱼来；用鱼网❼~；有人在天黑的时候~；从锅❽里~；往外~

1. basket 2. shrimp 3. tadpole 4. *Jiaozi* (dumpling with meat and vegetable stuffing) 5. crab 6. goldfish bowl 7. fishnet; fishing net 8. pot; pan; boiler

② gain; get by improper means〔~宾〕〈名〉上次赌❶输❷了，这次可得好好~~本儿❸了；这次他想多~点儿钱〔~补〕〈结〉他这几年钱可~够❹了〈趋〉好处❺都让他~走(~去)了；把本儿都~回来(~回去)了〈可〉在这件事情上我~不着(zháo)什么好处〈时〉~了半天也没把本儿~回来〈量〉~过一次；~一把❻〔状~〕一次就全~回来了；好好~；拼命❼~；狠狠地❽~〔习用〕~稻草❾

1. gambling 2. lose; be beaten; be defeated 3. win back lost wagers; recover one's losses; recoup oneself 4. though; sufficient; ample 5. good; benefit; advantage 6. reap some profit 7. with all one's might; for all one is worth 8. firmly; resolutely 9. (try to) take advantage of sth.

lào 烙 brand; iron 〔~宾〕〈名〉~饼❶；~烧饼❷；~衣服〔~补〕〈结〉饼~好了；~熟❸了没有？衣服没~平〈程〉烧饼~得真好；~得真香〈可〉这么多，一个小时~不出来(~不完／~不了(liǎo)；我一个人~不过来那么多；他只会做包子，~不了(liǎo)烧饼〈时〉~一会儿就熟了〈量〉我就~过一次饼〔状~〕第一次~；用平锅❹~；多(少)~一会儿；两面~

1. a round flat cake 2. sesame seed cake 3. done; cooked 4. frying-pan

lào 落 go down; set ≅下降
另见 luò 落 ①；②；③；⑤；⑥；⑦；⑧

lēi 勒 tie or strap sth. tight ≅ 系紧；扎紧〔~宾〕〈名〉领带❶系❷得太紧❸，有点儿~脖子❹；书包带儿❺太细❻~手；表带❼太紧，把胳膊❽~了一道印❾儿〔~补〕〈结〉~紧裤带❿；行李⓫~结实⓬了吗？孩子们把一只狗~死了〈趋〉从这边~过去，再从那边~回来〈程〉腰带太紧~得真难受⓭；~得太松⓮了；~得真疼〈可〉他手没劲儿⓯~不紧；~不动〈时〉~了半天也没勒紧；刚一会儿，手就疼了〈量〉多~几下儿比较结实〔状~〕用绳子~；使劲儿⓰~；用力；横着⓱~；竖着⓲~

1. necktie 2. tie; fasten 3. tight 4. neck 5. belt; girdle 6. thin 7. watch strap; watchband 8. arm 9.

mark; print 10. girdle 11. luggage 12. solid 13. feel unwell 14. loose 15. physical strength 16. exert oneself physically 17. horizontally 18. vertically

lěi 垒 build by piling up bricks, stones, earth, etc. ≅ 砌〔~宾〕〈名〉~墙；~砖❶〔~补〕〈结〉墙~高点儿；再~上一层❷砖就够高了〈趋〉墙半天就~起来了〈程〉~得真快；~得真齐❸；~得挺结实〈可〉这一面墙半天~得完~不完？技术❹不高~不直〈时〉~了三天才垒完；总说要垒可是~了一年还没垒上〈量〉你能帮我一下儿吗？我自己~过一次〔状~〕慢慢腾腾地~❺；往上~；一层一层地~❻；整整齐齐地~❼

1. brick 2. layer; stratum 3. neat; even; uniform 4. skill; technique 5. leisurely; unhurriedly 6. layer after layer 7. tidily

lèi 累 tire; strain; wear out ≅ 疲劳；疲倦；操劳〔~宾〕〈名〉在弱光下❶看书，~眼睛；这种工作太~脑子；孩子多了~心〔~补〕〈结〉走了一大段路~死我了；这两天把我~坏了；带这么多东西可把我~苦了；每天这么累，他都~怕了；她最近准备考试都瘦了❷〈程〉~得很利害❸；~得要命❹；~得慌❺；~得腰酸腿痛❻；~得睡不着觉〈可〉多拿点没关系，~不着(zháo)你〈时〉~了一天也该休息休息了；~了好几年，现在孩子大了，总算❼熬

❽出来了〔状~〕可~了；多~啊！不怎么~；特别~；实在❾太~

1. in a poor light 2. thin; emaciated 3. 4. 5.terrible; awful 6. aching back and legs 7. at last 8. endure; hold out 9. really; indeed

líkāi 离开 leave; depart from; deviate from ≅ 离〔~宾〕〈名〉他从小就~家了；我~大学已经五年了；一小时前，我~医院时，他还是好好的；发言❶的时候请不要~本题❷；孩子一天也没~过母亲；凡是生物❸都不能~阳光、空气和水〔~补〕〈程〉~得很早；~得比较晚〈时〉~好多年了；刚~两天就想得要命❹；~一会儿也不行❺〈量〉~过好几次；~一下儿马上就回来，一次都没~过〔状~〕一直没~过，一刻也别~；从来没~过；突然~了；擅自❻~；就要~；愉快地❼~〔习用〕三句话不离本行❽

1. speak; make a statement or speech 2. stray from the subject 3. living things 4. extremely; to death 5. won't do 6. without authorization 7. happily 8. can hardly open one's mouth without talking shop; talk shop all the time

lǐ 理 ① put in order; tidy up ≅ 整理〔~宾〕〈名〉头发长了，该~发❶了；需要冷静❷一下儿，~一~思路❸；星期日我要~一~书；~一~箱子❹和柜子❺；还

要~一~抽屉❻；~一~帐目❼〔~补〕〈结〉~完发了吗？等我把东西~好了就来；头发~短（~长）点儿〈趋〉他~出来的发型❽跟别人的不一样〈程〉她把家~得很有条理❾；她的头发~得很好看；抽屉里的衣服~得整整齐齐的〈可〉帐目老~不清❿；两书柜⓫的书，十分钟可能~不完；孩子自己~得了(liǎo)衣服~不了(liǎo)；他连抽屉都~不整齐，总是那么乱七八糟⓬的〈时〉~了一个多小时，还没理完〈量〉~过好几次了；东西太乱⓭了，好好儿一下儿吧〔状~〕经常~；不好~；精心地⓮~；有空的时候⓯~；在理发馆⓰~

1. haircut 2. sober; calm 3. thinking 4. chest; trunk; box; case 5. wardrobe 6. drawer 7. accounts; items of an account 8. hair style 9. proper arrangement or presentation; orderliness; method 10. not clear 11. bookcase 12. in disorder 13. in a mess; in confusion; in disorder 14. meticulously; carefully 15. at one's leisure 16. at the barber's

② pay attention to; acknowledge 〔~宾〕〈名〉她不爱~人〈代〉路上碰见❶了，谁也没~谁；这两个人吵过架❷，现在他们谁都不~谁〔~补〕〈量〉那个人态度❸很傲慢❹，从来不理人，好象~一下儿人就降低❻了自己的身份❼似的〔状~〕她一向不~人；从来不~人；一生气就不~人；连理都不~〔习用〕爱~不~❽

1. come across 2. quarrel 3. attitude 4. haughty; arrogant 5. it seems; it looks as if 6. reduce; cut down; drop; lower 7. status; capacity; identity 8. look cold and indifferent; be stand-offish

lǐjiě 理解 understand; comprehend ≅ 了解；知道〔~宾〕〈名〉~你的意思；~这个词的含义❶；~他的难处❷；~他们的处境❸；~我们的心情❹；~孩子的想法❺〈代〉你一点儿都不~我〔~补〕〈结〉~错了，不知道他对我们的困难~到什么程度❻；先把意思~透❼了再说〈趋〉~起来很困难〈程〉他对事物~得很深刻；~得很透彻❽；~得不太对〈可〉太难懂了，我真~不了(liǎo)；他的话我~不透；词的意思我~不好〔状~〕认真~；越来越~；逐渐~；难以~；不难~；着重❾~；充分❿~；真正~；非常~

1. meaning; implication 2. difficulty; trouble 3. unfavourable situation; plight 4. mood; state of mind 5. idea; opinion; what one has in mind 6. level; degree 7. fully; thoroughly; in a penetrating way 8. penetrating; thorough 9. emphatically 10. sufficiently; fully

lìyòng 利用 use; utilize; make use of; take advantage of ≅ 用〔~宾〕〈名〉~业余时间❶学英语；~一切❷有利条件❸；~空

间❹放东西；～他们之间的矛盾❺；～热空气❻把水份❼蒸发❽掉；～时机❾；～假期；～太阳能❿做饭；～他的弱点⓫；～职权⓬；～废料⓭；真会～人；～现有的人力、物力〔**～补**〕〈趋〉还可以继续～下去〈程〉他的时间～得真好〈量〉只好～一下儿上课的时间通知⓮了〔**状～**〕合理⓯～；大量⓰～；公开⓱～；广泛⓲～；充分⓳～；直接⓴～；间接㉑～；全部～；部分㉒～；好好儿～；被人～

1. spare time **2.** all **3.** favorable condition **4.** space **5.** contradiction **6.** hot air **7.** moisture content **8.** evaporate **9.** opportunity **10.** solar energy **11.** weak point **12.** powers or authority of office **13.** waste material **14.** notify; inform **15.** rationally **16.** largely; enormously **17.** openly; publicly **18.** widely **19.** fully; sufficiently **20.** directly **21.** indirectly **22.** partly

lián 连 ① link; join; connect ≃ 连接〔**主～**〕〈名〉骨头❶断❷了，筋❸还～着；我们两个人心～着心；坐在轮船❹上向外看真是天～着水，水～着天；他们两个人的感情❺真是藕断丝～❻〔**～宾**〕〈名〉把坏牙～根儿拔掉❼吧〔**～补**〕〈结〉～成一片；～在一起〈趋〉这座桥把南北两岸～起来了〈程〉～得很紧；～得不紧〈可〉～得起来～不起来？～得上～不上？～得紧～不紧〔**状～**〕紧紧地❽～；相～

1. bone **2.** be broken **3.** muscle **4.** steamer **5.** feeling; sentiment **6.** the lotus root snaps but its fibres stay joined **7.** extract **8.** tightly; closely

② including ≃ 包括在内〔**～宾**〕〈名〉别～皮❶儿吃啊！～皮带骨❷一共五十公斤〈代〉～你一共十二个人；～这些都算上也不够❸〔**状～**〕别～

1. skin **2.** bone **3.** not sufficient

liánxì 联系 integrate; relate; link; get in touch with.〔**～宾**〕〈名〉～工作；～思想〔**～补**〕〈结〉和他们～上了吗？明天参观的事～好了吗？这件事～晚了；～完了再说；把两件事～在一起考虑❶〈趋〉两件事～起来看就清楚了〈程〉～得很紧密❷；～得很好〈可〉不知道～得上～不上？什么事情让他去联系，准❸～不好；名字和人～不起来〈时〉～了半天；～了好长时间〈量〉～过一次；～一下儿看看〔**状～**〕多方❹～；好好～；认真～；紧密❺～；密切❻～；紧紧地～；一次一次地～；不断❼～；主动❽～；广泛❾～；跟他直接～；互相～

1. think over; consider **2.** closely; tightly **3.** certainly; surely **4.** in many ways; in every way **5. 6.** closely **7.** incessantly **8.** of one's own accord **9.** extensively; widely

liàn 练

practise; train; drill ≅ 练习, 训练 〔~宾〕〈名〉兵❶; ~长跑❷; ~球; ~气功❸; ~武术❹; ~杂技❺; 演员每天~功❻; ~~曲子❼; ~字; ~本领❽ 〈动〉~打球; ~游泳; ~跳舞; ~唱歌; ~打字; ~弹钢琴〔~补〕〈结〉一定要把身体~结实❾; 字~好了可有用了; 曲子~熟❿了〈趋〉本领~出来了; 你什么时候~起剑来了〈程〉他练功~得很刻苦⓫; 他武术~得不错〈可〉我的字~不出来(~不好)了; 年纪大了, 练什么也~不了(liǎo)了; 我怎么练也~不会游泳〈时〉~了那么多年也没学会; 每天都得(děi)~一会儿琴; ~过几天太极拳⓬, 后来就不练了〈量〉这个节目⓭~了十几次了; 再~一下儿吧〔状~〕苦⓮~基本功⓯; 努力~; 刻苦地~; 不停地~; 不间断地~; 起早贪黑⓰地~; 勤⓱~; 多~; 一遍一遍地~

1. troops 2. long-distance running 3. do breathing exercises 4. martial arts 5. acrobatics 6. do exercises in gymnastics; practise one's skill 7. song; tune; melody 8. practise one's skill 9. strong 10. skilful 11. assiduous; hardworking; painstaking 12. a kind of traditional Chinese shadow boxing 13. programme 14. assiduously; painstakingly 15. basic training; basic skill; essential technique 16. from dawn to dusk 17. diligently

liànxí 练习

practise ≅ 练 〔~宾〕 〈名〉~毛笔❶字; ~书法❷; ~速记❸; ~刺绣❹ 〈动〉弹钢琴; ~跑步❺; ~打字; ~讲英语; ~剪裁衣服❻〔~补〕〈结〉~好了; ~熟❼了; ~会了吗? ~完了再休息〈趋〉照❽这样~下去准❾能成功❿; ~出成绩⓫来了〈程〉~得很刻苦⓬; ~得很认真〈可〉时间不够~不了(liǎo); 他老~不会〈时〉~了五六年了; 刚~两个月; 多~一会儿〈量〉好好~一下儿就会了; ~了两次, 就不想学了〔状~〕刻苦地~; 努力~; 认真~; 经常~; 反复~

1. writing brush 2. calligraphy 3. shorthand; stenography 4. embroider; embroidery 5. run; march at the double 6. cut out (a garment) 7. skilled 8. according to; in accordance with 9. certainly; surely 10. succeed 11. result; achievement 12. assiduous

liàn 炼

temper (a metal) with fire; refine 〔~宾〕〈名〉~钢❶; ~铁❷; ~铜❸; ~油〔~补〕〈结〉把废铁❹~成有用的钢材❺; 刚~完一炉钢❻ 〈趋〉油都~出来〈可〉这种铁~得了(liǎo)好钢吗? 〈时〉他哥哥在炼钢厂❼~过五年钢〈量〉~过一次〔状~〕一连~三炉钢; 一共~了两斤猪油❽; 多~一会儿, 油就出净❾了 〔习用〕真金不怕火❿~

1. steel 2. iron 3. copper 4. scrap iron 5. steel products; steels; rolled steel 6. a heat of steel 7. steel mill; steel works 8. lard 9.

lián — liāo

completely 10. true gold does not fear the test of fire — a person of integrity can stand severe tests

liáng 量 measure 〔～宾〕〈名〉～～这间屋子有几米❶？～～这块地❷有多少亩❸？～～尺寸❹；～～这块布；～～身高；～～体温❺；～～长短；～～大小；～～多少；～～高矮❻；～～胖瘦❼；～～轻重；～～领子的高低〔～补〕〈结〉布～错了；体温～对了吗？尺寸～准❽点儿；裤子的长短～好了吗？〈趋〉一件衣服～过来～过去的〈程〉尺寸～得很准；～得很仔细❾；～得太马虎❿了；他们两个人～得不一样〈可〉我～不好，你来量吧；这个称⓫～不准；我不会量，～不了(liǎo)；他太马虎，量什么也～不对〈时〉体温～五分钟就差不多了吧？〈量〉～了两遍还不放心⓬，再～一下儿；～了好几回了〔状～〕用皮尺⓭～；按什么标准⓮～；照哪件衣服～；仔细(地)～；认真地～；草草地⓯～；比着⓰衣服～；一遍一遍地～；反复～；再三～；马马虎虎地～；赶快～；重新～

1. metre 2. land 3. *mu*(a unit of area) 4. size 5. temperature 6. height 7. the proportion of fat and lean 8. accurate 9. careful 10. careless 11. balance; steelyard 12. worry; feel anxious 13. tape measure 14. standard; criterion 15. carelessly; hastily 16. model after; copy

liàng 晾 dry in the air; dry in the sun ≅ 晒；吹〔～宾〕〈名〉～衣服；～被子❶；～毛巾❷；～渔网❸〔～补〕〈结〉大热天衣服一会儿就～干；把渔网～在海滩❹上了〈趋〉把毛巾～到绳子❺上去吧！把被子、毯子❻都～出来了〈程〉豆子～得很干〈可〉地方大极了，有多少都～得下；今天阴天❼～不了(liǎo)被；绳子太细❽了，～不了(liǎo)太重❾的东西〈时〉～了好几天了；～一会儿就可以了〈量〉～过好几次了〔状～〕在铁丝❿上～；在山坡上⓫～；多～几天；经常～

1. quilt 2. cotton-padded mattress 3. fishnet; fishing net 4. seabeach; beach 5. rope 6. blanket 7. cloudy day; overcast sky 8. thin 9. too heavy 10. iron wire 11. mountain slope; hillside

liāo 撩 ① sprinkle (with one's hand) 〔～宾〕〈名〉扫地的时候，最好～一点儿水，免得❶尘土飞扬❷；卖菜的时候❸往菜上～水，好保持❹菜的新鲜❺〔～补〕〈程〉水～得太多了〔状～〕多(少)～一点儿；往地上～一点儿；先～一点儿；别～水；轻轻地❻～

1. so as not to; so as to avoid 2. raise a cloud of dust 3. frequently; often 4. keep; maintain 5. fresh 6. slightly; gently

② hold up (a curtain, skirt, etc. from the bottom) 〔～宾〕〈名〉～

头发；～衣服；～裙子❶〔～补〕〈结〉把帘子❷～开；～起衣服给我看里边的毛衣〈趋〉把垂下❸的头发～了上去；地上都是水，把长裙子～起来点儿吧；把头发～到头顶❹上去了〈量〉向后～一下儿〔状～〕往上～

1. skirt **2.** curtain; screen **3.** hang down; droop **4.** the top of the head

liáo 聊

chat ≅ 闲谈〔～宾〕〈名〉～天；～考试的问题〔～补〕〈结〉昨天晚上～完天都十点多了；每天都～到很晚才睡觉〈趋〉他们两个人又～起小时候❶的事儿来了；～起天来没完没了❷(liǎo)；～起天来把正经事❸都忘了；～起天来把那么重要的事儿都耽误❹了〈程〉～得真热闹❺；～得太兴奋❻了；～得非常高兴❼；～得很有意思❽〈可〉他很能聊，谁也～不过他；我们两个人～不起来；～不出什么新内容❾来了；这个话题❿～不下去了，换⓫一个吧〈时〉～了半天，还不知道人家姓什么呢〈量〉我跟他～过两次〔状～〕漫无边际地⓬～；天南海北地⓭～；海阔天空地⓮～；信口开河地⓯～；闲⓰～；一边喝茶一边～；跟谁～？

1. when one was young **2.** endless **3.** serious affairs **4.** delay; hold up **5.** lively; bustling with noise and excitement **6.** be excited **7.** very happy **8.** interesting **9.** content; substance **10.** subject **11.** change **12. 13. 14.** straying far from the subject; discursively; rambling **15.** talk irresponsibly; wag one's tongue too freely **16.** chat

liǎojiě 了解

understand, know; grasp ≅ 知道〔～宾〕〈名〉～工作的进展❶情况❷；～大家的愿望❸和要求❹；～会议的主旨❺；～历史根源❻；～现实意义❼；～社会的❽现状❾；～他的思想；～她的性格❿；～内心世界⓫；～大会的精神⓬；我不～他的底细⓭；只～一个大概，不～细节⓮〔～补〕〈结〉～到很多情况；～完了再说⓯；这件事的经过我已经～清楚了〈趋〉等⓰～回来再研究⓱〈程〉～得很清楚；～得很细致⓲；～得不彻底；～得太马虎⓳；～得一清二楚〈可〉什么情况也～不到；～不出来〈时〉～了好长时间才弄明白⓴〈量〉多～一下儿，这究竟㉑是怎么回事㉒；你赶快去～一下儿吧〔状～〕好好～～；仔细～～；再多～～；彻底～；设法㉓～；一点儿也不～；真正～；互相～；全面～；深入㉔～；不太～；千方百计地㉕～；多方～；直接㉖～；反复～；间接㉗～；主动㉘～；及时～；随时㉙～；向谁～？深深～

1. make progress **2.** situation **3.** desire **4.** demand **5.** purport; substance; gist **6.** source; origin; root **7.** practical or immediate significance **8.** social **9.** present (current) situation **10.** nature;

disposition; temperament **11.** the inner world **12.** gist; spirit; essence **13.** ins and outs; exact details **14.** details **15.** put off until some later **16.** when; till **17.** study **18.** careful; meticulous **19.** careless **20.** be clarified **21.** actually; exactly **22.** what is all this about? **23.** do what one can **24.** deeply **25.** by every possible means; by hook or by crook **26.** directly **27.** indirectly **28.** on one's own initiative **29.** at any time; at all times

lièjǔ 列举 enumerate; list 〔～宾〕〈名〉～了大量❶事实❷；～了一些数字❸；～了许多生动❹的事例❺；～了几种药品❻；～了常见的疾病❼；～了很多人〔～补〕〈结〉事例～少了〈趋〉把有力的证据❽都～出来了〈程〉～得不够；～得很全〈可〉～不了(liǎo)几种；～不尽❾；～得完吗？〈量〉～一下儿让我们听听〔状～〕一共～了；大量～；详细❿～；一一～

1. a large number; a great quantity **2.** fact (a host of facts) **3.** figure; numeral; digit **4.** lively; vivid **5.** example; instance **6.** medicines and chemical reagents **7.** common disease **8.** evidence; proof; testimony **9.** endless; inexhaustible **10.** in detail

liè 裂 split; crack; rend 〔主～〕〈名〉烟囱❶～了，好几个月没下雨，地都～了；墙～了；碗～了一道缝❷；碗～了一道纹❸；手～了一个口子〔～补〕〈结〉地都～开了；竹竿～成两半儿了〔状～〕快～了；一下子就～了；容易～；一晒❹就～

1. chimney **2.** crack; crevice **3.** crack (on glassware or earthenware) **4.** be exposed to the sun

lín 淋 be caught in the rain; drench; pour ≅ 浇〔～宾〕〈名〉身上～了雨；～了一身雨〔～补〕〈结〉都被雨～湿❶了；～透❷了；～坏了〈趋〉从头顶❸一下来了〔状～〕一下子～病了；被雨～；别～着(zháo)；走到半路～了

1. wet **2.** through (wet through) **3.** the top of the head

lǐng 领 ① lead; usher ≅ 带领〔～宾〕〈名〉你在前边给我们～路；～兵打仗❶；～客人参观；～孩子去玩〔～补〕〈结〉别把路～错了；把孩子～走吧〈趋〉～来一位客人；把客人～过来（～过去）；～上楼来了；～进屋来（～进屋去）吧〈程〉那个小向导❷领路～得很好〈可〉他自己打仗很勇猛❸，可是～不了(liǎo)兵；这里的路我最熟❹，绝对❺不会给你们～错〈时〉～了三年兵〈量〉～过好几次路；需要有人～一下儿〔状～〕热情地～；积极地❻～；主动地❼～；往哪儿～？

1. fight **2.** guide **3.** bold and powerful **4.** familiar **5.** absolutely; definitely **6.** actively **7.** on one's own initiative

② receive; draw; get ≅ 领取〔~宾〕〈名〉~工资❶；~奖金❷；~现款❸；~东西；~文具❹；不~他的情❺；~抚恤金❻；~养老金❼；~工作服❽；~奖品❾；~毕业证书❿；~驾驶执照⓫；~护照⓬〔~补〕〈结〉你的工资已经~走了；东西~全⓭了吗？~多（~少）了；工作服没~错吧〈趋〉这个月的奖金已经~出来（~回去）了〈程〉文具~得太多了；护照~得很早〈可〉现在~得了(liǎo)工资吗？现在~不了(liǎo)，下午才发⓮呢〈量〉今年~过一次工作服了〔状~〕随便⓯~；冒⓰~；顺便⓱给我们~一下儿；一次~完；分三次~；由他一个人~；每月~；按什么标准⓲~；高高兴兴地~；马上~；立即⓳~

1. wage; salary 2. bonus; money award 3. cash 4. stationery; writing materials 5. kindness; favour 6. pension for the disabled or for the family of the deceased 7. old-age pension 8. work clothes 9. prize; award 10. diploma; graduation certificate 11. driving license 12. passport 13. complete 14. deliver; distribute 15. as one pleases 16. falsely; fraudulently 17. conveniently; in passing 18. standard; criterion 19. at once; immediately

lǐnghuì 领会 understand; comprehend ≅ 理解，懂〔~宾〕〈名〉还没~我的意思❶；~他的意图❷〔~补〕〈结〉~对了；~错了〈程〉~得很清楚；~得很好；~得很深刻❸；~得不对；~得很快〈可〉~不了(liǎo)你们的意图〔状~〕深刻~；认真~；进一步~；好好~；完全❹~

1. meaning; idea; wish; desire 2. intention 3. deep 4. completely; entirely

lǐngqǔ 领取 draw; receive ≅ 领〔~宾〕〈名〉~工资❶；~助学金❷；~生活费❸；~毕业证书❹；~护照❺；~执照❻〔~补〕〈结〉~到了〔状~〕替别人~；先~；后~；全部~；一次~

1. wage; salary 2. stipend grant-in-aid 3. living expenses 4. graduation certificate; diploma 5. passport 6. license

liū 溜 ① slide; glide ≅ 滑〔~宾〕〈名〉~冰❶〔~补〕〈结〉今天你们打算❷~到什么时候？〈趋〉孩子们在冰场❸上~过来~过去，玩得真高兴〈程〉~得真快；~得很好；~得不太好〈可〉年纪大了~不了(liǎo)冰了〈时〉一会儿就累了；~了一上午冰〈量〉~一下儿试试；今年已经~好几次了〔状~〕飞快地❹~过去了；弯着腰❺~；在溜冰场上~；来回❻~；转圈❼~；一直往前~；从小就~；从这边往那边~

1. skating 2. intend; plan 3. rink 4. very fast; at lightning speed 5. bend over to 6. to and fro 7. go round in a cycle

② sneak off; slip away 〔~补〕〈结〉他趁❶人没注意❷~走了〈趋〉他们从会场❸~出来（~出去）了；回来晚了，怕妈妈说，就偷偷地~进来了〈程〉~得真快，刚出去就没影儿❹了〈可〉门口有人看着~不进去；我有他的地址❺他想溜是~不掉❻（~不了(liǎo)）的〔**状~**〕偷偷地~了；果然❼~了；故意❽~了；一下子~了

1. take advantage of **2.** pay no attention to **3.** meeting-place; conference hall **4.** be seen no more; go out of sight **5.** address **6.** unable to sneak off (slip away) **7.** really; as expected; sure enough **8.** intentionally; purposely

liú 流 flow 〔**~宾**〕〈名〉热得直~汗❶；眼睛见❷风就~泪❸；手破❹了~了不少血；晒❺得都快~油了；感冒了，一个劲儿❻~鼻涕❼；那个孩子爱~口水❽〔**~补**〕〈结〉泪都~干了；血~多了；油管❾裂❿了，石油白白地⓫~走了〈趋〉水从门缝里⓬~出去了；血顺着⓭手指~下来了；接上⓮皮管子⓯以后，水就可以~过来了；~到河里去了〈程〉鼻涕~得真厉害；血~得太多了；~得真吓人⓰；~得止不住⓱；水管子太细⓲，水~得慢极了〈可〉~不出去；用沙袋⓳挡着⓴，水就~不过来了；看什么悲剧㉑我也~不了(liǎo)眼泪〈时〉伤风了，鼻涕~了好几天；~了半天汗，也找不着(zháo)干净毛巾㉒擦㉓一擦；~了一会儿血就不流了〈量〉这一个星期之内就~了两次鼻血；看一个电影~了好几次眼泪〔**状~**〕不停地~；一个劲地~；水哗哗地㉔~；血一滴一滴地㉕~；难过地㉖~泪；控制不住㉗地~；突然~；偶尔㉘~；经常~

1. sweat **2.** meet with; be exposed to **3.** tear **4.** cut **5.** (of the sun) shine upon **6.** continuously **7.** nasal mucus; snivel (have a running nose) **8.** saliva (slobber) **9.** oil pipe **10.** split; crack; rend **11.** in vain **12.** a crack between a door and its frame **13.** along **14.** connect; join; put together **15.** rubber tube **16.** frighten; scare; intimidate **17.** unable to stop **18.** thin **19.** sandbag **20.** keep off; ward off; block **21.** tragedy **22.** towel **23.** wipe **24.** go gurgling on **25.** drop by drop **26.** sadly **27.** lose control of **28.** occasionally; once in a while

liúlù 流露 reveal; betray; show unintentionally ≃ 露着〔**~宾**〕〈名〉脸上~出愉快的❶神色❷；~出掩不住❸的笑意❹〔**~补**〕〈结〉不安的❺神情❻~在脸上〈趋〉~出内心❼的想法；~出悲哀❽的感情❾；~出庄严❿的神情〔**状~**〕从脸上~；从嘴角⓫上~；明显地⓬~；自然地⓭~；不知不觉⓮~出了；从字里行间⓯~出

1. happy **2.** expression; look **3.** cannot conceal **4.** smile **5.** uneasy; disturbed; restless **6.** expression; look **7.** in one's heart **8.** grieved; sorrowful **9.** emotion; feeling; sentiment **10.** solemn **11.** corners of the mouth **12.** obviously **13.** naturally **14.** unconsciously; unwittingly **15.** between the lines

liú 留 ① remain; stay; ask sb. to stay ≃ 停留；挽留〔**～宾**〕〈名〉她毕业以后～校工作〈代〉你今天有事我就不～你了；他～我吃饭；叔叔❶～我住几天〔**～补**〕〈结〉孩子～在奶奶❷家了；你小时候的样子还深深地❸～在我的记忆❹中；你们都回去吧，我一个人～在这儿就行了；她非要走，谁也没～住她；到处都～下过他的足迹❺；给我～下了一个好印象❻；～下我一个人看(kān)家❼〈趋〉我们都劝❽她～下来，所以她决定❾不走了〈程〉他留客人～得很恳切❿；～得很热情〈可〉谁也～不住他；今年学校～不了(liǎo)太多毕业生〈时〉～了半天还是没留住〈量〉～过他两次了；会后请各班班长～一下儿〔**状～**〕热情地～；诚恳地⓫～；再三～；一共～；不能强⓬～

1. uncle **2.** grandmother **3.** deeply **4.** remembrance **5.** footmark; footprint; track **6.** good impression **7.** look after the house **8.** advise **9.** decide **10.** earnest; sincere **11.** sincerely; earnestly **12.** by force

② keep; reserve; save ≃ 保留〔**～宾**〕〈名〉给他～一个座位❶，他晚来一会儿；你～着这些钱自己用吧；～了一笔遗产❷；我去访问他，他不在家，只好给他～一个字条❸；她走的时候没～话❹；～地址❺；～电话号码；不用给他～饭了，他不回来吃了；作业后边～点空儿❻；这个人做事不～情面❼；他走的时候给我～了十块钱；～底稿❽；说话要～(有)余地❾；～头发；～胡子❿；～小辫⓫〔**～补**〕〈结〉电话号码～错了；她送我一张照片～做纪念⓬；～到明天再吃吧；饭～多了；时间～少了；头发～长点儿再去烫⓭；记事⓮本上的名字都～满了〈趋〉把礼物～下吧；～出地方来放东西；我把你喜欢吃的糖都～起来了；小胡子可别再～下去了；你能把车～下来给我用用吗？把他的座位先～出来；腿上～下来一块伤疤⓯；收据⓰先～起来吧〈程〉～得太多了；～得很少〈可〉天热了饭菜～不住；她的小辫儿总～不起来；头发～不长就剪掉⓱了〈时〉～了三年小辫〈量〉请你把地址～一下儿〔**状～**〕给他～个电话；替我～个座位；特意⓲～；只好～；不得不～；一直～；仍然～；仍旧～〔**习用**〕～得青山在，不怕没柴烧⓳；～后路⓴；手下～情㉑

1. seat **2.** legacy; inheritance; heritage **3.** brief note **4.** word (leave word) **5.** address **6.** space; blank space **7.** show no mercy **8.** draft; manuscript **9.** allow for unforeseen circumstances; leave some leeway 10. beard 11. plait 12. for a souvenir 13. perm 14. keep a record of events 15. scar 16. receipt 17. cut 18. specially; for a special purpose 19. as long as the green mountains are there, one need not worry about firewood — while there is life there is hope 20. keep a way open for retreat; leave a way out 21. show mercy or forgiveness

liú 遛 saunter; stroll ≅ 遛达；散步〔~宾〕〈名〉~马路❶；~大街❷；每天早上去公园~〔~补〕〈结〉每天~到小亭子❸那里就往回走；一直~到7点才回家；腿都~累了〈趋〉整天❹在马路上~来~去，一点正经事❺也不作；这两个人在公园里~过来~过去〈可〉这些日子太忙了，~不了(liǎo)马路了〈时〉那位退休❻的老人每天都要拄❼着手杖❽在住屋附近❾~一会儿；已经~了半天了，该回去了；天天都要~十几分钟〈量〉明天到哪儿去~一下儿？沿着❿湖边⓫~了一圈⓬〔状~〕沿着溪岸⓭~；在公园里~；陪着⓮他~；来回⓯~；整天~；独自⓰~；两个人一起~

1. 2. street 3. pavilion; kiosk 4. all day long 5. serious affairs 6. retired 7. lean on (a stick, etc.) 8. stick 9. nearby; neighbouring 10. along 11. the bank of a lake 12. in a circle 13. bank of a river 14. accompany 15. to and fro 16. alone; by oneself

lǒu 搂 hold in one's arms; hug; embrace ≅ 搂抱〔~宾〕〈名〉孩子~着妈妈的脖子❶；~着孩子的腰❷〔~补〕〈结〉~紧❸点儿；~松❹点儿；~住脖子；抱孩子的时候要~住腰；把孩子~在怀❺里〈趋〉把孩子~过去了；〈程〉~得很紧〈可〉这个柱子❻真粗❼，两个人都~不过来〔状~〕互相~；一只手~；一把~过来；紧紧地~；热情地❽~

1. neck 2. waist 3. close 4. loose 5. bosom 6. post; pillar 7. thick 8. warmly; enthusiastically; ardently

lòu 漏 ① leak〔主~〕〈名〉水壶❶~了；锅❷~了；房子~了；口袋❸~了；书包~了；鞋底~了〔~宾〕〈名〉照相机坏了，有些~光❹；窗帘❺没拉好，往外~光；房子~雨；水管子❻~水；钢笔~水儿；检查❼~不~煤气❽？油箱❾~油；锅坏了，炒菜❿时直~油；门牙⓫掉了，说话有些~风⓬〔~补〕〈结〉水都~光❸了；油都快~完了〈趋〉灯光从门缝⓮~出来了；口袋破了，钱都~出去了〈程〉水~得哪儿都是；房子~得一塌胡涂⓯；水龙头⓰坏了，水~得很厉害〈可〉窟窿⓱不大，东西~不出去〈时〉房子~了好多日子，也没人修理⓲〈量〉~过一次，现在修好了〔状~〕有点儿~；全~了；突然~了；又~了

1. kettle 2. pot; pan; boiler; cauldron 3. pocket 4. light 5.

curtain (window) 6. waterpipe 7. check up; examine; inspect 8. coal gas; gas 9. fuel tank 10. stir-fry; sauté 11. front tooth 12. speak indistinctly through having one or more front teeth missing 13. nothing left 14. a crack between a door and its frame 15. in an awful state 16. tap 17. hole 18. repair; mend

② be missing; leave out ≅ 遗漏〔～宾〕〈名〉这篇文章❶～了三行❷；抄❸的时候～了一段❹；～了两个人的名字；好象～了两个数字❺；～了几个号码❻〔～补〕〈结〉开车的时候～掉了一个人；书上～掉了一张图〔状～〕只～了一个字；在倒数第二行中间～了一个句号❼

1. essay; article 2. line 3. copy; transcribe 4. paragraph 5. figure 6. number 7. period; full stop

lòu 露 reveal; show 〔～宾〕〈名〉～脸；～头儿❶；～了马脚❷；想～一手儿❸；笑不要～齿❹；说话藏头～尾；他不愿意抛头～面❻〈形〉～丑❼〔～补〕〈结〉袜子❽破❾了，脚趾头❿～在外面；脸上～出了笑容；～出了一副可怜相⓫；大衣里～出白围巾⓬〈趋〉狐狸尾巴⓭～出来了〈可〉～不了(liǎo)马脚〔状～〕净⓮～丑；渐渐地⓯～出了笑容

1. head (show one's head) 2. sth. that gives the game away (show the cloven hoof; give oneself away) 3. proficiency; skill (make an exhibition of one's abilities or skills; show off) 4. tooth 5. show the tail but hide the head — tell part of the truth but not all of it 6. show one's face in public 7. disgraceful; shameful; scandalous (make a fool of oneself) 8. socks 9. broken 10. toe 11. pitiful appearance; a sorry figure 12. a white scarf 13. fox's tail — something that gives away a person's real character or evil intentions; cloven hoof 14. only; merely; nothing but 15. gradually

lù 录 tape-record 〔～宾〕〈名〉～音❶；～影❷；～了几首歌儿；～了一段讲话〔～补〕〈结〉这句话～错了；～完了；～好了吗？没～清楚；～在那盘磁带❸上了〈趋〉这个歌多好听啊，快～下来吧！〈程〉英语～得真清楚；他录音～得不错〈可〉这盘磁带～不了(liǎo)十课书；噪音❹太多，～不清楚；一个小时～不完；你～得好吗？〈时〉整整❺～了一个下午；能一个小时〈量〉～过好多次了；～一下儿试试〔状～〕在电台❻～；早就～了；马上～；用录音机～；用录影机～；正在～；已经～了；多～点儿；一次～完；分几次～

1. sound (sound recording) 2. video 3. magnetic tape 4. noise 5. whole 6. broadcasting (radio) station

lǚxíng 履行 perform; fulfil; carry out ≅ 实行; 执行〔**~宾**〕〈名〉~诺言❶; ~手续❷; ~合同❸; ~义务❹; ~职责❺; ~条约❻; ~公约❼〔**状~**〕认真~; 严格❽~; 从不~

1. promise 2. procedures; formalities 3. contract 4. duty; obligation; commitment 5. duty 6. treaty; pact 7. convention; pact 8. strictly

luò 落 ① fall; drop ≅ 掉下〔**主~**〕〈名〉花瓣❶~了; 秋天❷来了, 树叶都~了; 一阵风吹过, 花都~了〔**~宾**〕〈名〉桌子上~了一层尘土❸; ~了一身煤渣❹〔**~补**〕〈结〉雪花❺~在水里看不见了; 苹果~在地上了; 小路上~满了树叶〈趋〉一片羽毛❻~下来了; 降落伞❼~下来了〈程〉~得很快; ~得真慢〈可〉苹果还没熟❽呢, 如果不刮风~不下来〔**状~**〕飘飘摇摇地❾往下~; 一直往下~; 一夜之间树叶全~了

1. petal 2. autumn 3. dust 4. coal cinder 5. snowflake 6. feather; plume 7. parachute 8. not ripe 9. floating in the air

② go down; set ≅ 下降〔**主~**〕〈名〉潮水❶~了; 太阳~了; 价钱❷~了; 物价❸~了〔**~宾**〕〈名〉~价了; ~了不少; ~了一些〔**~补**〕〈趋〉石油价格❹~下来了〈程〉~得真快; ~得很慢〈可〉刚三点钟, 太阳还~不下去; ~不了(liǎo)〈时〉物价~了一个月, 又涨❺上去了〈量〉~过一次〔**状~**〕突然~; 一下子~; 慢慢~; 逐渐~; 很快~; 猛❻~

1. tidewater; tidal water 2. commodity prices 3. prices 4. oil price 5. rise; go up (of water, prices, etc.) 6. suddenly; abruptly

③ lower ≅ 放下〔**~补**〕〈趋〉把卷❶着的竹帘子❷~下来吧; 幕❸已经~下来了; 百叶窗❹~下来了〔**状~**〕赶快~; 慢慢地~; 幕徐徐地❺~

1. roll up 2. bamboo curtain 3. curtain; screen 4. shutter 5. slowly; gently

④ lag behind ≅ 遗留在后面〔**~补**〕〈结〉他在学习上进取心❶很强❷, 从不愿意~在别人的后面〔**状~**〕从未❸~; 一直~; 总是~
另见 là 落②

1. enterprising spirit 2. strong 3. never

⑤ decline; come down; sink ≅ 衰落〔**~补**〕〈结〉你怎么~到这种地步❶了〔**状~**〕一下子~; 居然❷~; 竟然❸~

1. get into such a mess 2. 3.unexpectedly; to one's surprise

⑥ leave behind; stay behind ≅ 停留; 留下〔**~宾**〕〈名〉屋顶上❶

~了很多鸽子❷；天黑了赶快找个地方~~脚吧❸；不~痕迹❹〔~补〕〈结〉喜鹊❺~在树上；海鸥❻~在沙滩❼上；他又给大家~(lào)下了一个笑柄❽〔状~〕已经~；正好~

1. roof 2. pigeon 3. let's stop for a rest 4. settle 5. magpie 6. sea gull 7. sandy beach 8. laughingstock; butt

⑦ fall onto; rest with 〔~补〕〈结〉这么重的任务❶都~在你一个人身上了；政权❷~在谁手里了？家庭重担❸都~在他哥哥肩上了；这个责任❹~在谁身上谁也受不了❺(liǎo)；〔状~〕只~；都~

1. hard task 2. political power 3. heavy burden 4. duty; responsibility 5. cannot bear; be unable to endure

⑧ get; have; receive ≅ 得到〔~宾〕〈名〉小时候❶得了小儿麻痹症❷，腿❸ ~了残疾❹〔~补〕〈结〉~下了一身毛病❺〔状~〕差点儿~〔习用〕~汤鸡❻

1. when one was young; as a child 2. infantile paralysis 3. leg 4. deformity 5. trouble; disease 6. like a drenched chicken; like a drowned rat; soaked through

M

mā 抹 wipe ≅ 擦〔～宾〕〈名〉～桌子；～玻璃❶；～了一把脸〔～补〕〈结〉用湿布❷抹，才能～掉❸〈趋〉用力抹能～下去吧。你怎么用我的洗脸毛巾❹～起桌子来了！〈程〉玻璃～得真亮；镜子❺～得不干净〈可〉椅子上粘❻了好多浆糊❼～不下去了；用脏布❽抹玻璃，～不干净〈时〉～了半天玻璃胳膊❾都酸❿了〈量〉用湿布～一下儿试试；桌子～过一遍了〔状～〕用干布～；用湿布～；好～吗？每天～

另见 mǒ 抹和 mò 抹

1. glass 2. wet cloth 3. wipe away 4. towel 5. mirror 6. glue; stick; paste 7. paste 8. dirty cloth 9. arm 10. ache; pain; sore

máfan 麻烦 put sb. to trouble; trouble sb; bother ≅ 打扰〔～宾〕〈代〉对不起，～您了；他已经够忙的了，不要再去～他了；你别去～人家❶了；没办法❷只好～你了；～你顺便❸告诉我家人一声，我今天可能回去晚一点儿；～你帮我打听❹打听他的住址❺；～你替我保存❻一下儿；～你去一趟吧；他是个大忙人❼，我们可不敢❽～他；这件事只好～他去办了〔～补〕〈结〉这件事又～上您了〈趋〉这件事变得～起来了〈可〉我只是顺便作这件事，～不了(liǎo)我什么；你不用躲着我们，我们～不着(zháo)你〈量〉～您一下儿，跟您打听一个人；～过他很多次了〔状～〕决不～别人；故意❾～人；屡次～；三番五次地～；自己能干的事何必❿～别人；尽量⓫不～别人；向来不～；不得不～；不用～；必须～；经常～

1. other people 2. it can't be helped 3. conveniently; in passing 4. ask about; inquire about 5. address 6. keep; preserve; conserve 7. busy person 8. dare not 9. on purpose; intentionally 10. there is no need; why 11. to the best of one's ability; as far as possible

mà 骂 abuse; curse; swear; call names〔～宾〕〈名〉～难听❶的话；他～人骂得真刺耳❷；这个人没有教养❸，一生气就～人；那个青年人没有礼貌❹，出口就～人；他喝醉了酒爱～人；这个人脾气❺太坏，动不动就～人〈代〉～我笨；～我糊涂❼；～我不求上进❽；～他没出息❾；～我不懂事❿〔～补〕〈结〉把我～急

⓫了；把她～哭了；孩子让他给～跑了；从早上一直～到现在〈趋〉～起人来真利害；那两个人不知为什么突然～起来了；他急了，什么难听的话都能～出来；一天到晚～过来～过去的〈程〉～得太凶⓬了；～得很难听；被～得抬不起头来了；被～得见不得人⓭了〈可〉那个人利害极了，可～不得；难听的话我可～不出来〈时〉整整～了一个晚上；～了一会儿，没人理⓮他，也就不骂了〈量〉～了一顿；～过几次；大～了一阵〔**状～**〕恶狠狠地⓯～；气势汹汹⓰地～；拍桌子瞪眼⓱地～；指着脸～；无缘无故地⓲～；破口大⓳～；边走边～；动不动就～；故意～；两个人对⓴～；暗地里㉑～；背后～；居然㉒～；一个劲儿㉓～；不停地㉔～；怪不得㉕～〔**习用**〕～大街㉖

1. unpleasant to hear **2.** ear-piercing; harsh **3.** education; **4.** politeness **5.** temper; disposition **6.** easily; frequently; at every turn **7.** muddled; confused; bewildered **8.** not strive to make progress **9.** spineless and sterile **10.** not intelligent; not sensible **11.** irritated; annoyed; nettled **12.** terrible **13.** shameful; scandalous **14.** pay no attention to; turn a deaf ear to **15.** fiercely; spitefully **16.** ferociously **17.** strike the table and glower at sb. (in anger) **18.** without cause or reason; for no reason at all **19.** shout abuse; let loose a torrent of abuse **20.** face to face **21.** in secret; behind; at the back **22.** unexpectedly; to one's surprise **23.** continuously; persistently **24.** ceaselessly **25.** no wonder **26.** shout abuses in the street

mái 埋 cover up; bury ≃ 埋藏

〔**～宾**〕〈名〉你蹲❶在那儿～什么东西？～珠宝❷；～财物❸；～地雷❹；～电线杆子❺〔**～补**〕〈结〉都被雪～上了；电线杆子～歪❻了；～斜❼了；小狗死了我把它～在树下了；～深❽点儿；～远❾点儿；～近❿点儿；他母亲就～在那个墓地⓫里〈趋〉骆驼队⓬被沙漠⓭～起来了；小路被落叶～起来了〈程〉～得很深；～得很浅⓮；～得很远；～得真快；路被大雪～得看不见了〈可〉土太少～不上；～得结实⓯～不结实？〈时〉这件文物⓰在地下～了三千多年才出土⓱；那具古尸⓲在地下～了两千多年，至今没有腐烂⓳；～了很长时间，也没被人发现〈量〉帮我～一下儿〔**状～**〕深深地～；深点儿～；结结实实地～；在山脚下⓴～；活㉑～人

1. squat on the heels **2.** pearls and jewels **3.** property; belongings **4.** mines (lay mines) **5.** (wire) pole **6.** askew; crooked; inclined **7.** oblique **8.** deep **9.** far **10.** near **11.** cemetry **12.** camel train; caravan **13.** desert **14.** shallow **15.** solid **16.** cultural relic **17.** be unearthed; be excavated **18.** ancient corpse **19.** decomposed; putrid **20.** at the foot of a hill **21.** alive

máicáng 埋藏 lie hidden in the earth; bury ≅ 埋〔~宾〕〈名〉地下~着丰富❶的石油❷；~着煤❸、铁❹、铜❺；~着有色金属❻；~着稀有金属❼〔~补〕〈结〉把话~在心里；把痛苦❽~在心底；~在心底的仇恨❾，像火山❿一样爆发⓫出来了〈趋〉已经~起来了〈时〉已经~了很多年了；~了几个世纪⓬了〔状~〕一直~在心里；树底下果然⓭~着一箱⓮珍宝⓯

1. rich; abundant 2. petroleum; oil 3. coal 4. iron 5. copper 6. nonferrous metal 7. rare metal 8. pain; suffering 9. hatred; hostility 10. volcano 11. erupt 12. century 13. really; as expected 14. chest; box; case 15. treasure

máimò 埋没 ①bury; cover up ≅ 掩埋〔~宾〕〈名〉泥石流❶~了一座城市〔~补〕〈结〉~在沙漠❷中了；~在地底下了〔状~〕被~；让土~了

1. mud-rock flow 2. desert

② neglect; stifle〔~宾〕〈名〉~了人材❶；~了天才❷〈代〉千万不要~了他〔~补〕〈可〉什么人才也~不了(liǎo)〈时〉~了一辈子❸〔状~〕被~；彻底~了；差点儿❹~；几乎❺~；千万❻别~

1. talented person 2. genius; talent; gift 3. the whole life 4. 5. almost; nearly; on the verge of 6. be sure to

máizàng 埋葬 bury ≅ 葬〔~宾〕〈名〉这个墓❶里~着一个皇帝〔~补〕〈结〉~在大海里；~在鱼腹中❷〈趋〉买了一块墓地把他~起来了〈程〉~得很深〈时〉~了两千多年的古尸❸最近出土❹了〔状~〕被~；在什么地方~

1. grave; tomb 2. become fish food; be swept to a watery grave 3. ancient corpse 4. be unearthed

mǎi 买 buy; purchase ↔ 卖〔~宾〕〈名〉~礼物❶；~零食❷；~衣服；~房子；~家具❸；~地毯❹；~书；~字画❺；~汽车〔~补〕〈结〉电影票~着(zháo)了吗？需要的东西都~齐❻了；苹果~少了；~通❼了海关人员❽；我的洗衣机和电视机都~贵❾了，现在比我买的时候便宜❿多了〈趋〉我把他那辆旧汽车~下来了；那个彩色电视机他刚~进来又卖出去了；把送人的礼物都~回来了〈程〉~得太多了，吃不下了(liǎo)；~得不满意⓫；~得不理想⓬；~得真便宜〈可〉大衣那么贵我~不起；这种东西现在你到那儿去买也~不到；去晚了就~不着(zháo)了〈时〉这种式样的毛衣⓭我~了好几年也没买着(zháo)；~了好久了〈量〉~过一次，尝了尝⓮不好吃，以后就再也没买〔状~〕多~点儿；这种药真难~；别乱⓯~；用现金⓰~；用支票⓱~；在小摊儿上⓲~；零⓳~；临时⓴~

1. present; gift 2. snacks (nibble between meals) 3. furniture 4.

carpet 5. calligraphy and painting 6. complete 7. bribe; buy over 8. customs officer 9. be dearly bought 10. cheap 11. unsatisfied 12. not ideal 13. woolen sweater 14. taste; try the flavour 15. casually; at random 16. in cash 17. in check 18. at vendor's stand; at a street booth 19. at retail 20. provisonally; at the time when sth. happens

mài 迈 step; stride ≃ 跨; 跨步 〔**～宾**〕〈名〉孩子刚学会～步❶; ～着矫健的步伐❷; ～着坚定的步伐❸; 他一步～了两级台阶❹; ～过一潭水❺; ～过这条沟❻; ～过小溪❼; ～过泥潭❽〔**～补**〕〈结〉～开大步往前走〈趋〉地上有一潭水, ～过去吧; 没看见, 一脚就～到水里去了; 栏杆❾很矮❿一迈就～过去了〈程〉步子～得太大了, 我跟不上⓫你; 他虽然步子～得小, 速度⓬却很快〈可〉门槛⓭太高～不过去; 人多得要命⓮, 连腿⓯都～不开〈量〉这条沟一天得～好几次, 赶快填死⓰就好了〔**状～**〕吃力地⓱～; 费劲儿⓲地～; 敏捷地⓳～; 往上～; 一下子就～了过去

1. take a step 2. vigorous strides 3. firm strides 4. two steps 5. mire 6. ditch 7. small stream 8. mire 9. railing; banisters; balustrade 10. low; short 11. not catch up with 12. speed 13. threshold 14. awfully; extremely 15. leg 16. fill up 17. strenuously 18. with great effort 19. agilely; nimbly

mài 卖 ① sell ↔ 买〔**～宾**〕〈名〉～菜; ～报; ～小吃❶; ～电影票; ～百货❷; ～书; ～了一所房子〔**～补**〕〈结〉菜都～完了; 票～光❸了; 屋子里的家具❹～空❺了; 货～错了; 这个月～亏❻了; ～惯❼了鱼, 就不怕腥味❽儿了; 把画～给书店了〈趋〉那本字典～出去了; 你原来不是理发❾的吗, 怎么现在～起百货来了? 〈程〉那个年轻的售货员❿～得挺快; 那种样式⓫的鞋～得比较慢; 打字机⓬～得太贵了; 这个牌子⓭的缝纫机⓮为什么～得那么便宜啊? 〈可〉这么多西瓜两天也～不完; 这一批⓯货⓰好长时间也～不掉〈时〉这是热门货⓱, 刚～一会儿, 就卖完了; ～了两三天, 才卖出去〈量〉～一下儿试试; 在大街上摆摊⓲～过两回〔**状～**〕容易～; 真难～; 零⓳～; 成批(地)～; 拍～⓴; 亏本㉑也～; 廉价㉒～; 高价㉓～; 摆摊～; 推车㉔～; 在店里～; 沿街叫～㉕

1. snack; refreshments 2. general merchandise 3. be sold out 4. furniture 5. empty 6. lose (money); have a deficit 7. be used to; be in the habit of 8. smelling of fish 9. barber 10. young shop assistant 11. pattern; style; form 12. typewriter 13. brand 14. sewing machine 15. batch; lot; group 16. goods; commodity 17. goods in great demands 18. set up a stall 19. retail 20. auction; selling off goods at reduced prices 21. lose money 22. at a low price; cheap

23. at a high price 24. push a cart 25. hawk one's wares in the streets

② exert to the utmost; not spare 〔～宾〕〈名〉小李今天工作得真～力气；士兵们没有人愿意为侵略战争❶～命❷的；他既然对你不好，你就别为他～命了了〔～补〕〈结〉～完了力气；～完了劲❸〔状～〕傻❹～力气；别～命了；不再～；猛❺～；为谁～？

1. war of aggression 2. work oneself to the bone; die for 3. spare no effort 4. think or act mechanically 5. with vim and vigour

màinòng 卖弄 show off; parade ≅ 炫耀，故意显示〔～宾〕〈名〉～才华❶；～才能❷；～学问❸；～辞藻❹；～小聪明❺；～风骚❻〔～补〕〈结〉～完了；～够了〈趋〉她又在人面前～起来了〈程〉～得太利害了；～得非常恶心❼〈可〉他在我面前～不起来；想卖弄可是肚里空空的又～不上来〈时〉～了半天〈量〉～过好几次；～了一番〔状～〕故意❽～；有意❾～；一再～；有机会就❿～；人越多他越～；从来不～；不由自主地⓫～

1. literary or artistic talent 2. ability; talent 3. learning; knowledge 4. flowery language; ornate phrases 5. smartness 6. coquettish; literary excellence 7. feel like vomiting; feel nauseated 8. 9. intentionally; on purpose 10. whenever the opportunity arises 11. involuntarily; cannot help

mányuàn 埋怨 blame; complain; grumble ≅ 抱怨〔～宾〕〈名〉～父母；～孩子〈代〉～自己；～人家❶；～谁？〔～补〕〈结〉这个录音机❷明明是他搞❸坏的，他却～上我了；你～错人了〈趋〉他们两个人为了一点小事又互相～起来了；还没找到真正的原因❹呢，就～起来了〈程〉～得让人心烦❺；～得让人受不了❻(liǎo)；～得一点道理也没有〈可〉这是你自己弄坏❼的，～不了(liǎo)我〈时〉为这件事他～了我很长时间〈量〉～过她两次〔状～〕总～；互相～；直～；千万❽别再～了；不好意思❾～

1. other people 2. tape recorder 3. do; work 4. cause; reason 5. be vexed; be perturbed 6. cannot bear 7. ruin; put out of order 8. be sure to; mind you 9. feel embarrassed

mán 瞒 hide the truth from ≅ 隐瞒〔～宾〕〈名〉～着他母亲；我没有～人的事情；不要～岁数❶〈代〉她孩子受伤❷的消息❸一直～着她〔～补〕〈结〉他家的丑事❹没～住，现在谁都知道了〈趋〉不要再继续～下去了；把真正的意图❺～起来了；因为怕家里人着急，所以把自己得❻了癌症❼的消息～了起来〈程〉～得一点风声❽都不透❾〈可〉什么也～不住他，他的消息最灵通⑩了；什么事儿也～不过她〈量〉先暂时⑪～一下儿她；～过他一次〔状～〕不用～；整整～了三年；一直～着他；有意地⑫～；千万⑬别～

1. year (of age) 2. be injured; be wounded 3. news 4. scandal 5. idea; opinion; what one has in mind 6. get 7. cancer 8. rumour 9. not leak out 10. well-informed 11. for the time being 12. purposely; intentionally 13. be sure to

mǎnzú 满足 ① satisfy; meet 〔～宾〕〈名〉～消费者❶的需要；～大家的要求；～了他多年的心愿❷；～了愿望❸；～了欲望❹；～了他的好奇心❺；～了他的求知欲❻〔～补〕〈可〉他的欲望老～不了(liǎo)〈量〉一下儿；我的合理❼要求，一次都没～过〔状～〕尽量❽～；尽可能❾～；无法❿～；很好地～；充分⓫～；适当⓬～

1. consumer 2. cherished desire; aspiration 3. desire; aspiration 4. desire; wish; lust 5. curiosity 6. thirst for knowledge 7. rational; reasonable 8. 9. to the best of one's ability; as far as possible 10. unable to; incapable of 11. sufficiently; completely; thoroughly 12. properly; suitably

② be satisfied with; be content with ≅ 满意〔～宾〕〈名〉～(于)已经取得❶的成绩❷；～(于)现有❸的水平❹；～(于)一知半解❺；～现状❻；～现在的生活〔状～〕决不～；从来不～；永远不～；很容易～；非常～

1. gain; acquire; obtain 2. result; achievement; success 3. existing; now available 4. level 5. (have) a smattering of knowledge; have scanty (half-baked) knowledge 6. present situation; status quo

mào 冒 ① emit; send out; give off〔～宾〕〈名〉工厂里的烟囱❶～黑烟❷；急❸得头上直～汗❹；香❺一直在～烟；热水❻～泡❼儿，马上就要开❽了；刚出笼的❾馒头❿还～热气⓫呢；从阴沟⓬往外～臭味儿⓭；眼睛～金星⓮；气得心里直～火⓯〔～补〕〈结〉烟囱里～出了浓烟〔状～〕往上～；从地下～；一阵阵地⓰～汗；一股股地～臭味儿；一缕缕地～烟⓱

1. chimney 2. black smoke 3. worry about; be anxious 4. sweat kept oozing out 5. incense 6. hot water 7. bubble (send up bubbles) 8. be about to boil 9. fresh from the food steamer 10. steamed bun 11. vapour; steam 12. sewer 13. offensive smell; stink 14. see stars 15. burn with anger 16. now ... now 17. a wisp of smoke

② risk; brave ≅ 不顾；顶着〔～宾〕〈名〉～着风浪❶出海捕鱼❷；～着大雨回家；～着大风雪❸去

追赶❹羊群；～着敌人的炮火❺前进；～着枪林弹雨❻；～着严寒❼；～着危险❽；～着生死来看我〈主-谓〉～着生命危险；〔状～〕经常～

1. the wind and the waves 2. go fishing on the sea 3. snowstorm; blizzard 4. run after; pursue 5. artillery fire; gunfire 6. a hail of bullets 7. severe cold 8. risk

③ assume false identity; act under false pretences ≅ 冒充〔～宾〕〈名〉～名❶；～牌儿❷

1. assume another's name 2. forge a trade-mark (of goods)

màochōng 冒充 pretend to be

〔～宾〕〈名〉～某公司经理❶；～警察❷；～名牌货❸；～好人〔～补〕〈时〉那个骗子❹冒充保安人员❺了好几年，最后终于被发现❻了〔状～〕竟然❼～；屡次❽～；一直～；多次～

1. director; manager 2. police 3. famous brand of goods 4. swindler; imposter 5. public security officer 6. be discovered 7. to one's surprise; unexpectedly 8. over and over again

mēn 闷 cover tightly

〔～补〕〈结〉茶已经～好了；有话说出来，别～在心里〈趋〉要多闷一会儿，才能把茶味儿❶～出来〈程〉茶味儿～得真香❷；～得真浓❸〈可〉不是刚开的水～不好茶；没有茶杯盖儿❹～不了(liǎo)〈时〉茶多～一会儿好喝；水不开❺，～了半天茶叶❻还漂在上面；多～一会儿再喝〔状～〕早一点儿～；有话别～在心里

1. smell; taste; flavour 2. fragrant 3. heavy; strong; dense 4. teacup lid 5. not boiled 6. tea; tea-leaves

méng 蒙 ① cheat; deceive; dupe

≅ 蒙骗；骗〔～宾〕〈名〉不要～人；他就爱～人〈代〉你可别～我〔～补〕〈结〉今天我可让你给～着(zháo)了，你说的话我居然❶信以为真❷了〈趋〉他～起人来可真有办法❸；这一次又被他～过去了〈程〉让他～得晕头转向❹〈可〉你～得了(liǎo)别人，可～不了(liǎo)我〈量〉她～过我好几次了，以后再也不要相信❺她了〔状～〕净❻～人；三番五次地❼～
另见 méng 蒙

1. unexpectedly; to one's surprise 2. accept sth. as true 3. have real skill 4. confused and disoriented; get sb. confused 5. believe 6. only; merely; nothing but 7. over and over again

méng 蒙 cover ≅ 盖；捂

〔～宾〕〈名〉睡觉时不要用被❶～头；尸体❷上～着一条白单子❸；用手～着她的眼睛，让她猜❹是谁；怕婴儿❺被风吹着，妈妈在孩子头上～了一条纱巾❻；昨天他～头大睡❼了一天〔～补〕〈结〉风刮过去以后，到处都～上了一层土；

～住眼睛；～住头；没～好〈趋〉〈程〉～得很严❽，一点风也进不来；～得不严，露❾了一条缝儿❿〈可〉这块布太小～不上〔状～〕用手～眼睛；在头上～；别～；往上一～就看不见了〔习用〕～在鼓里⓫
另见 mēng 蒙

1. quilt 2. corpse 3. white sheet 4. guess 5. baby 6. gauze kerchief 7. sleep heavily; sleep abundantly 8. tight; close 9. reveal 10. crack; crevice; fissure 11. be kept inside a drum — be kept in the dark

mī 眯 narrow (one's eyes) 〔～宾〕〈名〉～着眼睛笑；～着眼睛看〔～补〕〈结〉她笑得眼睛都～成一道缝❶了；～成一条线❷〈趋〉他有点近视❸，看什么都把眼睛～起来〈程〉眼睛～得很细❹〔状～〕使劲❺～着；总～着；故意❻～着

1. crack 2. shaped like a line 3. short-sighted 4. thin 5. exert all one's strength 6. on purpose; intentionally

míbǔ 弥补 make up; remedy; make good ≅ 填补〔～宾〕〈名〉～缺陷❶；～不足之处❷；～损失❸；～赤字❹；～亏损❺；～弱点❻〔～补〕〈结〉～上了〈可〉～得了(liǎo) ～不了(liǎo)？〔状～〕无法❼～；千万百计❽～；好好～；难以～；好容易才～上

1. 2. defect; drawback 3. loss; damage 4. deficit 5. loss 6. weakness; weak point 7. unable to; incapable of 8. by hook or by crook

mímàn 弥漫 fill the air; spread all over the place ≅ 充满；布满〔主～〕〈名〉山上雾气❶～；天上阴云❷～；空中烟雾❸～；烟尘❹～；风雪❺～；屋子里香气❻～；花房里花香～〔～宾〕〈名〉房间里～着中药❼味儿〔～补〕〈结〉忧愁❽象浓雾❾一样～在他的心头〔状～〕到处～；仍然❿～着

1. fog; mist 2. dark clouds 3. smoke; mist; vapour 4. smoke and dust 5. wind and snow 6. sweet smell 7. traditional Chinese medicine 8. anxiety; sorrow 9. dense fog 10. still; yet

mí 迷 ① be confused; be lost ≅ 迷失〔～宾〕〈名〉～路；～了方向❶〔～补〕〈可〉放心吧，我～不了(liǎo) 路〈量〉～过好几次路了〔状～〕几乎～；突然～；在森林中❷～；航海❸时～；夜里走路时～了路；在一个生疏的地方❹～了方向

1. (lose) one's bearings 2. in the forest 3. navigation 4. be unfamiliar with the place

② be fascinated by; be crazy about〔～补〕〈结〉孩子被橱窗❶

里的玩具❷～住了；她～上了京剧❸〔状～〕一下子把他～住了；简直❹让它给～住了

1. shopwindow; show window 2. toy 3. Beijing (Peking) opera 4. simply; at all

③ confuse; perplex; fascinate; enchant〔主～〕〈名〉景色❶～人；她的美貌❷～人；月光～人〔～宾〕〈名〉别让钱财～了心窍❸〔～补〕〈结〉把人～住了；被景色～住了〈程〉被～得神魂颠倒❹〔状～〕真～人；非常～；特别～〔习用〕～魂汤❺；～魂阵❻；财～心窍

1. scenery 2. good looks 3. be obsessed by a lust for wealth 4. be infatuated 5. sth. intended to turn sb's head; magic potion 6. a scheme for confusing or bewildering sb.; maze; trap

míhuo 迷惑 confuse; perplex; baffle〔～宾〕〈名〉～人；千方百计❶～敌人〈代〉休想❷～我〔～补〕〈结〉被她～住了；～上了〈程〉被他～得太利害❸了；让她给～得晕头转向❹〈可〉谁也～不了(liǎo)我〔状～〕用花言巧语❺～；使用各种办法❻～他

1. by hook or by crook 2. don't imagine that it's possible 3. terrible 4. confused and disoriented; get sb. confused 5. sweet words; blandishments 6. by every possible means

míxìn 迷信 superstition; superstitious belief; blind faith; blind worship〔～宾〕〈名〉～神❶；～鬼❷；～个人❸的权力❹；不要～名人❺〔～补〕〈程〉～极了；～得不得了(liǎo)〈可〉可～不得啊！〔状～〕特别～；决不～

1. god 2. ghost 3. individual; personal 4. power 5. famous person

miǎn 免 excuse sb. from sth.; exempt; dispense with ≅ 省去；去掉；除掉〔主～〕〈名〉这些手续❶可以～了；考试❷可不能～；礼节❸已经～了；结婚典礼❹是否可以～了〔～宾〕〈名〉～费❺；～了很多税❻；～了三年刑❼；他被～职❽了〈动〉他可以～试英语了❾；能不能～考；～服兵役❿〔～补〕〈结〉这些不必要的⓫手续都可以～掉；他的工作太重⓬，给他～掉几项吧〈量〉～了一次期中⓭考试〔状～〕一律⓮～费；全部～

1. procedures 2. examination 3. courtesy; ceremony 4. wedding; marriage ceremony 5. free charge 6. tax 7. exempt from punishment 8. remove sb. from office 9. be excused from an examination of English 10. exempt from military service 11. unnecessary 12. too heavy 13. midterm 14. all; without exception

miǎnlì 勉励 encourage; urge ≅ 鼓励〔～宾〕〈名〉～孩子好好学习

〈代〉~他继续努力〔~补〕〈时〉~了我半天〔~量〕~了他一番；~过我不少次〔状~〕临行前❶~；再三~；诚恳地❷~；热情地❸~；互相~

1. on departure; before leaving 2. sincerely 3. warmly

miǎnqiǎng 勉强 force sb. to do sth.
〔主~〕〈代〉这个手提包❶太重❷，你拿不动不要~〔~宾〕〈名〉最好不要~孩子〈代〉他吃不下就不要~他了；她不愿意去就不要~她了；我不想~你买这个；不应该~他去做他不愿意做的事情；不能~我跟她结婚❸；别人家那么早睡觉〔~补〕〈可〉婚姻❹大事❺是~不得的；什么事勉强是~不了(liǎo)的〔状~〕别~；再~；决不~

1. handbag 2. too heavy 3. marry 4. marriage 5. important matter

miáo 描 ① trace; copy
〔~宾〕〈名〉~图；~花；~一个样子❶；~一个轮廓❷；一个图案❸〔~补〕〈结〉样子~错了；图~走样❹了；颜色~深❺了；~浅❻了；描过一遍又描，～重❼(chóng)了；这种图案我都~熟❽了；清楚点儿就好了〈趋〉我~出来的图有点走样了；他~出来的图又快又好；看着很简单❾，~起来就不容易❿了〈程〉~得很清楚〈可〉这张图太复杂，我可能~不了(liǎo)；一个小时~得出来吗?〈时〉已经~了两个多小时了，刚

描完一半，这张画至少⓫要一个星期〔~量〕我~一下试试；~过两次〔状~〕细心⓬点儿~；耐心地⓭~；粗粗地⓮~；用彩色笔⓯~；一笔一笔地~；在玻璃⓰上~；重新~；真难~；专⓱~花鸟⓲

1. sample; model; pattern 2. outline; contour; rough sketch 3. pattern; design 4. lose shape 5. dark; deep 6. (of colour) light 7. repeat; duplicate 8. experienced; practised 9. simple 10. not easy 11. at least 12. carefully 13. patiently 14. roughly 15. colour pencil 16. glass 17. specially 18. flowers and birds

② touch up; retouch〔~宾〕〈名〉演员❶正在~眉❷；~字〔~补〕〈结〉~完了吗? ~坏了；~深❸了；~浅❹了；~粗❺了；~细❻了〈趋〉她对着镜子❼~起眉毛来了；写毛笔字别老~来~去的〈程〉~得很好〈可〉用这种笔描眉~不上吧〈时〉~了半天眉〈量〉用力~一下儿；~过一次〔状~〕写毛笔字一笔写下去，别来回❽~；淡淡地❾~；一笔一画地❿~

1. actor or actress; performer 2. eyebrow 3. deep 4. light (of colour) 5. thick 6. thin 7. mirror 8. back and forth 9. thinly 10. one stroke after another

miè 灭 ① go out ≅熄灭
〔主~〕〈名〉路灯❶~了；火~了；炉子❷~了；烟❸~了；火柴❹~了；

蜡烛❺；~了〔~宾〕〈名〉沙土❻可以~火，水也可以~火〔~补〕〈程〉路灯~得很晚〈可〉你看看，这炉子~得了(liǎo)~不了(liǎo)，〈量〉~过好几次了〔状~〕突然~；一下子~了；蜡烛被风一吹就~

1. street lamp 2. stove 3. cigarette 4. match 5. candle 6. sand

② destroy; exterminate; wipe ≅ 消灭；毁灭〔~宾〕〈名〉大家都来~蚊❶；~蝇❷；~虫；了敌人的威风❸〔~补〕〈可〉得了(liǎo)~不了(liǎo)？总~不彻底〈量〉~了很多次了；每年要~一次〔状~〕彻底~；尽早❹~；采取有效的措施❺~；自生自~❻

1. mosquito 2. fly 3. power and prestige (puncture the enemy's arrogance) 4. as early as possible 5. take effective measures 6. (of a thing) emerge of itself and perish of itself; run its course

míng 鸣 ① the cry of birds, animals or insects ≅ 叫〔主~〕〈名〉鸟❶~；蝉❷~；秋虫❸~

1. bird 2. cicada 3. autumn insects

② ring; sound〔主~〕〈名〉耳❶~；雷❷~〔~宾〕〈名〉~鼓❸；~锣❹；~笛❺；~枪❻；~礼炮❼；~了二十一响❽〔状~〕自~得意❾〔习用〕~锣开道❿；孤掌难~⓫

1. ear 2. thunder 3. drum 4. gong 5. whistle; bamboo flute 6. rifle; gun 7. salvo; (gun) salute 8. a 21-gun salute 9. be very pleased with oneself 10. beat gongs to clear the way (for officials in feudal times); prepare the public for a coming event 11. it's impossible to clap with one hand; it's difficult to achieve anything without support

mō 摸 ① feel; stroke; touch〔~宾〕〈名〉她爱抚地❶~了~孩子的头；我~了~他的脸，觉得有点发烧；你~~这块板子❷刨❸得多平；你~~我的头发洗得多松软❹；~~这块料子❺质量❻怎么样；让医生~~这里有没有肿块儿❼〔~补〕〈结〉这里长了一个瘤子❽，你~着(zháo)了没有？〈趋〉你能~出这种料子的好坏来吗？〈可〉我~不出来好坏，~不出来薄厚❾〈量〉他很有经验❿，~一下儿就知道质量如何〔状~〕用手~；轻轻地~；仔细地⓫~；爱抚地~；一遍遍地~

1. tenderly 2. board; plank 3. plane 4. soft; sponge 5. material for making clothes 6. quality 7. 8. tumour 9. thickness 10. experience 11. carefully; attentively

② grope; try to find out ≅ 摸索；找寻；掏；探取〔~宾〕〈名〉~鱼；~虾❶；~鸟蛋❷；他想~我们的底❸；~~他们对这个

问题的看法❹；～～她的脾气❺；～点经验❻；～点规律❼；电线❽被风刮断❾了，蜡烛❿也用完了，只好～黑儿了⓫〔～补〕〈结〉～着(zháo)一条大鱼；～透⓬了她的脾气；～清了他们的情况；～着(zháo)火柴⓭了吗？〈趋〉～上来不少鱼虾；从口袋⓮里～出一张纸条⓯来；从书包里～出一支钢笔来；～出不少好经验来〈程〉情况～得真详细⓰〈可〉～不清他是什么意思；～不透他是个什么样的人；对这件事我有点～不着(zháo)头脑⓱〈时〉～了一年多，才找着(zháo)窍门⓲；～了半天黑儿，电线好容易⓳修⓴好了〔状～〕在小河沟㉑里～鱼；在黑暗㉒中～；慢慢～着黑儿回去；始终㉓～不清

1. shrimp **2.** eggs **3.** not know the real situation **4.** view; a way of looking at a thing **5.** temper; temperament **6.** experience **7.** law **8.** electric wire **9.** be broken **10.** candle **11.** grope one's way on a dark night **12.** fully; thoroughly **13.** match **14.** pocket **15.** a slip of paper **16.** in detail **17.** be unable to make head or tail of sth. **18.** key (to a problem); knack **19.** with great difficulty **20.** repair; mend **21.** small stream **22.** in the dark **23.** from beginning to end

mófǎng 模仿 imitate; copy; model oneself on〔～宾〕〈名〉机器人❶～人的动作❷；口技❸演员能～火车行走的声音；孩子～大人走路；鹦鹉❹和八哥❺是否❻都能～人说话〔～补〕〈趋〉开始～起外国来了；～出来的产品跟原来❼的一样〈程〉～得真象❽；～得非常成功；～得跟原来的一模一样❾〈可〉～得了(liǎo)～不了(liǎo)？〈量〉想～一下儿；～过好几次都没成功〔状～〕专门❿～；精心⓫～；常常～；一遍一遍地～

1. robot **2.** action **3.** vocal mimicry; vocal imitation **4.** parrot **5.** myna **6.** whether; if **7.** original **8.** be very much alike **9.** as like as two peas **10.** specially; particularly **11.** meticulously; painstakingly; carefully

mó 磨 ① rub; wear ≃ 摩擦〔～宾〕〈名〉这双鞋有点儿～脚；脚上～了一个大泡❶；刀把儿❷太粗糙❸有点儿～手〔～补〕〈结〉鞋把脚都～红了；袜子❹～破❺了；鞋根❻～平了；鞋底❼～薄❽了；刚削❾的铅笔又～秃❿了；鞋钉⓫都～亮⓬了；我劝⓭了他半天，嘴皮子⓮都快～破了；绳子～断了；手～破了一点皮〈趋〉手都～出老茧⓯来了；～出大泡来了〈程〉脚～得真疼〈可〉～得破～不破？～不了(liǎo)〔状～〕容易～

1. blister **2.** handle **3.** coarse; rough; crude **4.** sock **5.** torn; worn-out **6.** heel (of a shoe) **7.** sole (of a shoe) **8.** thin **9.** sharpen **10.** blunt **11.** tack **12.** bright **13.**

mó — mǒ

advise 14. lips (of a glib talker) 15. callosity; callus

② grind; polish〔~宾〕〈名〉~刀；~冰刀❶；~剪刀❷；~墨❸写毛笔❹字；~大理石❺〔~补〕〈结〉刀子～快❻点儿；墨～稠❼了；把这块石头～圆了；磨刀石❽都～成月牙形❾了；把铅笔～尖点儿❿；先把石头～平了，再刻图章⓫〈程〉刀～得真快；墨～得太稠了〈可〉怎么磨也～不平；剪刀自己～不好〈时〉剪刀～了10分钟就好了〈量〉～过好几次了；～几下儿就行了〔状~〕好～；来回⓬～；用力～；在磨刀石上～

1. (ice) skates 2. scissors 3. Chinese ink 4. writing brush 5. marble 6. sharp 7. thick 8. grindstone 9. crescent moon 10. be sharpened 11. engrave a seal 12. back and forth; to and fro

③ trouble; pester; worry ≌ 纠缠〔~宾〕〈名〉这孩子真～人；这孩子净～大人〔~补〕〈结〉那孩子把他爸爸～急❶了；这孩子可把我～坏了；都快把人～死❷了〈趋〉这孩子平常很好玩❸，～起人来可真要命❹；～起人来真讨厌❺〈程〉把我～得一点办法也没有了；～得母亲干脆❻不理他了〈时〉孩子～了半天，爸爸才答应带他去动物园〔状~〕真～人；一个劲儿地～❼

1. irritated; annoyed; nettled 2. extremely; to death 3. be very cute 4. confoundedly; extreme-

ly; awfully 5. disgusting 6. simply; 7. persistently; continuously

④ wear down; wear out ≌ 折磨〔~宾〕〈名〉慢性病❶真～人〔~补〕〈结〉病把她～成这个样子❷了，这种病把人都～烦❸了；～急❹了；～死❺了〈程〉风湿病❻把他～得情绪❼很低❽；把他～得不象样子❾了；～得她见着(zháo)人就哭；～得她活不下去了〈时〉～了十几年；～了半辈子〔状~〕真～；被病～〔习用〕好事多～❿；～嘴皮子⓫；～牙⓬

另见 mò 磨

1. chronic disease 2. so; such; like this 3. be vexed; be annoyed 4. irritated; annoyed; nettled 5. extremely; to death 6. rheumatism 7. morale; feeling; mood 8. very low 9. worn to a mere shadow 10. the road to happiness is strewn with setbacks; the course of true love never did run smooth 11. jabber; blah-blah 12. indulge in idle talk

mǒ 抹 ① put on; apply; smear; plaster ≌ 涂抹〔~宾〕〈名〉～粉❶；～药膏❷；～了一层浆糊❸；～点胶水❹；～果酱❺；～蜂蜜❻；～口红❼；墙上～了一层油漆❽〔~补〕〈结〉浆糊～多了；果酱～少了；药膏别～厚❾了；药水❿～错了；粉没～匀⓫；浆糊～在邮票上〈趋〉紫药水⓬～上去，等一会儿才能干〈程〉粉～得太厚了；果酱～得真多〈可〉这种墙~不上浆糊，所以不能贴❸纸；她的皮肤❹怕刺激❺，~不了(liǎo)香粉❻〈量〉~一下儿试试〔状~〕在患处❼~药；用手~；厚厚地~了一层；薄薄地~了一层

1. powder 2. ointment; salve 3. paste 4. mucilage; glue 5. jam 6. honey 7. lipstick 8. paint 9. thick 10. liquid medicine 11. not evenly spread 12. gentian violet 13. paste; stick; glue 14. skin 15. stimulate 16. face powder 17. affected part (of a patient's body)

② cross (或 strike blot) out; erase ≅ 勾掉；除去〔~宾〕〈名〉~了一行❶字；~了一段❷录音❸；~了三个人的名字〔~补〕〈结〉~掉❹磁带❺上的歌曲❻；~错了，还得(děi)重写❼〈趋〉把没用的段落❽都~去了；刚录好的课文怎么就~下去了〈程〉~得乱七八糟❾；~得不干净；~得一塌糊涂❿〈可〉~得掉~不掉？〈时〉~了半天，还是能看出来；〈量〉~了好几下儿才抹下去〔状~〕用毛笔⓫~；全部~〔习用〕~了一鼻子灰⓬

1. line 2. part 3. sound recording 4. away; off 5. (magnetic) tape 6. song 7. rewrite 8. paragraph 9. in a mess; in a muddle 10. in a complete mess; in an awful state 11. writing brush 12. suffer a snub; meet with a rebuff

③ wipe ≅ 擦〔~宾〕〈名〉~了一把眼泪❶；用手巾❷~了~嘴；用抹布❸~桌子；~玻璃❹；用干毛巾❺~了~手〔~补〕〈结〉那个孩子眼泪还没~掉呢，就笑了；把手上的油都~在围裙❻上了〈趋〉墨水都~到脸上去了〈程〉~得哪儿都是；~得浑身❼都是；~得满脸满手都是〈可〉怎么抹也~不下去了〈时〉~了半天也没抹掉〈量〉那个孩子一天~好几次眼泪；随便❽~了几下桌子〔状~〕用湿❾抹布~；别往衣服上~；吃完饭把嘴一~就走了
另见mò抹和mā抹

1. tear 2. handkerchief 3. rag 4. glass 5. towel 6. apron 7. the whole body 8. casually; carelessly 9. wet

mò 没 overflow; rise beyond〔~宾〕〈名〉雪深❶~膝❷；~顶❸了〔~补〕〈结〉入水中；河水~过了马背❹〈可〉水那么浅，哪儿~得了顶啊！〔状~〕一下子~了；几乎~顶

1. deep 2. knee 3. above one's head 4. the back of a horse

mò 抹 daub; plaster〔~宾〕〈名〉~墙；~墙缝❶；~灰❷〔~补〕〈结〉把地~平；把墙缝~上；灰没~匀❸；树洞没~好〈程〉~得很平；~得真好；~得非常快〈可〉~得上吗？没有工具❹~不了(liǎo)〈时〉~了一上午也没抹完；~了两天〈量〉再~几下儿就行了；这条缝儿~过两次了〔状~〕用灰(泥❺/水泥❻)~；往墙

上～；多～点儿〔**习用**〕拐(转)弯～角❼
另见 mǒ 抹和 mā 抹

1. chink; crack 2. lime; mortar 3. not evenly spread 4. instrument 5. mud 6. cement 7. talk in a roundabout way; beat about the bush

mò 磨 mill; grind〔～宾〕〈名〉～面❶；～麦子❷；～豆腐❸〔～补〕〈结〉面～细点❹儿；豆子❺可以～成豆腐和豆浆❻〈趋〉电磨～起来比水磨❼快多了〈程〉～得很细；～得很粗糙；～得太碎了〈可〉这些麦子～得出10斤面粉来吗？今天没电～不了(liǎo)了〈时〉～了快一个小时了〈量〉需要～四五遍〔**状～**〕用电磨～；一道一道地❽～；连续❾～了三天；多～一点儿
另见mó磨

1. flour 2. wheat 3. bean curd 4. fine 5. bean 6. soya-bean milk 7. water mill 8. time and again 9. continuously; in succession

N

ná 拿 ① hold; take〔**～宾**〕〈名〉～钱；～钢笔；～东西；手里～(着)扇子❶〔**～补**〕〈结〉～住了，别掉❷了；谁把我的字典～走了？把没用的东西～开；东西～齐❸了再走；书都～全❹了吗？信已经～到了；他总把帽子❺～在手里〈趋〉把衣服～出来晒一晒❻吧；他从口袋❼里～出十块钱；要下雨了，快把窗台上❽的鞋～进去吧；这本小说，我现在不看，你先～去看吧；～起扇子来闻了闻❾是檀香木❿的，怪不得⓫扇⓬起来那么香⓭呢；这么重的东西，你一个人怎么～上来的？手提包⓮他已经替你～下去了〈程〉衣服～得太多了；手里～得满满的〈可〉这么重的箱子我～不动；针⓯太细⓰，我的手指⓱太粗⓲，所以一掉在地上，我～不起来了；我～不住了，要掉；没有借书证⓳，书是～不走的；把东西放高点儿，孩子就～不着(zháo)了；〈时〉～了半天，胳膊⓴都酸㉑了；～一会儿还不觉得累〈量〉这个月我从母亲那儿～过两次钱〔**状～**〕一只手～；勉强㉒～；干脆㉓～走；痛痛快快㉔地～走；按着次序㉕～；随便㉖～；快～；少～点儿

1. fan **2.** fall **3. 4.** whole; entire **5.** cap; hat **6.** dry in the sun **7.** pocket **8.** on the windowsill **9.** smell **10.** sandalwood **11.** no wonder **12.** fan **13.** fragrant; sweet-smelling **14.** handbag; suitcase **15.** needle **16.** thin **17.** finger **18.** thick **19.** library card **20.** arm **21.** ache; tingle **22.** reluctantly **23.** straightforwardly **24.** readily **25.** in good order **26.** casually; carelessly

② seize; capture ≃ 逮捕，捉〔**～宾**〕〈名〉猫～耗子❶；～贼❷〔**～补**〕〈结〉～住两个歹徒❸〈趋〉我们把那座城市从敌人手中～过来了；那座山～下来了〈程〉这只小花猫拿❹耗子～得真灵❺〈可〉那只老猫真笨❻，连耗子都～不着(zháo)；这么多人竟～不住一个小偷儿〈时〉～了半天连一只耗子都没拿着(zháo)〔**状～**〕一夜～了两只耗子

1. mouse; rat **2.** thief **3.** scoundrel; evil-doer **4.** seize; capture **5.** nimble; quick **6.** stupid; clumsy

③ have a firm grasp of; be able to do; be sure of〔**～宾**〕〈名〉你们那里谁～权❶？什么事都应该自己～主意❷〔**～补**〕〈结〉主意～准了（～定了）不要一会儿一变〈趋〉她年纪❸虽然不大，可是家里的事，样样都能～起来❹〈可〉

这件事能不能成功我可~不准；主意我可~不好，她在走不走的问题上一直~不定主意；遇事❺他总~不出主意来〈量〉这件事你可要替我~一下儿主意〔状~〕自己~；替别人~；一直~不定；赶紧~；赶快~〔习用〕~手好戏❻

1. power 2. (make) a decision 3. age 4. can do every kind of household chores 5. when anything comes up 6. a game or trick one is good at; one's speciality

nài 耐 be able to bear or endure 〔~宾〕〈名〉这种工作服❶~火；~高温❷；~油，~蒸气❸〈动〉我的那件衣服非常~穿；~洗；这种牙刷❹很~用；轮胎底的鞋❺~磨❻〈形〉这个人能吃苦~劳❼；这种建筑材料❽~热❾；深颜色的衣服~脏❿〈主-谓〉~人寻味⓫〔~补〕〈可〉这种植物⓬~不住热；~得了(liǎo)寒~不了(liǎo)？〔状~〕非常~；比较~；特别~

1. work clothes 2. high temperature 3. steam 4. toothbrush 5. shoe with a tyre sole 6. wear-resisting; wearproof 7. bear hardships and stand hard work 8. construction materials 9. heat-proof 10. dirt 11. afford food for thought 12. plant

nánwei 难为 ① embarrass; press ≅ 为难〔~宾〕〈代〉她不会唱歌你就别~她了；他既然不想去，你就别~他了；他不愿意说，你就别~他了〔~补〕〈趋〉你又~起我来了〈可〉~不了(liǎo)她〈时〉为这件事~了他半天〈量〉~一下儿他，~过我一次〔状~〕故意❶~；别~；总❷~；为这件事~

1. intentionally; on purpose 2. always

② be a tough job to〔~宾〕〈代〉她丈夫死得早，一个人把两个孩子带大了，真够❶~她的；一对盲人❷把家整理❸得干干净净，自己也收拾❹得整整齐齐，真够~他们的；~他在那么喧闹的环境❺里，用短短两个月的时间翻译出本小说来；作那么大手术❻，那个孩子连一声都没哼❼，也真够~他的了；这么远的道儿~您来〔状~〕真~；怪~的；真够~的

1. indeed; really 2. a blind couple 3. tidy up; put in order 4. put in order 5. condition; environment 6. operation; surgical operation 7. not even give one snort

nào 闹 ① make a noise; stir up trouble, dispute ≅ 吵；扰乱〔主~〕〈名〉疯子❶整天❷~；孩子一困❸了就~；他喝醉❹了酒就~；这件事他想不通❺，所以到处去~〔~宾〕〈名〉~名誉❻；~地位❼；~待遇❽〈动〉~出风头❾〔~补〕〈结〉他们又放录音❿又跳舞，~到夜里12点多；他们

两个人为了一点小事儿～翻⓫了〈趋〉再～下去也不会有什么结果；不知为什么他跟经理⓬～起来了；你要是不听话，～出事儿⓭来我可不负责⓮〈程〉～得不可开交⓯；又打雷⓰又闪电⓱～得我一夜没睡好觉；他们～得鸡犬不宁⓲；～得天翻地复⓳；～得无法工作；～得没有办法⓴了；～得真凶㉑；～个不休㉒〈可〉～不出什么名堂㉓来；～不好就得(děi)开除㉔〈时〉这群孩子在窗前～了两个多小时，吵得没法工作；外边的叫卖声㉕～了一个上午；昨天隔壁㉖来了好多客人，又说又笑，～了一个通宵㉗〈量〉～过好多次；他想～一下儿试探试探㉘；大～一场〔**状～**〕别～了；大吵大～；整天～；又吵又～；肆无忌惮地㉙～；毫无顾忌地㉚～；无法无天地㉛～；没完没了(liǎo)地㉜～；三番五次地～；为什么事～？

1. madman; lunatic **2.** the whole day **3.** sleepy **4.** be drunk **5.** not convinced **6.** be out for fame **7.** be out for position **8.** treatment **9.** seek or be in the limelight **10.** play back the recording **11.** fall out with sb. **12.** manager **13.** cause trouble **14.** not responsible for **15.** be awfully noisy **16.** thunder **17.** lightning **18.** even fowls and dogs are not left in peace **19.** heaven and earth turning upside down **20.** no way out **21.** awful **22.** endless **23.** (cannot achieve any thing) **24.** expel; discharge **25.** cry one's wares; peddle; hawk **26.** next door **27.** throughout the night **28.** sound out **29.** unscrupulously **30.** without scruple **31.** wantonly **32.** endlessly; without end

② suffer from; be trouble by ≃ 发生〔**～宾**〕〈名〉～病❶；～肚子❷；～眼睛❸；～水灾❹；～虫灾❺ ～饥荒❻；～灾荒❼；～笑话❽；～意见❾；～别扭❿；～纠纷⓫；～贼⓬；～鬼〔**～补**〕〈结〉闹病把身体～垮⓭了〈趋〉了解⓮清楚了再说，别～出笑话来；原来⓯这里很太平，怎么最近～起贼来了；两个人为了一点小事～起别扭来了〈程〉那时的瘟疫⓰～得太厉害⓱了〈可〉你放心⓲吧，我～不了(liǎo)笑话；〈时〉～了半年病，人瘦⓳得不象样子⓴了；～过一个时期㉑〈量〉～了一阵〔**状～**〕经常～；跟他～意见；从来没～过病；这孩子体弱㉒容易～病；连年㉓～灾荒；不懂装懂㉔就会～笑话；为什么事～别扭了？

1. fall ill; be ill **2.** belly; abdomen (have diarrhoea) **3.** have eye trouble **4.** flood; inundation **5.** insect pests (suffer from insect pests) **6.** famine **7.** famine due to crop failures **8.** make a stupid mistake **9.** be on bad terms because of a difference of opinion **10.** be difficult with sb.; be at odds with sb. **11.** dispute **12.** thief **13.** be broken down **14.** be clear about; understand **15.** formerly; originally **16.** pestilence **17.** terrible **18.** rest assured; set one's mind at rest **19.** thin; emaciated **20.** unpresentable; in no shape to be seen **21.** for some time **22.** weak **23.** in successive years; for years running **24.** pretend to understand when you don't

③ give vent (to one's anger, resentment, etc.) ≅ 发泄〔**～宾**〕〈名〉～情绪❶；～脾气❷〔**～补**〕〈结〉～完了脾气就后悔❸；情绪～大了〈趋〉～起脾气来真吓人❹；～起脾气来真让人讨厌❺；这两天不知为什么～起情绪来了〈程〉情绪～得很厉害；脾气～得太不象话❻了〈时〉～了半天情绪原来是为这件事〈量〉～了一通脾气；～过一次情绪；～了一顿〔**状～**〕无缘无故地❼～；莫明其妙地❽～；为一点小事就～；偶尔❾～

1. mood (be disgruntled) **2.** temperament; disposition **3.** regret; repent **4.** frightful; dreadful **5.** disagreeable; disgusting **6.** unreasonable **7.** without cause or reason; for no reason at all **8.** without rhyme or reason; unaccountably **9.** occasionally; once in a while

④ go in for; do; make ≅ 干；弄；搞〔**～宾**〕〈名〉～生产❶；～乱子❷；～事❸(儿)〔**～补**〕〈结〉把事情～坏了；他们两个人～僵❹了；我怕他们～翻❺了；别把关系❻～坏了；事情反而❼～复杂❽了〈趋〉～起罢工❾来了〈程〉～得满城风雨❿；～得人人皆知⓫；～得人心⓬惶惶⓭；～得鸡犬不宁⓮；～得乱七八糟⓯；～得一塌糊涂⓰；～得很别扭⓱；～得没脸见人⓲〈可〉谁都～不清⓳这是怎么回事⓴；～不好就要出人命㉑〈时〉罢工～了一年多〔**状～**〕大㉒～；不停地㉓～；连续地㉔～；此起彼伏地㉕～；接连不断地㉖～〔**习用**〕～了半天；～着玩儿㉗

1. production **2.** trouble (cause trouble) **3.** create a disturbance; make trouble **4.** be on bad terms **5.** fall out with sb. **6.** relation **7.** on the contrary; instead **8.** complicated **9.** strike **10.** become the talk of the town (create a sensation; create a scandal) **11.** it is known to all **12.** public feeling **13.** alarmed and bewildered **14.** even fowls and dogs are not left in peace **15.** at sixes and sevens; in a mess **16.** in a complete mess; in an awful (terrible) state **17.** be difficult with sb. **18.** too ashamed to face anyone **19.** not get the thing clear **20.** what's all this about **21.** involve human life **22.** greatly; fully **23.** without interruption **24.** in succession; in a row **25.** rise one after another **26.** on end; in a row; in succession **27.** joke

nǐdìng 拟定 draw up; draft; work out〔**～宾**〕〈名〉～一个学习计划❶；～一个切实可行的办法

❷；~条文❸；~草案❹；~方案❺；~章程❻；~一个教学大纲❼〔~补〕〈结〉~完了；~好了〈趋〉早就~出来了〈程〉~得很详细❽；~得很实际❾〈可〉~不出来；~得了(liǎo)吗？〈时〉~了不少日子了；~了一下午〈量〉~过一次；好好~一下儿〔状~〕先~；认真~；暂时❿~

1. study plan 2. practical method 3. article; clause 4. draft 5. scheme; plan 6. rules; regulations 7. teaching programme 8. detailed 9. practical 10. temporarily; for the moment

niǎn 撵 drive out ≅ 赶〔~宾〕〈名〉他们直往外~人〈代〉~他搬家❶〔~补〕〈结〉把屋里的人都~走了；把他~下台❷了〈趋〉天都这么晚了，你把他~到哪儿去啊？他嫌❸吵❹把孩子都~到外边去了；他一生气把我们都~出去了〈时〉~了半天，孩子就是不肯出去玩〈量〉~过两次了〔状~〕不客气地❺~；被他~了出来

1. move (house) 2. step down from the stage; be driven out of office 3. dislike 4. noisy 5. impolitely

niàn 念 ① read aloud ≅ 读；朗读〔~宾〕〈名〉~报；~台词❶；~诗；~英语；~课文；给妈妈~信；老和尚❷~经❸〔~补〕〈结〉~完了；把台词~熟❹点儿；~懂了吗？这个字没~对；请你~慢点儿；~清楚点儿〈趋〉继续~下去；~出声音❺来；他又起诗来了〈程〉~得很流利❻；~得真清楚；~得一点感情❼都没有；~得太快，我记不下来；~得不连贯❽；~得不熟〈可〉马上就要下课，这篇课文~不完了；这篇文章生词太多，我~不了(liǎo)；英语我可以念，但是~不好；这篇文章太难，我~不上来；嗓子❾哑❿了~不出声音来了〈时〉~了一上午也没念熟；~了半天也没念会；~了一辈子英语，直到⓫今天才知道这个词念错了〈量〉~了好儿遍，还是记不住；这个字~错过好几次了〔状~〕大声~；小声~；反复~；一遍一遍地~；从头儿⓬~

1. actor's lines 2. old monk 3. scripture 4. very well; skilful 5. read aloud 6. fluent 7. emotion; feeling; sentiment 8. incoherent 9. throat 10. hoarse 11. until 12. from the beginning

② study; attend school ≅ 上学；读〔~宾〕〈名〉~过大学吗？你的大孩子现在是~书呢，还是工作呢？她~文科❶〔~补〕〈结〉~完高中❷，一般人都想让孩子念大学；~到后年才能毕业❸〈程〉~得非常好；我弟弟念书~得不太好〈可〉他家里有负担❹，大学~不完就工作了；脑子❺不好~不好书；~不下去了，只好转系❻；那个孩子没毅力❼什么也不成〈时〉~了三年大学，没毕业就工作了；~了一阵子❽就不念

了〈量〉~一下儿试试吧〔状~〕正在~；还没~；已经~了；无法~；好容易~完了

1. liberal arts 2. senior middle school 3. graduation 4. burden 5. brain 6. transfer to another department 7. willpower 8. a period of time

niàng 酿
make (wine); brew (beer); make (honey); lead to; result in 〔~宾〕〈名〉~了一坛酒❶；蜜蜂❷~蜜❸〔~补〕〈结〉不注意❹就会~成大祸❺；小错❻不改❼就会~成大错❽〈趋〉这种花~出来的蜜特别甜❾〈时〉这坛酒~了十年〈量〉自己~过一次酒〔状~〕蜜蜂匆忙地❿~；辛勤地⓫~；分三次~

1. a jar of wine 2. bee 3. honey 4. not pay much attention 5. bring great disaster 6. trifling error 7. refuse to correct 8. make a gross error 9. rather sweet 10. hastily 11. hard-workingly

niào 尿
urinate; make water; pass water 〔~宾〕〈名〉~尿❶；~了一泡尿；~血❷；小孩子~床❸了；这孩子~了我一身〔~补〕〈结〉把尿布❹~湿❺了；~在床上了〈趋〉~出来了〈程〉~得很多；肾脏❻病人~得很频繁❼〈可〉有尿道❽结石❾的人往往~不出尿来；小孩子养成好习惯❿，夜里就~不了(liǎo)床了〈量〉那年他得了急性肾炎⓫~过一次血〔状~〕孩子夜里不~；经常~床

1. urine 2. haematuria 3. wet the bed 4. diaper 5. wet 6. kidney 7. frequent (frequent micturition) 8. urethra 9. stone; calculus 10. cultivate good habits 11. acute nephritis

niē 捏
①knead with the fingers; mould 〔~宾〕〈名〉~泥人❶；~饺子❷〔~补〕〈结〉泥人~好了；别~坏了；饺子要~住；~紧❸点儿；用胶泥❹能~成各种各样❺的东西〈趋〉那位老艺人❻~出来的泥人形象❼非常美〈程〉他捏饺子~得最快；泥人~得很象❽；~得维妙维肖❾；~得栩栩如生❿，~得优美⓫动人⓬；~得非常成功，~得很难看〈可〉没学过~不了(liǎo)；饺子~不住就破了；泥不粘⓭~不上〈时〉昨天我们~了一个多小时的饺子〈量〉饺子多~几下儿，就破不了(liǎo)了〔状~〕用手指~；用泥~

1. clay figurine 2. jaozi (dumpling) 3. tight 4. clay 5. all kinds of 6. artist 7. image; form; figure 8. much alike 9. remarkably true to life; absolutely lifelike 10. lifelike 11. graceful 12. moving; touching 13. not sticky enough

② hold between the fingers; pinch 〔~宾〕〈名〉从米里往外~沙子；~虫子；~稻壳❶〔~补〕〈趋〉把虫子~出来；把米里的沙粒~出去〈可〉虫子太小了，~

不出来；～不干净〔**状～**〕往外～；用手～；玩具❷猫一～就响❸；耐心地❹～〔**习用**〕～一把汗❺

1. rice husk **2.** toy **3.** make a sound **4.** patiently **5.** be breathless with anxiety or tension

níng 拧 ① pinch; tweak〔**～宾**〕〈名〉～人；～嘴；～胳膊❶；～腿❷；～耳朵〔**～补**〕〈结〉把腿都～青了；胳膊～肿❸了；把孩子～哭了；因为他把我～急❹了，所以我就打了他一巴掌❺〈趋〉她～起人来可狠❻了〈程〉～得真疼；～得太利害❼了；～得青一块紫一块的❽；～得直叫❾；～得直哭〈时〉～了半天也不撒手❿〈量〉你敢～吗？～一下儿试试！～了他一把⓫；～过一次他的耳朵〔**状～**〕狠狠地～；使劲～；拼命～

1. arm **2.** leg **3.** be swollen **4.** irritated; annoyed **5.** palm; give him a slap **6.** heartless **7.** too hard **8.** turn purple **9.** cry (with pain) **10.** not let go **11.** give him a pinch

② twist; wring〔**～宾**〕〈名〉～毛巾❶；～湿衣服❷；～麻绳❸〔**～补**〕〈结〉衣服没～干；～好了再晒❹；麻绳要～细❺点儿；～粗❻点儿；～紧❼点儿；～松❽点儿；～结实❾点儿；把这两股线～成绳❿〈趋〉她～出来的衣服总是湿漉漉的⓫〈程〉～得真干；～得太湿⓬；～得手都疼了〈可〉台布⓭太大，我一个人～不动；麻绳用手～不匀⓮〈时〉蚊帐⓯那么大，我～了半天都没拧干〈量〉帮我～一下儿可以吗？〔**状～**〕使劲儿～；两个人一起～
另见 nǐng 拧

1. towel **2.** wet clothes **3.** rope made of hemp, flax, jute etc. **4.** dry in the sun **5.** thin **6.** thick **7.** tight **8.** loose **9.** fast; solid **10.** twist a two-ply thread into rope **11.** extremely wet; rather wet **12.** too wet **13.** tablecloth **14.** not even **15.** mosquito net

nǐng 拧 twist; screw〔**～宾**〕〈名〉～螺丝❶；～墨水瓶盖❷；～灯泡❸；～自来水❹龙头❺〔**～补**〕〈结〉把瓶盖～上；～紧❻螺丝；把水龙头～开；～大点儿；把钢笔帽～好；盖儿～歪❼了；把灯泡～在那个灯口❽上；黄绿❾两种毛线❿～在一起织⓫好不好？这个螺丝钉太大，把木板都～裂⓬了；～错方向⓭了；两道浓眉⓮～在一起〈趋〉把螺丝钉～上去；把新壁灯⓯～到墙上去了〈程〉～得太松了；～得很结实⓰〈可〉瓶盖还～得上～不上了？笔帽～不开了；螺丝锈⓱住了，一点都～不动了；螺丝扣⓲坏了～不上了〈时〉～了好半天才拧下来〈量〉～了好几次才拧动；请你帮我～一下儿吧〔**状～**〕用手～；用钳子⓳～；使劲～；轻轻地～；顺着时针方向⓴～；倒着㉑～；别来回㉒～
另见 níng 拧

1. screw 2. cap of an ink-bottle 3. bulb 4. running water 5. tap 6. tighten up (a screw) 7. slanting 8. electric light socket 9. green 10. knitting wool 11. knit 12. split; open 13. direction 14. heavy eyebrows 15. wall lamp; bracket light 16. fast; solid 17. become rusty 18. thread of a screw 19. with pliers 20. clockwise 21. counterwise 22. to and fro; back and forth

niǔ 扭 ① turn round ≅ 扭转〔～宾〕〈名〉～着头向后看；坐好了，别～着身子〔～补〕〈结〉脖子❶都～酸❷了；身子都～累了〈趋〉她把头～过来了；～回去了〈程〉时间长了，身子～得真累〈量〉～了一下儿〔状～〕一～头就看见他了；很快地～过去了；突然～过头来；猛❸～

1. neck 2. ache; tingle 3. abruptly; suddenly

② sprain; wrench〔主～〕〈名〉腰❶～了；脖子❷～了〔～宾〕〈名〉～了腰了；搬东西时没注意❸～了腰了；追❹车的时候～了脚了；～了筋❺了〔～补〕〈结〉筋骨一伤❻了〈程〉～得可不轻❼；～得都肿❽了〈量〉脚～了一下儿，都肿了〔状～〕一下子～了；不小心～了

1. waist 2. neck 3. not pay much attention 4. chase after; catch up 5. muscle 6. be wounded 7. serious 8. be swollen

③ roll; swing〔主～〕〈名〉走路时腰❶一～一～的〔～宾〕〈名〉～了两步〔～补〕〈趋〉腰～来～去〈程〉腰～得真厉害；～得真难看 ❷〔状～〕来回❸～

1. waist 2. unsightly; displeasing to the eye 3. to and fro; back and forth

niǔzhuǎn 扭转 ① turn round ≅ 扭〔～宾〕〈名〉～身子；把天线❶一～一个方向❷〔～补〕〈趋〉把身子～过来〈量〉～了一下儿〔状～〕往哪边～?

1. antenna 2. direction

② turn back; reverse〔～宾〕〈名〉～局势❶；～乾坤❷；～局面❸；～时局❹〔～补〕〈趋〉把局面～过来了〈量〉要好好～一下局面〔状～〕一定要把局势～过来；不容易～；及时❺～；迅速～；立即～

1. situation 2. heaven and earth; the universe 3. state of affairs 4. the current political situation 5. in time

nòng 弄 ① play with; fool with ≅ 玩弄；摆弄〔～宾〕〈名〉他又～鸽子❶去了；别瞎❷～那个电视了，还是让内行(háng)的人❸给修理❹修理吧；他一天到晚就知道～家具❺；～～花呀草呀，也是一种休息〈代〉别～那个了，再弄就坏了〔～补〕〈结〉～裂❻了；～碎❼了；～断❽了；～

折❾(shé)了；～破❿了〈趋〉～来～去〈时〉～了半天也没弄好〈量〉我刚～一下儿就坏了〔**状～**〕别～了；不许再～了；怎么还～？

1. pigeon **2.** irresponsibly; to no purpose **3.** expert **4.** repair **5.** furniture **6.** split; cracked **7.** broken to pieces **8. 9.** snapped **10.** be torn

② do; manage; handle; get sb. or sth. into a specified condition ≃ 做；使〔**～宾**〕〈名〉我不会～鱼；～了不少菜；他就为了～个官儿❶作；摔倒❷了～了一身泥❸〔**～补**〕〈结〉鱼还没～好；别把孩子～醒❹了；饭菜都～多了；别把衣服～脏了❺；他的话把我～糊涂❻了；我把电话号码❼～错了；我的录音机❽被妹妹～坏❾了；你的意思❿我还没～清楚；钥匙⓫放好，别～丢⓬了；这句话把他～火儿⓭了；千万别把事情～糟⓮了；别把那条小金鱼～死；这两家人为了一点小事把关系～僵⓯了；这张画儿卷⓰得太厉害了，快把它～平了吧；纸都～皱⓱了；把他们两个人的名字～颠倒⓲了；书都让人给～乱⓳了；你怎么～成这副模样了⓴！别把好的和坏的～混(hùn)㉑了；把水都～混(hún)㉒了；刚削㉓好的铅笔又～断了；打起来了，把桌子都～翻㉔了；〈趋〉不知道他从哪儿～来那么多钱？把行李㉕都～上楼来吧；帮我把这些东西～上汽车去；好容易才把地毯㉖从楼上～下来了；那么重的东西，你一个人是怎么～过来的？〈程〉地～得这么脏㉗；一定要把事情～个水落石出㉘；屋子～得挺干净；～得非常整齐㉙；他讲了一大堆话～得我莫明其妙㉚；～得毫无办法㉛了；～得他们不知怎么办好了；～得他没话说；～得她脸通红㉜；～得她们非常不好意思㉝；～得满身是土㉞；～得我们措手不及㉟；〈可〉箱子㊱这么重㊲，我一个人～不动；塞子㊳掉在瓶子㊴里了，怎么弄也～不出来了；螺丝㊵锈住了㊶～不下来了；这件事到现在还～不出个结果来；～不清他有多少财产㊷；这些事情～不好就前功尽弃㊸了〈时〉这个句子的意思我～了半天，还是不懂〈量〉我来不及㊹了，你能不能帮我～一下儿午饭〔**状～**〕赶快～；在哪儿～？给我们～；一次～了不少

1. government official; officer **2.** tumble; trip and fall **3.** covered all over with mud **4.** be awake **5.** dirty **6.** confused; muddled **7.** telephone number **8.** tape-recorder **9.** out of work; out of order **10.** opinion; implication **11.** key **12.** lost **13.** flare up in anger **14.** make a mess of sth. **15.** be on bad terms **16.** roll **17.** roll up; crease **18.** transpose **19.** put out of order **20.** how did you get into such a mess? **21.** mix up; confuse **22.** mix together **23.** sharpen **24.** turn over **25.** luggage **26.** carpet **27.** dirty **28.** must get to the bottom of the matter **29.** tidy; neat **30.** be unable to make head or tail of sth. **31.** (become) helpless 32. blush scarlet with shyness 33. feel embarrassed 34. covered all over with dust 35. be caught unprepared 36. box; case 37. heavy 38. cork; plug 39. bottle 40. screw 41. become rusty 42. property 43. all that has been achieved is spoiled; all one's previous efforts are wasted 44. there is not enough time (to do sth.)

③ get; fetch〔~宾〕〈名〉你去~点水来；~点吃的；想办法~点儿钱；我给他~了一间房子〔补~〕〈结〉我新画好的那张画让我外甥❶给~走了；房子已经~到手了〈趋〉从河里~回一条活鱼来；他没有票，你能把他~进去吗？他真有办法❷，到外边转了一圈❸，鱼、肉什么的都~回来了〈程〉酒~得太少了；吃的东西~得太多了〈可〉天这么晚了，什么也~不到了；现在还~得着(zháo)吃的吗？〈时〉~了半天也没弄来〈量〉你自己去~一下儿吧〔状~〕设法❹~点儿去；随便~；马上~

1. nephew 2. method; way; 3. take a stroll 4. think of a way

nuó 挪 move; shift ≅ 搬；挪动

〔~宾〕〈名〉~柜子❶；~东西；~个地方；往前~了几步〔~补〕〈结〉把书架~开点儿❷；~远点儿；~走吧〈趋〉把床~过来；~到外边去〈可〉这东西太重❸，我一个人~不动；~不回来了〈量〉这个柜子~过好几次地方了；往后边~一下儿吧〔状~〕往外~一~；稍微❹~一~；经常~

1. cupboard; cabinet 2. a little bit away from 3. too heavy 4. slightly; a little

nuóyòng 挪用 divert (funds)

〔~宾〕〈名〉~公款❶；~资金❷；~现金❸〔~补〕〈可〉公款可~不得❹〈量〉~过一次〔状~〕偷偷地❺~；居然❻~

1. public money; fund 2. fund 3. cash 4. must not 5. stealthily; in secret 6. to one's surprise; unexpectedly

O

ōudǎ 殴打 beat up; hit ≅ 打〔~补〕〈量〉~了一顿；~了一阵〔状~〕互相~；被人~；无理❶~；寻衅❷~；故意❸~；起哄❹~

1. unreasonably 2. provokingly 3. intentionally; on purpose 4. gathering together to create a disturbance

ǒutù 呕吐 vomit; throw up; be sick ≅ 吐〔~补〕〈趋〉~出来了〈程〉~得真难受❶；~得很厉害❷〈量〉~了好一阵〔状~〕全部❸~出来了；经常~

1. feel unwell; feel ill 2. terrible; awful 3. completely; entirely; wholly

òu 怄 irritate; annoy〔~宾〕〈名〉不要~气❶；~了一肚子气❷；那天~了点气就病了〔状~〕净❸~气；跟谁~气了；经常~气

1. be difficult and sulky 2. have a bellyful of repressed grievances 3. only; merely

P

pā 趴 lie on one's stomach; lie prone〔**～补**〕〈结〉～在地上射击❶；～在桌子上写字；～在草地上照相；～在床底下找东西；快～下，子弹飞过来了〈可〉年纪太大，～不下了，请你帮我把钥匙❷捡❸起来吧〈时〉在海边儿～了半个多小时晒太阳；打完针先～一会儿再起来〔**状～**〕赶快～下；整天❹～；在沙滩上❺～；多～一会儿

1. bullet **2.** key **3.** pick up **4.** all day long **5.** on the beach

pá 爬 ① crawl; creep ≌ 爬行〔**主～**〕〈名〉蛇❶往洞❷里～；螃蟹❸横着❹～；孩子在床上～；壁虎❺～；吃了苍蝇❻～过的东西容易得❼肠炎❽〔**～补**〕〈结〉真危险❾，孩子已经～到床边了；蜈蚣❿～进了砖堆⓫〈趋〉青蛙从水里～出来了；孩子从铁丝网⓬底下⓭～过来了；乌龟⓮～到岸上来了；毛虫⓯在树叶上～来～去〈程〉～得很快；～得太慢了〈可〉人老了，梯子⓰～不上去了；门窗关得很紧⓱壁虎～不进来；洞堵死⓲了，蛇～不出来了〈量〉鳄鱼⓳～了几下儿，就停⓴下不动了〔**状～**〕迅速地㉑～；缓慢地㉒～；慢慢腾腾地㉓～；一直向前～；到处㉔～；蚂蚁从死苍蝇身上～过去；在草地上～；顽强地㉕～；吃力地㉖～；来回㉗～；满地～；横着～；密密麻麻地㉘～了一片蚂蚁

1. snake **2.** hole; cavity **3.** crab **4.** sideways **5.** gecko; house lizard **6.** fly **7.** be easily infected with **8.** enteritis **9.** how dangerous **10.** centipede **11.** heap of bricks **12.** wire netting; wire meshes **13.** from under **14.** tortoise **15.** caterpillar **16.** ladder **17.** very tight **18.** stop up **19.** crocodile **20.** stop **21.** promptly **22. 23.** slowly; sluggishly **24.** at all places **25.** stubbornly; obstinately **26.** strenuously **27.** back and forth; to and fro **28.** close and numerous

② climb; clamber; scramble ≌ 攀登〔**～宾**〕〈名〉他喜欢～山❶；孩子经常～树；消防队员❷都会～绳子❸；～云梯❹；动物园的猴子能～竹竿❺；墙上写着"不许～墙"；～桅杆❻；～楼梯❼；～栏杆❽〔**～补**〕〈结〉我们爬山～累了；他们终于～上了顶峰❾；～到了树尖❿；前边的～慢点儿吧，后边的跟⓫不上了；你们～快点儿好不好，这么慢，什么时候才能～到目的地⓬啊！〈趋〉大家都～上来了吗？我们比赛看

谁先～上去；你这么大年纪，一口气～上五层楼，真不容易⓭！小猴子在铁笼⓮子里～上来～下去，玩得很高兴〈程〉～得汗流浃背⓯；～得衣服都湿透了⓰；～得太慢了；～得累极了〈可〉她年轻时最喜欢爬山，现在老了，～不动了；～不上去了〈时〉～了两个多小时山，累得腰酸腿疼⓱的〔**状～**〕一连～了六层楼；气喘吁吁地⓲～；顽强地⓳～；终于～上来了；不停地⓴～；艰难地㉑～；勇敢地㉒～；迅速地㉓～；一级一级地㉔～

1. mountain **2.** fire fighter **3.** rope **4.** scaling ladder **5.** bamboo pole **6.** mast **7.** staircase **8.** railing; banisters **9.** the summit of the mountain **10.** top of a tree **11.** keep pace with; catch up with **12.** destination **13.** not easy **14.** iron cage **15.** streaming with sweat **16.** be wet through **17.** aching back and legs **18.** breathe heavily **19.** obstinately **20.** ceaselessly **21.** with difficulty **22.** bravely **23.** quickly **24.** step by step

pà 怕 ① fear; dread; be afraid of ≃ 害怕〔**～宾**〕〈名〉小偷❶～警察❷；那个孩子就～他爸爸；夜里一个人走路～流氓❸；你～不～疯子❹？她最～蛇❺；老鼠～猫〈动〉～打针；～打雷❻；～吃药❼；～挤❽；眼睛有毛病❾，～迎着光坐❿；～见生人⓫；～下雨，一下雨我全身的关节⓬就疼；～坐船，每次坐船我都吐⓭得很利害⓮〈形〉他从小就不～苦，不～累；我从不～麻烦⓯；他太～困难了；不要～艰苦⓰；他非常～热；你年纪轻轻的怎么那么～累啊！～咸⓱；～酸⓲；你们在这儿说话没关系，我一点儿也不～吵⓳；那个孩子见了生人～羞⓴〈主－谓〉～他罗唆㉑；～你捣乱㉒；～你们耽误时间；～别人把我的东西弄乱㉓〔**～补**〕〈程〉～得要命㉔；～得很利害㉕；～得不敢㉖出屋；～得发抖㉗；～极了〔**状～**〕最～蛇一类㉘的东西；非常～冷；特别～累；不～麻烦；只～一个人；一点也不～；绝不㉙～；不再㉚～；从来没～过；尤其㉛～

1. thief; pickpocket **2.** police **3.** rogue; hoodlum **4.** lunatic; madman **5.** snake **6.** thunder **7.** medicine **8.** squeeze **9.** eye trouble **10.** sit facing the light **11.** stranger **12.** joint **13.** vomit **14.** terrible; awful **15.** trouble **16.** hardship **17.** salty; salted **18.** acid; sour **19.** noisy **20.** feel bashful **21.** long-winded; wordy **22.** make trouble **23.** make a mess of; mess up; spoil **24. 25.** extremely; to death **26.** dare not **27.** shivered **28.** kind **29.** never **30.** not ... any more **31.** especially

② feel anxious; worry ≃ 担心〔**～宾**〕〈动〉～迟到❶；～不及格❷；～来不及❸；～生病❹；～迷路❺；～丢东西❻；～没钱；～浪费时间❼；～惹事❽；他

从来不～得罪人❾；～烫着❿(zháo)；～弄脏⓫衣服；～碰破⓬玻璃⓭；～冻病⓮孩子；～记不住生词；～找不着钥匙⓯；～考不上大学；～赶不上火车；～晚上回不来；～洗得不干净〈形〉演员⓰～胖⓱，不敢⓲多吃饭；他～脏，从来不用别人的茶杯；我不～瘦⓳，越瘦越好〈主－谓〉他～孩子闹⓴，拿好多玩具㉑哄㉒他；他～我不懂这个词的意思，又讲了一遍；～你明天来不了(liǎo)，所以先跟你说一说；～地震㉓〔**状～**〕真～；非常～；特别～；别～；就～

1. be late **2.** fail to pass (an exam) **3.** there's not enough time; it's too late (to do sth.) **4.** be taken ill **5.** lose one's way **6.** lose one's things **7.** waste time **8.** stir up trouble **9.** not be afraid of giving offence **10.** be scalded **11.** make dirty **12.** break **13.** glass **14.** be ill with cold **15.** key **16.** actor or actress **17.** put on weight **18.** dare not **19.** thin **20.** make a noise **21.** many toys **22.** coax **23.** earthquake

③ be unable to bear or endure ≃ 禁不住〔**～宾**〕〈名〉这种布～水，一下水就缩❶〈动〉孕妇❷～挤❸；瓷器❹～压❺；玻璃❻～碰❼；手～烫❽；这种植物❾～冻❿；孩子就～发高烧⓫；～着急⓬；～咳嗽⓭；我的牙不好，～吃酸⓮的；他胃不好⓯，～吃硬的⓰；他的病刚好，～累；〈主－谓〉木器⓱～雨淋⓲；花儿～水泡⓳〔**状～**〕只～；最～；特别～〔**习用**〕前～狼，后～虎⓴；不～不识货，就～货比货㉑；天下无难事，只～有心人㉒

1. shrink **2.** pregnant woman **3.** jostle; squeeze **4.** porcelain; chinaware **5.** press **6.** glass **7.** touch; bump **8.** scald **9.** plant **10.** freeze **11.** have a fever; run a high temperature **12.** anxiety; worry **13.** cough **14.** sour **15.** stomach trouble **16.**eat something hard **17.** articles made of wood **18.** be exposed to the rain **19.** soak in water **20.** fear wolves ahead and tigers behind (be full of fears) **21.** don't worry about not knowing much about the goods; just compare and you will see which is better **22.** nothing in the world is difficult for one who sets his mind on it.

pāi 拍 ① clap; pat; beat〔**～宾**〕〈名〉～巴掌❶；他～着我的肩膀❷说："好久不见了，最近怎么样啊？"；～蚊子❸；～球；～桌子大骂❹；～～身上的土；老鹰❺～～翅膀❻飞了〔**～补**〕〈结〉手都～肿了❼；用那么大劲❽，肩膀都被你～疼❾了；先把身上的土～掉再进来〈趋〉大家高兴地～起手来了〈程〉桌子～得真响❿；拍苍蝇～得很准⓫，一拍子就把苍蝇打死了〈可〉俗话说⓬："一个巴掌～不响"〈时〉～了半天，连一个苍蝇也没拍着(zháo)〈量〉我～了他一下儿〔**状～**〕轻轻地～；用拍子～；赶快～

1. palm 2. shoulder 3. mosquito 4. abuse; curse; swear loudly 5. eagle 6. wing 7. swollen 8. strength 9. pain; sore 10. loud 11. accurate 12. as the saying goes

② take (a picture); shoot ≅ 拍摄〔~宾〕〈名〉~电影；~照片；~记录片❶；~电视连续剧❷；~了几个惊险的场面❸；~了一个特写镜头❹；~内景❺；~外景❻〔~补〕〈结〉这个片子❼计划❽~到什么时候？〈趋〉赶快把这个动人的场景❾~下来吧；那张照片把路人❿也~进去了；她~出来的照片又清楚又漂亮；一个镜头要一来一去拍好几次〈程〉照片~得很多，~得非常清楚，~得模模糊糊的⓫〈可〉今天的天气不好，~不了电影了，照片也~不成了；刚学照相还~不好〈时〉这个片子~了三年才拍完；电视剧~两个月就差不多了；刚才在校园里~了一会儿照片〈量〉~过两次，都没拍好〔状~〕重新~；赶着~了一部电影

1. documentary film 2. telefilm in installments 3. thrilling scene 4. close-up shot 5. indoor setting; indoor scene 6. outdoor scene 7. film 8. plan; project 9. moving scene 10. passer-by 11. blurred; indistinct

③ send (a telegram, etc.) ≅ 发〔~宾〕〈名〉~电报❶〔~补〕〈结〉我刚~完一封电报〈趋〉电报已经~出去了〈程〉电文❷~得不清楚〈可〉那里没有电报局❸，~不了(liǎo)电报〈量〉~过一次电报〔状~〕给他女儿~；在电报局~〔习用〕~马屁❹

1. telegram 2. text of a telegram 3. telegraph office 4. lick sb's boots, flatter

pái 排 ① arrange; put in order 〔~宾〕〈名〉请你给我~一个代表团成员❶的名单❷；买电影票要~队❸；开学第一天老师给小学生~座位❹〔~补〕〈结〉好队，~错行(háng)了；~成单行❺；别把这两个淘气❻的孩子~在一起坐〈趋〉来晚的人都自动❼~到后边去了；请大家~过来点儿，那里妨碍交通❽〈程〉队~得很整齐，~得弯弯曲曲的❾；~得里出外进的❿；怎么总~不好啊；都三天了，连个参加比赛的名单都~不出来〈时〉光⓫排座位就~了半天；~了一个多小时的队才买上〈量〉开学头一天，老师让学生们先~一下儿座位〔状~〕一个挨着一个⓬地~；紧紧地⓭~；耐心地⓮~；有秩序地⓯~；整整齐齐地~

1. delegation members 2. list of names 3. line up 4. seat 5. in a single line 6. naughty; mischievous 7. voluntarily 8. block traffic 9. meandering; crooked 10. uneven 11. solely; only 12. one by one 13. tightly 14. patiently 15. in good order

② rehearse ≅ 排演〔~宾〕〈名〉~戏❶；~节目❷；~话剧❸

〔~补〕〈结〉昨天晚上~到几点❶；~累了〈趋〉~出来很多节目；刚从外地❹回来就~起节目来了〈可〉新年以前~得好~不好？演员❺病了，今天~不了(liǎo)节目了〈时〉这个话剧才~了两个月就公演❻了；昨天一连~了八个小时的戏；这个戏~了多久了？〈量〉~了无数❼次了；上演前还得再~一下儿〔状~〕认真~；积极地❽~；正在~；日夜❾不停地❿~；连续⓫~；反复⓬~；赶着⓭~

1. play; show 2. performance 3. modern drama 4. parts of the country other than where one is 5. actor (or actress) 6. perform in public 7. numberless; countless 8. actively 9. day and night 10. ceaselessly 11. continuously 12. repeatedly 13. hurry (rush) through

③ exclude; eject; discharge ≅ 除掉，排出〔~宾〕〈名〉~水；~脓❶；~气；~烟❷；~尿❸〔~补〕〈结〉气全部~完了；烟~净了再关窗；脓~出去就不疼了〈趋〉都~出去了〈程〉~得很快；~得很多〈可〉这一池子❹水三天也~不干〈时〉游泳池❺的水整整❻了一个星期才排净〔状~〕往外~；赶快~；日夜不停地❼~水；从烟囱❽里~

1. pus 2. smoke 3. urine 4. pool; pond 5. swimming pool 6. fully; whole 7. ceaselessly 8. chimney; stovepipe

páichú 排除 get rid of; eliminate〔~宾〕〈名〉~障碍❶；~干扰❷；机器~了故障❸又正常地❹运转起来❺了；~废水❻；~废气❼〔状~〕彻底❽~；及时❾~；立即❿~；设法⓫~；尽量⓬~；已被~

1. obstacle; barrier 2. obstruction 3. stoppage; trouble 4. normally 5. work; operate; function 6. waste water 7. waste gas or steam 8. thoroughly 9. in time 10. immediately; at once 11. think of a way; try 12. to the best of one's ability; as far as possible

pài 派 send; dispatch; assign; appoint ≅ 派遣〔~宾〕〈名〉~留学生；~代表❶；~工作；~兵；~代表团出国〔~补〕〈结〉把她~给你当秘书❷吧〈趋〉~去一个代表团；把他~到我们学校来了；~他到国外去工作了；把中年❸教师都~出去了；任务已经~下来了〈程〉人~得不合适❹〈可〉现在还~不出合适的人；~不了(liǎo)那么多人吧？~不到我头上来〈量〉~他去一趟；~过我一次了〔状~〕专~有经验的❺人去；特意❻~我来看看你；很难~；随便❼~谁都可以；多(少)~几个人去

1. representative 2. secretary 3. middle-aged 4. not suitable 5. experienced; skilled 6. for a special purpose; specially 7. casually

pāndēng 攀登 climb; clamber; scale〔~宾〕〈名〉~悬崖峭壁❶；~科学高峰❷；~世界最高峰——珠穆朗玛峰❸〔~补〕〈趋〉我不能一口气~上去，中途❹得多休息几次〈可〉这座山很高，我们~不上去〔状~〕无法~；飞速❺~；一步一步地~；努力~；充满信心地❻~；顽强地❼~；不停地~着；向顶峰❽~；一口气~上去；已经~上去了

1. sheer precipice and overhanging rocks 2. the heights of science 3. the world's highest peak — Mount Qomolangma 4. halfway; midway 5. at full speed 6. with full confidence 7. indomitably; staunchly 8. peak; summit

pán 盘 ①check; examine; interrogate ≅ 核对，清点〔~宾〕〈名〉~帐❶，~货❷〔~补〕〈结〉把帐~清了，货❸~完了吗?〈程〉盘货~得很仔细〈可〉货太多一天~不完，人少可~不了(liǎo)〔时〕昨天~了一天帐〈量〉一个月~一次货〔状~〕好好儿~；认真~；仔细~；定期❹~

1. accounts 2. make an inventory of stock on hand 3. goods 4. regularly

② coil; wind; twist ≅ 绕；卷；缠〔~补〕〈结〉一条蛇❶~在树上；把绳子❷~紧❸点儿〈趋〉把辫子❹~到头顶上❺去了；把头发~起来〈程〉~得很松〈可〉头发太短~不上去〈时〉蛇在树上~了一会儿就爬走了〔状~〕头发往头顶上一~；紧紧地~

1. snake 2. rope 3. tight 4. plait; braid; pigtail 5. on top of the head 6. loose

pàn 判 ① judge; decide ≅ 判断〔~宾〕〈名〉~案❶，~了无期徒刑❷，~罪❸〔~补〕〈结〉案子~错了，罪~重❹(zhòng)了〈程〉~得很公正❺，~得不合理❻；刑期❼~得真不短〈可〉这种罪~不了(liǎo)十年；~不成死刑❽吧?〈量〉已经~过一次刑了〔状~〕重(zhòng)~；重(chóng)新~；认真~；真难~；根据什么❾~? 不偏不倚地❿~

1. case 2. life imprisonment 3. crime 4. severe 5. just; fair 6. irrational 7. term of imprisonment 8. capital punishment 9. based on what 10. impartially

② give a mark; mark (students' paper; etc.) ≅ 评分〔~宾〕〈名〉老师给学生~卷子❶；~作业；~分❷〔~补〕〈结〉卷子~完了；这道题❸~错了；分数~少了〈趋〉两个人~出来的卷子不一样〈程〉卷子~得很快；~得很仔细❹；~得很认真❺；~得很马虎❻；判卷子~得头都疼了❼；~得太严❽了〈可〉这么多本子一个晚上可能~不出来；几千份卷子，我一个人哪儿~得过来啊〈时〉昨天我们~了一天卷子；昨

天晚上，他~了一会儿作业就睡觉了〈量〉我~过两次入学试卷❾〔**状~**〕认真~；仔细点儿~；粗略地❿~；挨着⓫~；一道一道地⓬~

1. examination paper 2. mark 3. problem 4. 5. careful 6. careless; rough 7. headache 8. too strict 9. entrance examination paper 10. roughly 11. one by one 12. one question after another

pànduàn 判断 judge; decide; determine

〔**~宾**〕〈名〉~是非❶；~对错，~好坏；~真假；~虚实❷〔**~补**〕〈结〉~对了〈趋〉我~出是谁错了〈程〉~得很正确〈可〉这件事我~不了(liǎo)；他老不出来〈时〉~了半天，也没判断出来〈量〉让我~一下儿看；经❸他~过几次了〔**状~**〕好好~；认真~；不易❹~；难以❺~；用什么办法~？仔细❻~；公正地❼~；无从~

1. right and wrong 2. true and false 3. by; through 4. not easy 5. difficult to 6. carefully 7. impartially

pàn 盼 hope for; long for; expect

≅ 盼望〔**~宾**〕〈动〉~(着)早点毕业❶，~放假；~过年；孩子~上学；~发工资❷；~考上大学〈主-谓〉~他平安地回来；~妈妈的病快好；~他学成❸回国〔**~补**〕〈时〉~了那么多年，愿望❹也没实现❺；~了那么多年最

后还是一场空❻〔**状~**〕一直~；长期~；好容易~来了；日夜~；殷切地❼~；总算❽把他~来了

1. graduate 2. pay out wages 3. succeed in one's study 4. wish; desire; hope 5. realize 6. all in vain 7. eagerly 8. at long last; finally

pāoqì 抛弃 abandon; forsake; cast aside

≅ 遗弃〔**~宾**〕〈名〉他~了结婚❶多年的妻子；我决不❷~真正的朋友〈代〉他~了她〔**状~**〕轻易❸~；无缘无故地❹~；无情无义地❺~；被他~

1. marry; get married 2. never; by no means 3. lightly; rashly 4. for no reason at all 5. heartlessly; mercilessly

páo 刨 dig; excavate

≅ 挖掘〔**~宾**〕〈名〉~一个坑❶；~树根❷；~花生；~胡萝卜❸；~地〔**~补**〕〈结〉~完了，~着(zháo)了〈趋〉把一个大树根~出来了〈程〉坑~得太深❹了；~得很浅❺〈可〉树根太大，~不出来；这一片地两天也~不完〈时〉~了一上午；刚~一会儿〈量〉~了几下儿就累了；我~过一次花生〔**状~**〕连续❻~；一下一下地~；好(不好)~〔**习用**〕~根儿问底❼
另见 bào 刨

1. pit 2. root of a tree 3. carrot 4. deep 5. shallow 6. continuously; successively 7. get to the root of the matter

pǎo 跑 ① run〔主～〕〈名〉兔子～了；火车在飞～；他腿有毛病❶不能～〔～宾〕〈名〉～圈儿❷；接力赛❸他～最后一棒❹；～步；～了一身汗；汽车～了五里路〔～补〕〈结〉～完了三圈儿了；他～慢了，让别人赶上去了；墙要倒❺了，快～开；他～在最前头，我～在最后头；他～出了新水平❻〈趋〉孩子从楼下～上来了；～回家来(去)了，～到前边儿去了〈程〉电表❼～得真快；～得上气不接下气❽；～得飞快〈可〉五分钟～不到那儿；年纪太大，有点儿～不动了；你～得过他吗？楼这么高，你～得上来吗？我现在连100米都～不下来了；跑道❾这么窄❿，人这么多，～得开吗？他～不出我的手心去⓫〈时〉～了十分钟；～了两天〈量〉～了几个来回⓬；～一趟；～一下儿试试；～了两圈儿〔状～〕赶快～；猛⓭～；一前一后地～；往前～；迎面⓮～来一个人；一瘸一拐地⓯～；出门就～；一边～一边喊；纷纷⓰～来；气喘吁吁地⓱～

1. trouble 2. track 3. relay race 4. the last relay baton 5. fall 6. new level 7. watt-hour meter; electric meter 8. breathe hard 9. track 10. narrow 11. He can't escape out of my hand 12. back and forth 13. violently 14. in one's face 15. with a limp 16. one after another; in succession 17. breathlessly

② run about doing sth. ≌ 奔走〔～宾〕〈名〉～码头❶；～买卖❷；～了很多地方；昨天～了几个商店〔～补〕〈趋〉后来他们就～起买卖来了〈程〉～得很勤❸；～得累死了〈可〉～得了(liǎo)那么远的路吗？〈时〉～了好几天也没跑到要用的材料❹〈量〉一年至少❺～三次码头；长途巴士❻一天只能～一个来回〔状～〕专❼～；来回❽～；一天～好几趟；白～了

1. wharf; dock; quay; pier 2. buying and selling; business; deal 3. frequent 4. material 5. at least 6. long-distance bus 7. specially 8. back and forth

③ escape; flee; leak〔主～〕〈名〉香味❶～了；热气～了；酒精❷～了〔～宾〕〈名〉这段电线❸有点～电，应该修一修；香皂❹～味儿了〔～补〕〈结〉茶叶放在外边，味儿都～光了；气都～光了〈趋〉热气都～出去了〈可〉放在玻璃瓶子❺里～不了(liǎo)味儿，把气球口儿系紧了❻，气就～不出来了；炸鱼❼味儿老～不出去，快把窗打开吧〔状～〕一下子～光了；太容易～了；往外～〔习用〕～了龙套❽；～了和尚～不了(liǎo)庙❾；一天到晚东～西❿颠

1. fragrance; scent 2. ethyl alcohol 3. electric wire 4. toilet soap 5. glass bottle 6. fasten tightly 7. fried fish 8. play a bit role; be a utility man 9. The Buddhist monk has run away but the temple remains — he can't escape 10. bustle about; run around here and there

pào 泡 steep; soak

〔~宾〕〈名〉~了一杯茶；喜欢用汤~饭吃；~豆芽❶；脸盆❷里~着一块新买来的花布〔~补〕〈结〉手叫肥皂水给~白了；菜都~烂❸了；手都~胀❹了；把该洗的衣服~在盆里；把床单❺用肥皂水~上；等~透了再洗〈趋〉再~下去就烂了；豆子~出芽儿来了〈程〉盆里的衣服~得太多了〈可〉盆小衣服多~不下〈时〉多~一会儿；~了好几天了〈量〉再~一下儿〔状~〕在水里~；用药水❻~；先~；用凉水~〔习用〕~磨菇❼

1. bean sprouts 2. wash basin 3. rotten 4. swell 5. sheet; bed cover 6. medicinal liquid 7. use delaying tactics; play for time; importune; pester

péi 陪 accompany; keep sb. company ≅ 陪伴

〔~宾〕〈名〉~客人；~外宾❶；~专家❷；~参观团❸；~病人；~母亲〈代〉~他吃饭；你先~她说说话，我一会儿就来；明天我~你去〔~补〕〈结〉~到下午5点；~烦了❹；~腻了❺〈可〉我有事~不了(liǎo)客人，你替我陪一陪吧〈时〉~了一个星期专家；在医院里~了一个月病人〈量〉~过几次外宾；你先在这里~一下他〔状~〕一直~；多次~；热情地❻~；主动❼~；勉强❽~；无可奈何地❾~；亲自❿~

1. foreign guest 2. expert; specialist 3. visiting group 4. be vexed; be annoyed 5. be bored with; be tired of 6. warmly; zealously 7. on one's own initiative 8. reluctantly 9. helplessly 10. personally

péi 培 bank up with earth; earth up

〔~宾〕〈名〉玉米❶长起来以后，根部要多~一点儿土〔~补〕〈结〉~上点儿土；~厚❷〈~高〉点儿〈状~〉多~点儿；结结实实❸地~；一层一层地❹~

1. maize; corn 2. thick 3. solidly; firmly; fast 4. layer after layer

péiyǎng 培养 foster; train; develop

〔~宾〕〈名〉~孩子；~下一代；~接班人❶；~人才❷；~感情❸；~兴趣❹；~疫苗❺；~细菌❻；~热带鱼❼〔~补〕〈结〉把他~成了科学家〈趋〉~出兴趣来了；~起感情来了；这个孩子很聪明，应该继续~下去〈程〉~得很好〈可〉我没有那么多钱，~不起一个大学生〈时〉~八年，才能成为一个医生〈量〉那个孩子有画画天才，应该好好~一下儿〔状~〕好好~；认真~；有计划地❽~；精心❾~；大力~；有目的地❿~

1. successor 2. a talented person; a person of ability 3. passion 4. interest 5. vaccine 6. germ; bacterium 7. tropical fish 8. systematically; in a planned way 9. with the best of care; elaborately 10. purposefully

péi 赔

① compensate; pay for ≅ 赔偿 〔~宾〕〈名〉碗❶是我打碎❷的，我应该~钱；昨天我得罪❸你了，今天特意❹向你~礼❺来了；~笑脸❻；快给他一个不是❼，他就不生气了；撕毁合同❽要~款❾〔~补〕〈结〉~上点儿钱就完了〈可〉~得起吗?，这么大的玻璃❿，要是打碎了，我可~不起〈量〉~过很多次钱了〔状~〕必须~；照原价⓫~；立即⓬~；替他~；加倍⓭~

1. bowl 2. break into pieces; smash 3. offend; displease 4. for a special purpose 5. offer an apology 6. smile obsequiously 7. apologize 8. tear up an agreement 9. pay an indemnity 10. glass 11. according to the cost 12. at once; immediately 13. redouble

② suffer a loss; run a business at a loss ↔ 赚〔~宾〕〈名〉做这笔买卖❶他~了很多钱；~本儿❷了〔~补〕〈结〉钱都~光了〈趋〉连本钱都~进去了〈程〉~得真惨❸；~得把房子都卖掉了〈量〉~了好几次钱，都赚❹回来了〔状~〕从来没~过钱；一次一次地~；钱统统❺~掉了

1. buying and selling; business; deal 2. capital 3. miserable; pitiful 4. gain; make a profit 5. all; completely; entirely

pèi 配

① compound; mix ≅ 掺合；混合〔~宾〕〈名〉~颜色❶；~药❷〔~补〕〈结〉颜色~深❸了；药~错了；~全❹了；把黄绿两盒油漆❺~在一起；这是三种原料❻~成的〈趋〉红颜色与白颜色~起来就是粉红色〈程〉药~得太多了；这两种颜色~得不好看〈可〉原料不全，这种药现在~不了(liǎo)；颜色总~不好；这两种东西~不到一起〈时〉~了很长时间才配好〈量〉这种药只~过一次，不知好用不好用〔状~〕多(少)~点儿；随便❼~；按一定比例❽~；大量❾~

1. colour 2. medicine 3. dark; deep 4. complete 5. paint 6. raw material 7. casually 8. in certain proportion 9. in a large number

② find sth. to fit or replace sth. else〔~宾〕〈名〉~零件❶；~螺丝❷；~钥匙❸；~锁❹；~眼镜❺；~镜框❻；~毛线❼；~纽扣❽；~一块花布〔~补〕〈结〉螺丝~上了吗?，钥匙~好了；书~成套❾；杂志都~全了；眼镜~晚了；纽扣~着(zháo)了；零件都~齐了❿〈程〉眼镜~得很合适⓫；~得跟原来的一样〈可〉不着(zháo)那种颜色的毛线；零件一时~不全了；慢慢配一定~得上；太贵了，我~不起〈时〉~了半年才配上；~了好长时间也没配上〈量〉~了三四次钥匙都丢⓬了；~过好多次了〔状~〕真难~；再~一个；赶快~；幸亏⓭~；在哪~?，在眼镜商店~

1. spare parts 2. screw 3. key 4. lock 5. a pair of glasses 6. picture frame 7. knitting wool 8. button

9. set; suit 10. complete 11. suitable 12. lost 13. fortunately; luckily

③ match ≅ 衬托; 陪衬〔~宾〕〈名〉黄~绿; 深蓝衣服~浅蓝边; 红花~绿叶; 他给这个曲子❶了歌词❷; 这个表应该~个金链❸〔~补〕〈结〉什么颜色~上白的都好看; 这两种颜色~在一起很调和❹; 这件大衣~上什么围巾❺好看; 〈趋〉这种家具❻和蓝颜色的地毯❼~起来显得❽很庄严❾〈程〉颜色~得很大方❿; ~得非常淡雅⓫; ~得太难看了〈可〉这两种蔬菜⓬~不到一起; 他的嗓子⓭和钢琴⓮~不上; 他说这首诗~不了(liǎo)音乐⓯〈时〉~了半天也没配好〈量〉~过一回; ~了几次都不理想⓰; 再~一下儿试试〔状~〕不好~; 不能乱⓱~; 精心地⓲~; 用艺术眼光~

1. song; tune 2. words of a song 3. golden chain 4. be in harmonious proportion 5. scarf 6. furniture 7. carpet 8. look; seem 9. solemn; stately 10. in good taste; tasteful 11. simple and elegant 12. vegetable; greens 13. voice 14. piano 15. music 16. not ideal 17. casually; at random 18. elaborately; meticulously

④ deserve; be worthy of; be qualified ≅ 够得上; 值得; 相称〔~宾〕〈动〉他不~当教师; 你不~说这种话; 他们俩不~当英雄❶; 我认为他不~当模范❷〔状~〕一点也不~; 完全~得上; 两个人不相~

1. hero 2. model

⑤ mate (animals)〔~宾〕〈名〉~种❶; ~马; 公驴❷~母马

1. breeding 2. jackass

pèibèi 配备 equip; allocate; furnish with 〔~宾〕〈名〉~一个秘书❶; ~几个助手❷; ~一套家具〔~补〕〈结〉~齐了❸〈趋〉设备❹已经~起来了〈程〉~得很齐全〈可〉一时可能~不齐; ~得了(liǎo)那么多吗?〈量〉给他~过一次助手〔状~〕必须~; 尽量❺~; 适当❻~; 及时❼~; 大量❽~; 合理❾~; 按一定标准❿~

1. secretary 2. assistant 3. complete; all in readiness 4. equipment; facilities 5. to the best of one's ability; to the full 6. properly 7. in time 8. in large number 9. rationally 10. according to certain standards

pèihé 配合 coordinate; concert; be in harmony with 〔~宾〕〈名〉~他们的工作; ~当前的❶形势❷和任务〈动〉~他们的行动❸; ~学习〔~补〕〈结〉和这项工作~上了〈程〉~得很好; ~得很融洽❹; ~得很和谐❺; ~得非常有默契❻; ~得很紧密❼; ~得不理想❽; ~得不太得力❾〈可〉力量❿~不上; 工作~不好〈时〉~了一段时间; ~了不少时候〈量〉~过很多次; 应该好好~一下儿〔状~〕认真~; 努力~; 主动⓫

~；积极❷~；紧密~；互相~；暗中❸~；尽力❹~

1. at present; current 2. situation 3. action 4. 5. harmonious; on friendly terms 6. tacit agreement; tacit understanding 7. close; intimate 8. not ideal 9. capable; competent 10. strength 11. on one's own initiative 12. actively 13. secretly 14. with utmost effort

pēn 喷 spurt; spout; spray 〔~宾〕〈名〉~点水再扫地；喷泉❶向空中~水；油井❷开始~油了；往果树上~农药❸；~杀虫剂❹；~油漆❺；火山往外~火；先往衣服上~点儿水再烫❻；蛇❼往外~毒液❽〔~补〕〈结〉把地都~湿❾了〈趋〉水~出来了；~到墙上去了；血从伤口❿~出来了；笑得把饭都~出来了〈程〉~得很高；~得真远〈可〉~得出来~不出来？〈时〉油只~了一天一夜〈量〉扫地前最好先~一下儿水〔状~〕往树上~药；从井口⓫~油；几个喷泉一齐~；往外~火；给花~点水；用喷壶⓬~水

1. fountain 2. oil well 3. agricultural chemical 4. insecticide; pesticide 5. paint 6. iron; press 7. snake 8. venom 9. wet 10. wound; cut 11. the mouth of the well 12. watering can

pěng 捧 ① hold or carry in both hands 〔~宾〕〈名〉~着肚子❶笑；~了一手花生米；母亲~着女儿的脸〔~补〕〈结〉~到他面前给他看〈趋〉他~出来一碗酒；~起泉水❷来就喝〈程〉花生~得太多了，直往下掉❸〈可〉孩子手小，~不了(liǎo)多少；花生米撒❹了一地，都~不起来了〈时〉~了半天也找不着(zháo)地方放〈量〉你先~一下儿，我拿个盘子❺去〔状~〕别~着了，快放下吧；一直~着；双手~着

1. belly 2. spring water 3. drop; fall 4. spill; drop 5. plate

② boost; exalt; flatter ≅ 吹捧 奉承〔~宾〕〈代〉~自己；~别人〔~补〕〈结〉~惯❶人了；简直❷把他朋友~上天了〈趋〉~起人来真肉麻❸；他没什么能力❹，是被人~上去的〈程〉他捧人~得实在❺恶心❻；~得太过分❼了〈时〉~了半天老李，老李也不喜欢他〈量〉我给他~过一次场〔状~〕专门❽~；从来不~；决不❾~；无须❿~

1. have the habit of 2. absolutely; virtually 3. nauseating; sickening; fulsome 4. capacity 5. trully; really 6. disgusting 7. excessive 8. for a special purpose 9. never 10. need not; not have to

pèng 碰 ① touch; bump ≅ 撞〔~宾〕〈名〉~杯；飞过来的球~了我的头；头上~了一个大包❶；石头~脚了；我不小心~了他的伤口❷；别~玻璃❸；一个人往里跑，一个人往外跑，两个人~

了一个满怀❹；别～这个箱子❺；汽车～人了；那个人非常厉害，谁也不敢～他一根毫毛❻； 在这件事情上他到处～壁❼〔～补〕〈结〉油瓶❽～倒❾了；头～晕❿了；茶～洒⓫了；腿～伤了；脚～破⓬了；我一跑把椅子～翻⓭了；手～破皮了；牙～流血⓮了；玻璃～碎⓯了；把我手里的书～掉⓰了；头～在墙上了〈程〉～得很利害；～得鼻青脸肿⓱〔可〕～不着(zháo)你，不用躲⓲〔时〕喝酒时～了半天杯〈量〉鸡蛋～一下儿就破〔状～〕不小心～了；差一点儿～了；可惜⓳～坏了；别～；没～；正好～；刚巧⓴～

1. protuberance; swelling 2. wound; cut 3. glass 4. bump right into sb. 5. box; chest 6. soft hair on the body 7. run up against a stone wall 8. oil bottle 9. fall 10. faint 11. sprinkle 12. cut; wound 13. turn over 14. bleed 15. break into pieces 16. fall 17. a bloody nose and a swollen face 18. hide 19. it's a pity 20. just right; just; exactly

② meet; run into; encounter ≃ 遇到〔～宾〕〈名〉明天上午10点～头❶；他们两个人没有一天不～头的〔～补〕〈结〉最近一直没～见他；～着(zháo)他替我说一声；带着钱去，～着(zháo)合适的❷就买点儿；刚才在路上～到一个熟人❸；第一次去就～上他家请客；～上好天气；今天去书店正好～到我要买的那本小说❹〈可〉一直～不到好的，所以没买〈量〉我们两个人在他家～过一次面；再安排❺一个日子～一下头吧〔状～〕在路上～见他了；偶然❻～；经常～；从未～过；正巧❼～；刚好❽～；万一❾～；难得❿～上

1. meet and discuss 2. suitable 3. acquaintance 4. novel 5. arrange 6. by chance; occasionally 7. 8. just at the right time; just 9. just in case; if by any chance 10. rarely

③ take one's chance ≃ 试探〔～宾〕〈名〉～～机会❶；～～运气❷〔～补〕〈量〉～一下儿看看〔习用〕～钉子❸；～一鼻子灰❹

1. chance; opportunity 2. fortune; luck 3. meet with a rebuff 4. be snubbed; meet with a rebuff

pī 批 write instructions or comments on (a report from a subordinate etc.)〔～宾〕〈名〉～文件❶；～签证❷；～条子❸；老师在作文❹本上～了几句话〈数〉一次就～了一万五〔～补〕〈趋〉怎么还没～下来啊！一个申请❺～过来～过去的，真费时间❻〈程〉～得很快；～得很及时❼；文章～得很认真；～得很仔细❽〈可〉签证老❾～不下来，真着急❿；他没那么大权力⓫，～不了(liǎo)文件〈时〉～了一年还没下来；～了那么长时间了，还没批完〈量〉～过一次了；请你～一下

儿〔状~〕认真~；及时~；亲自❷~；由别人代❸~；由院长~

1. document 2. visa 3. strip; a slip of paper; note 4. composition 5. ask; request 6. take a lot of time 7. in time 8. careful 9. for a long time 10. be anxious about; worry about 11. power 12. personally; in person; oneself 13. take the place of; replace

pīpíng 批评 criticize

〔~宾〕〈名〉~了他的错误；~了我的失职❶；~了报纸的单调❷和枯燥❸〈代〉他居然❹做出了这样的事情，真应该好好~~他〔~补〕〈结〉这件事跟他没关系❺，你~错人了；我把他~急了❻〈趋〉~起人来不留情面❼；~起人来真厉害❽；~起人来非常严肃❾；~起我来凶❿极了〈程〉~得很厉害；~得非常尖锐⓫；~得很有道理⓬〈可〉她这个人可~不得〈量〉~过两次；~了一顿〔状~〕好好~~；严厉地~；自我⓭~；净~别人；严肃地~；不留情面地~；语重心长地⓮~；诚恳地⓯~；适当地⓰~；婉转地⓱~；尖锐地~；直截了(liǎo)当地⓲~

1. neglect one's duty 2. monotonous; dull 3. dull and dry 4. unexpectedly; to one's surprise 5. have nothing to do with 6. irritated; annoyed 7. show mercy or forgiveness 8. stern; severe 9. serious; solemn 10. merciless 11. sharp 12. reasonable 13. self; oneself 14. sincere words and earnest wishes 15. sincerely 16. properly 17. tactfully; mild and indirect 18. straightforwardly; bluntly

pīzhǔn 批准 ratify; approve

〔~宾〕〈名〉~了我们的请求❶；~通航❷协定❸；~互不侵犯条约❹；会议~了他们的报告；~了城市建设❺的计划〈代〉~他去〔状~〕及时❻~；尚未❼~；由谁~？亲自❽~；不要草率地❾~；重新~；不易~

1. request; ask 2. be open to navigation or air traffic 3. agreement 4. nonaggression treaty 5. urban construction 6. in time 7. not yet 8. personally; in person; oneself 9. carelessly; perfunctorily; rushly

pī 披 ① drape over one's shoulders; wrap around

〔~宾〕〈名〉~着大衣；病人~着被❶坐在床上；蛇❷身上~着一层❸很小的鳞片❹；~着雨衣；~着羊皮的狼❺；~(散)着头发〔~补〕〈结〉建筑物❻~上了节日❼的盛装❽；夜深❾了，我把衣服给他~上；衣服没~好，眼看就滑❿下去了；他~上大衣就跑出去了；长长的头发~在肩上⓫〈程〉衣服~得很潇洒⓬；大衣~得真神气⓭〈时〉~一会儿衣服就暖和了；~了十分钟，才不哆嗦⓮了〔状~〕成天⓯~着；往身上~；从不~；赶快~上吧；替他~

1. quilt 2. snake 3. layer 4. scale 5. a wolf in sheep's clothing 6. building 7. holiday 8. splendid attire; rich dress 9. deep night 10. slip; slide 11. shoulder 12. natural and unrestrained 13. spirited; vigorous 14. tremble; shiver 15. all day long

② split open; crack ≅ 裂开〔主~〕〈名〉竹竿❶~了；指甲❷~了

1. bamboo pole 2. nail

pī 劈 ① split; chop; cleave〔~宾〕〈名〉~柴❶；~木头；一会儿就能~一大堆〔~补〕〈结〉~完了；~成两半了；~成一截❷一截的了；把木头~成碎片❸了；把木头~裂❹了；柴~多了〈趋〉一斧子❺就~下去了；一会儿的工夫就~出来一堆柴；你怎么用这把钝❻斧子~起柴来了？〈程〉~得很快；~得太多了〈可〉这么点儿时间~得完这一堆柴吗？斧子不快~得下来吗？你手没有劲儿❼，~得了(liǎo)吗？这么粗❽的木头一下子~不开；一上午~得出来这么多吗？〈时〉~了好几天；~一会儿就行了〈量〉你~一下儿试试；~了好几斧子才劈开；~过两次〔状~〕用斧子~；猛❾~；一气儿❿~了很多；分几次~；吃力地⓫~着

1. firewood 2. a section; one piece 3. pieces fragments 4. split; crack 5. axe; hatchet 6. blunt; dull 7. strength 8. thick 9. violently; suddenly 10. in one breath 11. strenously

② strike〔主~〕〈名〉一个孩子被雷❶~了；树被雷~了〔~补〕〈结〉~死了；~裂❷了；~倒了〈程〉有一个盲人❸被雷~得复明❹了〔状~〕被~；一下子~
另见pǐ 劈

1. thunder 2. split; crack 3. blindman 4. get the ability of seeing things again

pǐ 劈 ① strip off; break off〔~宾〕〈名〉一干树杈❶〔~补〕〈结〉把叶子都~掉了〈程〉她~得很快；~得很干净〈可〉~得下来吗？~不动；~不了(liǎo)那么多〈时〉~了半天〈量〉稍微❷~一下儿就行了〔状~〕多(少)~点儿；一层一层地❸~

1. withered crotch (of a tree) 2. slightly 3. layer after layer

② divide; split〔~宾〕〈名〉~线绳❶〔~补〕〈结〉把线绳~成三股❷〈程〉~得很快；~得不太匀❸〈可〉~得开~不开？绳子太细❹~不了(liǎo)〔状~〕用手~；用机器~
另见pī 劈

1. cotton rope 2. strand; ply 3. even 4. thin

piàn 骗 deceive; fool; cheat ≅ 欺骗〔~宾〕〈名〉~人；~东西；~钱〈代〉你可别~我〈动〉

~吃；~喝〔~补〕〈结〉把人~走了；把钱~光了〈趋〉越来越不学好；现在居然❶~起钱来了〈可〉你~得了(liǎo)谁也~不了(liǎo)我〈程〉~得很巧妙❷〈时〉~了很长时间了〈量〉~过无数❸次了〔状~〕用各种办法~；花言巧语❹地~；三番五次地❺~；千方百计地❻~；不择手段地❼~；被他~

1. unexpectedly 2. clever; ingenious 3. countless 4. sweet words; blandishments 5. time and again; over and over; repeatedly 6. in a thousand and one ways; by every possible means 7. by fair means or foul; unscrupulously

piànqǔ 骗取 gain sth. by cheating; cheat (或 trick, swindle) sb. out of sth.; defraud ≡ 骗得〔~宾〕〈名〉~别人的信任❶；~了大量❷财物❸；~钱财❹；荣誉❺〈动〉~别人的同情❻；大家对他的怜悯❼〔~补〕〈可〉~不到任何东西❽；眼泪❾也~不了(liǎo)人们对她的同情〔状~〕挖空心思❿地~；到处~；想方设法地⓫~

1. credit; trust 2. large quantity of 3. property; belongings 4. money and property 5. honour 6. sympathy 7. pity 8. anything 9. tear 10. rack one's brains 11. try every means

piāo 漂 float; drift〔~宾〕〈名〉水面上~着几片被风吹落的花瓣❶；海面上~着一只白帆船❷；死水❸池❹里~着一层❺污垢❻；汤里~着几片葱花❼〔~补〕〈结〉小船~走了；~到了对岸❽；一片树叶~远了〈趋〉死尸❾~上来了；皮球按❿到水里，一撒手⓫又~起来了〈程〉~得很慢；~得很远了〈可〉河里有水草挡⓬着，那张纸~不过来；石头太重，~不起来；那只鞋沉底⓭了，~不上来了〈时〉树叶在水上~了半天，后来被一个浪头⓮冲走了〔状~〕顺着风⓯~；顺着水⓰~；在水面上~；慢慢地~走了〔习用〕~洋过海
另见 piǎo 漂

1. petal 2. sailing boat 3. stagnant water 4. pool; pond 5. layer 6. dirt; filth 7. chipped green onion 8. the opposite bank 9. corpse; dead body 10. push; force 11. let go 12. block; keep off 13. sink to the bottom 14. wave; billow; breaker 15. with the wind 16. downstream; with the stream

piāo 飘 wave to and fro; float (in the air); flutter〔~宾〕〈名〉空气中~着花香❶；屋里~着饭菜的香味；天空~着雪花❷；蓝天上~着几朵白云；半山上~着一层薄雾❸；到处~着柳絮❹〔~补〕〈结〉~满了灰尘❺；一片羽毛❻随风❼~走了〈趋〉随风~过来一阵香水❽味❾；~来一股脂粉❿香；随着她的搧动⓫~来

了檀香⑫味；小纸片从楼上的窗口~下去了；片片落叶从树枝上~了下来；气球~上去了；他吐的烟慢慢地~上去了；裙子⑬被风吹得~了起来；一阵大风，把空中的风筝⑭吹得~来~去〈程〉~得很远；~得很慢；柳絮~得到处都是〈可〉~不上去；~不起来〈时〉断线⑮的风筝在空中~了半天才落地；肥皂泡⑯~了一会儿就破了〈量〉~了一阵；~了一下儿〔状~〕一阵一阵地~着香味；上午一直~着雪花；小木船在河面上慢慢地~着；满天~；任意⑰~；不时~来；轻轻地~着；旗子迎风⑱~；旗子呼啦呼啦地⑲~

1. fragrance of flowers 2. snowflake 3. mist; haze 4. catkin 5. dust 6. feather 7. with the wind 8. perfume 9. smell; aroma 10. rouge and powder; cosmetics 11. fan; flap 12. sandalwood 13. skirt 14. kite 15. (a kite) with a broken string 16. soap bubble 17. wantonly; arbitrarily 18. facing the wind 19. be flapping in the wind

piǎo 漂 bleach 〔~宾〕〈名〉~衣料❶；~衣服，~台布❷；床单❸；~毛线❹；~餐巾❺；~线❻；~线绳❼〔~补〕〈结〉白了；衣服都~糟❽了〈可〉原来❾的布太黑，可能~不白了〈时〉多~一会儿再拿出来〈量〉~过三次；~一下儿试试〔状~〕用漂白粉❿~；别~了；按照⓫使用说明⓬~；多~~；稍微⓭~

一~；经常~；第一次~
另见 piāo 漂

1. material for clothing; dress material 2. table cloth 3. sheet 4. knitting wool 5. table napkin 6. thread 7. cotton rope 8. rotten; poor; decayed 9. original 10. bleaching powder 11. according to 12. directions 13. slightly; a little

piē 撇 ① cast aside ≅ 抛弃〔~补〕〈结〉不能只做一件事，把别的事都~开不管❶；把客人~在一边了；~开这个问题不谈；父母双亡，~下了三个儿女〈程〉得远远的〈可〉~不下；~不开〔状~〕暂时❷~；必须~；完全~开了；无缘无故地❸~；无可奈何地❹~

1. show no consideration for 2. temporarily; for the moment 3. without cause or reason; for no reason at all 4. have no way out; have no alternative

② skim〔~宾〕〈名〉从肉汤❶上面~了一层油〔~补〕〈结〉~干净了吗?〈趋〉都~出去了；~到碗里去了〈程〉~得不干净；~得不彻底❷〈可〉~不出去；~不干净〈时〉~了半天也没撇干净〈量〉再~一下儿；~过两次了〔状~〕用勺子~；轻轻地~；从上面~；一层一层地❸~；慢慢地~
另见 piě 撇

1. broth 2. not thoroughly 3. layer after layer

piě 撇 throw; fling; cast ≅ 扔；掷〔~宾〕〈名〉~石子儿；~手榴弹❶〔~补〕〈趋〉迎面❷~过来一块砖头❸；从我头顶上~过去了；我刚走到窗前，正好从里边~出来一块西瓜皮；~到一边儿去了〈程〉石头~得很准❹；~得真远〈可〉我没劲儿❺，~不远；你~得到那棵树那儿吗?〈时〉孩子们~了一会儿石子儿就走开了〈量〉~了一下儿石子儿，把胳膊❻扭❼了；~过两次手榴弹〔状~〕使劲~；往远处~
另见piē撇

1. hand grenade 2. head-on; in one's face 3. fragment of a brick 4. accurate; exact 5. strength 6. arm 7. sprain; wrench

pīn 拼 ① put together; piece together ≅ 凑起来〔~宾〕〈名〉用小木条~了一个圆桌面；用黄瓜、香肠❶、鸡蛋~了一盘凉菜❷；零碎❸花布可以~一个小垫子❹〔~补〕〈结〉桌布~宽❺点儿；图案❻~成菱形❼好不好?〈趋〉两块木头~起来就够大了；可以把这块布条~上去；~出来的图案真漂亮〈程〉~得真好看；~得挺不错；~得非常艺术❽；~得十分雅致❾〈可〉材料❿不够~不了(liǎo)；这些碎布薄厚⓫不一样，~不起来〈时〉~了好长时间才拼完；~了三天〈量〉~过儿次；~一下儿〔状~〕耐心地⓬~；尽量⓭~；一块一块地~；随便⓮~；任意⓯~

1. sausage 2. a cold dish 3. scrappy 4. mat; cushion 5. large 6. design; pattern 7. rhombus; lozenge 8. conforming to good taste 9. refined; tasteful 10. material 11. thickness 12. patiently 13. to the best of one's ability; as far as possible 14. casually 15. wantonly; wilfully

② be ready to risk one's life (in fighting, work, etc.) ≅ 拼命〔~宾〕〈名〉他跟敌人~了命❶了；~刺刀❷〔~补〕〈趋〉~起刺刀来了〈程〉~得太厉害❸了；~得真凶❹〈可〉我可~不过他〈量〉~过好几次刺刀了；~了一阵子❺命〔状~〕跟敌人~；勇猛地❻~；不顾一切地❼~〔习用〕东西凑❽；七~八凑❾；~死~活地❿干

1. risk one's life; go all out regardless of danger to one's life 2. bayonet (bayonet-fighting) 3. 4. terrible; awful 5. a period of time 6. courageously 7. recklessly; regardless of the consequences 8. 9. scrape together; knock together 10. desperately; exerting the utmost strength

pìnqǐng 聘请 engage ≅ 聘〔~宾〕〈名〉~专家❶来作指导❷；我的同学为报幕员❸〈代〉~他当翻译;工会❹~她为兼职❺老师；~我为名誉会长；~谁为技术顾问❼? ~她当向导❽；~他为制片厂❾的导演❿〔~补〕〈结〉你们~着(zháo)合适⓫的人了没

有？～晚了，他已经离开这里了；已经～好了〈趋〉～来了〈程〉这次～得比较理想❷；～得不太满意❸〈可〉～得着(zháo)吗？～得到～不到。〈时〉～了很长时间才聘请到；～了三个多月〈量〉～过不少次了〔状～〕特意❹～；专门❺～；临时❻～；被～；多～几位；到处～；总算❼～到了；真不容易～

1. specialist; expert 2. guide 3. announcer 4. trade union 5. hold two or more posts concurrently (part-time teacher) 6. honorary president 7. technical adviser 8. guide 9. film studio 10. director 11. suitable 12. ideal 13. not satisfied 14. 15. specially; for a special purpose 16. at the time when sth. happens 17. at long last; finally

píng 平

① level (a piece of ground)〔～宾〕〈名〉～地；～土岗❶；～一～路面❷；把地一～，再播种❸〔～补〕〈结〉～掉一个小土堆；～过了〈程〉拖拉机❹平地～得又快又好〈可〉这块坑坑注注❺的地我一个人～不了(liǎo)；～不完〈量〉好好～一下儿；～过一遍了〔状～〕立即❻～；已经～了；用铁锹❼～；一锹一锹地❽～；用机器❾～

1. mound 2. road surface 3. sow 4. tractor 5. full of bumps and hollows 6. at once 7. shovel 8. shovel after shovel 9. by machine

② calm; peaceful; quiet ≅ 安定〔主～〕〈名〉两个人之间的误会❶消除❷后，气也就都～了〔～补〕〈趋〉先把气～下去再说〈可〉不这样处理❸就～不了(liǎo)气〈量〉～一下儿气〔状～〕先～～气

1. misunderstanding 2. clear up 3. handle; deal with

③ put down; suppress ≅ 平定〔～宾〕〈名〉～乱❶；～叛❷〔～补〕〈趋〉把一场骚乱❸～下去了〈程〉～得不彻底❹；～得很及时❺〈可〉～得下去吗？〈量〉派❻他带兵❼～过一次叛乱〔状～〕彻底～；及早❽～

1. 2. armed rebellion 3. disturbance; riot 4. not thorough 5. in time 6. send; dispatch 7. lead troops 8. at an early date; as soon as possible

píngxī 平息 calm down; quiet down; subside〔主～〕〈名〉一场风波❶渐渐地❷～了；怒气❸～了；叛乱❹～了〔～宾〕〈名〉～了一场叛乱；～了一场风波〔～补〕〈趋〉～下去了〈程〉～得很快〔状～〕已经～了；逐渐❺～了；尚未～；还没～

1. disturbance 2. gradually 3. anger 4. armed rebellion 5. little by little; gradually

píng 评 comment; criticize; judge〔～宾〕〈名〉你来给～～理❶；～分；～功过❷；～好坏；～是

非❸；～奖❹〈主－谓〉～～谁是谁非；～～他的话有没有道理❺〔～补〕〈结〉他被～为最佳演员❻了；物理卷子❼～完了〈趋〉谁好谁坏～出来看〈程〉分数～得不公平〈可〉我～不出好坏来〈时〉最佳售货员❽～了好几个月才评出来〈量〉今年～过两次了；大家～一下儿〔状～〕认真～；不知怎么～；真难～；重新～；反复❾～；根据❿什么～？按⓫什么标准⓬～？被～

1. (judge between) right and wrong 2. achievements and errors 3. judge between good and bad 4. award; praise 5. reason 6. the best actor (or actress) 7. an examination paper of physics 8. first-rate shop assistant 9. repeatedly; over and over again 10. 11. according to 12. standard; criterion

pō 泼 sprinkle; splash; spill 〔～宾〕〈名〉～水；水～了一身；～了一地〔～补〕〈结〉把水～远点儿；别～在门口儿；一杯水全～到我头上了〈趋〉不知是谁从窗口～下一盆❶水来；眼看❷一盆水从楼上～下来了；别把脏水❸～到院子❹里去〈程〉～得很远〈时〉天太冷，水刚～一会儿就冻上了〔状～〕泼水节❺时人们互相～水；差一点儿～了我一身脏水；猛地❻一～；别从窗口往外～〔习用〕～冷水❼

1. basin; tub; pot 2. soon; in a moment 3. dirty water 4. courtyard 5. the Water-Sprinkling Festival of the Dai and some other minority nationalities 6. violently; suddenly 7. pour (throw) cold water on; dampen the enthusiasm (spirits) of

pò 破 ① break; damage 〔主～〕〈名〉手～了；纸～了；鞋～了；袋子❶～了；书包～了；玻璃❷～了〔～宾〕〈名〉袜子❸～了一个洞❹；～了一个窟窿❺；衣服～了一个口子❻〔～补〕〈趋〉窟窿再～下去，就没法补❼了〈程〉～得越来越利害了；洞～得越来越大了；～得没法缝❽了〈可〉这种料子❾非常耐❿，穿十年八年都～不了(liǎo)〈时〉玻璃～了不少时候了，到现在还没安上⓫；～了很长时间了〈量〉～过好几次了〔状～〕这种纸不好，容易～；鞋又～了；这条裤子穿了十年，至今⓬还没～

1. bag; sack 2. glass 3. socks 4. 5. hole 6. cut; tear; opening; hole 7. mend; patch; repair 8. sew 9. material 10. durable 11. install; fix 12. up to now; so far

② split; break ≅ 劈开〔～宾〕〈名〉～浪❶前进❷〔～补〕〈结〉把那块厚板子❸～开；～成两半；～薄❹点儿；还没～完呢；没匀❺；把一块钱～成两张五毛的；〈趋〉这块木头太硬，～起来有点儿费劲❻〈程〉板子～得真薄；～得很匀；～得不一般厚❼〈可〉这块木板～得了(liǎo)～不了(liǎo)？

钱～得开吗？〈量〉把这块板子从中间～一下儿〔**状～**〕不好～，非常难～；用电锯❽～

1. wave **2.** advance; go forward; forge ahead **3.** thick board **4.** thin **5.** not even **6.** need or use great effort **7.** not of uniform thickness **8.** electric saw

③ break with ≃ 破除；突破〔**～宾**〕〈名〉今天他～例❶抽了一支烟；我也～～戒❷，喝点酒；～旧俗，立新风❸；游泳～了纪录❹；别～了人家的规矩❺〔**～补**〕〈可〉今天的比赛他～得了(liǎo)纪录吗？〈量〉她～过三次世界纪录❻〔**状～**〕又～了一项全国纪录❼

1. break a rule; make an exception **2.** break one's vow of abstinence **3.** break with outmoded customs and establish new ones **4.** break a record **5.** rule; custom **6.** world record **7.** national record

④ reveal; lay bare; solve ≃ 揭穿；揭露〔**～宾**〕〈名〉～案❶；～谜语❷；～密码❸〔**～补**〕〈趋〉密码～出来了；他们又～起谜语来了〈程〉这个案子～得很快；～得神速❹〈可〉这个凶杀案❺～得了(liǎo)吗？密码～得出来～不出来？〈时〉～了一晚上谜语；这个案子～了很长时间了〈量〉这个谜语请他～一下儿好不好？〔**状～**〕及时～案；认真～〔**习用**〕～罐儿～摔❻

1. case; lawcase **2.** riddle **3.** secret code; cipher **4.** marvellously quick **5.** a case of murder **6.** smash a pot to pieces just because it's cracked — write oneself off as hopeless and act recklessly

pòchú 破除 do away with; get rid of〔**～宾**〕〈名〉～迷信❶；～情面❷；～障碍❸；～顾虑❹；～隔阂❺〔**～补**〕〈程〉～得很好；～得很快；～得不彻底❻〈可〉～得了(liǎo)吗？〔**状～**〕必须～

1. superstition **2.** feelings; sensibilities **3.** barrier; obstruction; obstacle **4.** misgiving; worry **5.** estrangement; misunderstanding **6.** not thorough

pòhuài 破坏 destroy; wreck; sabotage〔**～宾**〕〈名〉～铁路❶；～大桥；～交通秩序❷；～建筑物❸；战争❹～了很多城市；～名誉❺；～协定❻；～旧习俗❼，建立新风尚❽；～团结❾；～友谊❿〔**～补**〕〈趋〉这座大楼盖⓫的时候费了很大的劲儿⓬，～起来真是易如反掌⓭；他在那儿～起我的名誉来了〈程〉～得很利害⓮；～得无法收拾⓯了〈可〉我们之间的友谊谁也～不了(liǎo)〔**状～**〕被～；已经～了；故意⓰～；有意⓱～；蓄意⓲～；三番五次地⓳～；屡次⓴～；暗中㉑～；公开㉒～；随意㉓～

1. railway 2. traffic order 3. building 4. war 5. fame; reputation 6. agreement 7. custom; convention 8. prevailing custom 9. unity 10. friendship 11. build 12. take a lot of effort 13. as easy as turning one's hand over 14. terrible; formidable 15. put in order; tidy; clear away 16. intentionally; purposely 17. 18. deliberately 19. 20. over and over again; repeatedly 21. secretly; in secret 22. openly; publicly 23. at will; as one pleases

pòmiè 破灭 be shattered; fall through 〔主～〕〈名〉幻想❶～了；梦想❷～了；美梦～了；理想❸～了；希望～了〔～补〕〈程〉～得很快〔状～〕又一次～了；彻底❹～了；早已❺～了；象肥皂泡似地❻～了；一下子就～了

1. illusion; fancy; fantasy 2. dream 3. ideal 4. thoroughly 5. long ago; for a long time 6. like soap bubble

pū 扑 ① throw oneself on; pounce on 〔～宾〕〈名〉～了一个空❶；和风～面❷；香气❸～鼻❹；一进门感到热气❺～脸〔～补〕〈结〉她一头～到妈妈怀里❻痛哭起来了；车窗外的景物❼～入了我的眼帘❽〈趋〉他虽然负了伤❾，但仍然英勇❿地向罪犯⓫～去；打开窗户一股冷风⓬迎面⓭～了进来；棕熊⓮向猎人⓯～过去了；〔状～〕猛地⓰～；向敌人～；激动地⓱～；勇敢地⓲～；从对面⓳～；一头～到

1. fail to get or achieve what one wants 2. the gentle breeze caressed one's faces 3. sweet smell 4. nose 5. steam; heat 6. bosom 7. scenery 8. eye (come into view) 9. be wounded; be injured 10. courageously 11. criminal 12. cold air 13. in one's face; head-on 14. brown bear 15. hunter 16. suddenly; violently 17. with excitement 18. bravely; courageously 19. opposite

② rush at; attack ≃ 扑打〔～宾〕〈名〉～蝴蝶❶〔～补〕〈结〉～着(zháo)一只大花蝴蝶❷；～火❸了一场大火；～灭蚊蝇❹〈趋〉他在捉蝴蝶，一会儿～过来，一会儿～过去〈可〉～不着(zháo)〔状～〕及时❺～灭了；用手～蝴蝶在花丛❻中～

1. butterfly 2. variegated butterfly 3. put out; extinguish 4. mosquitoes and flies 5. in time 6. flowering shrubs

③ flap; flutter ≃ 拍打〔～宾〕〈名〉海鸥❶～着翅膀❷〔～补〕〈结〉～上点儿粉❸；粉没～匀❹；～少点儿吧〈程〉～得太多；～得太厚了〈可〉～不匀〈时〉～了半天；～了一会儿〈量〉～了儿下儿；～了一阵❺〔状～〕厚厚地❻～了一层；薄薄地❼～了一层；往脖子❽上～；用粉扑儿❾～；给孩子～；经常～〔习用〕灯蛾～火❿

1. sea gull 2. wing 3. powder 4. not even 5. a spell; a period of time 6. thickly 7. thinly 8. neck 9. powder puff 10. a moth darting into a flame — bring destruction upon onself

pū 铺 spread; unfold; pave; lay 〔～宾〕〈名〉～被❶；～褥子❷；～床单❸；～毯子❹；～桌布❺；～铁轨❻；～石子儿；～柏油马路❼〔～补〕〈结〉为他～平道路；把桌布～在桌子上；褥子最好～厚❽一点儿；铁轨已经～到什么地方了? 地毯❾从房间一头～向另一头〈趋〉～到床上去〈程〉～得真平；铁路～得真快〈可〉床单太大，小孩子一个人～不上；草皮❿少，这块地～不满；今年年底以前，这段路～得完吗?〈时〉这段路～了半年多了〈量〉一天要～两次床，晚上～一次，午睡⓫时～一次〔**状**～〕正在～；将要～；平平整整地⓬～着；厚厚地～了一层⓭

1. quilt 2. cotton-padded mattress 3. sheet 4. blanket 5. tablecloth 6. rail 7. asphalt road 8. thick 9. carpet 10. sod; turf 11. nap 12. neatly 13. a layer

Q

qīfu 欺负 bully ≅ 欺负;欺凌 〔~宾〕<名>你是哥哥,不许❶~弟弟;不许~傻子❷;别~老实人❸;净❹~孩子;~弱者❺;~小国 <代>我~谁了?不能~人家〔~补〕<结>他把我~苦❻了;把她~急❼了;又把她~哭了;小李让他给~跑了;把人~到这种地步 <趋>他~起人来真可恨❽ <程>让人~得直哭;让她~得没法儿呆❾下去了 <可>有我在这儿,谁也~不了(liǎo)你 <时>她~了别人半天,自己也没得到好处❿ <量>~过我无数次⓫了 〔**状~**〕偏偏~;万一⓬~;别~;专门⓭~人;净~人;故意⓮~人;竟然⓯~;何苦⓰~;不能任意⓱~〔**习用**〕软的怕硬的⓲

1. not allow 2. fool; blockhead; simpleton 3. honest person 4. only; merely; nothing but 5. the weak 6. too much 7. irritated; annoyed; nettled 8. hateful; detestable; abominable 9. stay 10. advantage; good; benefit 11. innumerable 12. if by any chance; just in case 13. specially 14. intentionally; purposely 15. to one's surprise; unexpectedly 16. why bother 17. wantonly; wilfully; arbitrarily 18. bully the weak and fear the strong

qīpiàn 欺骗 deceive; cheat; dupe ≅ 欺诈〔宾〕<名>~群众❶;~人 <代>~别人;~自己〔~补〕<趋>连你也~起我来了 <可>谁也~不了(liǎo)他 <时>~了我一辈子❷;被他~了好多年 <量>~过我好多次〔**状~**〕总~人;一直~;经常~;从不~;决不❸~;三番五次地❹~

1. the masses 2. all one's life 3. never 4. again and again; over and over again

qī 漆 paint; coat with lacquer ≅ 涂〔~宾〕<名>~家具❶;~窗户〔~补〕<结>把门窗都~成绿色;颜色~深❷了;~浅❸了;~上一道边❹儿就好看了;这种漆❺看着很浅,~在木头上就深了 <趋>别着急❻;一~起来就快了;看着好看,~出来不一定好看<程>他~得真快;~得挺漂亮;~得太难看了;~得太厚❼;~得太薄❽;~得比较浅;~得不匀❾,有的地方厚,有的地方薄 <可>这个桌面太粗糙❿,可能~不上;我不会漆,怕~不好;我技术⓫不行,~不匀 <时>~了一下午,总算⓬漆完了;~了三天还没漆完 <量>~过两次;再~一遍;~一下儿试试〔**状~**〕前后~了一个

月；一律⓭~；用大刷子⓮~；多(少)~几道；重新~

1. furniture 2. deep; dark 3. light 4. margin; edge; brim 5. paint; lacquer 6. don't worry 7. thick 8. thin 9. not evenly spread 10. coarse; rough 11. technique; technology 12. after all; at long last; finally 13. all; without exception 14. brush

qí 骑 ride (an animal or bicycle); sit on the back of〔~宾〕〈名〉~牛；~骆驼❶；~摩托车❷；~着墙头❸〔~补〕〈结〉他~上马走了；车让他~走了；那个孩子~在牛背上吹笛子❹；车都~腻❺了〈趋〉这匹马很老实❻，你~上去试试；他把摩托车~出去了；也没问是谁的车，~起来就去追❼人了〈程〉~得很熟练❽；~得真快；~得时间太长了；骑车~得真累〈可〉这匹马不听话，我可~不了(liǎo)；车太高，孩子~不上去；摩托车坏了，~不回去了；坡儿太陡❾，~不上去，推❿着车走吧；前边修路，~不过去了，绕一下儿吧〈时〉我这辆车~了十年，还很新；~了一上午车，太累了；刚~一会儿〈量〉~过两次摩托车；刚~一下儿车就坏了〔**状~**〕快~；好~；别~；这车真难~；飞快地⓫~；第一次~〔**习用**〕~马找马⓬

1. camel 2. motor-cycle 3. the top of a wall 4. play the flute 5. be bored with 6. docile 7. chase (run) after; pursue 8. skilful 9. steep; precipitous 10. push 11. very fast; at lightning speed 12. looking for a horse while sitting on one — hold on to one job while seeking a better one

qǐtú 企图 attempt; try; seek ≅ 妄图〔**~宾**〕〈动〉~逃跑❶；~越狱❷；~破坏❸；~夺权❹；~发动❺新的进攻❻；~突围❼；~打开一个缺口❽；~掩盖❾事实真相❿；~掩饰⓫自己的缺点；~扇动⓬闹事⓭；~放毒药⓮；~下毒手⓯；~捣乱⓰会场⓱；~偷⓲越国境⓳；~叛国⓴投敌㉑〔**状~**〕多次~；再次~；时刻㉒~；一直㉓~

1.run away; escape; flee 2. escape from prison; break prison 3. destroy 4. seize power; take over power 5. start; launch 6. attack; offensive 7. break out of an encirclement 8. make a breach 9. cover; conceal 10. truth of the fact 11. conceal; cover up 12. instigate; incite; stir up 13. make trouble; create a disturbance 14. poison 15. resort to violent treachery; lay murderous hands on sb. 16. make trouble; create a disturbance 17. meeting-place; conference hall 18. stealthily; secretly 19. cross the boundary illegally 20. betray one's country; commit treason 21. go over to the enemy; defect to the enemy 22. always; constantly 23. continuously; always; all along

qǐfā 启发 arouse; inspire; enlighten

〔~宾〕〈名〉~人们的觉悟❶〈代〉~我们思考问题❷〔~补〕〈程〉~得很好〈时〉~了半天我也回答不出来〈量〉~一下儿；~了好几遍〔状~〕好好~~他吧；再三~；一遍一遍地~；反复~；多次~；用各种办法❸~；从各个角度❹~；耐心地❺~

1. consciousness; awareness 2. ponder a problem 3. by every possible means 4. from every respect 5. patiently

qǐ 起

① rise; get up; stand up ≅ 起来〔~补〕〈结〉今天我起床~晚了〈趋〉我每天6点钟~来〈程〉~得比较晚，每天都是爸爸~得最早〈可〉睡得太晚了，早上~不来；我睡得晚，所以早晨~不早；他每天~不了(liǎo)太早〈时〉这个孩子起床就~了半个小时，真磨蹭❶〈量〉孩子半夜~过两次〔状~〕按时❷~；准时❸~；赖着❹不~；醒❺了就~；快~；勉强❻~；早睡早~；每天几点~床?

1. move slowly; dawdle 2. 3. on time 4. hang in a place; drag out one's stay in a place; hold on to a place 5. wake up; be awake 6. reluctantly

② appear; raise ≅ 长出〔~宾〕〈名〉~了一身鸡皮疙瘩❶；脸上~了一个包儿❷〔~补〕〈结〉脖子❸上~满了痱子❹〈可〉勤洗着点儿就~不了(liǎo)痱子了〈量〉~过一次〔状~〕容易~；经常~；每年~；浑身上下❺都~；怪不得❻~

1. gooseflesh 2. swelling 3. neck 4. prickly heat 5. all over the body 6. no wonder; so that's why; that explains why

③ rise; grow ≅ 发生；发挥〔~宾〕〈名〉~风了；~火了；~歹念❶；~了黑心❷；~了不良之心❸；~了疑心❹；平地~风波❺；~了很大变化❻；~作用❼〔~补〕〈结〉不知能不能~到作用〈可〉他~不了(liǎo)什么好作用〔状~〕又~风了；没~变化；不~作用；动不动❽就~疑心；突然❾~风了

1. evil intention 2. 3. black heart; evil mind 4. suspicion 5. a sudden, unexpected turn of events; unforeseen trouble 6. great change 7. take effect 8. easily; frequently 9. suddenly

④ remove; extract; pull ≅ 取出〔~宾〕〈名〉~钉子❶；~图钉❷；~瓶塞❸；~地雷❹〔~补〕〈结〉把罐头❺盒❻~开；把啤酒❼瓶盖❽~掉❾〈趋〉把墙上的钉子~下来〈程〉~得很快；~得很好〈可〉~不开；~不下来；~了半天才起下来〈量〉你帮我~一下儿〔状~〕用钳子❿~钉子；用力~；小心地~

1. nail 2. drawing pin; thumbtack 3. cork; stopper 4. (land)

mine 5. tin; can 6. case; box 7. beer 8. bottle top 9. off; away 10. pliers; pincers

⑤ draft; work out ≅ 拟定 〔~宾〕<名>这篇文章我先~个草儿❶；谁给你~的名儿；给他~了一个外号❷(绰号)〔~补〕<结>文章已经~完草儿了；给孩子~好名字了<趋>他~出来的名字与众不同❸<程>名字~得很别致❹；~得很有诗意❺；~得太俗❻了；~得很好听；~得真怪；~得叫起来真拗口❼<可>名字我~不好<时>名字~了好长时间还没起满意❽<量>~过两次草稿，都不行〔状~〕先~；给孩子~；暂时❾~；随便❿~；重新

1. draft; draw up 2. nickname 3. out of the ordinary 4. unique; unconventional 5. very poetic 6. vulgar 7. hard to pronounce; awkward-sounding 8. satisfied 9. temporarily 10. casually; at random

qì 气 get angry; be enraged; enrage; make angry 〔~宾〕<名>学生不要~老师；那个孩子总~他妈妈〔~补〕<结>把他~急❶了；这个孩子真~死❷人；可把他~坏了；~炸了肺❸；把妹妹~哭了；把他~跑了；差点儿没把我~死；~晕❹了<趋>~出一场病来；孩子~起人来真要命❺<程>~得直哭；~得直哆嗦❻；~得吃不下饭；~得一句话也说不出来了；~得直跺脚❼<可>我~不过，就说了他几句<量>~了他一

下儿；~过我一次〔状~〕故意❽~；三番五次地❾~；让他~坏了；想方设法地❿~；净拿话~人

1. irritated; annoyed; nettled 2. extremely; to death 3. flare up; explode with rage 4. lose consciousness; faint 5. extremely; terribly; awfully 6. tremble; shiver 7. stamp one's foot with fury 8. intentionally; purposely 9. over and over again; repeatedly 10. try by hook or by crook; try every means

qì 砌 build by laying bricks or stones ↔ 拆〔~宾〕<名>~砖❶；~炉灶❷；~烟囱❸；~台阶❹；~台子❺〔~补〕<结>墙~矮❻了，烟囱~歪❼了，炉灶~好了，能用了；台阶~完了；灶~在厨房❽；烟囱~成方的了<趋>这么快就把墙~起来了<程>墙~得很直；台阶~得太高了<可>这个灶要是让我自己砌可~不上；他刚学，还~不好；我总~不直<时>这段围墙❾~了一年才砌完<量>~过两次〔状~〕第一次~；重新~；真难；慢慢腾腾地❿~；一层一层地⓫~；结结实实地⓬~

1. brick 2. cooking stove 3. chimney 4. stairs 5. platform; stage 6. low 7. oblique; slanting 8. kitchen 9. enclosure; enclosing wall 10. slowly 11. layer after layer 12. solidly

qiǎ 卡 wedge; get stuck 〔~补〕<结>鱼刺❶~在喉咙❷里了；东西

~在抽屉❸里了；头发~上点儿,就掉❹不下来了〈趋〉把头发~上去〈程〉鱼刺~得真疼；抽屉~得拿不出东西来了；~得怎么拉也拉不开了；头发~得真难看；~得太松❺了；~得太紧了〈可〉头发太短~不住；吃鱼时注点意,就~不了(liǎo)喉咙〈时〉鱼刺在喉咙里~了半天,才用水冲下去〈量〉头发这样~过一次；让鱼刺~了一下儿〔状~〕别~住；从来没~过；紧紧地❻~住了

1. fishbone 2. throat 3. drawer 4. drop; fall 5. loose 6. tightly; closely

qiānjiù 迁就 accommodate oneself to; yield to 〔~宾〕〈名〉~孩子；~犯错误的人；~病人〈代〉她〔~补〕〈结〉~惯❶了；~错了〈趋〉不能再~下去了；你怎么也~起孩子来了〈程〉他迁就人~得太过分❷了〈可〉孩子可~不得〈时〉~了一辈子❸人〈量〉~过他好几次了〔状~〕在小事上互相~；决不❹~；别再~了，一直~；千万❺别~；一味~❻

1. get used to; be used to 2. excessive 3. all one's life 4. never 5. be sure 6. make endless concessions; make one concession after another

qiān 牵 lead along (by holding the hand, the halter, etc.) pull ≅ 拉〔~宾〕〈名〉~着牛；~牲口❶；手~着手〔~补〕〈结〉把牲口~走了〈趋〉小牧童❷从对面~来一头牛；把牛~进牛棚❸里去了；把牲口~出来套❹车吧，把两头牛一块~过来了；~进牛棚里去了；耕❺完地把它又~回来了；~起来就走〈可〉孩子太小，~不了(liǎo)这头老牛〈量〉我来~一下儿；~过一次牛〔状~〕用绳子❻~；往地里~；从田里~〔习用〕顺手~羊❼；~肠挂肚❽

1. draught animals 2. shepherd boy; buffalo boy 3. stable 4. hitch up (an animal to a cart) 5. plough 6. rope 7. lead away a goat in passing — pick up sth. on the sly 8. feel deep anxiety about; be very worried about

qiān 签 sign; autograph〔~宾〕〈名〉~名；~字〈动〉~到❶〔~补〕〈结〉他~上字了；代表❷们~完名了；把名字~在书的扉页❸上了〈量〉请您先~一下儿名〔状~〕亲笔❹~名；到处~；按时❺~到；被迫❻~字；工工整整地❼~；在合同上❽~；主动地❾~；勉强❿~

1. register one's attendance at a meeting or at an office; sign in 2. deputy; delegate; representative 3. title page 4. in one's own handwriting 5. on time 6. be forced to 7. carefully and neatly done 8. in the contract 9. on one's own initiative 10. reluctantly; grudgingly

qiàn 欠

① owe; be behind with ≅ 该〔~宾〕〈名〉~帐❶；~债❷；我~他很多钱；~了点儿人情❸；~租❹；还~图书馆一本书没还〔~补〕〈结〉~下了一笔债；人情~多了〈趋〉没钱还，只好继续~下去；他也~起债来了〈程〉钱~得太多了；~得太久了；~得还(huán)都还(huán)不清了〈时〉这笔钱他~了三年才还清〈量〉他~了我两次钱，都忘记❺还了；钱先~一下儿，过两天再还〔状~〕少~点债吧；从不~；一向~钱不还；长期~；暂时❻~；偶尔❼~；经常~；照样❽~

1. account 2. debt 3. a debt of gratitude; human relationship 4. land rent; rent 5. forget 6. temporarily; for a moment 7. once in a while; occasionally 8. in the same old way; all the same; as before

② not enough ≅ 缺少；差〔~宾〕〈名〉这盘菜炒❶得有点~火❷了〈动〉这孩子~打；这句话~考虑❸；这些词语❹~斟酌❺〈形〉最近身体~佳❻；他说话~检点❼，所以常得罪❽人；这篇文章的文字~通❾；事情这么办~妥❿〔状~〕确实~考虑；有点儿~火

1. stir-fry; fry; *sauté* 2. fire (not long enough) 3. think over; ponder over 4. words and expressions; terms 5. consider; deliberate 6. poor 7. be careless about one's words 8. offend; displease 9. not grammatical 10. not proper

③ raise slightly (a part of the body ≅ 跷〔~宾〕〈名〉~着脚看；你再~~脚就够着(zháo)了；他只~了~身子，没站起来〔~补〕〈结〉脚再~高点儿〈趋〉你~起脚来就看见了〈程〉~得真高；~得不够高〈时〉~了半天什么也没看见〈量〉请你~一下儿身子，我要开抽屉❶〔状~〕向前~；拼命❷~；使劲❸~；稍微❹~了~；勉强❺~了~身子

1. drawer 2. with all one is worth; for all one is worth 3. exert oneself physically; exert all one's strength 4. slightly 5. reluctantly; grudgingly

qiāng 呛 choke

〔~宾〕〈名〉游泳时~了一口水；~了一口饭〔~补〕〈结〉差点儿没~死；~着(zháo)了吗? 可把他~坏了〈趋〉饭粒~进气管❶里去了；水~到气管里去了〈程〉~得真难受❷；~得直咳嗽❸〈可〉慢慢喝就~不着(zháo)了〈量〉~过好多次了；~一下儿真难受〔状~〕从鼻子❹里~进水去了；不小心~了；经常~；容易~；千万别~；难免❺~；差点儿~

另见qiàng呛

1. trachea 2. feel unwell 3. cough 4. nose 5. hard to avoid

qiángdiào 强调 stress; emphasize; underline

〔~宾〕〈名〉~困

难；～原因❶；～学习的重要性❷〈动〉～听；～说；～读；～写；～独立❸思考❹；～自学❺成才❻〈主－谓〉～情况特殊❼；～生活困难〔～补〕〈结〉她又～上困难了〈趋〉又～起他们的情况特殊来了〈时〉～了半天〈量〉需要～一下儿；～过好多次了〔状～〕一再～；反复～；屡次～；无须❽～；一味❾～；在讲话中～；在文章里❿～；着重⓫～；适当⓬～；特别～

1. cause 2. importance 3. independent; on one's own 4. ponder over; reflect on 5. study on one's own; study independently 6. capable person 7. particular; special 8. need not 9. blindly 10. essay; article 11. emphatically 12. suitably; properly; appropriately

qiǎng 抢 ① rob; loot; take by force ≅ 抢夺〔～宾〕〈名〉匪徒❶～银行❷；强盗❸～财物❹；地痞❺流氓❻～人；不要～座位❼；～地方〔～补〕〈结〉把钱～走了；把存折❽～走了；人让他们给～跑了；～到手了〈趋〉把孩子从火海❾里～出来了；把自己的衣物从小偷❿手里～回来了；把父母的遗产⓫～到自己手里来了〈程〉～得太可怕了；～得太凶⓬了〈可〉火势⓭太猛⓮，什么东西也～不出来〈时〉从小偷手里～了半天也没抢回来〈量〉那个罪犯⓯～过两次钱〔状～〕拼命⓰～；深更半夜⓱～；明目张胆地⓲～；里应外合地⓳～；肆无忌惮地⓴～；公开地㉑～；成帮结伙地㉒～；连续～；反复～；众目睽睽之下㉓～；拦路㉔～；在半路～；持刀㉕～；居然㉖～；竟然㉗～

1. bandit; gangster 2. bank 3. robber; bandit 4. property; belongings; effects 5. local ruffian; local riffraff 6. rogue; hooligan 7. seat 8. deposit book; bankbook 9. a sea of fire 10. thief 11. legacy; heritage; inheritance 12. terrible; awful 13. flame 14. violent 15. criminal 16. with all one's might; desperately 17. late at night 18. brazenly; flagrantly 19. collaborate from within with forces from without 20. unscrupulously 21. openly; publicly 22. in crowds; in throngs 23. in the public eye; in the public gaze 24. block the way 25. hold a sword 26. 27. to one's surprise; unexpectedly

② snatch; grab ≅ 抓取〔～宾〕〈名〉～球；下雨了，快往屋里～东西吧〔～补〕〈结〉一把就从我手里把像片～走了；别把书～撕❶了；～破❷了〈趋〉那个人真没礼貌❸，别人正在看报，他一把就把报纸～过来了；从人家手里～回来〈程〉～得真快〈可〉我跑得远远的，他抢也～不着(zháo)；你～得过去吗？～得回来吗？我总～不着(zháo)球〈时〉～了半天，也没抢过去；～了好长时间〈量〉～过好几次了〔状～〕一把就～过来了；拼命❹～；使劲❺～；

故意❻~；趁其不备❼~；趁❽她没注意~；从身后~；突然~；没礼貌地~

1. 2. torn 3. impolite 4. exerting the utmost strength 5. exert all one's strength 6. intentionally; on purpose 7. take sb. unawares 8. take advantage of

③ vie for; scramble for ≌ 竞争；争先〔~宾〕<名>不要~镜头❶；~时间〔~补〕<结>~在大雨来临❷之前修好；她什么事都~在前头<趋>大家都没开口，他~过来就说；这个月月底以前我要把这篇论文❸~出来；前边这辆车开得太慢，咱们~过去吧<可>这项任务三天之内~得完~不完？〈时〉一连~了五天才抢完〔状~〕连夜❹~；一连~了三天；专❺~；别~；拼命❻~

1. shot; scene 2. arrive; come 3. thesis; dissertation; treatise; paper 4. the same night; that very night 5. especially; particularly 6. for all one is worth; with all one's might

qiāng 呛 irritate (respiratory organs) 〔~宾〕<名>烟❶太~人；炸❷辣椒❸的味儿❹~鼻子❺〔~补〕<结>烟把人~死了；辣味儿~着(zháo)他了<程>~得直咳嗽❻；~得一个劲❼打喷嚏❽；~得眼泪❾都流❿出来了；~得睁不开眼⓫；~得要命⓬；~得慌⓭<可>烟往那边刮⓮，站在这边儿~不着(zháo)~一下

儿真难受⓯〔状~〕真~；多~啊！太~了
另见qiāng 戗

1. smoke 2. fry 3. chilli 4. smell; aroma 5. nose 6. cough 7. continuously; persistently 8. sneeze 9. tear 10. shed; flow 11. can't open one's eyes 12. 13. extremely; awfully; terribly 14. blow 15. feel ill; feel bad

qiāo 跷 ① lift up (a leg); hold up (a finger) ≌ 抬起〔~宾〕<名>~着腿坐❶；~着二郎腿❷；~着大拇指❸ 夸他〔~补〕<趋>他总喜欢❹把腿~起来<程>腿~得高高的〔状~〕总~；经常~

1. sit with one's legs crossed 2. sit with ankle on knee 3. hold up one's thumb in approval 4. like; be fond of

② on tiptoe ≌ 欠〔~宾〕<名>~着脚够❶上边的东西；~着脚往里看；~着脚也够不着(zháo)〔~补〕<结>脚~高点儿<趋>把脚~起来就看见了<程>脚~得那么高还是看不见<时>~了半天脚什么也没看见 <量>把脚~一下儿〔状~〕往上❷一~；高高地~

1. reach; be up to (a certain standard, etc.) 2. upwards

qiāo 敲 knock; beat; strike ≌ 打〔~宾〕<名>~门；~锣❶；~鼓❷；老和尚❸~木鱼❹；~警钟

❺；别用手~桌子；~玻璃❻〔~补〕〈结〉~错门了；鼓都~破❼了〈趋〉~起锣来了；快别敲了，再~下去耳朵都要震聋❽了〈程〉门~得太响❾了；~得太重了；鼓~得心烦❿；锣~得真乱⓫〈可〉门怎么~不开啊？〈时〉~了半天也没有人出来开门；多~一会儿就听见了〈量〉给他~了一次警钟；~了他一棍子〔状~〕轻轻地~；猛⓬~；有节奏地⓭~；不停地⓮~；再~~；多~一会儿〔习用〕~竹杠⓯；~门砖⓰；~骨吸髓⓱

1. gong 2. drum 3. Buddhist monk 4. wooden fish 5. alarm bell; tocsin 6. glass 7. damaged; broken 8. deafening 9. noisy; loud 10. be vexed; be perturbed 11. noisy 12. violently; vigorously 13. rhythmically 14. ceaselessly; incessantly 15. take advantage of sb.'s being in a weak position to overcharge him; fleece 16. a brick picked up to knock on the door and thrown away when it has served its purpose — a stepping-stone to success 17. break the bones and suck the marrow — cruel, blood-sucking exploitation; suck the lifeblood

qiào 撬 prize; pry〔~宾〕〈名〉~门；~锁❶；~保险柜❷；~着紧闭❸的牙往里灌药❹〔~补〕〈结〉门被小偷~开了；把锁~坏了〈可〉~不开箱❺子；石头太大，~不动；这种锁谁也~不了(liǎo)

〈时〉~了半天，纹丝不动❻〈量〉我家被~过两次〔状~〕用棍子❼~；大家一起~；使劲❽~；

1. lock 2. safe 3. tightly close 4. pour medicine down the throat 5. case; box 6. absolutely still 7. rod; stick 8. with great effort

qiào 翘 stick up; hold up; bend upwards; turn upwards〔~宾〕〈名〉狗~着尾巴❶〔~补〕〈趋〉铺板❷没放好，坐在一头儿，另一头儿就❸~起来了；豹的尾巴~起来了；气得胡子❹都~起来了；别把椅子的腿~起来〈程〉~得高高的〈可〉~不起来〔状~〕往上~；一得意❺就~尾巴❻

1. tail 2. bed board 3. leopard 4. beard 5. proud of oneself 6. be cocky; get stuck-up

qiē 切 cut; slice〔~宾〕〈名〉~菜；~肉；~苹果；~纸；~像片〔~补〕〈结〉把西瓜~开；把肉~成丝❶；把黄瓜❷~成片❸；都~碎了；~断❹敌人的后路❺〈趋〉从猪后腿❻上~下一块肉来〈程〉肉片~得真薄❼；~得真快；纸~得真齐❽；切肉~得手疼〈可〉我~不了(liǎo)他那么细；刀不快❾，~不动；~不下来〈时〉每天都要~好几个小时的菜；~一会儿还可以，时间长了手疼〈量〉~了三刀；用这把刀~一下儿试试〔状~〕斜着❿~；顺着丝~；一刀一刀地挨着⓫~；容易~；真难~；熟练地⓬~

qiē — qǐng

1. (cut into) slivers; shredded meat 2. cucumber 3. slice 4. cut off; stop 5. route of retreat 6. rear leg 7. thin 8. neat; even; uniform 9. not sharp 10. oblique; slanting 11. one after another; in turn 12. skilfully

qīnglǐ 清理 put in order; check up; clear; sort out 〔~宾〕〈名〉~房间；~床铺❶；~抽屉❷；~资料❸；~图书❹；~档案❺；~报纸；~文件❻；~讲义❼；~东西；~帐目❽；~债务❾；~仓库❿；~死者⓫遗留⓬下来的衣物；~贵重物品；~路面⓭；~河道⓮〔~补〕〈结〉已经~好了；把有用的东西都~到一起〈趋〉都~出来了〈程〉~得真快；~得不彻底〈可〉材料⓯太多，几天也~不完；一天的时间~不出来；我可~不了(liǎo)那么复杂⓰的帐目；他连自己的东西都~不好〈时〉~了一上午；~了一个多月〈量〉你把抽屉好好~一下儿吧；每月~一次仓库〔状~〕好好~~；及时~；认真~；彻底~；立即~

1. bed 2. drawer 3. material 4. books 5. files; archives; dossier 6. document 7. teaching materials 8. accounts 9. debt; liabilities 10. warehouse; storehouse 11. the dead; a dead person 12. remain 13. road surface 14. river course 15. material 16. complicated

qǐng 请 ① request; ask ≅ 请求〔~宾〕〈名〉~假❶〈代〉~人帮忙；~他给评评理❷〔~补〕〈结〉~准❸假了吗？〈趋〉假~下来了〈程〉假~得太多了〈可〉一直~不下假来〈时〉~了一个多月的事假❹〈量〉你替我~一下儿假；今年~过两次病假❺〔状~〕真难~；老~；再~几天假；三番五次❻地~；多~几天；必须~；提前❼~；及早❽~；动不动❾就~；断断续续❿地~；一连⓫~

1. leave of absence 2. judge (judge between right and wrong) 3. allow; grant; permit 4. leave of absence (to attend to private affairs) 5. sick leave 6. over and over again 7. ahead of time 8. as early as possible 9. easily; frequently 10. off and on; intermittently 11. successively; in succession; running

② invite; entertain ≅ 邀请；聘请；宴请〔~宾〕〈名〉~医生；~教练❶；~专家❷；~保姆❸；~客人〈代〉~他看电影；~他担任❹顾问❺；~谁当律师❻？~他来讲课〔~补〕〈结〉~着(zháo)了吗？教师已经~好了；~到一位专家〈趋〉把老师~到家里来教；把医生~到家里来看病；想把退休❼的老工人~出来当顾问；把客人都~过来坐吧！把那位老中医❽从外地~回来了〈程〉今天客人~得真不少〈可〉~不着(zháo)会做西餐❾的厨师；还是你亲自去吧，我们~不动他；你们几个人吃饭我还~得起；我家地方太

小~不了(liǎo)那么多客人〈时〉~了半年多才请着保姆〈量〉~了好几次人家也不来;这个月共~了三次客〔状~〕特意❿~;诚心诚意地⓫~;亲自~;经常~;好好~~他;随便⓬~了几个人;到处~;真难~

1. coach; trainer; instructor 2. expert; specialist 3. (children's) nurse 4. assume the office of 5. adviser 6. lawyer 7. retired 8. doctor of traditional Chinese medicine 9. western-style food 10. specially; for a special purpose 11. sincerely; cordially 12. casually; informally

③ please (polite expression)〔~宾〕〈动〉~进;~坐;~喝茶;~回电话;~勿吸烟❶;~快回信❷;~光临❸;~准时出席〈形〉~安静;~别客气

1. No smoking 2. write in reply; write back 3. presence (of a guest, etc.)

qìngzhù 庆祝 celebrate〔~宾〕
〈名〉~春节❶;~国庆❷;~元旦❸;~胜利❹〔~补〕〈结〉~完了;~过了〈可〉三天也~不完〈时〉一连❺~了好几天;~了一个星期〈量〉每年~一次;~了一番;~过两次〔状~〕提前❻~;按时❼~;热烈地❽~;隆重地❾~;热热闹闹地❿~;用各种形式⓫~

1. the Spring Festival 2. National Day 3. New Year's Day 4. victory 5. successively 6. ahead of time 7. on time 8. warmly 9. grandly; ceremoniously 10. lively; excitedly 11. in various ways; in all kinds of forms

qiú 求 ① beg; request; entreat
≌请求〔~宾〕〈名〉他不愿意~人;向她~婚❶;跟他~个情❷;~邻居❸照看❹一下儿门户❺〈代〉~你少说几句;~你顺便❻给我买一本书;~你帮帮忙〈动〉他直向我~饶❼〈形〉向交战国❽~和❾了〔~补〕〈结〉这件事你求他算是~对(着zháo)了,因为除了他谁也不会;那个人太不负责任了,我求他算~错了〈趋〉人家~上门来了,不好不答应;他又~起我来了〈程〉~得真可怜❿〈可〉我~不着(zháo)他〈时〉~了那么半天他都不答应〈量〉为这件事我~过他好几次;再好好~一下儿他〔状~〕苦苦哀⓫~;向他~;替谁~?白⓬~了;诚恳地⓭~;不得已只好~;为他的事~〔习用〕~之不得⓮

1. make an offer of marriage 2. plead; intercede; ask for a favour 3. neighbour 4. keep an eye on; look after 5. the house 6. in passing 7. beg for mercy; ask for pardon 8. belligerent countries 9. sue for peace 10. pitiful; pitiable; poor 11. piteously 12. in vain 13. sincerely 14. all that one could wish for

② strive for ≌ 要求〔~宾〕〈名〉他不~名,不~利❶〈动〉这个孩

子不~上进❷；~团结；~生存❸；~进步〔**状**~〕力❹~完善❺

1. seek neither fame nor gain 2. not strive to make progress 3. existence 4. do all one can; make every effort 5. perfect

③ seek ≅ 追求；寻求〔**~宾**〕〈名〉~知识❶；~学问❷；~答案❸〔**~补**〕〈趋〉数儿❹已经~出来了〈可〉答案~不出来〔**状**~〕真正~；认真~；多方~；努力~

1. knowledge 2. learning 3. answer; solution; key 4. number; figure 5. in many ways; in every way

qǔ 取 ① take; get; fetch〔**~宾**〕〈名〉到车站去~行李❶；到表店❷~修理❸好的表；去银行❹~点钱；到银行~款❺；唐僧❻去西天❼~经❽；到邮局去~包裹❾；~汇款❿〔**~补**〕〈结〉钱已经~走了；这一年的利息⓫都~完了；行李~错了〈趋〉她回家~东西去了；行李已经~回来了；请把挂⓬着的帽子替我~下来；把存⓭的钱都~出来〈程〉行李~得真快〈可〉邮局下班了，今天~不了(liǎo)包裹了〈时〉~了一上午才取回来；你怎么~了那么多时候啊？〈量〉明天请你替我~一下儿行李吧〔**状**~〕亲自~；我替你~；随时⓮~；一次~完；分几次~

1. luggage 2. watchmaker's shop 3. repair 4. bank 5. a sum of money 6. Buddhist monk of the Tang dynasty (Hsüan-chuang) 7. Western Paradise 8. go on a pilgrimage for Buddhist scriptures 9. parcel 10. a remittance 11. interest 12. hang 13. deposit 14. at any time; at all times

② aim at; seek ≅ 寻求〔**~宾**〕〈名〉他净❶拿别人~乐❷；只是为了~个笑儿❸〈动〉他们这样做是自~灭亡❹〈形〉不要投机~巧❺〔**状**~〕净拿我~笑；千方百计地❻~

1. only; merely 2. seek pleasure; find amusement 3. just for fun 4. court (invite) destruction; take the road to one's doom 5. seize every chance to gain advantage by trickery; be opportunistic 6. by every possible means; by hook or by crook

③ adopt; assume; choose ≅ 采取；选用〔**~宾**〕〈名〉给孩子~个名字；照像的时候她最会~景儿❶了；我们大家在学习上要互相~长补短❷；只~前三名；一共~了20名新生；这件事你打算~什么态度❸？〔**~补**〕〈结〉这次考试她又没~上；~好景儿了，就在这儿照吧；名额❹~满❺了；人没~够〈程〉景儿~得不错；名字~得很好听；这次人~得太少了〈可〉这次我可能~不上〈量〉他给我~过一次名字,我觉得不好,后来又改了〔**状**~〕从这个角度❻~景儿；只~30人；就~这么多；没~上；勉强❼~；最多~几名？暂时❽~个名字

1. find a view (to photograph, paint, etc.) 2. learn from others' strong points to offset one's weaknesses 3. attitude 4. the number of people assigned or allowed 5. full 6. angle; point of view 7. reluctantly; grudgingly 8. temporarily; for the moment

qǔdé 取得 gain; acquire; obtain ≅ 得到 〔～宾〕〈名〉～了很大成绩❶；～了巨大❷成就❸；～了显著的成果❹；～了丰富的经验❺；～了一致的意见❻〈动〉～了圆满成功；～了很大进步；～了各方面的支持❼；～了有关方面❽的协助❾；～了他的同意❿；又一次～了胜利；我们和他～了联系⓫〔～补〕〈可〉能～一致的意见吗？〔状～〕真正～；即将～；再次～；无法⓬～；不易～；基本⓭上～

1. success; achievement 2. huge; tremendous; immense 3. achievement; accomplishment; success 4. remarkable success 5. experience 6. consensus; unanimity 7. support 8. the parties concerned 9. assistance; help 10. agree; consent; approve 11. contact; connection; relation 12. unable; incapable 13. basically

qǔxiāo 取消 cancel; call off; abolish 〔主～〕〈名〉这个月的奖金❶～了；补贴❷～了；夜班贽❸～了；出差贽❹～了；去海滨❺度假❻的计划～了；期中考试❼～了〔～宾〕〈名〉参加比赛的资格❽；～一项禁令❾；～旧的借书规定❿；～以前的决定⓫；原来⓬想写三篇文章，后来～了一篇；～了一次会议〈动〉～了一次旅行；～了一次考察⓭〔～补〕〈结〉～早了；～对了〈程〉这项规定～得很好；～得很及时⓮〈可〉～得了(liǎo)吗？〔状～〕被～了；突然～；必须～；终于～了；尚未⓯～；即将⓰～

1. money award 2. subsidy; allowance 3. night shift pay 4. allowances for a business trip 5. seashore; seaside 6. spend one's holidays 7. mid-term examination 8. qualifications 9. prohibition; ban 10. rules; stipulations 11. decision 12. originally 13. inspection; investigation 14. in time 15. not yet 16. be about to; be on the point of

qǔ 娶 marry (a woman); take to wife 〔～宾〕〈名〉～妻；～亲❶；～媳妇❷；老奶奶❸要～儿媳妇了〔～补〕〈趋〉～来一个好儿媳妇〈可〉那个年轻人没有钱～不起❹媳妇〔状～〕早～几年就好了；给儿子～媳妇；早就～了；还没

1. (of a man) get married 2. son's wife; daughter-in-law 3. grandma 4. can't afford

qù 去 ① go; leave ≅ 离去 〔～宾〕〈名〉我～学校；～美国；～

医院；我给他~了一封信；~了一个电报❶；~了一个电话；~了三个人帮忙〈代〉你~哪儿？〔~补〕〈结〉~早了；~过了〈程〉~得不早不晚正合适❷；~得不巧❸〈可〉今天有事，~不了(liǎo)他家了；明天又~不成了吧？〈时〉我~一会儿就回来；~了那么久还没回来〈量〉我~一下儿就来；~了一趟〔状~〕坐车~；乘船~；怎么~？跟谁一起~？给谁~电话？什么时候~？从哪儿~？每天~图书馆；经常~；兴冲冲地❹~了一个电话

1. telegram 2. suitable; appropriate; right 3. unfortunately; as luck would have it 4. (do sth.) with joy and expedition; excitedly

② remove; get rid of ≅ 除去〔~宾〕〈名〉坚持❶锻炼❷能~病；喝点绿豆❸汤❹~~火❺；这段❻话~几个字就简练❼了；他叙述❽事情总爱掐头~尾❾〔~补〕〈结〉~掉皮再切；这衣服太长，~短点儿就好了〈趋〉这把椅子的腿儿太高，最好一下一截⓫去〈程〉~得还不够〈可〉衣服~不了(liǎo)那么多〈量〉稍微⓬~一下儿就行了；我给她~过一次头发〔状~〕不用~；随便⓭~；多~点儿；薄薄地⓮~一层皮就可以了；轻轻地~

1. persist in; keep up; stick to 2. have physical training 3. mung bean; green gram 4. soup 5. internal heat — one of the six causes of disease 6. paragraph 7. terse; succinct; pithy 8. narrate 9. break off both ends; leave out the beginning and the end 10. legs of a chair 11. section; chunk; length 12. slightly; a little 13. casually; at random 14. thinly

quān 圈 enclose; encircle〔~宾〕〈名〉~了一块地种花儿用；在文件❶上~一个圈儿❷表示看过了〔~补〕〈结〉把房前房后的空地都~上了〈趋〉不能把别人的地~进来〈程〉他那块地~得很大〈可〉绳子太短~不上〔状~〕用篱笆❸~；用铁丝❹~；用绳子❺~；从这头儿往那头儿~

1. document 2. circle 3. bamboo or twig fence 4. iron wire 5. rope

quàn 劝 advise; urge; try to persuade 〔~宾〕〈代〉她很难过❶，你好好~~她吧；~她别哭了；~他戒烟❷；~他每天坚持❸锻炼；~她好好休息；~他努力学习；~他们计划用钱；~她别生气〔~补〕〈结〉她闹情绪❹，我好容易❺才把她~好；他要打人，我把他~住了；他把那个故意捣乱❻的人~走了〈趋〉我把他从外边~回来了〈程〉~得口干舌燥❼；~得他回心转意❽了〈可〉谁也~不了(liǎo)他；~得回来吗？~不走〈时〉~了半天，她还是哭；~了他一个晚上；~了好几天，多~一会儿〈量〉~过好多次；好好~一下儿〔状~〕耐心地❾~；反复~；三番五次地~；一遍一遍

地～；苦口婆心地⑩～；诚心诚意地⑪～；左～右～⑫

1. feel unwell **2.** give up smoking **3.** persist in; keep up; stick to **4.** be disgruntled; be in low spirits **5.** with great difficulty **6.** make trouble; create a disturbance **7.** one's mouth and tongue are parched **8.** change one's views; come around **9.** patiently; with patience **10.** urge sb. time and again with good intentions **11.** earnestly and sincerely **12.** try again and again to persuade sb.

quē 缺 be short of; lack〔**～宾**〕〈名〉我们这儿～人；他老～钱花；这本书～了两页；～建筑材料❶房子就盖❷不了(liǎo)了；他～课太多；他这学期从来没～过席；这种东西市场❸上～货❹；做买卖～本钱；梳子❺～了两个齿儿❻〈数〉条件❼～一不可〈动〉不～吃；不～穿〔**～补**〕〈结〉钱～多了〈程〉课～得太多了〈可〉水一天也～不得〔**状～**〕常～；从来不～席；就是～钱；因病～课；无故❽～席；手头儿～钱〔**习用**〕～心眼❾

1. building materials **2.** build **3.** market **4.** be in short supply; be out of stock **5.** comb **6.** the teeth of a comb **7.** condition **8.** without cause or reason **9.** not alert and thoughtful

quēfá 缺乏 be short of; lack; be wanting in ≅ 缺少；缺〔**主～**〕〈名〉人力❶～；物资❷～；材料❸～；药品❹～；粮食❺～；工具❻～〔**～宾**〕〈名〉～人力；～物力❼；～资源❽；～经验❾；～勇气❿；～朝气⓫；～氧气⓬；～营养⓭；～信心⓮；～教养⓯；～涵养⓰；～起码⓱的道德观念⓲；～知识⓳；～高尚的情操⓴；～工具；～水源㉑；～确凿的证据㉒〔**状～**〕十分～；特别～；有点儿～；一直～；长期～；暂时㉓～；异常㉔～；极端㉕～

1. manpower **2.** goods; materials **3.** materials **4.** medicines and chemical reagents **5.** grain; cereals **6.** tool **7.** material resources **8.** resources **9.** experience **10.** courage **11.** vigour; vitality **12.** oxygen **13.** nutrition; nourishment **14.** confidence **15.** **16.** ability to control oneself; self-restraint **17.** minimum; rudimentary; elementary **18.** moral concepts **19.** knowledge **20.** lofty sentiments **21.** water-head; headwaters **22.** conclusive evidence; absolute proof **23.** temporarily **24.** unusually; extremely **25.** exceedingly; extremely

R

rǎn 染 dye〔~宾〕〈名〉~布；~衣服；~毛线❶；~头发；~指甲❷〔~补〕〈结〉衣服~花❸了；毛线~深❹了；颜色❺没~匀❻；指甲没~好；颜色没~上；~错了；应该~浅黄，怎么~成金黄了；〈趋〉这种料子❼~出来非常鲜艳❽；~出来比较暗淡❾；~出来的头发真黑〈程〉~得很好看；~得太深了〈可〉颜色~得上吗？这种毛线~不了(liǎo)；我给你染，一定~不坏〈时〉一件衣服得(děi)~一个小时；~一会儿就行了〈量〉她每月都要~一次头发；~过两次都没染好；~一下儿看看好不好；~一下儿试试吧〔**状~**〕用什么~？重新~；容易~；经常~；已经~好了；从来没~过；大批地❿~；大量地⓫~；单独⓬~

1. knitting wool 2. nail 3. unevenly 4. deep 5. colour 6. even 7. material for making clothes 8. bright-coloured; gaily-coloured 9. dull; dim; faint 10. 11. large quantities 12. alone; by oneself; on one's own

rǎng 嚷 ① shout; yell; make an uproar ≅ 嚷嚷 (rāng rang) 吵闹、喊〔**主~**〕〈名〉孩子们在院子❶里~〈代〉谁在那儿~？〔~**宾**〕〈代〉他们在外边~什么？〔~**补**〕〈结〉那个人又在马路上~上了；别~醒了孩子〈趋〉他们为了什么事~起来了；孩子夜里做梦突然~起来了〈程〉~得人们无法入睡；~得真讨厌；~得嗓子❷都哑❸了；~得真让人心烦❹；~得没法工作了〈可〉她这两天嗓子坏了，~不了(liǎo)了〈时〉~了一晚上，吵得大家无法休息；~了好几个钟头〈量〉他在外边~过好多次了；~了两三声；跟孩子~了一顿；~过好几回了〔**状~**〕大声~；在外边~；一声接着一声地~；不停地❺~；声嘶力竭地❻~；顺着风❼~；别~；故意❽~；他跟谁~？哇啦哇啦地❾~

1. courtyard 2. throat 3. hoarse; husky 4. be vexed; be irritated 5. ceaselessly; incessantly 6. shout oneself hoarse 7. with the wind 8. intentionally 9. in an uproar

② make widely known ≅ 声张；嚷嚷 (rāng rang)〔~**补**〕〈趋〉别把这件事~出去〈程〉他~得没有一个人不知道这件事的〔**状~**〕故意❶~；决不~；差点儿❷~出去

1. intentionally; on purpose 2. nearly; almost

ràng 让 ① give way; give ground; yield ≅ 退让〔~**宾**〕〈名〉教练

❶~了他五个球；~了他两步棋❷；~了他两个棋子；请一~路，她终于❸~了步❹〈代〉妹妹小，姐姐应该~着点儿她；这两个人吵❺起来谁也不~谁；那个人太利害了，谁都得(děi)~他三分〔~补〕〈结〉车来了，快~开〈趋〉看见车来了，她赶快~到一边去了〈程〉幸亏我~得快，否则❻就碰着(zháo)❼了〈量〉你就~他这一次吧；~过他好几次了〔状~〕给他~~路；快~开；赶快~一~；互相~；寸步不~❽；一直~着他；总~着他

1. coach; instructor; trainer 2. two moves in chess 3. at last 4. make a concession; give in 5. quarrel 6. otherwise 7. bump 8. refuse to yield an inch

② invite; offer ≅ 请〔~宾〕〈名〉每次去他家，他都是热情地❶~茶；~菜；~酒；~座❷；你怎么也不~~客人❸？〈代〉您要是真吃饱❹了，我就不~您了〔~补〕〈趋〉把客人~进来吧；~到里屋去了；他们两个人太客气了，你先走还是我先走的问题~起来没完❺；把同学~到客厅❻去坐吧；~上楼来吧〈程〉~得谁也没法吃了；~得很热情〈时〉~了半天才吃〈量〉向大家~了一遍；他吃什么东西都要~下儿别人，然后自己才吃；~过他好几次了〔状~〕先~；一次一次地~；从不~；主动~；挨个儿❼~；很有礼貌地❽~；客客气气地~；热情地~

1. warmly 2. invite guests to be seated 3. guest 4. be full; have eaten one's fill 5. without end 6. drawing room; parlour 7. one by one 8. courteously

③ let sb. have sth. at a fair price; cede; transfer ≅ 转让；出让〔~补〕〈结〉把我那架缝纫机❶~给他了；把房子~给她了；我把几张多余的票❷~给他们了〈可〉我家连一间房子都~不出来〔状~〕全部~；自动❸~；主动❹~；被迫❺~；勉强❻~；不得不~

1. sewing machine 2. several tickets to spare 3. voluntarily; of one's own accord 4. on one's own initiative 5. be forced to 6. reluctantly; grudgingly

④ let; allow; make ≅ 叫；听任〔~宾〕〈名〉要是~事情发展下去，会出大问题❶的；不能~个人受损失❷；不能~老张为难❸；别~人家看不起❹〈代〉谁~你不穿衣服的？感冒了吧！来晚了，~您久等❺了；~他说吧！~他考虑考虑；~我仔细❻想想；他拉着我，不~我走；医生不~她起床；她不~我看她的作文❼〈动〉展品❽不~摸❾；妈妈不~买〔状~〕只~；偏不❿~；是否⓫~；居然⓬~；终于⓭~

1. go wrong; get into trouble 2. sustain losses 3. feel embarrassed 4. look down upon; despise; scorn 5. wait for a long time 6. carefully 7. composition

8. exhibit; item on display 9. touch 10. against expectation 11. whether; if 12. to one's surprise; unexpectedly 13. at last; finally

ráo 饶 ① have mercy on; let sb. off; forgive ≅ 〔~宾〕〈名〉请您~命❶; 他说话不~人〈代〉~了他吧〔~补〕〈可〉他一定~不了(liǎo)我〈量〉~他这一次吧; 只~这一回〔状~〕只好~; 再~; 决不❷轻❸~

1. spare sb.'s life 2. never 3. easily

rǎoluàn 扰乱 disturb; create confusion; harass ≅ 搅扰; 打扰 〔~宾〕〈名〉~社会治安❶; ~市场❷; ~军心❸; ~人心❹; ~视线❺; ~课堂秩序❻; ~大会秩序; 别~他的学习〔状~〕存心❼~; 故意❽~; 一再~; 多次~; 拼命❾~; 决不~

1. public security of society 2. market 3. soldiers' morale 4. public feeling 5. line of vision; line of sight 6. order in the classroom 7. 8. intentionally; deliberately; on purpose 9. with all one's might; for all one is worth

rào 绕 ① wind; coil ≅ 缠; 缠绕〔~宾〕〈名〉~线❶; ~毛线❷; ~绳子❸; ~铁丝❹〔~补〕〈结〉把毛线~成团❺儿; 用绳子~上点儿; ~紧点❻儿; ~松点儿❼; 把线~在线轴❽上〈趋〉把抽屉里所有的线都~上去吧; 把这些零散❾的铁丝都~起来吧〈程〉别~得太紧; ~得慢极了〈可〉~得上; ~得了(liǎo)〈时〉~了一个多小时; ~了半天〈量〉~了几下儿; ~过一次〔状~〕紧紧地~; 多~几圈

1. thread 2. knitting wool 3. rope 4. iron wire 5. ball 6. tight 7. loose 8. a reel for thread; bobbin 9. scattered

② move round; circle; revolve ≅ 转圈儿; 围着转动〔~宾〕〈名〉飞机在机场❶上空一圈❷儿; 地球~着太阳转; 运动员❸~场❹一圈; 海鸥❺在海面上~圈儿〔~补〕〈结〉~完了三圈儿〈趋〉~过去了; ~回来了; ~到原来❻的地方去(来)了〈程〉~得真快; ~得慢极了; ~得太远了〈时〉~了半天〔状~〕在天空中~; 永远❼~; 一直~; 来回❽~; 缓缓地❾~; 不停地❿~

1. airport; aerodrome; airfield 2. circle 3. athletes; sportsmen 4. arena 5. sea gull 6. original 7. forever 8. back and forth; to and fro 9. slowly 10. ceaselessly; incessantly

③ make a detour; bypass; go round ≅ 迂回〔~宾〕〈名〉说话不要~弯儿❶, 怎么想就怎么说吧, 直❷着走, 不用~弯儿❸; 小船~过暗礁❹; 飞机~过山顶; 我怕遇到熟人❺, 故意~着道儿走; 走这条路有点儿~远❻; 前边修路, ~道儿走吧〔~补〕〈趋〉这

里有水，从那边~过来〈程〉~得太远了〈可〉~得过去~不过去？到了楼里~不出来了〈时〉~了半天也没绕出来〈量〉从那边~一下儿吧〔状~〕总是~；别~；不致❼~；从这边~；故意~

1. talk in a roundabout way; beat about the bush 2. straight 3. make a detour 4. submerged reef 5. run into an acquaintance 6. go the long way round 7. cannot go so far; be unlikely

④ confuse; baffle; befuddle〔~补〕〈结〉你的话把我~糊涂❶了〈趋〉这件事差一点儿把我~进去〈程〉把我~得糊里糊涂的；~得迷迷糊糊❷〈可〉~不糊涂〈时〉~了半天，都把我绕糊涂了〈量〉~过一次〔状~〕真~；一下子~；一时~住了；别净拿话~人〔习用〕~嘴❸；~脖子❹

1. confused; muddled 2. dazed; confused; muddled 3. (of a sentence, etc.) not be smooth; be difficult to articulate 4. involved; beat about the bush

rě 惹 invite or ask for (sth. undesirable); provoke; attract ≅ 招引；引起〔~宾〕〈名〉~事❶；~祸❷；~了一个乱子❸；~是非❹；~人注意❺；~人注目❻；~人讨厌❼〈代〉别~他，又~她不高兴了；没人敢~她〈形〉~麻烦❽〔~补〕〈结〉把他~急❾了；~烦❿了；~恼⓫了〈趋〉~出麻烦来了；~起他来可不得了(liǎo)

〈程〉他这句话~得大家议论纷纷⓬；~得他直哭；~得那些人对我恨之入骨⓭〈可〉人家有靠山⓮，你~得起吗？那个人利害极了，可~不得〈量〉~过他一次〔状~〕故意~；别~；净~；从来不~；不好~；经常~；几乎~；险些⓯；无意中⓰；实在~不起

1. 2. stir up trouble; court disaster 3. cause trouble 4. provoke a dispute 5. 6. attract attention 7. make a nuisance of oneself 8. ask for trouble 9. irritated; annoyed; nettled 10. 11. be vexed; be worried 12. everybody is talking about the matter 13. hate sb. to the very marrow of one's bones 14. backer; patron; backing 15. narrowly; nearly 16. accidentally; inadvertently; unwittingly

rěn 忍 bear; endure; tolerate; put up with ≅ 忍耐〔~宾〕〈名〉~着气❶；~气吞声❷；~着眼泪❸〈动〉~着疼，~饥挨饿❹〔~补〕〈结〉~住这口气❺；~住眼泪；~住笑；~住了悲痛❻；~住疼〈趋〉~下这口气去吧〈可〉我~不住，就笑出声音来了；我~不住骂了他一句；这种日子再也~不下去了〈时〉她~了半天眼泪，也没忍住；~一会儿就不疼了；~了好几年；~了好多日子没说〈量〉~过两次了；~一下儿，少说两句吧！〔状~〕一再~着；实在~不下去了；再~一段时间吧；只好~；不得不~；怎么~？无法~；

必须~；尽量❼~；难~〔**习用**〕~无可~❽

1. 2. swallow an insult; swallow an insult; submit to humiliation 3. hold back one's tears 4. (endure) the torments of hunger 5. refrain (quell) one's anger 6. sorrow; grief 7. as far as possible; to the best of one's ability 8. come to the end of one's patience

rěnshòu 忍受 bear; endure; stand 〔~宾〕〈名〉~（着）非人❶的生活；~（着）冤枉气❷；~（着）饥寒❸〈动〉~（着）侮辱❹；~（着）打骂，~（着）折磨❺；~（着）熬煎❻〈形〉~（着）痛苦❼；~（着）艰难❽；~（着）困苦❾；~（着）疼痛❿〔~补〕〈结〉~住了〈趋〉这种日子再也无法~下去了；她竟然⓫~下来了〈可〉再也~不住了；~不下去了〈时〉~了好多年；~了一辈子〈量〉~过许多次〔**状**~〕一直~；无法~；难以~；只好~；不得不~；痛苦地~；不再~了；居然⓬~

1. inhuman 2. wrong; treat unjustly 3. hunger and cold 4. insult 5. torment; cause physical or mental suffering 6. suffering; torture 7. pain; suffering; agony 8. hardship; difficulties 9. privation; hardship 10. ache; pain; sore 11. 12. to one's surprise; unexpectedly

rèn 认 ① recognize; know; make out 〔~宾〕〈名〉这个孩子已经~了不少字了；东西都放在这儿，过来~自己的东西吧；我不~路，你领❶我去吧；今天先来~~路，以后好来；~~地方，好找〔~补〕〈结〉~错门儿了；~清她的样子了；~准❷了这是我的东西〈趋〉~出这个字来了吗？字写得不清楚，~起来很费劲儿❸〈程〉这个孩子认字~得很快；~得很多〈可〉他戴着口罩❹，我都~不出来是谁了；字迹❺太模糊❻我都~不出来了；书上的字我还~不全呢〈时〉~了半天才认出他来〈量〉仔细❼~一下儿〔**状**~〕仔细~；好好~

1. lead; usher 2. accurate; exact 3. be strenuous; need or use great effort 4. gauze mask 5. handwriting 6. blurred; indistinct; dim; vague 7. carefully

② admit; recognize ≅ 承认〔~宾〕〈名〉~错儿；~了很多赔款❶；~罪❷〈动〉~输❸；~罚❹〈形〉~倒霉❺〔~补〕〈量〉他从没~过一次输〔**状**~〕只好~；不得不~；彻底~；刚~；从来不~

1. reparations; indemnity 2. crime 3. (admit) defeat 4. punishment 5. unlucky; bad luck

rènshi 认识 know; understand; recognize ≅ 认得〔~宾〕〈名〉你~那边站着的那个人吗？我以前不~去大使馆❶的路；玛丽已经~1000多个汉字了〔~补〕〈结〉通过❷这件事，我可~清楚他了；~到了自己的错误；没~到他自己的毛病❸〈程〉对他~得清清楚楚；对这件事~得还不十分清楚〈可〉对自己的缺点还~不到；对这个人还~不清〈时〉我们已经~二十多年了；~很长时间了〈量〉让我们好好~一下儿吧〔状~〕重新~；已经~了，还不~；简直不❹~；一点也不~；几乎不~

1. embassy 2. by means of; by way of; through 3. shortcoming; fault; defect 4. simply; at all

rènwéi 认为 think; consider; hold; deem ≅ 想；以为〔~宾〕〈动〉他~还是不去好，我~应该参加〈形〉我们两个人观点❶不一样，我~好的，他都~不好；这课书我~很难，他一点儿也不难；这个电影他~有意思，我~很无聊❷；那个话剧你们~怎么样？〈主-谓〉我~旅游❸可以增长知识❹；他~那样做是浪费❺；我们~她这篇文章写得不错；你~我说得不对吗？我们都~有必要❻开个座谈会❼〔状~〕总是~；一向~；不这样~；一直~；固执地❽~；仍然❾~；仍旧❿~

1. point of view 2. bored 3. travel; make a tour 4. broaden one's knowledge 5. waste 6. necessary 7. forum; symposium; informal discussion 8. stubbornly; obstinately 9. 10. still; yet

rēng 扔 ① throw; toss; cast ≅ 抛；掷〔~宾〕〈名〉~手榴弹❶；飞机~炸弹❷；~石子儿〔~补〕〈结〉球~歪❸了，没接着❹；~远一点儿；把书包~在桌子上就跑出去了；我~给他一块糖〈趋〉把钥匙❺从阳台❻上~下来吧；我要~过去了，接好了；我从这儿~上去你接着(zháo)吗？我把打火机❼给他~过去了；他们在操场上~起铅球❽来了；把球~到球场外边去(来)了〈程〉~得很远；~得真准❾〈可〉这些东西还有用，可~不得，胳膊❿疼，~不了(liǎo)；没劲儿，~不过去；你~得进篮里去吗？树挡⓫着，~不下去〈时〉~了一上午手榴弹；~了半天；~一会儿就行了〈量〉~多少次都扔不过去；再~一下儿试试；上午~了一阵球〔状~〕使劲儿⓬~；往远处~；赶快重新~；别乱⓭~；恰巧⓮~

1. hand grenade 2. bomb 3. oblique; slanting 4. catch 5. key 6. balcony 7. lighter 8. shot 9. accurate; exact 10. arm 11. block; get in the way of 12. exert oneself physically; put forth one's strength 13. at random 14. by chance; fortunately

② throw away; cast aside ≅ 丢掉；放在一边〔~宾〕〈名〉~花生壳❶；~果皮；~废纸❷；阳台❸上~着一堆破烂儿❹〔~补〕〈结〉快把这些没用的东西~掉吧；这件事她早就~在脑后了〈趋〉他又把果皮和糖纸从阳台上~下来了；把废纸~进了垃圾箱〈程〉~得到处都是瓜子皮❺；~得满地都是废纸〈可〉这些废品❻我想扔，他不让扔，所以总~不成；~

rēng 扔

不掉〈量〉这双皮鞋想~好几次都没舍得❼扔〔状~〕都~了；幸亏❽~了；已经~了；先别~；一起~；往外~；不要随处乱~❾；任意❿~；随便⓫~〔习用〕~到脖子后头去⓬了

1. peanut shell 2. waste paper 3. balcony 4. worthless stuff; rubbish 5. the skin of melon seeds 6. scrap; waste 7. grudge; hate to part with 8. fortunately; luckily 9. don't litter 10. wantonly; wilfully 11. casually; at random 12. be utterly forgotten

róngnà 容纳 hold; contain

≅容〔~宾〕〈名〉那个会议室❶只能~五十人；那个车厢❷可以~200人；这条路可以~三辆汽车并行❸；他不能~不同意见〔~补〕〈可〉这个教室~得下这么多人吗？〔状~〕最多~；至少❹~；一共~；简直❺~不下；实在❻~不了(liǎo)；不能~

1. meeting room; conference room 2. railway carriage 3. abreast 4. at least 5. at all; simply 6. really; truly

róu 揉 rub; knead

〔~宾〕〈名〉~眼睛；~~腿❶；用手~~头上碰❷的大包❸；她正在厨房里~面❹，把废纸❺~了一个团儿〔~补〕〈结〉把眼睛都~红了；面~好了，可以烤❻面包了；信在口袋❼里装的时间太长都~烂❽了；把衣服都~成团儿了；饼干❾都~碎❿了；别把纸~破⓫了〈程〉面~得不软不硬⓬正合适〈可〉我右手破⓭了，¹~不了(liǎo)面〈时〉~了半个小时；~了半天也没揉好〈量〉再~一下儿；多~几下儿〔状~〕自己~；我给你~；轻轻地~；来回⓮~；在盆⓯里面；使劲儿⓰~；用手~；好好~~；砂子进眼睛里可别~

1. leg 2. bump 3. protuberance; swelling; lump 4. knead dough 5. waste paper 6. toast 7. pocket 8. torn 9. biscuit 10. smashed; broken to pieces 11. broken; torn 12. neither soft nor hard 13. be cut on the right hand 14. to and fro 15. basin; tub; pot 16. exert oneself physically

S

sā 撒 ① cast; let go; let out ≅ 放开〔~宾〕〈名〉~传单❶；~网❷打鱼；小孩学走路，大人不能完全~手不管❸；他~腿就跑❹；一~手车票就让风刮跑❺了〔~补〕〈结〉传单都~完了〈趋〉把传单都~出去了〈程〉撒手~得太快了，把孩子摔❻了〈可〉一~手他就要倒〈时〉~了半天网，一条鱼也没打上来〔状~〕用力~网；一~线，风筝就上去了

1. leaflet 2. fishnet; fishing net 3. pay no attention 4. make off at once; scamper 5. blow away 6. fall; tumble

② throw off all restraints; let oneself go 〔~宾〕〈名〉~气❶、~酒疯❷〈形〉~赖❸；~娇❹；~野❺〔~补〕〈结〉~完酒疯就睡了；把气都~在我身上了〈趋〉~起娇来，真恶心❻；把气都~出来了〈程〉车胎❼里的气~得真快〈可〉怎么也~不了(liǎo)这口气〈时〉~了半天娇〈量〉~了一阵酒疯〔状~〕竟❽拿我~气；别~赖；在他面前~娇
另见 sǎ 撒

1. leak (of a ball, tyre, etc.); go soft; get a flat; vent one's anger or ill temper 2. be drunk and act crazy; be roaring drunk 3. make a scene; act shamelessly; raise hell 4. act like a spoiled child 5. act wildly 6. nauseating; disgusting 7. tyre 8. unexpectedly; actually

sǎ 洒 sprinkle; spray; spill; shed 〔主~〕〈名〉汤~了；墨水❶~了〔~宾〕〈名〉她身上~了不少香水❷；~了一桌子啤酒❸；碗没端❹好，~了一身汤〔~补〕〈结〉~上点儿水再扫地；院子❺里~满了水〈趋〉~出去了〈程〉~得太多了〈可〉盆❻端好了就~不了(liǎo)了〈时〉~了一会儿〈量〉~过两次〔状~〕多~点儿；往身上~；在院子里~

1. ink 2. perfume 3. beer 4. carry 5. courtyard 6. basin

sǎ 撒 scatter; sprinkle; spread 〔主~〕〈名〉面粉~了；书包里的东西全~了〔~宾〕〈名〉~种子❶；~盐❷；~胡椒粉❸〔~补〕〈结〉盐~匀❹点儿〈趋〉豆子装❺得太满，眼看就要~出来了〈程〉花生米~得哪儿都是〈可〉拿好了就~不了(liǎo)了；盖个盖儿❻就~不出来了〈量〉~过一次了〔状~〕别~了；再~点儿；往年糕❼上~白糖；用勺子❽~；一层

一层地～
另见 sā 撒

1. seed 2. salt 3. pepper 4. even 5. hold; contain 6. put on the lid 7. New Year cake (made of glutinous rice flour) 8. ladle; spoon

sāi 塞 fill in; squeeze in; stuff ≅ 填入；堵住〔～宾〕<名>箱子❶里还有地方，可以再～几件衣服；他怕吵，用棉花❷～着耳朵〔～补〕<结>瓷器❸怕压，包装❺的时候～上点草；牙都～疼了；把信～在枕头❻底下了；两个口袋❼都～满了东西；把窟窿❽～住<趋>把这本书也～进书包里去吧；从门缝❾里～进来一封信<程>手提包❿～得鼓鼓⓫的；～得一点地方都没有了<可>实在⓬～不下了<时>～了半天也塞不进去<量>～一下儿试试〔状～〕瓶口用塞子⓭～；鼓鼓地～了一书包；尽量⓮～；一点一点儿往里～；别使劲～；勉强⓯～；别往抽屉⓰里乱～

1. chest; trunk 2. cotton 3. porcelain; chinaware 4. press; push down; weigh down 5. pack; package 6. pillow 7. pocket; bag 8. hole 9. a crack between a door and its frame 10. handbag; bag 11. bulge; swell 12. really; truly 13. stopper; cork 14. to the best of one's ability; as far as possible 15. reluctantly; grudgingly 16. drawer

sài 赛 ① contest; compete ≅ 比赛〔～宾〕<名>～球；～马〔～补〕<结>～完了；～赢❶了；～输❷了；他们怎么又～开马了<趋>～出水平❸来了；～出成绩❹来了<程>～得很激烈❺；～得很猛❻<可>这匹马准❼～不赢；两个队的力量太悬殊❽，这场球～不起来<时>～了一个星期<量>～过五次〔状～〕A队跟B队～；准时❾～；一连❿～了两场；重新～；险些⓫～输

1. win 2. be defeated 3. level; standard 4. success; result; achievement 5. intense; sharp; fierce; acute 6. fierce; violent; energetic; vigorous 7. certainly; surely 8. great disparity; wide gap 9. on time 10. successively; in a row; running 11. narrowly; nearly

② be comparable to; surpass ≅ 胜〔主～〕<名>萝卜❶～梨❷〔～补〕<结>这些孩子做起事来～过大人；他一个人～过三个<可>不过<状～>简直❸～〔习用〕三个臭皮匠，～过诸葛亮❹

1. radish 2. pear 3. really; truly 4. three cobblers with their wits combined would equal Zhuge Liang the master mind — the wisdom of the masses exceeds that of the wisest individual; two heads are better than one

sǎn 散 come loose; fall apart ≅ 松开；分散〔主～〕<名>小辫儿❶～了；行李❷～了；队伍❸～了

〔~补〕〈可〉放心吧，我包的~不了(liǎo)〈量〉~过好几次了〔状~〕橡皮筋❹断❺了，小辫儿又~了；刚包好就~了
另见sàn 散

1. short braid; pigtail 2. luggage 3. ranks; contingent 4. rubber band 5. snapped

sàn 散 ① break up; disperse; ≅ 分开↔聚〔主~〕〈名〉乌云~了；会还没~呢；电影~了〔~宾〕〈名〉~戏了；他们早就~伙❶了〔~补〕〈结〉看热闹❷的人群都~开了；人走过去了，香水味❸还没有~尽❹〈程〉今天会~得比较早；云~得很快〈可〉这么早，会哪儿~得了(liǎo)啊〈时〉~了十多分钟了〔状~〕早就~了；什么时候~会？还没~呢；一直到5点半会议才~

1. (of a group, body or organization) dissolve 2. watch the excitement; watch the fun 3. smell of perfume 4. exhaustive

② dispel; let out ≅ 消除；排遣〔~宾〕〈名〉到外边去~~心；开开电风扇，~~屋子里的热气〔~补〕〈结〉~开了〈趋〉等屋里的烟都~出去，就不呛❶了〈程〉热~得比较慢〈可〉时间短了~不出去；热气~不了(liǎo)〈时〉到朋友家去~了一会儿心〈量〉~一下儿〔状~〕赶快~；多~~〔习用〕作鸟兽~❷
另见sǎn 散

1. choke 2. scatter like birds and beasts; flee helter-skelter; stampede

sànbù 散布 spread; disseminate; scatter; diffuse〔~宾〕〈名〉~谣言❶；~流言蜚语❷；~着许许多多的小岛屿❸；~种子；~病菌❹〔~补〕〈结〉羊群~在山坡上吃草〈趋〉谣言已经~出去了〈程〉消息~得很广❺；病菌~得真利害〈可〉什么消息也~不出去〈时〉~了很长时间〈量〉~过无数次谣言了〔状~〕到处~；故意❻~；经常~；从不~；屡次❼~；偶尔❽~；决不~

1. rumor 2. rumours and slanders 3. islet; small island 4. germs; pathogenic bacteria 5. wide; vast 6. intentionally 7. over and over again; repeatedly 8. occasionally

sànfā 散发 ① send out; send forth; diffuse; emit ≅ 发出〔~宾〕〈名〉花房❶里~着花的芳香❷；鱼市❸上~着腥味儿❹；阴沟❺里~着臭气❻〔~补〕〈结〉厨房里的炸油味儿还没~净〈趋〉从厨房窗口❼~出饭菜的香味❽〈程〉香味~得很远〈可〉汗~不了(liǎo)；腥味儿~不净〔状~〕从屋子里~出来；一阵阵地~；从早到晚~着；偶然❾~出；不时❿~

1. greenhouse 2. fragrant; aromatic 3. fish market 4. smelling of fish 5. sewer 6. bad smell;

stink 7. window 8. delicious smell; fragrance 9. accidentally; by chance 10. frequently; often; at any time

② distribute; issue; give out ≅ 分发〔~宾〕〈名〉~传单❶；~文件❷〔~补〕〈结〉~到每个人手里〈趋〉~出去了〈程〉~得很广❸；~得很及时❹〈可〉这么多材料一上午~不完〈时〉~了三天才散发完〈量〉~过一次传单〔状~〕从楼上~；向人群中~

1. leaflet 2. documents; papers 3. wide; vast 4. in time

sàngshī 丧失 lose; forfeit ≅ 失去〔~宾〕〈名〉~信心❶；~工作能力❷；~时机❸；~立场❹；~人格❺；~国土〔~补〕〈结〉不要~掉信心〈程〉~得一干二净❻〔状~〕完全~；将要~；几乎~

1. confidence; faith 2. ability 3. opportunity 4. stand (depart from the correct stand) 5. personality; character; moral quality 6. completely; wholly; entirely

sǎo 扫 ① sweep; clear away〔~宾〕〈名〉~土❶；~房；~楼梯❷；~马路❸；~墓❹；不要扫他的兴❺〔~补〕〈结〉快把身上的雪~掉吧；把垃圾❻~成一堆；把碎玻璃❼都~走吧〈趋〉土都~出来了；你这么用力扫，把灰尘❽都~起来了〈程〉~得真干净〈可〉没有扫帚❾~不了(liǎo)；这么多教室，我一个人~不过来〈时〉~了两个多小时了〈量〉~两下儿〔状~〕不要东一下西一下地乱~；轻轻地~；每年清明时❿~墓

1. dust 2. stairs 3. street; road 4. grave (pay respects to a dead person at his tomb) 5. have one's spirits dampened; feel disappointed 6. rubbish; refuse; garbage 7. bits of broken glass 8. dust 9. broom 10. Pure Brightness (5th solar term)

② eliminate; clear away ≅ 除去；消灭；消除〔~补〕〈结〉~光❶了；~掉了一批❷文盲❸〈程〉~得不干净〈可〉~得完~不完了？~得净吗？〈时〉~了三年文盲；~了半天地雷❹〈量〉~过两次〔状~〕认真~；彻底❺~；必须~

1. nothing left 2. numbers of 3. illiteracy 4. mine 5. thorough

③ sweep; pass quickly along or over〔~补〕〈结〉探照灯❶~过夜空❷〈时〉用眼睛向四周❸~了半天〈量〉~了一下儿；~了我一眼〔状~〕偷偷地❹~；向四下里❺一~；向台❻下~一眼；很快地~〔习用〕秋风~落叶❼

1. searchlight 2. night sky 3. on four sides; on all sides 4. stealthily; secretly 5. on four sides; on all sides 6. stage; platform 7. the autumn wind sweeping away the fallen (or dead) leaves — wipe out the corrupt and evil in an easy way

sǎochú 扫除
clear away; remove; wipe out ≅ 清除; 消除; 除去
〔~宾〕〈名〉~文盲❶; ~垃圾❷; ~路边的积雪❸; ~随地吐痰❹的恶习❺; ~封建思想残余❻〔~补〕〈结〉~干净; ~掉〈程〉~得很彻底; ~得很干净〈可〉~不了(liǎo)〔状~〕彻底~; 及时❼~; 一举❽~; 大力~

1. illiteracy 2. rubbish; refuse; garbage 3. piled snow 4. spitting 5. bad habit 6. survivals of the ideology of feudalism 7. in time 8. with one action; at one stroke; at one fell swoop

shā 杀
① kill; slaughter ≅ 弄死
〔~宾〕〈名〉这种药~虫效果❶很好; ~人要偿命❷; 勇敢❸~敌; 酒精❹可以~菌❺; ~猪宰羊❻〔~补〕〈结〉~死一个人〈程〉他杀鸡~得很内行❼; ~得很熟练❽; ~得很紧张❾; ~得鸡犬不留❿; 杀敌~得非常勇猛⓫〈可〉这种药~不死臭虫⓬〈量〉我只~过一次鸡〔状~〕残酷地⓭~人; 勇敢地~敌

1. effect; result 2. pay with one's life (for a murder); a life for a life 3. courageously; bravely 4. ethyl alcohol; alcohol 5. sterilize; disinfect 6. (slaughter) pigs and sheep 7. expert 8. skilful 9. nervous 10. even fowls and dogs are not spared 11. brave 12. bedbug 13. cruelly

② fight; go into battle ≅ 战斗
〔~补〕〈结〉~出重围❶; ~出包围圈❷〈趋〉~出一条路; ~到敌人营垒❸里去了〈程〉~得非常勇猛❹; ~得十分激烈❺; ~得敌人胆战心惊❻; ~得敌人望风而逃❼; ~得敌人抱头鼠窜❽; ~得敌人四处逃窜❾; ~得敌人丢盔弃甲❿; ~得他气喘吁吁⓫; ~得满身大汗〈可〉~得出去~不出去? 敌人~不进来; 防守很严⓬, ~不进去〈量〉猛⓭~一阵〔状~〕必须~, 已经~

1. fight one's way out of a heavy encirclement 2. ring of encirclement 3. barracks and the enclosing walls 4. bold and powerful; full of valour and vigour 5. intense; sharp 6. tremble with fear; be terror-stricken 7. flee at the mere sight of the oncoming force 8. cover the head and sneak away like a rat; scurry (scamper) off like a frightened rat 9. flee in all directions 10. throw away one's helmet and coat of mail; throw away everything in headlong flight 11. pant; puff hard 12. be strictly on guard against; take strict precautions against 13. violently; abruptly

③ weaken; reduce; abate ≅ 削弱; 消除〔~宾〕〈名〉不要拿孩子~气❶; ~~敌人的威风❷; ~他的傲气❸〔~补〕〈结〉~够了气〈趋〉把他们的威风~下去了〈可〉她的傲气一时还~不下去〈量〉好好~一下儿他的威风〔状~〕必须~; 好好儿~~〔习用〕

～风景❹；～人不见血❺

1. vent one's ill feeling 2. (deflate) the enemy's arrogance 3. air of arrogance; haughtiness 4. spoil the fun; be a wet blanket 5. kill without spilling blood

shā 刹 put on the brakes; stop; check ≌ 止住〔**～宾**〕〈名〉～车；〔**～补**〕〈结〉～住这股歪风❶〈程〉～得很及时❷；～得太慢了〈可〉汽车闸❸坏了，差一点～不住车〈时〉～了半天也没刹住〈量〉猛地❹～了一下儿〔**状～**〕急～车❺；突然～；快～

1. evil wind; unhealthy trend 2. in time 3. brake 4. suddenly; abruptly 5. slam the brakes on

shài 晒 (of the sun) shine upon; dry in the sun 〔**～宾**〕〈名〉～粮食；～被❶；～太阳；～图纸❷；～烟叶❸；～盐❹〔**～补**〕〈结〉粮食～干了；脸～红了；车胎❺～爆❻了；人都快～晕❼了；真～死人；～变色了；竹椅子～裂❽了；把被～在铁丝❾上〈趋〉这里开始～起来了，咱们换个地方吧〈程〉～得很暖和；～得真舒服❿；～得很好受⓫；～得懒洋洋⓬的；～得真难受⓭；～得要命⓮；～得太厉害⓯了；真～得慌⓰；～得直流汗；～得快晕倒⓱了〈可〉衣服挂在那儿～不着(zháo)；她皮肤⓲好，怎么晒也～不黑〈时〉她～一会儿头就晕〈量〉衣服有点潮⓳，拿出去～一下儿吧〔**状～**〕在绳子⓴上～被；彻底～；多(少)～一会儿；一～就干；差点儿～晕了〔**习用**〕三天打鱼，两天～网㉑

1. quilt 2. blueprint 3. sun-cured tobacco 4. salt (evaporate brine in the sun to make salt) 5. tyre 6. burst; explode 7. dizzy; giddy 8. split 9. iron wire 10. 11. comfortable 12. languid; listless 13. feel unwell 14. 15. 16. extremely; awfully 17. faint 18. skin 19. wet 20. rope 21. spend three days fishing and two days drying nets — work by fits and starts

shān 删 delete; leave out ≌ 去掉〔**～宾**〕〈名〉～了几个字；～了一行❶；～了一小段❷；～了几篇文章❸；～了两个逗号❹〔**～补**〕〈结〉～掉〈趋〉这样～下去，就剩❺不了(liǎo)多少了〈程〉～得不多；～得真狠❻〈可〉这一段话～不掉〈时〉～了半天，还有点啰嗦❼；～了半天，字数❽还不少〈量〉～过一次；需要～一下儿〔**状～**〕必须～；不好～；真难～；适当地❾～；一字不漏❿地～；大刀阔斧地⓫～；整句⓬～；整段⓭整段地～

1. a line 2. a small paragraph 3. article; essay 4. comma 5. remain 6. resolute; heartless 7. long-winded; wordy 8. number of words 9. properly; suitably 10. without leaving out a word 11. boldly and resolutely 12. whole sentence 13. whole paragraph

shān 扇 fan (up)〔~宾〕〈名〉~扇子❶；~蚊子❷；~炉子❸；~烟；~火〔~补〕〈结〉把火~灭❹了；把炉子~旺❺点儿；别把蜡烛❻~灭了；火已经~着❼(zháo)了〈趋〉把烟~出去；那个大蚊子藏❽在黑暗的地方，快把它~出来〈程〉~得太猛❾了；~得手都酸❿了〈可〉火~不着(zháo)〈时〉~一会儿就累了〈量〉使劲⓫~一下儿；猛地⓬~了一下儿〔状~〕多~几下儿；一个劲儿地~；不停地⓭~；用电风扇⓮~；母亲给孩子~；一下儿接着一下儿地~

1. fan 2. mosquito 3. stove 4. go out 5. burn briskly 6. candle 7. on 8. hide 9. violent; vigorous 10. tingle; ache 11. with strength 12. suddenly; violently 13. ceaselessly; incessantly 14. electric fan

shāndòng 扇动 ① flap; fan ≅ 扑动〔~宾〕〈名〉小鸟~着翅膀❶〔~补〕〈量〉~了几下儿翅膀〔状~〕上下~着；呼啦呼啦地❷~

1. wing 2. be flapping (in the wind)

② incite; instigate ≅ 鼓动〔~宾〕〈名〉~学潮❶；~反抗精神❷〈动〉~闹事❸；~罢工❹；~罢课❺；~叛乱❻〔~补〕〈趋〉把坏人~起来了〈程〉他在那里~得很厉害❼〈可〉~不起来〈时〉~了半天也没扇动起来〔状~〕专门❽~；屡次❾~；一再~；拼命❿~；竭力⓫~

1. student strike 2. rebellious spirit 3. create a disturbance; make trouble 4. strike 5. students' strike 6. armed rebellion 7. terrible 8. especially 9. over and over again; repeatedly 10. with all one's might 11. do one's utmost

shǎn 闪 ① dodge; get out of the way ≅ 躲避；躲闪〔~宾〕〈名〉~一~身〔~补〕〈结〉~开点儿，别蹭❶一身油；听见我来了，他故意❷~在门后边想吓❸我一下儿〈趋〉很快地~过去了〈程〉~得很快〈可〉~不开〈量〉请你往旁边~一下儿〔状~〕猛地❹一~；赶快~开

1. be smeared with 2. intentionally; purposely 3. frighten 4. suddenly; violently

② flash; sparkle; shine ≅ 突然出现〔~宾〕〈名〉脑子里~了一个念头❶〔~补〕〈结〉窗外~过一个人影❷〈趋〉山后~出一条小路来〈量〉一个奇怪❸的念头在我的脑子里~了一下儿〔状~〕往旁边一~；一~而过；下意识地❹~；立刻~出

1. thought; idea; intention 2. the shadow of a human figure 3. strange; odd; surprising 4. subconsciously

shànyú 善于 be good at; be adept in

〔～宾〕〈名〉～歌舞；～辞令❶〈动〉～结交朋友；～团结❷人；～做生意❸；～经营❹；～拍马❺；～奉承❻别人；～辨别真假❼；～识别好坏❽；～发现别人的优点❾；～学习别人的好经验❿；～模仿⓫；～察言观色⓬；～钻研⓭；～画山水〔状～〕不～；特别～；一向～

1. language appropriate to the occasion (gifted with a silver tongue) 2. unite 3. do business 4. manage; run 5. lick sb.'s boots; flatter; soft-soap; fawn on 6. flatter; fawn upon; toady 7. distinguish true from sham 8. distinguish good from bad 9. merit; strong point 10. good experience 11. imitate; copy; model onself on 12. carefully weigh up a person's words and closely watch his expression; watch a person's every mood 13. study intensively; dig into

shàncháng 擅长 be good at; be expert in; be skilled in

〔～宾〕〈名〉～游泳；～绘画❶；～音乐❷〈动〉～烹调❸；～缝纫❹；～织毛衣❺〔状～〕只～；不～；尤其❻～

1. drawing (painting) 2. music 3. cooking 4. sewing; tailoring 5. knit a woolen sweater 6. especially; particularly

shāng 伤 injure; hurt ≅ 伤害

〔～宾〕〈名〉出口❶；～人；在光线不足的地方看书～眼睛；人千万别～感情❷；～了筋骨❸；吃辣椒❹容易～胃❺；～了他的心〈形〉彼此❻～了和气❼〔～补〕〈结〉～透❽心了〈程〉她说话太刻薄❾，伤人～得非常厉害；骨头❿～得不轻⓫〈量〉～过一次〔状～〕别～感情；故意⓬～人；容易～；特别～〔习用〕～脑筋⓭

1. speak; utter 2. feelings 3. bones and muscles 4. eat chilli 5. stomach 6. mutual; each other 7. (hurt sb.'s) feelings 8. fully; thoroughly; in a penetrating way 9. unkind; harsh; mean 10. bone 11. serious 12. intentionally; purposely 13. knotty; troublesome; bothersome

shānghài 伤害 injure; harm; hurt ≅ 损害；损伤；伤

〔～宾〕〈名〉不许❶～珍奇动物❷；别～孩子的心灵❸；～感情❹；毒蛇❺常常～人；不要～身体；～眼睛；别～他的自尊心❻〔～补〕〈程〉～得很厉害〈可〉～不着(zháo)〈量〉我无意中❼～过一次他的自尊心〔状～〕容易～；不致❽～；故意❾～；无意中～；别～；难免❿～；屡次⓫～

1. not allow 2. rare animals 3. soul; heart 4. feelings 5. poisonous snake 6. pride; self-esteem 7. inadvertently; unwittingly; accidentally 8. cannot go so far;

be unlikely 9. intentionally; on purpose 10. hard to avoid 11. time and again; repeatedly

shāngliang 商量 consult; discuss; talk over ≅ 讨论，研究〔~宾〕〈名〉~事情；~对策❶；~办法，~做法〔~补〕〈结〉把时间~好了再发通知；事情~晚了，我们两个人~过了，这件事就算❷~定了❸；~妥❹了〈趋〉他们~来~去，也没~出个好办法来〈程〉~得很仔细❺〈可〉他是个没主意❻的人，什么事情跟他都~不了(liǎo)；对策怎么商量也~不好〔时〕~了那么多时候，还商量不出结果来〈量〉先~一下儿；~过好几次了〔状~〕跟谁~？事先❼~；反复❽~；三番五次地❾~；好好儿~~；暗地里❿~；认真~一下儿；叽叽咕咕⓫地~

1. the way to deal with a situation; counter measure 2. consider; regard as 3. fixed; decided 4. settled; finished 5. careful 6. idea; plan 7. beforehand; in advance 8. 9. repeatedly; time and again 10. secretly; in secret 11. gabble; whisper

shǎng 赏 ① grant (bestow) a reward; award ≅ 赏赐，奖赏〔~宾〕〈名〉主人~她很多钱；国王~他一匹马〔~补〕〈结〉他嫌❶钱~少了〈程〉~得真多〈可〉~不了(liǎo)多少钱〈量〉~过几次〔状~〕很大方地❷~给我了；从来没~

过；又~你一件衣服；偶尔❸~；一连❹~了好几件；一古脑儿❺都~给我了

1. dislike; mind; complain of 2. generously; liberally 3. occasionally; once in a while 4. in succession; in a row; running 5. completely; root and branch; lock; stock and barrel

② admire; enjoy; appreciate ≅ 欣赏，观赏〔~宾〕〈名〉~菊花❶；~金鱼；~月〔~补〕〈趋〉一个人站在那里~起雪了〈时〉~了一晚上月〔状~〕一边喝酒一边~雪；在公园~菊花，兴致很高地❷~；跟朋友一起~

1. chrysanthemum 2. full of zest

shàng 上 ① go up; mount; board; get on ≅ 登〔~宾〕〈名〉~山；~楼；~汽车；~树；~台阶❶；~船；~岸❷；~飞机〔~补〕〈结〉~错车了〈趋〉他已经~到山顶❸上去了；快~去吧，她在家等❹着你呢〈程〉年轻人❺上车~得快；老年人~得慢〈可〉年纪大了，~不了山了〔状~〕顺利地❻~；吃力地❼~；别人扶❽着~；送他~飞机；气喘吁吁地❾~；一口气❿~；好容易⓫~

1. stairs 2. shore; bank; coast 3. the top of a mountain 4. wait 5. young people 6. smoothly; successfully; without a hitch 7. strenuously; painstakingly 8. support with the hand 9. gasping for breath; panting 10. in one

shàng 331

breath; without a break **11.** with great difficulty

② enter; appear on the stage; enter the court or field ≅ 出场〔~宾〕〈名〉双方❶运动员❷已经~场❸了；他已经化好妆❹，就等着~场了〔~补〕〈结〉演员出场时差点儿~错了门〈程〉~得太早；~得很快〈可〉运动员受伤❺了，这一场~不了(liǎo)了〈量〉这次比赛，他一共~过三次场〔状~〕慢点儿~；先~；别~；一起~；一个人~

1. both sides; the two parties **2.** athletes; players; sportsmen or sportswomen **3.** arena; sports field **4.** (of actors) make up **5.** be injured; be wounded

③ go to ≅ 到，去〔~宾〕〈名〉~街❶；~餐馆；~哪儿去？~美国〔~补〕〈趋〉昨天晚上他~朋友家去了；~餐馆去吃一顿❷吧；~这儿来，我给你看一个东西〈可〉今年还~不了(liǎo)美国〈量〉一趟邮局〔状~〕西瓜大量❸~市❹；赶紧~医院；急急忙忙地~❺

1. street **2.** have a meal **3.** a large number; a great quantity **4.** go (appear) on the market **5.** in a hurry; hastily

④ fill; supply; serve ≅ 增加，添补〔~宾〕〈名〉锅炉❶里再~点水；~了一盘菜；货架子❷上~了不少货❸〔~补〕〈结〉锅炉里的水~满了〈程〉~得太多了；~得不够〈可〉水已经满了，再也~不 了(liǎo)了〈量〉~过好几次水了〔状~〕多~些；一次~满；慢慢~；分几次❹~

1. boiler **2.** goods shelves **3.** goods; commodity **4.** in several times

⑤ place sth. in position; set; fix ≅ 安装〔~宾〕〈名〉~刺刀❶；~螺丝❷；~领子❸；~鞋底❹；~袖子❺〔~补〕〈结〉螺丝~紧点❻儿，领子别~歪❼了〈程〉螺丝~得太松❽了；领子~得不合适❾〈可〉袖子~不上了〈时〉~了半天才上上〈量〉请你帮我~一下儿〔状~〕不太好~；容易~吗？第一次~

1. bayonet **2.** screw **3.** collar **4.** sole (of a shoe) **5.** sleeve **6.** close; tight **7.** oblique; slanting **8.** loose **9.** not suitable

⑥ apply; paint; smear ≅ 涂；搽；擦；抹〔~宾〕〈名〉颜色；~药；~漆❶；~油〔~补〕〈结〉没~匀；颜色~重❷了；已经~完药了；油~多了，都流❸出来了〈程〉颜色~得太浓❹了；~得太浅❺了，药~得太厚❻了；颜色~得不匀❼〈可〉漆~不匀；没有刷子❽，今天~不了(liǎo)〈量〉一天要~两次妆❾；一天~好几次药〔状~〕多~一点儿；往门上~漆；一层一层地❿~；等干了再~

1. lacquer; paint **2.** deep; heavy **3.** flow **4.** dense; thick; concentrated **5.** light (of colour) **6.** thick **7.** not even **8.** brush **9.** make up **10.** layer after layer

⑦ be put on record; be carried (in a publication) ≅ 登载〔～宾〕〈名〉英雄事迹❶～报了；这笔款❷～帐❸了吗？名字～了光荣榜❹；他～了电影镜头❺〔～补〕〈可〉这个消息❻～不了(liǎo)报〈量〉～过三次电视了〔状～〕第一次～；从来没～过

1. heroic deeds 2. a sum of money 3. make an entry in an account book 4. honour roll 5. appear in a film 6. news

⑧ wind; screw; tighten ≅ 拧紧〔～宾〕〈名〉～闹钟❶；～发条❷；～弦❸；～螺丝❹〔～补〕〈结〉～紧❺了；闹钟～好了；发条～满❻了〈程〉～得真紧〈可〉上满了就～不动了〈时〉～了一分钟才才上满〈量〉今天～过一次表了，用不着❼再上了〔状～〕多～几下；别～了；轻轻地～

1. alarm clock 2. 3. spring (of a watch, etc) 4. screw 5. tight, close 6. full 7. need not

⑨ lock (a door, etc) ≅ 关〔～宾〕〈名〉天太晚了，铺子❶～门了；十二点以后门就～锁❷了〔～补〕〈结〉～早了；～晚了〈程〉大门～得太早了〈可〉旅馆二十四小时都有人进进出出，所以大门～不了(liǎo)锁〔状～〕早点儿～；按时～❸；在门外边～了一把锁

1. shop; store 2. lock up 3. on time

⑩ be engaged (in work, study, etc) at a fixed time 〔～宾〕〈名〉～课了；你每天几点～学？他都～大学了！～夜校❶；～补习班❷；～速成班❸；～训练班❹；～英语；～工；～夜班〔～补〕〈结〉今天的课就～到这儿吧〈趋〉后来因为家里出了事情，他没有再继续～下去〈程〉他上学～得比较晚〈可〉一上午连上四节课你～得了(liǎo)～不了(liǎo)？今年～不完这本书了〈时〉～了四年大学〈量〉你先在这个班～一下儿，不行再换❺班〔状～〕从几点到几点～？在哪个学校～学？继续～；一个月至少～一次中班❻

1. night school 2. continuation class 3. accelerated course; crash course 4. training class; training course 5. change 6. middle shift

⑪ up to ≅ 达到；够〔～宾〕〈名〉～了年纪❶；～了岁数❷；走了～百里路；～万人〔～补〕〈可〉这次考试我～不了(liǎo)80分〈量〉我的数学❸就～过一次95分〔状～〕真～岁数了，腿脚都不灵便❹了〔习用〕～圈套❺；～贼船❻

1. 2. age (advanced in years) 3. mathematics 4. have difficulty walking 5. fall into a trap; play into sb's hands 6. board the pirate ship — join a reactionary faction

shāo 烧

① burn ≅ 燃烧〔～宾〕〈名〉把信～了；～柴❶；～煤❷；～煤气❸；森林❹着火，～了很多树〔～补〕〈结〉火～旺❺了；木

柴~焦❻了；煤~红了；煤气~完了；~伤❼了两个人；把干树叶都~掉了；锅❽底~黑了；划火柴❾别~着(zháo)手〈趋〉这火再~下去，损失❿更大了；这些煤能~到年底〈程〉炉火~得正旺；这把火~得太猛⓫了；~得太惨⓬了；煤气~得太快了，刚十天就烧完了〈可〉这木柴被雨淋湿⓭了，怎么烧也~不着(zháo)；这罐煤气~得了(liǎo)一个月吗？木柴~得成炭吗？〈时〉这场大火整整⓯~了一个星期〈量〉~一下儿试试；~过两次〔状~〕老~不着(zháo)；整整~了三天；这种煤好~不好~？一下子~起来了；连续~

1. firewood 2. coal 3. gas 4. forest 5. burn briskly 6. burnt 7. burn 8. pan; pot 9. scratch a match 10. loss 11. violent; fierce 12. miserable; pitiful; tragic 13. be drenched with rain 14. charcoal 15. whole; complete

② cook; bake; heat 〔~宾〕〈名〉~饭；~水；~炭❶；~砖❷；~窑❸〔~补〕〈结〉水~开❹了；炉子的铁❺都~红了；砖都快~裂❻了〈程〉水~得不够，再烧一点儿吧〈可〉煤气❼快用完了，连水都~不开了〈时〉一窑石灰❽要~多长时间？刚~一会儿，屋子就暖和了〈量〉~一下儿试试〔状~〕赶紧~点水吧

1. make charcoal 2. bricks 3. kiln 4. boil 5. iron 6. split 7. gas 8. lime

③ stew after frying or fry after stewing 〔~宾〕〈名〉~茄子❶；~海参❷；红~鲤鱼❸；红~排骨❹〔~补〕〈结〉肉~烂❺了〈趋〉她~出来的鸡好吃极了〈程〉菜~得好香❻啊！〈可〉我什么菜也~不好；时间短~不烂；~不熟❼〈时〉多~一会儿就可以吃了〈量〉我~过一次鱼〔状~〕用电炉❽~；用酱油❾~；经常~；偶尔❿~

1. eggplant; aubergine 2. sea cucumbers 3. carp stewed in soy sauce 4. spareribs stewed in soy sauce 5. tender 6. really appetizing 7. not thoroughly cooked 8. electric stove 9. soy sauce 10. occasionally; once in a while

④ run a fever; have a temperature 〔~补〕〈结〉~到40°C；人都~糊涂❶了；快~死了；嘴唇❷都~干了；把孩子都~坏了〈趋〉早上退烧❸了，现在又~起来了；连❹着烧了几天，嘴唇都~出泡❺来了；再~下去，身体可吃不消❻了〈程〉孩子~得真可怜；~得直说胡话❼；~得滚烫❽；脸~得通红❾；~得实在❿受不了(liǎo)了；~得昏迷⓫了；~得连人都不认识⓬了〈可〉早点儿吃药⓭就~不起来了〈时〉断断续续地⓮~了半年；整整~了十天〔状~〕这个孩子体质⓯太差⓰，一感冒就~；从来没~过；动不动⓱就~

1. dazed; confused; muddled 2. lips 3. bring down a fever 4.

running; in succession 5. sth. shaped like a bubble 6. be unable to stand 7. ravings 8. boiling hot; burning hot 9. very red 10. really; indeed; honestly 11. stupor; coma; unconscious 12. can not recognize 13. medicine 14. off and on; intermittently 15. physique; constitution 16. very poor 17. frequently

⑤ turn yellow; corrode 〔~宾〕〈名〉上的肥料❶太多，把根儿❷都~了；盐酸把衣服~了一个窟窿❸〔~补〕〈结〉药水❹把手~掉一层皮❺；白菜叶子都让肥料给~黄了；~焦❻了〔趋〕~下一层皮；~出一个泡❼来〔程〕~得真疼；~得真利害〈量〉我的手被硝酸❽~过一次，到现在还有疤❾〔状~〕被什么~的? 小心别~着(zháo)；又~了一个洞❿

1. fertilizer 2. root 3. hole 4. lotion 5. skin 6. burnt 7. sth. shaped like a bubble 8. nitric acid 9. scar 10. hole; cavity

shāo 捎 take along sth. to or for sb.; bring to sb. ≌ 顺便带〔~宾〕〈名〉请你给他~一封信；~个口信❶；~点儿吃的，~点儿钱〔~补〕〈结〉请把这些东西~给他〔趋〕把这包点心❷替我~回家去吧；有什么口信，再给我~回来〈程〉钱~得真不少〈可〉怕口信~不到，所以又赶紧写了这封信〈量〉我给他~过三次〔状~〕顺便❸~；请你替我~；又~什么? 没完没了(liǎo)地~东西

1. oral message 2. a package of light refreshments 3. conveniently; in passing

shǎo 少 be short; lack; lose; be missing ≌ 短少，缺↔多〔~宾〕〈名〉我们这里~两张票；这本新书~了两页；我们那儿~一个打字员❶；先别开车，还~两个人呢；羊群里~了几只羊；我回家一数❷~了两块钱〈数〉4比10~6〔~补〕〈结〉头发比年轻时~多了〈程〉~得太多了〈可〉每次去旅行❸都~不了(liǎo)他; 以后有事~不了(liǎo)麻烦你〈量〉分什么东西也没~过他一次〔状~〕经常~; 只~两个人; 又~了一把椅子〔习用〕~来这一套❹; ~给我装蒜❺; ~管闲事❻

1. typist 2. count 3. travel; journey 4. cut it out; quit that 5. stop pretending 6. none of your business

shé 折 break; snap ≌ 断〔主~〕〈名〉木棍❶~了；扁担❷~了；眼镜腿❸~了；粉笔❹~了；绳子❺~了；毛线❻~了；表带❼~了；铁丝❽~了〔~宾〕〈名〉梳子❾~了几根齿❿; 树~了一个杈儿⓫〔~补〕〈程〉~成一截⓬一截的了〈可〉挑⓭这么重⓮的东西，扁担~得了(liǎo)~不了(liǎo)? 这么细⓯的绳子晒⓰衣服~得了(liǎo)~不了(liǎo)?〈时〉眼镜腿~了半年了，也没地方去修〈量〉~过两次了，再折就没法修了〔状

~〕一摔⑰就~；喀嚓一声⑱~了；突然~了；差一点儿~

1. rod; stick 2. shoulder pole; carrying pole 3. the side (bow) 4. chalk 5. rope 6. knitting wool 7. watchband; watch strap; watch bracelet 8. iron wire 9. comb 10. teeth 11. branch (of a tree) 12. chunk 13. shoulder; carry on the shoulder with a pole 14. heavy 15. thin 16. dry in the sun 17. cast; throw; fling 18. with a crack

shěde 舍得 be willing to part with; not grudge 〔~宾〕〈动〉~吃；你~买吗？ ~扔❶吗？ ~花钱；~离开❷他吗？ ~花时间；下工夫❸吗？〔状~〕真~；非常~；完全~；一向❹~吃

1. throw away 2. leave; depart from 3. put in time and energy 4. all along; consistently

shěbude 舍不得 hate to part with or use; grudge 〔主~〕〈名〉孩子去当兵❶，妈妈有点~〔~宾〕〈代〉要分手❷了，两个人你~我，我~你〈动〉~说❸他两句；~打孩子；~花那么多钱买；那条新裤子❹他老~穿；鞋都那么破❺了，她还~扔掉❻；~给我吃〔状~〕真~；就是~；有点儿~；怎么也~；实在❼~

1. join the army 2. part company; say good-bye 3. scold; criticize 4. new trousers 5. torn; worn-out 6. throw away 7. really; truly

shè 设 set up; establish; found ≅ 设置；设立〔~宾〕〈名〉那个学院❶一共~了五个系❷；工业部❸下面~了十个局❹；~了专门机构❺；~了几门新课程❻；~了重重障碍❼〔~补〕〈结〉经销处❽~在全国各大城市❾〈程〉机构~得太多了；~得太细❿了〈可〉师资⓫不够，~不了(liǎo)那么多课程〔状~〕为儿童~；专⓬为成人⓭~；根据⓮需要~；新~的；打算⓯再~一个

1. college 2. department 3. the Ministry of Industry 4. bureau 5. special agency; special organ 6. new subject; new course 7. one obstacle after another 8. agency 9. city 10. minute; trifling 11. persons qualified to teach; teachers 12. especially; particularly 13. adult; grown-up 14. on the basis of 15. intend; plan

shèjì 设计 design; plan 〔~宾〕〈名〉~一个新方案❶；~了一座旅馆❷；~园林❸；~电影院❹；~体育馆❺；~一种儿童玩具；~服装❻样式❼；~图案❽；~花样❾；~皮鞋样式；~版面❿；~包装纸⓫〔~补〕〈结〉~好了；他已经开始~了〈趋〉~出来一个很漂亮的样式；大家立即⓬着手⓭~起来了〈程〉~得很好；~

得很适用❶❹；～得美观❶❺大方❶❻；～得不太合理❶❼〈可〉我～不了(liǎo)；你～得出来吗？给你一个月的时间～得完～不完？〈时〉～了好长时间；光❶❽设计就～了半年〈量〉～过好几次了；好好～一下儿〔状～〕精心❶❾～；按❷⓿希腊❷❶的建筑❷❷样式～；根据❷❸我的提议❷❹～；初步❷❺～；重新～；为这次演出❷❻～；为国际❷❼比赛～；老工程师❷❽亲自❷❾～

1. scheme; plan; programme 2. hotel 3. gardens; park 4. cinema 5. gymnasium; gym 6. dress; clothing; costume 7. pattern; type; style; form 8. pattern; design 9. pattern; variety 10. layout of a printed sheet 11. wrapping paper 12. at once; immediately 13. start; begin 14. suit; be applicable 15. pleasing to the eye; beautiful; artistic 16. tasteful in good taste 17. not reasonable enough 18. solely; only; merely 19. elaborately; painstakingly; meticulously 20. according to 21. Greek 22. architecture 23. on the basis of 24. proposal; motion 25. preliminary; initial 26. performance 27. international 28. old engineer 29. personally

shèxiǎng 设想 ① imagine; envisage; conceive; assume ≅ 想象；假想〔～宾〕〈名〉我们可以～一个方案❶；～一种情况；～一个场景❷〈动〉～不费力❸就能成功❹；不能～轻而易举地❺成为❻学者❼〔～补〕〈结〉～错了〈趋〉～出来的一切都极端❽可笑〈程〉～得很不实际❾；～得有点不着边际❶⓿；～得太顺利❶❶了〈可〉～不出来那将是什么样子〈时〉～了半天，又有什么用呢？〈量〉可以好好～一下儿；先随便❶❷～一下儿；～过几次了〔状～〕大胆❶❸～；曾经～；不妨❶❹～；不堪❶❺～；凭空❶❻～；从最坏的方面去～；事前❶❼～；反复～

1. scheme; plan; programme 2. scene (in drama; fiction, etc.) 3. not needing an effort 4. succeed 5. easy to do 6. become 7. scholar; learned man; man of learning 8. extremely; exceedingly 9. unpractical 10. not to the point; irrelevant 11. smooth; successful 12. casually; at random 13. boldly 14. there is no harm in; might as well 15. cannot bear; cannot stand 16. without foundation 17. beforehand

② have consideration for ≅ 着想〔～补〕应该为孩子～一下儿〔状～〕为学龄前儿童❶～；为老年人～；为残废人❷～；为这一带居民❸～；替大家～

1. preschool children 2. the disabled 3. resident

shèjí 涉及 involve; relate to; touch upon ≅ 牵涉到；关系到〔～宾〕〈名〉不要～其他❶问题；不要～别人的私生活❷；～许多领域❸〔～补〕〈结〉～到如何教育

❹下一代❺的问题；～到还能不能坚持❻学下去的问题〈可〉～不了(liǎo)那么广❼〔**状**～〕从未～；仅仅❽～；不曾～；不免～；不得不～；多次～

1. other 2. private life 3. field; sphere; domain 4. educate; teach; inculcate 5. future generation 6. persist in; persevere in; insist on 7. wide 8. only; merely

shè 射 shoot; fire; send out (light, heat, etc.) ≅ 发出〔**～宾**〕〈名〉～箭❶；～了一颗子弹❷〔**～补**〕〈结〉子弹～中(zhòng) 了靶心❸；用猎枪❹～着(zháo)一只麻雀❺；箭～穿了一片树叶；月光从树梢❻的空隙里❼～到地上；电影院里放映机❽的强烈❾光柱❿～在幕布⓫上〈趋〉～进一个球去；一连⓬～出去三发炮弹⓭；从门缝⓮～进来一道灯光；他很敏捷地⓯ 躲开⓰ 了～过来的子弹〈程〉～得正好，～得非常远；～得很集中⓱〈可〉鸟飞得那么快，我～不着(zháo)〈时〉～了半天，一只也没射着(zháo)〈量〉～一下儿试试；～了好几下儿都没射着〔**状**～〕从耳朵旁边～过来了；用鸟枪⓲～；向空中～；猛烈地⓳～；连续～；从四面八方⓴～来

1. arrow 2. bullet 3. hit the bull's-eye 4. shot-gun; hunting rifle 5. sparrow 6. the tip of a tree; treetop 7. hole; small opening 8. projector (film) 9. strong; intense 10. light column 11. screen; curtain 12. in succession; in a row 13. shell (artillery) 14. a crack between a door and its frame 15. quickly; nimbly; agilely 16. avoid; dodge 17. concentrate 18. fowling piece 19. fiercely; violently 20. from all directions

shēnqǐng 申请 apply for ≅ 请求〔**～宾**〕〈名〉～助学金❶；～奖学金❷；～出境签证❸〈动〉～加入工会❹；～出国；～免税❺；～调动❻工作〔**～补**〕〈结〉他说他～晚了，要是早两年申请就好了〈程〉我～得太晚了；～得不是时候，～得不多不少正合适❼；～得不合理❽〈可〉她不够条件❾，～不了(liǎo)〈时〉～了好几年才批准❿，刚～几天就批下来了〈量〉～过两次；～一下儿试试〔**状**～〕多次～；从去年就～；从未～过；一直～；不好意思⓫～；一再～；向有关部门⓬～；向政府⓭～；重新～；尽快～；相继⓮～；在哪儿～？用什么方式⓯～？

1. stipend; grant-in-aid 2. scholarship 3. housing; lodgings 4. trade union; labour union 5. exempt from taxation 6. transfer sb. to another post 7. suitable; appropriate; right 8. unreasonable 9. condition 10. ratify; approve 11. feel embarrassed; find it embarrassing 12. the department concerned 13. government 14. one after another 15. way; fashion; pattern

shēn 伸 stretch; extend ≅ 展开 ↔缩 〔~宾〕〈名〉他不习惯❶~手跟别人要钱；坐得时间长了，应该站起来~~胳膊❷~~腿，活动活动❸；你~着脖子❹往里看什么呢？向我~大姆指❺；他常在别人背后~舌头❻做鬼脸❼；狗热得~着舌头〔~补〕〈结〉这儿有地方，可以把腿~开轻松❽一下儿〈趋〉坐汽车和火车时都不要把头~出窗外去；这个孩子又把舌头~出来了；~起大姆指来夸❾他；别把腿~出去，那样容易把人绊倒❿；小偷又把手~到人家皮包里去了〈程〉她跳水⓫时腿~得很直；体操运动员⓬的胳膊~得很平；树枝从墙头⓭~到墙外来了〈可〉他的腿有毛病⓮，~不直；手一抽筋⓯就~不开；他老得连腰⓰都~不直了〈时〉了半天舌头〈量〉~一下儿腿〔状~〕向上~；向前~；从窗户外边~进来

1. not be used to; not be accustomed to 2. arms 3. move about 4. neck 5. hold up one's thumb 6. tongue 7. make a wry face; make faces; make grimaces 8. relax 9. praise 10. stumble over 11. dive 12. gymnast 13. the top of a wall 14. trouble 15. have a cramp 16. waist

shēnrù 深入 go deep into; penetrate into 〔~宾〕〈名〉~实际❶才能了解情况；~生活才能写出好的作品❷来；~群众，才能了解人们的想法；~敌后❸；~病房；~人心〔状~〕真正~进去；自觉地❹~；主动❺~；不断❻~；多次~；一点也不~

1. reality; practice 2. good works 3. enemy's rear area 4. conscientiously 5. on one's own initiative 6. ceaselessly; incessantly

shěn 审 ① examine; go over ≅ 审查〔~宾〕〈名〉~稿件❶；~节目〔~补〕〈结〉稿子~完了吗？〈趋〉~起乱稿子来真头疼❷〈程〉他审稿子~得很仔细❸；~得真严❹；~得极慢❺；~得太马虎❻了〈可〉这么一大堆❼稿子，我一个人可~不过来；时间太短，~不出来了；~不仔细〈时〉这篇稿子我整整❽了三天〈量〉稿子多~几遍，错误就少了，你要是不忙，帮我~一下儿稿子吧〔状~〕多~几遍；认真地~；反复~；一遍一遍地~；马马虎虎地~；白❾~了；集体❿~

1. manuscript 2. headache 3. careful 4. strict 5. extremely slow 6. careless 7. heap; pile 8. whole 9. in vain 10. collectively

② interrogate; try ≅ 审问；讯问〔~宾〕〈名〉~案❶；~俘虏❷；~贼❸；~流氓❹；~罪犯❺；你说话象~犯人❻似的〔~补〕〈结〉~清楚了没有？〈趋〉~出口供❼来了；犯罪动机❽还没~出来；这个案子太复杂，~下来至少❾要半年；这个案子牵涉❿的面⓫太广⓬，~起来比较困难〈程〉~得很详细⓭；~得很合理⓮；~得不令人心服⓯〈可〉什么重要的口

供也没～出来；这个案子没经验的⓰法官⓱～不了(liǎo)〈时〉～了十年；刚～一会儿他就招供⓲了〈量〉好好～一下儿他〔**状～**〕尚未⓳～；反复～；一次一次地～；慎重地⓴～；严肃地㉑～；严格地㉒～；一丝不苟地㉓～；公正地～；公开地㉔～

1. case; law case **2.** prisoner **3.** thief **4.** rogue; hooligan **5. 6.** criminal **7.** a statement made by the accused under examination **8.** criminal motive **9.** at least **10.** involve **11.** side; aspect **12.** wide **13.** detailed **14.** reasonable **15.** not persuasive **16.** inexperienced **17.** judge **18.** confess **19.** not yet **20.** cautiously; prudently **21.** solemnly; seriously **22.** strictly; rigorously **23.** not be the least bit negligent **24.** openly; publicly

shěnchá 审查 examine; investigate

≌ 查〔**～宾**〕〈名〉～计划❶；～经费❷；～剧本❸；～电影；～节目；～内容❹；～书；～证件❺；～档案❻；～文凭❼；～学历❽；～历史；～这件事〔**～补**〕〈结〉～完了；～清楚了；～严❾了；～松❿了〈趋〉一个剧本～下来需要一年吗？已经审查很长时间了，还要继续～下去吗？～出什么问题来了吗？～起来至少⓫要半年〈程〉～得很仔细；～得非常马虎⓬〈可〉他没经验⓭，～不出问题来〈时〉～了好长时间；整整～了三个月〈量〉～过两遍了；再请他～一下儿吧〔**状～**〕认真～；严格⓮～；一遍又一遍地～；从头至尾地⓯～；从各方面～；重新～；彻底～；亲自⓰～；一丝不苟地⓱～；暗中⓲～；暗地里⓳～；严密地⓴～

1. plan **2.** funds **3.** drama; play **4.** content **5.** certificate **6.** files; archives; dossier **7.** diploma **8.** record of formal schooling **9.** strict **10.** loose **11.** at least **12.** careless **13.** inexperienced **14.** strictly **15.** from beginning to end **16.** personally **17.** not be the least bit negligent **18. 19.** secretly; in secret **20.** closely

shèn 渗 ooze; seep

≌〔**主～**〕〈名〉血往外～；水往外～〔**～宾**〕〈名〉直往纱布❶外～血〔**～补**〕〈结〉池子❷里的水都～完了；雨水～透❸了泥土〈趋〉这么多层❹纱布血都～过来了；雨水都～到土里去了；花盆❺里的水很快就～进去了〈程〉水～得真快；～得太慢〈可〉下水道❻堵❼了，水～不下去了；流血❽不多，～不过来〈时〉～了半天也没渗下去〔**状～**〕一点一点地～；又～出来了；慢慢儿地～；多～～

1. gauze **2.** sink; pool **3.** fully; thoroughly; in a penetrating way **4.** layer **5.** flowerpot **6.** sewer **7.** stop up; block up **8.** bleed

shēng 升 ① rise; hoist; go up; ascend

≌升起↔降，落〔**主～**〕〈名〉太阳～起来了；温度❶～高

shēng

了〔~宾〕〈名〉~旗❷〔~补〕〈结〉今天气温❸又~高了一度❹〈趋〉旗子~上来了；气球~上去了〈程〉温度~得真快〈可〉绳子❺断❻了，旗子~不上去了〔状~〕风太大，旗子不好~；太阳从东方~起来了；慢慢地~；逐渐❼~；温度一下子~高了；突然~；很快地~上去了

1. temperature 2. flag 3. air temperature 4. degree 5. rope 6. snapped 7. gradually

② promote ≅ 提升↔降职〔~宾〕〈名〉徒工❶一级❷了；孩子~学❸了〔~补〕〈结〉老李~为校长了〈程〉她这几年~得真快；现在她的地位❹已经~得很高了〈可〉他孩子几次考试都不及格，今年恐怕又~不了(liǎo)级了〈时〉~了半天才是个副教授❺〈量〉~了好几次了〔状~〕他又高~了；一级一级地往上~；连❻~三级

1. apprentice 2. grade 3. go to a school of a higher grade 4. status 5. associate professor 6. in succession; in a row; running

shēng 生 ① give birth to; bear

≅ 生育〔~宾〕〈名〉她又~了一个女孩子〔~补〕〈结〉刚~下的婴儿❶怕冷〈趋〉这个孩子刚~下来的时候才2500克〈程〉孩子~得太多了；孩子~得很顺利❷〈可〉她有病~不了(liǎo)孩子〈时〉那位产妇❸生孩子~了三天三夜〈量〉她只~过一次孩子〔状~〕有心脏病❹的人不宜❺~孩子；哪一年~的?

1. baby 2. smoothly; successfully 3. lying-in woman 4. heart disease 5. not suitable

② grow; get; have ≅ 生长；发生；产生〔~宾〕〈名〉~根儿❶；~芽儿❷；~病；条约❸什么时候~效❹；菜刀老不用，都~锈❺了；~气；米里~了虫子〔~补〕〈结〉~满了锈；~够了气〈趋〉不知她跟谁~起气来了〈可〉精神病人❻~不得❼气；那个孩子真结实❽，怎么折腾❾都~不了(liǎo)病;买药真贵❿，连病都~不起了；抹点油⓫就~不了(liǎo)锈了〈时〉~了半年多的病〈量〉~过一次大病〔状~〕三天两头地⓬~病；容易~气

1. root 2. bud; sprout 3. treaty 4. go into effect; become effective 5. rusty 6. mental patient 7. must not 8. strong; healthy 9. fiddle with 10. expensive; dear 11. smear oil 12. almost every day

③ light (a fire) ≅ 点火〔~宾〕〈名〉~火做饭；~炉子❶取暖❷〔~补〕〈结〉火~旺❸点儿〈趋〉天这么冷，快把炉子~起来吧〈程〉火~得真快；炉子~得真早〈可〉他连炉子都~不着(zháo)〈时〉~了两个小时，才把炉子生着(zháo)〈量〉炉子总灭❹，一天要~好几次〔状~〕用劈柴❺~；大家轮流❻~炉子；重新~

1. stove 2. warm oneself 3. burn briskly 4. go out 5. fire-wood; kindling 6. by turns

shēngchǎn 生产 produce; manufacture ≌ 出产；制造〔**～宾**〕〈名〉～电子计算机❶；～摩托车❷；造船厂❸～轮船❹；～望远镜❺；纺织厂❻～棉布；～地毯❼；制药厂❽～各种药品❾；～水稻❿；～棉花⓫〔**～补**〕〈结〉～多了；～少了〈趋〉～出来一批小型打字机⓬；这种东西再～下去就过剩⓭了；～出来很多新品种〈程〉～得太少了；～得过量了⓮〈可〉他们现在还～不了(liǎo)导弹⓯；最新的样式⓰我们还～不出来〈时〉这批产品⓱才～了三个月就全部交货⓲了〔**状～**〕大量⓳～；成批⓴～；成套㉑～；按计划㉒～；按比例㉓～；盲目㉔～；有目的地㉕～

1. calculator **2.** motor-car **3.** shipyard; **4.** steamer **5.** telescope **6.** textile mill **7.** carpet **8.** pharmaceutical factory **9.** medicines and chemical reagents **10.** paddy (rice); rice **11.** cotton **12.** small-sized typewriter **13.** over production **14.** excessive; over **15.** guided missile **16.** pattern; type; style; form **17.** product **18.** delivery **19.** a large number; a great quantity **20.** in batches **21.** whole set; complete set **22.** according to the plan **23.**in proportion **24.** blindly **25.** purposefully

shěng 省 ① economize; save ≌节省；节约↔费；浪费〔**～宾**〕〈名〉～钱；～时间；～力气；～事儿❶；～心❷；这样可以～劳动力❸〈动〉这个人总是～吃～喝的〔**～补**〕〈结〉～下一笔钱；时间～多了〈趋〉～下来很多汽油❹〈程〉～得太过分❺了；～得很利害〈可〉自己做衣服也～不了(liǎo)多少布；～不下多少汽油；～得出3个小时来吗？〈时〉～了很多时间〈量〉〔**状～**〕在吃上～；从各方面～；一点一滴地❻～；尽量❼～

1. (save) trouble **2.** (save) worry **3.** (save) labour force **4.** gasoline; petrol **5.** excessive; over **6.** bit by bit **7.** to the best of one's ability; as far as possible

② omit; leave out ≌省略；减去〔**～宾**〕〈名〉～了许多繁琐手续❶；～两个字〔**～补**〕〈结〉这一段❷可以～掉三个逗号❸；这样改比较❹好，～掉了一段与主题无关❺的话〔**状～**〕尽量❻～；尽可能❼～

1. overelaborate procedure; tedious formalities **2.** paragraph **3.** comma **4.** relatively **5.** have nothing to do with the subject **6. 7.** to the best of one's ability; as far as possible

shèng 剩 be left; remain ≌ 剩下；余下〔**～宾**〕〈名〉～了一盘菜；～了三个馒头❶；屋子里就～他一个人了；毛衣就～一个边儿没织❷了；别的事都做完了，就～信没写了〈代〉饭菜都吃完了，没～什么〈动〉她发现❸钱全丢了，急得一句话也说不出来，就～哭了；到了山顶❹只～喘气❺

了〔~补〕〈结〉~下的都给他；~下的时间自己复习吧；上次买的纸没用完，还~下很多张〈趋〉好的都卖出去了，~下来的都有点毛病❻〈程〉~得太多了〈可〉分给大家以后，也就~不了(liǎo) 多少了；天太热，饭菜可~不得❼〈量〉昨天又~了一次菜〔状~〕只~他没去过了；千万❽别~；今后不要再~了

1. steamed bread 2. knit 3. find 4. the top of a mountain 5. breathe; pant; gasp 6. defect; shortcoming; imperfection 7. must not 8. be sure

shībài 失败 fail; be defeated; lose (a war, etc.) ↔ 胜利〔主~〕〈名〉战争❶~了；比赛~了；考试~了；试验❷~了〔~补〕〈可〉他准备得很好，这次考试~不了(liǎo) 〈量〉这么多次比赛，她只~过一次〔状~〕彻底~了；屡次❸~；万一❹~了；必定❺~

1. war 2. experiment; test 3. over and over again; repeatedly 4. just in case; if by any chance 5. certainly

shīchuán 失传 not be handed down from past generations; be lost〔主~〕〈名〉秘方❶~了；这种技术❷~了；古代❸科学著作❹~了；古筝❺的曲谱❻~了〔~补〕〈时〉~很多年了〔状~〕全部~了；已经~了；早已❼~了

1. secret recipe 2. technique; technology 3. ancient times; antiquity 4. scientific works 5. a 21-or 25-stringed plucked instrument in some ways similar to the zither 6. song; tune; music score of Chinese operas 7. long ago; for a long time

shīdiào 失掉 lose; miss ≌ 失去；错过〔~宾〕〈名〉~信心❶；~了勇气❷；~了作用❸；~权力❹；~了理智❺；~国籍❻；~了知觉❼；~了机会❽〈动〉~了联系❾〔~补〕〈量〉~了一次很好的机会〔状~〕完全~了；已经~了；白白❿~一次机会

1. confidence; faith 2. courage 3. function; action 4. power; authority 5. reason; senses 6. nationality 7. consciousness 8. chance; opportunity 9. contact; connection; relation 10. in vain

shīlíng 失灵 (of a machine, instrument, etc.) not work or not work properly; be out of order ≌ 不好用〔主~〕〈名〉开关❶~；发动机❷~了；锁❸锈❹得太利害，都~了；这个办法~了；听觉❺~了〔状~〕完全~了；经常~

1. switch 2. engine; motor 3. lock 4. rust 5. sense of hearing

shīxiào 失效 lose efficacy; cease to be effective〔主~〕〈名〉

药受潮❶以后就~了；条约❷~了；法律❸条文❹~了；契约❺~了〔状~〕完全~；已经~；尚未❻~

1. be affected with damp 2. treaty 3. law 4. article; clause 5. contract 6. not yet

shī 施 ①apply; use〔~宾〕〈名〉给苗圃❶里的树苗❷~点儿肥❸〔~补〕〈结〉肥~多了不好；~过肥了没有？〈程〉花盆❹里的肥不能~得太勤❺〈量〉已经~过两次了〔状~〕经常~；按时❻~；隔❼一段时间再~

1. nursery (of young plants) 2. sapling 3. fertilizer; manure 4. flowerpot 5. frequent 6. on time 7. after or at an interval of

② execute; carry out〔~补〕〈结〉在一个地方~完工❶，就要换❷到另一个地方去〔状~〕日夜~工；认真❸~；不负责任地❹~；即将❺~

1. construction 2. change 3. all the same 4. irresponsibly 5. soon

shí 识 know ≌认；认识；知道〔~宾〕〈名〉这个人不~货❶；俗话说❷："不怕不~货，就怕货比货❸。"；不~字；不~好歹❹；不~真假；不~美丑❺〔~补〕〈结〉~破❻了他的阴谋❼；~破了坏人的伪装❽；~破骗局❾〈可〉他自作聪明❿，以为⓫别人~不破他的诡计⓬〔状~〕多少几个字；真不~货

1. goods 2. as the saying goes 3. "Don't worry about not knowing much about the goods; just compare and you will see which is better." 4. good and bad 5. beautiful and ugly 6. see through 7. conspiracy 8. disguise; guise 9. fraud 10. think oneself clever (in making suggestions, etc.) 11. think 12. crafty plot

shíxiàn 实现 realize; achieve; bring about〔主~〕〈名〉计划❶~了；目标❷~了；愿望❸~了；预言❹~了；理想❺~了；梦想~了〔~补〕〈趋〉~起来还有不少困难〈可〉这个计划~得了(liǎo)~不了(liǎo)？〔状~〕终于~；如何~？即将❻~；尚未❼~；逐步❽~；难以~

1. plan 2. objective; target 3. desire; wish 4. prophecy; prediction 5. ideal 6. soon 7. not yet 8. gradually

shíxíng 实行 put into practice; carry out; implement〔~宾〕〈名〉~政策❶；~新的法令❷；~八小时工作制❸〔~补〕〈结〉~晚了；~对了；~坏了〈趋〉这种错误政策不能再继续~下去了；~起计件工资❹制来了〈程〉~得很晚；~得ь很快〈可〉这种方案❺~不了(liǎo)；计划~不下去了〈时〉已经~了一段时间；~三个多月了〈量〉~一下儿试试；~过一次〔状~〕认真~；早就❻~了；不易❼~；立刻~

1. policy 2. laws and decrees 3. eight-hour day 4. piece rate wage 5. scheme; plan; programme 6. long ago 7. not easy

shí 拾 pick up(from the ground)
≅ 捡〔~宾〕〈名〉~了一个钱包；~了一个存折❶；~了一张支票❷；~了一串钥匙❸；~柴❹；农村的孩子背着筐❺~牛粪❻〔~补〕〈结〉~到一百元钱〈趋〉把地上的钥匙~起来〈程〉得真不少〈可〉我怎么老~不着(zháo)啊！〈时〉~了一上午也没拾多少〔状~〕弯腰❼~起；偶然❽~到；在马路上~的

1. deposit book 2. cheque; check 3. a bunch of keys 4. firewood; faggot 5. basket 6. cow dung 7. bend over to 8. by chance; accidentally

shíduo 拾掇 ① tidy up; put in order ≅ 收拾；整理〔~宾〕〈名〉~屋子；~抽屉❶；你头发那么乱❷还不~~〔~补〕〈结〉屋子已经~干净了；把头发~好了再照像〈趋〉这个人~起屋子来真利索❸；把手边不用的工具❹都~起来吧〈程〉屋子~得干干净净；他的床总是~得那么整齐〈可〉那么大的人连屋子都~不干净〈时〉~了半天也不显❺干净〈量〉一天要~好几遍；好好~一下儿吧〔状~〕一遍一遍地~；彻底~；成天❻~；随便❼~；随时❽~；随手❾~；从不~；不停地❿~

1. drawer 2. in disorder 3. agile; nimble 4. tools 5. appear; look; seem 6. all day long; always 7. casually; at random 8. at all times; at any time 9. conveniently; without extra trouble 10. ceaselessly; incessantly

② repair; fix ≅ 修理〔~宾〕〈名〉他自己能~手表；~藤椅❶；你会~收音机❷吗？〔~补〕〈结〉~好了〈趋〉这些儿童玩具❸~起来很麻烦❹〈程〉~得跟原来❺的一样；~得比原来的还好用〈可〉~得了(liǎo)吗？〈时〉~了半天也没拾掇好〈量〉这个东西就请你给~一下儿吧〔状~〕给邻居❻~；赶快~；不好~

1. cane chair; rattan chair 2. radio 3. children's toy 4. troublesome 5. original 6. neighbour

shǐ 使 ① use; employ; apply ≅ 用；使用〔主~〕〈名〉这块橡皮❶好~；那支圆珠笔❷不好~〔~宾〕〈名〉你会~中文打字机❸吗？她右手不会~剪刀❹；先~湿抹布❺擦一下儿玻璃❻；~红笔改卷子❼；她直跟我~眼色❽，让我别说了〔~补〕〈结〉圆珠笔芯❾~完了；炒菜的铲子❿~薄⓫了；笔尖⓬都~秃了⓭〈趋〉把全身的力量都~出来了；把你的劲儿都~上去吧；看着不好，~起来不错；~出来最后一点力气〈程〉橡皮~得太快了；她使剪刀~得最利索⓮〈可〉我的皮肤⓯过敏⓰，~不了(liǎo)这种香皂；她总~不好

电熨斗⓱；她～不惯⓲这种香水；有本事⓳～不上；这个办法可～不得⓴！做一件大衣～得了(liǎo)这么多料子㉑吗？〈时〉这把剪刀～了快十年了；先借我～一会儿〈量〉这种眼药㉒我～过一次；你～一下儿试试〔**状～**〕好～；难～；偷偷地～眼色；暗中～劲儿

1. rubber; eraser 2. ballpen 3. typewriter 4. scissors 5. wet rag 6. glass 7. examination paper 8. tip sb. the wink 9. refill (for a ball-point pen) 10. slice 11. thin 12. nib 13. blunt 14. agile; nimble 15. skin 16. allergy 17. electric iron 18. not get used to 19. ability; skill 20. undesirable 21. material for making clothes 22. medicament for the eyes; eye ointment or eyedrops

② make; cause; enable ≅ 让；叫；使得〔**～宾**〕〈名〉他办事❶～人满意❷；～人信心❸倍增❹；～顾客❺满意；洗澡❻可以～毛孔❼、汗腺❽保持❾通畅❿；别～人讨厌⓫；～人郁闷⓬压抑⓭；虚心～人进步，骄傲～人落后⓮；～计划⓯能实现⓰；～企业⓱蓬勃⓲发展⓳；他做事～人佩服⓴；这话并不～人感到意外㉑；这个消息㉒～大家非常高兴；经常锻炼身体～人身体健康〈代〉～我对他更了解了；～他失去了信心〔**状～**〕真～人讨厌；千万别～人腻烦㉓；尽量～人满意

1. handle affairs; work 2. satisfied 3. confidence; faith 4. double 5. customer; client 6. have a bath 7. pore 8. sweat gland 9. keep; maintain; preserve 10. unobstructed 11. disagreeable; disgusting; repugnant 12. gloomy; depressed 13. constrained 14. Modesty helps one to go forward, whereas conceit makes one lag behind 15. plan 16. realize; come true 17. enterprise; business 18. vigorous; flourishing; full of vitality 19. develop 20. admire 21. be surprised; be taken by surprise 22. news 23. be bored; be fed up

shǐyòng 使用 make use of; use; employ; apply ≅ 使；用〔**～宾**〕〈名〉～种种手段❶；～新机器；～新设备❷；～资金❸；～几名工人；禁止❹～核武器❺〔**～补**〕〈结〉～完了请放回原处；～惯了〈趋〉～起来不顺手❻；～起来很方便❼〈程〉～得很熟练❽〈可〉～不了(liǎo)〈时〉这台机器才～了三十年就坏了〈量〉～过很多次；～一下儿〔**状～**〕初次～；正在～；广泛❾～；普遍❿～

1. by hook or by crook; resort to every means (trick) 2. new equipment 3. fund 4. prohibit; ban; forbid 5. nuclear weapons 6. not smooth; with difficulty 7. convenient 8. skilful 9. widely 10. generally

shì 试 try; test〔**～宾**〕〈名〉衣服什么时候可以～样子❶？演员～～镜头❷；先让他来～～工❸〈主

－谓〉～～衣服长短；～～两个人的能力❹高低；～～这双手套大小；～～她能不能回答；～～这张桌子放得下放不下；～～这根绳子❺结实❻不结实；～～裤子❼合适❽不合适；～～这双鞋小不小；～～水烫不烫❾〔**～补**〕〈结〉衣服～过样子了吗？〈趋〉一件新衣服～来～去；我～过才知道这种肥皂的泡沫❿多〈程〉～得次数太多了；～得烦死了⓫〈可〉我～不出来哪支钢笔好使⓬；没有穿衣镜⓭，在这里～不了(liǎo)衣服〈时〉～了半天；～一会儿〈量〉再～一下儿；已经～过两遍了〔**状～**〕孩子高高兴兴地～新衣服；一遍一遍地～；左～右～

1. fitting **2.** camera lens; shot; scene **3.** test sb.'s conduct, abilities, qualities, etc., before he is finally accepted for a position **4.** ability **5.** rope **6.** solid **7.** trousers **8.** suitable **9.** very hot; boiling hot **10.** foam **11.** be extremely bored with **12.** be convenient to use; work well **13.** full-length mirror

shì 是 ① to be〔**～宾**〕〈名〉她姐姐～医生；我昨天看的～话剧，不～电影；鲸鱼❶～哺乳动物❷；我说的～以后的事儿；她们俩～夫妻；那个姑娘～个哑吧❸；不管你信不信，事实总～事实；诗～好诗，就是长了点儿；你来的不～时候；火车开车时间～晚上十二点；赶❹到那儿已经～九点了〈代〉人活着为的～什么？嚎啕大哭❺的那个人～谁？〈动〉不说话～默认❻了；他昨天真的～病了，不～装病❼；那天我没去真～有事，不～偷懒❽；反复地说～想引起❾你们的重视❿；不懂就～不懂，不要装懂⓫；说了半天才知道他～跟我开玩笑⓬〈形〉你这种行为⓭～鲁莽⓮，不～勇敢⓯；这东西好～好，就～太贵⓰〈主－谓〉那个青年走上犯罪⓱道路的原因就～平时家长太溺爱⓲他了；麻烦⓳的～他生病来不了；可气⓴的～他不肯帮忙；可恨㉑的～他一再说谎㉒；遗憾㉓的～他没参加；值得㉔庆幸㉕的～这次事故㉖没有伤人㉗；不～我讲错了，～他记错了〈数〉9～3的三倍〈介〉我第一次看见她～在舞台㉘上；我看电影不～为了消遣㉙〈……的〉这些书都～图书馆的；这是演戏㉚，不～真的；这些青菜～新鲜㉛的；你亲自去一趟～必要㉜的；那本词典不～我的；他们都～看热闹㉝的；那本书～从国外寄来的；我～坐飞机来的；我买的这些都～你爱吃的；那篇文章～她以前写的；昨天～我最后走的；早上～谁锁的门？〔**状～**〕他就～张教授；他好象～来过；都不～；净～胆小鬼㉞；总～勤勤恳恳地㉟工作；特别～胃㊱不好

1. whale **2.** mammal **3.** mute; a dumb person **4.** try to catch; make a dash for; rush **5.** cry loudly; wail **6.** give tacit consent to **7.** pretend to be ill **8.** loaf on the job; be lazy **9.** give rise to;

arouse; cause 10. attach importance to; pay attention to; think highly of 11. don't pretend to know 12. crack a joke; joke; make fun of 13. deed 14. crude and rash; rash 15. courageous 16. dear; expensive 17. criminal 18. spoil (a child); dote on (a child) 19. troublesome 20. annoying; exasperating 21. hateful 22. tell a lie 23. regret; pity 24. be worth; merit; deserve 25. rejoice 26. accident 27. injure; hurt 28. stage; platform 29. divert oneself; while away the time 30. playacting 31. fresh 32. necessary 33. watch the excitement; watch the fun 34. coward 35. diligently and conscientiously 36. stomach

② 〔indicating existence〕〔～宾〕〈名〉前面～一条河；马路上全～人；靠❶窗～一个写字台❷；地上全～水；山坡❸上净～果树〔状～〕全～；到处❹～

1. near; by 2. writing desk 3. slope 4. everywhere

③ 〔indicating agreement〕A：你明白了吗？B：～，我明白了。A：你为什么要离开❶呢？B：～啊，我要是不离开就好了〔习用〕有❷的～；多的❸～；不～味儿❹

1. leave; part from; be away from 2. 3. have plenty of; there's no lack of 4. not the right flavour; feel bad; be upset

shōu 收 ① collect 〔～宾〕〈名〉～水电费❶；～会费❷；这部词典共～了五千个词；时间到了，老师来～卷子❸了；班长❹替老师～练习本〔～补〕〈结〉～完报贺了；卷子～走了，练习本～齐了；把钱～在抽屉❺里吧〈趋〉衣服～进来了；把这些东西都～到箱子❻里去吧〈程〉这本词典的词～得太少了吧；〈可〉本子总～不齐；我不会算帐❼，～不了(liǎo)钱；衣服还没干，现在还～不进来；话说出去就～不回来了〈时〉～了一个星期还没收齐〈量〉一个月～一次房租❽；老师没时间，让我替他～一下儿本子〔状～〕每月～一次；总～不齐；一时❾～不完；多(少)～点儿；从来不～；好好儿地～

1. charges for water and electricity 2. membership dues 3. examination paper 4. monitor 5. drawer 6. chest; case; trunk 7. do accounts; make out bills 8. rent 9. temporarily; for the moment

② harvest; gather in ≅ 收割；收获〔～宾〕〈名〉～稻子❶；～庄稼❷；今年～了五千斤〔～补〕〈结〉地里❸的麦子都～干净了吗？〈趋〉～下来的粮食放在粮仓❹里了；今年遇到❺了水灾❻，～上来的粮食不多〈程〉今年玉米～得很多〈可〉今年有风灾❽，～不了(liǎo)多少水果；灾情❾很严重❿，今年恐怕连种子⓫都～不回来了〈时〉麦子～了一个多星期就收完了〈量〉一年～两次庄稼〔状～〕天阴了⓬，赶快～麦子吧；多～；没～多少斤；抢～⓭

1. paddy; rice 2. crop 3. in the field 4. granary; barn 5. run into; encounter; come across 6. flood; inundation 7. maize; corn 8. disaster caused by a windstorm 9. the condition of a disaster 10. serious 11. seed 12. the sky is overcast 13. rush in the harvest

③ receive; accept ≅ 接受〔~宾〕〈名〉不~礼物❶；~了三个徒弟❷；~他一瓶酒❸；~了一批研究生❹；~了一封信〔~补〕〈结〉请把礼物~下吧；~到一封挂号信❺〈趋〉你先把礼物~下来再说〈程〉今年研究生~得真不少；钱~得不合理❻〈可〉老~不着(zháo)家里的信；早上发出去的电报❼晚上~得到~不到？〈量〉只~过别人一次礼物〔状~〕决不❽~；果然~到了；主动❾~；被迫❿~；不得不⓫~；只好~；一次~到三封信

1. gift 2. apprentice 3. wine; liquor 4. postgraduate 5. registered letter 6. unreasonable; irrational 7. telegram 8. never 9. on one's own initiative 10. be forced; be compelled 11. have no choice but

④ bring to an end; stop ≅ 结束；停止〔~宾〕〈名〉时间到了，该~工❶了；这件事看你怎么~场❷；不获全胜，决不~兵❸；要下雨了，~摊❹吧〔~补〕〈结〉今天收工~晚了〈程〉今天收工~得比昨天早点儿〈可〉跑得太快，都~不住脚；天黑以前~不了(liǎo)工〔状~〕急急忙忙地❺~；圆满地❻~了场；赶快~；提前❼~；马上~

1. stop work for the day 2. wind up; end up; stop 3. we will not withdraw our forces till complete victory. 4. pack up the stall — wind up the day's business or the work on hand 5. in a hurry; hurriedly 6. satisfactorily 7. in advance; ahead of time

shōumǎi 收买 purchase; buy over〔~宾〕〈名〉~旧书；~废品❶；~破衣服；~人心❷；~了两个坏蛋〔~补〕〈结〉用钱把那两个人~住了〈可〉我们是~不了(liǎo)的〈时〉~了半天人心，也没有一个人肯跟他走的〈量〉他用金钱~过我一次，被我拒绝❸了〔状~〕专门❹~；竭力❺~；暗中❻~；偷偷地❼~；三番五次地❽~；大量❾~；直接❿~；间接⓫~

1. scrap; waste 2. buy popular support 3. refuse 4. especially 5. do one's utmost; with all one's might 6. secretly; in secret 7. stealthily 8. over and over again; repeatedly 9. a large number; a great quantity 10. directly 11. indirectly

shōushi 收拾 ① put in order; tidy; clear away ≅ 整顿；整理；拾掇〔~宾〕〈名〉~残局❶；~屋子；~碗筷❷；~床铺❸；出诊❹前~~药箱❺；~书包；~皮

箱❻； ～行李❼； ～衣服； ～抽屉❽； 该收工❾了， ～～工具❿吧〔～补〕〈结〉刚说完，大家就立即～上了； 快把屋子～干净； 把床铺～好〈趋〉平时不太乱， ～起来很快； 一会儿的工夫就～好了〈程〉屋子～得真干净； ～得井井有条⓫〈可〉他的屋子老～不好，总是乱七八糟⓬的； 我一个人～不过来〈时〉～了一上午才收拾完〈量〉快来帮我～一下儿〔状～〕刚刚～好； 一天到晚～； 随时⓭～； 从不～； 好好～～； 稍微⓮～～； 赶紧～； 亲自⓯～

1. (clear up) a messy situation 2. the bowls and chopsticks 3. the bed 4. (of a doctor) visit a patient at home 5. medical kit 6. leather suitcase; leather trunk 7. luggage 8. drawer 9. stop work for the day (it's time to knock off) 10. tools 11. in perfect order 12. at sixes and sevens; in a mess; in a muddle 13. at any time; at all times 14. slightly; a little 15. personally

② repair; mend ≅ 修理〔主～〕〈代〉椅子腿❶不一般❷高，麻烦❸你给～一下儿〔～宾〕〈名〉他会～录音机❹〔～补〕〈结〉～好了还能用〈趋〉这个破沙发❺， 扔了有点可惜❻， ～起来又很麻烦〈程〉～得跟新的一样； ～得比原来的还好〈可〉坏到这样子了，已经～不了(liǎo)了〈时〉～了一下午也没收拾完〈量〉～过两次了，还是不行； ～一下儿试试吧〔状～〕替我～； 早点儿～； 彻底～； 赶快

～； 立即～； 不用～

1. legs of a chair 2. same as; just like 3. trouble; disturb 4. tape recorder 5. ragged (worn-out) sofa 6. it would be a pity

③ settle with; punish ≅ 弄死； 整治； 惩治〔～宾〕〈名〉把那个坏蛋～了〈代〉绝不能轻饶❶， 一定要好好儿～～他〔～补〕〈结〉一会儿的工夫就把一连❷敌人～掉了〈程〉～得真痛快❸； ～得真过瘾❹； ～得大快人心❺〈可〉你一个人可～不了(liǎo)他〈量〉非得好好～他一下儿不可〔状～〕早晚❻把他～了； 及早❼～； 齐心合力❽地～； 暗暗地❾把他～了； 赶快～

1. not let him off so easily 2. a company 3. to one's great satisfaction 4. to one's heart content 5. (of the punishment of an evildoer) affording general satisfaction; most gratifying to the people; to the immense satisfaction of the people 6. sooner or later 7. early; in advance 8. work as one; make concerted efforts 9. in secret

shǒu 守 ① guard; defend ≅ 把守〔～宾〕〈名〉～边疆❶； ～着球门❷； 战士～着阵地❸〔～补〕〈结〉把球门～住了〈程〉守门员～得真好〈可〉他不行，～不了(liǎo)大门； 阵地还～得住～不住了？〈时〉～了一天一夜〈量〉～过好几次〔状～〕死死地❹～着； 紧紧地

❺～着；目不转睛地❻～着；全神贯注地❼～；聚精会神地❽～着；严❾～阵地

1. border area; frontier region **2.** keep goal **3.** position; front **4.** obstinately; to the last **5.** firmly; tightly; closely **6.** look with fixed eyes; watch with the utmost concentration **7.** with rapt attention; be all ears **8.** be all attention; concentrate one's attention **9.** in full battle array

② keep watch ≅ 守候〔**～宾**〕〈名〉医生～着病人；护士❶～着伤者❷；妈妈～着发烧❸的孩子〔**～补**〕〈结〉～在旁边〈时〉～了一夜病人；你先在这儿～一会儿〈量〉你替我在这儿～一下儿〔**状～**〕整夜地❹～着；一连～了好几天；连续～了三天三夜；焦急地❺～着；担心地❻～着；轮流❼～着

1. nurse **2.** the wounded; wounded personnel **3.** have a fever **4.** all night long **5.** impatiently **6.** anxiously **7.** by turns

③ observe ≅ 遵守〔**～宾**〕〈名〉每个公民❶都应该～法❷；学生都要～纪律❸；他非常～规矩❹；与人约会❺一定要～时❻；那个人不～信用❼〔**状～**〕一向❽～纪律；一直❾很～；一贯❿不～；从来不～；严格⓫～法；必须～；绝对⓬～

1. citizen **2.** law **3.** discipline **4.** rule; established practice (abide by the rules) **5.** appointment; engagement **6.** be on time; be punctual **7.** confidence; faith **8.** **9.** **10.** consistently; all along **11.** strictly **12.** absolute

shòu 受 ① receive; accept ≅ 接受〔**～宾**〕〈名〉～教育❶；～奖❷；～权❸发表❹声明❺〈动〉～训❻；～降❼；～贿❽；～表扬❾〈主－谓〉～坏人指使❿；～他指挥⓫；～大家欢迎〔**～补**〕〈程〉受贿～得太多了〈时〉～了四年大学教育⓬〈量〉～过很多次表扬〔**状～**〕没～过教育；在哪儿～训？经常～表扬；从不～贿；是否⓭～过别人的礼

1. education **2.** be rewarded **3.** be authorized **4.** issue; make **5.** statement **6.** training **7.** surrender **8.** bribes **9.** be praised **10.** instigate; incite **11.** command **12.** higher education **13.** whether; if

② suffer; be subjected to ≅ 遭受〔**～宾**〕〈名〉～灾❶；～难❷；～罪❸；～气❹〈动〉～蒙蔽❺；～骗❻；～欺骗❼；～威胁❽；～压迫❾；～剥削❿；～监督⓫；～侮辱⓬；～审⓭；～批评⓮；～批判⓯；～损失⓰；～埋怨⓱；～罚⓲；～伤；～害；～冻⓳；～折磨⓴；马～惊㉑了〈形〉～凉㉒了；～热㉓了；～窘㉔了；别怕～累㉕；～委屈㉖；让你～苦了〔**～补**〕〈结〉他小时候受罪～大了；受气～够㉗了；受骗～急㉘了；～尽了苦；～到法律制裁㉙〈程〉她受气～得忍耐不下去㉚了〈可〉她一点委屈也～不得；我可

~不了(liǎo)这种气；这个人~不得冷，也~不得热；这种气我再也~不下去了〈时〉~了好几年罪；~了一辈子苦〈量〉~过一次骗；~过两次伤〔状~〕连年㉛~灾；太~罪了；总~气；小时候一直~苦；可则~风㉜；凭㉝什么~欺负？〔习用〕~气包㉞

1. calamity; disaster 2. (suffer) calamities or disasters 3. hardships 4. (suffer) wrong; be bullied 5. be fooled; be hoodwinked 6. 7. be deceived 8. be threatened 9. be oppressed 10. be exploited 11. be controlled 12. be insulted; be disgraced 13. be tried; be on trial 14. 15. be criticized 16. (suffer) losses 17. be blamed 18. be punished 19. suffer from cold 20. cause physical or mental suffering 21. be frightened; be startled 22. catch cold 23. be affected by the heat 24. be embarrassed 25. be put to much trouble 26. be wronged 27. enough 28. irritated; annoyed; nettled 29. be dealt with according to law 30. cannot stand any more 31. year after year 32. catch a chill 33. base on 34. a person whom anyone can vent his spite upon; one who always gets blamed (takes the rap)

shòu 售 sell〔~宾〕〈名〉~票；~货❶〔~补〕〈结〉票已~完；货已~出〔状~〕零~❷；成批地❸~；陆续❹~出了

1. goods; commodity 2. retail 3. group by group; in batches 4. one after another; in succession

shū 梳 comb one's hair, etc.〔~宾〕〈名〉~头；~小辫❶儿；~羊毛〔~补〕〈结〉把头发~通❷；把羊毛~顺❸了；把辫子~高点儿〈趋〉把头发~到耳朵后边去吧〈程〉头发~得很漂亮；~得很高雅❹；~得很大方❺；~得很别致❻；~得真难看；~得很光滑❼；头发总是~得光光的〈可〉头发太乱❽，怎么梳也~不通〈时〉你的头发怎么~了那么多时候还没梳完啊。〈量〉~过一次羊毛〔状~〕轻轻地❾~；用梳子❿~；精心地⓫~；对着镜子⓬~

1. short braid; pigtail 2. comb out 3. smooth 4. elegant; refined 5. in good taste 6. unique; unconventional 7. smooth; sleek 8. dishevelled 9. gently 10. comb 11. carefully; meticulously 12. facing a mirror

shū 输 ① convey; transport ≅ 运输〔~宾〕〈名〉给病人~血；赶快~氧❶；管子❷安装❸好就可以~油了〔~补〕〈结〉把电~给各用户❹使用❺；血~错了可不得了❻(liǎo)〈趋〉把葡萄糖❼~到静脉❽里去了；每年都要~出去很多大米；~往国外〈程〉血不能~得太快〈可〉人快死了，氧气都~不进去了〈量〉我~过两次血〔状~〕给病人~；马上❾~；立即❿~；快点~；已经~；从来没~过；还得再~点儿；一直⓫~

1. oxygen 2. pipe; tube 3. install 4. consumer; user 5. use; make use of 6. disastrous; desperately serious 7. glucose; grape-sugar 8. vein 9. 10. at once; immediately 11. continuously; all along

② lose: be defeated ↔ 赢〔**～宾**〕〈名〉～了两个球；～了一盘棋❶；～了一着❷(zháo)儿；～了一局❸；～了两场❹〔**～补**〕〈结〉这次可～惨❺了；棋子❻～多了；他～急❼了；～给对方❽了；～在配合❾不好上了〈趋〉从那个球以后，就不停地❿～下去了〈程〉球～得太惨了；～得真气人；～得多可惜⓫啊！～得打不起精神⓬来了〈可〉这盘棋～不了(liǎo)〈量〉～过一次〔**状～**〕从未～过；偶尔⓭～；果然⓮～；彻底⓯～；一下子就～了；经常～

1. chess 2. a move in chess 3. game; set; innings 4. a measure word (for sports and recreation, etc.) 5. miserable; wretched 6. a piece (in a board game) 7. irritated; annoyed; nettled 8. the other party 9. cooperate; coordinate; concert 10. ceaselessly; incessantly 11. it's a pity 12. unable to bestir oneself (brace up) 13. once in a while; occasionally 14. really; as expected, sure enough 15. thoroughly

shú 赎 redeem; ransom; atone for (a crime) 〔**～宾**〕〈名〉～衣服；～房子；～地；～首饰❶；～字画；～罪❷〔**～补**〕〈结〉他已经把皮衣服～走了〈趋〉把房子～回来了；东西都～出来了〈程〉～得很快〈可〉现在还没有钱，～不出来；～不完的罪〔**状～**〕从当(dàng)铺❸～回来；分几次～；将功～罪❹

1. ornaments; jewelry 2. crime 3. pawnshop 4. atone for a crime by good deeds; expiate one's crime by good deeds

shúxī 熟悉 know sth. or sb. well; be familiar with ≅ 了解；知道 ↔ 生疏〔**～宾**〕〈名〉～情况❶；～内情❷；～老百姓❸的语言；～那里的环境❹；～他的声音；～她的样子；～你的脾气❺；～老孙的性格❻；～那条小路〔**～补**〕〈趋〉他和大家～起来了；小狗和主人～起来了〈程〉我们彼此❼～极了〈可〉他跟大家总～不起来；那里的情况太复杂，一时恐怕～不了(liǎo)〈量〉应该先一下儿那里的情况〔**状～**〕彼此很～；逐渐❽～起来了；一天一天地～起来了

1. situation 2. the ins and outs of the matter 3. common people; ordinary people 4. environment; surroundings; circumstances 5. temperament; disposition 6. nature; disposition 7. each other 8. gradually

shǔ 属 belong to ≅ 属于〔**～宾**〕〈名〉你知道海南岛❶～热带气候❷还是～亚热带气候❸？〔**状～**〕

都~他管❹；这话纯❺~造谣❻；直接❼~；完全~；是否❽~

1. Hainan Island 2. tropical climate 3. subtropical climate 4. in his charge 5. simple; pure; sheer 6. rumour; fabrication 7. directly 8. whether; if

shǔyú 属于 belong to ≅属〔~宾〕〈名〉光荣❶~攀登❷上珠穆朗玛峰❸的勇士❹；蓝❺、深绿❻、紫❼等颜色~冷色❽；猿猴❾~灵长类动物❿〈代〉这笔财产⓫~谁?〔状~〕完全~；一直~；部分~；暂时~；永久~

1. glory 2. climb 3. Mount Qomolangma 4. a brave and strong man; warrior 5. blue 6. dark green 7. purple; violet 8. cool colour 9. apes and monkeys 10. Primates 11. property; estates

shǔ 数 ① count〔~宾〕〈名〉小孩用手~着天上的星星；~钱〈动〉~~来了几个人；~~有多少把椅子；~~还剩❶多少钱〔~补〕〈结〉数儿~错了；数着数着就~乱了❷；~糊涂❸了；把数儿~准❹了；从1~到10〈趋〉把这5块钱~进去就对了；手里拿着名单❺从上边一个一个地~下来；把工资❻一份一份地~出来了；这点钱~过来~过去还是数不对〈程〉他数钱~得真快〈可〉怎么数也~不清；这么几个就~不过来了!〈时〉~了半天也没数对

〈量〉多~几遍；再~一下儿〔状~〕应该好好~~；仔细~~；大概~了一下儿；马马虎虎地❼~；按次序❽~；顺着❾~；一个一个地~；从东往西❿~；从头⓫~；怎么也~不清；多得简直⓬~不过来；无法⓭~

1. remain 2. 3. confused; muddled 4. accurate 5. name list 6. wage; salary 7. carelessly 8. by order 9. in proper sequence 10. from east to west 11. from beginning 12. simply; at all 13. unable; incapable

② be reckoned as exceptionally (good, bad, etc.) ≅算〔~宾〕〈名〉最温顺❶的动物要~大象了；他们班上跑得最快的要~李丽了〈数〉就能力❷说，他在我们班~第一〈主-谓〉论❸成绩~他最好；论年龄❹~我最大；发音~他最清楚；我们家~我妈的身体最差❺〔~补〕〈可〉论拉小提琴❻我们学校可~不着❼(zháo)我；也~不上❽他〔状~〕可~不上我；就~他行❾〔习用〕~一~二❿

1. docile; meek 2. ability 3. by; in terms of 4. age 5. poor 6. play violin 7. 8. not count as outstanding, important, etc. 9. capable; competent 10. count as one of the very best; ranking very high

shùfù 束缚 tie; bind up; fetter ≅约束；限制〔~宾〕〈名〉~着我们的手脚；~人们的思想〔~补

〈结〉不能让这种思想～住我们的手脚〈趋〉封建意识❶把她的行动～起来了〈程〉～得紧紧❷的〈可〉～得住～不住？〈时〉那个老奶奶❸被封建思想～了一辈子〔**状～**〕被这种思想～住了；紧紧地～着

1. feudal consciousness **2.** tight; close **3.** aunty; granny

shùlì 树立 set up; establish〔**～宾**〕〈名〉～榜样❶；～远大理想❷；～雄心壮志❸；～好的作风❹；～典范❺；～信心❻〔**～补**〕〈结〉～起了雄心壮志〈趋〉好的社会风气❼已经～起来了〈程〉～得很牢固❽；这个典型❾～得好〈可〉～不起来〔**状～**〕牢固地～；尚未❿～；必须～；逐步⓫～

1. example; model **2.** lofty ideas **3.** lofty aspirations and great ideals **4.** style; style of work; way **5.** model; example; paragon **6.** confidence; faith **7.** general mood of society **8.** firm; secure **9.** typical case; type **10.** not yet **11.** step by step; progressively

shù 竖 set upright; erect; stand ≃立↔横〔**～宾**〕〈名〉～电线杆子❶；～一个路标牌❷；～一个广告牌❸；～一个旗杆❹〔**～补**〕〈结〉杆子❺没～好；没～直❻〈趋〉杆子～起来了〈可〉～不直；～不起来〔**状～**〕一根一根地～；高高地～

1. (wire) pole **2.** road sign **3.** billboard **4.** flagpole **5.** pole; staff **6.** straight

shuā 刷 brush; clean; daub〔**～宾**〕〈名〉用牙刷❶～牙；用鞋刷❷～鞋；～碗筷❸；用白灰❹～墙；往家具❺上～油漆❻〔**～补**〕〈结〉锅～干净了；墙～白了；～完牙再洗脸；把牙～流血❼了；油漆～厚❽点儿；颜色～深❾了；～满了浆糊❿；桌子～成奶油色⓫的了〈趋〉这次考试～下来⓬不少人；这一桶漆都～上去也不够；～过来～过去〈程〉油漆～得太厚了；锅～得不干净；鞋油⓭～得不匀⓮；墙～得挺⓯白〈可〉木头太粗糙⓰～不了(liǎo)漆；他的牙怎么刷也～不白了；锅底的黑不用去污粉⓱就～不掉；～不干净〈时〉星期日我在家～了一天墙〈量〉再～几刷子；～了两遍了；刚～几下儿就把衣服弄脏了〔**状～**〕用硬毛刷子⓲～；等⓳干了再～第二道；一层一层地～；一刷子挨着一刷子～；别东一下儿西一下儿地⓴乱㉑～

1. tooth brush **2.** shoe brush **3.** bowls and chopsticks **4.** lime **5.** furniture **6.** lacquer; paint **7.** bleed; shed blood **8.** thick **9.** dark; deep **10.** paste **11.** milk white **12.** eliminate **13.** shoe polish **14.** not even **15.** very **16.** coarse; rough; crude **17.** household cleanser **18.** stiff brush **19.** when; till **20.** one brush here and another there **21.** at random

shuǎ 耍 ① play with; flourish ≃玩；玩弄〔**～宾**〕〈名〉男孩子们最喜欢～刀❶～枪❷玩；他在杂

技团❸里～坛子❹；我在杂技团里～盘子❺〔**～补**〕〈结〉耍坛子都～熟❻了〈趋〉～起龙灯❼来很有节日气氛❽〈程〉～得很熟练；～得很有意思〈可〉胆子小❾的人～不了(liǎo)蛇〈时〉～了两个小时猴子，连一分钱都没得着(zháo)；～了半天白❿耍了〈量〉～过好几次；再～一遍；～一下儿让我们看看〔**状～**〕在街上～；熟练地～；每逢春节⓫都～；一遍一遍地～

1. toy sword **2.** toy gun **3.** acrobatic troupe **4.** juggling with jars **5.** plate **6.** skilful **7.** dragon lantern **8.** atmosphere **9.** timid **10.** in vain **11.** on Spring Festival

② play (tricks); juggle ≅ 施展〔**～宾**〕〈名〉～脾气❶；～威风❷；～花招儿❸；～鬼把戏❹；～心眼儿❺；～嘴皮子❻；～手腕❼；～笔杆子❽；～流氓❾；～贫嘴❿〈形〉～无赖⓫〔**～补**〕〈结〉～尽⓬了花招儿；～惯⓭了贫嘴；～够了威风〈趋〉～起贫嘴来没完没了(liǎo)；～起心眼儿来，谁也比不过他〈可〉在我们这里他～不了(liǎo)威风；在这儿～不起贫嘴来，因为没人理他〈时〉～了半天脾气〈量〉他～过好几次花招儿，都被我们戳穿⓮了；他总想在我面前～一下儿威风；～了一阵脾气〔**状～**〕别～；经常～；在我面前～；动不动⓯就～

1. get into a huff **2.** make a show of authority **3. 4.** tricks **5.** pull a smart trick **6.** talk glibly **7.** tricks; artifices **8.** wield a pen **9.** behave like a hoodlum; take liberties with women; act indecently **10.** garrulous; loquacious **11.** act shamelessly **12.** exhausted **13.** be used to **14.** puncture; expose; uncover; disclose **15.** easily; frequently; at every turn

shuāi 摔

① fall; tumble; lose one's balance ≅ 跌；栽〔**～宾**〕〈名〉不小心～了一交❶；～了一个跟头❷(筋斗)；头上～了一个大包❸〔**～补**〕〈结〉人～倒了；腿～瘸❹了；头～破❺了；～着(zháo)了没有？骨头❻～断❼了；～折❽(shé)了；～碎❾了；～裂❿了；～披⓫了；～成两截⓬了；他摔交都～怕了；胳膊⓭～伤⓮了；～肿⓯了；牙～掉了；嘴～流血⓰了；孩子～哭了；～破了一块皮；～晕⓱了；～昏迷⓲了；险些⓳～死〈趋〉扶⓴好了，别～下来；～到台阶㉑下边去了〈程〉～得真疼；～得不轻㉒啊！～得站不起来了；～得鼻青脸肿㉓〈可〉扶好了就～不着(zháo)了〈量〉年轻人～一下儿没关系；老年人～一下儿可不得了㉔(liǎo)〔**状～**〕不小心～了；从床上～下来了；扑通一声㉕～倒了；老人小孩都容易～

1. 2. tumble; trip and fall **3.** a swelling **4.** be lame; limp **5.** cut; wounded **6.** bone **7. 8.** snapped **9.** break to pieces **10. 11.** split **12.** in two halves **13.** arm **14.** be wounded **15.** be swollen **16.** shed blood; bleed **17.** dizzy; giddy **18.** lose consciousness **19.** narrowly;

② cause to fall and break ≅ 打破〔**主~**〕〈名〉茶杯~了；眼镜❶~了；镜子❷~了；茶壶❸~了；脸盆❹~了〔**~宾**〕〈名〉~了一个烟灰缸❺；~了一个灯泡❻〔**~补**〕〈结〉瓶子~碎了；盘子❼~成两半儿了；手表~坏了；罐头❽~瘪❾了；粉笔❿~折⓫(shé)了；~成两半了；~成两截⓬了〈程〉盘子和碗~得精光⓭〈可〉放在这儿~得了(liǎo)~不了(liǎo)？这东西很结实⓮，~不坏〔**状~**〕险些儿⓯~；可惜⓰~了！万一⓱~了；小心别~了；哐啷一声⓲~了

1. glasses 2. mirror 3. teapot 4. washbasin 5. ashtray 6. (electric) bulb 7. plate 8. tin; can 9. dented 10. chalk 11. snapped 12. in two halves 13. with nothing left 14. strong; solid 15. narrowly; nearly 16. it's a pity 17. just in case; if by any chance 18. crash

③ cast; throw; fling ≅ 扔〔**~宾**〕〈名〉他脾气❶特别不好，一生气就~东西；把门一~就出去了；把书包往桌子上一~就走了；~碗❷〔**~补**〕〈结〉~坏了；~碎❸了；~裂❹了；~折❺(shé)了；~断❻了；~在桌子上〈趋〉又一起东西来了；~到外边去了〈程〉~得太凶❼了；~得太可惜❽了〈时〉~半天了〈量〉~过好几次了；~了一阵〔**状~**〕往地上~；用力~；故意❾~；气呼呼地❿~；白白地⓫~了；一连~了好几个；经常~；吵吵嚷嚷地⓬~；丁当一声⓭~了

1. temperament; disposition 2. bowl 3. smashed to pieces 4. split 5. 6. snapped 7. awful; terrible; fearful 8. it's a pity 9. intentionally; on purpose 10. in a huff; panting with rage 11. in vain; for nothing 12. shout in confusion 13. with a clatter

shuǎi 甩 ① swing; crack (a whip) ≅ 摆动，抡〔**~宾**〕〈名〉~胳膊❶；~鞭子❷；马~尾巴❸；~辫子❹〔**~补**〕〈趋〉跑起来小辫子~来~去〈程〉体操队的运动员胳膊~得一样❺齐❻；鞭子~得真响〔**状~**〕往后~辫子；一前一后地~着胳膊；来回❼~

1. arm 2. whip 3. tail 4. braid 5. same as; just like 6. uniform; even 7. back and forth; to and fro

② throw; toss; fling ≅ 扔；摔〔**~宾**〕〈名〉~小石子儿；~墨水❶；~了我一身水；~手榴弹❷〔**~补**〕〈结〉手上的水都~干了〈趋〉孩子把小石子儿~出去了；把鞋~到很远；没注意❸把墨水都~到墙上去了〈程〉~得到处都是墨水儿〈可〉体温表❹的水银❺总~不下来；药片❻卡❼在小瓶❽子里~不出来〈时〉~了半天也甩不

出来; 水银柱❾~了半分钟才甩下去〈量〉~一下儿试试; ~了好几次〔状~〕使劲❿~; 用力~; 别到处乱⓫~

1. ink 2. hand grenade 3. through neligence; inattentively 4. (clinical) thermometer 5. mercury; quicksilver 6. (medicinal) tablet 7. block; check 8. bottle 9. mercury column 10. exert all one's strength 11. at random

③ leave sb. behind; abandon; throw off ≅ 丢开; 抛弃〔~宾〕〈名〉把多年的朋友们都~了; ~掉包袱❶〔~补〕〈结〉把盯梢❷的人~掉❸; 把他~开; 别把她一个人~在后边〈趋〉~到一边去了〈程〉~得很干脆❹; ~得很利索❺; ~得很痛快❻〈可〉那个坏蛋怎么甩也~不掉〈时〉~了半天才把那个密探❼甩掉〈量〉~了好几次都甩不掉〔状~〕尽快❽~; 立即~; 很难~; 不易~; 必须~; 终于~; 千方百计地❾~; 好容易~

1. cast off a burden 2. shadow sb. tail sb. 3. away; off 4. clear-cut; straightforward 5. agile; nimble 6. without hesitation 7. secret agent; spy 8. as quickly as possible 9. by hook or by crook

shuān 拴 tie; fasten ≅ 系↔解〔~宾〕〈名〉~一根绳子❶晒❷衣服; 树上~着一匹马; 用绳子~东西; ~船〔~补〕〈结〉~绳子结实❸点儿; 把狗用铁链子❹~

上吧, 别让它乱跑; 把船~住; 把马~在树上; 铁丝❺没~直; 没~紧❻; ~松❼了; 把两条船~在一起〈趋〉把牛~起来吧, 免得❽它跑了〈程〉绳子~得太松; ~得很紧〈可〉绳子不结实, ~不住; 没有柱子❾~不了(liǎo)铁丝; 她手劲大❿, 绳子总~不紧; 我从来没拴过, 怕~不好〈时〉~了十几分钟才拴上〈量〉~了好几次; 帮我~一下儿; 随便⓫~一下儿〔状~〕赶快~; 往哪~? 多~几道; 不能那样~; 紧紧地~

1. rope 2. dry in the sun 3. fast; strong 4. iron chain 5. iron wire 6. tight; close 7. loose 8. so as not to; so as to avoid 9. pillar; post; column 10. strength 11. casually; at random

shuàn 涮 ① rinse〔~宾〕〈名〉~~手; ~盘子❶; ~茶壶❷; ~锅❸; ~衣服〔~补〕〈结〉把衣服~干净了再晾❹; 把瓶子~干净再装❺东西; 杯子里的茶叶❻~掉了吗?〈趋〉她特别爱干净, ~起杯子来没完〈程〉~得真干净〈可〉瓶子里的脏东西~不出来了; ~得干净~不干净?〈时〉~了一会儿; ~了好半天〈量〉再~一下儿; 又~了一遍〔状~〕多~; 在净水里~; 用开水❼~; 一遍一遍地❽~

1. plate 2. kettle 3. pot; pan 4. dry in the air 5. hold; pack; load 6. tea 7. boiling water 8. over and over again

② scald thin slices of meat in boiling water; instant-boil 〔~宾〕〈名〉~羊肉；~锅子❶〔~补〕〈结〉肉❷~熟❸了吗？〈趋〉再~下去肉就老❹了〈程〉~得太多了；~得时间不够〈可〉这个火锅❺~不了两斤肉〈时〉~了半天；再~一会儿〈量〉~一次尝尝❻〔状~〕用开水❼~；在火锅里~

1. instant-boil of meat and vegetables in a chafing dish 2. meat 3. cooked; done 4. tough 5. chafing dish 6. taste; try the flavour of 7. boiling water

shuì 睡 sleep↔醒〔~宾〕〈名〉~午觉；~了一个大觉〔~补〕〈结〉~着❶(zháo)了；~醒❷了；今天可~够❸了；还没~足❹啊？~过站了；都快~迷糊❺了；你~糊涂❻了吧？昨天早上~过头❼了，差点儿迟到❽〈趋〉一觉~下去了，连饭都没吃；他~起觉来多大的声音都吵不醒❾〈程〉~得真实❿；~得真沉⓫；~得真香⓬；~得很安稳⓭；心里有事⓮，~得不踏实⓯；~得迷迷糊糊的〈可〉我老~不够；他总~不醒；~不上两个小时就醒了〈时〉~了一天一夜；刚~一会儿；每天中午只~十分钟〔状~〕总~不着(zháo)；经常~不好；早~早起；从来不~午觉；早点儿~吧；蒙头大~⓰；坐着~了一会儿；他喜欢仰着⓱（侧着⓲／趴着⓳）~；整整~了一天；安安稳稳地~；踏踏实实地~；安然地⓴~

1. fall asleep 2. wake up; be awake 3. 4. enough 5. dazed with sleep 6. muddled; confused; bewildered 7. sleep in 8. be late 9. not awoke 10. 11. 12. soundly 13. peacefully 14. have sth. on one's mind 15. not quietly 16. tuck oneself in and sleep like a log 17. on one's back 18. on one's side 19. on one's stomach 20. peacefully; quietly

shùn 顺 arrange; put in order 〔~宾〕〈名〉把这些筷子❶~一~，不要这么横七竖八❷的；一~书架❸上那些乱七八糟❹的书；~一~卡片❺；~一~这篇文章里不通❻的句子〔~补〕〈结〉把筷子~好了〈趋〉把船一只一只地~过来〈可〉~不过来了〔状~〕再~一~；好好~一~

1. chopsticks 2. in disorder; at sixes and sevens 3. book-shelf 4. in disorder; in a mess; in a muddle 5. cards 6. not make sense; be illogical; be ungrammatical

shuō 说 ① speak; talk; say〔主~〕〈名〉天气预报❶~；报上~；社论❷~；广播❸~；心里~〔~宾〕〈名〉你怎么不~话？~实话❹；不要~空话❺；我最怕人~大话❻；你可真爱~笑话；她专会~俏皮话❼；那个人只会~漂亮话❽；我从来没~过一句假话；妈妈一边~着话，一边收拾❾东西；我一向是~话算数❿的；他净~瞎话⓫；别~谎话⓬；别~梦话⓭了；我只会~英语，不会~日语；他会~哪几种外语？你会~普通话⓮吗？你给大家~一个故事吧；怕别人~闲话⓯；~相声⓰〈代〉你~怎么样？有什么~什么，别客气〈动〉我~买，他~不买〈形〉我~冷，他~不冷〈主-谓〉他母亲~他不在家；医生~她得了肝炎⓱〔~补〕〈结〉话~错了；他们~好了明天早上八点见；两个人的意见~拧⓲(nǐng)了；应该把话~清楚；~穿⓳了也没什么；他们两个人话都~绝⓴了；~尽㉑了；嘴都快~破㉒了，他还是不听；~死㉓了也不去；~走嘴㉔(~漏嘴)了；~快了听不懂；还没~上两句就吵起来了；她又滔滔不绝地㉕~开了；故事~到哪儿了？这话简直~到我们心坎㉖上了；把话先~在前头；把他的心都~活㉗了；把人都~烦了〈趋〉~起来容易做起来难；~起来话长；把你想到的都~出来吧；这件事情你可别~出去；话又~回来了，就是你马上走也来不及啊！~来~去还是那么几句话〈程〉她说话~得真快；事情经过~得很详尽；话~得非常有分寸㉘；理由~得不十分充足；~得很圆滑㉙〈可〉他的名字我一时~不上来了；这种话可~不得；骂人㉚的话我~不出口；这个我可~不清，哭得~不下去了；这东西~不上是好还是坏；我跟他认识，但~不上熟悉；跑得直喘气㉛一句话也~不上来了；感动得一句话也~不出来了；她的嘴很利害，谁也~不过她〈时〉两个人在门口~了一夜；~了两个小时〈量〉~过两遍了；把情况给我们~一下儿吧〔状~〕准确地~；按理㉜~；傲慢地㉝~；诡秘地㉞~；懊悔地㉟~；旁敲侧击地㊱~；有气无力地㊲~；实~㊳了吧；真诚地㊴~；假装㊵~；一边哭一边~；声音沙哑地㊶~；厉声㊷对我~；无可奈何地㊸~；冷冷㊹地~；假惺惺地㊺~；娇滴滴地㊻~；恶狠狠地㊼~；装腔作势地㊽~；赌气地㊾~；委屈地㊿~；蛮不讲理地51~；强词夺理地52~；瞪着眼睛53~；哭哭啼啼地54~；唉声叹气地55~；眉飞色舞地56~；细声细气地57~；笑嘻嘻地58~；手舞足蹈地59~；严肃地~；热情地~；温和地~；主动地~；耸耸肩膀60~；慢条斯理地61~；慢吞吞地62~；绘声绘色地63~；大大方方地64~；口口声声地65~；咬牙切齿地66~；婆婆妈妈地67~；暗地里~；私下68~；鬼鬼祟祟地69~；一五一十地70~；滔滔不绝地71~；口若悬河地72~；信口开河地73~；怒气冲冲地74~；不慌不忙地~；咬文嚼字地75~；交头接耳地76~；羞羞答答地77~；夸夸其谈地78~

1. weather forecast **2.** editorial **3.** broadcast **4.** truth **5.** empty talk **6.** big talk **7.** witty remark; witticism **8.** fine words; high sounding words **9.** tidy; put in order; clear away **10.** mean what one says **11. 12. 13.** words uttered in one's sleep **14.** common speech (of the Chinese language) 15. complaint 16. comic dialogue 17. hepatitis 18. differ; disagree 19. tell what sth. really is 20. leaving no leeway 21. without reserve 22. cut (take a lot of talking) 23. no matter (what, how, etc.); in any case; anyway 24. inadvertently blurt out 25. talk on and on in a flow of eloquence 26. the bottom of one's heart 27. movable; flexible 28. proper limits for speech or action 29. oily; slippery; cunning 30. swear (at people) 31. pant; gasp; breathe deeply 32. according to reason; normally 33. arrogantly 34. surreptitiously 35. regretfully 36. make oblique references 37. weakly 38. to tell the truth 39. sincerely; honestly 40. pretend; feign 41. hoarsely; huskily 42. in a stern voice 43. have no way out; have no alternative 44. coldly 45. hypocritically; unctuously 46. affectedly sweet; delicately pretty 47. fiercely; ferociously 48. be affected or pretentious; strike a pose 49. feel wronged and act rashly 50. feel wronged 51. be impervious to reason 52. use lame arguments; reason fallaciously 53. open (one's eyes) wide 54. endlessly weep and wail 55. have deep sighs; moan and groan 56. with dancing eyebrows and radiant face; exultantly 57. in a soft voice 58. smiling broadly 59. dance for joy 60. shrug one's shoulders 61. leisurely; unhurriedly 62. at a leisurely pace 63. lively; vividly 64. generously 65. say again and again 66. gnash one's teeth 67. womanishly fussy 68. privately 69. furtively; stealthily 70. systematically 71. talk on and on in a flow of eloquence 72. let loose a flood of eloquence 73. talk irresponsibly 74. angrily 75. pay excessive attention to wording 76. speak in each other's ears; whisper to each other 77. feel embarrassed; shyly 78. indulge in exaggerations

② explain ≡ 解释〔**~宾**〕〈名〉~~你昨天没来的原因❶；~~你不去的理由❷；~一~这个词的含义❸；~~这段话的意思❹；~一~风的起因❺；~一~开会的目的；~一~学好语音❻的重要性；~一~这种药❼的使用方法❽；~一~打太极拳❾的好处❿；~一~你的想法；~一~油画儿⓫的特点⓬〈主－谓〉~一~你昨天为什么没做练习〔**~补**〕〈结〉请你把道理~清楚；他没~明白；他终于把我~服⓭了；把道理~透⓮了；这个词的用法我~错了〈趋〉这个道理太深奥⓯，我~出来恐怕你也不懂；一~起体育锻炼⓰的好处来，他就滔滔不绝⓱〈程〉~得非常清楚；~得乱七八糟的；~得太详细⓳了；~得头头是道⓴〈可〉这样做有点儿~不过去；道理我懂了，但是~不出来〈时〉我~了半天，你一点儿都没懂啊？〈量〉~了好几遍，他

才领会❷❶；请你～一下儿〔状～〕不必❷❷～了；仔细～～；从头～～；白❷❸～了；随便❷❹～了～

1. cause 2. reason 3. meaning; implication 4. meaning 5. cause; origin 6. pronunciation 7. drug; medicine 8. usage 9.*taijiquan*, a kind of traditional Chinese shadow boxing 10. benefit; good; advantage 11. oil painting 12. characteristic 13. persuade 14. thoroughly (explained) 15. abstruse; profound 16. physical training 17. talk on and on in a flow of eloquence 18. at sixes and sevens; in a mess 19. too detailed 20. clear and logical 21. understand; comprehend; grasp 22. need not; not have to 23. in vain 24. casually

③ scold ≃ 批评；责备〔～宾〕〈代〉你明明知道他说谎❶也不～～他〔～补〕〈结〉把他～急❷了；话～重(zhòng)❸了〈程〉～得我哑口无言❹；～得他很不好意思❺；～得她满脸通红❻〈时〉～了他半天〈量〉～了他一顿；～了很多遍〔状～〕狠狠地❼～；耐心地❽～；严厉地❾～；当面❿～；私下⓫～；个别⓬～

1. tell a lie; lie 2. irritated; annoyed; nettled 3. too strongly 4. dumb-founded 5. feel embarrassed 6. blush scarlet 7. fiercely; ferociously 8. patiently 9. severely 10. in the face of; face to face 11. privately 12. individually

shuōmíng 说明 explain; illustrate; show ≃ 解释〔～宾〕〈名〉～原因❶；～情况；～用法；～理由❷；～事实真相❸；～问题；～自己的意见；～我们的主张❹；～机器的性能❺；～去向❻〈主－谓〉事实～她做的完全对；他字写得这么好，～他一定用了不少时间练习〔～补〕〈可〉这个例子～不了(liǎo)问题〈量〉～一下儿〔状～〕简单地❼～；反复～；耐心❽～；详细❾～；用文字～；口头❿～；向大家～；充分～

1. cause 2. reason 3. the truth of the fact 4. view; position; stand; proposition 5. function; property 6. the direction in which sb. or sth. has gone 7. concisely 8. patiently; with patience 9. in detail 10. orally

sī 撕 tear; rip ≃ 扯〔～宾〕〈名〉小心点儿，别～了衣服；～了两张照片；～了一张画儿；衣服～了一个大口子❶；～了一堆废纸❷；～了几封旧信〔～补〕〈结〉把信～开了；把旧衣服～碎❸了；把纸～成碎片❹了；～下了他的假面具❺；把纸折❻好，～齐❼点儿；～直❽点儿；怎么把书皮❾～掉了？别把纸～破❿了〈趋〉把今天的日历⓫～下来了；从本子上～下一页纸来〈程〉～得真齐；～得粉碎⓬〈可〉～不直，还是剪⓭吧；布要先剪一个口儿⓮，才～得开〈时〉～了半天也没撕下来〈量〉不用剪，～一下儿就行了〔状～〕用手～；使劲～；先剪个口子再～；急急忙忙地⓯～；不小心～了；故意⓰～；幸亏⓱～了；实在⓲～不动；差一点儿～了；气呼呼地⓳～

1. cut **2.** waste paper **3.** torn to pieces **4.** slices **5.** mask **6.** fold **7.** neat; even uniform **8.** straight **9.** book cover **10.** torn **11.** calendar **12.** torn to pieces **13.** cut **14.** opening; tear **15.** in a hurry **16.** intentionally **17.** fortunately; luckily **18.** really; truly **19.** angrily

sǐ 死 die↔生；活〔**主～**〕〈名〉这棵树～了；庄稼❶～了；狗吃了有毒❷的药～了；喷❸了药以后虫子都～了；你走的这个棋❹已经～了〔**～宾**〕〈名〉动物园里～了一只老虎；她三岁就～了母亲；她对这件事还没～心❺〔**～补**〕〈结〉亲属❻都～光了；～在战场❼上了；～于非命❽〈趋〉痛❾得～过去❿了〈程〉他～得真惨⓫；～得太可怜⓬了；～得真奇怪⓭；～得莫明其妙⓮；～得糊里糊涂⓯；～得很突然；～得很干脆⓰；～得真受罪⓱〈可〉这棵树～得了(liǎo)～不了(liǎo)？〈时〉她母亲～了二十年了〔**状～**〕眼看⓲就要～了；他父母早就～了；痛苦地⓳～；差点儿～；突然～了；莫明其妙地～了〔**习用**〕～马当作活马医⓴

1. crop **2.** poisonous **3.** spray; sprinkle **4.** chess **5.** have no more illusions about the matter **6.** relatives **7.** battlefield; battleground **8.** die a violent death **9.** pain; ache **10.** lose consciousness **11.** miserable **12.** pitiful; pitiable; poor **13.** strange; surprising **14.** without rhyme or reason **15.** muddled **16.** quickly; rapidly **17.** endure hardships **18.** soon; in a moment **19.** painfully; bitterly **20.** doctor a dead horse as if it were still alive — not give up for lost; make every possible effort

sòng 送 ① deliver; carry 〔**～宾**〕〈名〉～货❶；～杂志❷；～信；～报；你去给她～个信儿❸；～情报❹；～雨伞；给病人～菜；～牛奶〔**～补**〕〈结〉货还没～到；电报已经～到了；东西～到他手里了；今天报纸～晚了；信～错了；文件❺～给秘书室❻了〈趋〉这种中药❼不好吃，用了半杯水还没～下去；把产品❽用传送带❾～上来了；把信～到信箱❿里去吧！〈程〉牛奶～得特别早；货～得不全〈可〉信明天～得到～不到？这么多牛奶，一上午～得完吗？秘密文件⓫～得出去～不出去？〈时〉～了二十多年信；～了一上午报纸〈量〉～了三趟；～过两次〔**状～**〕按时⓬～；定期⓭～；立即⓮～；顺便⓯～；特意⓰～；每天～；偶尔⓱～；及时～；往哪儿～？给我们～；风雨无阻地⓲～；认真⓳负责⓴地～；挨家挨户地㉑～

1. goods **2.** magazine **3.** message; word; information **4.** information 5. documents; papers 6. secretary office 7. traditional Chinese medicine 8. product 9. conveyor belt 10. letter box 11. secret papers; confidential document 12. on time 13. at regular intervals 14. at once; immediately 15. conveniently; in passing 16. specially 17. occasionally; once in a while 18. stopped by neither wind nor rain; rain or shine 19. seriously; conscientiously 20. responsibly 21. from door to door

② give as a present ≅ 赠送〔~宾〕〈代〉她~我一张画儿；我~他一首诗；我想~你一套❶茶具❷；~她一个项链❸；~你什么礼物？~个人情❹〔~补〕〈结〉他不懂法文，我却送给他一本法文小说，真是~错人了〈趋〉把礼物~到他家去了〈程〉~得不合适❺；~得太贵重❻了〈可〉我~不起那么贵的东西〈量〉~了三次礼都被他退❼回来了〔状~〕从来不~礼；多~点儿；无须~；偷着❽~；暗中❾~；一次一次地~；热情地❿~；主动⓫~；白⓬~

1. a set 2. tea set 3. necklace 4. gift; favour 5. not suitable 6. valuable; precious 7. return send back 8. stealthily; secretly 9. secretly; furtively 10. warmly 11. on one's own initiative 12. in vain

③ see sb. off or out〔~宾〕〈名〉~客人❶；~孩子去幼儿园❷；~病人去医院；~亲戚❸上火车〈代〉~你几步；~了她一段路❹〈动〉明天我要去给朋友~行❺；给谁~葬❻？~殡❼〔~补〕〈结〉把客人~走了；~完了朋友就回来了；~出了大门；~上了火车〈趋〉把孩子~到托儿所❽去了；~进幼儿园去了吗？~下楼去了；~到屋里去了；我把小王~回去了；把骨灰盒~到墓地❿去了；~到哪儿去？〈程〉~得太远了〈可〉我今天没有时间，~不了(liǎo)你了；一天的时间~不到〈量〉~过两次朋友；~过好几趟了〔状~〕热情地⓫~；主动地⓬~；一直~到家；别~了，请回吧；为他~葬；勉强⓭~；只好~

1. guest 2. nursery school 3. relatives 4. a section of road 5. see sb. off; wish sb. bon voyage 6. 7. take part in a funeral procession 8. nursery; child-care centre 9. cinerary casket 10. graveyard 11. warmly 12. on one's own initiative 13. reluctantly; grudgingly

sōu 搜 search ≅ 搜查〔~宾〕〈名〉~身❶；~腰包❷；~赃款❸；~赃物❹；~罪证❺；~毒品❻；~武器❼〔~补〕〈结〉都~遍❽了；没~着(zháo)〈趋〉~出来毒品就没(mò)收❾〈程〉~得很仔细❿；~得很彻底⓫；~得太马虎⓬；~得非常严⓭〈可〉~着(zháo)吗？谁也~不出来〈时〉~了半天；~了好长时间〈量〉~过一遍，再~一下儿；~了一阵〔状~〕仔细~；来回~；浑身上

下⓮～；一遍一遍地～；挨个儿⓯～；到处～

1. search the person; make a body search 2. search sb.'s pockets; search sb. for money and valuables 3. money stolen; embezzled or received in bribes; illicit money 4. stolen goods 5. evidence of a crime 6. narcotic drugs 7. weapon; arms 8. everywhere 9. confiscate 10. careful 11. thorough 12. careless 13. strict 14. all over the body 15. one by one

sōubǔ 搜捕 track down and arrest 〔～宾〕〈名〉～杀人凶手❶；～逃犯❷；～小偷；～流氓❸；～坏人〔～补〕〈结〉～着(zháo)了；～到了〈趋〉开始～起来了；继续～下去〈可〉～得到吗？〈时〉～了很长时间；～了一个多星期〈量〉好好～一下儿；再～一遍〔状～〕到处～；积极～；彻底～；连夜❹～；连续❺～；全面～；大～

1. murderer; manslayer 2. escaped criminal 3. rogue; hoodlum 4. the same night; that very night 5. continuously; in succession

sōuchá 搜查 search; ransack ≅查；搜寻〔～宾〕〈名〉～小偷；～流氓❶；～逃犯❷；～走私犯❸；～枪弹❹；～毒品❺；～赃物❻；～凶器❼；～血衣❽；～罪证❾〔～补〕〈结〉～遍❿了；～到了；～错了〈趋〉继续～下去；在他家里～起来了〈程〉～得很严⓫；～得很急⓬；～得很细⓭；～得很及时⓮〈可〉一上午～不完；人少了～不了(liǎo)；就是～不出来〈时〉～了好几个月；多～一会儿〈量〉～了好几遍；再～一下儿〔状～〕好好～～；不便⓯～；无须⓰～；连日～；彻底～；四处～；大胆～；细心⓱～；别马马虎虎地⓲～；严密⓳～；挨户⓴～

1. rogue; hoodlum 2. escaped criminal 3. smuggler 4. cartridge 5. narcotic drugs 6. stolen goods; booty 7. tool or weapon for criminal purposes 8. blood-stained garment 9. evidence of a crime 10. everywhere; all over 11. strict; severe; stern 12. urgent 13. careful 14. in time 15. inconveniently; inappropriately 16. needlessly 17. carefully 18. carelessly 19. closely 20. one by one

sōuguā 搜刮 ≅ 掠夺 extort; plunder; expropriate; fleece 〔～宾〕〈名〉～钱财❶；～财物❷；～地皮❸〔～补〕〈结〉～净了；～光了〈趋〉都～到自己腰包❹里去了〔状～〕拼命❺～；千方百计地❻～；绞尽脑汁地❼～；不择手段地❽～；毫无顾忌地❾～；明目张胆地❿～

1. wealth; money 2. property 3. land for building 4. purse; pocket 5. with all one's might 6. by every possible means; by hook

or by crook 7. rack one's brains 8. by fair means or foul; unscrupulously 9. without any scruples; brazenly 10. in a barefaced way; before one's very eyes

sōují 搜集 collect; gather ≅ 汇集〔～宾〕〈名〉～情报❶；～民间歌谣❷；～民间传说❸；～民间故事❹；～意见❺；～了很多种贝壳❻；～材料❼；～史料❽；～文物❾ ～各种标本❿；～各种邮票⓫；～废铜烂铁⓬〔～补〕〈结〉标本都～全了，情报～到了〈趋〉把意见～起来，好好研究研究⓭〈程〉标本～得很全〈可〉～得到那么多吗？～不着什么重要的情报；品种太多，一时⓮～不齐〈时〉～了很多年才把标本搜集全了〈量〉好好～一下儿，看看有多少〔状～〕经常⓯～；从各方面⓰～；耐心地⓱～；一点一滴地⓲～；不辞辛苦地⓳～；广泛⓴～

1. intelligence; information 2. folk song 3. folk legend 4. folk story 5. opinion 6. shell 7. material 8. historical data 9. cultural relic 10. all kinds of specimen (sample) 11. stamp 12. scrap 13. study 14. for the moment 15. frequently; often 16. from every respect 17. patiently 18. little by little 19. make nothing of hardships 20. widely

sōuluó 搜罗 collect; gather; recruit〔～宾〕〈名〉～了大量史料❶；～人才❷；～了不少残兵败将❸〔～补〕〈结〉史料～齐了；没～全〈趋〉都～进来了；～到他名下来❹了〈可〉～得全吗？〈时〉～了很多年〔状～〕广泛地❺～；从全国各地～；多方～；一点一点地～；四处～

1. historical data 2. a person's ability; qualified personnel 3. remnants of a routed army 4. under sb.'s name 5. widely

sōusuǒ 搜索 search for; hunt for; scout around〔～宾〕〈名〉～残敌❶；～枯肠❷也想不出一句好诗来〔～补〕〈结〉～遍了〈趋〉～出来了好几个残敌；开始～起来了〈程〉～得敌人无处藏身❸；～得小偷无处躲藏❹；～得很仔细❺；～得很彻底❻〈可〉～不出好句子来〈时〉～了半天；～了一个星期〈量〉～过两次；～了一遍〔状～〕认真～；四处～；挖空心思❼地～词句❽

1. surviving enemy 2. rack one's brains 3. find no shelter 4. have no place to hide 5. careful 6. thorough 7. rack one's brains 8. words and phrases; expressions

sōuxún 搜寻 search for; seek; look for ≅ 搜查〔～宾〕〈名〉～敌人❶；～罪犯❷；～逃犯❸；～材料❹〔～补〕〈结〉～到了；～着(zháo)了〈趋〉在附近～起来了〈程〉～得很仔细❺；～得太马虎❻了〈可〉～得出来吗？〈时〉～了

不少时候❼了〈量〉~了两遍；好好~一下儿〔状~〕在哪儿~？正在~；反复❽~；到处~；尽快❾~；必须~

1. enemy 2. criminal 3. escaped criminal or convict 4. material 5. careful 6. careless 7. a long time 8. over and over again 9. as soon as possible

sùkǔ 诉苦 vent one's grievances; pour out one's woes ≅ 诉委屈〔~补〕〈结〉诉完了苦❶〈趋〉有什么苦都诉出来吧；她诉起苦来就没完没了〈可〉他有诉不完的苦〈时〉诉了半天苦〈量〉诉了一通苦；诉过好几次苦〔状~〕没完没了(liǎo)地~；眼泪汪汪地❷~；偷偷地~；一遍一遍地~；从来不~

1. hardship; suffering 2. tearfully

sùqīng 肃清 eliminate; clean up; mop up ≅ 清除〔~宾〕〈名〉~不良影响❶；~封建思想❷；~残余势力❸；~土匪❹；~残匪❺；~暗藏的敌人❻〔状~〕必须~；彻底~；完全~；逐步❼~；逐渐❽~；尚未❾~；及早❿~

1. harmful effects 2. feudal ideology 3. remaining forces 4. bandit 5. surviving bandit 6. hidden enemy 7. 8. gradually 9. not yet 10. as soon as possible

sùzào 塑造 model; mould; portray〔~宾〕〈名〉~石膏像❶；~铜像❷；~了一个英雄形象❸；~大理石❹像〔~补〕〈结〉头像~坏了；~成半身像了〈趋〉他~出来的人物都很威武❺〈程〉~得很成功〈可〉~不好石膏像〈时〉~了半年多〈量〉~过一次〔状~〕第一次~；专门❻~；特意❼~；成功地~；大胆❽~；精心❾~

1. plaster figure 2. bronze statue 3. image of hero 4. marble 5. powerful; mighty 6. 7. specially 8. boldly 9. elaborately; painstakingly

suàn 算 ① calculate; reckon ≅ 计算〔~宾〕〈名〉~帐❶；~钱；~水电费❷；~~成本❸〈动〉~~需要❹多少钱；~~花❺了几块钱；~~浪费❻了多少时间〔~补〕〈结〉帐~错了；钱~多了；题都~完了；旅费❼~清了吗？~到哪一天为止〈趋〉他~起帐来真是一清二楚❽；这道题非常难，我~了半天才算出来；这笔住院费❾~下来得(děi)二百多块；不算了，再一下去我头都疼了〈程〉~得真快；~得清清楚楚；~得乱七八糟❿；帐~得糊里糊涂⓫；~得太马虎⓬了，~得非常仔细⓭；~得很精确⓮〈可〉这道题你~得上来~不上来？这笔帐怎么~都~不对；用电子计算机⓯就不会~错了；该交多少钱，我~不出来〈时〉~了一个小时才算

出来；～了一天帐〈量〉～过两遍了；又仔细地～了一下儿，我还欠⓰你五块钱〔**状～**〕细心地～马马虎虎地～；多～几遍；一笔一笔地～；一齐⓱～；埋头⓲～；用心～；用算盘⓳～；认真～；反复～；从头儿～；一遍一遍地⓴～；重新～

1. account **2.** charges for water and electricity **3.** cost **4.** need **5.** spend **6.** waste **7.** travelling expenses **8.** clear **9.** hospitalization expenses **10.** in confusion; in a mess **11.** muddled **12.** careless **13.** careful **14.** exact **15.** calculator **16.** owe **17.** at the same time; simultaneously **18.** immerse oneself in **19.** abacus **20.** over and over again

② include; count ≃ 包括〔**～宾**〕〈代〉～她一份；～这个不～？〔**～补**〕〈结〉～上我一共三个人；～上下星期日，一共还有十天；把她～在内〈趋〉把他～进来了；把假日❶也～进去了〔**状～**〕别～我；必须～；统统❷～进去；只好～

1. holiday **2.**completely; all; entirely

③ consider; regard as ≃ 算作；当作〔**～宾**〕〈名〉我～什么专家❶，比起别人来差远了；这点小病不～回事；她可以～一个好管家❷〈名〉谁做～谁的；你们挑❸剩下❹的都～我的〈动〉有人说；偷❺书不～偷；你～是打听❻对了〈形〉这不～太贵❼；一个业余歌唱家❽唱得这样，就～不错了；年纪虽然大了，身体还～结实❾；那个孩子不～笨❿〈主－谓〉今天～我请客；～你说对了；说了你不听就～我白⓫说了；今天遇⓬到你了，～我倒霉⓭〔**～补**〕〈结〉把他～成专家了〈可〉这点缺点⓮～不了(liǎo)什么；你打了人家，也～不得什么英雄⓯；他～不上才子⓰；这一点不顺利⓱～不上什么打击⓲〔**状～**〕勉强⓳～；千万别～她；不～什么；一律⓴～；仍旧㉑～；当然～

1. specialist **2.** good manager **3.** choose; select **4.** be left over; remain **5.** steal **6.** ask about; inquire about **7.** expensive; dear **8.** amateur singer **9.** strong **10.** cuckoo **11.** in vain; for nothing **12.** meet **13.** have bad luck; be out of luck **14.** shortcoming **15.** hero **16.** gifted scholar **17.** not smoothly **18.** blow **19.** might **20.** all; without exception **21.** still

④ think; suppose; divine ≃ 推测；料想〔**～宾**〕〈名〉～命❶；～卦❷〈主－谓〉～～他哪天回来？我～着你今天该来了〔**～补**〕〈结〉我～准❸了你今天来，果然来了〈程〉他～得很准；～得一点也不错〈可〉我～不出他什么时候回来〈时〉那个瞎子❹给我们～了半天命〈量〉小时候别人给我～过一次命〔**状～**〕从来不～；用扑克牌❺～；自己给自己～；偷偷地～

1. fortune-telling **2.** divinatory symbols **3.** exact; accurate **4.** blind man **5.** playing cards

⑤ hold; stand ≅ 算数〔~宾〕〈名〉说话~话; 说一句~一句〔状~〕必须~; 他说了不~; 一定~〔习用〕~了, 别说了

sǔnhài 损害 harm; damage; injure〔~宾〕〈名〉不能~别人的利益❶; ~集体❷的事情绝对❸不能做; 光线❹太弱❺, 看书容易~视力❻; 污浊的空气❼会~健康; 肥料❽用多了反而❾要~庄稼❿〔~补〕〈趋〉这种光线~起眼睛来非常利害〈程〉庄稼被虫子~得一塌糊涂⓫〈可〉~不了(liǎo)我们一根毫毛⓬〔状~〕容易~; 被冰雹⓭~; 无意中⓮~; 严重地⓯~

1. interest 2. collective 3. absolutely 4. light 5. dim 6. eyesight 7. foul air 8. fertilizer; manure 9. on the contrary 10. crops 11. in an awful state 12. single hair 13. hail 14. inadvertently; accidentally 15. seriously

sǔnhuài 损坏 damage; injure〔~宾〕〈名〉~公物❶; 糖吃多了容易~牙齿❷; 不能~庄稼❸; 不要~家具❹〔状~〕故意❺~; 完全~; 部分❻~

1. public property 2. tooth 3. crops 4. furniture 5. on purpose 6. partly

sǔnshī 损失 lose〔~宾〕〈名〉~了很多东西; ~了一点儿钱财❶; ~了一大笔❷财产❸; ~了不少粮食❹; ~了一船货❺〔~补〕〈程〉~得不太多〈可〉~不了(liǎo)多少钱〈量〉~过两次〔状~〕统统❻~了; 只~了一部分; 所有的财物❼都~了; 无意中❽~; 险些❾~; 差点儿~; 几乎~; 万一❿~

1. wealth; money 2. a large sum 3. property 4. food 5. cargo 6. wholly; totally 7. property; belongings 8. inadvertently; accidentally 9. narrowly; nearly 10. just in case; if by any chance

suō 缩 ① contract; shrink ≅ 抽〔~宾〕〈名〉这种布不~水❶; ~了一大截❷〔~补〕〈结〉衣服~短了; 都~成什么样子了！〈趋〉再~下去就穿不了(liǎo)了〈程〉衣服缩水~得太多了; ~得太短了; ~得没法儿穿了〈可〉这种料子❸怎么洗也~不了(liǎo)〈量〉洗一次~一次〔状~〕一洗就~

1. (of cloth through wetting) shrink 2. length 3. material

② draw back; withdraw; recoil ↔伸〔~补〕〈结〉乌龟❶的头老~在壳儿里〈趋〉快把腿❸~回去, 不然❹会把人绊倒❺的; 开开门左右❻看了一下儿, 又把头~进去了; 刚伸手❼要拿, 想了想又把手~回去了〈程〉头~得真快〈可〉小偷刚一伸手偷东西就被人抓住❽〔状~〕老鼠又~进洞❾里去了; 蜗牛❿很快就~回壳里

去了；冷得脖子⓫直往大衣领子⓬里~

1. tortoise 2. shell 3. leg 4. otherwise 5. stumble; trip 6. right and left 7. stretch out one's hand 8. catch 9. hole 10. snail 11. neck 12. the collar of the coat

suǒ 锁 ① lock〔~宾〕〈名〉~箱子❶；~抽屉❷；~保险柜❸；紧~着双眉❹〔~补〕〈结〉把门~上；钱都~在保险柜里了；把钥匙❺~在屋子里了〈趋〉狗被~起来了〈程〉柜子❻~得很结实❼〈可〉锁坏了，~不了(liǎo)了；~不住〈量〉我手里拿的东西太多了；请你帮我~一下儿门〔状~〕好好~上；这种锁好不好~？真难~；紧紧地~；一道一道地~；咔嚓一声❽~上了；随手❾~

1. box; case 2. drawer 3. safe 4. the eyebrows 5. key 6. cupboard; cabinet 7. firm; fast; durable 8. with a crack 9. conveniently; without extra trouble

② lockstitch ≅ 缝〔~宾〕〈名〉~边儿❶；~扣眼❷〔~补〕〈结〉~快点儿；~整齐❸点儿；~歪了❹；~大了〈趋〉她~出来的扣眼不一般大〈程〉~得太慢；~得挺❺不错〈可〉~不好；~不整齐〈时〉~一会儿就完了〈量〉~过一次；~一下儿试试〔状~〕用缝纫机❻~；用手~；一个一个地~；别~歪了

1. border 2. buttonhole 3. neat and tidy 4. askew; crooked; slanting 5. very; rather; quite 6. sewing machine

T

tā 塌 ① collapse; fall down; cave in; sink ≅ 下陷〔主~〕〈名〉桥❶~了；楼要~；地~了一个坑❷；地板❸~了一块；防空洞❹可别~了；房顶❺~了；墙~了一段❻；积木❼~了〔~补〕〈趋〉这条马路年久失修❽，有的地方都~下去了〈程〉房子~得没办法修了〈可〉踩❾上去房顶得了(liǎo)~不了(liǎo)；那么结实❿，~不了(liǎo)吧；〈时〉房子~了好几年了也没有人管〈量〉防空洞~过一次〔状~〕容易~；全部~了；墙哗啦一声⓫~了；突然~了

1. bridge 2. hole 3. floor 4. air-raid shelter 5. roof 6. a section 7. toy bricks; building blocks 8. have long been out of repair; fall into disrepair 9. step on; trample 10. solid; durable 11. with a crash

② sink; droop ≅ 凹下；下垂〔~补〕〈趋〉她瘦❶得两腮❷都~下去了；~进去了〔状~〕一下子~；转眼就~

1. be emaciated 2. cheeks

tái 抬 ① lift; raise ≅ 举；提高〔~宾〕〈名〉~头看月亮；她坐在那里看书，半天连头都没~；他一手就打人；~腿就跑；~~胳膊❶，你压❷住我的东西了〔~补〕〈结〉商人❸千方百计地❹~高物价❺；她总是打击别人，~高自己❻〈趋〉她一起头来看着黑板〈程〉正步❼走时腿~得比较高〈可〉胳膊疼得~不起来了；羞❽得头都~不起来了〈量〉一下儿腿❾让我过去〔状~〕多~一会儿；一直~着；慢慢地~

1. arm 2. press 3. businessman; merchant; trader 4. by every possible means; by hook or by crook 5. enhance (rise) prices 6. attack others so as to build up oneself 7. parade step 8. shy 9. leg

② (of two or more persons) carry〔~宾〕〈名〉~担架❶；~柜子❷；~东西〔~补〕〈结〉把桌子~高点儿；把这堆❸土~走吧〈趋〉请把床~到二楼去吧；地毯❹已经~上去了；把沙发❺~进来了；煤气罐❻太重，请你帮我~下去吧；洗衣机❼拿去修理❽的时候，是他跟我一起~下来的；担架从救护车❾里~出来了；这边比较亮❿，把桌子~过来吧；〈程〉~得太远了；~得太累了；担架他~得最稳⓫〈可〉柜子太

tái — tān

大，门那么窄⓬，～得出去吗？钢琴⓭那么重，两个人哪儿～得上去？这么沉⓮你～得起来～不起来？〈时〉我已经～了半天了；我～一会儿，你去休息休息〈量〉～了三趟；～过两次〔状～〕轮流⓯～；一口气⓰～；真难～；两个人～；用担架～；从这儿往那儿～

1. stretcher; litter 2. cupboard; cabinet 3. pile; heap 4. carpet 5. sofa 6. gas container 7. washing machine 8. repair 9. ambulance 10. bright 11. steady 12. narrow 13. piano 14. heavy 15. by turns 16. in one breath; without a break

tān 贪 be greedy for; have an insatiable desire for ≅ 贪图〔～宾〕〈名〉～财❶〈动〉～玩儿；～吃；～睡〈形〉～多；～便宜❷，～热闹❸，～小失大❹〔～补〕〈程〉这孩子贪玩～得厉害❺〈量〉～过无数次❻便宜〔状～〕太～了；有点儿～；特别～；非常～〔习用〕～多嚼不烂❼；～心不足❽

1. wealth; money 2. small advantages; pretty gains (anxious to get things on the cheap; keen on gaining petty advantages) 3. the fun; the excitement 4. covet a little and lose a lot; seek small gains but incur big losses 5. terrible; awful 6. innumerable 7. bite off more than one can chew 8. insatiably greedy

tān 摊 ① spread out ≅ 摆开〔～宾〕〈名〉衣服～了一床（～了一床衣服）；书～了一桌子（～了一桌子书）〔～补〕〈结〉把绿豆❶～开晒❷一晒；东西～在那里没人管〈趋〉把问题～到桌面上来谈❸〔状～〕快～开晒晒吧；把几本字典往桌子上一～；乱七八糟地❹～；全部～出来

1. mung bean; green gram 2. dry in the sun 3. thrash out 4. in a mess; in a muddle

② take a share in ≅ 分担〔～宾〕〈名〉～钱买礼物❶〔～补〕〈可〉一个人～不了(liǎo)多少钱〔状～〕一次一次地～钱买东西；经常～；偶尔❷～

1. gift 2. once in a while; occasionally

③ fry batter in a thin layer〔～宾〕〈名〉～鸡蛋；～煎饼❶〔～补〕〈结〉煎饼～破❷了；把煎饼～薄❸点儿〈趋〉煎饼刚～出来很好吃〈程〉～得真好；～得真薄；～得真熟练❹〈可〉他连鸡蛋都～不好〈量〉我只～过一次〔状～〕经常～；熟练地～

1. thin pancake made of millet flour, etc. (make pancakes) 2. be torn 3. thin 4. skilful

④ meet with; suffer ≅ 碰到；落到〔～补〕〈结〉这种事情～在谁头上❶，谁也受不了❷；这种事谁～上谁倒楣❸〔状～〕差点儿～在我头上；可别～上

1. befall; happen 2. cannot bear; be unable to endure 3. have bad luck; be out of luck

tán 谈 talk; chat; discuss ≅ 说

〔**～宾**〕〈名〉～天儿❶；～家常❷；～心❸；～恋爱❹；～点儿事儿；～生意❺；～条件❻；～一～事情的经过；～一个问题〔**～补**〕〈结〉事先❼把话～清楚；事情～妥❽了吗？～明白了吗？～急❾了；他都把我～糊涂了，不知道他到底要说什么；话～远❿了；～到科学的前景⓫；他们一见面就～开了〈趋〉把心里话～出来吧；～过来～过去就是那点儿事；他～起话来非常幽默⓬；你的这一席⓭话～到我的心坎⓮里去了〈程〉～得很融洽⓯；～得很投机⓰；～得非常高兴；～得很别扭⓱；～得非常生气；～得口干舌燥⓲〈可〉他跟我比较～得来⓳；～不拢⓴；他们两个人～不来㉑；我虽然懂，但～不上㉒是什么专家㉓；跟他～不明白，因为他不讲理㉔；我们两个人不对脾气㉕，～不了两句话就～不下去了；这个人嘴笨㉖，心里有话～不出来；那个孩子心太浮㉗，跟他谈什么也～不进去〈时〉昨天晚上，他在我这儿～了一会儿就走了；我想跟您～十分钟，可以吗？〈量〉我跟他～过两次；你找他～一下儿吧〔**状～**〕详细㉘～～吧；不慌不忙地㉙～；好好～～；随便～；认真～一～；不好意思㉚～；闭口不～㉛；你一言我一语地㉜～；单独㉝～；个别㉞～；公开㉟～；偷偷地㊱～；当面㊲～；背地里㊳～；不约而同地㊴～；不假思索地㊵～；喊喊喳喳地㊶～；痛痛快快地㊷～；一点一滴地㊸～；从头到尾地㊹～；一五一十地㊺～；嬉皮笑脸地㊻～；耐心地㊼～；理直气壮地㊽～；再三地～；～；简单地～；亲切地㊾～；热情地～；严肃地㊿～；诚恳地(51)～；从来不～；苦口婆心地(52)～；语重心长地(53)～；海阔天空地(54)～；口若悬河地(55)～；漫无边际地(56)～〔**习用**〕～情说爱(57)

1. chat 2. talk about everyday matters 3. heart (heart-to-heart talk) 4. be in love; have a love affair 5. business 6. condition 7. beforehand 8. ready; settled; finished 9. irritated; annoyed; nettled 10. far 11. prospect; future 12. very humorous 13. a measure word (for talk, banquet, etc.) 14. the bottom of one's heart 15. harmonious; on friendly terms 16. very congenially 17. awkward; uncomfortable 18. one's mouth and tongue are parched 19. get along well 20. 21. not get along very well 22. out of the question 23. expert; specialist 24. be unreasonable 25. be on bad terms with 26. inarticulate; clumsy of speech 27. too superficial 28. in detail 29. unhurriedly 30. feel embarrassed 31. refuse to say anything about; avoid mentioning 32. with everybody joining in 33. alone 34. individually 35. publicly 36. stealthily 37. in

sb.'s presence; to sb.'s face **38.** behind sb's back **39.** take the same action or view without prior consultation; happen to coincide **40.** without thinking; without hesitation **41.** chatter away; jabber **42.** to one's heart's content; to one's great satisfaction **43.** by little and little **44.** from beginning to end **45.** systematically and in full detail **46.** grinning cheekily; smiling and grimacing **47.** patiently **48.** with perfect assurance; justly and forcefully **49.** kindly; cordially **50.** in all earnestness; solemnly **51.** sincerely **52.** urge sb. time and again with good intentions **53.** sincere words and earnest wishes **54.** as boundless as the sea and sky; unrestrained and far-ranging (have a rambling chat about everything under the sun) **55.** let loose a flood of eloquence **56.** ramblingly; discursively **57.** be in love; have a love affair

tán 弹 ① shoot (as with a catapult, etc.); send forth 〔～宾〕〈名〉小孩子喜欢～球❶玩；～石子儿❷容易伤人❸〔～补〕〈结〉别把球～掉❹了；～丢了〈趋〉把球～过来了〈程〉～得真远；～得真准❺〈可〉～得着(zháo)吗？～不出去；～得过去～不过去？〈时〉～了半天也没弹着(zháo)；再一会儿就不弹了〈量〉孩子们你一下儿，我～一下儿，玩得很热闹❻；我小时候❼～过一次石子儿，把一块橱窗❽玻璃❾给打碎❿了，以后再也不敢⓫弹石子了，〔状～〕在地板上～；用拇指⓬～；使劲儿～；对准了⓭～

1. (play) marbles 2. cobblestone; cobble; pebble 3. hurt 4. fallen 5. accurate 6. lively 7. in one's childhood 8. shopwindow 9. glass 10. broken to pieces 11. dare not 12. thumb 13. aim at

② flick; flip 〔～宾〕〈名〉～～烟灰❶；～～尘土❷〔～补〕〈结〉把帽子❸上的土～掉❹了〈趋〉把烟灰～到烟灰缸里❺去了〈程〉～得很干净〈可〉～不下去；～不干净〈量〉烟灰都那么多了，快一下儿吧〔状～〕使劲～；轻轻地～；用拇指和中指❻～

1. tobacco or cigarette ash 2. dust 3. headgear; hat; cap 4. off 5. ashtray 6. middle finger

③ fluff; tease 〔～宾〕〈名〉～棉花❶；～被套❷〔～补〕〈结〉棉花～匀❸点儿；～松❹点儿；～软❺点儿；～薄❻了；被套～厚❼点儿；～完了吗？什么时候可以～好〈趋〉这种次❽棉花～出来的被套不好〈程〉棉花～得很松软；机器～得匀还是手工❾～得匀？〈·可〉这点儿棉花太少，～不了(liǎo)一个被套〈时〉那里的工作太多，我送去的被套～了一个多月才弹好〈量〉～过两次〔状～〕已经～了；什么地方～？

1. cotton 2. quilt padding 3. even 4. 5. soft; spongy; loose 6. thin 7. thick 8. second-class 9. by hand

④ play (a stringed musical instrument); pluck 〔~宾〕〈名〉~钢琴❶；~琵琶❷；~吉他❸；~了一个优美的❹曲子❺〔~补〕〈结〉曲子~完了，大家热烈地❻鼓起掌❼来；有的地方~错了；一直~到很晚〈趋〉她~出来的曲子非常好听；他一~起钢琴来什么烦恼❽都忘了；接着❾~下去吧〈程〉~得很熟练❿；~得很好听；~得不熟；~得真不错〈可〉琴坏了，~不了(liǎo)了；不看着乐谱⓫我~不下来；老~不对，我刚学，还~不好；心乱⓬得很，~不下去了；这个曲子太难，我~不上来；他~不出什么优美动听⓭的曲子来〈时〉整整~了一个晚上；再~一会儿〈量〉教我~一下儿吉他可以吗？这支曲子~过无数⓮遍了〔状~〕经常~；偶尔⓯~；连续~；反复~；熟练地~；随便⓰~；任意⓱~

1. piano 2. *pipa*, a plucked string instrument with a fretted fingerboard 3. guitar 4. graceful; fine 5. song; melody 6. warmly; enthusiastically; ardently 7. clap one's hands 8. worry 9. go on 10. skilful 11. music score 12. be confused and disconcerted 13. interesting or pleasant to listen to 14. innumerable; countless 15. occasionally; once in a while 16. casually; at random 17. wantonly; wilfully

⑤ spring; leap 〔~补〕〈趋〉从跳板❶上~起来了；球碰❷到墙上又~回来了；门~回来打了我一下儿〈程〉~得很高；~得很远〈可〉~得起来~不起来？〔状~〕自动~；使劲❸~；一下子~了出去〔习用〕重~老调❹；老调重~❺

1. springboard 2. hit 3. exert all one's strength 4. 5. harp on the same string; sing the same old tune

tàn 探 ① explore; try to find out ≃ 寻求；寻找；试探；探听〔~宾〕〈名〉你先去给我们~~路❶；好好~~她的口气❷；我先去~~消息；到深山❸去~宝❹；用竹竿❺~~水的深浅❻〔~补〕〈结〉~着(zháo)矿❼了吗？路线~清了吗？〈趋〉~出她的口气来了没有〈可〉从她那里~不着(zháo)任何消息；~不到什么情况〈时〉~了好几年，也没探出矿来〈量〉我们一起去~过两次；再~一次试试〔状~〕用什么机器~？用什么办法~？再~~

1. (explore) the way 2. ascertain (find out) sb.'s opinions or feelings 3. remote mountains 4. treasure 5. bamboo pole 6. depth 7. mineral resources

② visit; pay a call on ≃ 看望〔~宾〕〈名〉~亲❶；~亲访友❷；~监❸有一定的时间❹，不是随便什么时候都可以探的；每星期二、四下午是~病时间〔~补〕〈时〉回家探亲~了半个月；~监只能~一会儿〈量〉在外地工作的人，每年可以回家~一次亲

〔状～〕多少日子～一次监；在规定的时间内❺～

1. go home to visit one's family or go to visit one's relatives 2. visit (call on) one's relatives and friends 3. visit a prisoner 4. at a fixed time 5. within the fixed time

③ stretch forward ≅ 伸〔～宾〕〈名〉～头❶向外看；他总是把门打开一条小缝❷，～头～脑❸地往里看；为了不把衣服弄脏，她～着身子吃西瓜〔～补〕〈趋〉车行驶❹时，不要把身子～出去〈量〉～了一下儿头〔状～〕向前；往外～；千万❺别～；不时地❻～；鬼鬼祟祟地❼～了一个头儿

1. pop one's head 2. crack 3. pop one's head 4. (of a vehicle, ship, etc.) go; ply; travel 5. be sure 6. frequently; often 7. sneakingly; furtively

tānfīng 探听 make inquiries; try to find out ≅ 探〔～宾〕〈名〉～孩子的下落❶；～～消息❷；～虚实❸；～真假❹；～情况❺；～敌人的动静❻；～～他的口气❼；～～他的真实❽意图❾；～别人的秘密❿〈主-谓〉～他有什么打算⓫；～～她对这件事有什么看法⓬〔～补〕〈结〉～着(zháo)什么好消息了吗？至今⓭没～到她的下落〈趋〉～出来了吗？〈程〉～得很仔细〈可〉～不到任何消息；～不出真假来〈时〉～了好几天；～过不少日子〈量〉～过好几

次了；再去～一下儿〔状～〕好好～～；已经～到了；到处～；间接⓮～；向他～

1. whereabouts 2. news 3. try to find out about an opponent, etc. 4. true or false 5. situation 6. movement; activity 7. what is actually meant; implication 8. real 9. intention 10. secret 11. intention 12. a way of looking at a thing; view 13. up to now; to this day 14. indirectly

tǎng 躺 lie; recline ↔ 起〔～宾〕〈名〉路边儿～着一棵枯树〔～补〕〈结〉我～下就睡着了；～在草地上晒太阳；病人吃完药就～下了；一棵小树被风刮断，～在水池❶边上〈趋〉吃完药刚出了一身汗❷快～下去吧；～到床上去吧〈程〉～得头都晕❸了；～得不舒服❹；～得真难受❺；～得腿❻都软❼了〈可〉病刚好就～不住了；事情那么多，我可～不下去了〈时〉～了三个小时也没睡着，只好起来；在医院里整整～了五个月〈量〉～一下儿就起来〔状～〕横❽着～；～在床上；斜❾着～；侧身❿～；仰面朝天地⓫～；直挺挺地～⓬着；蜷缩着⓭～；在长椅子上～；一天到晚～着〔习用〕横～竖卧⓮

1. pond; pool 2. sweat; perspiration 3. dizzy; giddy 4. uncomfortable 5. feel unwell 6. leg 7. weak; feeble (feel like jelly) 8. horizontally 9. slantingly 10. on one's side 11. lie on one's back

12. stiff; straight 13. roll up; huddle up; curl up 14. lie in disorder

tàng 烫 ① scald; burn 〔~宾〕〈名〉这个锅把儿❶真~手；刚沏❷的茶真~嘴；汤❹这么热，把舌头❺都~了；开水❻把手~了一个大泡❼；火柴❽差点儿~了手〔~补〕〈结〉手~肿了❾；嘴~疼了❿；脚~伤了⓫；可把我~坏了；~掉⓬（~破）了一层皮⓭；怎么~成这个样子⓮了？〈趋〉~起一个大泡〈程〉~得厉害；~得要命；真~得慌；~得没法儿喝（吃）⓯〈可〉~不着(zháo)手〈量〉我被开水~过一次；拿好了，不然一下儿可受不了⓰(liǎo)〔状~〕真~；好~啊；让开水~了；被锅里溅⓱出来的油星儿⓲~了

1. handle of a pot 2. infuse 3. mouth 4. soup 5. tongue 6. boiling water 7. blister 8. match 9. be swollen 10. pain; ache 11. scald 12. lose; come off 13. skin 14. to such an extent 15. too hot to drink (eat) 16. unbearable 17. splash; spatter 18. drops of oil

② heat up in hot water; warm; iron 〔~宾〕〈名〉天太冷了，~点儿酒喝；用热水~~脚解除乏❶；用热水~~手就不冷了；用电熨斗❷~衣服〔~补〕〈结〉衣服上的褶子❸都~开了；手脚都~暖和了；裙子❹~好了；~上一壶酒；衣服能~平吗？〈趋〉你怎么连一块布都不垫❺就~起衣服来了〈程〉衣服~得真平，裤线❻~得真直❼〈可〉这么一大堆衣服十分钟可~不完；熨斗❽不热，褶子~不开；不喷水❾~不平〈时〉多~一会儿就好了；~了半天，酒还不热〈量〉裤子压❿得皱极了，赶快~一下儿吧；她每星期集中⓫~一次衣服〔状~〕自己~衣服；从来没~过；用热水~；用熨斗~；至少⓬~；熟练地⓭~；铺⓮上一块湿布⓯再~

1. recover from fatigue 2. electric iron 3. pleat 4. skirt 5. put sth. under sth. else 6. creases of trousers 7. straight 8. iron 9. sprinkle water 10. press; exert pressure on 11. concentrate; put together 12. at least 13. skillfully 14. spread; pave 15. wet cloth

tāo 掏 ① draw out; pull out 〔~宾〕〈名〉~钱买东西；从书包里~钥匙❶；出入大门要~工作证❷；舍不得❸~腰包❹；从麻雀窝❺里~麻雀❻；从炉子❻里~炉灰❼；从腰❽里~手枪❾〔~补〕〈结〉耳朵~干净了；口袋~空了以后，再把衣服放进水里去；~着(zháo)两只麻雀〈趋〉孩子们~起鸟来，什么都不顾❿了；他~出手枪来吓唬⓫人〈程〉炉灰~得真干净〈可〉铅笔让别的东西压在书包底下~不出来了，炉子里的灰怎么掏也~不干净〈时〉那个孩子~了一晚上麻雀〈量〉一天要~好几次〔状~〕从口袋里~；往外~；用煤铲⓬~炉灰；用挖耳

勺⓭～耳朵；轻轻地～；经常～；从来不～；乖乖地⓮把钱～出来

1. key **2.** employee's card **3.** hate to part with or use; grudge **4.** pay out of one's own pocket **5.** sparrow's nest **6.** stove **7.** ash from the stove **8.** waist **9.** pistol **10.** show no consideration **11.** frighten; menace **12.** coal shovel **13.** earpick **14.** obediently

②dig (a hole, etc.); hollow out; scoop out ≅ 挖〔**～宾**〕〈名〉在墙上～一个洞；在门上～一个窟窿❶装锁❷〔**～补**〕〈结〉山洞～通了❸；老鼠把粮食袋❹都快～空❺了〈可〉木板太厚❻，～不过去；没有工具❼～不了(liǎo)〈时〉～了半天才掏通〔**状～**〕在门上～；用什么工具～？

1. hole **2.** install a lock **3.** open; through **4.** sack **5.** empty **6.** too thick **7.** tool

táo 逃 run away; escape; flee

〔**～宾**〕〈名〉～荒❶；～难❷；～学；～命❸〔**～补**〕〈结〉他已经～走了；刚～出了虎口❹，又进了狼窝❺〈趋〉从监狱❻里～出去了；～到别的地方去了；～到山上来了〈程〉～得很快；～得很远；～得无影无踪❼了〈可〉～不出我们的手心❽；这回敌人～不了(liǎo)了；监狱的看守❾很严❿，～不出来；学校和家长管⓫得都很严，想逃学是～不成的；去了就～不回来；你应负的责任⓬是～不脱的⓭〈时〉～了三天学〈量〉小时候～过两次难〔**状～**〕从监狱里～出来了；法网难～⓮；插翅难～⓯；无法⓰～；无故⓱～学；千方百计地⓲想～出去；跳墙～跑⓳了；借故⓴～走；趁人不备㉑～走了

1. flee from famine; get away from a famine-stricken area **2.** flee from a calamity; be a refugee **3.** run for one's life **4.** tiger's mouth — jaws of death **5.** wolf's lair **6.** prison **7.** not a trace left; untraceable **8.** the palm of the hand; control **9.** guard **10.** strict; severe **11.** subject sb. to discipline **12.** assume the responsibility **13.** can't get rid of **14.** be unable to escape the net of justice **15.** unable to escape even if given wings **16.** unable; incapable **17.** without cause or reason **18.** in a thousand and one ways; by every possible means **19.** escape by climbing over the wall **20.** find an excuse **21.** catch sb. off guard

táo 淘 ① wash in a pan or basket〔**～宾**〕〈名〉～米做饭；以前很多人被骗❶到国外去～金❷〔**～补**〕〈结〉把米～干净点儿；～完了米再切菜〈程〉米～得不干净〈可〉水少了～不干净〈时〉～了半天了〈量〉～过好几遍了〔**状～**〕好好～～；一遍一遍地～

1. deceive **2.** gold (panning)

② clean out; dredge〔**～宾**〕〈名〉～阴沟❶；～井❷；～水缸❸；

～厕所❹〔～补〕〈结〉还没～干净呢；把井～干了〈趋〉把水缸里的水都～出来了；快把鱼缸❺里的雨水～出去吧〈时〉～了三天〈量〉这条沟每年都得～一次〔状～〕不好～；用机器～；一下一下地～；往外～

1. clean out a drain (or sewer) 2. dredge a well 3. water vat 4. lavatory; toilet; W. C. 5. goldfish bowl

táotài 淘汰 eliminate through selection or competition; die out; fall into disuse〔主～〕〈名〉他在最后的比赛中被～了；这种机器太老了，已经被～了；这种方法被～了；有些词语❶被～了；〔～补〕〈趋〉A队和B队都被～下去了〈可〉～得了(liǎo)～不了(liǎo)〔状～〕逐渐❷被～了；日趋❸～；几乎❹被～了；就要全部～了

1. words and expressions 2. gradually; by degrees 3. day by day 4. nearly; almost

tǎo 讨 ① beg for; demand; ask for ≅ 索取；要〔～宾〕〈名〉他小时候～过饭❶；～债❷；他象～帐❸似地逼着❹我要钱〈动〉那个孩子被打得直～饶❺；我愿意向有学问的❻人～教❼〈形〉～便宜❽〔～补〕〈结〉他说，他可～够了饭了，想起来就难过❾〈趋〉那个孩子一起饶来，嘴可甜❿了；有的人一起债来真凶⓫〈可〉我们什么便宜⓬也～不着(zháo)；反正⓭怎么做也～不了(liǎo)好儿〈时〉～过三年饭；～了半天饶〈量〉～过好多次便宜了〔状～〕专门⓮～便宜；就会～好别人；小时候～过饭；千方百计地⓯～好

1. beg for food; be a beggar 2. debt 3. demand the payment of a debt 4. force 5. beg for mercy; ask for forgiveness 6. learned 7. ask for advice 8. seek undue advantage; try to gain sth. at the expense of others 9. feel unwell 10. sweet 11. terrible 12. small advantages; petty gains 13. anyhow; anyway; in any case 14. specially 15. by every possible means; by hook or by crook

② incur; invite ≅ 招惹〔～宾〕〈名〉～人喜欢；～人嫌❶〈形〉自～没趣❷；自～苦吃❸〔～补〕〈可〉这个人的性格❹永远也～不着(zháo)别人的喜欢；～不了(liǎo)人家的欢心〔状～〕特别❺～；实在❻～；别～人嫌了〔习用〕费力不～好❼

1. disagreeable; annoying 2. ask for a snub; court a rebuff 3. ask for trouble 4. character; personality 5. specially 6. really; truly 7. put in much hard work, but yet very little result; undertake a thankless task

tǎoyàn 讨厌 dislike; loathe; be disgusted with ≅ 不喜欢↔喜欢〔～宾〕〈名〉～虚伪的❶人；我

真～这家伙❷；～蚊蝇❸；～她的庸俗作风❹；～那里的炎热❺气候❻〈代〉～他来罗嗦❼；～她爱打听❽别人的私事❾；～她爱显示❿自己〈动〉～刮风；～下雨；～说谎⓫〔～补〕〈结〉～死⓬那个人了；～到无法生活下去的程度⓭〈趋〉大家慢慢地都～起他来了〈程〉～得不得了⓮(liǎo)；～得要命⓯；～极了⓰〔状～〕非常～；特别～；真～

1. sham; false; hypocritical 2. fellow 3. mosquito and fly 4. the vulgar ways 5. sorching; blazing; burning hot 6. climate 7. long-winded; wordy 8. ask about; inquire about 9. private (personal) affairs 10. show off 11. tell a lie 12. extremely; to death 13. degree; level 14. 15. 16. extremely; awfully; terribly

tào 套 ① put (nooses) around; interlink〔～宾〕〈名〉孩子～着救生圈儿❶在游泳池里玩；脖子❷上～了一个花环❸；钥匙环❹上～了一串钥匙❺；锁链子❻一个环儿～着一个环儿❼；钢笔上没～着笔帽儿❽〔～补〕〈结〉把花环～在贵宾❾的脖子上〈趋〉三把钥匙都～到钥匙环儿上去了〈程〉笔帽～得太紧❿〈可〉～不了(liǎo)那么多把钥匙〈时〉～了半天才套上〈量〉～一下儿试试，套得上套不上〔状～〕刚好～上；不见得⓫～不上；一连⓬～了好几个；热情友好地⓭给客人～上花环；往脖子上～

1. life ring 2. neck 3. garland; floral hoop 4. key ring 5. a bunch of keys 6. chain 7. all linked with one another 8. the cap of a pen 9. honoured guest 10. tight 11. not necessarily; not likely 12. in succession; in a row 13. warmly and friendly

② cover with; slip over; encase in ≅ 罩上〔～宾〕〈名〉棉袄❶外面～一件罩衣❷；打字机❸上～了一个人造革的罩儿❹；床上～着一个绿底白花的床罩❺；沙发上～了一个新沙发套儿❻；我脚冷，所以又多～了一双袜子❼；词典上～了一个塑料书皮儿❽〔～补〕〈结〉电视机～上一个罩儿，可以防尘❾；短大衣～在外面；笔帽～错了〈趋〉把刚做好的椅套～上去，试试合适❿不合适〈可〉椅套儿⓫太小～不上；东西太滑～不住〔状～〕在外边～；做小了，好容易才～进去；一直～着

1. cotton-padded jacket 2. dustcoat; overall 3. typewriter 4. artificial leather cover 5. bedspread with white flowers on a green background 6. new sofa cover 7. a pair of socks 8. plastic cover 9. keep out the dust 10. suitable 11. chair cover

③ harness (an animal); hitch up (an animal to a cart)〔～宾〕〈名〉～车；～马；～牲口❶〔～补〕〈结〉把牲口～上；把车～好了；绳子❷～紧❸点儿；～结实❹了

吗？把马～住，别让它跑了〈趋〉马已经～上去了；把车～过来吧〈程〉～得太紧了；～得真结实〈可〉我～不了(liǎo)，请你帮我套一下儿；怎么～不紧呢？〈时〉～了半天也没套上〈量〉再重新～一下儿吧〔～状〕用绳子～；使劲～；从这边～

1. draught animals **2.** rope **3.** tight; close **4.** solid

④ model on (after); copy ≅ 模仿；照抄〔～宾〕〈名〉～公式❶〔～补〕〈趋〉这句话是从别人的文章上～下来的〔状～〕生搬硬～❷别人的；机械地❸～；盲目地❹～

1. formula **2.** copy mechanically in disregard of specific conditions **3.** mechanically **4.** blindly

⑤ coax a secret out of sb.; trick sb. into telling the truth ≅ 引出〔～宾〕〈名〉她总想～我的话〔～补〕〈趋〉终于把他的话～出来了〈时〉她～了半天，也没把我的话套去〈量〉他～过我好几次话，我都没说〔状～〕专门❶～；故意❷～；三番五次地❸～；想方设法地❹～；用各种办法❺～；连哄带骗地❻～

1. specially **2.** intentionally; on purpose **3.** over and over again; repeatedly **4. 5.** by every possible means; by hook or crook **6.** coaxingly

⑥ try to win (sb.'s friendship) ≅ 拉拢〔～宾〕〈名〉～交情❶〔～补〕〈趋〉他一见面就跟人家～起交情来了〈量〉他跟主任❷～了好几次交情了，真恶心❸〔状～〕总～；故意❹～；从不～；决不～

1. friendship; friendly relations **2.** director; head **3.** disgusting; nauseating **4.** intentionally; purposely

téng 疼 ① ache; pain; sore〔主～〕〈名〉头～；牙～；喉咙❶～；胃❷～；腰❸～；胳膊❹～；浑身❺～；关节❻～；伤口❼～〔～补〕〈结〉牙～死❽了；～晕❾了〈趋〉人们常常说“牙疼不算病，～起来真要命”❿〈程〉～得真厉害⓫；～得睡不着觉；～得吃不下饭去；～得在床上打滚⓬；～得满地翻滚⓭；～得直哭；～得受不了⓮(liǎo)；～得直流汗⓯；～得没办法了⓰；～得上不了班了；～得哎哟，哎哟⓱地叫⓲；～得支持不住了⓳〈时〉整整～了一夜；～一会儿就过去了〈量〉一个月胃要～好几次〔状～〕经常～；有点儿～；从来没～过；不停地～；忍不住⓴（忍不了(liǎo)）地～；一个劲儿地㉑～；不时地㉒～；一阵一阵地～；剧烈地㉓～；简直㉔～死了；差一点～晕了；象针扎似地㉕～

1. throat **2.** stomach **3.** waist **4.** arm **5.** all over the body **6.** joint **7.** cut; wound **8.** extremely; to death **9.** lose consciousness **10.** “An ache in a tooth can't be counted as an illness; but it seems impossible to stand the ache." 11. terrible; awful 12. 13. writhe with pain 14. cannot bear; unable to endure 15. perspire; sweat 16. can't be helped 17. ouch! ouch! 18. cry out 19. cannot endure 20. unable to bear 21. continuously; persistently 22. frequently; often 23. acutely 24. absolutely; virtually 25. as if the prick of a needle

② dote on; love dearly; be fond of〔～宾〕〈名〉外婆❶最～外孙子❷〔状～〕十分～；真～；多～孙子啊！〔习用〕好了疮疤忘了❸～

1. (maternal) grandmother 2. daughter's son; grandson 3. forget the pain after the wound is healed — forget the bitter past when we are relieved of our suffering

téngxiě 誊写 transcribe; copy out ≌ 誊清，抄写〔～宾〕〈名〉按照❶底稿❷再～一份〔～补〕〈结〉那篇文章还没～完呢；把作文～清楚❸以后再给我；稿子一律❹～在稿纸上〈趋〉底稿太乱了，～起来也困难〈程〉～得很清楚〈可〉这么乱的底稿我可～不了(liǎo)；〈时〉这么多得(děi)～两天〈量〉这稿子太乱❺，需要～一遍〔状～〕好好～；仔细❻点儿～；认真❼～；照原稿～；多～几份

1. according to 2. manuscript 3. make a fair copy of 4. all; without exception 5. messy; confused 6. carefully 7. seriously; conscientiously

téng 腾 make room; clear out; vacate ≌ 空出来〔～宾〕〈名〉～房子；～地方；～箱子❶；～抽屉❷，～座位❸；我要一个书架给他放书〔～补〕〈结〉把房子都～空了；地方已经～好了〈趋〉钱～出来买什么？这几间屋子都得(děi)～出来；～出时间来学英语；～出工夫❹来好好整理整理房子❺；～出地方来放东西；～出房子来给客人住〈程〉房子～得很及时❻〈可〉～不了(liǎo)那么多间房；～不出来那么多地方〈时〉～了一个星期才腾出来〈量〉～过一次了〔状～〕给谁～？什么时候～？一时～不了(liǎo)；暂时❼～；先别～；赶快～；热情地～；主动❽～；勉强❾～；不得不～

1. chest; box; case 2. drawer 3. handbag; bag 4. find time 5. put a room in order 6. in time 7. temporarily; for a moment 8. on one's own initiative 9. reluctantly

tī 剔 pick; clean with a pointed instrument〔～宾〕〈名〉～牙❶；～骨头❷，～指甲❸〔～补〕〈结〉把骨头上的肉～干净〈趋〉把塞❹在牙缝❺里的东西～出去了；他原来❻不需要剔牙，现在老了，也～起牙来了〈程〉骨头～得真干净；肉～得真快；～得真熟练❼

〈可〉刀不快❽；骨头上的肉~不下来〈时〉牙里塞的东西我~了半天也没剔出来〈量〉牙签得很难受❾；想找一根牙签❿~一下儿〔**状~**〕用牙签~牙；用刀~肉，一点一点儿地~；往外~；每顿饭后都~；必须~

1. tooth 2. bone 3. nail 4. stuff 5. crack; crevice 6. originally; formerly 7. skilful 8. not sharp; blunt 9. feel unwell 10. toothpick

tī 踢 play (football); kick〔**~宾**〕〈名〉~足球；~毽子❶；孩子走路爱~石子儿；这马~人不踢? 他~中锋❷〔**~补**〕〈结〉凳子❸~倒❹了；椅子~翻❺了；门让他给~开了；~破❻了；鞋都~坏了；把毽子~丢❼了；球~高了；马~把人~死了；~伤❽了；~紫❾了；~晕❿了；脚~疼了；~肿⓫了〈趋〉球~到球门⓬里去了；我们刚~过去又被他们~回来了〈程〉球~得太高；~得太远了；~得真准⓭；这个球~得真漂亮⓮〈可〉马~不着(zháo)人? 毽子我~不好；球~得进去~不进去?〈时〉~了一下午球，腿都疼了；再~一会儿吧〈量〉这一个星期他~了好几次足球了；~一下儿毽子〔**状~**〕用左脚⓯~；使劲儿~；往高处~；在足球场⓰~；别~了〔**习用**〕~皮球⓱

1. shuttlecock 2. centre forward 3. stool 4. fall 5. turn over (up) 6. broken 7. lost 8. wounded 9. purple 10. faint; lose consciousness 11. swollen 12. goal 13. accurate 14. remarkable; brilliant; splendid 15. left foot 16. (football) field 17. kick a ball; kick sth. back and forth like a ball; pass the buck; shift the responsibility

tí 提 ①carry (in one's hand with the arm down)〔**~宾**〕〈名〉~着篮子❶；~着书包；~着一条鱼〔**~补**〕〈结〉把东西~走了〈趋〉把篮子~进屋来了；你先把这一摞书❷~回去吧；把鱼~到厨房去吧〈程〉~得很费劲儿❸；~得很吃力❹〈可〉~得动；~不起来；~不了(liǎo)那么多〈时〉~了半天，胳膊❺都提累了〈量〉我来~一下儿吧〔**状~**〕吃力地~；勉强❻~；一下子就~起来了

1. basket 2. a stack of books 3. 4. need or use great effort 5. arm 6. reluctantly; with difficulty

② put forward; bring up; raise ≌ 提出〔**~宾**〕〈名〉~意见❶；~问题❷；~条件❸；~建议❹；~名❺〈动〉~抗议❻；~要求❼〔**~补**〕〈结〉意见~多了；问题~完了；要求~早了〈趋〉把名单❽~上来了；有什么意见可以~出来；他~起意见来很尖锐❾〈程〉问题~得很多；意见~得很尖锐；建议~得很好；要求~得不合理❿；口号⓫~得很响亮⓬〈可〉意见~不完，明天接着⓭提〈时〉~了半天意见，他们也不改〈量〉~过多少遍了；~了好多次〔**状~**〕

先～；尽量⓮～；重新～；反复～；三番五次地～；多～；愤怒地⓯～；慎重地⓰～名；严肃地⓱～；认真～条件；诚恳地⓲～意见；一时⓳～不完；主动⓴～；适当地㉑～

1. opinion **2.** question **3.** condition **4.** suggestions **5.** nomination **6.** protest **7.** requirement; demand **8.** name list **9.** sharp; incisive; penetrating **10.** irrational **11.** slogan **12.** loud and clear **13.** continue **14.** to the best of one's ability **15.** angrily **16.** cautiously; prudently; carefully **17.** seriously; solemnly **18.** sincerely **19.** temporarily; for a short while **20.** on one's own initiative **21.** suitably; properly

③ draw (take) out; extract ≃ 提取〔**～宾**〕〈名〉到仓库❶去～点儿货❷；从银行❸里～了一笔款❹；到车站❺～行李❻〔**～补**〕〈结〉把货～走了〈趋〉从银行里把存款全部～出去了〈程〉货～得太多了〈可〉款～得出来吗？货一次～不全〈量〉～了两次〔**状～**〕一共～了多少？不好～

1. warehouse **2.** goods **3.** bank **4.** a sum of money **5.** railway station **6.** luggage

④ mention; refer to; bring up〔**～宾**〕〈名〉不愿意～往事❶；别再～那些伤心❷事了；怎么还～那件事啊？〔**～补**〕〈结〉～起往事我就难受❸；～到他，他就来了；～到那篇小说❹，很多人都知道〈趋〉她又～起那段辛酸❺的往事来了〈可〉往事～不得，提起来她就哭〔**状～**〕重新～；一再～；不轻易❻～

1. past events **2.** painful memory; old sore **3.** feel unwell **4.** novel **5.** sad; bitter; miserable **6.** not rashly

tíbá 提拔 promote〔**～宾**〕〈名〉好好～～小李〈代〉我想～他当❶主任❷〔**～补**〕〈趋〉把他～上来了；～起来了〈程〉～得真快〈量〉～过他三次了〔**状～**〕好好～～；一再❸～；被～

1. work as **2.** director; head **3.** again and again; repeatedly

tíchàng 提倡 advocate; promote; encourage; recommend〔**～宾**〕〈名〉～民主❶；～刻苦❷学习的精神❸；～晚婚❹；～计划生育❺；～自学❻〈动〉～勤俭节约❼〔**～补**〕〈结〉～晚了〈趋〉～起来了〈程〉～得很好〈可〉～不了(liǎo)〈量〉～过不少次了〔**状～**〕大力❽～；认真～；必须～

1. democracy **2.** assiduous; hardworking **3.** spirit; gist **4.** late marriage **5.** birth control; family planning **6.** study independently; teach oneself **7.** hardworking and thrifty **8.** vigorously; energetically

tíchū 提出 put forward; advance; pose; raise ≅ 提〔**～宾**〕〈名〉～一个建议❶；～一个办法；～一种设想❷；～一种新理论❸；～一个问题；～意见；～一种口号❹；～一种观点❺；～了一个新课题❻；～了竞选❼的条件；～一个初步❽名单❾〈动〉～警告❿；～抗议⓫；～要求；～申请⓬〔**～补**〕〈时〉～半年多了；～很长时间了〈量〉～过不少次了〔**状～**〕又一次～；毫不隐讳地⓭～；大胆⓮～设想；愤怒地⓯～抗议；勇敢地⓰～自己的观点；不断地⓱～建议；一再～要求；进一步⓲～

1. suggestion 2. tentative plan; tentative idea 3. new theory 4. slogan 5. point of view 6. new task 7. enter into an election contest; campaign for (office); run for 8. preliminary 9. name list 10. warning 11. protestation 12. application 13. not avoid mentioning at all 14. boldly 15. angrily; indignantly 16. courageously 17. constantly 18. further

tígāo 提高 raise; heighten; enhance; improve; increase ↔ 降低〔**主～**〕〈名〉工作能力❶～了；产品质量❷～了；工作效率❸～了；警惕性❹～了；地位❺～了；欣赏❻水平❼～了；生活标准❽～了〔**～宾**〕〈名〉～警惕；～在人们心目中❾的地位；～表达❿能力；～对这个问题的认识⓫；～觉悟⓬；～勇气⓭；～战斗力⓮；～工作效率；～技术⓯；～产品质量；～产量⓰；～整个民族⓱的文化水平⓲〔**～补**〕〈结〉～到一定的水平〈程〉她的英文水平～得很快；下雨以后水位⓳～得真快〈可〉他的办事能力总也～不了(liǎo)〈时〉～了半天，也没提高多少〈量〉需要再～一下儿〔**状～**〕认真～；逐步⓴～；日益㉑～；不断㉒～

1. working ability 2. quality of product 3. efficiency 4. vigilance 5. status 6. appreciate; admire 7. level 8. living standard 9. in people's eyes 10. express 11. understanding; knowledge 12. consciousness; awareness 13. courage 14. fighting capacity; combat effectiveness 15. technology; technique 16. output; yield 17. whole nation 18. cultural level; educational level 19. water level 20. gradually 21. day by day 22. continuously

tígōng 提供 provide; supply; furnish; offer ≅ 供给〔**～宾**〕〈名〉～原料❶；～粮食❷；～市场❸；～贷款❹；～费用❺；～援助❻；～枪支❼；～弹药❽；～武器❾；～了有利条件❿；～了可靠的情报⓫；～两种可能性⓬；～了重要的线索⓭；～了科学依据⓮；～了很有价值的资料⓯〈形〉～了方便⓰〔**～补**〕〈可〉～不了(liǎo)贷款；～不出经验⓱来〈量〉～过

两次情报〔**状~**〕为他们~；已经~；必须~；一直~；大量⓲~

1. raw material 2. grain 3. market 4. loan 5. cost 6. assistance; help 7. firearms 8. ammunition 9. weapon 10. favourable condition 11. reliable information 12. possibilities 13. important clue 14. scientific basis 15. valuable data 16. convenience 17. experience 18. a great quantity

tíxǐng 提醒 remind; warn; call attention to
〔**~宾**〕〈代〉幸亏❶你~我，不然❷我就忘❸了；一定要~他明天早点儿来〔**~补**〕〈程〉他~得很及时；~得太好了〈量〉请你~我一下儿；~过他好几次了〔**状~**〕主动❹~；经常~；再三~；多次~；反复~

1. fortunately; luckily 2. if not, otherwise 3. forget 4. on one's own initiative

tíyì 提议 propose; suggest; move
〔**~宾**〕〈动〉我~写信去安慰安慰❶她；我~为我们的友谊❷干一杯❸〔**~补**〕〈时〉我~了半天，没人响应❹〈量〉我~过好几次了，谁都不同意❺〔**状~**〕在会上~；向大家~

1. comfort; console 2. friendship 3. drink a toast 4. respond; answer 5. agree

tǐtiē 体贴 show consideration for; give every care to ≅ 关心〔~宾〕〈名〉~老人；~病人；~父母〔**~补**〕〈程〉~极了；~得很〔**状~**〕一向~；非常~；特别~；从不~；对他很~

tì 剃 shave
〔**~宾**〕〈名〉~胡子❶；~头发；~眉毛❷〔**~补**〕〈结〉~干净❸了；~光❹了；~掉❺了〈趋〉~下来一撮❻头发〈程〉~得很好；~得挺快；~得真干净〈可〉我技术❼不高❽，~不好，刀子不快❾~不下来〈时〉很快，~一会儿就完了；一个头~了十多分钟〈量〉~过一次，又长起来了；应该~一下儿了〔**状~**〕给别人~；小心点儿~；慢慢~；一刀一刀地~；第一次~；用剃头刀❿~；用刮脸刀⓫~；涂⓬点肥皂⓭再~

1. beard, moustache or whiskers 2. eyebrow 3. clean 4. bare; nothing left 5. away; off 6. a handful of 7. skill 8. unskilled 9. not sharp; blunt 10. 11. razor 12. apply 13. soap

tì 替 take the place of; replace; substitute for ≅ 代替
〔**~宾**〕〈名〉我来~工❶；他来~班❷；我是来~我爸爸的〈代〉今天他没来，谁~他？你休息一会儿，我来~你〔**~补**〕〈结〉5号上场❸~下了8号〈趋〉张师傅身体不好，你去把他~回来吧〈可〉这种手术❹只有张医生能作，别人谁也~不了(liǎo)；他工作正紧张❺，现在还~不下来；大家都请我替工，我有点儿~不过来了〈时〉明天她~我一天；我替工~了好几个月了〈量〉一时❻还找不到合适❼的人，你能不能先~一下儿他〔状~〕先~；暂时❽~；由他~；从去年就~〔习用〕~死鬼❾，~罪羊❿

1. work as a temporary substitute 2. shift 3. enter the court or field 4. operation 5. intense 6. temporarily; for a moment 7. suitable 8. temporarily 9. scapegoat; fall guy 10. scapegoat

tìhuàn 替换 replace; substitute for; displace; take the place of ≅ 替；换〔~宾〕〈名〉5号运动员❶~12号；~值班❷的人〈代〉我~他，谁~我？〔~补〕〈结〉~晚了〈趋〉快把他~下来吧，他太累了；我能不能把他~出来，〈程〉~得很及时❸〈可〉~得了(liǎo)吗？~不下来吧？〈量〉我~你一下儿吧，他~过我一次了〔状~〕赶快~；立即❹~；按时❺~

1. athlete; sportsman 2. be on duty 3. in time 4. at once; immediately 5. on time

tiān 添 add; increase ≅ 加；增加 ↔ 减；减少〔~宾〕〈名〉这个工作还需要~人吗？还应该~一点儿燃料❶，~煤❷，~水，~柴❸；再~一碗饭；今天天冷，出去时我又多~了一件衣服；工厂还要~机器；~设备❹；~零件❺；年纪大了容易~病，又~

了很多毛病❻；再~点儿钱就够了；家里~了新家具❼；给学校~了不少光彩❽〈形〉给您~麻烦❾了〔~补〕〈结〉再~上点儿就够了；~足❿了；需要的东西都~齐⓫了；工厂~起了很多新设备〈趋〉那个小饭馆开始~起新家具来了〈可〉料~得太多了〈可〉水~不满；这种坏习惯⓬可~不得〈时〉他光添煤就~了十分钟〈量〉~过一次饭了；还得再~一次〔状~〕慢慢地~；一点一点地~；容易~病；可别~坏毛病；给他们~；不用~；打算⓭再~；陆续⓮~；经常~

1. fuel 2. coal 3. firewood 4. equipment 5. spare parts 6. trouble; fault; defect 7. furniture 8. splendour; lustre 9. sorry to have troubled you 10. enough 11. complete 12. bad habit 13. intend 14. one after another; in succession

tián 填 ① fill; stuff〔~宾〕〈名〉~沟❶；~海❷；~坑❸；给鸭子~食❹；往坑里~土❺〔~补〕〈结〉把沟~上；把坑~平；把枕头~鼓❻点儿；~满❼了；给鸭子~饱了〈趋〉快把沟~起来吧，太危险❽了；把土都~进去了〈程〉枕头~得真鼓；鸭子~得太饱了〈可〉这个沟怎么老~不平啊？不用机器~不了(liǎo)这么大的海；他老说~不饱肚子〈时〉再~两天也完不了(liǎo)；再一会儿就差不多了〈量〉~一下儿

〔**状～**〕满满地～；鼓鼓❾地～；用机器～土

1. ditch **2.** sea **3.** hole; pit; hollow **4.** feed **5.** earth; soil **6.** swollen **7.** filled; full **8.** dangerous **9.** bulge; swell

② fill in; write ≃ 填写〔**～宾**〕〈名〉～表❶；～统计表❷；～登记表❸；～空儿❹；～歌词❺；～了一首词❻；～日期；～号码❼；～姓名〔**～补**〕〈结〉表都～满❽了；歌词～好了；日期～上了；号码～对了吗？那几个空儿都～对了吗？〈趋〉把日期～上去；表上各项❾都～出来了吗？〈程〉她填词～得非常好；日期～得不清楚；号码～得不对；表～得很详细❿〈可〉这张表太复杂了，十分钟也～不完；她不懂英文，这张表～不了(liǎo)〈时〉～了半天也没填上来〈量〉～过一次〔**状～**〕细心地⓫～；用钢笔～；按着次序⓬～

1. table; form **2.** statistical graph **3.** registry; register **4.** blank **5.** words of a song **6.** a poem of classical Chinese verse **7.** number **8.** full **9.** all items **10.** detailed **11.** carefully **12.** in order; by order

tiāo 挑 ① choose; select; pick ≃ 选；挑选〔**～宾**〕〈名〉～心爱的东西；～最好的给你；把那筐❶苹果～一～；～个好日子举行婚礼❷；～毛病❸；专爱～别人的不是❹；～演员❺；～运动员❻〈动〉这个孩子总是～吃～喝的〔**～补**〕〈结〉～满❼了一筐；这次可～错人了；～上一个好演员；～着(zháo)一把满意的❽提琴❾；东西太多，我都～花眼❿了；她买东西挑得太厉害，把售货员都～烦⓫了；～火⓬儿了〈趋〉那个人～起毛病来可厉害了；他～起东西来最有眼力⓭了；～过来～过去，把眼睛都挑花了；把好的都～到他自己那儿去了；把米里的稻壳⓮都～出来了；从豆子里～出不少砂子⓯来〈程〉～得很仔细⓰；～得太厉害了〈可〉老～不着(zháo)合适的⓱；～不满一筐；你怎么老～不完啊？〈时〉～了半天也没挑着(zháo)满意的；～了半天，越挑越不知道哪个好了；～了好一会儿才决定下来〈量〉～过一次了；好好～一下儿〔**状～**〕仔细～一～；可以随便⓲～；任意⓳～；故意⓴～；翻来复去地㉑～；左～右～㉒；反复㉓～；专～；总～；由谁来～？精心㉔～

1. basket **2.** hold a wedding ceremony **3. 4.** fault **5.** actor or actress **6.** sportsman; athlete **7.** full **8.** satisfied; pleased **9.** violin **10.** blurred; dazzled **11.** be vexed **12.** flare up **13.** eyesight; judgment **14.** rice husk **15.** sand **16.** careful **17.** suitable **18.** casually; at random **19.** wantonly; wilfully **20.** intentionally; purposely **21. 22. 23.** repeatedly; over and over again **24.** meticulously

② shoulder; carry (tote) on the shoulder with a pole ≃ 担〔～

宾〕〈名〉～水；～行李❶；～东西；～菜〔～补〕〈结〉缸❷里～满❸了水；小黄把行李～走了〈趋〉我帮他把东西～到他家去了；把货❹～上山去了；他没劲儿❺，～起担子❻来左右摇晃❼；把行李～到火车站❽去了；～起扁担❾来一颤一颤❿的〈程〉东西～得真多；他一口气儿～得真远；～得很累；～得一点也不费劲⓫，～得太吃力⓬了；水～得满满的〈可〉太沉⓭我可～不动；～不起来；平时⓮缸里的水总～不满〈时〉你累了，我～一会儿吧〈量〉～了五趟；～过两次；你来一下儿〔状～〕从来没～过；一直～到家；勉强⓯～；自己～；用扁担～；换换⓰肩膀⓱再～；两个人轮着⓲～；多一点儿；吃力地～；摇摇晃晃地⓳～〔习用〕横～鼻子竖～眼⓴

另见 tiǎo 挑

1. luggage 2. vat 3. full; filled 4. goods 5. strength; energy 6. a carrying pole and the loads on it; load; burden 7. shake from side to side; stagger 8. station 9. carrying pole; shoulder pole 10. shaky 11. not needing the slightest effort 12. entail strenuous effort; be a strain 13. heavy 14. at ordinary times; in normal times 15. reluctantly 16. change 17. shoulder 18. in turn 19. with faltering steps 20. find fault in a petty manner; pick holes in sth.

tiáo 调 mix; adjust ≅ 调整，调和〔～宾〕〈名〉～味儿❶；～弦❷；～(颜)色；～音❸；～电视；～一一座位❹；～一一照相机❺的光圈❻和距离❼〔～补〕〈结〉～音好了吗？把颜色～匀❽；把弦～准❾；把光圈～大点儿〈趋〉她做菜～出来的味儿真香❿；弦～过来～过去总调不准〈程〉颜色～得很好看；味道⓫～得真香〈可〉音～得准吗？颜色～不匀；味儿不香〈时〉～了半天还是调不好，多～一会儿就好了〈量〉～过一次座位了；用白颜色～一下儿〔状～〕慢慢～；用哪种颜色～？胡乱⓬了～；随便⓭了～；一下子就～好了

1. flavour; season 2. string 3. tuning 4. seat 5. camera 6. diaphragm; aperture 7. distance 8. even 9. accurate 10. delicious 11. taste; flavour 12. at random; carelessly 13. casually; at random

tiáojié 调节 regulate; adjust〔～宾〕〈名〉～空气❶，～气候❷，～水流❸〔～补〕〈结〉～好了〈程〉～得很合适〈可〉～不了(liǎo)了〈时〉～了半天才调节好〈量〉～过一次；～一下儿〔状～〕自动❹～；适当❺～；可以随意❻～

1. air 2. climate 3. regulate the flow of water 4. automatically 5. suitably; properly 6. at will; as one pleases

tiáojiě 调解 mediate; make peace ≅ 解决〔～宾〕〈名〉～纠纷

❶〔～补〕〈结〉他把两个人的纠纷～好了〈程〉他给～得很好；～得不错〈可〉谁也～不了(liǎo)〈量〉已经～过好几次了；再～一下儿〔状～〕给他们两个人～；热心地❷～；多次～；无法❸～

1. dispute 2. warm-heartedly 3. unable; incapable

tiáozhěng 调整 adjust; regulate; revise ≅ 调〔～宾〕〈名〉～工资❶；～速度❷；～价格❸；～计划❹；～人力❺；～作息时间❻〔～补〕〈量〉价格～过好多次了〔状～〕按时❼～；及时❽～；按比例❾～；必须～；好好～～；适当地❿～；积极⓫～；普遍⓬～；个别⓭～；及早⓮～

1. wages; pay 2. speed 3. price 4. plan 5. manpower; labour power 6. work schedule 7. on time 8. in time 9. in proportion 10. suitably 11. actively 12. generally; in common 13. individually 14. at an early date; as soon as possible

tiāo 挑 ① push sth. up with a pole or stick; raise ≅ 掀；打开〔～宾〕〈名〉～门帘❶；～着旗子❷；～着灯笼❸；～着白旗❹投降❺；他的行为❻让人～大拇指❼〔～补〕〈结〉把帘子❽～开〈趋〉把帘子～起来〈程〉帘子～得太高了〈可〉帘子太厚❾，～不动〈时〉我～了半天帘子等你，你还不快进来〈量〉她轻轻地～了一下儿窗外的帘子〔状～〕往上～；高高地～；用竹竿❿～

1. door curtain 2. flag 3. lantern 4. white flag 5. surrender; capitulate 6. deed; conduct 7. thumb 8. curtain 9. thick 10. bamboo pole

② poke; pick ≅ 拨〔～宾〕〈名〉篝火❶烧❷得不旺❸，快用木棍❹～一～木柴❺；～刺❻；把这个水泡❼～了吧〔～补〕〈结〉把火～旺点儿；刺～断❽了；水泡破❾了；问题～明❿了；矛盾⓫～开了；把我手都快～烂⓬了，刺也没挑出来〈趋〉刺～出来了〈程〉她挑刺～得不疼〈可〉这个刺扎⓭得太深⓮了，～不出来；这根针太粗⓯，～不了(liǎo)刺〈时〉～了半天也没挑出来〈量〉刚～两下儿，刺就出来了〔状～〕轻轻地～；别使劲～；掐⓰着肉～刺；用针～；用铁钩子⓱～火；
另见 tiǎo 挑

1. bonfire 2. burn 3. not roaring 4. rod; stick 5. firewood 6. pick out a splinter 7. blister 8. snapped 9. pricked 10. clear; distinct 11. contradiction 12. festered 13. pricked 14. deep 15. thick 16. pinch; nip 17. poker

tiǎobō 挑拨 instigate; incite; sow discord〔～宾〕〈名〉～是非❶；不要～人家夫妻❷关系❸；～两家人打架❹；～婆媳❺不和〔～补〕〈结〉那个坏蛋又～上了〈趋〉她企图❻～是非，结果没～起来〈程〉～得几个人之间都有矛盾；～得两个人产生了隔阂❼

〈可〉只要自己做得对，谁也～不了(liǎo)我们的关系〈时〉～了半天也没达到目的❽〈量〉～过好多次了〔**状～**〕专门❾～；一次次地～；得机会❿就～；三番五次地⓫～；一再～；故意⓬～；存心⓭～；从中～

1. foment discord **2.** husband and wife **3.** relation **4.** come to blows; fighting **5.** mother-in-law and daughter-in-law **6.** attempt **7.** estrangement; misunderstanding **8.** achieve the goal **9.** specially **10.** whenever occasion offered **11.** over and over again; repeatedly **12. 13.** intentionally; purposely; deliberately

tiào 跳 ① jump; leap; spring; bounce〔**主～**〕〈名〉麻雀❶～；运动员～〔**～补**〕〈趋〉～过这条沟❷去；～到水里去游泳；从窗台上～下来了；她高兴得～起舞来了；从篱笆❸那边～过来了；你能～过这条小河去吗？别看她那么胖❹，～起舞来倒❺很轻巧❻；大家急忙❼～下船去〈程〉～得很高；～得真好；～得多高兴啊！她是我们班跳远❽～得最远的；跳水❾～得真漂亮❿〈可〉这么宽⓫的河我～不过去；这么高的竹竿我～不过去；车太高遇到⓬危险⓭临时⓮～不下来〈时〉～了半天也没跳过去；孩子们每天做完功课都去～一会绳⓯〈量〉～过一次伞；刚～一下儿就把脚扭伤⓰了〔**状～**〕痛痛快快地～⓱；他高兴得直～；从跳板⓲上～；往下～；不慌不忙地⓳～；扑地一声⓴～进水里去了；从这边往那边～；两条腿㉑一块～；单脚㉒～；纵身㉓～；猛㉔～；腾身㉕～；青蛙一～就不见了

1. sparrow **2.** ditch **3.** bamboo or twig fence **4.** fat **5.** but; yet; on the contrary **6.** agile; nimble **7.** in a hurry **8.** long jump **9.** dive **10.** wonderful; splendid **11.** large **12.** run into; encounter; come across **13.** danger **14.** at the time when sth. happens **15.** rope skipping **16.** sprain one's foot **17.** to one's heart's content **18.** diving board; spring board **19.** unhurriedly **20.** with a splash **21.** with both legs **22.** with one foot **23.** jump; leap **24.** suddenly; abruptly **25.** jump; prance

② skip (over); make omissions〔**～宾**〕〈名〉～了一班；～了一级；怎么～了一个格儿❶啊？～一针❷再织❸；这本书我～过第二章去没看〔**～补**〕〈结〉～错针了；从第一页～到第十页〈趋〉～过一行❹字去〔**状～**〕连续❺～了两级；上小学时～过一班

1. square **2.** drop a stitch **3.** knit **4.** row; line **5.** in succession; in a row; running

③ move up and down; beat ≃ 跳动〔**主～**〕〈名〉心～；眼皮～；心惊肉～❶〔**～补**〕〈趋〉眼皮～起来不停❷〈程〉心～得太快了；眼皮～得真难受❸〈时〉～了半天了；～一会儿就好〈量〉心又猛❹

～了一阵❺〔**状～**〕吓❻得心直❼～；一个劲儿地❽～；一阵一阵地❾～；不停地～；没完没了❿(liǎo)地～；怦怦地⓫～〔**习用**〕狗急～墙⓬

1. palpitate with anxiety and fear; be filled with apprehension **2.** ceaseless; incessant **3.** feel unwell **4.** violently **5.** a fit **6.** frighten **7. 8.** continuously **9.** in fits and starts **10.** without end **11.** pit-a-pat **12.** a cornered beast will do sth. desperate; (of evils) will take desperate measures if pushed to the wall

tiē 贴 ① paste; stick; glue ≃ 粘〔**～宾**〕〈名〉～邮票❶；～一张画儿；工作证❷上要～像片；～广告❸；～布告❹；～海报❺；～通知❻；～膏药❼；墙上～着墙纸❽；往脸上～金❾〔**～补**〕〈结〉布告牌❿上～满⓫了广告；画儿～歪⓬了；～斜⓭了；～反⓮了；邮票～多了；把纸～平点儿；纸都～皱⓯了；邮票最好～在信封正面⓰〈趋〉你怎么也～起膏药来了；地图～到对面⓱墙上去了〈程〉墙纸～得真平；墙上的画儿～得乱七八糟⓲的，一点也不艺术⓳；广告～得不是地方⓴〈可〉我的皮肤㉑～不了(liǎo)膏药，贴上就过敏㉒；这种砖墙㉓～不上纸〈时〉～了半天；～一会儿就完了〈量〉～过三次；～过好几回了〔**状～**〕在正面～；结结实实㉔地～；一张挨着㉕一张地～；整整齐齐地～

1. stamp **2.** employee's card **3.** advertisement **4.** notice **5.** playbill **6.** notice **7.** plaster **8.** wall paper **9.** prettify (put feathers in one's own cap) **10.** notice board **11.** full **12. 13.** oblique; slanting **14.** inside out **15.** wrinkle; crease **16.** front; frontage; the obverse side; the right side **17.** opposite **18.** in disorder; in a mess **19.** not conforming to good taste **20.** not on the proper place **21.** skin **22.** allergy **23.** brick wall **24.** solid **25.** get close to; be next to

② keep close to; nestle closely to ≃ 挨近；紧靠；靠近〔**～宾**〕〈名〉这件衣服紧❶～身❷；他总～着墙走；嘴～着耳朵说〔**～补**〕〈结〉孩子紧紧地～在妈妈身边；把孩子的头紧紧～在自己的胸前❸〈趋〉～上去了〈程〉～得很紧〔**状～**〕紧紧地～着

1. closely **2.** next to the skin **3.** bosom

tīng 听 ① listen; hear〔**～宾**〕〈名〉～音乐❶；他最喜欢～流行歌曲❷；我喜欢～地方戏❸；明天我要去～课；孩子最爱～故事；医生给病人～心脏❹；等着～我的回话❺吧；～新闻广播❻；～录音❼；～收音机❽；～天气预报❾〔**～补**〕〈结〉～明白了吗？～懂了没有？我把她的意思～错了；老说这些我们都～腻❿了；～烦⓫了；孩子听故事～出神⓬了；～呆⓭了；听小说～上瘾⓮了；

有点儿~糊涂❶了；孩子听大人说话都~困❶了；这一句我没~清；把话~完了再发表意见❶；昨天我~到一个可怕的消息❶〈趋〉别捣乱❶好好一下去；这个消息我是从我妹妹那儿~来的；仔细❷~来，窗外好象有人；~出他话里的意思来了吗？她的话~起来多亲切❷啊！这话~起来倒很有道理❷；我没~出来他是哪儿的人，虽然开着收音机，可是她脑子❷在想别的事，所以讲的是什么她一点也没~进去；他虽然坐在一边织❷毛衣❷，可是你们说的话她都~进去了；这孩子非常懂事❷，大人嘱咐❷他的话，他都~进去了；给他讲那么多道理，他都没~进去〈程〉~得很兴奋❷；~得非常激动❷；~得紧张❸极了；~得太难过❸了；~得直哭〈可〉报告的内容❸太没意思，我听了一半就~不下去了；她事情太多，每星期连一节课都~不了(liǎo)；这两个音❸的区别❸，我~不出来；电台这么多好听的节目❸，我都~不过来了；声音太小，我~不清；她的话我~不懂;谣言❸可~不得啊!〈时〉~了一年课；~过两年英语；~了半天也没听懂〈量〉这件事我~过三遍了，这个歌儿我~过无数次❸了〔状~〕注意~；专心❸~；细心地~；耐心地❸~；聚精会神地❹~；全神贯注地❹~；恭恭敬敬地❹~；不便❹~；偷偷地~；安安静静地~；一声不响地~着；每天~新闻广播；按时~英语讲座；偶尔❹~；虚心地❹~；不耐烦地❹~；不屑❹一~；

洗耳恭❹~；三心二意地❹~；心不在焉地❺~；一边看书一边~；堵着耳朵❺不~

1. music 2. popular song 3. local opera 4. heart 5. reply; answer 6. newscast 7. tape recording 8. radio 9. weather forecast 10. be bored with; be tired of 11. be vexed 12. be spellbound; be in a trance; be lost in thought 13. be stupefied 14. be addicted to sth. 15. confused 16. sleepy 17. express an opinion 18. news 19. make trouble; create a disturbance 20. carefully 21. cordial; kind 22. reasonable 23. brains; mind 24. knit 25. woolen sweater 26. sensible; intelligent 27. exhort; enjoin; tell 28. 29. excited 30. nervous 31. feel unwell; grieved 32. content 33. sound 34. difference 35. programme 36. rumour 37. innumerable 38. with concentrated attention 39. patiently 40. 41. with rapt attention; with concentrated attention 42. respectfully 43. inconvenient 44. occasionally; once in a while 45. modestly 46. impatiently 47. disdain 48. with respectful attention 49. half heartedly 50. absent-mindedly 51. stuff one's ears

② obey ≅ 听从；接受〔~宾〕〈名〉你怎么总不~我的话啊？~我的命令❶行事❷；这匹马不~话〈动〉他总不~劝❸；一切行动❹要~指挥❺；人老了，腿脚❻

tīng — tíngliú 393

都不～使唤❼了；为什么要～他的指使❽〔～补〕〈结〉这件事听你的算～对了〈可〉跟他讲多少道理❾他都～不进去；什么意见她也～不进去〈量〉应该好好～一下儿别人的劝告〔状～〕必须～；幸亏❿～了

1. order 2. act; handle affairs 3. advise; exhort 4. act; take action 5. command 6. legs and feet — ability to walk 7. not nimble 8. instigation 9. reason 10. fortunately; luckily

tīngjiàn 听见 hear〔～宾〕〈名〉我～她的脚步声❶了；你～我说的话了没有？〈动〉我～打雷❷了；你～放鞭炮❸了吗？〈主-谓〉我～他们在吵架❹；我～铃响❺了；～孩子哭〔～补〕〈可〉他耳朵聋❻了，什么也听不见了〈量〉～过一次〔状～〕一点也没～；偶然❼～了；假装❽着～了；几乎听不见；隐隐约约地❾～了；模模糊糊地❿～了；差点被他～；声音那么小他都～了

1. footfall; footsteps 2. thunder 3. let off firecrackers 4. quarrel 5. the bell goes 6. deaf 7. accidentally; by chance 8. pretend 9. 10. indistinctly; faintly

tīngshuō 听说 be told; hear of〔～宾〕〈主-谓〉我～他回来了；～她瘫痪❶了；～老李的孩子已经考上大学了；～他买了一辆汽车〔状～〕早～；确实❷～；

尚未❸～；不曾❹～；好象～过；仿佛❺～过；或许❻～了

1. be paralysed 2. indeed; really 3. not yet 4. never 5. seem; as if 6. perhaps

tíng 停 stop; cease; halt; pause ≌ 停止〔主～〕〈名〉风～了；钟～了；机器～了〔～宾〕〈名〉～水；～电；杂志～刊❶了；交战❷双方已经～火❸了；～工了；现在已经～课了〈动〉这个报纸已经～办❹了〔～补〕〈结〉等❺船～稳❻了再下；前边的车怎么～住了？船～到对岸❼了；～在江心❽了；汽车～在大门口了〈趋〉车慢慢地～下来了〈程〉车～得太猛❾〈可〉～不住了；～不了(liǎo)了〈时〉～了一个小时电；火车在小站只～几分钟〈量〉今天一晚上～了好几次电；请～一下儿车〔状～〕突然～；渐渐❿～下来了；风一下子～了；一直～了三年

1. stop publication (of a newspaper, magazine, etc.) 2. belligerent 3. cease fire 4. close down 5. till; when 6. steady 7. the opposite bank 8. the heart of a river 9. abruptly; suddenly 10. gradually

tíngliú 停留 stay for a time; stop; remain ≌ 逗留〔主～〕〈名〉马车❶不许❷在这里～；大家没有～，又继续前进了〔～补〕〈结〉～在我原来❸站的地方；科学技术❹不能～在目前❺的水平❻

上；他们的实验❼还只是～在实验室❽里；～在原有❾的基础❿上〈时〉希望你们多～一些时候；火车在这个站⓫只～一分钟；只～了几个小时就走了〔状～〕不要在这儿；多～一会儿；必须～；只好～；不得不～

1. (horse-drawn) carriage 2. not allow 3. original 4. scientific technology 5. at present 6. level 7. experiment 8. laboratory 9. original; former 10. basis 11. station

tíngzhǐ 停止 stop; cease; halt; suspend; call off ≅ 停〔主～〕〈名〉战争❶～了；罢工❷～了；呼吸❸～了；消防演习❹～了〔～宾〕〈名〉～工作；～学习；～营业❺〈动〉～供应❻；～活动❼；～宣传❽；～试验❾；～演习❿；～通行⓫；～广播⓬；～使用⓭；～发球⓮；心脏⓯～了跳动，大家～了说笑〔～补〕〈结〉不要～在原有的水平⓰上〈可〉怎么也～不了(liǎo)了；～不下来了〔状～〕刚刚～；已经～了；必须～；不得不～；主动⓱～；被迫⓲～

1. war 2. strike 3. breathe 4. fire drill 5. business 6. supply 7. activity 8. propaganda 9. experiment; test 10. exercise; drill 11. pass (go) through 12. broadcast 13. use 14. serve a ball 15. heart 16. original level 17. on one's own initiative 18. be forced to

tǐng 挺 ① stick out; straighten up (physically) ≅ 伸直；凸出〔～宾〕〈名〉～胸❶；～着脖子❷；～着肚子〔～补〕〔结〕把身子～直❸了〈趋〉～起胸膛来❹；腰❺再不～起来，就变成驼背❻了；他胖❼得肚子都～起来了〈程〉她身子～得很直，走起路来真精神❽那个人脖子～得那么硬❾，得的是什么病啊？〈可〉身子～不直〔状～〕直直地～着

1. chest 2. neck 3. straight 4. throw out one's chest 5. waist 6. hunchback 7. fat 8. lively; spirited 9. hard; straight

② endure; stand; hold out〔～补〕〈趋〉有点感冒也没休息，硬❶～下来了；再一下去病就更厉害❷了〈可〉她身体真不好，连两个小时都～不下来〈时〉硬～了半天，最后还是不行了；～一会儿还可以，时间长了就受不了❸(liǎo)了〔状～〕别硬～着；勉强❹～着；总算～下来了

1. manage to do sth. 2. serious 3. cannot bear; unable to endure 4. with difficulty

tōng 通 ① open; through〔主～〕〈名〉路～了；管子❶～了；车～了；地道❷～了；山洞❸～了〔～宾〕〈名〉打开窗户～～风❹；鼻子❺不～气❻了〔～补〕〔状～〕还没～啊？终于～了；好容易❼～了，已经～

1. tube; pipe 2. tunnel 3. cave; cavern 4. ventilate (the room) 5. nose 6. stuffy 7. with great difficulty

② connect; communicate〔～宾〕〈名〉～商❶；～车❷；这条小路～后山〈结〉火车已经～到边境❸了〈可〉年底以前这段路～得了(liǎo)车吗？〈时〉车都～了半个多月了，你还不知道呢。〔状～〕我们两国一直❹～商；刚刚～车

1. (of nations) have trade relations 2. be open to traffic 3. frontier 4. all the time

③ notify; tell ≌ 传达〔～宾〕〈名〉～电话；～信，互❶～消息❷；互～姓名〔～补〕〈量〉～过两次电话了〔状～〕经常～；不～

1. each other 2. news; information

tōngguò 通过 ①pass through; get past; traverse ≌ 穿过〔主～〕〈名〉前面正在修路❶，车辆一律❷不能～〔～宾〕〈名〉小船～了桥洞❸；火车～了大桥，电流❹～了导线❺；战士～了敌人的封锁线❻；勘探队❼～了沙漠❽；～了好几道难关❾；仪仗队❿～了检阅台⓫；游行队伍⓬～了广场⓭；火车～了隧道⓮〔状～〕缓慢地～⓯；步伐整齐地～⓰；高呼⓱着口号～；迅速⓲～；顺利地⓳～；运动员英姿勃勃地⓴～

1. build a highway 2. all; without exception 3. bridge opening 4. electric current 5. lead; (conducting) wire 6. blockade line 7. prospecting team 8. desert 9. difficulty; crisis 10. guard of honour; honour guard 11. reviewing stand 12. contigents of paraders or marchers; procession 13. square 14. tunnel 15. march in step 16. shout; cry out 17. slogans 18. rapidly; quickly 19. smoothly; successfully; without a hitch 20. with heroic bearing

② adopt; pass; carry〔主～〕〈名〉考试❶～了；考查❷没～；测验❸～没～？毕业论文❹～了；决议❺～了；预算❻～了；代表名单❼～了；提案❽已经～了；这个报告❾是否❿～了〔～宾〕〈名〉～决议；～了一项决定⓫；～计划⓬；～议案⓭；～名单⓮〔～补〕〈程〉～得很快；～得非常顺利⓯〔状～〕已经～了；还没～；一致⓰～；庄严地⓱～；一次～；在会上～

1. examination; test 2. examination; check 3. test 4. graduation thesis; dissertation 5. resolution 6. budget 7. list of representatives 8. motion; proposal 9. report 10. whether 11. decision 12. plan 13. motion; proposal 14. name list 15. very smoothly 16. unanimously 17. solemnly

tōngzhī 通知 inform; notify; give notice ≌ 告诉〔主～〕〈名〉学校～星期三下午开全校大会〔～宾〕〈名〉～一件事；～一个好消息❶〈代〉请你～他；你都～谁了？～他明天8点开会；～她在门口集合❷〔～补〕〈结〉～晚了，大家都回家了；～早了不行，到

tóngyì 同意 agree; consent; approve ≅ 赞成，准许 ↔ 反对

时候都忘了；这件事要~到每个人〈趋〉出发时间都~下去了吗？住得太分散❸，~起来很麻烦❹〈程〉~得太慢了；~得比较早〈可〉太晚了，~不了(liǎo)了，怕~不到，所以写了一封信〈时〉~了两个小时才通知完〈量〉~了好几遍；你走的时候~我一声；请替我~他一下儿〔状~〕马上~；预先❺~；事先❻~；挨家挨户地❼~；一起~；早点~；没法~；口头❽~；书面❾~；个别❿~

1. news 2. gather; call together 3. scattered 4. troublesome 5. 6. in advance 7. from door to door 8. orally 9. in written form 10. individually

tóngyì 同意 agree; consent; approve ≅ 赞成，准许 ↔ 反对

〔~宾〕〈名〉~你的意见❶；~他的看法❷；~这种观点❸；~这项建议❹；~他们提的方案❺；~那个计划❻；~这种办法；~了我的要求〈主-谓〉~他当校长；不~我一个人去；~你买录音机了吗？〔状~〕不~；真~了！完全~；勉强❼~了；一致❽~；无可奈何地❾~了，只好~；不得不~；终于~了；居然❿~了；大概~了；好象~了；早就~了

1. opinion 2. 3. point of view 4. propose; suggest 5. scheme 6. plan 7. reluctantly 8. unanimously; showing no difference 9. have no way out 10. to one's surprise; unexpectedly

tǒng 捅 poke; stab ≅ 戳；扎；刺

〔~宾〕〈名〉~了他一刀❶；在窗户纸❷上~了一个窟窿❸〔~补〕〈结〉把那个人~死了；~伤❹了；~昏迷❺了；~流血❻了；注意别把窗纸~破❼了；那个孩子不小心用棍儿❽把眼睛~瞎❾了；罪犯❿的凶器⓫正好~到他的肺⓬上〈趋〉他家大门锁着⓭，只好把报纸从门缝⓮里~进去；邻居⓯家的小孩把我的信从门缝~进来了〈程〉这一刀~得真深⓰；~得真狠⓱；窟窿~得太大了〈可〉纸太厚，~不破；~不过去；多注意一点就~不了(liǎo)眼睛了〈量〉~一下儿；被流氓⓲~了一刀〔状~〕是用什么凶器~的？狠狠地~；猛⓳~；突然~；往胸口~；别~了眼睛；差点儿~破；到处乱~

1. stab 2. window paper 3. hole 4. wounded 5. lose consciousness 6. shed blood 7. through 8. rod; stick 9. blind 10. criminal 11. tool or weapon for criminal purposes 12. lung 13. lock up 14. crack between a door and its frame 15. neighbour 16. deep 17. ruthless; relentless 18. rogue; hooligan 19. abruptly; violently

tōu 偷 ① steal; pilfer

〔~宾〕〈名〉~东西；~钱，~衣服〔~补〕〈结〉东西都被人~光❶了；差点儿把他~穷❷了〈趋〉再~下去就得抓❸起来了；那个孩子真没出息❹，把家里的东西都~出来卖了；那个青年受了坏人的引

诱❺，也～起东西来了；小偷把～来的表卖了；工厂的木头都叫人给～去了〈程〉～得太凶❻了；东西～得太多了〈可〉那个人凶极了，～不着(zháo)就抢❼〈时〉～了好几年；～了一辈子❽〈量〉～了无数次❾了；刚～一次就被人抓住了〔状～〕一贯❿～；经常～；从小就～；从监狱⓫里放出来还～；到处～；专⓬～；顺手⓭～；仍旧⓮～；单独⓯～；合伙⓰～；不停地～；一次一次地～

1. nothing left 2. poor 3. arrest; take into custody 4. be a good-for-nothing 5. lure; seduce 6. fearful; terrible 7. rob 8. all one's life 9. innumerable 10. consistently; persistently; all along 11. prison 12. specially; particularly 13. in passing; without extra trouble 14. still 15. alone; by oneself 16. in league with; in collusion with

② find (time); take time off (from work) 〔～宾〕〈名〉～空儿❶去了一次〈形〉～闲❷〔～补〕〈时〉～了一会儿空儿〔状～〕幸亏❸～空儿去了一次〔习用〕忙里～闲；～鸡不成蚀把米❹；～～摸摸❺

1. time (take time off from work to do sth. else) 2. spare time; leisure (snatch a moment of leisure) 3. fortunately 4. try to steal a chicken only to end up losing the rice; go for wool and come back shorn 5. furtively; surreptitiously; covertly

tóu 投 ① throw; fling; hurl ≅ 扔；掷〔～宾〕〈名〉～篮❶；～铅球❷；～手榴弹❸；～标枪❹；～石子儿〔～补〕〈结〉～中❺了；～偏❻了〈趋〉把球～进篮去了；～进来一颗石子；过来一颗手榴弹〈程〉～得非常远；～得很准❼〈可〉我基本功❽太差❾，球～不进去；胳膊❿没劲儿⓫～不远〈时〉～了半天也没投进去〈量〉我～过一次铅球；～了好几下儿才进去〔状～〕站在线外边⓬～；使劲儿⓭～；不慌不忙地⓮～

1. (shoot) a basket 2. shot (put the shot) 3. hand grenade 4. javelin 5. hit 6. inclined to one side; missed 7. accurate 8. basic skill 9. poor 10. arm 11. strength; energy 12. standing on the outside of the line 13. exert all one's strength 14. unhurriedly

② put in; drop〔～宾〕〈名〉～了一笔资金❶；～了一笔款❷〔～补〕〈结〉把选票❸～进了票箱❹；把信～进了邮筒❺；信～错信箱了；票已经～完了，但是还不知道选举结果❻〈可〉～不进去；～不了(liǎo)那么多〈量〉～过一次票；在这个邮筒里～过一次信〔状～〕多一点儿资金；一次～了三封信；先后共～；大量❼～资

1. fund 2. a sum of money 3. vote; ballot 4. ballot box 5. letter box 6. election results 7. a great quantity

③ throw oneself into (a river, well etc. to commit suicide) ≅

跳〔~宾〕〈名〉~河❶；~井❷；~海❸〔~补〕〈量〉她以前~过一次井，后来被救上来了〔状~〕几乎~；曾经~过；突然~；千万别~；为什么~？

1. commit suicide by throwing oneself into a river 2. commit suicide by throwing oneself into a well 3. commit suicide by throwing oneself into the sea

④ project; cast ≙ 投射〔~补〕〈结〉把目光❶~到她身上；树影❷~在窗户上〈趋〉大家的眼光一齐❸~了过来〔状~〕一齐~；全部~

1. sight; vision; view 2. shade (of a tree) 3. at the same time; in unison

⑤ send; deliver ≙ 寄；送〔~宾〕〈名〉~稿❶〔~补〕〈结〉把稿子~到报社❷去了；稿子~给那个出版社❸算~对了〈趋〉稿子已经~出去了；~到哪儿去了？连她都~起稿来了〈量〉~过两次；~一下儿试试〔状~〕多次~；经常~；第一次~

1. manuscript 2. newspaper office 3. publishing house

tóurù 投入 throw into; put into〔~宾〕〈名〉~了大量资金❶；~一些力量；~了几十万兵力❷；~不少人力❸；~了紧张的工作❹；~了生产〈动〉已~使用❺〔~补〕〈趋〉~进来不少劳动力❻；一大笔资金都~进来了〔状~〕全部~；积极~；大量~；大规模地❼~；纷纷❽~；陆续❾~

1. large fund 2. military strength; armed forces 3. manpower 4. intense work 5. be put into operation 6. labour force 7. on a large scale 8. 9. one after another; in succession

tòu 透 ①penetrate; pass through; seep through ≙ 通过；穿过〔~宾〕〈名〉暗室❶的门没关好❷，有点儿~光❸；窗缝❹太大，有点~风；把门打开~~气❺；今天真热，开开窗户~~风吧〔~补〕〈结〉~过车窗❻可以看见前面的村子；阳光~过窗户照❼进来了〈趋〉纸太薄❽，墨水~过去了〈可〉挡❾得这么严❿，~不了(liǎo)光；这种布很厚⓫，光线~不过去；这棵树枝叶很密⓬，阳光一点儿也~不进来〈时〉~一会儿气吧〔状~〕一点儿也不~；往外~；从门缝~

1. dark room 2. not closely shut 3. light 4. a crack between the window and its frame 5. air 6. carriage window 7. shine 8. thin 9. fend; blind 10. tight; close 11. thick 12. dense; thick

② tell secretly ≙ 泄露〔~宾〕〈名〉~个消息❶；~个信儿❷；~个一句半句的〔~补〕〈趋〉把消息~出来了；一点儿情况也没出来〈量〉她给我~过一次信儿〔状~〕早点~个信儿；给他~；务必❸~；怎么~？没法儿❹~

1. news 2. message; news 3. must; be sure to 4. unable; incapable

③ appear; show ≅ 显露〔~宾〕〈形〉~出哀怨❶；她的皮肤❷白里~红〔~补〕〈结〉脸上~出一副高兴的样子；~出幸福❸的样子；那个人~出一脸凶相❹；~出了得意❺的神态❻

1. sad; plaintive 2. skin 3. happy 4. fierce look; ferocious features 5. complacent; proud of oneself 6. expression; manner

tú 图 pursue; seek ≅ 谋取〔~宾〕〈名〉他不~名❶，不~利❷，什么也不图；她这样做的目的❸是~钱❹〈动〉~享受❺；~省事❻〈形〉~安静❼；~一时痛快❽；~舒服❾；~方便❿；~凉快⓫；~宽敞⓬〔~补〕〈趋〉她以前不在乎⓭，现在也~起钱来了〔状~〕明明⓮~；只~；不~；总是~；别~；一向~

1. fame 2. gain 3. objective; purpose; aim 4. money 5. enjoyment 6. save trouble; simplify matters 7. quiet 8. momentary satisfaction 9. comfortable 10. convenient 11. nice and cool 12. spacious; roomy; commodious 13. not mind; not care 14. obviously; plainly

tú 涂 ①spread on; apply; smear ≅ 抹〔~宾〕〈名〉门上~绿漆❶；腿❷上~点儿药膏❸；机器上~油；演员脸上~了油彩❹；嘴上~口红❺；地板~蜡❻吗?〔~补〕〈结〉漆没~匀❼；螺丝❽上~满❾了油；颜色~深❿了〈趋〉这一桶漆都~上去了；这种颜色~出来不太好看〈程〉~得太厚；~得不匀；~得真快；~得哪儿都是〈可〉没有刷子⓫~不了(liǎo)；墙太脏~不上；桌面不平~不匀；这盒药膏一个月也~不完；油漆这么贵，我可~不起⓬；后边~不着(zháo)〈时〉了一个星期药伤⓭才好；别着急再~一会儿就完了〈量〉一天~两次药；~了两遍〔状~〕一层一层地⓮~；干了以后再~；按次序⓯~；别瞎⓰~；净乱⓱~；给机器零件⓲~；往脸上~；用刷子快~；每天~

1. green paint 2. leg 3. ointment 4. greasepaint 5. lipstick 6. wax 7. even 8. screw 9. all over 10. deep; dark 11. brush 12. cannot afford 13. wound 14. layer upon layer 15. in order 16. 17. at random 18. spare parts

② scribble; scrawl ≅ 划〔~补〕〈结〉快把写错的字~掉❶吧；把橡皮擦❷都~黑了〈程〉他把簿子❸~得不象样儿了❹！~得太脏了；~得乱七八糟的❺；~得看不清了〈可〉用这种橡皮擦~不掉；怎么涂也~不干净；这种纸很结实❻，~不破❼〈时〉~了半天也没涂掉〈量〉多~几下儿就行了〔状~〕轻轻地~；使劲儿❽~；真难~；慢慢~；一点一点地~〔习用〕~脂抹粉❾

1. away; off 2. eraser 3. exercise book 4. unpresentable 5. in disorder; in a mess 6. durable 7. not easily torn 8. with strength 9. apply powder and paint; prettify; whitewash

tǔ 吐 ① spit〔~宾〕〈名〉~核儿❶；~葡萄皮儿❷；~了一地瓜子皮；~痰❸；~唾沫❹；~舌头❺；壁炉❻~着火舌❼；蚕❽~丝❾，~鱼刺❿〔~补〕〈结〉把核儿~净⓫了；蚕~完了丝；痰要~在纸里〈趋〉把瓜子儿~出来〈程〉瓜子皮儿~得太多了；~得满地都是〈可〉鱼刺卡⓬在嗓子⓭里~不出来了〈时〉这条蚕~了两天丝〔状~〕往外~；大口地~；不要随地~痰⓮；别乱⓯~〔习用〕狗嘴里~不出象牙来⓰

1. stone; pit; core 2. grape skins 3. sputum 4. saliva 5. tongue 6. fireplace 7. tongues of fire 8. silkworm 9. silk 10. fishbone 11. complete 12. block; check 13. throat 14. no spitting 15. at random 16. a dog's mouth emits no ivory; a filthy mouth can't utter decent language

② say; tell; pour out ≃ 说出来〔~宾〕〈名〉他唱歌~字清楚；不~实话❶，~苦水❷；问了半天他也不~口❸；~了一口气❹〔~补〕〈趋〉把一肚子冤屈❺都~出来了〈程〉字~得真清楚〈可〉一肚子怨气❻~不出来；~不完的苦水〔状~〕一向~字清楚；从来不~实话；向谁~苦水？总算❼

~了一口气；终于❽把怨气都~出来了
另见 tù 吐

1. truth 2. grievance; suffering 3. tell the truth 4. feel elated and exultant 5. full of pent-up injustice 6. grievance; complaint 7. 8. at long last; finally

tù 吐 vomit; throw up〔~宾〕〈名〉~血❶；~白沫❷；~苦水❸；~酸水❹〔~补〕〈结〉~完了觉得舒服❺一些；胃里的东西全~干净了〈趋〉把刚喝下去的中药❼全~出来了；一坐船就~个没完；再~下去人都要支持不住❽了〈程〉~得真难受❾；~得两腿脚软⓫了；~得一点力气都没有了；~得无精打采⓫〈可〉恶心⓬想吐，可又~不出来；吃完汤药⓭，赶快吃一块糖，就~不了(liǎo)了〈时〉她怀孕⓮的时候，整整⓯~了八个月；~一会就好了〈量〉~过一次；~了一阵〔状~〕哇哇地⓰~；一口一口地~鲜血；全部~出来了；突然连续⓱~了半年；差点儿~出来，酒⓲喝多了，直~
另见 tǔ 吐

1. (spitting) blood 2. foam 3. 4. gastric secretion etc. rising to the mouth 5. feel well 6. stomach 7. traditional Chinese medicine 8. cannot hold out any longer 9. feel unwell 10. one's legs feel like jelly 11. in low spirits; out of sorts 12. feel nauseated; feel sick

13. a decoction of medicinal ingredients 14. be pregnant 15. whole; as long as 16. bursting out 17. in succession; in a row 18. liquor; wine

tuán 团 roll sth. into a ball; roll 〔~宾〕〈名〉~一个纸团儿❶；~煤球❷；~药丸❸；~肉丸子❹〔~补〕〈结〉把雪球❺小点儿；把煤球~紧点❻儿；把纸~成团儿；把雪~成球；药丸~大了；肉丸子~完了就下锅炸❼；~坏了再重新团〈程〉纸团~得真紧，打都打不开〈可〉泥❽不粘❾~不上，就把它扔❿了〈量〉我来~一下儿试试〔状~〕好~吗？ 使劲儿⓫~；用手~

1. (roll paper into) a ball 2. (egg-shaped) briquet 3. pill 4. meatball 5. snowball 6. closely; tightly 7. put into pan for frying 8. mud 9. not sticky 10. throw away 11. with strength

tuánjié 团结 unite; rally ↔ 分裂〔~宾〕〈名〉~朋友；~一切可以团结的力量❶〔~补〕〈结〉一致❷；~紧❸；~在一起〈趋〉大家~起来〈程〉~得很好；~得紧紧的〈可〉~得起来吗？ ~不紧〔状~〕好好~；主动❹~；他们之间有点儿不~；紧密地~；必须~；互相~

1. unite with all the forces that can be united 2. unite as one 3. closely; tightly 4. on one's own initiative

tuī 推 ① push; shove ↔ 拉〔~宾〕〈名〉~着一辆独轮车❶；护士❷~着病人；~了一车青菜；~了一车石灰❸；用手~了~门；驴❹能~磨❺；她正在~铅球❻〔~补〕〈结〉我一开门一看，屋子里没有人，把椅子~倒❼了，桌子被他一翻❽了〈趋〉把没用的东西都~到旁边去了；病人被护士从手术室里❾~出来了；把菜~过来卖吧；把子弹❿~上膛⓫去了〈程〉车~得很远了，~得真费劲儿⓬〈可〉手推车⓭上装的东西太多了，我一个人~不动；门关得很紧⓮，~不开；子弹~不上去；责任⓯是~不掉⓰的；五个人也~不倒这棵树〈时〉~了半天也没推开〈量〉轻轻地~了一下儿；使劲儿~了他一把〔状~〕用力~；一把就把她~开了；往后~；真难~；慢点儿~；冷不防地⓱~了他一下儿；用轮椅⓲~病人

1. wheelbarrow 2. nurse 3. lime 4. ass; donkey 5. mill 6. shot 7. fallen 8. turned over 9. operating room 10. bullet 11. bore of a gun 12. need or use great effort 13. handcart; wheelbarrow 14. tightly closed 15. responsibility 16. unable to shirk 17. suddenly; by surprise 18. wheelchair

② cut; pare〔~宾〕〈名〉~头❶；用推草机❷~草❸〔~补〕〈结〉把

头发~短点儿；头发~完了，显得❹更年轻了；用刨子❺把木板~光〈趋〉用推草机~起草来可快了〈程〉头发~得真不错〈可〉~不了(liǎo)那种样子；~不出那种发型❻来〈时〉~了半个小时；再~一会儿就完了〈量〉~过一次平头，再用力~几下儿，板子就平了〔状~〕不好~吧₂随便❼~；有时候；仔细❽~

1. have a haircut or cut sb.'s hair
2. mower 3. mow 4. look; seem; appear 5. plane 6. hair style 7. casually; at random 8. carefully

tuīchí 推迟 put off; postpone; defer

〔~宾〕〈名〉~婚期❶；~开会❷的日期〔~补〕〈结〉~到下个月举行❸〈趋〉别再~下去了〈可〉~不到那么晚；~不到那个时候吧₂〈时〉~了三天；~了一年〈量〉已经~过一次了〔状~〕一再~；再三~；连续❹~；往后~；又再~

1. wedding day 2. hold a meeting 3. hold 4. in succession; in a row; running

tuīguǎng 推广 popularize; spread; extend

〔~宾〕〈名〉~汉语拼音❶；~优良品种❷〔~补〕〈趋〉要把这种好方法~开来〈时〉~了一个时期❸〈量〉应该~一下儿〔状~〕认真~；向大家~；大力❹~；普遍~；部分~

1. The Chinese phonetic alphabet 2. fine variety 3. a period of time 4. energetically; vigorously

tuījiàn 推荐 recommend

〔~宾〕〈名〉~两本书；~优秀作品❶；~一篇好文章❷；~一个电影；~广播员❸；~老师；~保姆❹；~厨师❺〈代〉~他去当教练❻〔~补〕〈结〉~错了人；~过了〈趋〉把他~上去了；是谁把那个人~进来的₂〈程〉~得很及时❼〈可〉~得出来~不出来？~得了(liǎo)吗₂〈量〉~过一次；~一下儿试试吧〔状~〕向学生~；认真~；好好~；大力❽~；经常~

1. works of excellence 2. article; essay 3. announcer; broadcaster 4. (children's) nurse 5. cook 6. coach; instructor; trainer 7. in time 8. energetically; vigorously

tuīqiāo 推敲 weigh; deliberate

〔~宾〕〈名〉~词句❶；~文字❷〔~补〕〈结〉这些词我都认真~过了〈趋〉~出好词句来了〈时〉~了半天也没找到合适的❸词句〈量〉~过好几次；再好好~一下儿〔状~〕认真~；反复~；一句一句地~；字斟句酌地❹~；仔细❺~；尽量❻~

1. words and phrases; expression 2. characters; words 3. suitable; proper 4. choose one's words with great care; weigh every word 5. carefully 6. to the best of one's ability; as far as possible

tuīxíng 推行 carry out; pursue; practise

〔~宾〕〈名〉~奖励❶办

法〔~补〕〈结〉~开了〈趋〉~开来〈可〉~得了(liǎo)~不了(liǎo)？~不下去了〈时〉~过一个时期❷〈量〉~过一次〔状~〕极力❸~；大力❹~

1. award; reward 2. a period of time 3. do one's utmost 4. energetically; vigorously

tuì 退 ① move back; retreat ↔ 进〔主~〕〈名〉敌人~了〔~宾〕〈名〉请你向后~一步；为了加宽马路❶，临街的房子❷要往后~一米〔~补〕〈结〉~远点儿；~到门口〈趋〉人们都~出门外去了；队伍❸从前线❹~下来了；敌人已经~下去了；人们都从屋里~出来了；向前走了几步，又~回来了；她~到后边去了〈程〉敌兵❺~得很快；队伍一天一夜也~不完〈时〉~了三天才退完〔状~〕向后~；倒❻~；赶快~吧

1. widen a road 2. house overlooking the street 3. troops 4. front 5. enemy troops 6. backwards

② withdraw from; quit ≅ 退出〔~宾〕〈名〉~席❶；~职❷；~伍❸；~役❹；~伙❺；~学❻；~会❼(工会)；皇帝❽~位❾了〔~补〕〈程〉退伙~得很早〈可〉现在还~不了(liǎo)伙，再过几天才行❿〈量〉他~过一次学〔状~〕中途⓫~学(席)；还没~伍；已经~伙了，只好~职

1. leave a banquet or a meeting 2. resign or be discharged from office; quit working 3. retire or be discharged from active military service 4. retire or be released from military service (on completing the term of reserve) 5. cancel an arrangement to eat at a mess; withdraw from a mess 6. leave school 7. trade union 8. emperor 9. give up the throne; abdicate 10. O.K.; all right 11. halfway; midway

③ return; give back; refund ≅ 退还〔~宾〕〈名〉~钱；~货❶；~火车(飞机/船)票；~赃款❷〔~补〕〈结〉钱~错了；把瓶子钱~给我了〈趋〉把货~回去了，钱都~回来了；他把赃物全部~出来了吗？〈程〉货~得真快；~得很及时❸〈可〉毛衣❹弄脏了❺，~不了(liǎo)了；这种票~不出去〈量〉~过好几次票了〔状~〕一次~完；分批❻~；一点一点地~；一共~；不用~；弄坏了没法儿❼~了；纷纷~

1. goods 2. money stolen 3. in time 4. woollen sweater 5. get dirty 6. in batches 7. unable; incapable

④ decline; recede; ebb; fade ≅ 减退，下降〔主~〕〈名〉潮水❶~了，高烧❷已经~了，洪水❸~了〔~宾〕〈名〉~潮❹了；~烧了；这布~色❺了；电镀❻东西~光❼了；那个孩子学习~步了〔~补〕〈结〉颜色都快~没了〈趋〉潮水~下去了；~起烧来很慢〈程〉~得真快；颜色~得不象样

子❽了〈可〉吃了多少药也~不了(liǎo)烧〈量〉这种布洗一次~一次颜色〔**状**~〕不容易~；很快就~了〔已经~了；还没~呢；逐渐❾~下去了；就要~了

1. tide; tidal water 2. high fever 3. flood 4. tide 5. fade; colourfast 6. electroplate 7. nothing left 8. unpresentable; in no shape to be seen 9. gradually

⑤ cancel; break off ≅ 撤销〔~宾〕〈名〉~婚❶；~亲❷；~订货❸〔~补〕〈结〉~掉全部❹订货〈程〉~得比较晚；~得很及时❺〈可〉~得了(liǎo)吗？〈时〉~了半天；~了好久〈量〉~过一次〔**状**~〕已经~了；早就~了；正在~；必须~；及时~

1. 2. break off an engagement 3. cancel an order 4. whole; all 5. in time

tuìchū 退出 withdraw from; secede; quit〔~宾〕〈名〉~战场❶；~会场❷；~教室；~试验❸小组❹〈动〉~比赛；~试验〔~补〕〈趋〉从试验小组里~来了〈程〉~得比较晚；~得很早〈量〉~过一次〔**状**~〕当场❺~；立即❻~；只好~；必须~；莫明其妙地❼~

1. battlefield; battleground 2. meeting-place 3. experiment; test 4. group 5. on the spot; then and there 6. at once; immediately 7. without rhyme or reason

tuì 煺 scald (a pig, chicken, etc.) in order to remove hairs or feathers〔~宾〕〈名〉~鸡毛；~猪毛〔~补〕〈结〉先把鸡毛~干净了，再放在锅❶里烧❷；毛~完了再洗〈程〉~鸭毛~得很干净；~得真快〈可〉用冷水~不了(liǎo)毛；用开水❸一浇❹就~下来了〈时〉吃鸡~真麻烦❺，光煺毛儿就要~半天〈量〉~过一次鸡毛，没煺过鸭毛〔**状**~〕好不好~？怎么~？用开水~

1. pot; pan 2. cook; bake; stew 3. boiling water 4. pour on 5. troublesome

tuì 褪 shed (feathers) ≅ 脱〔~宾〕〈名〉小鸡~毛了〔~补〕〈结〉毛都快~完了；~干净了没有？〈趋〉那只小白鸡也~起毛来了〈程〉~得真快〈时〉~了一个星期就全褪完了〔**状**~〕一点一点地~；一下子~完了；正在~；已经~完了，还没~呢

另见 tùn 褪

tūn 吞 swallow; gulp down ↔ 吐〔~宾〕〈名〉~中药丸❶；大鱼~了很多小鱼〔~补〕〈结〉一口就~掉了；雾气❷把远山~没(mò)了〈趋〉把一块肥肉❸~下去了；把中药丸~进肚子❹里去了；~到胃❺里去了〈可〉整个❻的药丸我~不下去〔**状**~〕往下~；不费劲儿❼就~下去了；钱财❽他想一个人独❾~

1. pill of Chinese medicine 2. fog; mist; vapour 3. fat 4. belly 5. stomach 6. whole 7. not needing the effort 8. wealth; money 9. alone; by oneself

tùn 褪 slip out of sth. 〔~宾〕〈名〉那匹马~套儿❶了〔~补〕〈趋〉把绳套儿❷~下来了；把(手)表从胳膊❸上~下来了；~下一只袖子❹来量❺血压❻〈可〉袖子太瘦❼~不下来；绳套系❽得很结实❾，~不了(liǎo)〈时〉那么多人等着检查身体❿可是我的袖子~了半天也没褪下来，真急⓫人〔状~〕好~吗？往下~；使劲~

另见 tuì 褪

1. break loose 2. loop; noose 3. arm 4. sleeve 5. measure 6. blood pressure 7. thin; emaciated 8. tie; fasten 9. fast 10. have a physical examination 11. annoying

tuō 托 ① hold in the palm; support with the hand or palm 〔~宾〕〈名〉饭馆的侍应生❶一只手~着盘子❷送菜；她两手~腮❸，坐在那儿想心事❹〔~补〕〈结〉~住了；~好了，别把盘子摔❺了〈趋〉轻轻一托，就把球~过网❻去了〈程〉她托球~得多好啊！〔状~〕一只手~着；好好~着

1. attendant; waiter 2. plate 3. cheek 4. sth. weighing on one's mind; worry 5. fall; 6. over the net

② ask; entrust ≅ 委托〔~宾〕〈名〉~个人情❶；~一个人〈代〉~她照看❷孩子；这事儿~他办吧〔~补〕〈结〉把孩子~给人家了〈趋〉孩子~到人家家里去了〈可〉孩子太小了，现在还~不了(liǎo)〈时〉~半天人情也没办成❸〈量〉~过他好几次了；~一下儿他〔状~〕不便❹~；不好❺~人情；没法儿❻~；过些日子再~

1. ask an influential person to help arrange sth. 2. look after 3. succeed 4. 5. inconvenient 6. unable; incapable

tuō 拖 ① pull; drag; haul ≅ 拉〔~宾〕〈名〉大船~着小船；脑后❶~着一条大辫子❷；彗星❸~着一条大尾巴〔~补〕〈结〉是那个坏蛋把他~下水❹的；长裙❺~在身后；把地~干净点儿；把那辆破汽车~走了〈趋〉把小船~上岸来了；把打死的猎物❻从山坡上~下来了〈程〉地板~得真干净〈可〉这头野牛❼真沉❽，三个人都~不动；她连地都~不干净；小船~不回来了〈时〉两间屋子的地~了半个小时〈量〉一天~两次地板；试~一下儿但没拖动〔状~〕使劲~；用绳子~；从床底下~出一个皮箱❾；往外~；往后~；只好~着走

1. behind the head 2. plait; braid 3. comet 4. get sb. into hot

water; get sb. into trouble 5. long skirt 6. bag 7. wild ox 8. heavy 9. leather suitcase (trunk)

② delay; drag on ≅ 拖延〔～宾〕〈名〉～时间❶〔～补〕〈结〉他的病拖久了，都把身体～垮❷了〈趋〉再～下去病就不好治❸了〈程〉时间～得太长了；病～得太久了〈可〉身体～不垮；这件事再也～不下去了；病可～不得❹〈时〉～了半年没去看，结果看不了(liǎo)了；她干什么事都是～一会儿是一会儿的；再一一会儿就来不及❺了〔状～〕一直～了半年；别再～了〔习用〕～泥带水❻；～后腿❼

1. play for time 2. wear oneself down 3. not easy to cure 4. must not; cannot afford 5. there's not enough time (to do sth.) 6. messy; sloppy; slovenly 7. hinder (impede) sb.; hold sb. back; be a drag on sb.

tuō 脱 ① (of hair, skin) shed; come off ≅ 脱落〔～宾〕〈名〉晒❶得～了一层皮；那只骆驼❷～毛了；得了伤寒❸以后容易～头发；脚被石头砸❹坏了，现在开始～趾甲❺了〔～补〕〈结〉头发～光了；毛～完了〈趋〉～下一层皮去〈程〉头发～得很厉害；～得都露❻头皮❼了〔量〕每年～一次毛〔状～〕一下子～光了；一层一层地❽～皮

1. be exposed to the sun 2. camel 3. typhoid fever 4. pound; tamp 5. toenail 6. reveal 7. scalp 8. layer after layer

② take off ↔ 穿〔～宾〕〈名〉～鞋；～袜子❶；～衣服；～裤子❷；～手套❸〔～补〕〈结〉孩子把衣服～光去洗澡❹了；～掉❺手套再跟朋友握手〈趋〉回屋以后把皮鞋～下去换❻上了拖鞋❼；袜子都湿❽了，快～下来吧〈程〉～得真快；～得太多了〈可〉我～不开身❾；脚肿❿了，鞋都～不下来了；一只手～不了(liǎo)衣服〈时〉冬天穿得太多，脱衣服～半天也没脱下来〈量〉帮她～一下儿大衣〔状～〕一件一件地～；妈妈给孩子～；快～；先别～；自己～；马上～；

1. socks; stockings 2. trousers; pants 3. gloves 4. take a bath 5. away; off 6. change 7. slippers 8. wet 9. can't get away 10. swollen

③ get out of; escape from ≅ 脱离〔～宾〕〈名〉已经～险了❶；那匹马～缰❷了〔状～〕幸亏❸～险了；好容易❹～险了；终于❺～险了；怎么～缰了？

1. danger (escape danger) 2. reins; halter 3. fortunately; luckily 4. with great difficulty 5. at last; in the end

tuōlí 脱离 separate oneself from; break away from; be divorced from〔～宾〕〈名〉～实际❶；～了虎口❷；～了家庭❸；～关系❹；病人～了危险❺；人不能～社会

❻〔～补〕〈结〉～开烦恼 ❼〈可〉～不了(liǎo),～不开〔状～〕暂时 ❽～;永远 ❾～;好容易 ❿才～;不能～;无法 ⓫

1. reality; practice (lose contact with reality) 2. tiger's mouth — jaws of death 3. family 4. relation 5. danger 6. society 7. vexation; worry 8. temporarily; for the moment 9. always; forever 10. with great difficulty 11. unable; incapable

tuó 驮 carry on the back 〔～宾〕〈名〉小毛驴 ❶能～粮食 ❷;骆驼 ❸～行李 ❹;～了五里路〔～补〕〈结〉把东西～走了;～在驴背 ❺上〈趋〉把煤～进来;～到山上去了〈程〉～得真多;～得很远〈可〉～不了(liǎo)那么多东西;太沉 ❻～不动;一趟～不完;太远～不到;～得上来/～得过去/～得起来吗?〈时〉～了好长时间;～一会儿就累了〈量〉～过两趟;～了好几次〔状～〕一共～;一趟一趟地～;吃力地 ❼～;往哪儿～?

1. donkey 2. food 3. camel 4. luggage; baggage 5. back 6. heavy 7. strenuously

W

wā 挖 dig; excavate; tap (potentialities)〔**~宾**〕〈名〉~沟❶；~隧道❷；~防空洞❸；木板上~了一个槽❹儿；墙上~了一个窟窿❺〔**~补**〕〈结〉山洞~通❻了；沟~深了；槽儿~浅❼了；窟窿~大了；隧道~斜❽了；~宽❾了；~窄❿了；防空洞~塌⓫了；游泳池~深了〈趋〉把土一锹一锹地⓬~上来了；还不够深，再~下一尺去〈程〉~得真快；~得很深；槽儿~得很合适〈可〉没有工具⓭~不了(liǎo)；这个山洞一个月~得通~不通？门上要装⓮一把锁⓯，可是窟窿我~不好；~不圆；池塘⓰里的泥~得上来~不上来？〈时〉~了三个月才挖通；多~一会儿就行了〈量〉多~几下儿；~过好多次了；再往下~一下儿〔**状~**〕用什么工具~？深点儿~；人工~⓱；用机器~；从东往西~；白⓲~了；别乱⓳~；一气儿⓴~；断断续续地㉑~；一锹挨着一锹地~〔**习用**〕~墙脚㉒

1. ditch **2.** tunnel **3.** air-raid shelter **4.** slot **5.** hole; opening **6.** open; through **7.** shallow **8.** oblique; slanting **9.** wide **10.** narrow **11.** collapse **12.** shovel after shovel **13.** tool **14.** install **15.** lock **16.** pond; pool **17.** manual work; by hand **18.** in vain **19.** at random **20.** at a stretch; without a break; at one go **21.** off and on; intermittently **22.** undermine the foundation; cut the ground from under sb.'s feet

wān 弯 bend; flex ↔ 直〔**主~**〕〈名〉腰❶别~着；腿~着呢〔**~宾**〕〈名〉~着腰插秧❷；~着身子捡❸东西〔**~补**〕〈结〉那个孩子总弯着腰，都~成驼背❹了；腰~习惯❺了，就不好改了；杂技演员❻的头能~到脚面❼；腰都~累❽了〈趋〉~下腰去捡起一串钥匙❾来；把铁丝❿头儿~过来〈程〉弯腰~得很累；~得都直不起来了〈可〉手指的关节⓫坏了，~不了(liǎo)了；腰~不下去了；铁丝太粗⓬~不过来；~不成那种形状⓭〈时〉~了半个多小时，腰都直不起来了；~一会儿还可以，时间长了可受不了⓮(liǎo)〈量〉把铁丝往那边~一下儿〔**状~**〕深深地⓯~着腰；向下~；往回⓰~；人老了腰逐渐⓱~了

1. waist **2.** transplant rice seedlings (shoots) **3.** pick up; collect; gather **4.** hunchback; humpback **5.** get used to; get into the habit **6.** acrobat **7.** instep **8.** tired **9.** a bunch of keys **10.** iron wire **11.**

joint **12.** thick **13.** form **14.** unbearable; cannot bear; be unable to endure **15.** deeply **16.** backwards **17.** gradually

wánchéng 完成 accomplish; fulfil〔**～宾**〕〈名〉～任务❶；～计划❷〔**～补**〕〈程〉～得不好；～得很出色❸〈可〉计划～不了(liǎo)；任务总～不好〔**状～**〕认真～；按时❹～；终于～了；如期❺～；限期❻～；想方设法地❼～；顺利地❽～；部分❾～；基本上❿～

1. task **2.** plan **3.** outstanding; remarkable; splendid **4.** on time **5.** as scheduled; by the scheduled time; on schedule **6.** within a definite time **7.** by every possible means; by hook or by crook **8.** smoothly; without a hitch; successfully **9.** partly **10.** basically; fundamentally; on the whole

wánr 玩儿 ① play; have fun; amuse oneself ≃ 玩耍〔**主～**〕〈名〉孩子们常在一起～；小猫跟老猫～；你有空儿到我家来～〔**～宾**〕〈名〉他爱～足球；我们～一盘棋❶；～牌❷；～朴克❸；他敢～蛇❹；～鸟；小孩子～火柴❺很危险❻；小孩子都喜欢～水；男孩子最爱～枪❼；～秋千❽；～滑梯❾；谁～捉迷藏❿？他们在～堆雪人⓫；～跳绳⓬儿；～跷跷板⓭〔**～补**〕〈结〉手枪～腻⓮了，又要玩汽车；～高兴了，唱起来了；孩子们刚打完架又～开了；这盘棋～赢⓯了；牌～输⓰了；他们～到天黑还没回家；玩牌～上瘾⓱了，到时候就想玩〈趋〉这些日子又～起汽枪⓲来了；再～下去，考试就得(děi)不及格⓳；这孩子前两天玩弹弓⓴，这两天又～起空竹㉑来了〈程〉他玩牌～得真精㉒；玩朴克～得很痛快㉓；玩龙灯㉔～得真高兴；～得什么也不顾㉕了；～得连饭都不想吃了；～得真起劲㉖〈可〉兴趣㉗不一样～不起来；大人和孩子～不到一块儿〈时〉什么玩具㉘到他手里，～一会儿就坏；这孩子非常文静㉙，一个人静静坐在那儿～了一个上午；一玩牌就得(děi)～三、四个小时，太浪费时间㉚了〈量〉小红对小英说："你的娃娃借我～一下儿吧？"〔**状～**〕整天～；高高兴兴地～；在公园～；痛痛快快地～；孩子们吵吵嚷嚷地㉛～；彻夜不眠地㉜～；根本㉝不～；偏㉞要～；偷偷地～；连续～；偶尔㉟～；一年一度地㊱～；决不～；适当地㊲～；随便㊳～

1. chess **2. 3.** card **4.** snake **5.** match **6.** dangerous **7.** toy gun **8.** swing **9.** (children's) slide **10.** hide-and-seek **11.** make (build) a snowman **12.** skipping **13.** seesaw **14.** be bored with; be tired of **15.** win **16.** lose; be beaten; be defeated **17.** be addicted (to sth.) **18.** air gun; pneumatic gun **19.** cannot pass an examination, etc. **20.** catapult;

slingshot 21. diabolo 22. smart; sharp; clever; shrewd 23. very happy; 24. dragon lantern 25. show no consideration 26. energetical; vigorous; enthusiastical 27. interest 28. toy 29. gentle and quiet 30. waste time 31. noisily 32. awake all through the night 33. at all; simply 34. wilfully; against expectation 35. once in a while; occasionally 36. once a year 37. suitably; appropriately; properly 38. casually; at random

② employ; resort to ≅ 使用〔~宾〕〈名〉~手腕❶儿；~阴谋手段❷；~花招儿❸；~绝招儿❹；〔~补〕〈结〉花招儿都~绝❺了；~尽❻了各种手法❼〈趋〉他又~起花招儿来了〈程〉他手腕~得真绝〈可〉那么老实的人~不了(liǎo)花招儿〈时〉~了半天手腕儿〈量〉~过好几次花招儿了〔状~〕总~；专门❽ ~；别~；跟大家~〔习用〕可不是~的❾；~命❿

1. artifice; finesse; stratagem 2. conspiratorial means 3. trick; game 4. unique skill; unexpected tricky move (as a last resort) 5. exhausted; matchless 6. try one's best; put to the best use 7. trick 8. specially; especially 9. this is no joking matter 10. gamble (play) with one's life; risk one's life needlessly

wánnòng 玩弄 ① dally with ≅ 戏弄〔~宾〕〈名〉~女性❶；~人〔~补〕〈量〉~过无数次❷〔状~〕经常~；一向❸ ~；一贯❹ ~；肆无忌惮地❺ ~；公开❻ ~；暗中❼ ~；决不~；多次~

1. the female sex; woman 2. innumerable 3. 4. consistently; all along 5. unscrupulously; brazenly 6. openly; publicly 7. secretly; in secret

② play with; juggle with ≅ 搬弄〔~宾〕〈名〉~词句❶；~辞藻❷〔~补〕〈趋〉又~起辞藻来了〔状~〕一再~；故意❸ ~；仍旧❹ ~

1. words (juggle with words) 2. rhetoric; flowery language 3. intentionally 4. still; yet

③ employ; resort to ≅ 施展；使用 (见 wánr 玩儿②)

wǎn 挽 ① pull; draw ≅ 拉；拉住〔~宾〕〈名〉手~着手；胳膊~着胳膊❶〔~补〕〈趋〉大家把手~起来〈程〉胳膊~得很紧❷〔状~〕紧紧地~着胳膊

1. arm in arm 2. close; tight

② roll up ≅ 卷〔~宾〕〈名〉~袖子❶〔~补〕〈结〉把袖子~上〈趋〉~起袖子来工作方便❷；~起袖子来要打架❸〈程〉袖子~得真高〈时〉~了半天也没挽上去〈量〉帮我往上~一下儿〔状~〕往外~；真难~；勉强❹ ~；别~高高地~；少~点儿

1. sleeve 2. convenient 3. come to blows 4. with difficulty

wǎnhuí 挽回 retrieve; redeem 〔~宾〕〈名〉~败局❶；~面子❷；~劣势❸；~损失❹；~僵局❺；~残局❻；~几乎不可收拾的❼局面❽；~局势❾；~名誉❿〔~补〕〈量〉需要~一下儿〔状~〕立即⓫~；及时⓬~；无法~；竭力⓭~；千方百计地⓮~

1. lost game; losing battle 2. face 3. inferiority; inferior strength or position 4. loss 5. deadlock; impasse; stalemate 6. the final phase of a game of chess; the situation after the failure of an undertaking or after social unrest 7. irremediable; unmanageable; out of hand; hopeless 8. aspect; phase; situation 9. situation 10. fame; reputation 11. at once; immediately 12. in time 13. do one's utmost; energetically 14. by every possible means; by hook or by crook

wǎnjiù 挽救 save; remedy; rescue ≅ 救〔~宾〕〈名〉~病人的生命；~了他的性命❶；~堕落❷的人；~失足❸的人；~生命垂危❹的人；~庄稼❺〔~补〕〈趋〉终于把那个青年人~过来了；从泥坑❻里~出来〈程〉~得还比较及时〈可〉谁也~不了(liǎo)他了〈时〉~了半天，全白费❼了〈量〉~一下儿|他吧；~过两次，还是没挽救过来〔状~〕无法~了；竭力❽~；热情地❾~；千方百计地❿~；一再~；及时⓫~；从危险⓬中~；从火坑⓭中~；尽量⓮~；尽力⓯~；奋不顾身地⓰~

1. life 2. degenerate 3. take a wrong step in one's life 4. critically ill; at one's last gasp 5. crop 6. mud pit; mire 7. in vain 8. do one's utmost 9. warmly 10. by every possible means; by hook or by crook 11. in time 12. from danger 13. fiery pit; pit of hell; abyss of suffering 14. 15. to the best of one's ability; as far as possible 16. dash ahead regardless of one's safety

wǎnliú 挽留 urge (persuade) sb. to stay ≅ 留〔~宾〕〈名〉~客人；~朋友；~亲戚❶〈代〉~她多坐一会儿〔~补〕〈结〉怎么也没把他~住〈趋〉终于把他~了下来〈可〉~不住客人〈时〉~了半天，他还是要走〈量〉好好~一下儿她〔状~〕被主人~；热情地❷~；真诚地❸~；再三❹~；实在❺~不住

1. relative 2. warmly 3. sincerely; truly; genuinely 4. over and over again; repeatedly 5. really; truly

wǎngluó 网罗 enlist the services of ≅ 搜罗〔~宾〕〈名〉~人材❶；~坏蛋；~亲信❷；~党羽❸；~了一帮❹人；~了一伙❺〔~补〕〈结〉~在一起〈趋〉~起来；~进来〈可〉~不着(zháo)有用的人材〈时〉~了很长时间；~了半天〈量〉~一下儿〔状~〕到处~；拼命❻~；竭力❼~

1. a person of ability; a talented person 2. trusted follower 3. members of a clique; adherents; henchmen 4. gang; band; clique 5. company; band 6. for all one is worth; with all one's might 7. do one's utmost

wàng 忘 forget ≅ 忘记〔~宾〕〈名〉我~了一件重要的事儿；永远别~了在困难中帮助过你的人；~了她的名字；我~了他的电话号码❶了；饮水❷不~掘井❸人；我永远不~接到录取通知书❹那一天；不能只看到优点❺而~了缺点❻〈动〉~了通知❼他；他~了叫醒❽我；我~了带钢笔；别~了关灯；他紧张地❾工作，~了去吃饭〈主-谓〉~了他是哪一天去的了；你~了那次我们一起去旅行了；~了这本词典是什么时候买的了〔~补〕〈结〉把不愉快❿的往事⓫~掉吧；把钥匙⓬~在家里了〈程〉~得一干二净⓭；~得一点儿也想不起来了〈可〉这件事交给他办吧! 他~不了(liǎo)；永远也~不了(liǎo)你对我的好处〈量〉这几个词查⓮一次~一次；~了好几次了〔状~〕一下子~了；完全~了；很难~；这件伤心事⓯好容易才~了；没~；别~；全~了；一辈子也~不了(liǎo)；差一点儿~了；一时⓰~了；不致⓱~；偏偏⓲把他给~了；已经~；又~了；彻底~；〔习用〕~乎所以⓳

1. telephone number 2. drink water 3. dig a well (never forget where one's happiness comes from) 4. admission note 5. merit 6. demerit 7. notify 8. wake up; awaken 9. intensely; tensely 10. unhappy 11. past events; the past 12. key 13. be utterly forgotten 14. look up; consult 15. old sore; painful memory 16. temporarily; for a moment 17. cannot go so far; be unlikely 18. by coincidence 19. forget oneself in a moment of excitement; lose all bearings in moment of pride and satisfaction

wàng 望 gaze into the distance; look over ≅ 看〔~宾〕〈名〉~着前方；~着对岸❶；~着远处驶❷来的汽车；~着天上的彩虹❸；〔~补〕〈结〉水很清，一眼能~到底〈趋〉向远处~去；一眼~过去〈程〉站在高处~得比较远〈可〉天连水，水连天❹，一眼~不到边儿❺；~不到头儿❻〈时〉~了半天也不见人影〈量〉他~了我一眼〔状~〕放眼❼~去；仰头❽~；抬头❾~；登高远~❿；焦急地⓫~着

1. the opposite bank 2. drive; speed 3. rainbow 4. the sky and the water seem to merge 5. limit; bound 6. end 7. take a broad view; scan widely 8. 9. raise one's head 10. ascend a height to enjoy a distant view 11. impatiently

wēihài 危害 harm; endanger; jeopardize ≅ 破坏；损害〔~宾〕

〈名〉～健康❶；～着他的生命财产❷；～社会治安❸〈动〉～儿童的健康成长〈主-谓〉～生命安全；～庄稼❹生长〔状～〕严重❺～；必然❻～；的确❼～；仍然❽～；随时❾～；已经～；始终❿～；一直⓫～

1. health 2. life and property 3. social security 4. crops 5. seriously 6. certainly; inevitably 7. indeed; really 8. still; yet 9. at any time; at all times 10. from beginning to end; all along; throughout 11. always; continuously; all along

wēixié 威胁 threaten; menace; imperil〔～宾〕〈名〉大气污染❶～着这个城市❷人民的健康❸；经济危机❹正在～着那个国家；扩军备战❺～着邻国❻的安全❼；地震❽灾害❾～着人们的生命财产❿；～生命安全；～着困守⓫在山上的敌人；～世界和平⓬〈代〉你不用～我，我不怕这个〔～补〕〈趋〉～起人来真凶⓭〈量〉～过我一次；他想～一下儿我〔状～〕多次～；经常～；别～人；直接⓮～；间接⓯～；持刀⓰～；一直～；时时刻刻⓱～着；仍旧⓲～

1. air pollution 2. city; town 3. people's health 4. economic crisis 5. arms expansion and war preparations 6. neighbouring country 7. security 8. earthquake 9. calamity; disaster 10. life and property 11. defend against a siege; stand a siege 12. world peace 13. fierce; ferocious 14. directly 15. indirectly 16. holding a sword 17. constantly; always 18. still; yet

wéi 为 ① do; act ≅ 做〔～宾〕〈名〉不许❶他～非作歹❷〔状～〕我一定尽力❸而～；敢作敢～❹；大有可～❺

1. not allow 2. do evil; commit crimes 3. do one's best 4. decisive and bold in action; act with daring 5. be well worth doing; have bright prospect

② act as ≅ 当；做〔～宾〕〈名〉拜❶你～师；选❷她～代表❸；以什么～凭❹；以他～榜样❺；以这棵树～标准❻〈形〉以友谊～重❼；不能什么文章都以短～好；生活以安定❽～好

1. take you as my teacher 2. elect; choose 3. representative 4. evidence; proof 5. example; model 6. standard 7. heavy; important 8. stability

③ become ≅ 变成；成为〔～宾〕〈名〉变沙漠❶～良田❷；大家都转❸悲❹～喜❺〈动〉转败❻～胜❼〈形〉转弱❽～强❾

1. desert 2. arable land 3. turn; change; transform 4. sad; sorrowful; melancholy 5. happy; pleased; delighted 6. defeat 7. victory 8. weak 9. strong

④ be; mean ≅ 是〔~宾〕〈名〉服役期限❶~五年；年产量❷~八十亿公斤

1. term of military service 2. annual output

wéibèi 违背 violate; go against; run counter to ≅ 违反〔~宾〕〈名〉~良心❶；~道德❷；~了自己的感情❸；~愿望❹；~意愿❺；~心愿❻；~意志❼；~意旨❽；~原则❾；~历史事实❿；~自己的诺言⓫；~誓言⓬；~公约⓭；~条约⓮；~协定⓯；~规定⓰〔~补〕〈量〉~过一次〔状~〕竟然⓱~；只好~；已经~；完全~；决不~

1. conscience 2. moral 3. feeling; sentiment; emotion 4. 5. 6. desire; wish; aspiration 7. will 8. intention; will 9. principle 10. historical fact 11. one's own promise 12. oath; pledge 13. convention; pact 14. treaty; pact 15. agreement; accord 16. stipulation 17. unexpectedly

wéifǎn 违反 violate; go against; infringe〔~宾〕〈名〉~政策❶；~了一条重要的规定❷；~交通规则❸；~原理❹；~社会发展规律❺；~历史潮流❻；~原则❼；~集体的利益❽〔状~〕严重地❾；屡次❿；一再⓫；故意⓬~；净⓭~；又~了；从不~；决不~；初次⓮~

1. policy 2. important stipulation 3. traffic regulations 4. principle 5. law of the development of society 6. historical trend 7. principle 8. collective interest 9. seriously 10. 11. over and over again; repeatedly 12. intentionally 13. always 14. the first time

wéi 围 surround; circle; enclose ≅ 绕〔~宾〕〈名〉~了一条围巾❶；妈妈做饭的时候总要~围裙❷；~着炉子❸坐；大家~着小李问长问短❹；房子外边~了一圈铁丝网❺；~了一道人墙❻；警察❼旁边~了好多人〔~补〕〈结〉外边冷，快把围巾~上吧；学生们把老师~住了，要问考试成绩〈趋〉一下子就~上来了；他刚一进来，孩子们就把他~起来了，让他讲故事〈程〉人~得水泄不通❽；~得风雨不透❾；头巾~得很紧；~得严严实实❿的〈可〉铁丝⓫太短~不过一圈来〈时〉~了半天也没围好〈量〉~几次就习惯⓬了；~一下儿试试〔状~〕用篱笆⓭~上；用铁丝~；团团~住；一下子~过来了，紧紧地~；一层一层地~；从四面八方~了过来

1. scarf; muffler 2. apron 3. stove 4. take the trouble to make detailed inquiries 5. wire netting; wire entanglement 6. wall (formed by men) 7. policeman 8. not even a drop of water could trickle through 9. not penetrated by neither wind nor rain 10.

close; tight 11. iron wire 12. get used to 13. bamboo or twig fence

wéirǎo 围绕 go round; centre on; revolve round ≌ 环绕〔~宾〕〈名〉地球~着太阳转；~湖边❶跑一圈❷；~节约❸问题讨论❹一下儿〔状~〕永远❺~；一直~；每天~

1. the bank of a lake 2. a circle 3. save; economise; practise thrift 4. discuss 5. forever

wéikǒng 惟恐 only fear; for fear that ≌ 只怕〔~宾〕〈动〉~对我们照顾❶得不好；~打扰❷了他；~睡过头；~误❸了火车；~受到父亲的责骂❹〈主-谓〉~带的衣服不够；~他找不到住处；~人家不知道；~天下不乱❺；~考试通不过；~她忘了；~我们不满意❻；~我们吃不惯❼她做的菜

1. give consideration to; care for; look after 2. disturb; trouble 3. miss 4. scold 5. desire to see the world plunged into chaos; desire to stir up trouble 6. not satisfied 7. not be used to certain food

wéichí 维持 maintain; keep; preserve ≌ 保持〔~宾〕〈名〉~现状❶；~秩序❷；靠❸什么~生活？~生命〔~补〕〈结〉能~住现状就不错了；生活~在中等❹水平❺；这些粮食还能~到

月底〈趋〉生活很难~下去；一家人的生活勉强❻~下来了〈程〉秩序~得很好；~得井井有条❼〈可〉挣❽这么一点儿钱，生活~得下去吗？现状都快~不下去了〈量〉请帮我~一下儿秩序〔状~〕勉强~；主动❾~；难以❿~；足以⓫~；靠什么~？无法⓬~；尽量⓭~；竭力⓮~

1. present situation; status quo 2. order 3. rely on; depend on 4. medium 5. standard; level 6. reluctantly; with difficulty 7. in perfect order 8. earn; make 9. on one's own initiative 10. difficult to 11. enough; sufficient 12. unable; incapable 13. to the best of one's ability; as far as possible 14. do one's utmost; with all one's might

wéihù 维护 safeguard; defend; uphold〔~宾〕〈名〉~人民的利益❶；~国家的主权❷；~人类的尊严❸；~她的名誉❹；~世界和平；~民主❺；~自由❻；不能~封建礼教❼；~社会道德❽〈动〉~团结❾；~民族的统一❿；~封建统治⓫〔~补〕〈结〉她的名誉能~住吗？〈可〉~不住；~得了(liǎo)吗？〔状~〕积极⓬~；主动⓭~；千方百计地⓮~；竭力⓯~；大力~；大胆⓰~

1. people's interest 2. national sovereignty 3. the dignity of mankind 4. fame; reputation 5. democracy 6. freedom 7. the

Confucian or feudal ethical code 8. social morality 9. unity 10. national unity 11. feudal rule 12. actively 13. on one's own initiative 14. by every possible means; by hook or by crook 15. do one's utmost; with all one's might 16. boldly

wéixiū 维修 keep in (good) repair; maintain〔~宾〕〈名〉~房屋；~汽车；~机器；~设备❶〔~补〕〈结〉房子~完了才能搬进去住〈趋〉用的太不仔细❷，~起来比较麻烦❸；这是进口❹零件❺，~起来比较困难〈程〉~得不错；~得很好〈时〉几辆汽车整整~了三个月〈量〉每年都要~一次〔状~〕彻底~；多次~；汽车公司❻的汽车轮流❼~；一起~；定期❽~；专门❾~；及早❿~；无法⓫~

1. equipment; installation; facilities 2. too carelessly 3. troublesome; inconvenient 4. import 5. spare parts; spares 6. company; corporation 7. in turn 8. at regular intervals 9. especially; specially 10. at an early date 11. unable; incapable

wěizào 伪造 forge; falsify; fabricate; counterfeit ≅ 假造〔~宾〕〈名〉~证件❶；~证据❷；~供词❸；~帐目❹；~历史；~字画❺；~文件❻；~货币❼；~钞票❽；~签名❾〔~补〕〈趋〉~出来的钞票，有经验❿的人一眼就能看出来〈程〉~得太象了；~得跟真的一样；~得一点儿也看不出来；~得不象〈量〉那个犯人⓫供认⓬，他~过一次帐目〔状~〕竟然⓭~；经常~；曾经~；肆无忌惮地⓮~；明目张胆地⓯~；屡次⓰~；挖空心思地⓱~；竟敢⓲如此大胆地⓳~

1. certificate; papers; credentials 2. evidence; proof; testimony 3. a statement made under examination 4. accounts; item of an account 5. calligraphy and painting 6. documents; papers; instruments 7. money; currency 8. bank note; paper money; bill 9. signature 10. experience 11. criminal 12. confess 13. unexpectedly; to one's surprise 14. unscrupulously; brazenly 15. flagrantly; brazenly 16. time and again; repeatedly 17. rack one's brains 18. have the audacity; have the impertinence 19. boldly

wěizhuāng 伪装 pretend; feign; disguise ≅ 假装〔~宾〕〈动〉~中立❶〈形〉~积极❷；~善良❸〔~补〕〈趋〉~起来了〈程〉~得一点破绽❹也没有〈量〉需要~一下儿〔状~〕一贯❺~；一向❻~；用什么办法~?

1. neutrality 2. active 3. good and honest 4. weak point; flaw 5. 6. continuously; persistently; all along

wěituō 委托 entrust; trust 〔～宾〕〈名〉～我的同事❶〈代〉这件事就～你了；～她代办❷了；～你负责❸这项工程❹；～你去完成招生❺任务〔～补〕〈结〉没想到他这么不负责任，委托他算❻错了；我把钥匙❼～给邻居保管❽〔状～〕诚恳地～❾；幸亏❿～；分别⓫～；正式⓬～；特意⓭～；已经～；曾经～过；暂时⓮～；必须～；郑重地⓯～

1. fellow worker 2. do sth. for sb.; act on sb.'s behalf 3. be responsible for; be in charge of 4. engineering; project 5. enrol new students; recruit students 6. at last indeed 7. key 8. keep; take care of 9. sincerely 10. fortunately; luckily 11. separately 12. formally; officially 13. for a special purpose; specially 14. temporarily; for the moment 15. solemnly

wèi 喂 feed 〔～宾〕〈名〉护士给病人～饭；妈妈给孩子～奶；小孩子可以～牛奶；他～鸡；给牲口❶～草料❷，动物园的工作人员每天要～野兽❸吃生肉❹；～猴子❺水果〔～补〕〈结〉水～呛❻了，孩子直咳嗽❼；奶嘴❽太松❾，牛奶都～洒❿了；鸡食⓫～够了；把一只快死的小鸟～活了；我没经验⓬，把猪给～瘦⓭了〈趋〉我～出来的鸡又小又瘦，还不爱下蛋〈程〉小猪～得真肥⓮，孩子～得挺胖⓯〈可〉那个孩子不饱，老哭；她吃得少，一顿～不了(liǎo)多少饭；吃那么多，我们可～不起⓰；这么小的鸡～得活吗?〈时〉刚～一个月，鸡就长得那么大了〈量〉一天～三次；隔四个小时～一次〔状～〕给病人～；用奶瓶⓱～；用勺子～；一口一口地～；慢慢地～；夜里～草料；精心地～

1. draught animals; beasts of burden 2. forage; fodder 3. wild beast; wild animal 4. raw meat 5. monkey 6. choke 7. cough 8. nipple (of a feeding bottle) 9. loose; slack 10. spill; spray; sprinkle 11. chicken feed 12. inexperienced 13. thin; emaciated 14. 15. fat 16. can't afford 17. feeding bottle; baby's bottle

wèiwèn 慰问 express sympathy and solicitude for; extend one's regards to 〔～宾〕〈名〉～病人；～灾区❶人民；～病人家属❷；～死者❸家属〔～补〕〈结〉～完了；～过了〈可〉那么多病人，我一个人哪儿～得过来啊! 一个星期也～不完〈时〉～了半天，还不知道人家是谁〈量〉应该去～一下儿〔状～〕特意❹～；热情地❺～；及时❻～；挨家挨户地❼～；主动❽～；按时❾～

1. disaster area 2. family members 3. the dead; a dead person 4. for a special purpose; specially 5. warmly 6. in time 7. from door to door 8. on one's own initiative 9. on time

wēn 温

① review; revise ≅ 复习；温习〔~宾〕〈名〉~书；~功课；~台词❶〔~补〕〈结〉功课都~熟❷了；~完了吗？〈程〉功课~得很好〈可〉总~不会〈时〉~三天了，多~一会儿〈量〉~好几遍了〔状~〕好好~~；努力~；从头到尾❸~；一遍又一遍地~；反复~；经常~；按时❹~

1. actor's lines 2. practised; familiar 3. from beginning to end 4. on time

② warm up ≅ 加热〔~宾〕〈名〉~酒❶；~药❷；~牛奶〔~补〕〈结〉把酒~热点儿〈程〉水~得够❸热的了〈可〉塑料盆❹~不了(liǎo)水，酒怎么还~不热啊？〈时〉~五分钟就行了；多~一会儿〈量〉药~过好几次了；再~一遍〔状~〕在火上~；放在开水❺里~；多一~；早点❻~；逐渐❼~热了

1. wine; liquor 2. medicine 3. enough 4. plastic basin 5. boiling water 6. early 7. gradually

wén 闻

① smell ≅ 嗅〔~宾〕〈名〉~味儿❶〔~补〕〈结〉~见糊味❷儿了吗？~着(zháo)酒味❸儿了；~到一股浓烈❹的酒精味❺儿〈趋〉你~出汽油味❻儿来了吗？这种茶叶❼~起来很香❽，喝起来并不香〈程〉~得直恶心❾；~得直要吐❿；~得头晕⓫〈可〉我怎么~不见糊味儿？我~不出来是哪一种香味儿〈时〉我~了半天也没闻见有什么异常⓬的气味儿〈量〉你~一下儿香不香？警犬⓭的嗅觉⓮特别灵⓯，只要~过一次罪犯⓰留下⓱的某种气味儿，就能跟踪追击⓲〔状~〕好~吗？难~；别~；突然~

1. smell; odour 2. smell of burning 3. smell of drink 4. strong 5. smell of ethyl alcohol 6. smell of gasoline 7. tea 8. fragrant; sweet-smelling 9. feel nauseated; feel like vomiting; feel sick 10. vomit; throw up 11. dizzy; giddy 12. unusual; abnormal 13. police dog 14. (sense of) smell; scent 15. acute; sensitive; keen; agile 16. criminal; offender 17. leave 18. go in hot pursuit of

② hear ≅ 听见〔状~〕听而不~❶；充耳不~❷〔习用〕耳~不如眼见❸；久❹~大名❺；百~不如一见❻

1. hear but pay no attention 2. stuff one's ears and refuse to listen; turn a deaf ear to 3. seeing for oneself is better than hearing from others 4. for a long time 5. your name 6. it is better to see once than hear a hundred times

wěn 吻

kiss ≅ 亲〔~宾〕〈名〉~手；~脸；~了~孩子的额头❶〔~补〕〈时〉~了好长时间〈量〉~了她一下儿；~过很多次〔状~〕热情地❷~；文静地❸~；疯狂地❹~；粗鲁地❺~；长时间地~；爱抚地❻~；礼节性地❼~

1. forehead 2. affectionately; passionately 3. gently 4. madly 5. rudely; roughly 6. tenderly 7. by courtesy

wèn 问 ① ask; inquire ↔ 答

〔**～宾**〕〈名〉我举手～了老师一个问题；到前边去～～路吧；～电话号码❶；法官❷～了一个案子❸；一定要～个究竟❹〈代〉你～谁呀？是～我吗？～～他我们什么时候出发❺；～～他现在几点了；～～他住在哪儿〈动〉～～行不行？～～明天去得了(liǎo)去不了(liǎo)〈形〉他见了我总是～长～短❻；～寒～暖❼〔**～补**〕〈结〉～准❽了他明天来不来？路～清楚了吗？事情～明白了吧？他嫌❾我问题～多了；这个问题不该问；～完了电话号码，就马上记在本子上了；她突然提出❿这个问题，都把我～糊涂⓫了；～傻⓬了；～成死罪⓭〈趋〉再～下去，她就要哭了；她生气的原因～出来了吗？明明你知道，怎么反而⓮～起我来了？〈程〉～得很清楚；问题～得很有意思；～得我糊里糊涂的；～得我无法回答；～得哭笑不得⓯；～得很仔细⓰〈可〉～不清原因；～不出什么结果来；他知道的事儿很多，什么问题也～不住他；这个问题可～不得⓱；他们到底为什么吵架⓲，我怎么问也～不明白；这个案子很复杂，他～不了(liǎo)〈时〉～了半天，才找到去他家的路〈量〉这个词～过好几遍，都没记住〔**状～**〕举手～问题；轻易⓳不～；有礼貌地⓴～；恭恭敬敬地㉑～；严肃地㉒～；生气地～；生硬地㉓～；不懂就～；没完没了(liǎo)地～；勤㉔～着点儿；不耻下～㉕；故意㉖～；好奇地㉗～了一句；他耳背㉘，跟他说话，他总要一遍一遍地～

1. telephone number 2. judge 3. case; law case 4. get to the bottom of a matter 5. set out; start off 6. take the trouble to make detailed inquiries 7. ask after sb.'s health with deep concern; be solicitous for sb.'s welfare 8. accurate; exact 9. dislike; mind; complain of 10. put forward; advance; pose; raise 11. muddled; confused; bewildered 12. be dumbfounded; be stunned 13. capital offence (crime) 14. on the contrary; instead 15. not know whether to laugh or to cry; find sth. both funny and annoying 16. meticulous; careful 17. must not 18. quarrel; wrangle; have a row 19. lightly; rashly 20. courteously; politely 21. respectfully 22. seriously; solemnly 23. stiffly; be stiff in manner 24. frequently; regularly 25. not feel ashamed to ask and learn from one's subordinates 26. intentionally; purposely 27. curiously 28. hard of hearing

② send one's respect (regards) to; extend greetings to ≌问候〔**～宾**〕〈形〉向你～好❶；给他～安❷〔**状～**〕热情地❸～；主动❹

~；彬彬有礼地❺~；客客气气地❻~

1. send one's regards to; say hello to 2. pay one's respects (usu. to elders) 3. warmly 4. on one's own initiative 5. courteously 6. politely

wò 卧 ① lie ≅ 趴〔主~〕〈名〉狗~在门口；鸡~在窝❶里〔~补〕〈结〉动物园的老虎在假山旁边~下了〈时〉猫~了半天，一点也不动〔状~〕一直❷~在那儿；老老实实地❸~着；一动不动地❹~着

1. hencoop 2. all along 3. honestly; conscientiously 4. motionlessly

wò 握 hold; grasp〔~宾〕〈名〉~手，~着枪❶；~着拳头❷〔~补〕〈结〉~紧❸拳头；两个人的手~在一起〈趋〉两个老朋友刚一见面就紧紧地~手来了〈程〉~得不太紧〈可〉手麻❹了，~不住把❺了；手肿❻得~不紧了〈时〉两个人~了半天手也不撒开❼〈量〉轻轻地❽~了一下儿〔状~〕热情地❾~手；紧紧地~着手

1. gun 2. fist 3. tightly 4. have pins and needles; tingle 5. handlebar (of a bicycle) 6. swelling; swollen 7. let go one's hold; let go 8. slightly; gently 9. warmly

wù 误 ① miss ≅ 耽误〔~宾〕〈名〉差点儿~了事；别~了工作❶；别~了学习；差点儿~了这班船；几乎~了火车；~了自己的前程❷〈动〉别~了上课；别~了看病〔~补〕〈可〉~得了(liǎo)你上班~不了(liǎo)？〈量〉火车~过好几次点儿了〔状~〕差点儿~；险些❸~；千万❹别~；又~了

1. work 2. future; prospect 3. narrowly; nearly 4. be sure

② harm ≅ 损害〔~宾〕〈名〉~人子弟❶；~了下一代〔状~〕别~；已经~了〔习用〕聪明反被聪明❷~

1. harm the younger generation; lead young people astray 2. clever people may be victim of their own cleverness

wùhuì 误会 misunderstand〔~宾〕〈名〉你~了我的意思❶〔状~〕别~；被他~了；完全❷~了

1. meaning; opinion 2. completely; wholly

wùjiě 误解 misunderstand; misread〔~宾〕〈名〉~了我的话；~了我的意思〈代〉~我了〔~补〕〈可〉不知他~得了(liǎo)~不了(liǎo)？〈量〉他~过我一次〔状~〕完全~；真~了；别~；没~；被他~

X

xī 吸 ① inhale; breathe in; draw ↔ 呼〔**～宾**〕〈名〉～烟； ～毒❶； ～一口气； ～点新鲜空气； 婴儿❷～奶； 蚊子❸～人血❹〔**～补**〕〈结〉烟～多了头晕❺； ～多了中毒❻； ～足❼了一口气〈趋〉把尘土❽都～进肺里去了〈程〉烟～得真过瘾❾； ～得牙都黑了； ～得手指都黄了〈可〉老在屋子里活动❿，连新鲜空气都～不着(zháo)； 毒品可～不得⓫啊！〈时〉他～过一个时期烟，后来戒了⓬； ～一会儿，头就疼⓭〈量〉烟刚～一口就咳嗽⓮； ～一下儿尝尝⓯； ～过两次〔**状～**〕深深地⓰～了一口气； 大量地⓱～毒； 她一～冷空气就咳嗽； 多～新鲜空气对身体有好处⓲

1. narcotics (take drugs) 2. baby 3. mosquito 4. blood 5. dizzy; giddy 6. poisoning 7. sufficient; enough 8. dust 9. satisfy a craving; enjoy oneself to the full; do sth. to one's heart's content 10. activity 11. must not 12. give up 13. headache 14. cough 15. taste; try the flavour of 16. deeply 17. a great quantity 18. good; benefit; advantage

② absorb; suck up ≅ 吸收〔**～宾**〕〈名〉这种纸～墨❶； 药棉花❷～血； 吸尘机❸能～尘❹〔**～补**〕〈结〉粉笔把洒在桌子上的墨水～干了〈趋〉海绵❺把水都～进来了； 尘土都～到吸尘机里去了〈程〉～得真干净； ～得真快〈可〉实心砖❻～不了(liǎo)热； 吸尘机坏了，一不起尘土来了； 这块海绵能把这一碗水都～进去吗?〈时〉刚～一分钟，就全干了〈量〉用粉笔～过一次； 再～一下儿〔**状～**〕用吸墨纸❼～； 一下子就～干了； 赶快～

1. ink 2. absorbent cotton 3. dust catcher; dust collector 4. dust 5. sponge 6. solid brick 7. blotting paper

③ attract; draw to oneself ≅ 吸引〔**～宾**〕〈名〉吸铁石❶能～铁❷； 磁铁❸能～铁〔**～补**〕〈结〉用吸铁石能把一个空铁盒❹～走〈趋〉把钥匙❺～上来了； 医生把断针❻从肉❼里～出来了〈程〉～得真结实❽〈可〉磁性❾小～不起来〈时〉～了半天也没吸起来〈量〉～了好几下儿才吸起来〔**状～**〕一下子就～住了； 果然❿～起来了

1. magnet 2. iron 3. magnet 4. an empty iron box 5. key 6. broken needle 7. flesh 8. not easily to separate; fast; solid 9. magnetism 10. really; as expected; sure enough

xīqǔ 吸取 absorb; draw; assimilate〔～宾〕〈名〉～成功❶的经验❷；～失败❸的教训❹；～精华❺；～别人的长处❻；～人家的优点❼；～各家❽之长；～养料❾；～营养❿；～水分⓫〔～补〕〈程〉教训～得还不够䠄〈可〉这个人总～不了(liǎo)别人的优点〈量〉应该好好～一下儿〔状～〕大量⓬～；努力～；认真～；尽量⓭～

1. successful 2. experience 3. unsuccessful; failing 4. lesson 5. quintessence 6. 7. merit; strong points; good qualities 8. a specialist in a certain field 9. 10. nutriment; nourishment 11. moisture 12. a great quantity 13. to the best of one's ability; as far as possible

xīshōu 吸收 ① absorb; suck up; assimilate; imbibe〔～宾〕〈名〉植物❶的根❷可以～水分❸和无机盐❹；～各民族的文化❺；从食物❻中～营养❼；叶子～阳光；～有用的知识❽；～古代文化遗产❾；海绵❿能～水；粉笔可以～墨水；吸尘机⓫可以～尘土⓬；深颜色⓭的衣服～热量⓮；植物由根～养分⓯〔～补〕〈趋〉把别人的优点都～进来了；水分都被～进去了；青年人～起知识来很快〈程〉～得很好〈可〉他的肠胃⓰功能⓱不好，什么营养也～不好，营养太多了也～不了(liǎo)，好的经验和方法总～不进来〔状～〕好好～；很难～；一点一点地～；大量⓲～；无法⓳～；从食物里～

1. plant; flora 2. root 3. moisture 4. inorganic salt 5. national culture 6. food 7. nutriment; nourishment 8. useful knowledge 9. cultural heritage 10. sponge 11. dust catcher; dust collector 12. dust 13. deep (dark) colour 14. heat 15. nutriment 16. intestines and stomach 17. function 18. a great quantity 19. unable; incapable

② recruit; enrol; admit ≅ 接受〔～宾〕〈名〉乐队❶～新队员❷；～新来的教师入工会❸；～老工程师❹参加这项设计❺〔～补〕〈结〉～够了；～多了〈趋〉合唱队❻～起新队员来了〈程〉～得太多了；～得还不够〈可〉～不满❼；～不着(zháo)满意的❽；～得着(zháo)合适❾的吗？暂时❿还～不进来〈量〉～过一次〔状～〕前后～了，大量⓫～；至少⓬～

1. orchestra; band 2. member 3. trade union 4. old engineer 5. design; plan 6. chorus 7. not sufficient 8. satisfied 9. suitable 10. temporarily; for the moment 11. a great quantity 12. at least

xīyǐn 吸引 attract; draw; fascinate〔～宾〕〈名〉她打扮❶得花枝招展❷，～了人们的注意（力）；电影的内容❸很～人；展览会丰富多彩❹，～了很多观众❺；橱窗❻里的玩具❼～了孩子们；一个疯子❽～了一群人〈代〉～了我〔～补〕〈结〉她被手里的小说～住了〈趋〉一声喊叫把人们都~到他身边来了；把敌人的火力~过来了；音乐声把人们都~上来了〈可〉现在什么东西都~不了(liǎo)他了；~不到他的注意力〈量〉~一下儿〔**状**~〕被~；为…所~；互相~；故意❾~；有意❿~；曾经~；竭力⓫~；千方百计地⓬~；逐渐⓭~；日益⓮~；深深地⓯~

1. dress up; make up 2. (of women) be gorgeously dressed 3. content 4. rich and varied; rich and colourful 5. spectator; audience 6. show window 7. toys 8. madman 9. 10. intentionally; purposely 11. do one's utmost; with all one's might 12. by every possible means; by hook or by crook 13. gradually 14. day by day 15. deeply

xīwàng 希望 hope; wish; expect ≅ 期望；盼望↔失望〔~宾〕〈动〉~出国留学❶；~接❷到家里的信；~快一点学好英语；~长大当一个医生〈主-谓〉~你明天能来；~她的病快好；~他能考上大学〔~补〕〈程〉~得很好，最后都失望❸了〔**状**~〕衷心❹~；真诚地❺~；多么~你来啊；非常~；特别~；成天❻~；殷切地❼~；始终❽~着

1. go abroad for study 2. receive 3. disappointed 4. wholeheartedly; sincerely 5. honestly 6. all day long 7. earnestly; sincerely; ardently 8. from beginning to end; always

xīshēng 牺牲 sacrifice; give up; do sth. at the expense of〔~宾〕〈名〉为了营救❶别人而~了宝贵❷的生命❸；~休息时间；~个人利益❹；~了无数❺钱财❻〈代〉~了自己的一切〔**状**~〕暂时❼~；英勇❽~；壮烈❾~；完全~；光荣地❿~；为国~

1. save; rescue 2. valuable; precious 3. life 4. interest; benefit; gain; profit 5. innumerable 6. wealth; money 7. temporarily 8. courageously 9. heroically; bravely 10. gloriously

xī 熄 extinguish; put out〔~宾〕〈名〉学校每天晚上十一点~灯❶〔**状**~〕按时❷~灯；准时❸~灯；快~灯了；已经~灯了

1. light 2. 3. on time

xíjī 袭击 make a surprise attack on; surprise; raid〔主~〕〈名〉敌机❶~；台风❷~了沿海❸一带❹〔~宾〕〈名〉~敌人的阵地❺；~了敌人的最后一道防线❻；~敌人的据点❼〔~补〕〈程〉~得很猛〈量〉~了很多次〔**状**~〕突然~；猛烈❽~；乘敌不备❾~；连夜❿~；乘⓫黑夜~

1. enemy's plane 2. typhoon 3. along the coast; inshore;

offshore 4. area; surroundings 5. front; position 6. defence line 7. stronghold; fortified points; foothold 8. fiercely; violently; furiously 9. take the enemy unawares 10. that very night 11. seize the opportunity; take advantage of

xíguàn 习惯 be accustomed to; be used to; be inured to〔~宾〕〈名〉渔民❶~海上生活；她还不~演员❷生活；我很快就~这种工作了；他~了自己的学习方法〈动〉你~吃辣椒❸了吗？她不~用冷水冲凉❹；不~连续❺开夜车❻；~早晨跑步；他~早起，我~晚睡；猫头鹰❼~夜间出来活动；我可不~在这种嘈杂❽的环境❾中写东西〈主-谓〉他已经~一个人单独生活❿了；我们已经~假日全家出去玩了〔~补〕〈趋〉开始~起来了〔状~〕完全~；逐渐~；还没~；实在不~；必须~

1. fisherman 2. actor or actress 3. hot pepper 4. shower bath 5. running; in succession; in a row 6. work late into the night 7. owl 8. noisy 9. surroundings; environment 10. live in solitude

xǐ 洗 ① wash; bathe〔~宾〕〈名〉~脸；~澡❶，~衣服，用冷水❷~血迹❸；给小孩~尿布❹；〔~补〕〈结〉手~干净了；血迹~掉了〈趋〉她母亲~出来的衣服真干净；尿布~来~去都洗破了；

小孩喜欢玩水，在澡盆❺里~起澡来就不愿意出来〈程〉~得真干净；~得太慢；洗澡~得真舒服❻；洗衣服~得太累了；尿布~得手疼，孩子们洗澡~得可高兴了〈可〉衣服太旧❼，~不白了；~不干净了；这一大堆❽衣服，半天也~不完；小孩子太小，自己~不了(liǎo)脸；我的头发太干，用什么洗也~不亮❾〈时〉再~一会儿就完了；多~一会儿，才能洗干净〈量〉用洗衣机❿~过好多次了；~一下儿看看，能不能洗掉〔状~〕用凉水~还是用热水~？我用肥皂⓫~；她用肥皂粉⓬~；用手~太累；在盆⓭里~；干~⓮；在河里~；单⓯~；经常~；重新~；赶快~；别~了；不停地~；真难~；一遍又一遍地⓰~

1. bath 2. cold water 3. bloodstain 4. diaper 5. the washtub 6. comfortable 7. old 8. pile; heap 9. not bright 10. washing machine 11. soap 12. soap powder 13. washbasin 14. dry cleaning 15. alone; singly 16. once and again

② develop (a film)〔~宾〕〈名〉~相片；~了三张底片❶；~黑白的；~半身的〔~补〕〈结〉照片还没~好，可能已经~完了〈趋〉那个照像馆❷~出来的照片好，你怎么自己~起相片来了？〈程〉~得真快；~得不错；~得太糟糕❸了；~得不清楚；颜色~得太深❹；~得太浅❺了〈可〉一个小时~不完；你自己~得好吗？

照片太多～不过来了；没有暗室❻～不了(liǎo)；放心吧，我～不坏；自己～得清楚～不清楚？～不出光泽❼来〈时〉～过一个时期〈量〉你自己～过几次照片？明天我也～一下儿试试〔**状～**〕我不常❽～；一张一张地～；从来没～过；多～几张；正在～

1. negative **2.** photo studio **3.** too bad **4.** too dark; too deep **5.** (of colour) light **6.** darkroom **7.** lustre; gloss **8.** not often

③ shuffle (cards etc.)〔**～宾**〕〈名〉～牌❶；这次该你～牌了〔**～补**〕〈结〉牌还没～好〈趋〉他～出来的牌跟没洗一样〈可〉我～不好扑克牌❷〈时〉～了这么半天还不行呀！多～会儿吧〈量〉这次你～一下儿〔**状～**〕多～～；彻底❸～～；好好～～

1. cards; dominoes **2.** playing cards **3.** thoroughly

xǐ'ài 喜爱 like; love; be fond of; be keen on ≌ 喜欢↔讨厌〔**～宾**〕〈名〉～这首歌曲；～这首诗；～这幅画；～这些古玩❶；～户外活动❷；～她的钢琴❸；～自己的小孙子❹；～那座别墅❺〈动〉～打猎❻〔**状～**〕最～；专门❼～；一向❽～

1. antique; curio **2.** outdoor activities **3.** piano **4.** grandson **5.** villa **6.** hunting **7.** especially; particularly **8.** always; all along

xǐhào 喜好 like; love; befond of; be keen on ≌ 喜欢；爱好↔厌恶〔**～宾**〕〈名〉～音乐；～体育；～文艺〈动〉～打猎❶〔**状～**〕一向❷～；从小就～；特别❸～；非常～；不太～

1. hunting **2.** always; all along **3.** especially; particularly

xǐhuan 喜欢 like; love; be fond of; be keen on ≌ 喜爱；爱↔讨厌〔**～宾**〕〈名〉他～物理；我不～这种花布；孩子们都～大气球；大家都不～骄傲自大❶的人；～那个地方风景❷秀丽❸〈代〉我～他聪明；他～我老实❹；～他诚实❺；～他憨厚❻；～他勤快❼；我们都～她作事认真❽；她长得真好玩❾，大家都～她〈动〉他～去，就让他去吧；她妹妹最～游泳；我最不～吃羊肉；他～早睡早起；～看推理小说❿；不～看古装片⓫〈形〉我这个人最～热闹⓬；她最不～罗嗦⓭；我就～干脆利索⓮，不～拖拖拉拉⓯；小王～清静⓰；谁～吹吹拍拍⓱啊！〔**～补**〕〈结〉她突然～上吉他⓲了〈程〉～得不得了⓳(liǎo)；～得要命⓴〈可〉他对什么都没兴趣，什么也～不起来；这孩子太讨厌㉑，我怎么也～不上他〔**状～**〕特别～；就～；只～；多么～啊；极端㉒～；一向㉓；一直～

1. swollen with pride; conceited and arrogant **2.** scenery; landscape **3.** beautiful; pretty **4. 5.** honest **6.** straightforward and good-natured; simple and honest 7. diligent; hardworking 8. serious 9. cute 10. detective story 11. film in ancient costume 12. fun; excitement 13. long-winded; wordy 14. clear-cut; straightforward 15. dilatory; slow; sluggish 16. quiet 17. boasting and toadying 18. guitar 19. 20. extremely; exceedingly 21. disgusting 22. extremely; exceeding 23. always; consistently; all the time

xiā 瞎 blind〔主～〕〈名〉眼睛～了〔～宾〕〈名〉～了一只眼〔～补〕〈程〉～得什么也看不见了；～得一点亮儿❶都看不见了〈可〉这眼睛早点治❷就～不了(liǎo)了〈时〉～了很多年了〔状～〕生下来就～；后来才～的；差点儿～；已经～了；怎么～的？

1. light 2. cure

xià 下 ① descend; alight; get off ↔ 上〔～宾〕〈名〉～山；～坡❶；～楼；～车；～船；～飞机；～床；病好了，可以～地❷了；又一艘新船～水❸了；你自己做坏事还不够，还要拖人～水❹；这一站有两个人～车〔～补〕〈结〉还没到站就下来了；～错了〈趋〉她在楼上看书没～来；太阳都～去了；任务❺～来了；你最好自己～去看看；演员❻刚从台❼上～来；你的气还没～去呢？脸上的汗❽都～去了；一学期～来能

记❾两千个词；她已经～楼去了；从电梯❿上～来了〈程〉他下车～得真利索⓫；下楼～得真快〈可〉太高，我～不去了〈时〉车太挤⓬了，～了半天也没下去〈量〉今天一天我才～了一趟楼〔状～〕河水顺流⓭而～；挨着次序⓮～；一个一个地～；车上人太多，真不好～；好容易才～来（好不容易才～来）；扶着⓯门框⓰～；慢慢～；病刚好，拄着拐杖⓱儿～床；孩子们跑着～山了；并排⓲～；一前一后地～

1. slope 2. leave a sickbed 3. be launched; enter the water 4. involve sb. in evildoing 5. task; assignment; mission 6. actor or actress 7. stage; platform 8. sweat; perspiration 9. learn by heart 10. lift; elevator 11. agile; nimble 12. crowded; packed 13. with the stream 14. in order 15. place a hand on sb. or sth. for support 16. doorframe 17. lean on a stick 18. side by side

② (of rain, snow, etc.) fall ≅ 降落〔～宾〕〈名〉～雨；～雪；～霜❶；～雾❷；～冰雹；～半旗❹〔～补〕〈结〉今年的雪～晚了；这个地区雨一～多了就闹水灾❺；～完了一阵冰雹庄稼❻都毁❼了；这样的大雨再～上三天，就要发大水❽了；这场雨要～到什么时候才能停啊！〈趋〉这场大雪再～下去，交通❾都要停止了；今天晚上外边一起大雾来了，明天准❿是晴天⓫〈程〉雨～

得很急❷；霜~得很薄❸；雪~得多么厚啊；〈可〉冰雹~不了(liǎo)多少时候；看样子雨~不起来〈时〉大雨~了一天一夜才停；雪刚~一会儿，地就白了〈量〉傍晚❷又~了一阵❺小雨；去年这里~过一次冰雹〔**状**~〕淅淅沥沥地❻~雨，哗哗地❼~雨，一阵一阵地❽~雨，断断续续地❾~；噼哩啪啦地❷~了一阵冰雹；按规定❷~半旗，又~雾了，快~点雨吧，太旱❷了；突然~；眼看就~；连续❷~；果然❷~；经常~；好久不~了；真该~点儿了；这雨可真难~啊!

1. frost 2. mist 3. hail 4. fly a flag at half-mast 5. suffer from flood 6. crop 7. ruin; destroy; damage 8. flood 9. traffic 10. certainly; surely 11. fine day; sunny day 12. violent; rapid; fast 13. thin 14. toward evening; at nightfall 15. a spell of 16. pattering 17. gurgling 18. by fits and starts 19. off and on; intermittently 20. crackling and spluttering 21. according to the rule 22. droughty 23. in succession; in a row; running 24. really; as expected; sure enough

③ issue; deliver; send ≅ 发布；投递〔**~宾**〕〈名〉~命令，~战书❶，~请帖❷；~聘书❸〔**~补**〕〈结〉~完了命令，首长❹就走了；请帖~晚了，人都没来齐❺〈趋〉他居然❻也~起命令来了〈程〉命令~得很及时❼〈可〉录取通知这个星期还~不来〈量〉~过两次命令〔**状**~〕早点~；赶快~；给谁~？往哪儿~？及时~；马上~；立即~

1. letter of challenge 2. invitation card 3. letter of appointment 4. leading cadre 5. all present 6. to one's surprise; unexpectedly 7. in time

④ go to ≅ 到…去〔**~宾**〕〈名〉~乡，~厨房❶，~餐馆❷吃饭〔**~补**〕〈可〉今天家里有事~不了(liǎo)地❸了〈时〉~过三年乡〔**状**~〕经常~乡；从来不~餐馆吃饭；以前~过乡；隔一段时间❹~一次

1. kitchen 2. restaurant 3. field 4. at intervals

⑤ leave; exit ≅ 退场〔**主**~〕〈名〉下❶一场球赛❷，7号上，10号~〔**~宾**〕〈名〉运动员❸~场❹了；演员❺~台❻了；总统❼~台❽了〔**~补**〕〈结〉下场~错了〈趋〉~来了〔**状**~〕从左边的门~；在热烈❾的掌声❿中~；怀⓫着激动⓬的情绪⓭~；高高兴兴地~；兴冲冲地⓮~；垂头丧气⓯地~；无精打采⓰地~

1. next 2. match (ball) game 3. sportsman 4. enter the arena (sports field) 5. actor or actress 6. stage; platform 7. president 8. fall out of power; leave office 9. warm; enthusiastic; ardent 10. clapping; applause 11. keep in mind; cherish 12. excited 13. feeling; mood; morale 14. excitedly; with joy and expedition

15. crestfallen; dejected 16. listlessly; in low spirits

⑥ put in; cast ≌ 放入；投入〔～宾〕〈名〉花生上星期刚～了种❶；～网❷捕鱼；牛奶里～了毒药❸；～本钱❹；在学习上～了不少工夫❺；学外语不～苦功❻不行；～料❼；～鱼饵❽；～面条❾〔～补〕〈结〉～完种了；已经把网～好了；本钱～多了；苦功再～大点儿；料没～够〈趋〉他要是～起工夫来谁也比不上他〈程〉本钱～得太少了；鱼饵～得太晚，鱼都游走了；种子～得很匀❿〈可〉工夫～不够，就学不好；这个锅⓫太小，～不了(liǎo)一斤面(条)〈时〉好好～几年工夫，准能学成〈量〉～了两次网，一条鱼都没打上来〔状～〕分几次～；狠⓬～；白⓭～；多～点儿；刚～在这儿～网；在写方面再～点工夫

1. seed 2. fishnet 3. poison; toxicant 4. capital 5. put in time and energy 6. hard work 7. material; stuff 8. (fish) bait 9. noodles 10. even 11. pan; pot 12. firmly; resolutely 13. in vain

⑦ have a game of chess ≌ 比赛〔～宾〕〈名〉～了一盘象棋❶〔～补〕〈结〉棋又～输❷了；～赢❸了没有？〈趋〉他们～起棋来什么也不管❹了；她现在也～起围棋❺来了〈程〉他的围棋～得最好；下棋～得连饭都忘了吃了；棋～得真高明❻〈可〉我～不好国际象棋❼，你教教我吧；他什么棋也～不了(liǎo)；他们两个人的水平❽相差❾太多，～不起来；心里惦记❿去幼儿园⓫接孩子，这盘棋我～不下去了；他棋艺⓬太差⓭，怎么也～不赢老王〈时〉一盘棋竟～了两个小时；还想～一会儿〈量〉跟他～过一次；咱们两个人～一下儿试试〔状～〕经常～；跟谁～？痛痛快快地⓮～；一盘接着一盘地⓯～；别～了；以后再～吧

1. a game of chess 2. be defeated 3. win 4. show no consideration for 5. a game played with black and white pieces on a board of 361 crosses 6. wise; brilliant 7. chess 8. level 9. differ 10. remember with concern 11. kindergarten; nursery school 12. skill in a game of chess 13. poor; not up to standard 14. to one heart's content; to one's great satisfaction 15. one after another

⑧ take away (off); dismantle; unload ≌ 卸掉〔～宾〕〈名〉演员❶～装❷了；～了一扇❸窗户〔～补〕〈结〉她～完装就回家了〈趋〉把那扇破窗户❹～下来了〈程〉演员们下装都～得很快〈可〉那扇窗～不下来了〈时〉每次下装就得❺(děi)～半个小时〔状～〕快点儿～；这扇窗真不好～；怎么～？没法❻～；别～了

1. actor or actress 2. remove theatrical makeup and costume 3. a measure word (for window, door, etc.) 4. broken window 5. must; have to 6. unable; incapable

xià

⑨ form (an opinion, idea, etc.) ≌ 做；做出〔~宾〕〈名〉~注解❶；~保证❷；~定义❸；~结论❹；~狠心❺；~决心〔~补〕〈结〉注解都~全了吗？要把定义~准确❻；结论~错了；决心~定❼了〈趋〉她要是~起决心来，谁也动摇❽不了(liǎo)〈程〉结论~得太早了；注解~得不够❾；定义~得很确切❿〈可〉想戒烟⓫，可是总~不了(liǎo)决心；这个词我~不好定义；一时⓬还给他~不了(liǎo)结论；注解老~不全〈时〉~了半天决心，还是没把烟戒掉〈量〉他~过好几次决心了，可是结果怎么样呢？〔状~〕不要匆忙⓭~结论；一时~不了(liǎo)；很难~；准确地~；详细地⓮~注释；不能过早地~结论；不能轻率地⓯~结论；不要轻易⓰~结论；研究⓱以后再~；调查⓲清楚了再~；不能随便⓳~；应该怎么~？不知怎么~？暗⓴~决心

1. note; annotation 2. pledge; guarantee; assure 3. definition 4. conclusion 5. cruel-hearted; heartless 6. accurate 7. fix; decide 8. shake 9. not enough 10. definite; exact; precise 11. give up smoking 12. temporarily; for a moment 13. in a hurry 14. in detail 15. rashly; hastily 16. lightly; rashly 17. consider; discuss; deliberate 18. investigation 19. casually; at random 20. secretly; inwardly; to oneself

⑩ apply; use ≌ 使用〔~宾〕〈名〉刚学牙雕❶的时候真不知从哪儿~刀；这个字应该先~哪一笔❷？她身体太虚弱❸了，医生有点儿不敢❹~药；他要~毒手❺了〔~补〕〈结〉第一笔就~错了；刀子~歪❻了；药~少了〈趋〉她~起毒手来真狠❼〈程〉这种药~得太多了；刀子~得太深❽了；这个字下笔❾~得不对〈可〉你们看着我写，我紧张❿得都~不了(liǎo)笔了〈量〉这种药我只给他~过一次〔状~〕先~哪一笔？竟然⓫~了毒手；几乎⓬~错了药

1. ivory carving 2. stroke 3. weak; poor 4. dare not 5. violent treachery; murderous scheme 6. oblique 7. heartless; cruel 8. deep 9. put pen to paper; begin to write or paint 10. nervous 11. to one's surprise; unexpectedly 12. almost; nearly

⑪ (of animals) give birth to; lay〔~宾〕〈名〉~了两窝❶兔子❷；这只老母鸡~了十个蛋〔~补〕〈结〉老母猪~完了小猪就睡觉了〈趋〉那只大黑鸡也~起蛋来了〈程〉鸭蛋~得真多〈可〉那只鸡快死了，~不了(liǎo)蛋了〈量〉一天~一次蛋；一年~两次猪仔❸〔状~〕一下儿~了那么多；天天~；隔一天❹一~

1. sow 2. rabbit 3. piglet 4. every other day

⑫ finish (work, etc.); leave off〔~宾〕〈名〉~班；~课〔~补〕〈结〉今天的课~早了〈程〉今天的课~得太晚了〈可〉下午不到六点

~不了(liǎo)|班〈时〉课已经~了十分钟了〔状~〕早就~;还没~;就要~;刚~;马上~;快~了;什么时候~?怎么还不~?

⑬ be less than ≅ 少于;低于〔~宾〕〈名〉昨天参加会❶的不~三千人;不~五百斤❷

1. attend a meeting 2. *jin*, a unit of weight

xià 吓 frighten; scare; intimidate〔~宾〕〈名〉他摔倒了❶,流❷了一地血,真~人;那只疯狗❸跑出来了,真~人;昨天夜里我们隔壁❹着(zháo)火了❺,真~人〔~补〕〈结〉注意!别~着(zháo)孩子;一条蛇❻爬❼到我脚边儿,可把我~坏了;我们不能让困难给~倒;听到这个消息都把他~傻了;~楞❽了;那次真把我~死了〈趋〉把我~出一身汗❾来;~出一身鸡皮疙瘩❿来了;把她~出病来了〈程〉~得哆嗦⓫起来了;~得要命⓬;~得又哭又叫;~得不知道往哪儿躲⓭了;~得不得了⓮(liǎo);~得魂都没了⓯;~得魂不附体⓰〈可〉放心吧,~不着(zháo)她;多大的困难也~不倒他〈量〉他用玩具蛇⓱~过我一次;咱们藏在门外边~一下儿她,看她叫不叫〔状~〕真~人;千万别~着(zháo)他;实在⓲~人;简直⓳~死了〔习用〕~了一跳

1. stumble; fall 2. shed 3. mad dog 4. neighbour 5. catch fire; be on fire 6. snake 7. crawl; creep 8. be dumbfounded; be stunned 9. sweat all over 10. be gooseflesh all over 11. tremble; shiver 12. awfully; extremely 13. hide 14. extremely; exceedingly 15. be scared out of one's wits 16. as if the soul had left the body 17. toy snake 18. 19. really; truly; simply

xiàhu 吓唬 frighten; scare; intimidate ≅ 恫吓;吓〔~宾〕〈名〉不要用"老虎来了"~孩子;不许~动物园的动物〈代〉别~她,她胆儿小❶〔~补〕〈结〉把那个孩子~哭了〈可〉你~不了(liǎo)我,我不怕〈时〉~了半天,孩子还是哭〈量〉~过他两次;~一下儿他〔状~〕别~他;净❷~人;何苦❸~她;老~我;故意❹~

1. timid; cowardly 2. always 3. why bother; is it worth the trouble 4. on purpose; intentionally

xiān 掀 lift (a cover, etc.) ≅ 揭开〔~宾〕〈名〉~窗帘❶;~(开)蚊帐❷;~(开)锅盖❸;~(开)被❹;~(开)衣襟❺〔~补〕〈结〉~开窗帘往外一看,下雪了;~开锅盖往里放面条❻;微风❼~动了他的衣襟;壶❽里的蒸气❾把壶盖都~动了;一阵急风❿把我的帽子~掉⓫了;~开课本,~起学习英语的高潮⓬;~起了罢工⓭的怒潮⓮;~起节约⓯运动;~起了一场激烈的辩论⓰;

大海～起了波涛⑰〈趋〉把褥子～起来找东西；～起一张日历⑱来；她～起衣角⑲来让我看里边的毛衣⑳〈程〉～得声音真大〈可〉书页都粘在一块儿～不开了〈时〉～了半天也没掀开；我在这儿～了半天帘子了，快进来吧！〈量〉你这么一会儿～了多少次锅盖了〔状～〕狗用嘴㉑～门帘㉒；给我～；被风～；迅速㉓～起

1. window curtain 2. mosquito net 3. cover of a cooker 4. quilt 5. the one or two pieces making up the front of a Chinese jacket 6. noodles 7. breeze 8. kettle 9. steam 10. a gust of wind 11. fall 12. high tide 13. strike 14. angry tide 15. thrift 16. heated argument 17. great waves; billows 18. calendar 19. corner of clothes 20. woollen sweater 21. by mouth 22. door curtain 23. rapid; swift; speedy

xiánliáo 闲聊 chat ≌ 聊天；闲谈；闲扯〔～宾〕〈代〉你们每天都～些什么〔～补〕〈结〉他们又～上了❶；～开了❷；～成习惯❸了〈趋〉又～起来了；每天这样～下去，什么正经事❹也干不成了〈程〉～得很热闹❺；～得满有兴趣❻〈可〉～不完〈时〉～了一个晚上；每天吃完饭都～一会儿〈量〉我跟他～过几次〔状～〕天南海北❼地～；没事儿就～；凑在一起～；成天❽～；经常～；整晚上❾～；海阔天空地❿～；从不～

1. 2. start 3. get into habit 4. serious affairs 5. lively 6. take a great interest 7. discursive; rambling 8. all day long; all the time 9. the whole night 10. as boundless as the sea and sky; unrestrained and far-ranging

xián 嫌 dislike ≌ 讨厌；嫌恶〔～宾〕〈名〉他～小孩子闹❶；～那个青年人不懂事❷；～这篇文章❸不精练❹；～衣领❺太高；你要是～这个地方不好，就换❻一个地方〈代〉你不～我，我就常来；没有人～你，你就安心在这里呆着❼吧；这个人总挑毛病❽，不是～这，就是～那；～他讲话罗嗦❾；～我脾气❿不好；～他没礼貌⓫；～我笨⓬；～她爱多嘴⓭；～他窝囊⓮；～自已发音不好〈形〉她～贵，没买；我不～麻烦⓯；给你那么多，你怎么还～少；她～冷，没去游泳；给他多少钱，他都不～多；你不～吵，我～吵；～乱⓰〔状～〕一点儿也不～；总～；别～

1. stir up trouble 2. sensible; intelligent 3. article; essay 4. not concise; not succinct 5. collar 6. change 7. stay 8. pick faults 9. long-winded; wordy 10. temperament; disposition; temper 11. courtesy 12. stupid 13. speak out of turn; shoot off one's mouth 14. good-for-nothing 15. troublesome 16. disorder; confusion

xiǎn 显 ① look; seem; appear ≃ 显得; 看起来〔**～宾**〕〈形〉他都五十岁了,可是一点也不～老; 深色❶衣服不～脏❷; 洗完了也不～白; 他一点儿也不～年轻❸; 身体不好的人, 头发往往～干; 你最近可～瘦❹了; 因为他瘦, 所以不～矮❺〔**～补**〕〈趋〉他的外表就～出伶俐❻的样子来了; 那个孩子～出笨❼来了〈程〉～得很干净; ～得非常凉快❽〈可〉这个人皮肤❾太黑, 怎么洗也～不出干净来; 一点儿也～不出慌乱❿来; ～不出紧张⓫来; 你看我～得出病容⓬来吗?〔**状～**〕真～苍老⓭; 有点儿～旧⓮; 特别～亮⓯; 不怎么～矮

1. dark colour **2.** dirty **3.** young **4.** thin **5.** short **6.** clever; bright **7.** stupid **8.** nice and cool; pleasantly cool **9.** skin **10.** flurried; alarmed and bewildered **11.** nervous **12.** sickly look **13.** old; aged **14.** old; out of date **15.** bright

② show; display; manifest ≃ 夸耀; 炫耀〔**～宾**〕〈主－谓〉～他有钱; ～他能干❶; ～他识多❷见广❸; ～他无所不知❹〔**～补**〕〈结〉看他～完了还有什么可显的〈趋〉～起来就没完; 又～起他那段光荣历史来了〈程〉～得太利害了; ～得真讨厌; ～得腻❺死了; ～得真无聊❻〈可〉他跟我～不了(liǎo), 我不听他的〈时〉～了半天没人听; 再～一会儿, 人就都走了〈量〉那点儿东西～了好多次了; ～了好几遍了〔**状～**〕看见谁就跟谁～; 翻来覆去地❼～; 一个劲儿地❽～; 没完没了(liǎo)地～; 变着法子❾～; 有什么可～的? 随时❿都～; 有意地⓫～; 不自觉地⓬～

1. able; capable; competent **2.** one's knowledge is broad **3.** one's experience is wide **4.** omniscient **5.** be bored **6.** senseless; silly **7.** again and again, repeatedly **8.** continuously; persistently **9.** try different ways **10.** at any time **11.** intentionally; on purpose **12.** unconsciously

xiǎnde 显得 look; seem; appear ≃ 显〔**～宾**〕〈形〉今天夜里没有月亮, 所以天上的星星～特别亮❶; 她已经快五十了, 可是还～那么年轻❷; 因为墙❸特别白, 所以～屋子很亮; 雨后, 树～特别绿❹; 今天她～格外❺漂亮❻; 会场❼的气氛❽～得非常严肃❾; 他穿上这身衣服～真神气❿; 他爸爸～很有派头⓫; 那个女孩子～非常活泼⓬; 屋子～很宽绰⓭(宽敞)⓮; 他的举止⓯～很大方⓰; 这种布置⓱～很小气⓲; 那种衣料⓳穿起来～很高贵⓴; 文章㉑的结构㉒～很松散㉓; 内容㉔～不完整㉕; 她～又凄凉㉖又孤单㉗; 对老年人称㉘"您"～尊敬㉙〈主－谓〉～他比谁都高; ～他声音最大; ～她精神㉚最好; ～他很懂礼貌㉛; ～她认识人最多; ～我很有办法; ～我很无能㉜〔**状～**〕一下子～; 特别～; 一向㉝～

1. very bright 2. young 3. wall 4. green 5. all the more 6. beautiful 7. meeting-place 8. atmosphere 9. serious; solemn 10. spirited; vigorous 11. style; manner 12. alive 13. 14. spacious 15. manner; bearing 16. easy; unaffected 17. arrangement 18. mean; niggardly 19. material for clothing 20. noble 21. article; essay 22. structure 23. loose 24. content 25. incomplete 26. dreary; desolate; miserable 27. alone 28. call 29. respect; honour; esteem 30. spirit 31. courtesy; politeness 32. incapable; incompetent 33. always; all along; consistently

xiǎnlù 显露 become visible; appear; manifest itself ≅ 现〔主~〕〈名〉缺点❶~出来了；影响❷~出来了〔~宾〕〈名〉脸上~出亲切的❸笑容❹；~出一种不安的❺神态❻；~出激动的❼神情❽；~出喜色❾；雾❿散⓫了，~出了远处⓬的山峰⓭；~出了晨光⓮〔~补〕〈趋〉~出病容⓯来了〈可〉缺点一时还~不出来〈量〉~过一次〔状~〕全部~出来了；在各方面⓰~出来了；必然⓱~；突然~；从未~过

1. shortcoming 2. influence 3. kind 4. smiling expression; smile 5. anxious; worried 6. expression; manner 7. excited 8. expression; bearing 9. joyful look 10. fog 11. lift 12. distant 13. mountain peak 14. the light of the early morning sun 15. sickly look 16. in every way 17. surely

xiǎnshì 显示 show; display; manifest ≅ 表现〔~宾〕〈名〉~了不可战胜的❶力量❷；~了巨大❸威力❹；~了超人❺的智慧❻；~了高度❼的文化❽程度❾；~出了高超❿的艺术⓫水平⓬；~了强大⓭的生命力⓮；~（出）了无比的优越性⓯；~（出）了青春的活力⓰〔~补〕〈结〉图象⓱~在荧光屏⓲上〈趋〉~出来了〈程〉~得很清楚〈可〉~得出力量来吗?〈量〉~了一次威力；好好地~一下儿我们的战斗力⓳〔状~〕充分⓴~；一再~；在哪方面~?用什么~? 故意㉑~；又一次~

1. invincible 2. power; force 3. huge; tremendous 4. power; might 5. be out of the common run 6. wisdom; intelligence 7. high level 8. civilization; culture 9. level; degree 10. superb; excellent 11. art 12. level 13. big and powerful; powerful 14. lifeforce; vitality 15. incomparable superiority 16. youthful vigour 17. picture; image 18. fluorescent screen 19. combat effectiveness; fighting capacity 20. full; ample; abundant 21. intentionally; on purpose

xiàn 现 show; appear ≅ 显露〔~宾〕〈名〉~了原形❶〔~补〕〈结〉~出了原形〔状~〕终于~

出了；一下子儿~出了；突然❷~；完全~

1. original shape; the true shape under the disguise 2. suddenly

xiàn 限 set a limit; limit; restrict ≅ 限制；限定〔~宾〕〈名〉~三天完成❶；~数儿❷；~人数；~字数；~年龄❸；~时间，~范围❹〈动〉每人~购❺两张〔~补〕〈结〉别把条件~死❼了〈趋〉买这种东西也一起数儿来了〈程〉别~得太多；这种东西限数儿~得没道理❽〔可〕用这种办法是~不住人的行动❾的，这~得了(liǎo)谁？〔状~〕别~；不必❿；严格地⓫~；都~；从来不~；一律⓬~

1. accomplish; complete 2. number; figure 3. age 4. scope; limits; range 5. buy 6. condition 7. fixed; rigid; inflexible 8. unreasonable; irrational 9. action; activity 10. need not; not have to 11. strictly; rigorously; rigidly 12. same; alike; uniform; without exception

xiàndìng 限定 prescribe (或 set) a limit to; limit; restrict〔~宾〕〈名〉~时间，~人数；~字数；~数目❶；~范围❷；~地点；~方式❸；~期限❹〔~补〕〈结〉别~死了；~多了大家不高兴〈程〉范围~得太窄；时间~得太死〈可〉人数~不了(liǎo)〈量〉应该~一下儿〔状~〕严格❺~；必须~；何必❻~

1. number; amount 2. scope; limits; range 3. fashion; form; way 4. allotted time; time limit; deadline 5. strictly 6. there is no need; why

xiànyú 限于 be confined to; be limited to〔~宾〕〈名〉~条件❶，还不能录取❷那么多人；~水平❸，只能理解到这一步；~能力，只能承担❹一部分；~篇幅❺，稿件❻不能全文❼刊登❽；~时间，不能详细❾说明；月票❿的有效期⓫只~当月⓬；~时间只能简单地⓭介绍一下儿；我的外语水平，现在还不能翻译；~现有的条件，也只能做到这个程度⓮了〔状~〕不~；仅~

1. condition 2. enroll; recruit; admit 3. level 4. bear; undertake; assume 5. space (on a printed page) 6. manuscript; contribution 7. full text 8. publish in a newspaper or magazine; carry 9. in detail 10. monthly ticket 11. term of validity; time of efficacy 12. instant 13. simply 14. degree; level

xiànzhì 限制 place (或 impose) restrictions on; restrict; limit; confine ≅ 限〔~宾〕〈名〉~年龄❶；~岁数儿❷；~性别❸；~数量❹；~字数❺；~篇幅❻；~版面❼；~时间，~他们的权力❽；~范围❾；不要~孩子们的行动❿；不能~思路⓫；~购

买力⑫〈动〉～工业的发展；～才智⑬的发挥⑭〈形〉～民主⑮；～自由⑯〔～补〕〈结〉被年龄～住了；～到五十岁；～在一定范围内〈趋〉～起人数来了；不能再～下去了〈程〉～得太多；～得非常利害〈可〉～不住；～得了(liǎo)～不了(liǎo)？〈时〉～了半天，全白费⑰；～过一个时期〈量〉～过很多次；需要～一下儿〔**状～**〕竭力⑱～；拼命⑲～；一再～；千方百计地⑳～；无法㉑～；从各方面㉒～；必须～；在一定范围内～

1. 2. age **3.** sexual distinction; sex **4.** quantity **5.** number of words **6.** space (on a printed page) **7.** space of a whole page **8.** power; authority **9.** scope; limits **10.** action; activity **11.** train of thought; thinking **12.** purchasing power **13.** ability and wisdom **14.** bring into play; give play to **15.** democracy **16.** freedom **17.** waste **18.** do one's utmost; with all one's might **19.** for all one is worth; desperately **20.** by hook or by crook; by every possible means **21.** unable; incapable **22.** in every respect; in all respects

xiàn 陷 ① get stuck or bogged down ≃ 陷入〔**～补**〕〈结〉汽车～在泥❶里了；～在烦恼❷里了〈趋〉脚～进泥坑❸里去了；～到黑暗❹的深渊❺里去了〈程〉～得很深❻；～得不能自拔❼；～得拔❽不出脚来了〈可〉～不进去；～不下去〔**状～**〕又～进去了；一点一点地～进去了；往下～；深深地～；日益❾～；逐渐❿～；突然～；长期～

1. mud **2.** be vexed; be worried **3.** mud pit; mire; morass **4.** dark **5.** abyss **6.** deep **7.** free oneself (from pain or evildoing); extricate oneself **8.** pull out; pull up **9.** day by day **10.** gradually

② sink; cave in〔**主～**〕〈名〉病好以后，两颊❶～下去了；地基❷～下去了；那里的地势❸有些向下～了；路面～下去了；地板～下去了；整个城市～下去了〔**～补**〕〈趋〉～下一个角❹去；～下一块去〈程〉～得很深❺〔**状～**〕已经～；一下子～；深深地～；全部～；部分～

1. cheek **2.** ground; foundation **3.** physical features of a place **4.** corner **5.** deep

xiànhài 陷害 frame (up); make a false charge against〔**～宾**〕〈名〉～好人〈代〉～人家；～我〔**～补**〕〈结〉把人～死了；把她～疯❶了；～成这个样儿了；～致死；～成残废❷〈趋〉她～起人来，真是心毒手狠❸〈程〉被她～得家破人亡❹；～得无处栖身❺；～得有口难辩❻〈可〉谁也～不了(liǎo)他；他跟我没仇❼，～不着(zháo)我〈时〉被他们～了十年〈量〉～过我三次〔**状～**〕随便❽～人；无缘无故地❾～；故意❿～；莫明其妙

地⑪～；多次～；净～；专门⑫～；别～；千方百计地⑬～；竟然⑭～；几乎～；差一点儿～；被她～

1. mad 2. maimed; crippled; disabled 3. cruel and evil; wicked and merciless 4. with one's family broken up, some gone away; some dead 5. have no place to stay 6. find it hard to vindicate oneself 7. hatred; enmity; hostility 8. casually; at random 9. without cause or reason; for no reason at all 10. intentionally; wilfully 11. without rhyme or reason 12. specially 13. by every possible means; by hook or by crook 14. to one's surprise; unexpectedly

xiànrù 陷入 sink into; land oneself in; get bogged down in ≃ 掉进〔**～宾**〕〈名〉～困境❶；～停滞❷状态❸；～罪恶❹的深渊❺；～敌人的重围❻；谈判❼～了僵局❽；～绝境❾；～不能自拔❿的境地⓫；～无休止⓬的争论⓭；～没膝⓮的泥⓯里；～火坑⓰；暴风雨⓱使交通⓲～混乱⓳状态〈动〉匪徒⓴～了我军的包围㉑；～沉思㉒〔**状～**〕一下子～；完全～；渐渐～；深深地㉓～

1. difficult position; predicament; straits 2. stagnant; be at a standstill; bog down 3. state 4. crime; evil 5. abyss 6. tight encirclement 7. negotiations; talks 8. deadlock; impasse; stalemate 9. hopeless situation; impasse; blind alley 10. free oneself (from pain or evildoing) 11. condition; circumstances 12. ceaseless; endless 13. controversy; dispute; debate 14. knee-deep 15. mud 16. fiery pit; pit of hell; abyss of suffering 17. storm 18. traffic; communication 19. confusion; chaos 20. bandit; gangster 21. surround; encircle 22. ponder; meditate; be lost in thought 23. deeply; profoundly

xiànmù 羡慕 admire; envy〔**～宾**〕〈名〉～黄先生；～有权有势的人❶；～有学问的人；～有知识的人❷；～有地位的人❸；～生活比自己好的人；～优越的❹生活；～她的新家具〈代〉～他有一个和睦的家庭❺；～她能出国深造❻；～他会五种语言；～他常出差❼；～他写文章写得快〔**～补**〕〈结〉她～上我们家的房子了；真让人～死了〈趋〉他以前看不起我，现在又～起我来了〈程〉她对优越的物质生活❽～极了❾；～得不得了❿(liǎo)；～得要命⓫；～得垂涎三尺⓬〔**状～**〕非常～；真～；特别～

1. influential person 2. learned man 3. a man of high rank 4. superior; favourable 5. harmonious family 6. take a more advanced course of study or training abroad 7. be on a business trip 8. material life 9. 10. extremely 11. awfully; con-

xiàn 献 ① offer; present; dedicate; donate 〔～宾〕〈名〉小朋友跑到台上去～花；向代表团❶～礼品；向死难烈士❷～花圈❸；为科学事业❹～身❺〔～补〕〈结〉～完了花，代表和演员❻热烈❼地握手❽；把自己珍藏❾多年的文物❿～给了国家〈趋〉～上来一束鲜花；把祖传的宝物～出去了〈程〉花圈～得真多〈可〉你们的好计策、好办法～得出来～不出来？〔状～〕往墓地⓫～；全部～出来了；英勇地⓬～出

1. delegation 2. martyr 3. (floral) wreath 4. cause; undertaking 5. devote oneself to; give one's life for 6. actor or actress 7. warmly; enthusiastically; ardently 8. shake hands 9. collect (rare books, art treasures, etc) 10. cultural relic; historical relic 11. graveyard; burial ground; cemetery 12. courageously

② show; put on; display 〔～宾〕〈名〉当众～技❶〈动〉～媚❷〈形〉～丑❸；～殷勤❹〔～补〕〈结〉他～够❺了殷勤；～尽了❻丑〈趋〉他～起殷勤来，真讨厌❼；有什么技能❽都～出来吧〈程〉献媚❾～得真利害❿；献殷勤～得真恶心⓫；献丑～得还不够啊！〈可〉跟我～不了(liǎo)殷勤，我不买他的帐⓬〈量〉～过一次丑〔状～〕当众～技；别～丑了；竭力⓭～殷勤

1. show one's skill in public 2. flatter; fawn on 3. show oneself up; show one's incompetence 4. pay one's addresses to; do everything to please 5. enough 6. to the utmost; to the limit 7. annoying; disgusting 8. skill; ability 9. try to ingratiate oneself with; make up to 10. terrible; awful 11. disgust 12. acknowledge the superiority or seniority of him; show respect for him 13. do one's utmost

xiāng 相 see for oneself (whether sb. or sth. is to one's liking) 〔～宾〕〈名〉～亲❶；～女婿❷；～媳妇❸〔～补〕〈结〉～上一个好媳妇，好容易❹～中❺(zhòng)了；～着(zháo)了没有？〈可〉～得中(zhòng)～不中(zhòng)？〈量〉～过好几次也没相中一个；应该好好～～；仔细地～～〔状～〕一次又一次地～；在家里～；偷偷地～；暗中❻～；不好意思❼～

1. bride 2. son-in-law 3. daughter-in-law 4. with great difficulty 5. be to one's liking 6. secretly; on the sly 7. feel embarrassed; be ill at ease

xiāngchǔ 相处 get along (with one another) 〔～补〕〈结〉邻居❶～好了，跟一家人一样；亲密地❷～在一起〈趋〉他的脾气❸这么暴躁❹，今后还怎么～下去啊！〈程〉我们两家～得很好；～得十分亲密；～得跟一家人一样；～

得不分彼此❺；～得很和睦❻；～得十分融洽❼〈可〉她脾气那么坏，谁跟她也～不下去；我们两个人～不来〈时〉我们在一起～了二十年〈量〉你跟他～一下儿，就知道他是什么人了〔状～〕无法❽～；不好～；亲切地❾～；热情地❿～；友好～；怎么～；真难～；长期～；和睦地～

1. neighbour 2. closely; intimately 3. temperament; disposition; temper 4. irascible; irritable 5. make no distinction between one's own and another's 6. harmony 7. on friendly terms; harmonious 8. unable; incapable 9. cordially; kindly; warmheartedly 10. warmly

xiāngxìn 相信 believe in; be convinced of; have faith in ↔怀疑〔～宾〕〈名〉～真理❶；～科学❷；不～神鬼❸〈代〉～我吧，我不会骗❹你的〈主–谓〉～他一定能学好；不～这种药这么灵❺〔～补〕〈结〉我相信她可～错了〈程〉～极了；～得不得了(liǎo)〈可〉那个人可～不得〔状～〕真正～；非常～；别～；从来不～；就是不～；完全～；一直～；只好～；必须～

1. truth 2. science 3. ghosts and gods; spirits 4. cheat 5. effective

xiāng 镶 inlay; set; mount; rim; border〔～宾〕〈名〉～牙；项链❶上～着一颗宝石；给窗户～一块玻璃❷；塔顶❸上～了一颗闪闪发光的金星〔～补〕〈结〉牙～上了；玻璃～好了；金星～歪了❹〈趋〉她的牙早就～上去了；玻璃已经～起来了；把这颗珠子❺～到戒指❻上去吧！〈程〉牙～得真快；花边～得很好看〈可〉一个星期～得上吗？那个新来的牙医～得好牙吗？镜框❼小，玻璃大，～不进去；我们这个医院只能拔牙❽，～不了(liǎo)牙〈时〉那块玻璃整整❾～了半年才镶上〈量〉～过一次牙〔状～〕好不好～；还没～；刚～；已经～；早点～；在裙子❿边上～

1. necklace 2. glass 3. on the top of the tower 4. slanting; askew 5. pearl; bead 6. finger ring 7. picture frame 8. pull out a tooth 9. whole; full 10. skirt

xiǎngshòu 享受 enjoy〔～宾〕〈名〉～助学金❶；～奖学金❷；～退休金❸；～合法的权利❹；～平等待遇❺；～幸福❻〈形〉～精神上的❼快乐；～家庭的温暖❽〔～补〕〈结〉～到了晚年的❾欢乐〈趋〉他从今年起也一起助学金来了〈可〉～不到精神上的快乐；～不着(zháo)应得的❿权利〈量〉你也好好～一下儿晚年的幸福吧〔状～〕从未～过；尽情地⓫～；尽量⓬～；总算⓭～到了；充分⓮～；正在～；白白⓯～；一律⓰～；仍然～

1. bursary; grant-in-aid 2. scholarship 3. pension 4. lawful rights 5. equal treatment 6. happiness 7.

spiritual **8.** the warmth of family **9.** old age; one's remaining years **10.** deserved; due **11.** to one's heart's content; as much as one likes **12.** to the full **13.** at long last; finally **14.** fully **15.** without paying **16.** all; without exception

xiǎng 响 sound; make a sound; ring〔**主～**〕〈名〉枪～；炮❶～；爆竹❷～；锣❸～；鼓❹～；喇叭❺～；扩音器❻～；铃～；雷❼～；钟摆❽～；哨子❾～；闹钟～；汽笛❿～；海浪拍打岩石⓫～〔**～补**〕〈结〉各种声音～成一片〈趋〉剧场里⓬～起了暴风雨般的掌声⓭；远处的炮声⓮～起来了〈程〉雷声⓯～得真吓人⓰；～个不停⓱；～得震耳朵⓲〈时〉掌声～了十分钟；～了好半天〈量〉～了一阵；电话铃一会儿就～一次；闹钟刚～一下儿，我就醒⓳了〔**状～**〕一直～；不停地～；断断续续地⓴～；一阵一阵地㉑～；突然～；还～呢？别让它再～了；雨哗哗地㉒～；风呼呼地㉓～；水滴滴答答地㉔～；噼里啪啦㉕地～；呜呜地㉖～

1. gun **2.** firecracker **3.** gong **4.** drum **5.** trumpet **6.** megaphone **7.** thunder **8.** pendulum **9.** whistle **10.** steam whistle; siren **11.** rock **12.** in the theatre **13.** thunderous applause **14.** the report of a gun in the distance **15.** thunderclap **16.** frightening **17.** endless **18.** deafening **19.** wake **20.** off and on **21.** in fits and starts **22.** The rain is gurgling on. **23.** The wind is whistling. **24.** The water keeps pitter-pattering. **25.** cracking **26.** hoot; toot; zoom

xiǎng 想 ① think〔**～宾**〕〈名〉～办法；～问题；～主意❶；～事情；～心事❷；～答案❸；多～～困难；～～他的优点❹；～～自己的缺点❺〈动〉她在～放假以后到哪儿去旅行；～应该怎么回答他〈主－谓〉～一～他说得对不对？～下一步棋❻怎么走；我刚才～这句话有没有道理〔**～补**〕〈结〉话～好了再说；问题～通❼了没有？答案～清楚了吧？事前❽把问题～周到❾点儿；我跟你讲的道理，你～明白了吗？把困难都～到了，就不致于❿措手不及⓫了；什么事情都应该～开⓬点儿；这个问题你可～错了；她想孩子都快～疯了⓭；～到什么时候才完呢？〈趋〉她～出来一个好办法；一点儿小事就～过来～过去的没完〈程〉这个办法～得很好；答案～得很快；困难～得太多了；你～得不对；他们～得很周到；～得真细致⓮〈可〉头都晕⓯了，～不下去了；老～不出好主意来；～不周到就会出问题；她还～不通吗？这个人什么事都～得开；我～不了(liǎo)那么快；～不了(liǎo)那么多；答案一时～不起来；这么多事都让我一个人想着，我哪儿～得过来啊！这个道理你怎么老～不明白（～不清楚）啊！〈时〉～了好几天也没想通；再～一会儿，看能不能想出来〈量〉好好儿～一下儿；～过两遍了〔状～〕多～～；认真❶⑥～～；仔细❶⑦～～；再～～；赶快～办法，反复❶⑧～；前后～；从头❶⑨～

1. idea 2. something weighing on one's mind; a load on one's mind 3. key; solution 4. merit; strong point 5. shortcoming; demerit 6. chess 7. straighten out 8. in advance; beforehand 9. thoughtful 10. cannot go so far; be unlikely 11. be caught unprepared; be caught unawares 12. open-minded 13. go mad 14. careful; meticulous 15. dizzy; giddy; faint 16. seriously; conscientiously 17. carefully; attentively 18. repeatedly 19. from beginning

② think back; recall; recollect ≅ 回想〔～宾〕〈名〉～往事❶；～～过去❷；～以前的生活〈动〉你好好～～这句话他到底说过没有？你仔细❸～～这本词典我是什么时候买的；你帮我～～我的钥匙❹放在哪儿了〔～补〕〈结〉～起了过去；又～到他了〈趋〉我突然～起一个老同学来；～起那件事我就生气；她～起死去的孩子就哭；他又～起童年❺的生活来了〈程〉～得很难过❻；～得很兴奋❼〈可〉这个人好象在哪儿见过，一时～不起来了；你还～得起来我叫什么名字吗？〈时〉～了半天也想不起来他是谁；多～一会儿就想起来了〈量〉那件往事，他～过无数❽遍❾了；应该好好～一下儿〔状～〕怎么也～不起来了；多～一会儿；再～一～；一直～着；不断地～；一幕一幕地❶⓪～；痴痴地❶⓫～

1. past events 2. the past 3. carefully 4. key 5. childhood 6. feel sorry 7. excited 8. countless 9. times (a measure word) 10. one scene after another 11. crazily

③ suppose; think ≅ 认为〔～宾〕〈主－谓〉我～他一定会去的；你～晚饭以前我们写得完吗？她～，哥哥知道了一定要生气；我～他可能买不着(zháo)；我在～我该走了〔～补〕〈结〉你～错了，他不是那样的人；没～到她也来了〈程〉我～得一点儿也没错，他真的来了〈可〉我去看她，你～不到吧？〈时〉～了半天也没想对〔状～〕一点儿也没～到；完全没～到

④ remember with longing; miss ≅ 想念〔～宾〕〈名〉～家；～亲人❶；～孩子；～祖国〈代〉谁也不～〔～补〕〈结〉你可～死我们了，把母亲～坏了；你把大家～苦了❸〈趋〉她又～起家来了〈程〉孩子想妈妈～得直哭；想家～得睡不着(zháo)觉；奶奶❹想你～极了❺〈时〉从来的时候到现在整整❻～了一年的家；～了好长时间；～了一会儿〈量〉一天要～好几次〔状～〕净❼～；老❽～；别～；从来不～；一直～；无时无刻❾不～；时时刻刻❶⓪都在～；

一遍一遍地❶~；不停地❷~；日夜~

1. one's parents, spouse, children, etc.; one family members 2. motherland 3. cause sb. suffering; give sb. a hard time 4. grandma; grandmother 5. extremely 6. whole 7. only; merely 8. always 9. 10. all the time; incessantly 11. time and again 12. endlessly

⑤ bear in mind ≅ 记住〔~宾〕〈名〉~着这件事，千万别忘了〈代〉~着我们，可别把我们忘了〈动〉到了那儿~着给我们写信；~着买火柴❶〔~状〕好好~着；一直~着；总~着；时刻❷~着

1. match 2. all the time

xiàng 向 ① face; turn towards ≅ 对着〔~宾〕〈名〉面❶~讲台❷；脸~观众❸；屋门~西；葵花❹~着太阳〔~状〕一直~着总是~着太阳；正好~东

1. face 2. platform 3. audience 4. sunflower

② take sb.'s part; side with; be partial to ≅ 偏袒〔~宾〕〈名〉妈妈~着妹妹〔~状〕总~着；谁也不~着；当然~着；必然❶~着

1. inevitably; certainly

xiàng 象 ① resemble; be like; take after〔主~〕〈名〉他们姐妹两个的模样❶很~；你们母女二人说话的声音❷真~；他们几个人的脸型❸很~；神态❹~；他们两个人写的字有点儿~〔~宾〕〈名〉她的两只大眼睛真~她妈妈；她~一个护士❺；他的身体不~七十岁的人；那个演员演❻谁~谁；健壮❼得~头小牛；我不~你那么有福气❽；人群~潮水❾一样涌❿向广场⓫；今天还~那天那样走着去吧！我们的校园~公园一样美丽〔~补〕〈程〉他们两个人长得~极⓬了，她学得~极了〔~状〕真~；非常~；特别~；太~了，一点儿也不~；哪儿~? 完全~；没有比他们两个人更~的了；全然⓭不~一个军人⓮

1. appearance 2. sound; voice 3. the shape of face 4. expression; manner; bearing 5. nurse 6. perform; play 7. healthy and strong 8. happy lot; good fortune 9. tidewater 10. pour; surge 11. square 12. extremely; to death 13. completely; entirely 14. armyman

② like; such as ≅ 例如〔~宾〕~苹果、梨❶、桔子❷、葡萄❸等，都是我爱吃的水果

1. pear 2. orange 3. grape

xiāo 削 pare (peel) with a knife〔~宾〕〈名〉~果皮；~铅笔；~藤条❶〔~补〕〈结〉把皮~薄❷点儿；把藤条~细❸点儿；别把铅❹~折❺(shé)了；主人把~好的苹果递❻给了客人〈趋〉把皮~

下来以后，放在垃圾箱❼里；她一次~出好几根铅笔〈程〉~得很好；皮~得太厚❽了；皮~得很干净；铅笔~得太尖❾了〈可〉他~不好铅笔，一削就断；这把刀~不了(liǎo)果皮〈时〉他真笨❿，~了半天还没削完一个梨⓫；那个孩子~了半天苹果，好容易⓬削好了又掉地下了〈量〉那把刀不快⓭，用这把~一下儿试试；~过好几次了〔**状**~〕真难~；我替你~；用小刀~；慢慢地~；薄薄地⓮~

1. rattan 2. thin; flimsy 3. thin; slender 4. lead in a pencil 5. broken; snapped 6. pass 7. dustbin 8. thick 9. pointed 10. clumsy; awkward; stupid 11. pear 12. with great difficulty 13. not sharp 14. thinly

xiāo 消 eliminate; dispel; remove ≌ 除去〔**主**~〕〈名〉气❶~了；红肿❷已经~了，云~雾❸散❹〔**~宾**〕〈名〉~痰❺；~毒❻；~~气〈形〉~愁❼；~肿❽〔**~补**〕〈趋〉肿已经~下去了〈程〉气~得很快〈可〉不上药~不了(liǎo)肿；这个大包❾一时~不下去了〔**状**~〕逐渐❿~；慢慢地~；老不~；很快~；一下子就~；全~了

1. anger 2. red and swollen 3. fog 4. lift 5. phlegm; sputum 6. disinfect 7. divert oneself from boredom 8. swollen 9. protuberance; swelling; lump 10. gradually

xiāochú 消除 eliminate; dispel; remove〔**~宾**〕〈名〉~彼此间的隔阂❶；~我们两个人之间的分歧❷；~顾虑❸；~误会❹；~疾病❺〈形〉~疲劳❻〔**~补**〕〈结〉~掉〈程〉~得很快〈可〉~得了(liǎo)~不了(liǎo)？〔**状**~〕努力~；彻底❼~；终于❽~了

1. clear up the misunderstanding of each other 2. differences 3. misgivings; worries 4. misunderstanding 5. disease 6. fatigue; weary 7. thoroughly 8. at last; finally

xiāohào 消耗 consume; use up; expend ≌ 耗费〔**~宾**〕〈名〉~精神❶；~力量❷；~热量❸；~精力❹；~能量❺；~能源❻；~武器❼弹药❽；~粮食❾；~人力物力❿〔**~补**〕〈结〉把能源都~完了；力量~尽了；粮食~没⓫了〈程〉精神~得太利害了；~得太多了〈可〉~不得；~不起〔**状**~〕大量~；完全~；几乎~；一再~；直接⓬~；间接⓭~

1. spirit 2. strength 3. quantity of heat 4. energy; vigour 5. energy 6. the sources of energy 7. weapon; arms 8. ammunition 9. grain 10. material resources 11. exhausted 12. directly 13. indirectly

xiāohuà 消化 digest〔**主**~〕〈名〉吃的食物都没~；学的东西

没很好地～〔～补〕〈结〉中午吃的东西都～完了〈趋〉都～下去了〈程〉年轻人～得快〈可〉胃不好❶，吃这么硬的❷东西～得了(liǎo)吗？所学的知识❸都～得了(liǎo)吗？〔状～〕容易～；难～；全～了；学的知识一点儿都没～

1. have some trouble with one's stomach 2. hard 3. knowledge

xiāomiè 消灭 perish; exterminate; die out; wipe out〔～宾〕〈名〉～苍蝇❶；～文盲❷；～传染病❸；～敌人❹；～匪徒❺〈形〉～贫困❻〔～补〕〈结〉把蚊蝇❼～干净❽；把敌人统统❾～掉〈程〉～得很干净；～得不彻底❿〈可〉～得了(liǎo)～不了(liǎo)？～不完〔状～〕已经～；几乎～了；彻底～；终于⓫～了；赶快～；差不多～；基本上⓬～了；想方设法地⓭～；从地球上～；不能自行⓮～

1. fly 2. illiterate 3. infectious disease 4. enemy 5. bandit 6. poverty 7. mosquito and fly 8. completely 9. all; entirely 10. thoroughly 11. at last 12. basically; on the whole; fundamentally 13. by every possible means 14. by oneself

xiāomó 消磨 fritter away〔～宾〕〈名〉～时间；～岁月❶；～意志❷；～志气❸；～锐气❹〔～补〕〈结〉～完了；～掉了很多宝贵的❺时光〔状～〕白白地❻～；用什么办法❼～时间；故意❽～

1. years 2. will 3. aspiration; ambition 4. dash; drive 5. valuable; precious 6. in vain; to no purpose 7. by what means 8. on purpose; intentionally

xiāohuǐ 销毁 destroy by melting or burning〔～宾〕〈名〉～罪证❶；～证据❷；～核武器❸；～文件❹；～记录❺；～日记❻；～资料❼；～档案❽；～信件；～赃物❾〔～补〕〈结〉想把所有罪证都～干净❿，那是不可能的〈趋〉他有便利⓫条件⓬，～起证据来不易⓭被人发现〈程〉～得不彻底⓮；～得一点痕迹⓯都不露〈可〉销毁是～不完的；～不净⓰的〈量〉～过好多次信件了〔状～〕彻底～；暗中⓱～；及早⓲～；不易～；必须～；全部～；部分⓳～；已经～；无须⓴～；明目张胆地㉑～

1. evidence of a crime 2. proof; testimony; evidence 3. nuclear weapon 4. document 5. record 6. diary 7. data; material 8. files; archives; record 9. stolen goods; booty 10. completely 11. convenient; easy 12. condition 13. not easy 14. not thorough 15. mark; trace 16. not complete 17. in secret 18. as early as possible 19. partly 20. needlessly 21. brazenly; flagrantly

xiào 笑 ① smile; laugh↔哭〔**～补**〕〈结〉～死❶我了；把人都～坏了❷〈趋〉～出眼泪❸来了；再～下去肚子都要疼❹了；三个月的婴孩❺就能～出声音❻来了〈程〉那个孩子～得真高兴；～得直不起腰❼来了；～得直流眼泪❽；～得止不住❾了；～得前仰后合的❿；～得真甜；～得莫明其妙⓫〈可〉他难过⓬得～不出来了〈时〉整整～了两分钟〈量〉～了一阵；～了一通⓭〔**状～**〕歇斯底里地⓮～；微微地⓯～；狂⓰～；不怀好意⓱地～；爽朗地⓲～；抿着嘴⓳～；嘻嘻地～⓴；尖声㉑～；偷偷地～；捂着嘴㉒～；裂着嘴～㉓；捧腹大～㉔；叽叽嘎嘎地～㉕；忍不住地㉖～；格格地～㉗；嫣然一～㉘

1. extremely; to death **2.** awfully; badly **3.** tear **4.** pain; ache **5.** baby **6.** sound **7.** unable to straighten one's back **8.** shed tears **9.** cannot stop **10.** rock (with laughter) **11.** unable to make head or tail of sth.; be baffled **12.** sorrowful **13.** a period of time **14.** hysterically **15.** slightly **16.** violently **17.** harbour evil designs; harbour malicious intentions **18.** heartily **19.** with closed lips **20.** giggle **21.** in a shrill voice **22.** cover one's mouth with one's hand **23.** grinningly **24.** be convulsed with laughter **25.** crackle **26.** unable to bear; can't hold back (one's laughter) **27.** chuckle; titter **28.** give a winsome smile

② laugh at; ridicule≃笑话；讥笑〔**～宾**〕〈代〉他刚学跳舞，别～他；～他不懂事❶；～他少见多怪❷；～他没礼貌❸；～他糊涂❹〔**～补**〕〈结〉别让人～掉大牙〈趋〉自己不怎么样，倒～起别人来了〈程〉笑人～得可利害了〈可〉他～不着(zháo)我，他自己也不行〈时〉～了半天别人，自己也错了〔**状～**〕净❺～；总(是)～；从来不～；别～；故意❻～〔**习用**〕～面虎❼

1. ignorant **2.** consider sth. remarkable (or queer) simply because one has not seen it before **3.** impolite **4.** muddle **5.** only; merely **6.** intentionally; on purpose **7.** smiling tiger — an outwardly kind but inwardly cruel person

xiē 歇 have a rest〔**～宾**〕〈名〉～工❶；～～腿❷；～口气儿〔**～补**〕〈结〉～够❸了吧？这么多天没上班，在家都～腻❹了〈趋〉睡了一夜觉，可～过来了；累得我都～不过来了；还～不够啊？〈时〉一连❺～了一个月；～一会儿就不累了〈量〉～一下儿就行了〔**状～**〕稍微❻～一会儿；多～一会儿；痛痛快快地❼～；在树底下～；轮班❽～；别总～着

1. stop work; knock off **2.** leg **3.** enough **4.** be tired of **5.** in succession; in a row; running **6.** a little; slightly **7.** to one's heart's content; to one's great satisfaction **8.** in shifts; in relays

xiě 写 ① write ≃ 书写；记〔**～宾**〕〈名〉你喜欢用什么笔～字？～了一封信；你的字真好，请你给我～一幅对联❶可以吗？～地址❷；～帐❸；～了两篇❹〔**～补**〕〈结〉～上名字；老人～惯❺了毛笔❻字，不愿意用钢笔；对联～好了，你拿走吧；～到夜里两点；纸上～满❼；名字～错了；这一行字～歪❽了；把号码～在右上角吧！这张纸太小，那么多字能～下吗？帐～清楚了吗？把字～整齐❾〈趋〉就按❿这种格式⓫～下去吧；听写的生词你都～上来了吗？把这笔帐也～进来了；她又～起信来了；他把电话号码～到墙上去了〈程〉他的字～得真漂亮⓬；地址～得太潦草⓭了，看不清楚；帐一笔一笔的～得真清楚；字～得龙飞凤舞⓮〈可〉她手破⓯了，～不了(liǎo)字；玻璃⓰太滑⓱，～不上字；我想添⓲上几个字，还～得进去吗？他的地址，你现在～得出来吗？一个小时～不完；你的字怎么总～不整齐〈时〉这封信～了两个小时；不会用毛笔的人，～一会儿手就酸⓳了〈量〉请～一下儿通讯处⓴；你的电话号码我～了好几遍了〔**状～**〕在书皮㉑上～；用圆珠笔㉒～；一笔一划地㉓～；重新～；偶然㉔～；经常～；轻易㉕不～；随便㉖～；马上㉗～；一遍一遍地㉘～；细心点儿㉙～；白㉚～了；一边说一边～；一连㉛～了三篇；一时㉜～不上来；实在㉝～不好；简直㉞～不下去了；没法儿㉟～；容易～

1. antithetical couplet (written on scrolls, etc.) **2.** address **3.** account **4.** a measure word (for an article, etc.) **5.** be used to **6.** writing brush **7.** full; filled **8.** oblique; slanting **9.** neat **10.** according to **11.** form; pattern **12.** remarkable; pretty; beautiful **13.** (of handwriting) hasty and careless; illegible **14.** like dragons flying and phoenixes dancing — lively and vigorous flourishes in calligraphy **15.** cut; wounded **16.** glass **17.** slippery; smooth **18.** add **19.** tingle; ache **20.** address **21.** book cover **22.** ball pen **23.** one stroke after another **24.** accidentally; by chance **25.** lightly; rashly **26.** casually; at random **27.** at once **28.** time and again **29.** carefully; meticulously **30.** in vain **31.** in succession; running; in a row **32.** temporarily; for a moment **33.** really; truly **34.** simply; at all **35.** unable; incapable

② write; compose ≃ 写作〔**～宾**〕〈名〉～文章❶；～论文❷；他擅长❸～悲剧❹，还是～喜剧❺？～报道❻；～总结❼；～个计划❽；～日记❾；～传记❿；～摘要⓫；～人物的心理⓬活动⓭；～景⓮；～事〔**～补**〕〈结〉文章～好了吗？人物～活⓯了；把散文⓰～成诗了〈趋〉把她～进小说里去了；总

结报告❶已经~出来了；这篇报道~出水平❶来了；说着容易，~起来可就难了；那个孩子~起作文❶来很认真；把摘要~到小黑板上去；这个细节❷也应该~进去〈程〉人物~得很生动❷；故事~得很感人❷；那个剧本的结构❷~得太松散❷；故事情节❷~得很紧凑❷；文章~得太呆板❷〈可〉心情❷不好，~不下去了；想得不错，就是~不出来；半年的时间~得完~不完？〈时〉这部著作❷他前后一共~了十年；那位作家每天差不多要~十几个小时〈量〉我~过好多次总结了；先~一下儿看看行不行〔状~〕特意❷~了一首；专门❸~诗❷；试着~；重新~；夜以继日地❸~；认真~；一篇一篇地❷~；及时❸~出；接着❸~；用第一人称❸~；真难~；笼统地❸~；具体地❸~；简直❹~不下去了；想起来就~；从来不~；没法儿❹~；净❷~；合❸~；随时❹~

1. article, essay 2. thesis 3. be good at; be expert in; be skilled in 4. tragedy 5. comedy 6. report (news) 7. summary 8. plan 9. diary 10. biography 11. abstract 12. psychology; mentality 13. activity 14. view; scenery; scene 15. lively; vivid 16. prose 17. report 18. level 19. composition 20. details; particulars 21. lively; vivid 22. move; touch 23. structure; construction; organisation 24. loose 25. plot 26. well-knit 27. stiff; rigid; inflexible 28. state of mind; mood 29. work; writings 30. specially; for a special purpose 31. specially; specialize 32. poem 33. day and night 34. one after another 35. in time 36. follow 37. the first person 38. in general terms 39. concretely 40. simply; at all 41. unable; incapable 42. only; merely 43. jointly 44. at any time; at all times

xiè 卸 ① unload; discharge ↔ 装〔~宾〕〈名〉~货❶；~担子❷；~任❸〔~补〕〈结〉三船货都~完了；把煤❹ 先~到门外边吧！〈趋〉火车刚进站，工人们就~起货来了〈程〉货~得真快〈可〉时间短了~不完；没有工具❺，煤~不下去〈时〉都~二十分钟了，还没卸完一半呢〈量〉帮我~一下儿装❻〔状~〕在哪儿~？大家一起~；七手八脚地❼~；乱❽~

1. goods 2. burden 3. be relieved of one's office 4. coal 5. tools; instruments 6. remove stage make up 7. with everybody lending a hand 8. at random; in disorder

② remove; strip ≌ 拆〔~宾〕〈名〉~螺丝❶；~零件❷；~锁❸；~玻璃❹〔~补〕〈结〉不是那把锁，你~错了〈趋〉把窗❺下来修理❻修理吧！〈程〉~得太慢；~得很利索❼〈可〉锈❽得太利害❾，~不下来了；你~得动~不动？〈时〉~了半天也没卸下来〈量〉再~一下儿试试看能不能卸下来〔状~〕怎么~？用什么工

具❿~；不容易~；差点儿~不下来；点⓫一点儿油⓬再~；赶快~；没法儿⓭~

1. screw 2. spare parts 3. lock 4. glass 5. window 6. repair; mend 7. agile; nimble 8. rust 9. terrible; awful 10. tool; instrument 11. drip 12. oil 13. unable; incapable

xiè 谢 thank〔~宾〕<名>~~你的好意❶<动>~~你的帮助；~你的款待❷<代>~~大家；不知道到底❸应该~谁〔~补〕<可>这件事~不着(zháo)他，不是他做的<时>我~了她半天<量>应该好好儿~一下儿他〔**状**~〕诚心诚意地❹~；再三地❺~；不用~；怎么~？赶快~

1. kindness 2. treat cordially; entertain 3. after all; to the end 4. sincerely; earnestly; cordially 5. over and over again; repeatedly

xìn 信 ① believe ≌ 相信〔~宾〕<名>你~不~这件事？我真~她说的话了；我们既不~神❶，也不~鬼❷<代>我什么也不~了<动>不~闹鬼❸<主-谓>我不~他这盘棋❹能赢❺〔~补〕<结>我~错人了<可>这个人你~得过信不过？〔**状**~〕一点儿也不~；千万别~；完全~；别轻易❻~

1. god 2. ghost 3. haunt 4. a chess 5. win 6. rashly; lightly

② believe in ≌ 信仰〔~宾〕<名>他~佛教❶；我们什么教也不~

〔~补〕<趋>他老了以后~佛佛教起来了<时>他外祖父❷~了一辈子❸基督教❹〔**状**~〕居然❺~；不~，笃❻~，虔诚地❼~；依然❽~

1. Buddhism 2. (maternal) grandfather 3. all one's life 4. Christianity 5. unexpectedly; to one's surprise 6. 7. sincerely; devoutly 8. still; yet

xīng 兴 prosper; rise; prevail; become popular ≌ 时兴〔~宾〕<名>前几年~短发；现在的衣服~长的，不~短的；我们那里不~这一套儿❶<动>~旅行结婚了；这几年又~跳舞了；现在又~练气功❷了；~火葬❸了〔~补〕<结>皮凉鞋❹也~开了<趋>衣服样子又~回来了<可>~得开~不开？<时>旗袍❺~过一个时期，现在不怎么兴了〔**状**~〕已经不~了；一阵风似地❻~起来了

1. convention; formula 2. do breathing exercises 3. cremation 4. leather sandals 5. a close-fitting woman's dress with high neck and slit skirt 6. like a gust of wind

xíngchéng 形成 take shape; form〔~宾〕<名>~一种好的社会风气❶；~习惯❷；~了自己的独特❸风格❹；多年的独居生活❺~了他的古怪脾气❻；两个人的处境❼~了鲜明的对比❽；谈判❾~了僵局❿；~了今天这种局面⓫；~一种学派⓬〔**状**~〕由

什么原因〕~的; 很快~; 逐渐❸ ~; 日益❹~; 自然❺~的; 天长日久❻必然❼~; 早已~

1. the general mood of society 2. habit 3. particular; characteristic 4. style 5. a solitary life 6. eccentric character 7. unfavourable situation; plight 8. a sharp contrast 9. talks; negotiations 10. deadlock; impasse 11. aspect; phase; situation 12. school of thought; school 13. gradually 14. day by day 15. naturally 16. after a considerable period of time 17. inevitably

xǐng 醒 ① wake up; be awake ↔睡〔主~〕〈名〉孩子~了〔~补〕〈结〉今天早晨~晚了, 差点儿迟到〈趋〉这孩子刚睁开眼睛还没~过来呢, 就跟妈妈去上班了〈程〉我每天~得太早〈可〉累得我都不过来了〈时〉孩子~了半天也没哭〈量〉一夜要~好几次〔状~〕刚~; 一直~着; 突然~了

② regain consciousness; sober up; come to ≅ 清醒〔主~〕〈名〉那个醉汉❶的酒~了; 麻药❷劲儿❸过去以后, 病人~了; 刚才她昏倒❹了, 现在~了〔~补〕〈趋〉病人从昏迷❺中~过来了; 听了他的一番教诲❻, 那个迷途❼青年才~过来〈程〉~得很快; ~得很慢〈可〉他醉❽得太利害了, 今天晚上~不过来了〈量〉~了一下儿, 又昏迷了〔状~〕还没~; 逐渐❾~; 一下子~; 刚(刚)~

1. drunkard; drunken man 2. anaesthetic 3. effect 4. fall into a swoon; go off into a faint 5. stupor; coma 6. teaching 7. go astray 8. drunk; intoxicated; tipsy 9. gradually; by degrees

xǐng 擤 blow (one's nose) 〔~宾〕〈名〉~鼻涕❶〔~补〕〈结〉把鼻涕~干净; ~在纸上〈趋〉把鼻涕~出来〈程〉那个孩子鼻涕~得很干净〈可〉~不出来〈时〉~了半天也没擤干净〈量〉他感冒了, 一会儿~一次(鼻涕); 使劲❷~一下儿〔状~〕赶快~; 用纸~; 使劲~

1. nasal mucus; snivel 2. exert all one's strength

xiū 休 stop; cease ≅ 歇; 停〔~宾〕〈名〉~假❶; ~学❷; ~会❸〔~补〕〈结〉你的假~到什么时候截止❹?〈趋〉不能再~下去了〈程〉~得时间太长了〈可〉看样子今年的假又~不成了, 你的假怎么老~不完哪! 〈时〉休学~了一年多; 他~了两个星期病假❺〈量〉每两个星期~一次, 一次休两天〔状~〕争论不~❻; 按时❼~; 轮流着❽~; 从来不~; 因病~学; 以后再~; 一次~完; 分期❾~; 集中~; 分散❿~; 长期~; 暂时⓫~

1. holiday 2. suspend one's schooling without losing one's status as student 3. adjourn 4.

end; close 5. sick leave 6. an endless debate 7. on time; to schedule 8. in turn 9. by stages 10. decentralizedly 11. temporarily; for the moment

xiūxi 休息 have a rest; rest ≅ 歇〔～补〕〈结〉他真懒❶，没做多久又～上了；～腻❷了〈趋〉下火车以后，整整❸睡了一天，可～过来了〈程〉～得真舒服❹；～得不够〈可〉家务事❺太多，～不好；你在家休息了那么长时间还～不腻吗？睡上三天三夜也～不过来〈时〉～了一个多月；～一会儿就好了〈量〉累了就～一下儿；这一年，你一共～了多少次〔状～〕好好～～；准时～；想再～一下儿；无法❻～；因病～；整天❼～；差不多～了半年

1. lazy 2. be bored with 3. whole 4. comfortable 5. household duties 6. unable; incapable 7. all day long

xiū 修 ① repair; mend ≅ 修理；修补〔～宾〕〈名〉～收音机❶；～电冰箱❷；～钟表❸；～房子；～家具❹〔～补〕〈结〉打字机❺～好了没有？这么多日子还没～完哪？〈趋〉～出来跟新的一样〈程〉～得挺快；～得跟原来一样；～得很认真❻；～得非常马虎❼〈可〉修了好几次也～不好；跑了好几家❽都说～不了(liǎo)，太贵我可～不起；半年还～不好吗？遇到❾困难～不下去了；零件❿不全⓫，

～不了(liǎo)了〈时〉～了两个多月才修好〈量〉～过不少次了；～一次多少钱？〔状～〕正在～；不好～；容易～；立即⓬～；当场⓭～；彻底⓮～；勉强⓯～；认真～；专门⓰～；细心⓱～；马马虎虎地⓲～；赶着⓳～；赶紧～；别～

1. radio 2. refrigerator 3. clocks and watches 4. furniture 5. typewriter 6. serious 7. careless 8. run about to several shops 9. meet with; encounter 10. spare parts; parts 11. not complete 12. at once 13. on the spot 14. thoroughly 15. reluctantly; barely 16. specially 17. carefully; meticulously 18. carelessly 19. hurry through; rush

② build; construct ≅ 修建；修筑〔～宾〕〈名〉～铁路❶；～纪念碑❷；～机场〔～补〕〈结〉铁路～完了；机场～好了没有？码头❸～小了〈趋〉这条铁路～下来，至少❹得❺(děi)三年；～起一个水库❻来，可不是容易的事情；又～起来一个新机场〈程〉机场～得真漂亮；～得不够高〈可〉这里的地基❼不好，～不了(liǎo)铁路；这个工程两百万也～不下来；前面有山挡❽着，公路～得过去吗？一两年之内还～不起来〈时〉再～一年差不多能交工❾了〈量〉这条路不平，需要好好～一下儿〔状～〕太难～了；用什么材料❿～？按⓫什么图纸⓬～？

1. railway 2. monument; memorial 3. wharf 4. at least 5. must;

have to 6. reservoir 7. ground; foundation 8. block; get in the way 9. hand over a completed project 10. material 11. according to 12. blueprint; drawing

③ trim; prune ≅ 修剪；修整〔~宾〕〈名〉~树枝；~指甲❶〔~补〕〈结〉把指甲~齐❷点；松墙❸~好了；脚~破❹了〈趋〉老园丁❺~出来的松树真齐〈程〉脚~得一点儿也不疼❻了〈可〉学徒❼~不了(liǎo)；怎么还~不完哪？〈时〉指甲~了半天才修好〈量〉半个月就得~一次〔状~〕好好~；白❽~了；用刀子~；仔细点儿❾~；轻轻地❿~；很难~；给别人~；自己~

1. nail (fingernail) 2. even 3. pine wall 4. cut; wounded 5. old gardener 6. ache; pain; sore 7. apprentice 8. in vain 9. carefully 10. slightly; gently

xiūgǎi 修改 revise; modify; amend; alter 〔~宾〕〈名〉~宪法❶；~计划❷；~文章❸；~章程❹；~契约❺；~条文❻〔~补〕〈结〉~完了；~到夜里12点〈趋〉文章~起来不容易〈程〉~得比原来❼具体❽；~得还不如❾原来的好呢〈可〉这么多文章，一位编辑❿哪儿~得过来啊！〈时〉~了不少时间了；~半年了〈量〉好好~一下儿；已经~好几遍了〔状~〕没法⓫~；一句句⓬~；认真~；反复⓭~；马马虎虎地⓮~

1. constitution 2. plan 3. article; essay 4. rules; regulations; statute 5. contract 6. clause; article 7. original 8. concrete 9. not as good as; inferior to 10. editor 11. unable; incapable 12. one sentence after another 13. repeatedly; over and over again 14. carelessly

xiūjiàn 修建 build; construct; erect ≅ 修筑；建造〔~宾〕〈名〉~铁路❶；~地铁❷；~码头❸；~纪念馆❹；~了一条通往山顶❺的游览❻公路❼；~了一个体育馆❽；~疗养院❾；~了一个歌舞❿剧院⓫；~工厂〔~补〕〈结〉~在山坡上；~到今年年底竣工⓬〈趋〉土质⓭不好，不能再继续~下去了；很短时间就~起来了〈程〉~得太慢了；别墅~得小巧玲珑⓮；样式~得很新颖⓯〈可〉技术不行⓰，目前还~不了(liǎo)；这项工程⓱太大，三年也~不完；短期内~得起来吗？〈时〉~了十个月；~了不少时候〔状~〕为旅游⓲~；刚~；特地⓳~；重新~；日夜不停地⓴~；赶着㉑~

1. railway 2. underground; subway 3. wharf 4. memorial hall 5. attain the top of a mountain 6. tour; go sight seeing 7. highway 8. stadium 9. sanatorium 10. song and dance 11. theatre 12. completed 13. properties of soil 14. small and exquisite 15. new and original; novel 16. be no

good; not work 17. engineering; project 18. tourism 19. especially; particularly 20. day and night 21. hurry through; rush

xiūlǐ 修理 repair; mend; overhaul; fix ≅ 修〔~宾〕〈名〉~机器；~手表；~钢琴❶；~桌椅；~鞋〔~补〕〈结〉几天才能~完？反而❷给~坏了〈趋〉这个电视要是~下来比买新的还贵〈程〉~得又快又好；~得比原来❸的还好用；~得真粗糙❹〈可〉太贵我可~不起，一个星期哪儿~得出来呀〈时〉整整❺~了半年〈量〉这个电视买了不到一年~过两次了〔状~〕仔细❻~；定期❼~；按时❽~；马马虎虎地❾~；不负责任地❿~；彻底~；专门~；提前⓫~

1. piano 2. on the contrary 3. original 4. coarse 5. whole 6. carefully 7. at regular intervals 8. on time 9. carelessly 10. irresponsibly 11. ahead of time

xiù 绣 embroider〔~宾〕〈名〉~花❶；~枕头套❷；~了几个字〔~补〕〈结〉~好了；~上几个字；~在枕头上〈趋〉把这几个字也一起~上去好不好？~到台布❸上去吧！〈程〉~得太漂亮了！~得真快。~得不好看〈可〉两天~得完~不完？〈时〉这条床单❹~了半年多〈量〉~过好多次了；~一下儿试试〔状~〕从很小的时候就~；刚刚~好；试着~；一针一

线地❺~；耐心地❻~；这种图案❼难~；密密地❽~；稀稀地❾~

1. embroider 2. pillowcase 3. tablecloth 4. sheet 5. one needle after another 6. patiently 7. pattern; design 8. densely 9. sparsely

xūyào 需要 need; want; require; demand〔~宾〕〈名〉他~一本字典；我们现在就~时间；国家~人才❶；建设❷~资金❸〈代〉我们这儿的工作~你〈动〉产妇❹~休息；孩子~照顾❺；我们~研究一下儿，才能决定；这座楼❻~修理❼；这种情况~立即采取措施❽〈形〉病人~安静❾；在紧要关头❿~冷静⓫；速度⓬~快一点儿；~沉着⓭〈主-谓〉果园~专人⓮管理⓯；这件事~老张亲自去办〔状~〕非常~；特别~；十分~；哪儿也不~；真正~；谁都~；极端⓰~

1. man of ability; gifted person 2. construction 3. fund 4. lying-in woman 5. take care of 6. building 7. repair 8. take action; take steps 9. quiet 10. critical moment 11. sober; calm 12. speed 13. cool-headed; steady 14. person specially assigned for a task or job 15. manage; run 16. extremely

xù 续 add; supply more〔~宾〕〈名〉往锅❶里再~一点儿水；已经休息三天了，还想再~几天假〔~补〕〈结〉~水~满❷了；她嫌❸

我续假~多了〈趋〉往壶里再~进点儿冷水❹去〈程〉水~得不够〈可〉水怎么还~不满啊?〈时〉~了一个小时假〈量〉~过两次假了〔状~〕多~点儿;别~了;一次次地~;再~

1. pot; cooker 2. full 3. dislike; 4. cold water

xuānbù 宣布 declare; proclaim; announce ≅ 宣告〔~宾〕〈名〉~一件事;~三条纪律❶;~注意事项❷;~罪状❸〈动〉~开会;~解散❹;~戒严❺;独立❻〈主-谓〉~会议结束❼;~条约❽无效❾了;~筹备委员会❿成立⓫〔~补〕〈结〉~完了;~早了〈程〉~得比较晚〈可〉这几天还~不了(liǎo)〈量〉~过好几次了;~一下儿〔状~〕郑重⓬;及时⓭~;严肃地⓮~;向大家~;正式⓯~;当场⓰~

1. discipline 2. matters needing attention; points for attention 3. facts about a crime 4. dismiss 5. enforce martial law; impose a curfew 6. independence 7. the end of a conference 8. treaty; pact 9. invalid; null and void 10. preparatory committee 11. found; set up 12. solemnly; seriously 13. in time 14. seriously 15. formally; officially 16. at the spot

xuānshì 宣誓 take (swear) an oath; make a vow; make a pledge 〔状~〕庄严❶~;向谁~;举手❷~;单独❸~;集体❹~;在什么地方~?

1. solemnly 2. raise up one's hand 3. alone; by oneself 4. collectively

xuǎn 选 ① select; choose ≅ 挑选;挑〔~宾〕〈名〉~稿子❶;~演员❷;~运动员❸;~一个合适的❹时间;~一种你喜欢的样式;~民歌❺;~场地❻〔~补〕〈结〉稿子都~好了;那个女孩子被导演❼~上了;时间定了;这本文集❽里少数民族❾的文章~少了〈趋〉把好文章~上来了;把好画都~进来了;~过来~过去也没选中〈程〉~得不理想❿;~得太多了;~得挺快〈可〉~不出来〈时〉~了半天才选中〈量〉~过两遍了;~了三次〔状~〕集体⓫~;认真⓬~;按什么标准⓭~?在什么地方~?初步~;最后一次~;公开⓮~;暗中⓯~

1. manuscript 2. actor or actress 3. sportsman 4. suitable 5. folk song 6. space; place; site 7. director 8. collected works 9. national minorities 10. not ideal 11. collectively 12. seriously; carefully; attentively 13. standard 14. publicly 15. in secret

② elect ≅ 选举〔~宾〕〈名〉~班长❶;~总统❷;一共~了五名代表❸〈代〉他们~你为本届❹学生会主席❺;~他当班长〔~补〕

〈结〉她这次没被～上〈趋〉代表已经～出来了〔程〕人～得不理想❻；～得很顺利❼〈可〉～得上～不上都没关系❽；～不出理想的人来〈时〉～了很长时间才选出来〈量〉～了两次了〔状～〕一致❾～；没～上；重新～；直接❿任⓫～一个；随便⓬～；不记名⓭～；在哪儿～? 用什么方式～?

1. monitor 2. president 3. representative 4. this year 5. the chairman of the student union 6. not ideal 7. successfully; without a hitch 8. It doesn't matter 9. unanimously 10. directly 11. 12. casually; as you like; as you see fit 13. secretly

xuǎnjǔ 选举 elect ≅ 选〔～宾〕

〈名〉～代表❶；～工会主席❷；～了三名；～自己满意的❸人〔～补〕〈结〉～过了，～到哪一天截止❹? 〈趋〉～来～去还是那么几个人〈程〉～得很顺利❺；～得不理想❻〈可〉～不出什么合适❼的人来；有本领❽的人都～不上来；半天的时间～不完〈时〉整整～了三个小时；～了一会儿就完了〈量〉需要重新～一次〔状～〕直接❾；间接❿；无记名⓫～；投票⓬～；定期⓭～；四年一～；重新～

1. representative 2. chairman of labour union 3. satisfied 4. end; close 5. smoothly; successfully; without a hitch 6. not ideal 7. suitable; appropriate 8. skill;

ability 9. directly 10. indirectly 11. secretly 12. vote; cast a vote 13. regularly

xuǎnzé 选择 select; choose; opt ≅ 选〔～宾〕〈名〉～日期；～地点；～商品❶；～合适的人❷；～保姆❸；～什么样子的衣服? ～一种发型❹；～对象❺；～职业❻；～哪种类型❼的?〔～补〕〈结〉～好了吗? ～对了〈趋〉他起来可麻烦了〈程〉～得不错，～得不够理想〈可〉我可～不好〈时〉～了好几年，最后还是不满意❽〈量〉要好好～一下儿〔状～〕慎重地❾～；严格❿～；精心⓫～

1. goods; commodity 2. suitable person 3. children's nurse 4. hair style 5. boy or girl friend 6. occupation; profession 7. type 8. not satisfied 9. prudently; cautiously 10. strictly 11. meticulously; elaborately

xuàn 旋 turn sth. on a lathe; lathe; pare 〔～宾〕〈名〉在车床❶上～一根车轴❷；给他～一个苹果吃〔～补〕〈结〉～完了皮再吃〈趋〉你怎么用菜刀～起水果来了? 把那块烂的地方❸～掉再吃〈程〉～得真快，～得不错〈可〉这把水果刀不快，连皮都～不了(liǎo)〈时〉我真笨❹，一个梨❺～了十分钟〈量〉他给我～过好几次水果了，今天我该给他～一次了〔状～〕用水果刀～；薄薄地❻～；往外～；太难～了

1. lathe 2. axle 3. that rotten part 4. clumsy; awkward 5. pear 6. thinly

xué 学 ① study; learn ≅ 学习〔**～宾**〕〈名〉～技术❶;～文化❷;～外语; ～科学; ～别人的长处❸〈动〉～画画儿; ～滑冰❹; ～管理❺经济; ～写毛笔❻字〈形〉那个孩子不～好;～聪明❼了〔**～补**〕〈结〉游泳❽～会了吗？外语没～好; 一个人要活到老, ～到老❾; 还没～会管理企业❿; 学了一辈子⓫也没～成〈趋〉我～起来感到吃力⓬; 他总算～出成绩(本领⓭／本事⓮)来了〈程〉～得很好; ～得比谁都快〈可〉笨⓯极了, 怎么教也～不会; 看样子今天又～不成了; 该学的东西太多了, 有点～不过来了; 太难我～不会〈时〉小时候～过三年毛笔字; 他想多～一会儿〈量〉我想～一下儿雕塑⓰; ～过几次, 后来还是放弃⓱了〔**状～**〕认真～; 刻苦(地)⓲～; 一点一滴地⓳～; 不间断地⓴～; 虚心㉑～; 有计划地㉒～; 有目的地～; 难～; 贪婪地㉓～; 勤奋地㉔～; 盲目地㉕～; 如饥似渴地㉖～; 孜孜不倦地㉗～; 心不在焉地㉘～; 反复㉙～

1. technology 2. an elementary education; how to read and write 3. merit; good point 4. skating 5. manage; run 6. writing brush 7. intelligent; clever 8. swimming 9. live and learn 10. enterprise; business 11. all one's life 12. entail strenuous effort; be a strain 13. 14. skill; ability 15. stupid; foolish; dull 16. sculpture 17. give up 18. painstakingly; assiduously 19. bit by bit 20. ceaselessly; incessantly 21. modestly 22. systematically 2. greedily 24. diligently 25. blindly 26. as if thirsting or hungering for sth.; eagerly 27. diligently; assidously 28. absentmindedly 29. over and over again; repeatedly

② imitate; mimic ≅ 模仿〔**～宾**〕〈名〉他会～鸡叫; ～他爸爸走路的样子〈代〉～谁象❶谁〈主－谓〉鹦鹉❷～人说话〔**～补**〕〈趋〉那个孩子模仿力❸很强, ～起人来真象〈程〉～得不象〈可〉我～不上她那个可笑的样子❹来; 你～得出她那种刺耳的❺声音来吗？〈时〉～了半天也学不象〈量〉再～一下儿让我们听听; 他又～了一遍〔**状～**〕专门❻～; 故意❼～; 一遍一遍地❽～; 再～他就生气❾了

1. be like; resemble; take after 2. parrot 3. power of imitation 4. laughable appearance 5. ear-piercing; harsh 6. specially 7. intentionally; on purpose 8. over and over again 9. get angry

xuéxí 学习 study; learn; emulate ≅学〔**～宾**〕〈名〉～新技术❶; ～艺术❷; ～文学; ～别人的优点❸; ～他的高尚❹品质❺〔**～补**〕〈结〉技术还没～到手❻〈趋〉本领

❼已经～出来了；她从美国～回来了〈程〉～得很有成绩❽〈可〉她手指受伤❾以后再也～不了(liǎo)钢琴❿了；这么复杂的⓫内容他哪儿～得下来啊！小提琴⓬没有人指导⓭是～不出来的〈时〉～了好长时间〈量〉～过几次；～了一阵就放下⓮了〔**状～**〕认真⓯～；按部就班地⓰～；诚心诚意地⓱～；成年累月地⓲～；踏踏实实地～⓳；孜孜不倦地⓴～；如饥似渴地㉑～；心不在焉地㉒～；马马虎虎地㉓～；盲目地㉔～；随便㉕～；勤奋地㉖～

1. new technique **2.** art **3.** merit; strong point **4.** noble; lofty **5.** character; quality **6.** in one's hands; in one's possession **7.** skill; ability **8.** achievement **9.** be wounded **10.** piano **11.** complicated **12.** violin **13.** give directions **14.** put down **15.** seriously; carefully **16.** keep to conventional ways of doing things **17.** earnestly and sincerely **18.** year in year out; for years on end **19.** be steadfast in one's study **20.** with indefatigable zeal; painstakingly **21.** with great eagerness; eagerly **22.** absent-mindedly **23.** carelessly **24.** blindly **25.** casually **26.** diligently

xūn 熏 smoke; fumigate〔**～宾**〕〈名〉药味❶～人；～蚊子❷；用茉莉花❸～茶叶❹〔**～补**〕〈结〉汽油味❺把我～恶心❻了；药味儿把人～坏了；一根檀香❼就把屋子～香❽了〈趋〉天刚黑就～起蚊子来了〈程〉这味儿～得真难受❾；沥青❿味儿～得我直想吐⓫〈可〉蚊香⓬～不死蚊子，只能把它熏晕〈时〉昨天～了一夜蚊子；～一会儿就头疼〈量〉用这种药水⓭～一下儿试试；～过几次都不管事〔**状～**〕用蚊香～；被烟～得直呛⓮；整夜地⓯～
另见xùn 熏

1. smell of medicine **2.** mosquito **3.** jasmine **4.** tea **5.** smell of petrol **6.** disgust **7.** sandal incense **8.** fragrant; sweet-smelling **9.** feel unwell; feel ill **10.** pitch; asphalt **11.** vomit; throw up **12.** mosquito-repellent **13.** liquid medicine **14.** irritate (respiratory organs) **15.** the whole night

xún 驯 tame and docile〔**～宾**〕〈名〉～兽❶〔**～补**〕〈结〉把虎❷～服了❸〈趋〉把熊❹～出来以后可以登台表演❺了〈时〉一只虎要～很多年吧？〈量〉一天要～好几次吧？〔**状～**〕专门❻～；严格地❼～；耐心地❽～；每天～；在哪儿～？用什么方法～？不间断地❾～

1. beast **2.** tiger **3.** docile; tame **4.** bear **5.** can take the stage and perform **6.** specially **7.** strictly **8.** patiently **9.** continuously; incessantly; ceaselessly

xùn 训 lecture; teach; train〔**～宾**〕〈名〉～人；～话❶〔**～补**〕〈结〉把他～烦了❷；～哭了；他

~完了话就走了〈趋〉那个人~起话来就没完;他爸爸一起人来可真凶❸啊!〈程〉~得他脸都红了;把她~得直哭〈时〉~了半天话,没人听〈量〉他~过几次人以后,大家对他很反感❹〔**状~**〕经常~;专门❺~;老❻~人;偶尔❼~;狠狠地❽~;毫不客气地❾~

1. give an admonitory talk to subordinates 2. be vexed; be irritated 3. fierce 4. be disgusted with; be averse to 5. especially 6. always 7. occasionally 8. 9. ruthlessly; mercilessly

xùnliàn 训练 train; drill 〔**~宾**〕〈名〉~军队;~跳伞员❶;~警犬❷〔**~补**〕〈结〉把她~成了一个优秀的飞行员❸;~成功了没有?〈趋〉有些杂技演员❹从三岁就开始~起来了〈程〉~得非常熟练❺;~得很成功;警犬~得非常精❻〈可〉岁数大了就~不好;工夫❼不到是~不出来的〈时〉整整~了十年;~了好多日子〈量〉需要~一下儿〔**状~**〕严格❽~;有计划地❾~;坚持不懈地❿~;有意识地⓫~;在困难条件下⓬~;采取各种办法⓭~;反复⓮~;一遍一遍地⓯~;好好地~;终于⓰~出来了;亲自⓱~;集中~

1. parachutist; parachuter 2. police dog 3. excellent pilot 4. acrobat 5. skilled 6. clever 7. time; effort 8. strictly 9. systematically 10. unremittingly 11. consciously 12. under difficult conditions 13. by every possible means 14. 15. repeatedly; time and again; over and over again 16. at last 17. by oneself

xùn 熏 be poisoned or suffocated by coal gas〔**~宾**〕〈名〉煤气❶~人〔**~补**〕〈结〉他的朋友就是被煤气~死的;头都~晕了❷〈趋〉~死过去了❸〈程〉~得很利害❹;~得不省人事❺了〈可〉~不着(zháo);怎么能~不死呢?〈量〉我让煤气~过一次;~一下儿就不得了❻(liǎo)〔**状~**〕差点儿~死;别~着;最~人了
另见 xūn 熏

1. coal gas 2. dizzy; faint 3. pass out 4. serious 5. be unconscious; be in a coma 6. desperately serious

Y

yā 压 ① press; push down 〔~宾〕〈名〉上面~了一块大石头；大雪❶~着树枝；玻璃板❷底下~着两张照片〔~补〕〈结〉肩膀❸~红了；把衣服~平❹点儿；这块布都~皱❺了；果子把树枝~弯❻了；别把纸盒❼~扁❽了；房子倒❾了，把他~伤❿了〈趋〉不能把工作都~到他一个人身上去；那个人的声音真洪亮⓫，他一说话把别人的声音都~下去了〈程〉~得他直不起腰来⓬；工作~得她喘不过气来⓭〈可〉那块木头太轻⓮，~不住；衣服干了就~不平了〈时〉他被地震⓯倒塌⓰的房子~了两天居然⓱没死；多~一会儿衣服就平了〈量〉~一下儿试试能不能平〔状~〕往下~；使劲⓲~；结结实实地⓳~；用砖头⓴~；一齐~

1. snow 2. glass plate 3. shoulder 4. flat 5. crease 6. bend 7. paper box 8.(be) crushed 9. fall down 10. be wounded 11. loud and clear; sonorous 12. be unable to straighten one's back 13. be out of breath 14. light 15. earthquake 16. fall down 17. to one's surprise; unexpectedly 18. exerting all one's strength 19. solidly 20. brick

② keep under control; keep under; quell ≅ 制止〔~宾〕〈名〉喝点热水把咳嗽❶~一~；说几句好话给他~~气〔~补〕〈结〉~住心头怒火❷；她值了一夜班❸现在刚睡，你说话~低点儿嗓门❹〈趋〉刚要发作❺，冷静❻一想不应该，就把气~下去了〈可〉会场❼的嘈杂声❽一时❾~不下来；~不住心头的怒火〈时〉~了半天才把火儿❿压下去〔状~〕勉强⓫~；竭力⓬~；拼命⓭~

1. cough 2. one's anger; one's rage 3. be on night duty 4. lower one's voice 5. have a fit of anger; flare up 6. sober; calm 7. meeting-place; conference hall 8. hubbub of voices 9. for the time being 10. anger; rage 11. reluctantly 12. with all one's might; energetically; actively 13. with all one's might; for all one is worth

③ bring pressure to bear on; suppress; intimidate ≅ 镇压；压制〔~宾〕〈名〉别拿势力~人❶；一个劲儿❷往下~价❸；~敌人投降❹〔~补〕〈结〉把对方~垮❺；~低价钱〈趋〉他刚要寻衅❻闹事❼，被我们给~下去了；用机关枪❽把敌人的火力❾~下去了；她总想把别人都~下去，自己出风头❿〈程〉他压人~得太利害了

〈可〉想用武力⓫压人是～不服⓬的〈量〉得(děi)～他一下儿〔状～〕往下～; 拼命⓭～; 拿权势⓮～; 一再～

1. take advantage of one's or sb. else's power to bully people 2. continuously; persistently 3. force prices down 4. surrender 5. collapse 6. provoke; pick a quarrel 7. create a disturbance; make trouble 8. machine gun 9. fire power; fire 10. seek or be in the limelight 11. by force 12. unable to persuade 13. with all one's might 14. by power

④ pigeonhole; shelve ≅ 积压〔主～〕〈名〉这件事得赶快办，别～着〔～补〕〈结〉文件❶到了他那里又～下了〈趋〉文件到了他那里就～起来了〈程〉～得时间太长了〈可〉事情到他手里～不下，他办事很快〈时〉这个案子❷在他手里～了三年〔状～〕一直❸～着; 别～着; 老～着; 从不～

1. document 2. case; law case 3. all along; always; all the time

yāpò 压迫 oppress; repress

〔～宾〕〈名〉～老百姓❶; ～弱小民族❷〈代〉～我们〔～补〕〈结〉可把老百姓～苦了; 快把我们～死了, 不知要～到什么时候才算完〈程〉～得太利害了❸; ～得没活路❹了〈时〉～了很长时间; 被他～了一辈子❺〔状～〕残酷地❻～; 曾经～过; 一直～; 拼命❼～; 被～; 任意❽～

1. common people; ordinary people 2. small and weak nations 3. awful; terrible 4. means of subsistence; way out 5. a life time; all one's life 6. cruelly; ruthlessly 7. exerting the utmost strength; with all one's might 8. wantonly; arbitrarily; wilfully

yāsuō 压缩 compress; condense; reduce; cut down

〔～宾〕〈名〉～开支❶; ～篇幅❷; ～字数❸〔～补〕〈结〉～到1,000字以内〈程〉～得不够〈可〉再也～不了(liǎo)了〈时〉～了半天还是不行〈量〉好好～一下儿〔状～〕适当～; 必须～

1. pay; expenses; expenditure 2. length (of a piece of writing) 3. the number of words

yāzhì 压制 suppress; stifle; inhibit

≅ 压抑; 抑制〔～宾〕〈名〉～不同意见❶; ～愤怒❷的情绪❸; ～着自己的感情❹〈动〉～心中的不满❺〈形〉～内心的激动❻〔～补〕〈结〉～住心中的痛苦❼〈趋〉把涌上心头的怒火❽～下去了〈程〉～得太利害了; ～得过火了〈可〉～不住悲愤❾的感情〈时〉不同意见被他们～了很多年〔状～〕竭力❿～; 尽力⓫～; 拼命⓬～; 长期～; 一再～; 尽量⓭～; 被～

1. differing opinions 2. indignation; anger; wrath 3. feeling; sentiments 4. emotion; feeling;

sentiment 5. be discontented 6. excited 7. pain; suffering 8. fury; anger 9. grief and indignation 10. 11. with all one's might; energetically 12. for all one is worth; desperately 13. as far as possible; to the best of one's ability

yā 押 detain; take into custody ≡拘留〔~宾〕<名>~流氓❶；~小偷；~犯人❷〔~补〕<结>把小偷~走了<趋>把犯人~回监狱❸去；把犯人~上来了；把小偷~到警察局❹去了<可>人少了~不了(liǎo)<量>~过几次〔状~〕往刑场❺~；往法庭❻~

1. rouge 2. prisoner; convict 3. prison 4. police station 5. execution ground 6. court; tribunal

yà 轧 roll; run over〔~宾〕<名>~路；~面条❶〔~补〕<结>把路面❷~平；用机器❸把钢管❹~断❺了；压路机❻把石子儿~碎❼了；手指❽被机器~折❾(shé)了；腿❿被~成残废⓫了<趋>~到泥土⓬里去了；没小心⓭把手指~下去了<程>骨头⓮~得粉碎；腿~得走不了⓯路了<可>小心点儿~不着(zháo)了；路不用压路机就~不平<量>来回⓰~了好几趟〔状~〕用压路机~；被~；一趟一趟地~

1. noodles 2. road surface 3. machine 4. steel tube 5. snapped 6. road roller 7. broken to pieces 8. finger 9. break; snap 10. leg 11. maimed 12. mud 13. through negligence 14. bone 15. unable to walk 16. back and forth; to and fro

yān 淹 flood; submerge; inundate〔主~〕<名>房屋、树木、人、畜❶等都被~了；整个村子都~了〔~宾〕<名>~了三个村子〔~补〕<结>~死了很多人<程>我们村子~得最利害；~得灾民❷四处逃难❸<可>修❹了堤❺以后就~不了(liǎo)了；她游泳技术❻非常高❼，在一般情况下❽~不着(zháo)<时>大水~了两个月才退❾<量>那里隔❿一年就要~一次〔状~〕差点儿~死；万一⓫~了怎么办？可别再~了；一夜之间⓬~；难怪⓭年年~

1. domestic animals 2. victims of a natural calamity 3. flee from a calamity 4. build; construct 5. dam 6. technique 7. high level 8. in general 9. recede; decline; ebb 10. after or at an interval of 11. just in case; if by any chance 12. overnight 13. no wonder

yān 腌 preserve in salt; salt; pickle; cure〔~宾〕<名>~菜；~肉；~鸭蛋〔~补〕<结>~多了；~咸❶了<趋>有人喜欢冬天把菜~起来慢慢吃<程>~得不算❷多；鸭蛋~得时间太长了<可>坛子❸太小~不了(liǎo)<时>~几天就能吃了；已经~一个月了<量>我~过一次，没腌好，以后就再

也没腌〔状～〕每年都～；很容易～；立刻就～；从来不～

1. salty; salted 2. consider; regard as 3. earthern jar

yáncháng 延长 lengthen; prolong; extend ≅ 缩短

〔～宾〕〈名〉～时间，～距离❶；铁路❷～了二百公里❸；～了一截❹〔～补〕〈结〉会议～到下星期二〈趋〉会议可别再～下去了〈时〉展览❺～了三天；只能～十分钟〈量〉时间能不能再～一下儿？会议又～了一次〔状～〕一直～；从这里往前～；不许任意❻～考试时间；不能无限❼～

1. distance 2. railway 3. kilometre 4. section; chunk; length 5. exhibition 6. wantonly; arbitrarily; wilfully 7. indefinitely; *sine die*

yánqī 延期 postpone; defer; put off

〔主～〕〈名〉会议❶～了；比赛❷～了；考试～了〔～宾〕〈动〉～举行❸，～付款❹，～交工❺，～偿还❻〔～补〕〈结〉～到下周进行〈时〉～三天，～十年偿还债务❼〔状～〕不能无限地❽～；一再～；无故❾～；因雨～

1. meeting; conference 2. match; competition 3. hold; take place 4. pay a sum of money 5. hand over a completed project 6. repay; pay back 7. debt; liabilities 8. infinitely 9. without cause or reason

yǎngài 掩盖 cover; conceal

〔～宾〕〈名〉～矛盾❶；～缺点❷；～错误；积雪❸～着大地；～事实真相❹；～自己的罪行❺；～丑恶面目❻〈动〉～内心的恐惧❼〔～补〕〈结〉想用谎话❽把事实～住，那是办不到的〈趋〉想把丑恶面目～起来；丑事❾不能再～下去了〈可〉缺点是～不住的；矛盾掩盖是～不了(liǎo)的，罪行再也～不下去了〈时〉～半天也没掩盖住〈量〉我替他～了一下儿，才算过去〔状～〕无须～；竭力❿～；拼命⓫～；一再～；想方设法地⓬～；难以～；有意识地⓭～；故意⓮～；严严实实地⓯～

1. contradiction 2. weakness; shortcoming; defect 3. heaped snow 4. the real facts 5. crime; guilt 6. ugly features 7. fear; dread 8. lie 9. scandal 10. with all one's might 11. risk one's life; desperately; exerting the utmost strength 12. by hook or by crook 13. consciously 14. intentionally; purposely 15. closely; tightly

yǎnhù 掩护 screen; shield; cover

〔～宾〕〈名〉～战友❶；～战士进攻，～老百姓❷撤退❸〈代〉我～他〔～补〕〈程〉～得很好〈可〉我～不了(liǎo)你，你还是走吧〔状～〕用身体～战友；主动❹～；积极❺～；多次～；用机枪❻～

1. comrade-in-arms; battle companion 2. common people; ordinary people 3. retreat 4. on

one's own initiative **5.** actively **6.** machine gun

yǎnshì 掩饰 cover up; gloss over; conceal〔**~宾**〕〈名〉~错误；~他的真实❶意图❷；~缺点❸；~自己的感情❹〈形〉~内心的空虚❺；~心中的不安〔**~补**〕〈趋〉其实❻我们已看出了他的慌乱❼，可是他还想继续~下去；她想把自己的错误~过去〈可〉~不住内心的恐慌❽；~不了(liǎo)不安的心情〈时〉~了半天也没掩饰过去〈量〉~了好几次；替他~一下儿〔**状~**〕毫不❾~；竭力❿~；用各种办法~

1. real; true **2.** intentions; intent **3.** defect; weakness; shortcoming **4.** feeling; sentiment **5.** hollow; void (lack mental or spiritual ballast) **6.** as a matter of fact; in reality **7.** flurried; flustered; confused **8.** panic **9.** not...at all **10.** with one's might

yǎn 演 play; act; perform; put on〔**~宾**〕〈名〉~电影；~话剧❶；~节目❷；一共~五场❸；我一直~反派人物❹；~小丑❺；~主角❻；~配角❼〔**~补**〕〈结〉电影~完了吗？今天可~糟❽了；~成功了；~到几点才完？〈趋〉说错了台词❾也别紧张❿，继续~下去；这个戏~出来效果⓫不错；这个话剧刚~出去就轰动⓬了；老是那几个片子，~过来~过去的真没意思⓭；这个孩子真聪明，导演⓮教他的动作⓯，他一演就~上来了〈程〉~得很逼真⓰；~得多精采⓱啊！〈可〉话剧两个小时~不完；有的演员就是~不象；这个动作我老~不上来；台⓲下的观众⓳老说话，演员都有点儿~不下去了；词儿不熟⓴，现在还~不下来；好多制片厂㉑都邀请㉒她去拍片㉓，她真有点~不过来了；这几个人~不出一场戏来〈时〉~了一辈子京剧㉔；这个话剧连续㉕~了半年〈量〉这个节目~过好多遍了；他去年到我们学校来~过一次舞蹈〔**状~**〕特㉖为毕业生㉗~；这个角色㉘好~；第一次~；多~几场就好了；多~点有教育意义㉙的；临时㉚~；从很小就~；老~坏蛋

1. modern drama **2.** programme **3.** scene **4.** negative character (role); villain **5.** clown; buffoon **6.** lead; protagonist **7.** supporting role **8.** too bad **9.** actor's lines **10.** nervous **11.** effect; result **12.** make a stir; cause a sensation **13.** not interesting **14.** director (of a film, play, etc.) **15.** movement; motion; action **16.** true to life; lifelike **17.** brilliant; splendid; wonderful **18.** stage; platform **19.** audience **20.** unfamiliar; unskilled **21.** plant for production of a film **22.** invite **23.** act in a film; shoot a film **24.** Beijing opera **25.** in succession; successively **26.** especially; specially **27.** graduate **28.** part; role **29.** instructive **30.** provisionally; temporarily

yǎnchū 演出 perform; show; put on a show ≅ 表演〔~宾〕〈名〉~了一场话剧❶；~了很多精采❷节目❸；~了两场芭蕾舞❹；为毕业生❺~了一场杂技❻〔状〕首次~；公开❼~；照常❽~；在礼堂~

1. modern drama; stage play 2. brilliant; splendid; wonderful 3. programme 4. ballet 5. graduate 6. acrobatics 7. publicly; openly 8. as usual

yàn 咽 swallow 〔~宾〕〈名〉~唾沫❶；~口水❷；他爷爷刚~气❸；病得连水都不能~；~了一口痰❹〔~补〕〈趋〉吃鱼要小心，千万别把鱼刺❺~下去；话到嘴边又~下去❻〈程〉他这口气~得真慢〈可〉嗓子❼疼得什么东西也~不下去〈时〉这块干面包他~了半天也没咽下去〈量〉我轻轻地❽~了一下儿试试，嗓子不疼了〔状〕多嚼嚼❾再~；细嚼慢~❿；吃东西狼吞虎~⓫；千万别~

1. saliva; spittle 2. saliva 3. breathe one's last; die 4. phlegm; sputum 5. fishbone 6. check oneself 7. throat 8. slightly; lightly 9. chew carefully 10. chew carefully and swallow slowly 11. devour ravenously; gobble up

yàn 验 examine; check; test; ≅ 化验；检验〔~宾〕〈名〉~血❶；~尿❷；~痰❸；~货❹；眼睛不好，需要去~~光❺；~护照❻；~票❼；~尸❽〔~补〕〈结〉护照~完了，可以走了〈趋〉验尿~出什么病来了？验尸~出什么问题来了吗〈程〉验票~得很认真❾；~得太马虎❿；~得很仔细⓫；~得很勤⓬〈可〉今天~不了(liǎo)血，明天空腹⓭来验；从痰里~不出什么问题来〈时〉~了半天；~了十几分钟〈量〉~过两次血了，也没找出病因⓮来〔状~〕在化验室⓯里~；仔细~；马马虎虎地⓰~；一遍一遍地~

1. blood 2. urine 3. phlegm; sputum 4. goods 5. (test) the refractive power and visual range of the eye 6. passport 7. ticket 8. postmortem 9. serious 10. careless 11. careful 12. frequent 13. on an empty stomach 14. cause of disease 15. laboratory 16. carelessly

yǎng 养 ① support; provide for ≅ 供养；抚养〔~宾〕〈名〉~一家老小❶；~公婆❷〈形〉~老❸〔~补〕〈结〉我从小儿没有父母，是姑姑❹把我~大的；父母把子女~大成人❺〈趋〉那个孤儿❻没人要，我就把他~起来了〈可〉钱挣❼得太少，~不了(liǎo)家❽；他老要吃好的穿好的，我可~不起他了〈时〉儿子虽然死了，儿媳❾却心甘情愿❿地~了她那么多年〔状~〕不得⓫~；心甘情愿地~；从小把他~大；父母由几个子女轮流⓬着~

1. grown-ups and children 2. husband's father and mother; parents-in-law 3. live out one's life in retirement 4. father's sister 5. be grown to manhood 6. orphan 7. earn 8. unable to support one's family 9. daughter-in-law 10. be most willing to 11. have no choice but 12. by turns

② raise; keep; grow ≃饲养；培植〔**～宾**〕〈名〉～猪；～鸡；～鱼；～蜜蜂❶；～蚕❷；～花〔**～补**〕〈结〉今年蚕～少了；鱼都让他给～死了；他舅舅❸退休❹以后～开❺花了〈趋〉养鸡真脏❻，我不想～下去了，过两天都宰❼了吃；她～出来的花老❽那么茂盛❾；养蜜蜂～出经验❿来了〈程〉养这几口猪～得人都累死了〈可〉小鸟伤⓫得这么利害还～得活吗？〈时〉那个老工人～了一辈子蜜蜂；在鸭场⓬～了五年鸭〔**状～**〕决不～；专门⓭～；精心⓮～；一直～；已经～了；从未～过；不适宜⓯～；在笼子⓰里～；纷纷⓱～

1. bee 2. silkworm 3. mother's brother; uncle 4. retire 5. begin (to do sth.) 6. dirty 7. slaughter 8. always 9. flourishing; luxuriant 10. experience 11. be wounded 12. duck farm 13. especially 14. meticulously; elaborately 15. unsuitably 16. a large box or chest 17. one after another; in succession

③ rest; convalesce; recuperate one's health; heal ≃修养〔**～宾**〕〈名〉正在家～病；～伤❶；别操心❷了，好好～～神❸吧；病刚好，要好好～～身体；俗话❹说"～兵千日，用兵一时❺"〔**～补**〕〈结〉他在医院里住了半年，都～胖了；伤～好了才能出院〈趋〉我的病养得差不多了，不能再这样～下去了，给我点儿事儿做吧；他又坐在那儿～起神来了〈程〉伤～得差不多了；在医院里养病～得真着急❻；养伤～得不耐烦❼了〈可〉她心事太重❽，～不好病；现在住院费❾昂贵❿，我哪里～得起病啊！我吃什么有营养⓫的东西都～不胖；这个婴儿⓬早产⓭了两个月，不知道～得活～不活〈时〉在疗养院⓮～了半年肺病⓯〈量〉这身体还需要好好～一下儿〔**状～**〕一直～；在医院～；彻底～；被迫～；安心静⓰～；踏踏实实地⓱～；无忧无虑地⓲～；成年累月地⓳～；在这种环境⓴里不适于㉑～

1. wound 2. worry about 3. rest to attain mental tranquility; repose 4. common saying; proverb 5. maintain an army for a thousand days to use it for an hour 6. become impatient 7. impatient 8. sth. weighing on one's mind; a load on one's mind; worry (be laden with anxiety; be weighed down with care) 9. hospitalization expenses 10. expensive 11. nourishing; nutritious 12. baby 13. premature delivery 14. sanatorium 15. tuberculosis 16. quietly 17. having peace of mind 18. carefree;

yǎng

free from all anxieties 19. year in year out; for years on end 20. circumstance 21. unsuitable for

④ cultivate; form; acquire ≅ 培养〔主～〕<名>得了伤寒❶以后,头发都掉光❷了,得(děi)好好～～了〔～补〕<结>要～成不随地吐痰❸的好习惯❹;把头发～长了梳❺小辫❻<趋>她打算把头发～起来去烫❼了<程>头发～得不短了<可>好习惯老～不起来<时>头发～了一年才长(zhǎng)这么长(cháng)〔状～〕不是一朝一夕❽～成的;逐渐～成了,从小儿～成的习惯;有意识地❾～;无意❿中～成了

1. typhoid 2. nothing left 3. spit; expectorate 4. good habit 5. comb 6. short braid 7. perm 8. in one morning or evening; in one day 9. consciously 10. inadvertently; accidentally; unwittingly

yǎng 痒 itch; tickle ≅ 痒痒

〔～主〕<名>头皮❶～;浑身❷～;因药物过敏❸皮肤❹～〔～补〕<结>～死我了<趋>又～起来了<程>～得不停地❺挠❻;～得睡不着觉;～得坐立不安❼;～得受不了❽〔状～〕真～;特别～;太～了

1. scalp 2. all over the body 3. drug allergy 4. skin 5. incessantly 6. scratch 7. feel uneasy whether sitting or standing; be fidgety; be on tenterhooks 8. cannot bear; be unable to endure

yāoqiú 要求 ask; demand; require

〔～宾〕<名>我们应该严格❶～学生;做手术❷～医生精神❸高度❹集中❺<代>只能～自己,不能～人家;～别人不要太苛❻;～他亲自完成;～大家注意听<动>～参加比赛;～赔偿❼;～及时❽记帐❾;～调动工作❿<形>这个工作～细心⓫;～大胆⓬;～勇敢⓭;～迅速⓮〔～补〕<结>对他～高了<程>～得很严;～得有点儿脱离实际⓯;～得不太合理⓰<可>自己做得不好就～不了(liǎo)别人<量>我只向经理⓱～过一次;～一下儿试试〔状～〕严格～;再三～;合理地～;非法⓲～;竟然⓳～;无理⓴～;大胆～

1. strictly; severely 2. perform or undergo an operation 3. spirit; mind 4. highly; a high degree of 5. concentrate; centralize 6. severe; harsh; stern 7. compensate 8. in time 9. keep accounts 10. transfer sb. to another post 11. careful; attentive 12. bold; audacious 13. brave; courageous 14. quick 15. lose contact with reality 16. irrational 17. manager; director 18. illegally 19. unexpectedly; to one's surprise 20. unreasonably

yāoqǐng 邀请 invite; request

〔～宾〕<名>～了三个人;我们根本❶没～张先生,是他自己来的;～代表团❷来我国访问❸;～客

人到我家来吃饭；～球队❹来比赛❺〔～补〕〈结〉～晚了，他已经离开❻这里了〈趋〉把朋友～到家里来玩玩；被他们～去喝酒了〈程〉～得不是时候；～得不凑巧❼；～得非常真诚❽；～得不热情❾〈可〉地方小～不了(liǎo)那么多人；我面子❿小～不到〈时〉～了半天也不肯来〈量〉替我～一下儿他；～了他好几次，他都不来〔**状～**〕热情(地)～；再三⓫～；已经～了；替我～；多～些人；主动⓬～；虚情假意地⓭～；礼节性地⓮～

1. at all; simply **2.** delegation **3.** visit **4.** (ball game) team **5.** match; competition **6.** leave **7.** bad luck **8.** sincere; true **9.** not warm **10.** reputation; prestige; face **11.** time and again; over and over again **12.** on one's own initiative **13.** hypocritically **14.** by courtesy

yáo 摇 shake; wave; rock; turn 〔**～宾**〕〈名〉他站在她背后直❶向我～手；她什么也不说只是～头儿；～铃了；他从小儿就会～橹❷；那条狮子狗❸～着尾巴跑过来了；～着手巾❹向岸❺上的朋友告别❻；～着小旗❼去欢迎；使劲❽～着帽子向到机场来接❾的人打招呼❿〔**～补**〕〈趋〉她远远地就向我～起手来了〈程〉弟弟是我家摇橹～得最好的，他～得又快又稳⓫〈时〉我向岸上～了半天手巾，你都没看见吗？〈量〉她向我～了一下儿手，我也不知道她是什么意思〔**状～**〕来回～；不停地⓬～；一个劲儿地⓭～；一上一下地～；左右～；猛～⓮；拼命⓯～；轻轻地～〔**习用**〕～钱树⓰

1. continuously **2.** scull **3.** the pug-dog **4.** handkerchief **5.** bank **6.** farewell **7.** flag **8.** exert all one's strength **9.** meet; welcome; greet **10.** greet; say hello **11.** steady **12.** incessantly **13.** continuously; persistently **14.** vigorously **15.** with all one's might **16.** a legendary tree that sheds coins when shaken — a ready source of money

yǎo 咬 ① bite; snap at 〔**～宾**〕〈名〉～苹果；～馒头❶；恨❷得直❸～牙；狗～了他的腿❹；老鼠净～粮食❺袋；他刚才吃得太急❻～了舌头❼；疯狗❽～了一个过路的人〔**～补**〕〈结〉被毒蛇❾～死了；疼得把嘴唇❿都～破了；他用牙把线⓫～断⓬了；这孩子真淘气⓭，把铅笔上的橡皮⓮头儿都～掉⓯了；没带蚊帐⓰，身上都快被蚊子～烂⓱了；别老～住那句话不放⓲；他一口～定⓳是我弄丢⓴的；他喜欢把水果糖～碎㉑了吃；我们要～紧牙关㉒〈趋〉不知谁把桌子上的梨㉓～下一口去；这条恶狗㉔～起人来真凶㉕〈程〉～得真疼㉖；被蛇～得昏迷不醒㉗〈可〉面包太硬㉘了我～不动；离它远点就～不着(zháo)你了〈时〉昨天没挂蚊帐，被蚊子～了一夜〈量〉被蛇～了一口；被狗～过一次了〔**状～**〕猛地㉙～；

狠狠地❸0~了一口；追着❸1~；拼命❸2~；往腿上~；差一点儿~；一口一口地~；直~牙

1. steamed bread 2. hate 3. continuously 4. leg 5. grain 6. fast; rapid 7. tongue 8. mad dog 9. poisonous snake; viper 10. lip 11. thread 12. snapped 13. naughty 14. rubber 15. fall; come off 16. mosquito net 17. festered 18. not making a concession; not yield 19. insist; assert emphatically 20. lose 21. broken to pieces 22. grit one's teeth 23. pear 24. a ferocious dog 25. awful; terrible 26. ache; pain; sore 27. remain unconscious 28. hard 29. suddenly; violently 30. ruthlessly; relentlessly 31. chase (run) after 32. with all one's might

② pronounce; articulate 〔~宾〕〈名〉这个演员❶~字很清楚〔~补〕〈程〉每个字的发音都~得清清楚楚〈可〉很多音❷她都~不准❸〔状~〕别老~文嚼字❹的了

1. actor or actress 2. sound; tone 3. not accurate 4. pay excessive attention to wording

yǎo 舀 ladle out; spoon up 〔~宾〕〈名〉~汤；~菜；~油；~了一碗；~了一勺❶儿〔~补〕〈结〉~满一勺汤；粥~多了怕吃不了(liǎo)，~少了又怕不够吃；别~洒❷了；多~上点油，炒❸出来的菜才能好吃；锅❹里的汤干净了吗？〈趋〉桶里的水都~出去了；把锅里的油~出来一点儿〈程〉~得太多了〈可〉碗里的汤少得都~不上来了；孩子自己~不了(liǎo)汤〈时〉~了半天才这么一点儿啊？〈量〉又~了两下儿；再~一勺儿〔状~〕从锅里~；妈妈给孩子~；满满地❺~；一勺接着一勺地❻~

1. spoon 2. spill 3. fry; stir-fry 4. pot 5. fully 6. spoon after spoon

yào 要 ① want; ask for; wish; desire 〔~宾〕〈名〉这里有两张电影票❶谁~？这些邮票❷小玲还~呢，别扔❸；他小时候到处去~饭❹；妈妈问我~多少钱；我那天差一点儿❺被汽车撞着❻(zháo)，司机❼骂❽我；"你不~命❾了？"那个人真不~脸❿，净⓫做一些见不得人的⓬事；她非常~面子⓭；在饭馆~了一桌菜〔~补〕〈结〉菜~多了〈趋〉好容易⓮才从爸爸那儿~出点儿钱来；把我借给他的书~回来了〈程〉钱~得太多了；菜~得不够〈可〉钱怎么老~不够啊？那么贵我可~不起；书借给他，再也~不回来了〈时〉孩子~了半天洋娃娃⓯，妈妈也没给买〈量〉我跟他~过一次，他没给我〔状~〕勉强⓰~；早晚⓱得(děi)~；真~吗？什么时候~？必须~；多~点，一共~了多少？

1. film ticket 2. stamp 3. throw away 4. beg food 5. almost; nearly 6. bump against; run into 7. driver 8. scold 9. risk one's life

10. have no sense of shame; shameless 11. only; merely; nothing but 12. shameful; scandalous 13. be keen on facesaving 14. with great difficulty 15. doll 16. reluctantly 17. sooner or later

② ask (want) sb. to do sth. ≌ 让〔～宾〕〈代〉～我替他寄一封信；～我早点儿回来；～她别迟到；～他们好好念书；～她念出声音❶来；～他遇事❷要沉着❸；～我陪❹他去一趟〔状～〕他没～我给他买药❺；他一定～我明天去看他

1. read aloud 2. when anything crops (comes) up; when matters arise 3. calm; cool-headed; composed 4. accompany 5. buy drugs (medicine)

yē 噎 choke

〔～补〕〈结〉～死我了；慢点吃，别～着(zháo)；～着(zháo)了，快喝一口水吧〈程〉～得真难受❶；～得直❷打嗝❸儿；～得直瞪眼❹〈可〉慢点吃就～不着(zháo)了〔量〕他特别容易❺噎，吃一顿饭也要～好几次〔状～〕老❼～；经常❽～；从来没～过；容易～；怎么又～了？

1. feel unwell 2. continuously 3. belch 4. open one's eyes wide 5. be apt to 6. have a meal 7. always 8. frequently; often

yī 依 yield to; listen to; comply with

≌ 听任；由着〔～宾〕〈名〉当时❶要是～了你的主意❷就糟❸了〈代〉不能因为孩子小，就什么都～着他〔～补〕〈程〉依他～得太利害❹了；～得太过分❺了〈可〉孩子可～不得啊〈时〉～了他一次就会有第二次〔状～〕不能什么都～他；千万别～；怎么能这样～着孩子呢？〔习用〕～样画葫芦❻；～葫芦画瓢❼

1. at that time 2. opinion; idea 3. too bad 4. awful; terrible 5. excessive 6. copy mechanically 7. draw a dipper with a gourd as the model — copy; imitate

yīkào 依靠 rely on; depend on

≌ 依赖〔～宾〕〈名〉～朋友；～自己的力量❶；～父母〈代〉你的生活～谁？不要什么事情都～别人〔～补〕〈可〉谁也～不了(liǎo)谁；他比我还忙，一点也～不上他〔状～〕互相❷～；紧紧❸～；完全～；必须～

1. one's own force 2. each other; mutually 3. closely; tightly

yǐ 倚 lean on or against; rest on or against; rely on

≌ 靠〔～宾〕〈名〉～着墙；别～着车门；～着栏杆❶；～势欺人❷〔～补〕〈结〉～住了，别掉下去〔状～〕往后～；舒舒服服地❸～；悠闲地❹～着；悠然自得地❺～着；别～；使劲❻～着

1. balustrade; railing; banisters 2. take advantage of one's position

to bully people 3. 4. 5. at ease 6. with strength

yìlùn 议论 comment; talk; discuss ≅ 评论〔~宾〕〈名〉大家都~这件事；～他们的行为❶；～他的为人❷〈代〉~他们〔~补〕〈结〉对这件事～开了〈趋〉别议论了，再一下去让他听见就不好了〈可〉这件事老～不完；～不下去了〈时〉～了好长时间才完；让他们议论去吧，～几天也就完了〈量〉这个问题这样处理❸行不行，大家好好～一下儿〔状~〕纷纷❹～；到处～；悄悄地❺～；暗地里❻～；私下❼～；背后❽～；别～；随便❾～；指手画脚地❿～

1. action; behaviour; conduct 2. behave; conduct oneself 3. deal with; handle 4. one after another; in succession 5. quietly 6. in secret; secretly 7. privately 8. behind sb.'s back 9. as one pleases 10. with animated gestures

yǐn 引 ① lead; guide ≅ 引导；带领〔~宾〕〈名〉我来～路；～水灌田❶〔~补〕〈结〉～入❷歧途❸；把敌人～走〈趋〉把水～上山去了；从国外～进来一些新技术❹〈可〉水～得上来吗？〔状~〕给他们～路；往山上～；故意❺～

1. channel water to irrigate the fields 2. lead into; draw into 3. wrong road; astray 4. technology; technique 5. intentionally; on purpose

② cause; attract ≅ 引起〔~宾〕〈名〉~火生炉子❶〔~补〕〈结〉火~着❷(zháo)了吗？由于❸一个烟头❹~起了一场火灾❺〈趋〉把火种❻~过来；~起火灾来就麻烦❼了〈可〉柴火❽太湿❾，火老~不着(zháo)〈时〉~了半天火，炉子也没着(zháo)〔状~〕用纸~；用汽油~

1. light a stove 2. burn 3. owing to; due to 4. cigarette end 5. fire (as a disaster); conflagration 6. kindling material 7. troublesome; inconvenient 8. fire wood; faggot 9. wet

yǐnjìn 引进 introduce from elsewhere〔~宾〕〈名〉~新品种❶；～新技术❷；～军事装备❸；～外国资本❹；～几种珍贵的动物❺；～技术资料❻；～科学管理❼方法〔~补〕〈结〉~多了〈程〉~得不够〔状~〕大量❽~；大胆~；从国外~

1. new variety; new assortment 2. new technique (technology) 3. military equipment 4. foreign capital 5. rare animals 6. technical data; technological data 7. scientific management 8. in large quantities

yǐnqǐ 引起 lead to; give rise to; set off; arouse; cause ≅ 导致〔~

yīnqǐ 引起

宾〕〈名〉~不堪设想❶的后果; ~连锁反应❷; ~强烈❸的反响❹; ~公愤❺; ~火灾; ~兴趣❻〈动〉一场热烈的讨论❼; ~怀疑❽; ~注意; ~争论❾; ~共鸣❿; ~暴动⓫; ~动乱⓬; ~骚动⓭; ~爆炸⓮〔状~〕必然⓯~; 不致⓰~; 已经~; 逐渐⓱~; 易⓲~; 一再~

1. dreadful to contemplate 2. chain reaction 3. strong; intense; violent 4. repercussion; echo 5. public indignations; popular anger 6. interest 7. lively discussion 8. doubt; suspect 9. dispute 10. sympathy 11. insurrection; rebellion 12. disturbance; turmoil; upheaval 13. tumult; disturbance; commotion 14. explode 15. inevitably; certainly 16. cannot go so far; be unlikely 17. gradually 18. easily

yǐnyòu 引诱 lure; seduce ≅ 诱惑

〔宾〕〈名〉~无知❶青年; ~幼稚的孩子❷; ~意志薄弱❸的人〔~补〕〈结〉~坏了〈趋〉~到邪路❹上去了〈程〉被坏人~得走了犯罪❺的道路; 被~得无法自拔❻了〈可〉~不了(liǎo)意志坚强❼的人〔状~〕故意❽~; 一再~; 用各种办法~; 暗中❾~

1. ignorant 2. naive child 3. weak-willed 4. wrong path 5. commit a crime 6. unable to extricate oneself 7. strong-willed 8. intentionally; on purpose 9. secretly; in secret

yǐnmán 隐瞒 conceal; hide; hold back

〔~宾〕〈名〉~自己的错误; ~不光彩❶的事; ~事实真相❷; ~缺点❸; ~消息❹; ~情况❺; ~病情❻; ~财产❼; ~原因❽〔~补〕〈结〉能~住吗? 你还想~到什么时候?〈趋〉别再~下去了; 把事实~起来了〈程〉~得很严; ~得谁也不知道〈可〉想隐瞒是~不住的; 再也~不下去了〈时〉~了好多年; ~了十几年〈量〉~过一次〔状~〕一直~; 长期~; 多次~; 故意❾~; 无须❿~; 何必⓫~; 毫不⓬~

1. not honourable; not glorious 2. the truth of the facts 3. shortcoming; weakness 4. news; information 5. situation 6. patient's condition 7. property 8. cause 9. intentionally; on purpose 10. need not; not have to 11. there is no need 12. not ... in the least

yìn 印 print

〔~宾〕〈名〉~书; ~杂志❶; ~讲义❷; ~封面❸; ~邮票❹; ~表格❺; ~入场券❻; ~包装纸❼; ~名片❽〔~补〕〈结〉讲义~完了; 电话号码❾~上了没有? 图案❿~清楚了吗? 字~歪⓫了; ~反⓬了; 封面没~好; 地址~在信封左上角〈趋〉把这几个缩写字母⓭也~上去; 看着不太好, ~出来还不错〈程〉~得很清楚; ~得很漂亮; ~得不理想⓮; ~得歪歪斜斜⓯的〈可〉我们这儿~不了(liǎo), 请你到别的印刷厂⓰去问问; 相片照得不好，所以~不清楚；这么多字哪儿~得下啊；机器坏❶了，今天~不成了〈时〉刚~一会儿就印完了；需要~多少时候；〈量〉今年~过好几次纪念邮票❶了〔状~〕往布上~；多~点；深深地~在脑子里了；一并❶~；正在~；已经~完了；一次一次地~

1. magazine 2. teaching materials 3. front cover 4. stamp 5. form; table 6. (admission) ticket 7. wrapping paper 8. visiting card 9. telephone number 10. pattern; design 11. oblique; slant 12. in reverse; in an opposite direction 13. abbreviation 14. not ideal 15. crooked; askew 16. other printing house 17. trouble; breakdown; mishap 18. commemorative stamp 19. together

yíngjiē 迎接 meet; welcome; greet

〔~宾〕〈名〉~客人；~外宾❶；~代表团❷；~国庆❸〔~补〕〈时〉~了半天，他们没来〈量〉~过三次外国贵宾❹〔状~〕在机场❺~；亲自❻~；热情地❼~；高兴的~

1. foreign guest 2. delegation 3. National Day 4. honoured guest of foreign countries 5. airport 6. personally 7. warmly

yíng 赢 win; beat ≗ 胜 ↔ 输

〔主~〕〈名〉棋❶又~了；这场球没~〈动〉打赌❷~了；比赛~了；玩扑克❸~了〔~宾〕〈名〉~了两个球；~了一场❹；~了一局❺；~了一盘棋❻〔~补〕〈程〉这个球~得真费劲❼；~得真漂亮；~得真痛快❽；这盘棋~得真快〈可〉看这意思❾，他们今天~不了(liǎo)了〈量〉只~过一次〔状~〕反倒❿~了；果然⓫~了；大概⓬~不了(liǎo)了；一直没~过；很难~了；怎么也~不了(liǎo)；轻而易举地⓭就~了

1. chess 2. bet; wager 3. play cards 4. 5. one game 6. a game of chess 7. use great effort 8. to one's great satisfaction 9. it seems; it looks as if 10. instead; on the contrary 11. really; as expected; sure enough 12. probably; most likely 13. easy to do

yíngdé 赢得 win; gain

〔~宾〕〈名〉~时间；~了喘息之机❶；~了最大的荣誉❷；~观众的掌声❸〈动〉~全场❹的喝采❺；~了大家的赞扬❻；~了学生们的信任❼；~胜利〔状~〕已经~了；多次~；连续❽~；尚未❾~；必须~

1. breathing spell 2. honour; credit; glory 3. clapping; applause 4. the whole audience 5. acclaim; cheer 6. acclaim; praise 7. trust; have confidence in 8. in succession; in a row; running 9. not yet

yǐngxiǎng 影响 affect; influence

〔~宾〕〈名〉~质量❶；~

产量❷；～进度❸；～情绪❹；健康❺；～睡眠❻〈代〉我吸烟不～你吧? 〈动〉～学习；～消化❼；～建设； ～思考❽； ～看书〔～补〕〈结〉灯光❾不好，就会～到演出❿效果⓫〈可〉这样做谁也不着(zháo)〔状～〕实在⓬～；经常～；已经～了； 别～他；用模范行为⓭～孩子；逐渐⓮～；潜移默化地⓯～着

1. quality 2. quantity 3. rate of progress 4. morale; feeling; mood; sentiments 5. health 6. sleep 7. digest 8. think carefully; meditate 9. the light of lamp 10. perform 11. effect; result 12. really; truly 13. exemplary deeds 14. gradually 15. imperceptibly

yìngfù 应付

① deal with; cope with; handle ≅ 对待〔～宾〕〈名〉他知道如何❶～复杂❷的局面❸；能够～临时❹发生❺的事情；让我来～那个坏蛋；～突然事变❻〔～补〕〈趋〉能把这么复杂的局面～过去就很不容易了〈程〉什么事情来了，他都能～得很好〈可〉这么多事情我一个人真～不过来〔状～〕不好～；难以～；很有把握地❼～；有信心地❽～；满有经验❾地～着一切；想方设法地❿～；顺利地⓫～；从容不迫地⓬～

1. how 2. complicated 3. aspect; situation 4. at the time when sth. happens; temporarily 5. occur; happen; take place 6. emergency 7. with assurance 8. with confidence 9. experience 10. by hook or by crook 11. smoothly; successively; without a hitch 12. calmly and unhurriedly

② do sth. perfunctorily; do sth. after a fashion ≅ 敷衍了事；对付〔主～〕〈名〉他又来了，你去～～吧〔～宾〕〈名〉～考试；～了他几句〔～补〕〈结〉好容易❶把他～走了〈趋〉她～起人来真有一套❷儿〈程〉～得很自如❸；～得很好〈可〉我～不了(liǎo)他, 你去吧〈时〉～了十几分钟〈量〉～过他一次； 我随便❹～了他一下儿； ～了一阵❺〔状～〕简直❻～不了(liǎo); 难以～；经常～；不假思索地❼～

1. with great difficulty 2. convention; formula 3. free; smooth 4. casually; informally 5. a period of time 6. simply; at all 7. without thinking; without hesitation; readily

yōngbào 拥抱

embrace; hug; hold in one's arms 〔～补〕〈结〉两个老朋友一见面就紧紧地❶～在一起〈趋〉胜利消息传❷来，大家不由得❸互相～起来了；一下飞机他们就热情地❹～起来了〔状～〕互相～；热烈地～； 紧紧地～； 跟来迎接❺的亲人～

1. closely 2. spread 3. can't help; cannot but 4. warmly; enthusiastically 5. greet; meet; welcome

yōnghù 拥护 support; uphold

〔**～宾**〕〈名〉～这个决定；～一项决议❶〈代〉～他作我们的代表❷；～他当组长〔**状～**〕热烈❸～；真正～；衷心❹～；完全～

1. resolution **2.** representative **3.** warmly; enthusiastically **4.** whole-heartedly; from the bottom of one's heart

yǒng 涌 gush;pour; well; surge

〔**～补**〕〈结〉许多往事❶～上了心头〈趋〉热泪❷从眼眶❸里～了出来；人们从电影院～了出来；东方～出一轮红日；酸水❹从胃❺里～上来了；伤口❻～出很多血；清澈❼的水～进水渠❽里去了；油井❾～出石油来了；泉水❿从地里～了出来；放学的时候学生们～出校门去了〔**状～**〕一齐⓫～；一下子～；向外～；一窝蜂似地⓬～；不断地⓭～；一股一股地～

1. past events; the past **2.** tears **3.** eye socket; orbit **4.** hydrochloric acid in gastric juice **5.** stomach **6.** wound; cut **7.** limpid; clear **8.** ditch; canal **9.** oil well **10.** spring water **11.** at the same time; simultaneously **12.** like a swarm of bees **13.** ceaselessly; incessantly

yòng 用 ① use; employ; apply

≃使用〔**～宾**〕〈名〉你还～不～这本词典了？他这两天要～钱；我要～这个地方，你到那边去看书好不好？孩子刚一岁正是～人的时候；日本人和中国人都会～筷子❶；～火烤一烤❷再吃；～水煮❸着吃；～开水沏茶❹；～油炸❺；～力拉❻门；听讲❼的时候～点儿心❽；两个词之间应该～顿号❾；～平时节省❿的钱买了一台录音机⓫〔**～补**〕〈结〉词典我～完了，还给⓬你；笔尖⓭都～秃了；不要把精力⓮都～在打扑克⓯上；刚买的热水瓶⓰就～上了；有人把汽油桶⓱～作乐器⓲来演奏⓳；在中药⓴里甘草㉑常～作润喉㉒止咳㉓剂〈趋〉酒精㉔可以～来消毒㉕；把自己学的那点知识全～上去了〈程〉这项工程㉖用人～得很多；用油～得比较省；～得太快了，两天就没了〈可〉这颗螺丝㉗太小～不上；一瓶香水㉘半年也～不完；把～不了(liǎo)的钱都存到银行里 ㉙ 去了；写一篇报道 ㉚ ～不了(liǎo)一个星期；这么贵我可～不起；把～不着(zháo)的书放回书架㉛去吧；有力量～不出来；有～得着(zháo)我帮忙的地方尽管㉜说，别客气！～不着(zháo)请别人帮忙，自己完全可以做；毛笔㉝我～不惯㉞〈时〉电视机刚～三年就坏了；我～一会儿就给你；足足㉟～了二十分钟〈量〉刚～一下儿就坏了〔**状～**〕仔细点儿～；经常～；一直～；从来没～过；已经～了；随便㊱～；仍旧㊲～；天天～；偶尔㊳～；真难～；一次～光；别～；先～；等一会再～

1. chopsticks **2.** bake; roast; toast **3.** boil; cook **4.** infuse tea; make tea 5. fry in deep fat or oil 6. pull 7. attend a lecture 8. pay attention to 9. a slight-pause mark used to set off items in a series (、) 10. save 11. tape recorder 12. give back; return 13. nib; pen point 14. energy; vigour 15. play cards 16. thermos 17. petrol drum 18. musical instrument 19. perform 20. traditional Chinese medicine 21. licorice root 22. moisten one's throat 23. relieve a cough 24. ethyl alcohol; alcohol 25. sterilize 26. engineering; project 27. screw 28. perfume 29. deposit money in a bank 30. report 31. bookself 32. not hesitate to 33. writing brush 34. not in the habit of 35. full; as much as 36. as one pleases 37. still; yet 38. occasionally; once in a while

② need ≅ 需要〔～宾〕〈动〉不～开灯；不～准备；不～重新写；不～怕；不～感谢我；不～生气；不～操心❶；不～担心❷；不～叫醒❸他；天那么冷不～去了；晚饭不～等我〈形〉不～着急❹；不～难过❺；不～悲伤❻；不～后悔❼〔状～〕千万不～；真不～；都不～

1. 2. worry about 3. wake up; awaken 4. worry; feel anxious 5. feel sorry; feel bad 6. sad; sorrowful 7. regret; repent

yóu 游 ① swim ≅ 游泳〔～补〕〈结〉～完了；～累❶了；～到了对岸❷；她已经～远了〈趋〉他～过来了；天刚暖和❸他就～起泳来了〈程〉～得真快；～得多费劲❹儿啊；～得很轻松❺的样子〈可〉我可～不过去，年纪大了～不了(liǎo)泳了；你一口气～得到对岸～不到？她累了，～不回来了；现在真～不动了〈时〉～了三十年泳；～～一会儿就上来了〈量〉天热的时候一天～好几次泳；你下来～一下儿试试〔状～〕在游泳池❻里～；来回～；绕圈❼～；轻松愉快地❽～；别在深水❾区里～；猛❿～；万一⓫～不到；勉强⓬～

1. tired 2. the opposite bank 3. warm 4. take a lot of effort 5. easily; with ease 6. swimming pool 7. circle; go round and round 8. happily 9. deepwater 10. vigorously 11. if by any chance 12. reluctantly

② tour; travel; wander; rove around ≅ 游逛；游览〔～宾〕〈名〉他最喜欢～山玩水❶〔～补〕〈结〉名山大川❷他几乎都～遍❸了；〈趋〉他一个人～到后边又～回来了〈程〉～得很高兴；～得真累❹；～得没意思〈可〉明天如果下雨就～不了(liǎo)了；一个人没意思，～不下去了〈时〉～了一天；～了三个多小时〔状～〕到处～；信步❺～来；无目的地❻～；兴冲冲地❼～；随旅游团❽～；冒(着)雨❾～

1. travel from place to place enjoying the beauties of nature; go on trips to different scenic

spots 2. famous mountains and great rivers 3. all over; everywhere 4. be bored with; be tired of 5. take a leisurely walk; stroll 6. aimlessly 7. excitedly; in high spirits 8. with tour group 9. braving the rain

yóulǎn 游览 go sight-seeing; tour; visit ≃ 游〔**～宾**〕〈名〉～名胜古迹❶；～了很多地方〔**～补**〕〈结〉有名的地方都～遍❷了〈趋〉老是那么几个地方，～过来～过去的，都有点儿腻❸了〈程〉那天～得不错；～得不痛快❹〈可〉没有汽车～不了(liǎo)；一天～不完；那个地方太好了，我总～不够〈时〉只～了三个小时，就急急忙忙地❺走了；今天可以多～一会儿〈量〉这次我得❻(děi)好好～一下儿〔**状～**〕多～几个地方；单独❼～；兴致勃勃地❽～；兴冲冲地❾～；四处～；随旅游团❿到处～；初次～；不妨⓫～一下儿

1. places of historic interest and scenic beauty; scenic spots and historical sites 2. all over; everywhere 3. be bored with; be tired of 4. feel bad 5. hurriedly; in a hurry 6. must; have to 7. alone; by oneself 8. full of zest 9. in high spirits 10. with tour group 11. there is no harm in; might as well

yǒu 有 ① have; possess ≃ 具有 ↔无〔**～宾**〕〈名〉他～两个孩子；谁～汉英词典，借我用用；我们～一个好邻居❶；这个人就是～个坏脾气❷；她神经❸～毛病❹；她很～朝气❺；那个人一点热情❻都没～；这孩子很～艺术天才❼；你真～办法！那个作家❽很～名；那位老教授很～学问❾；他比我～经验❿；你～什么困难吗？做什么工作都应该～个计划；这个工作应该什么时候完成，～期限⓫吗？你昨天找我～事吗？看见你来了，我又～了希望；孩子死了，她没～指望⓬了；做坏事的人总不会～好结果；吃了半年药也没～什么显著的效果⓭；最近忙得一点时间都没～；我们两个人～缘⓮，走到哪儿都能碰上⓯；请你出来一下儿，我～一句话要问问你；他弟弟～了很大进步〈动〉情况～了变化；他们思想上～没～波动⓰？他对考古很～研究；那个孩子没～救了；我还～什么盼望⓱？幸亏⓲我们～防备⓳〔**状～**〕曾经～过；肯定⓴～；大概～；确实～；也许～；好容易㉑～〔**习用**〕那个人真～两下子㉒；～奶便是娘㉓

1. neighbour 2. bad temper 3. nerve 4. trouble 5. vigour; youthful spirit 6. enthusiasm; zeal; warmth 7. artistic talent; a gift for art 8. writer 9. learning; knowledge 10. experience 11. time limit; deadline 12. hope; prospect 13. notable effect 14. lot or luck by which people are brought together 15. meet; run into 16. in an anxious state of mind 17. prospect; hope 18.

fortunately; luckily 19. be on guard; take precaution 20. affirmatively; definitely 21. with great difficulty 22. know one's stuff 23. whoever suckles me is my mother; submit oneself to anyone who feeds one

② [indicating existence] ≅ 存在there is; exist〔～宾〕〈名〉树上～一只麻雀❶；墙上～一幅❷风景画儿❸；推开门一看屋子里没～人；那个教室里～没～地图❹？我问旁边一个小孩："这个座位❺～人吗？"窗外～人说话〔状～〕大约❻～；大概～；也许～；真～；的确❼～

1. (house) sparrow 2. a measure word 3. landscape painting 4. map 5. seat 6. approximately; about 7. really; truly

③ [indicating estimation or comparison] ≅ 相当〔～宾〕〈名〉这棵树～碗口❶那么粗❷；我的大孩子已经～我那么高了；谁也没～他认识❸的人多；你回来～一个星期了吧？〔状～〕大约～；足足❹～；明明～；至少～；确实～；简直❺～〔习用〕隔墙～耳❻；善有善报，恶～恶报❼；大～人在❽

1. the mouth of a bowl 2. thick 3. recognize; know 4. full; as much as 5. simply; at all 6. walls have ears; beware of eavesdroppers 7. good will be rewarded with good and evil with evil 8. there are plenty of such people; such people are by no means rare

yùbèi 预备 prepare; get ready

≅ 准备〔～宾〕〈名〉～功课；～点儿酒菜招待客人❶；～了两桌酒席❷〔～补〕〈结〉明天要考试了，你功课都～好了吗？〈趋〉钱都～出来了，快去买吧〈程〉饭菜～得太多了；功课～得不太好〈可〉～不了(liǎo)太多菜，因为没人做〔状～〕多～点儿；提前❸～；临时❹～

1. entertain guests 2. feast 3. in advance; ahead of time 4. temporarily; at the time when sth. happens

yùfáng 预防 prevent; take precautions against; guard against

〔～宾〕〈名〉～扒手❶；～火灾❷；～疾病❸；～传染病❹；～肝炎❺〈主－谓〉～煤气中毒❻；～鼠疫❼蔓延❽〔～补〕〈结〉～晚了〈程〉～得很好；～得比较及时❾〈可〉这种病怎么预防也～不了(liǎo)〈时〉～了半天还是传染上❿〈量〉还是～一下儿好〔状～〕必须～；及早⓫～；想方设法地⓬～；千方百计地⓭～；认真⓮～；不易⓯～

1. pickpocket 2. fire (as a disaster) 3. disease 4. infectious (contagious) disease 5. hepatitis 6. carbon monoxide poisoning; gas poisoning 7. the plague 8. spread; extend 9. in time 10. be infected 11. at an early date; as soon as possible; before it is too late 12. 13. by every possible

yù 遇 meet ≅ 相逢; 遭遇 〔~补〕〈结〉在马路上~见了一个熟人❶; ~上了坏人就麻烦❷了; ~到了敌人设下的埋伏❸; 小船在海上~到了暗礁❹; ~到了风暴❺; ~到了危险❻; ~到了灾难❼; ~到了一些棘手的问题❽; ~到了意外❾; 今天在车上~上了麻烦〈可〉我们都在一个城市里工作, 可是老~不见〔状~〕偶然❿相⓫~; 经常~见; 从未~见过; 总~不上; 不期而~⓬

1. acquaintance 2. too bad 3. lay an ambush 4. submerged reef 5. storm 6. danger 7. calamity; disaster 8. a knotty problem 9. accident; mishap 10. by chance 11. each other; mutually 12. meet by chance

yuàn 怨 blame; complain ≅ 怪 〔~宾〕〈名〉怎么能~你母亲呢? 〈代〉这件事不能~他; 就~你多嘴❶; 都~他不听话; ~她不准时❷来〔~补〕〈结〉这件事你可错人了, 根本❸不是他干的〈趋〉你怎么又~起孩子来了? 〈可〉这~得了(liǎo)谁啊! 这可~不着(zháo)我, 我根本就不知道〈时〉~了半天人家, 结果还是他自己的问题〔状~〕总是~人家; 别~孩子; 动不动❹就~别人; 只~自己

1. speak out of turn; shoot off one's mouth 2. on time 3. simply; at all 4. easily; frequently

yuē 约 ① make an appointment; arrange 〔~宾〕〈名〉~一个大家都有空的时间; ~一个地方见面 〔~补〕〈结〉我们~定了, 后天早上六点出发❶; ~在哪一天?〈程〉时间~得不合适❷; ~得比较晚了点儿〈可〉时间总~不好, 不是你有事, 就是他有事〈量〉~过一次她〔状~〕预先❸~好; 主动❹~; 热情地❺~他到我家来玩

1. start off; set out 2. convenient 3. in advance; beforehand 4. of one's own accord; on one's own initiative 5. warmly

② ask or invite in advance ≅ 请 〔~宾〕〈名〉~几个朋友〈代〉~他去看电影; 你们~谁来吃饭了? 〔~补〕〈结〉人都~齐❶了吗? 平时❷大家都上班不容易❸~到一起 〈趋〉把同学都~到我家来了; 把她~出来谈谈吧; 大家住得太分散❹, ~起来很不容易〈程〉~得太晚了, 人家都走了; ~得不是时候〈可〉大家工作时间不一致, 老~不到一起〈时〉~了半天好容易❺约齐了〈量〉~了好几次他, 他都不肯来〔状~〕专门❻~; 特地❼~; 经常~; 三番五次地❽~; 先后❾~; 预先❿~; 主动⓫~; 热情地⓬~

1. complete; all 2. at ordinary times; in normal times 3. not easy 4. disperse; scatter; decen-

tralize 5. with great difficulty 6. 7. especially; particularly 8. again and again; over and over again 9. successively; one after another 10. beforehand; in advance 11. on one's own iniative 12. warmly

yūn 晕 swoon; faint〔～补〕〈结〉～倒❶了；～在马路上了〈趋〉疼❷得～过去❸了〈程〉～得站不起来了；～得天旋地转❹；～得直吐❺；～得只能躺在床上〈可〉我不怕晒，怎么晒也～不了(liǎo)〈时〉～了一秒钟就好了〈量〉～过一次〔状～〕差点～了；几乎一倒 另见yùn晕

1. fall; topple 2. ache; pain; sore 3. lose consciousness; faint; swoon 4. (feel as if) the sky and earth were spinning round; very dizzy 5. continuously vomit

yǔnxǔ 允许 permit; allow ≅ 许可〔～宾〕〈代〉～他看吗？请～我代表❶学校向你致谢❷；不～任何人破坏纪律❸；不～别人这么对待❹他；不～任何人偷看别人的日记❺〔～补〕〈量〉～过他一次〔状～〕决不～；无可奈何地❻～；早已～；居然❼～；倘不❽～

1. on behalf of; in the name of 2. express thanks 3. permit no breach of discipline 4. treat; handle 5. diary 6. have no alternative; have no way out 7. unexpectedly; to one's surprise 8. if not

yùn 运 carry; transport ≅ 运输，搬运〔～宾〕〈名〉～货❶；～粮食❷；～了两车〔～补〕〈结〉～完了没有？用小船～走了；这些东西～给谁；〈趋〉把药材❸都～出去了；货～回来了；行李❹都～上去了吗？〈程〉～得挺多吧？～得真快〈可〉时间短了～不完；我一个人～不了(liǎo)；两天也～不到〈时〉这点儿东西整整❺～了两天〈量〉～了两趟；一天～好几次〔状～〕一次～完；分批❻～；多～几趟；从这往仓库❼～；全部～走；一趟一趟地❽～；不停地❾～

1. goods 2. grain 3. medicinal materials 4. luggage 5. whole; full 6. in batches; in turn 7. warehouse; store house 8. one after another 9. incessantly; ceaselessly

yùn 晕 dizzy; giddy; faint 〔～宾〕〈名〉～车❶；～船❷〔～补〕〈程〉～得很利害❸；～得起不来床；～得直恶心❹〈时〉～了好长时间了；眩晕❺病弄得我～了半年才好〈量〉坐一次车～一次〔状～〕容易～；经常～；从来不～；有时候～；又～了，有一点儿～ 另见yūn晕

1. carsickness 2. seasickness 3. terrible; awful 4. feel sick 5. dizziness

yùn 熨 iron; press 〔～宾〕〈名〉～衣服；～台布❶；～领带❷〔～补〕〈结〉裤子还没～完吧？裙子

❸的褶儿❹不要~斜❺了; 熨斗不热皱褶❻不容易~开〈趋〉怎么没喷水❼就~起来了; 喷水以后~出来比较平〈程〉~得真平; ~得很快; 裤线❽~得笔直❾; ~得笔挺❿〈可〉~不平; 熨斗不热~不了(liǎo)〈时〉一条裤子~了半天〈量〉洗一次~一次; 这件衣服压⓫得太皱了, 应该好好~一下儿〔**状~**〕用电熨斗~; 来回⓬~

1. tablecloth **2.** tie; necktie **3.** skirt **4.** crease; pleat; wrinkle **5.** oblique; slant **6.** wrinkle; crease; pleat **7.** sprinkle; spray **8.** creases (of trousers) **9. 10.** straight as a ramrod; perfectly straight **11.** press **12.** to and fro

Z

zā 扎 tie; bind ≃ 捆；束；↔解〔**～宾**〕〈名〉～小辫儿❶；～腰带❷；在绳子上❸～了一个结❹，作记号❺；～蝴蝶结❻〔**～补**〕〈结〉把腰带～紧❼点儿；把两条辫子～在一起了〈趋〉头发长了，可以～起小辫来了〈程〉皮带❽～得真紧；～得不好看〈可〉头发太短小辫儿还～不起来；这么细❾的带子❿～不紧；小辫我自己～不了(liǎo)〈时〉他真笨⓫，～了半天也没扎上〈量〉～过一次；往上～一下儿〔**状～**〕把蝴蝶结往上～一～；用各种颜色⓬的绸子⓭～彩球⓮；紧紧地～
另见zhā扎

1. plait, braid, pigtail **2.** waistband; belt **3.** on the rope **4.** knot **5.** mark a sign **6.** bow **7.** tight **8.** leather belt **9.** thin **10.** girdle; ribbon; belt **11.** stupid **12.** various colours **13.** silk fabric **14.** coloured balloon

zá 砸 ① pound; tamp ≃ 打；敲〔**～宾**〕〈名〉～地基❶；孩子用石头把玻璃❷～了；锤子❸把手～了；孩子们扔❹砖头❺把头～了；头上～了一个大窟窿❻〔 **～补** 〕〈结〉一定要把地基～实❼；房子倒了把人都～伤了；锤子把手～肿了❽；把脚趾❾～紫了❿；把腿～瘸了⓫；地震⓬～死了不少人；～流血⓭了；骨头⓮～折⓯(shé)了；这颗钉子⓰又～歪了；被球～晕了⓱；把铁丝⓲～扁⓳了再用；～残废⓴了〈趋〉快躲开㉑，这座楼要～下来可不得了㉒(liǎo)；用大石头朝㉓坏蛋㉔头上～了下去；他们要盖房子㉕，已经～起地基来了〈程〉～得真疼；～得走不了(liǎo)路了；～得昏迷不醒㉖了；～得站不起来了；～得直叫；～得快死了〈可〉别过来了，站在那儿～不着(zháo)〈时〉屋里的人都哪儿去了，门～了半天也没砸开〈量〉地基～过一遍了；脚被石头～过一次；核桃～了好几下儿，都没砸开〔**状～**〕核桃不好～；轻轻地㉗～；用力～；一手扶着㉘一手～；在地上～；猛㉙～

1. foundation **2.** glass **3.** hammer **4.** throw **5.** fragments of bricks **6.** hole **7.** solid **8.** be swollen **9.** toe **10.** turn purple **11.** become lame **12.** earthquake **13.** bleed **14.** bone **15.** broken **16.** nail **17.** faint **18.** iron wire **19.** flat **20.** maimed; crippled; disabled **21.** get out of the way; jump aside **22.** disastrous **23.** toward **24.** bad egg **25.** build a house **26.** unconscious 27. softly; lightly 28. hold 29. violently

② break; smash ≅ 打破; 打坏〔主~〕〈名〉碗~了; 玻璃❶~了〔~补〕〈结〉碗~碎了❷; 盘子~两半了〈趋〉玻璃被石子儿~了一个角儿〈程〉~得粉碎❸〈可〉玻璃杯放在抽屉❹里就~不了(liǎo)了〔状~〕差点儿~了, 险些❺~了, 连续❻~; 万一❼~了〔习用〕~了饭碗❽; 这件事办~了❾

1. glass 2. be broken 3. smashed to pieces 4. drawer 5. nearly; narrowly 6. successively; in a row; in succession 7. if by any chance 8. be out of work; lose one's job 9. make a mess of; be bungled

zāi 栽 ① plant; grow ≅ 种〔~宾〕〈名〉~秧❶; ~了三百棵树苗❷〔~补〕〈结〉把花~到花盆❸里了; 马路两边都~满了树〈趋〉把这些树苗都~到山坡上去吧; ~进坑❹里去了〈程〉~得太密❺了; ~得真齐❻〈可〉现在天太冷, 还~不了(liǎo)树苗; 一天~不完〈时〉这些树一共~了四天〈量〉每年~一次〔状~〕往坑里~; 一棵挨着一棵地~; 已经~; 全部~

1. seedling; sprout 2. sapling 3. flower pot 4. hole; pit; hollow 5. too close 6. neat

② stick in; insert ≅ 插〔~宾〕〈名〉~电线杆子❶; ~一个木桩子❷; ~牙刷〔~补〕〈结〉这里不知什么时候~上了一个木桩子; 电线杆子~斜❸了; 路标❹~结实❺了吗?〈趋〉~起来了〈程〉~得非常结实〈可〉坑❻太浅❼, 杆子~不住〈时〉~了一会儿〔状~〕别马马虎虎地❽~; 匆匆忙忙地❾~; 结结实实地❿~; 刚~好就被大风刮倒⓫了

1. wire pole 2. stake 3. oblique; slanting 4. road sign 5. solid 6. pit; hole 7. shallow 8. carelessly 9. hastily; hurriedly 10. firmly 11. be blown down

③ tumble; fall ≅ 跌倒; 摔倒〔~宾〕〈名〉~了一交❶; 头上~了一个大包❷〔~补〕〈结〉~倒❸; 鼻子❹~流血❺了; ~晕❻; ~伤了❼; 她有高血压病❽, 栽了一交, 就~死了; 扶~倒(dǎo)了〈趋〉从上边~下去了; ~到泥❿里去了〈程〉~得不轻⓫; ~得很重⓬; ~得鼻青脸肿⓭; ~得鼻子直流血〈可〉他腿脚⓮很灵便⓯~不着(zháo), 扶好了栏杆⓰~不下去〈量〉~了一下儿〔状~〕突然~; 狠狠地⓱~; 一头~下去了; 向前~; 差点儿~

1. have a fall 2. swelling 3. fallen 4. nose 5. bleed; shed blood 6. faint 7. be wounded 8. high blood pressure 9. hold; support with the hand 10. mud 11. 12. rather serious 13. a bloody nose and a swollen face; badly battered 14. legs and feet 15. nimble 16. railing; banisters 17. violently

④ force sth. on sb; impose ≅ 安；安上〔~宾〕<名>~赃❶；~罪名❷〔~补〕<结>把罪名~到我头上了<可>~不到我头上〔状~〕往他身上~；给我~赃；硬❸~；居然❹~；偷偷地❺~

1. plant stolen or banned goods on sb. 2. frame sb.; fabricate a charge against sb. 3. forcibly 4. unexpectedly 5. secretly

zǎi 宰 slaughter; butcher ≅ 杀；屠宰〔~宾〕<名>~鸡；~牲畜❶〔~补〕<结>刚~完鸡；十几只兔子都~光了<趋>怎么用那把刀~起鸡来了，那把刀不快❷<程>他宰鸡~得很内行❸<可>你一个人~得了(liǎo)羊吗?<时>我没经验❹，那只鸡~了好半天<量>他~过好多次猪了〔状~〕顺利地❺~；经常~；哆哆嗦嗦地❻~

1. cattle 2. not sharp 3. expert 4. experience 5. smoothly; successfully 6. in fear and trembling

zài 在 ① exist; be living ≅ 存在〔主~〕<名>昨天我去找他，他不~；你给我的那个书签❶现在还~；你父母都还~❷吗? 中国有句名言❸叫做"留得青山~，不怕没柴烧"❹〔~宾〕<名>研究这个问题时，我不~场❺；那天开会~座❻的有我，还有小黄；烟灰缸❼~茶几❽上呢；她现在~食堂呢〔状~〕经常~；刚才还~；早就不~了；什么时候~? 多半不❾~；大概不❿~；也许~

1. bookmark 2. be still living 3. well-known saying; celebrated dictum 4. as long as the green mountains are there, one need not worry about firewood 5. I wasn't there 6. be present 7. ashtray 8. tea table; side table 9. 10. probably not

② rest with; depend on ≅ 在于；决定于〔~宾〕<名>这一次能不能获得❶冠军❷，就~这一场球了；一个人能否❸成功，不完全~才智❹；诗❺主要~意境❻<代>去不去~你；这件事能不能办成❼就~她了<动>贵❽~坚持❾；得肠胃炎❿的原因，多半⓫~平时⓬不注意饮食卫生⓭；词汇⓮完全~平时的积累⓯〔主-谓〕不~钱多少；学习好主要~自己努力；问题就~自己怎么看〔习用〕事~人为⓰；身~福中不知福⓱

1. gain; obtain; win 2. champion 3. whether or not 4. talent 5. poem 6. artistic conception 7. do; handle; manage 8. be valued for 9. persistence 10. enterogastritis 11. most likely 12. at ordinary times 13. dietetic hygiene 14. words and phrases; vocabulary 15. accumulate 16. it all depends on human effort 17. growing up in happiness; one often fails to appreciate what happiness really means

zàihu 在乎 ① care about; mind; take to heart 〔~宾〕<名>我不~

什么报酬❶；他既不~名，也不~利；那个人最~钱；她非常~衣着❷；你那么有钱还~这么点东西；他非常~营养❸〈动〉只要事情能办成，我不~多跑点腿❹；他从来也不~吃得怎么样〈主-谓〉我不~他背后说我什么；他不~别人怎么看他，她不~手工如何，只~样子是否❺新颖❻；他不~东西贵不贵，只要喜欢，他就买〔~补〕〈结〉以前他多花点儿钱，少花点儿钱都不在乎，现在也~上了〈趋〉这一次连她也~起钱来了〔状~〕一向~；一点也不~；特别~；非常~；并不~；毫不~❼；什么也不~；不怎么~② 见→在 zài ②

1. reward 2. clothing; headgear and footwear 3. nutrition 4. do much legwork 5. whether or not 6. new and original 7. not care in the least

zànchéng 赞成 approve of; agree with ≅ 同意 ↔ 反对〔主~〕〈名〉五票❶~，两票反对❷；别人都~，就我不~〔~宾〕〈名〉我们都~你的意见〈代〉我可不~他〈动〉我不~瞎闹❸；她不~骑车去〈主-谓〉不~你们这样做〔状~〕都~；就是不~；完全~；一致❹~；非常~

1. five votes 2. oppose 3. run wild; be mischievous 4. unanimously

zàng 葬 bury ≅ 埋葬〔~补〕〈结〉~在老家❶了；~在山坡上了；~在墓地❷

1. native place; old home 2. graveyard

zàngsòng 葬送 ruin; spell an end to ≅ 断送〔~宾〕〈名〉~了幸福❶；~了前途❷；~了一生；~了青春❸〔~补〕〈结〉~掉了；~在他的手里〔状~〕白白❹~；完全~；几乎~

1. happiness 2. future; prospect 3. youth 4. for nothing

zāo 遭 meet with (disaster, misfortune, etc.); suffer ≅ 遭受；遇到；碰到〔~宾〕〈名〉~殃❶；~灾了❷；~劫❸；~难❹；~毒手❺〈主-谓〉~人暗算❻；~人白眼❼；~人欺侮❽；~水淹了❾〔~补〕〈结〉~到了不幸❿；~到了不测⓫〔状~〕差一点儿~；屡次~挫折⓬；一再⓭~；险些⓮~；万一⓯~

1. suffer disaster 2. be hit by a natural calamity 3. 4. meet with catastrophe 5. violent treachery; murderous scheme 6. fall a prey to a plot 7. be treated with disdain 8. bully 9. suffer from inundation 10. misfortune 11. accident; mishap; contingency 12. setback 13. again and again 14. narrowly 15. if by any chance

zāodào 遭到 suffer; meet with encounter ≅ 遭受〔~宾〕〈名〉~解雇❶的厄运❷；~很大挫折❸〈动〉~迫害❹；~拒绝❺；~失败❻；~破坏❼；~袭击❽；~扼杀❾；~打击❿；~镇压⓫〈形〉~困难；~危险⓬；~不幸⓭〔状~〕几乎~；差点儿~；险些⓮~；屡次⓯~；万一⓰~；也许~；大概~

1. be dismissed 2. adversity; misfortune 3. setback; reverse 4. persecution 5. refusal 6. defeat 7. destruction 8. attack 9. strangulation 10. hit; strike 11. suppression 12. danger 13. misfortune 14. narrowly 15. repeatedly 16. if by any chance

zāotà 糟蹋 ① waste; ruin; spoil ≅ 浪费；损坏〔~宾〕〈名〉碗里剩那么多米粒就洗了，真~粮食；算好了尺寸❶，别把料子❷~了〔~补〕〈结〉粮食可~多了〈趋〉~起东西来一点儿也不心疼〈程〉~得太可惜❸了；~得真让人心疼❹〈可〉~不了(liǎo)多少〈量〉~好多次了〔状~〕真~；多~啊！白白地❺~；净❻~；都被老鼠~了

1. measurement; size 2. material for making clothes 3. it's a pity; it's too bad 4. make one's heart ache 5. in vain; to no purpose 6. always

② insult; trample on; ravage ≅ 蹂躏〔~宾〕〈名〉~人〔~补〕〈结〉战争把城市~成什么样子❶了〈程〉~得太利害了；~得没法活下去了；~得不象样子❷了〔状~〕没有人性地❸~；肆无忌惮地❹~；简直❺~；被…~

1. be seriously damaged 2. be in ruins 3. inhumanly; brutally 4. unscrupulously 5. simply; really

záo 凿 chisel; dig〔~宾〕〈名〉~石头；~土块；~钉子❶；这个人哪儿是敲门，简直❷是~门；别~了手；~山；~洞；~了一个窟窿❸〔~补〕〈结〉别把屋顶❹~漏❺了；钉子那么长，墙都快~穿❻了；宁可❼把船~沉❽，也不能让敌人抢❾去；把石头~裂❿了；把土块~碎⓫了；把手~破⓬了；用劲儿⓭太猛⓮，把凿子⓯~坏了〈趋〉从山上~下一块石头来；~起来声音⓰吵⓱死人；这颗钉子出来了，快把它~进去吧！〈程〉~得太响⓲了；窟窿~得太大了；手~得真疼〈可〉钉子太大~不进去；木头太硬⓳~不进去；她~不动；手往后点儿就~不着(zháo)了〈时〉~了半天也没凿穿；我先~一会儿你再凿〈量〉我来~几下儿，你去休息休息〔状~〕用锤子⓴~；使劲㉑~；往下~；不好㉒~；一下儿一下儿地~

1. nail 2. simply; at all 3. hole; cavity 4. roof 5. leak 6. through; pass 7. would rather; better 8. sunk 9. rob 10. split 11. break to pieces; smash 12. cut; wounded 13. put forth one's strength 14.

violently; abruptly 15. chisel 16. voice; sound 17. make a noise 18. noisy; loud 19. hard 20. hammer 21. exert all one's strength 22. not easy

zào 造 ① make; build ≅ 做；制作；盖〔~宾〕〈名〉~机器❶；~飞机；~房子；~纸；~句子；~舆论❷；~预算❸；~林❹〔~补〕〈结〉这个句子~对了吗？预算~完了；句子~错了；桥~好了〈趋〉这幢楼❺~下来要多少钱啊；一座楼刚三个月就~起来了；舆论~出去了〈程〉~得真快；~得不错〈可〉二十年前还~不了(liǎo)飞机；三个月~得起来一幢楼吗？〈时〉大概❻要~多长时间？一个句子~了五分钟〈量〉这一节课我~了好几次句子了〔状~〕这个句子不好~；按❼什么图纸❽~？模仿别人❾~；到处~舆论

1. machine 2. public opinion 3. budget 4. forest 5. building 6. probably 7. according to 8. blueprint 9. imitating other people

② ≅ 捏造 fabricate; invent; cook up〔~宾〕〈名〉~谣❶；~假帐❷〔~补〕〈趋〉她又在那里~起谣来了；谣言❸~到我头上来了〈程〉那个人造谣~得可利害❹了；~得满城风雨❺；~得人人皆知❻〈可〉大家互相监督❼，谁也~不了(liǎo)假帐〈量〉~了好多次假帐了；他~过好多次谣了〔状~〕从来没~过假帐；净❽~谣；专门❾~；居然❿~到我头上了；凭空⓫~；无缘无故地⓬~；故意⓭~；无中生有地⓮~

1. cook up a story and spread it around 2. counterfeit account 3. rumour 4. terrible 5. become the talk of the town 6. be known by everybody 7. mutually supervise 8. always 9. specially 10. unexpectedly 11. out of the void; without foundation 12. for no reason at all 13. on purpose 14. fictitiously

zēngjiā 增加 increase; raise; add ↔ 减少〔~宾〕〈名〉~收入❶；~工资❷；~困难；~面积❸；~体重❹；~百分比❺；~了一倍❻；~产量❼；~项目❽；~人；~内容❾；~光彩❿；~高度；~长度；~热量⓫；~时间；~次数；~名额；~麻烦⓬〔~补〕〈结〉~到一万二千斤；~多了〈程〉~得太少了〈可〉还~得了(liǎo)吗？〈时〉~了半天才增加这么一点儿〈量〉~过两次〔状~〕逐渐⓭~；急剧⓮~；一点一点地~；日益⓯~；突然⓰~；从未~过；适当地~

1. income 2. wages; salary 3. area 4. weight 5. percentage 6. times; -fold 7. output; yield 8. item 9. content 10. lustre; splendour 11. quantity of heat 12. trouble 13. gradually 14. rapidly; sharply 15. day by day; increasingly 16. suddenly

zēngqiáng 增强 strengthen; heighten; enhance ↔ 减弱〔**～宾**〕〈名〉～体质❶；～信心❷；～抵抗力❸；～兵力❹；～实力❺；～斗志❻；～防御力量❼〔**状～**〕必须～；大大地～

1. physique **2.** confidence **3.** resisting capacity (strength) **4.** military strength **5.** actual strength **6.** will to fight; fighting will **7.** defence capabilities

zēngtiān 增添 add; increase ≌增加 ↔ 减少〔**～宾**〕〈名〉～设备❶；～力量❷；～了信心❸；～了许多桌椅和教学用具❹；要注意～衣服；～了光彩❺；～了勇气❻；～麻烦❼；～了烦恼❽〔**～补**〕〈结〉～够了〈趋〉慢慢～起来了〈程〉～得不多〈可〉～不了(liǎo)什么光彩〔**状～**〕及时❾～衣服；顿时❿～了光彩；给您～了麻烦；为学校～仪器⓫

1. facilities **2.** strength **3.** faith **4.** instruments for teaching **5.** splendour **6.** courage **7.** trouble **8.** vexation **9.** in time **10.** suddenly **11.** instrument; apparatus

zēngzhǎng 增长 increase; rise; grow〔**～宾**〕〈名〉～知识❶；～见识❷〈数〉～了百分之四十；～了两倍❸〔**～补**〕〈趋〉～起来了〈程〉～得很快；～得比较慢〈可〉～得了(liǎo)～不了(liǎo)？〔**状～**〕多～一些；今年比去年～；连续❹～；逐年❺～；日益❻～；稳步❼～

1. knowledge **2.** experience; knowledge **3.** two times **4.** in succession; in a row **5.** year by year **6.** day by day; increasingly **7.** steadily

zhā 扎 ① prick; run or stick (a needle, etc.) into ≌ 刺〔 **～宾** 〕〈名〉手上～了一个刺❶；医生给病人～针❷；差点儿被毛衣针❸～了眼睛；玫瑰花❹有刺，小心～手；～了一个大窟窿❺〔**～补**〕〈结〉把手～破了；～流血了；把他～伤❻了；流氓❼一刀就把他～死了；针灸❽必须～在穴位❾上；把肺❿都～穿⓫了；爸爸的胡子楂儿⓬把孩子～疼⓭了〈趋〉医生的技术⓮真高，那么长的针，～进来我都不知道；针灸的时候针刚～进去没什么感觉⓯，过一会就感到有些酸麻⓰；手上～进去一个刺〈程〉～得一点儿也不疼；～得直流血；扎针～得晕过去⓱了；这根刺～得真深；这一刀～得可不轻⓲〈可〉我手哆嗦⓳，～不了(liǎo)针；别着急慢慢缝⓴～不了(liǎo)手〈量〉～了一刀；～了一针〔**状～**〕给病人～；往腿上～；木头粗糙㉑容易～刺；熟练地㉒～
另见zā扎

1. thorn **2.** give an acupuncture treatment **3.** knitting needle **4.** rose **5.** hole **6.** wounded **7.** rogue; hooligan **8.** acunpuncture

9. acupuncture point 10. lung 11. pierce through 12. father's stubble 13. ache; pain; sore 14. medical skill; art of healing 15. not sensible 16. feel a tingling sensation 17. lost consciousness 18. serious 19. shiver; tremble 20. sew 21. hoarse 22. skilfully

② plunge into; get into ≅ 钻〔**～补**〕〈结〉他一头～进❶了图书馆；～到屋子里就不出来了〈趋〉～进水里去了〔**状～**〕头朝下❷～；一头～进去了；勇敢地❸～；扑通❹一声～下去了

另见zā扎

1. directly; plunge headlong into 2. downwardly 3. bravely 4. flop; thump; splash

zhá 炸 fry in deep fat or oil〔**～宾**〕〈名〉～鱼；～馒头❶；～花生米〔**～补**〕〈结〉～焦了❷〈趋〉～出来焦黄❸焦黄的，真好〈程〉～得真香；～得挺❹脆❺〈可〉油少～不焦〈时〉用不着～那么长时间；鱼要不要多～一会儿？〈量〉一斤油～两次鱼就用完了〔**状～**〕大火～；稍微❻～一下儿；刚～好

1. steamed bread 2. burnt; scorched; charred 3. brown 4. rather 5. crisp 6. slightly

zhǎ 眨 blink; wink〔**～宾**〕〈名〉不～眼地看着我；他向我～了～眼；星星～着眼〔**状～**〕不停地❶～；一个劲儿地❷～；灯光晃❸得我直❹～眼

1. ceaselessly 2. continuously; persistently 3. dazzle 4. continuously

zhà 炸 ① blow up; blast; bomb〔**～宾**〕〈名〉～碉堡❶；～火药库❷；～军舰❸；～桥；～楼；～坦克❹；～山；～建筑物❺；～飞机场〔**～补**〕〈结〉～掉了敌人❻很多碉堡；桥被～断❼了；楼～塌❽了；坦克～坏了；～死～伤❾很多人；～掉❿一只胳膊⓫；～沉⓬了一艘军舰；～平了一条街；～开一个缺口⓭；～毁⓮了一辆卡车⓯；眼睛～瞎⓰了；城市～成了焦土⓱〈程〉～得寸草不留⓲；～得粉碎⓳；～得敌人狼狈逃窜〈时〉～了一夜〔**状～**〕猛⓴～；拼命㉑～；疯狂地㉒～；盲目地㉓～；轰隆一声㉔～；狂轰滥～㉕；被～

1. pillbox; blockhouse 2. magazine 3. warship 4. tank 5. building 6. enemy 7. be broken 8. collapse; fall down 9. wounded 10. blast away 11. an arm 12. bomb and sink 13. breach; gap 14. blow up; blast to pieces 15. a truck 16. blind 17. scorched earth — ravages of war 18. leave not even a blade of grass 19. smashed to pieces 20. fiercely 21. 22. desperately 23. blindly 24. with a bang 25. wanton and indiscriminate bombing

② explode; burst〔**主～**〕〈名〉茶杯～了；玻璃板❶～了一个大口

子❷；这瓶子❸一灌❹开水就～〔～补〕〈结〉～开一道裂纹❺；～成了碎片❻〈程〉～得粉碎❼〈可〉没关系❽，～不了(liǎo)〔状～〕一冷一热容易～；突然～

1. glass plate; plate glass 2. cut; opening 3. bottle; flask 4. fill; pour 5. crack 6. bits and pieces 7. smashed to pieces 8. it doesn't matter

zhāi 摘 pick; pluck; take off 〔～宾〕〈名〉～一串葡萄❶；～一朵花；～帽子；～围巾❷；～手套❸；～眼镜❹〔～补〕〈结〉～满了一筐❺梨❻；把帽子～掉❼了〈趋〉把眼镜～下来擦❽了擦；把灯泡❾～下来；把墙上那张旧画～下来了；一会儿的工夫❿就～下来那么多葡萄〈程〉～得很快〈可〉眼镜戴⓫了十几年，现在可～不了(liǎo)了；～不满一筐；今天～不完〈时〉我们一起～过两天棉花⓬〔状～〕随便⓭～；往下～；轻易⓮不～眼镜；愉快地⓯～；高高兴兴地～

1. a cluster of grapes 2. muffler; scarf 3. gloves 4. glasses 5. basket 6. pear 7. take off 8. wipe; clean 9. light bulb 10. for a short while 11. wear 12. cotton 13. freely; at will 14. generally; in normal case 15. merrily

zhān 沾 ① be stained with 〔～宾〕〈名〉手上的伤口❶还没好，先别～水；鞋底上～了一张糖纸；嘴角上～了一粒芝麻❷；手套❸上～了很多油漆❹；衣服上～了一点墨水；～了一身泥❺〔～补〕〈结〉双手～满了鲜血❻〈量〉～了一次水，现在伤口又化脓❼了〔状～〕在哪儿～的？怎么～上的？一直～着；差点儿～

1. wound; cut 2. sesame 3. gloves 4. paint 5. mud 6. blood 7. fester

② touch ≅ 接触〔～宾〕〈名〉他跑得真快，好象脚不～地似的；我每天晚上一～枕头❶就睡着(zháo)了；贪污❷行贿❸的事，听说她也～了点边儿；他烟酒不～〔状～〕轻轻地～〔习用〕～光❺

1. pillow 2. corruption; graft 3. bribe 4. softly; lightly 5. benefit from association with sb. or sth.

zhān 粘 glue; stick; paste ≅ 贴〔～宾〕〈名〉～信封；这种糖～牙；玻璃❶破了❷，先用纸把它～一～〔～补〕〈结〉浆糊❸～多(少)了；把信封～上；玻璃上～满了纸条；牙都快～掉了〈趋〉手上有浆糊把纸屑❹都～起来了；纸条～到袖子❺上去了〈程〉～得真结实；～得很严❻；粘牙～得太利害❼了〈可〉浆糊干❽了，～不上了；没有胶水❾～不了(liǎo)〈时〉浆糊太少了，～了半天才粘上〈量〉～过一次〔状～〕这糖真～牙；用胶水～；一层一层地❿～

1. glass 2. broken 3. paste 4. oddments of paper 5. sleeves 6. tight 7. terrible 8. dried 9. glue 10. layer after layer

zhǎnkāi 展开 spread out; unfold; open up

〔~宾〕〈名〉雄鹰❶~翅膀❷;把画卷❸~〈动〉~竞赛❹;~攻势❺;~讨论❻;~辩论❼〔状~〕向敌人~进攻❽;多次~辩论;全面~竞赛

1. eagle 2. wings 3. picture scroll 4. contest; competition 5. offensive 6. discussion 7. argument 8. attack

zhàn 占 occupy; seize; take

〔~宾〕〈名〉~优势❶;~上风❷;~地方;~座位❸;~多数❹;统治地位❺;不能~别人的房子〈数〉海洋几乎~地球表面的四分之三;女学生~一半〈形〉~便宜❻〔~补〕〈结〉人没来就先把座位~上了,真不应该〈趋〉这些孩子又~起座位来了〈程〉便宜~得太多了〈可〉~不了(liǎo)上风;~不了(liǎo)便宜〈时〉~了半天座位,人都没来〈量〉从来没~过一次上风;你给我~一下儿地方〔状~〕少~点便宜吧;一直~上风;差不多~;不必❼~座位;强❽~;硬❾~;给别人~

1. superiority; dominant position 2. advantage; upper hand 3. seat 4. majority 5. dominant position 6. gain extra advantage by unfair means; profit at other people's expense 7. needlessly 8. 9. forcibly

zhàn 站 ① stand; be on one's feet ≅ 立

〔~宾〕〈名〉~岗❶;~讲台❷〔~补〕〈结〉~累了;~上半天,腿❸就乏了❹;~好了,别掉下去;~错队了;~惯了❺;~好最后一班岗❻;~完了八个小时,脚跟❼还没~稳❽〈趋〉有胆量❾的~出来;~到桌子那儿去〈程〉~得很直;队伍❿~得很整齐⓫;~得高,看得远〈可〉累得~不住了;要晕倒⓬~不稳了;那个醉汉⓭站都~不稳了;这个孩子总~不直;他~不惯,总想坐着〈时〉~了半天才站起来;~了三个小时岗〈量〉你替我~一下儿柜台⓮,我出去一下儿;一天两次岗〔状~〕替我~一会儿;轮流⓯~;整天~;一连~了三个小时;靠边⓰~;笔直地⓱~;一动不动地⓲~;规规矩矩地⓳~

1. stand guard 2. platform; dais 3. legs 4. tired; weary 5. get used to 6. (of one who is about to leave his job) continue working hard till the last minute 7. heel 8. gain a firm foothold 9. a man with plenty of guts 10. ranks 11. in good order 12. fall into a swoon 13. drunkard 14. counter 15. by turns 16. keep on one side 17. perfectly straight 18. motionlessly 19. well-behaved

② stop; halt ≅ 停〔~补〕〈结〉前边那个人怎么走着走着~住了?别跑了,站住❶!等汽车~稳❷了再下〈可〉他跑得太快,一下子~不住〔状~〕猛然❸~住了,突然❹~住了,一下子~住了〔习用〕不怕慢,就怕~❺

1. halt! 2. steady 3. abruptly 4.

suddenly 5. it's better to go slowly than just to mark time

zhāng 张 open; spread; stretch ↔闭〔~宾〕〈名〉医生让病人~嘴，看看喉咙❶红不红；我想找她帮忙，又不好意思❷～嘴❸；孩子~着胳膊❹让妈妈抱〔～补〕〈结〉~开了翅膀❺；～开手，让我看看里边有什么〈程〉嘴~得真大〈可〉想跟老王借点钱，可是又~不开嘴❻〈时〉我跟他~了半天嘴，他一分钱都不肯借给我〔状～〕不好~嘴要东西

1. throat 2. feel embarrassed; be ill at ease 3. bring the matter up 4. arm 5. the wings 6. find it embarrassing to ask; feel embarrassment in asking

zhǎng 长 ① grow; develop ≅ 生长〔～宾〕〈名〉树都~虫子了；脸上~癣❶了；~了一颗黑痣❷；~了一脸雀斑❸；铁锅❹老不用都~锈❺了，孩子~牙了〔～补〕〈结〉她最近~胖❻了；他又~高了；头发~长(cháng)了；牙~歪❼了；伤口❽~好了〈趋〉胡子❾~起来了；新芽❿~出来了；竹子又~出一个节儿⓫来〈程〉个子~得真快；花~得太慢了；孩子~得很胖；身体~得很结实⓬；那个姑娘~得挺漂亮⓭；牙~得不整齐⓮；花~得很茂盛⓯〈可〉他都二十了，~不高了；头发剪⓰得太短了，两个月也~不起来；树让虫子给咬坏了，叶子~不出来了〈时〉~了半年多才长出来〈量〉我也~过一次癣〔状~〕一天一天地~大了；突然~；猛⓱~

1. tinea; ringworm 2. nevus; mole 3. freckle 4. pan; pot 5. become rusty 6. fat 7. oblique 8. cut; wounded 9. beard 10. bud 11. knot 12. strong 13. beautiful; pretty; good-looking 14. not neat and tidy 15. flourishing; luxuriant 16. cut 17. vigorously; energetically

② acquire; enhance; increase ≅ 增长〔～宾〕〈名〉到各处去旅游❶可以~不少见识❷；~志气❸；~能力❹了；~本领❺了〈量〉经一次事，~一次见识〔状～〕多~点儿

1. go on a tour; make a tour 2. knowledge; experience 3. aspiration; ambition 4. 5. capacity; skill; ability

zhǎng 涨 (of water, prices, etc.) rise; go up ≅ 上涨 ↔ 落；下跌〔主～〕〈名〉河水~了；物价❶~了〔～宾〕〈名〉~价了，~了三尺；~了四倍〔～补〕〈趋〉物价又~上去了；河水~上来了〈程〉~得太多了；~得快极了〈可〉物价可能~不了(liǎo)了〈量〉~过好几次了〔状～〕可别再~了；猛❷~；一点一点地~；偷偷地❸～；潮水❹正在~

1. prices 2. rapidly 3. secretly 4. tidewater; tidal water

zhǎng 掌 hold in one's hand; be in charge of; control 〔~宾〕〈名〉~舵❶；~权❷〔~补〕〈结〉一定要~好舵〈可〉你~得好舵吗？我可~不好舵〔状~〕由谁~舵？

1. be at the helm 2. be in power

zhǎngwò 掌握 ① grasp; master; know well ≅ 了解、会〔~宾〕〈名〉~技术❶；~理论；~原则❷；~规律❸；~特点；~两门外语；~科学知识〔~补〕〈结〉~住政策〈趋〉入了门以后❹，~起来就快了〈程〉外语~得很熟练❺；政策~得不错；语法~得很好〈可〉理论太高深，我~不了(liǎo)；规律~不住；技术~不熟〔状~〕好好~；尽快❻~；熟练地~；彻底❼~；终于❽~了；一点一点地~；逐渐~；基本上❾~；直接❿~；难以⓫~

1. technique 2. principle 3. law; regular pattern 4. after crossing the threshold; after learning the rudiments of a subject 5. skilled 6. as quick as possible 7. thoroughly 8. at last 9. on the whole; by and large; basically 10. directly 11. difficult to

② have in hand; take into one's hands; control ≅ 主持、控制〔~宾〕〈名〉~时间；~局势❶；~保险柜的钥匙❷；~自己的命运❸；~国家的财政大权❹；~经济命脉❺；~会议；~政权❻；~时机❼〔~补〕〈结〉要~住时机；~准❽方向〈程〉时间~得很好；火候~得不错，炒出来的菜非常香〈可〉政权~得稳❾吗？时局~得住吗？连自己的命运都~不了(liǎo)；什么也~不起来；会议她~不好〔状~〕好好~；适当❿~；难以~；容易~；认真~；仍旧⓫~

1. situation 2. key to the safe 3. destination; fate 4. financial power of a state 5. economic lifeline 6. regime 7. opportunity 8. accurate 9. steady 10. properly 11. still; yet

zhàng 胀 ① expand; distend ≅ 膨胀〔主~〕〈名〉淋雨❶以后，门窗都~了；铁轨❷~了〔~补〕〈结〉~大了〈趋〉~起来了〈程〉门~得关不上了〔状~〕容易~；一热就~

1. rain-drenched 2. rail

② swell; be bloated〔主~〕〈名〉肚子❶~；胃❷~；脸有点儿~〔~补〕〈趋〉肚子~起来真难受❸〈程〉眼睛~得酸痛❹；~得都攥不上拳头❺了；肚子~得鼓鼓的❻；胃~得吃不下饭〔状~〕经常~；有时~；有点儿~

1. belly 2. stomach 3. feel unwell; unbearable 4. ache 5. can't clench one's fist 6. bulging

zhàng 涨 ① swell after absorbing water, etc.〔主~〕〈名〉豆子

泡❶在水里就～了〔～补〕〈趋〉豆子都～起来了；河里的水都快～出来了〈程〉豆子～得很大；水～得很快〈可〉～得起来～不起来？～得出来～不出来？〔状～〕多泡一会儿就～了；河水又～了

1. steep; soak

② (of the head) be swelled by a rush of blood 〔主～〕〈名〉头昏脑～❶〔～补〕〈结〉气得～红了脸❷〈趋〉头又～起来了〈程〉～得真难受❸；～得很利害❹；～得脸通红❺

1. feel one's head swimming 2. redden with anger 3. feel unwell; feel ill; unbearable 4. terrible 5. very red; red through and through

zhāo 招 ① beckon 〔～宾〕〈名〉我一～手❶，那个孩子就过来了；他～手让我进去〔～补〕〈趋〉我不认识他，他怎么向我～起手来了〈时〉他向我～了半天手，我也没看见〈量〉我向他～了一下儿手〔状～〕远远地❷～；不停地～；一个劲地❸～；微笑着❹～手

1. wave; beckon 2. from distance 3. continuously; persistently 4. smilingly

② recruit; enlist; enrol ≅ 招募〔～宾〕〈名〉～打字员❶；～兵；～新生；～售货员❷；～研究生❸；～护士❹；～翻译人员❺；～司机❻〔～补〕〈结〉他弟弟被招兵～走了；今年研究生～少了；打字员～够数❼了吗？名额❽已经～满了〈趋〉今年～上来的新兵都不错〈程〉今年招兵～得比较晚；电工❾～得太多了；大学生～得还不够多〈可〉有的系每年人数都～不满；～不了(liǎo)那么多人；～不着(zháo)理想的演员❿；名额～得满吗？〈时〉～了好几个月〈量〉～过两次了〔状～〕少～点；净⓫～女的；在几个大城市～；提前⓬～生；同时～；盲目地⓭～；公开⓮～；内部～；按比例⓯～

1. typists 2. shop assistants 3. postgraduates 4. nurses 5. translators 6. drivers 7. enough; sufficient in quantity 8. the number of people assigned or allowed 9. electrician 10. ideal actor or actress 11. only; merely 12. ahead of time 13. blindly 14. publicly; openly 15. in proportion

③ attract; incur; court ≅ 引〔～宾〕〈名〉垃圾❶要及时❷处理❸，不然的话❹容易～苍蝇❺；不知为什么我那么容易被蚊子咬，可能我的血❻～蚊子；他净❼在外边～灾惹祸❽；灯光～蛾子❾；每天都～一大帮孩子来听故事；～了一圈人❿围观⓫〔状～〕容易～；净～；总～；又～了

1. rubbish; garbage 2. in time 3. deal with; dispose of 4. otherwise 5. fly 6. blood 7. always 8. court disaster; invite trouble 9. moth 10. a crowd of people 11. watch sth. in a circle

④ provoke; tease ≅ 招惹〔～宾〕

〈名〉这种人特别❶~人恨❷；有才能的人❸容易~人忌妒❹；这个人不~人同情❺；这孩子一点儿也不~人爱；他的样子真~人笑〈代〉谁也没~他，他就不高兴了；我又怎么~你了？净❻~他嚷嚷❼；我们快走吧，别在这儿~人家讨厌❽了；不要~人家不痛快〔~补〕〈结〉又把孩子~哭了；把他爸爸都~笑了〈程〉~得她直哭；~得她骂❾起来没完〈可〉我~不起别人的忌妒来〔状~〕特别~人讨厌；就是~人爱；非常~人同情；一点儿也不~人喜欢；别~

1. especially 2. hate 3. capable man 4. be jealous of; envy 5. sympathy 6. only; merely 7. shout; yell 8. dislike; disgust 9. abuse; curse; swear

⑤ confess; own up 〔~宾〕〈名〉~供❶〔状~〕老老实实地~❷；已经~；完全~；彻底~；都~〔习用〕树大~风❸

1. make a confession of one's crime 2. honestly 3. a tall tree catches the wind — a person in a high position is liable to be attacked

zhāodài 招待 receive (guests); entertain; serve (customers) 〔~宾〕〈名〉~外宾❶；~客人；~老师；~顾客❷〔~补〕〈结〉我回来晚了，我的同屋❸替我~上朋友了〈趋〉他帮助我一起~客人来了〈程〉~得很周到❹；~得非常热情❺；~得很冷淡❻；~得很有礼貌❼〈可〉~不周，请原谅❽怕~不好〔时〕帮他~了半天客人〈量〉~过好几次外宾；好好替我~一下儿客人〔状~〕热情地~；殷勤地❾~；很有礼貌地~；用什么吃的❿~？主动⓫~；特意⓬~；不知该怎么~

1. foreign guest 2. customer 3. roommate 4. thoughtful 5. warm; enthusiastic 6. cold; indifferent 7. courteous; polite 8. excuse; forgive 9. solicitously; eagerly 10. food 11. initiatively; on one's own initiative 12. especially

zháo 着 ① touch ≅ 接触；沾〔~宾〕〈名〉手上的伤口❶一~水就疼❷；扶❸好了梯子，等他脚~了地，你再撒手❹；上不~天，下不~地❺；这个人好象~了魔❻似的；她说话总是不~边际❼〔~补〕〈可〉伤没好，现在还~不了(liǎo)水；车座❽太高骑❾上去脚~不了(liǎo)地〈量〉~了一次水又发炎❿了〔状~〕别~水

1. wound; cut 2. pain 3. hold 4. let go one's hand 5. touch neither the sky nor the ground 6. seem to be bewitched 7. not to the point 8. seat of a bike 9. ride 10. inflame

② feel; be affected by (cold, etc.) ≅ 受〔~宾〕〈名〉他前天晚上没盖好❶被，~风❷了，两肩❸酸疼❹〈动〉他有点~迷❺了〈形〉

衣服穿少了，～凉❻了；一摸❼口袋❽发现忘了带❾钱包，当时心里就～了慌❿；别～急⓫〔～补〕〈趋〉又～起急来了〈程〉着急～得连饭都吃不下了〈可〉你血压高⓬，可～不得急啊！〈量〉为了这件事我～过多少次急了〔**状～**〕容易～凉；瞎⓭～急；千万别～急；一点也不～急；果然⓮～；不必⓯～

1. didn't cover himself up well 2. become unwell through being in a draught 3. two shoulders 4. ache 5. be fascinated 6. cold 7. feel 8. pocket 9. forget to bring along 10. get alarmed 11. worry; feel anxious 12. high blood pressure 13. blindly 14. really; as expected; sure enough 15. needlessly

③ burn ≅ 燃烧〔**主～**〕〈名〉炉子❶～了；灯笼❷～了；汽油❸～了；纸～了；你点❹了半天，蚊香❺～了没有？蜡烛❻～了；木头差一点～了〔**～宾**〕〈名〉小心，～了火可不得了❼(liǎo)；孩子玩火柴，容易～火〔**～补**〕〈结〉香❽都～完了；火～旺了❾〈趋〉火～起来了〈程〉香～得很慢〈可〉不放纸和劈柴❿炉子～不了(liǎo)；煤不好，火～不旺〈时〉蚊香～了一夜；一只蜡烛能～多长时间？〈量〉化工厂⓫～过两次火了〔**状～**〕容易～火；柴湿不好～；一点就～；立刻⓬就～；还～着呢；连续⓭～

1. stove 2. lantern 3. gasoline; petrol 4. light 5. mosquito-repellent incense 6. candle 7. desperately serious; disastrous 8. incense 9. vigorously 10. firewood 11. chemical plant 12. at once; immediately 13. continuously; in succession

zhǎo 找 ① look for; try to find; seek ≅ 寻找 ↔ 丢〔**～宾**〕〈名〉我在～车钥匙❶；到图书馆去～点材料❷；他们要～房子；她正在～门牌号码❸；替我～个座位❹；她真能～机会❺；在这儿～出路❻很不容易；～～失败的原因；～～地震的规律❼；～一个准确的❽答案❾；～个合适的工作；你真是没事～事❿，动它干什么？他就爱～毛病⓫；我在地上～我掉的钱呢；～个地方休息休息吧〈代〉你～谁？他蹲⓬在哪儿～什么？〈形〉～麻烦⓭；～别扭⓮〔**～补**〕〈结〉～到帽子了吗？找来找去都把他～烦⓯了；门牌～错了；原因没～对；～到天黑也没找着(zháo)；所有的地方都～遍了⓰，也没找到你〈趋〉去年丢的那辆车已经～回来了；他～上门来了〈程〉～得很仔细⓱，哪儿都找到了；～得很马虎⓲〈可〉～不着(zháo)就别找了；东西丢了就～不回来了〈时〉～了好几天都没找着(zháo)；多～一会儿〈量〉～了好多遍了；好好～一下儿〔**状～**〕随便⓳～了～；四处～；来回⓴～；仔细～；粗略地㉑～；从头到尾地㉒～；一遍又一遍地㉓～；翻箱倒柜地㉔～；里里外外地㉕～；不容易～；自～麻烦；净～别扭；别瞎㉖～；没完没了(liǎo)地㉗～；想方设法㉘～

1. bicycle key 2. data; information 3. house number 4. seat 5. chance; opportunity 6. way out; outlet 7. law of earthquake 8. correct; right; proper 9. answer; key; solution 10. ask for trouble 11. find fault; pick a quarrel 12. squat on the heels 13. look for trouble 14. awkward; uncomfortable; difficult 15. vexed 16. all over 17. careful 18. careless 19. casually; at random 20. to and fro 21. roughly 22. from beginning to end 23. again and again 24. rummage through chests and cupboards 25. inside and outside 26. at random 27. without end 28. try every means

② give change〔~宾〕〈名〉~钱，~零钱❶；~你两毛（钱）；~了一把❷；~了一堆❸〔~补〕〈结〉应该~给你多少钱？~多了；别~错了〈趋〉我给他两块，~回来一块三；她把一张五块的当作一块的~出去了〈程〉钱~得不对〈可〉没零钱，~不开〔状~〕还没~钱呢，你怎么就走了〔习用〕骑马~马❹

1. change 2. a handful 3. a heap; a pile 4. look for a horse while sitting on one — hold on to one job while seeking a better one

zhào 照 ① shine; illuminate; light up ≅ 照射〔~宾〕〈名〉用手电❶筒~~路〔~补〕〈结〉阳光~在身上，懒洋洋的❷；闪电❸把屋子都~亮了，阳光~到白墙上特别晃眼❹〈趋〉手电筒~出来一条光柱❺；刚换❻的电池❼~出来真亮〈程〉~得什么都看得见；火光把脸~得通红❽〈可〉这个角落❾太阳~不着(zháo)；灯光~不着(zháo)她〈量〉请你用手电筒给我~一下儿亮儿〔状~〕用手电筒~；从玻璃窗上~；太阳~；给他~亮；往远处~；对着他的脸~；向上~

1. electric torch; flashlight 2. languid; listless 3. lightning 4. dazzle 5. light column 6. change 7. (electric) cell; battery 8. very red; red through and through 9. corner

② reflect; mirror ≅ 反射〔~宾〕〈名〉~镜子❶〔~补〕〈结〉平静的❷湖面❸~出了岸边❹杨柳❺的倒影❻；镜子的光~到屋里墙上；这面镜子把人都~走样❼了；哈哈镜❽把人都~成奇形怪状的❾了〈趋〉水里~出我的影子❿来了；她总在镜子那儿~来~去的〈程〉小镜子~得也很清楚；河水~得人影直动〈可〉镜子太脏，都~不见人了；镜子挂⓫得太高，~不着(zháo)〈时〉她每天光照镜子就得(děi)~一个小时〈量〉一天~好几次镜子；你好好~一下儿吧〔状~〕从前面~；一遍一遍地~；从来不~；翻来覆去地⓬~；对着镜子~；在玻璃窗⓭上~

1. mirror 2. calm; quiet 3. the surface of the lake 4. bank; coast

5. poplar and willow 6. inverted reflection in water 7. lose shape; go out of form 8. distorting mirror 9. grotesque or fantastic in shape or appearance 10. shadow 11. put up; hang 12. again and again; repeatedly 13. glass window

③ take a picture (photograph); shoot 摄影，拍摄〔～宾〕〈名〉我给他～了一张相；～夜景❶；～彩色的；～X光❷〔～补〕〈结〉这张相～坏了；那么好的镜头没～上；～完了X光再去验血❸〈趋〉这个孩子刚才笑得多好玩啊，真应该给他～下来〈程〉～得真好；～得挺清楚；～得非常漂亮；～得太难看了；～得不满意❹；～得不怎么样❺〈可〉孩子老动，～不了(liǎo)；太远了，～不清楚；脸上的伤疤❻～得出来～不出来？你靠近❼点儿，要不然❽就～不上你了；～不出有什么病来〈时〉照X光的时候，医生给他～了十几分钟；他怎么～那么半天啊〈量〉～过好几次X光了〔状～〕再～几张；摆好了姿式❾再～；一连～了三卷❿；随便～〔习用〕～猫画虎⓫；～葫芦画瓢⓬；～妖镜⓭

1. night scene 2. X-ray 3. blood test 4. not satisfied 5. not up to much; very indifferent 6. scar 7. approach 8. otherwise 9. assume a posture 10. three reels 11. draw a tiger with a cat as a model — copy; imitate 12. draw a dipper with a gourd as a model — copy; imitate 13. monster-revealing mirror; demon-detector

zhàogu 照顾 ① give consideration to; show consideration for ≅ 考虑到〔～宾〕〈名〉～全局❶；～大家的实际需要❷；～他家的困难；～面子〔～补〕〈结〉～到两国关系；～到各个方面〈程〉～得很周到❸〈可〉～不了(liǎo)那么多了；一时～不到就要出问题〔状～〕合理❹～；适当❺～；尽量❻～；经常～；过分❼～；不必～；无须～；必须～

1. overall situation 2. real need (demand) 3. very thoughtful; considerate 4. rationally 5. suitably 6. to the best of one's ability; as far as possible 7. excessively

② look after; care for; attend to ≅ 看管〔～宾〕〈名〉～孩子；～病人；～残废人❶；～穷人❷〔～补〕〈结〉要把病人～好〈趋〉她～起人来真热情❸〈程〉对病人～得很周到❹〈可〉他连自己都～不好，还能照顾❺病人吗？那么小的孩子～得了(liǎo)一群羊吗？护士少，病人多，～不过来〈时〉她为我～了好几年孩子〈量〉请你好好儿～一下儿他〔状～〕主动地❻～；耐心地❼～；细心地❽～；精心❾～；热情地～；热心地❿～；对病人～得很好；请你多～；一直～；由他～

1. maimer; disabled man 2. the poor 3. warm 4. thoughtful; considerate 5. look after; care for 6. on one's own initiative 7. patiently 8. 9. carefully; meticulously 10. warmly

zhào 罩 cover; overspread; wrap〔～宾〕〈名〉钟上～着一个玻璃罩儿❶；山坡上～着一层薄雾❷〔～补〕〈结〉～上玻璃罩就不进土了；～在外面〈趋〉把切好的西瓜用纱罩❸；～起来了〈可〉太小了～不上〔状～〕在外面～；用什么～？从上面；薄薄地❹～着一层雾

1. glass cover 2. a thin mist 3. gauze covering 4. thinly

zhēteng 折腾 ① turn from side to side; toss about〔～补〕〈结〉昨天夜里他茶喝多了，睡不着(zháo)觉，又～上了〈趋〉～过来～过去地睡不着(zháo)；刚躺下❶就～起来了〈程〉～得一夜没睡；～得别人也没法睡了；～得要命❷〈时〉那个孩子又哭又闹❸～了半天好容易❹睡着(zháo)了；～了一夜〔状～〕来回❺～；翻来覆去地❻～；刚躺下就～；没完没了(liǎo)地❼～

1. lie down 2. extremely 3. make a tearful scene 4. with great difficulty 5. back and forth 6. toss from side to side 7. continuously; endlessly

② do sth. over and over again ≌反复做〔～补〕〈结〉一会要，一会不要把人都～腻了❶〈趋〉一会把家具❷这么摆❸，一会儿那么摆，～来～去地真没意思；机器❹拆❺了又安❻，安了又拆，～起来没完〈程〉～得太利害了；～得烦死了〈可〉怎么折腾也～不好；三天也～不完〈时〉～了好几个钟头；～了半天也没买〈量〉～了好几回；～好几次〔状～〕来回❼～；净❽瞎❾～；别乱❿～

1. be tired of 2. furniture 3. place; put; arrange 4. machine 5. disassemble; take apart 6. install; fix 7. back and forth 8. only; merely 9. groundlessly; foolishly; to no purpose 10. recklessly

③ cause, physical or mental suffering; get sb. down ≌折磨〔主～〕〈名〉牙疼❶真～人；孩子真～大人〔～补〕〈结〉病人都快把人～死了；把精神～垮❷了；把人～苦了〈程〉～得太凶❸了；～得很利害❹；～得受不了(liǎo)❺了；～得活不下去了〈可〉～不死；～不垮〈时〉～了一个多星期；～了好长时间；～好多年〈量〉～过无数❻次〔状～〕真～；故意❼～

1. toothache 2. collapse; break down; fall 3. terrible 4. awful 5. unbearable 6. innumerable; countless 7. on purpose

zhē 蜇 sting〔主～〕〈名〉蝎子❶～人；蜜蜂❷～人〔～宾〕〈名〉～

了我的手;头上被马蜂❸~了一个大包❹〈代〉蜜蜂你不碰❺它,它是不~你的〔~补〕〈结〉小心点,别让蝎子~着(zháo);眼睛都被~肿了❻;把孩子~哭了〈程〉~得真利害❼;~得直哭〈可〉躲❽到屋子里去就~不着(zháo)了〈量〉让马蜂~了一下儿;小时候被蝎子~过一次〔状~〕突然❾~;被~;几乎~;差点儿~

1. scorpion 2. bee 3. hornets; wasp 4. swelling 5. provoke; touch 6. be swollen 7. terrible 8. hide 9. suddenly

zhē 遮 hide from view; block; obstruct; impede ≅ 挡;掩盖〔~宾〕〈名〉草帽边儿❶大一点好,可以挡❷雨,又可以~阳光;他这样做是为了~人耳目❸〈形〉我帮他说了一句话,替他~~羞❹〔~补〕〈结〉那块云彩❺把月亮都~住了;阳光被前面的大楼~住了;头发太长,把眼睛都~上了〈趋〉我怕光,所以用很厚的窗帘❻把窗~起来了〈可〉山再高也~不住太阳〈时〉~了半天也没遮好〈量〉用灯罩❼~一下儿就不晃眼❽了〔状~〕被什么东西~住了;严严实实地❾~;完全~;故意❿~;稍微⓫~一下儿就可以了

1. edge of a strawhat 2. keep from 3. deceive the public 4. hush up a scandal; cover up one's embarrassment 5. cloud 6. heavy curtain 7. lampshade 8. not dazzling 9. tightly; closely 10. on purpose 11. slightly

zhéhé 折合 convert into; amount to ≅ 合〔~补〕〈结〉从日元~成新币❶〈可〉这钱应该怎么折合,我可~不好〈时〉~了半天也不对〈量〉你帮我~一下儿吧!〔状~〕按照❷什么牌价❸~呢?请给我~一下儿

1. currency of Singapore 2. according to 3. list price

zhémó 折磨 cause physical or mental suffering; torment〔主~〕〈名〉疾病❶~人;贫穷❷~人;痛苦❸~人〔~宾〕〈名〉~人〈代〉别~我了〔~补〕〈结〉把人都快~死了;~疯❹了;病把他~得不象样子❺了;这么折磨都没把他~怕〈程〉把人~得死去活来❻的;~得骨瘦如柴❼〈可〉他很坚强❽,怎么折磨也~不死;~不垮❾〈时〉~了那么长时间;~了好几年〈量〉~过我好多次〔状~〕从精神上❿~;用各种办法~;故意⓫~;残酷地⓬~

1. disease 2. poverty 3. suffering 4. mad 5. extremely thin; worn to a mere shadow 6. half dead; half alive 7. thin as a lath; worn to a shadow 8. strong; firm 9. break down; wear down 10. spiritually 11. intentionally; on purpose 12. cruelly

zhēnduì 针对 be directed against; be aimed at〔~宾〕〈名〉~这个问题进行研究;我是~他的

话说的；~这种倾向❶；~这种观点❷；~这种缺点；~这种现象❸；~那篇文章；~现实〈代〉这句话我不是~你说的；不知你是~什么而言；这段❹话~谁?〔状~〕专门❺~；一向~；一直~；始终~；好象~；全部~

1. tendency; trend 2. point of view 3. phenomenon 4. paragraph 5. specially

zhēnxī 珍惜 treasure; value; cherish ≅ 重视〔~宾〕〈名〉~时间；~财富❶；~人力物力❷〔状~〕好好儿~；异常❸~；过分❹~；分外❺~；十分~

1. wealth; riches 2. manpower and material resources 3. extremely; exceedingly 4. excessively 5. particularly; especially

zhēnzhuó 斟酌 consider; deliberate ≅ 考虑；掂量〔~宾〕〈名〉~词语❶；~字句❷；~情况❸〔~补〕〈结〉~过了，还要~到什么时候啊〈趋〉这些词语~起来还得(děi)费一番思索❹〈可〉~不出好词儿来〈时〉~了半天也没找到一个满意的❺词〈量〉应该好好~一下儿〔状~〕一起~；再~；再三~；仔细~；需要~；反复~

1. 2. weigh one's words 3. situation 4. take a lot of time to think deeply 5. satisfactory

zhěn 枕 rest the head on 〔~宾〕〈名〉~枕头❶；~着胳膊睡❷；~着一摞书睡❸；~着被❹睡〔~补〕〈结〉~高点儿；头没在枕头上〈程〉~得太不舒服了；~得脖子疼❻〈可〉书那么硬❼~不了(liǎo)〔状~〕舒舒服服地❽~；随便❾~

1. pillow 2. sleep with one's head resting on one's arm 3. sleep with one's head resting on a pile of books 4. quilt 5. uncomfortable 6. pain in the neck 7. hard 8. comfortably 9. casually

zhènzuò 振作 bestir (exert) oneself; display vigour ≅ 打起〔~宾〕〈名〉大家要~精神❶〔~补〕〈趋〉把精神~起来❷〈可〉他的精神总❸~不起来〈量〉把精神~一下儿〔状~〕突然❹~起来了；必须~起来；总算~起来了

1. bestir oneself 2. brace up 3. always 4. suddenly

zhèn 震 shake; shock; vibrate 〔主~〕〈名〉鼓声❶~人；玻璃器皿❷怕~；瓷器❸不能~〔~宾〕〈名〉声音太大~耳朵〔~补〕〈结〉你的耳朵是怎么~聋❹的? 这一声雷❺可把我~坏了；把耳膜❻都快~破了；心最快~裂了〈趋〉隔壁❼往墙上钉钉子把我家墙上的镜框❽(给)~下来了〈程〉鼓声~得心慌❾；坦克❿开过去~得地都颤⓫了；楼上敲⓬东西~得

楼下天花板⓭上的灰⓮直往下掉；他捶⓯了一下儿桌子，上面的火柴盒⓰都被～得跳起来了；～得耳朵嗡嗡⓱响〈时〉～一会儿我就受不了(liǎo)了〔**状～**〕被爆炸声⓲～；差点儿～聋；容易～坏

1. drumbeats **2.** glass **3.** chinaware; porcelain **4.** deaf **5.** thunder **6.** tympanic membrane **7.** neighbour **8.** picture frame **9.** be flustered; be nervous **10.** tank **11.** vibrate; quiver; tremble **12.** knock; beat; strike **13.** ceiling **14.** lime **15.** beat; pound; thump **16.** match box **17.** drone; buzz; hum **18.** explosion; detonation

zhēng 争 ① contend; strive; vie ≃争夺〔**～宾**〕〈名〉～权❶；～名❷；～利❸；～名次❹；～地盘❺；别人看不起❻你，你好好干，一定要～一口气❼；这个运动员❽又得了一个世界冠军❾，真给祖国～光❿；父母都很好，就是孩子不～气〈数〉他一心想～个第一〈动〉～挑重担⓫〔**～补**〕〈结〉冠军～到了〈趋〉那个老实人⓬也跟人～起名次来了；为了名和利～来～去的，真没意思〈程〉～得很利害⓭；～得很激烈⓮；～得很凶⓯〈可〉～不着(zháo)；～不到〈时〉～了好几年；～了很长时间〈量〉～过无数次⓰；～了一阵⓱〔**状～**〕终于⓲～到了；始终⓳没～到手；居然⓴也～起来了；为祖国～光；拼命㉑～；你死我活地㉒～；怎么也～不着(zháo)；一直～；明着㉓～；暗中㉔～；千方百计地㉕～；三番五次地㉖～；挖空心思地㉗～；不顾一切地㉘～；力㉙～上游

1. power; right **2.** fame **3.** gain; wealth **4.** position in a name list; place in a competition **5.** territory under one's control; domain **6.** look down upon **7.** try to make a good showing; try to win credit for **8.** sportsman; athlete **9.** world champion **10.** win honour (glory) for **11.** rush to carry the heaviest load; vie with each other for the hardest job **12.** honest man **13.** terrible; awful **14.** intense; sharp; acute **15.** terrible; fearful **16.** innumerable; countless **17.** a period of time **18.** at last; finally **19.** from beginning to end **20.** to one's surprise; unexpectedly **21.** with all one's might; desperately **22.** life-and-death **23.** openly **24.** secretly; in secret **25.** by every possible means; by hook or by crook **26.** over and over again; repeatedly **27.** rack one's brains **28.** recklessly **29.** work hard for; do all one can do

② argue; dispute ≃ 争执；争论〔**～宾**〕他们在～什么问题？〔**～补**〕〈结〉他们为打球犯规❶的事又～上了；一直～到现在还没～完〈趋〉不知为什么事两个人又～起来了；这个问题还要再～下去吗？为这点儿小事～过来～过去的没有必要❷〈程〉为了一个棋子❸，两个人～得面红耳赤❹；～

得气呼呼的❺〈可〉这两个人的脾气❻都很温和❼，～不起来；这个问题他们几个人～不下去了，只好暂时❽停一停；～不出结果来，只好去请教别人；这个问题争也～不清楚〈时〉两个人～了半天；这个问题一直～了好几年〈量〉非～一下儿不可〔状～〕必须～个水落石出❾；不善于❿跟人～；有节制地⓫～；不屑⓬与他～；为这点小事～；激烈地⓭～；据理力～⓮；有根有据地⓯～；蛮不讲理地⓰～

1. foul 2. there's no need 3. piece (in a board game) 4. be red in the face; be flushed 5. panting with rage; in a huff 6. temperament; disposition 7. gentle; mild; temperate 8. temporarily 9. (argue) a matter out; (get) to the bottom of the matter 10. be bad at 11. moderately 12. disdain to do sth. 13. intensely; sharply; bitterly 14. argue strongly on just grounds 15. having good grounds 16. be impervious to reason; persist in being unreasonable

zhēngduó 争夺 fight for; contend for ≅ 争〔～宾〕〈名〉～领导权❶；～地盘❷；～势力范围❸〔～补〕〈结〉～上领导权了；～到手❹了〈趋〉不要再～下去了；～起领导权来什么都不顾❺了〈程〉～得不可开交❻；～得太激烈❼了〈可〉谁也～不着(zháo)〈时〉～了半天；～了好长时间〈量〉都想～一番❽〔状～〕拼命❾～；为什么事情～？跟谁～？在这个问题上～；互相～

1. leadership 2. territory under one's control; domain 3. (scramble) for spheres of influence 4. in one's hands; in one's possession 5. casting all caution to the winds; recklessly 6. be engaged in a heated argument 7. intense; sharp; acute 8. one time 9. for all one is worth; with all one's might; desperately

zhēngqǔ 争取 strive for; fight for; win over〔～宾〕〈名〉～自由❶；～民主❷；～胜利❸；～选票❹；～和平；～时间〈动〉～独立❺；～提前❻完成任务❼；～一次解决问题；～早点把病养好；～演❽主角❾〈形〉～主动❿〔～补〕〈结〉～在下星期去〈趋〉～过来了〈可〉这么好的机会⓫我怎么～不到哇；〈时〉～了半天，才给我一张参观券⓬〈量〉我也想～一下儿试试，不知行不行；～过一次〔状～〕积极⓭～；好容易⓮～上了；尽量⓯～；主动～；无法～；无须⓰～；不妨⓱～一下儿试试；始终⓲～不到；终于⓳～到了；勇敢地⓴～

1. freedom 2. democracy 3. victory 4. vote; ballot 5. independence 6. ahead of time 7. task 8. perform; play; act 9. leading role; protagonist 10. initiative 11. good chance 12. visiting

ticket 13. actively 14. with great difficulty 15. to the best of one's ability; as far as possible 16. need not 17. there is no harm in; might as well 18. from beginning to end 19. at last; finally 20. courageously

zhēng 征 ① levy (troops, taxes) ≅征收；征募〔~宾〕〈名〉~兵❶；~粮❷；~税❸〔~补〕〈结〉兵已经~齐❹了；税~完了〈可〉~得来那么多粮吗？〈时〉出去~了几个月兵〈量〉每年~一次兵〔状~〕按时❺；隔一年❻一~

1. soldier (conscription; call-up) 2. impose grain levies 3. levy taxes 4. complete 5. on time 6. every other year

② ask for; solicit〔~宾〕〈名〉~文❶；~稿❷〔状~〕向教授❸~稿；登报❹~文

1. articles or essays 2. contributions (to a journal, etc.) 3. professor 4. publish in the newspaper

zhēngfú 征服 conquer; subjugate〔~宾〕〈名〉~自然❶；~一个部落❷；~敌人；~一个国家；~一个民族❸〔~补〕〈趋〉终于❹把他的心~过来了〈可〉~不了(liǎo)我的心〔状~〕已经~；难以~；用武力❺~；再次~❻；始终❼~不了(liǎo)

1. nature 2. tribe 3. nation 4. at last; finally 5. by force of arms 6. again 7. from beginning to end

zhēngqiú 征求 solicit; seek; ask for〔~宾〕〈名〉~意见❶；~订户❷〔~补〕〈结〉意见都~遍❸了；所有的人我都~过了〈趋〉组长又向大家~起意见来了；~过来~过去〈程〉~得很广泛❹〈可〉~不着(zháo)订户〈时〉~了半天意见也没有人提❺〈量〉~过两三次了；~过一回〔状~〕及时❻~；一再❼~；再三❽~；多次~；口头❾~；书面❿~；广泛~；诚心诚意地⓫~

1. opinions 2. subscriptions 3. all over; everywhere 4. wide 5. put forward; bring up; raise 6. in time 7. 8. over and over again; repeatedly 9. orally 10. in written form 11. earnestly and sincerely

zhēngzhá 挣扎 struggle〔~补〕〈结〉人民~在水深火热之中❶；~在死亡线上❷〈趋〉从痛苦❸里~出来；那狗从水里~上来了；给他上手铐❹的时候，他~起来了〈程〉那个小偷~得很利害❺〈可〉捆上❻以后，他就再也不了(liǎo)了〈时〉~了半天也没把绳子❼弄掉〈量〉使劲❽~了一下儿；~了好几次都没挣扎上来〔状~〕拼命❾~；终于~出来了；多次~；竭力❿~；在死亡线上~；在困境中⓫~；垂死⓬~

1. in an abyss of misery 2. for existence on the verge of death 3. pain; suffering 4. handcuffs 5. awful; terrible 6. tie up; bundle up 7. rope 8. exert all one's strength 9. with all one's might; desperately 10. do one's utmost 11. (be) in a fix; (be) in a tight place 12. be in one's death throes; put up a last-ditch struggle

zhēng 睁 open (the eyes) ≅ 张 ↔闭〔~宾〕〈名〉~眼看一看；你别~着眼睛说瞎话❶了〔 ~补 〕〈结〉~开眼睛向四处一看，一个人都没有〈程〉眼睛~得大大的；眼睛~得真圆〈可〉困❷得眼睛都~不开了〔状~〕使劲❸~；惊恐地❹~大了眼睛；还没睡醒，勉强❺~开眼睛了；蒙蒙胧胧地~❻；迷迷糊糊地~❼；硬❽~〔习用〕~一只眼，闭一只眼❾

1. tell a barefaced (或 out and out) lie 2. sleepy 3. exert all one's strength 4. in a great panic; alarmingly 5. reluctantly 6. 7. somnolently; drowsily 8. with difficulty 9. turn a blind eye to sth.; wink at sth.

zhēng 蒸 steam 〔~宾〕〈名〉~馒头❶；~蛋糕〔~补〕〈结〉包子已经~上了；肉~熟❷了没有？〈趋〉这种面粉❸~出来的馒头真白；~出油来了〈程〉肉~得很烂❹；馒头~得不熟〈可〉肉一个小时~得烂~不烂？锅❺太小，~不下这么多饭，馒头十分钟~不熟〈时〉多~一会儿〈量〉熟肉❻吃的时候再~一下儿〔状~〕多~会儿；用旺火❼~；容易~；不好~

1. steamed bread 2. done 3. flour; wheat flour 4. soft enough 5. pot 6. cooked meat 7. a roaring fire

zhènglǐ 整理 put in order; arrange ≅ 收拾〔~宾〕〈名〉~房间；~东西；~笔记；~图书；~资料❶；~民歌❷；~行装❸；~抽屉❹；~~被风吹乱的头发〔~补〕〈结〉把屋子~干净；材料都~完了吗？把书~成一摞❺一摞的了〈趋〉把要带的东西都~出来了吗？又一起抽屉来了〈程〉屋子~得很整齐❻〈可〉材料一时❼还~不出来；笔记~不全❽〈时〉~了半天还是不显❾干净〈量〉你的东西真需要好好~一下儿了；隔一段时间就要~一次〔状~〕经常~；从不~；再~~；提前❿~；一点一点~；彻底⓫~

1. materials 2. folk song 3. outfit for a journey 4. drawer 5. a stack 6. tidy; neat 7. for the moment; temporarily 8. not complete 9. look; appear 10. ahead of time 11. thoroughly

zhèngmíng 证明 prove; testify; bear out 〔~宾〕〈动〉~不是他说的；~是我错了；~是他写

的〈主-谓〉~她是好人；我~他不知道这件事；~她没迟到；~那个孩子没说谎❶〔~补〕〈可〉我~不了(liǎo)这件事〈量〉请你给我~一下儿〔状~〕互相~；完全~；充分❷~；有力地❸~；已经~；事实~；一再❹~；反复❺~；无可辩驳地❻~

1. tell a lie 2. fully 3. forcefully 4. 5. over and over again; repeatedly 6. indisputably

zhèng 挣

① earn; make ≅ 赚〔~宾〕〈名〉你每月~多少钱？只能~饭吃❶；没有什么富余〔~补〕〈结〉这几年他的钱可~足❷了；他这一辈子❸钱可~多了〈趋〉他孩子都~起钱来了〈程〉钱~得很多；~得勉强❹能维持一家人的生活〈可〉~不了(liǎo)多少钱〔状~〕辛辛苦苦地❺~；好不容易❻才~；到底❼~了多少钱？用这个办法果然❽~了不少钱；至少~

1. earn a living 2. enough 3. all one's life 4. reluctantly; grudgingly 5. laboriously; painstakingly 6. with great difficulty 7. in the end; at last 8. to one's surprise; unexpectedly

② struggle to get free; try to throw off ≅ 挣脱；摆脱〔~补〕〈结〉把捆绑的❶绳子❷~开了❸；~断❹了；把千年的铁锁链❺~开了〈可〉~不脱；~不断〈时〉~了半天也没挣开〈量〉~了好几下儿都没挣折❻(shé)〔状~〕用尽全身力量~；拼命❼~；往外~；一下子~开了

1. bound 2. rope 3. loose 4. snapped 5. shackles 6. snapped 7. for all one is worth

zhī 支

① prop up; put up ≅ 支撑〔~宾〕〈名〉~帘子❶；~帐蓬❷；~一个临时的棚子❸；两只手~着头；婴儿车❹上~了一个布蓬❺〔~补〕〈结〉帐蓬很快就~好了；把帘子~高点儿〈趋〉要吃饭了，把桌子、椅子都~起来吧〈程〉棚子~得真高；帐蓬~得快极❻了〈可〉你们两个人~得起一个帐蓬来吗？木棍太细~不住〈量〉请帮我~一下儿窗〔状~〕在哪儿~？大家一起~；用竹竿❼~还是用木棍~？不用~；别~了；用的时候再~；临时❽~

1. curtain; screen 2. tent 3. provisional shed 4. bassinet 5. cloth shed 6. extremely 7. bamboo pole 8. temporarily; for a short time

② protrude; raise ≅ 伸出；龇；竖起〔主~〕〈名〉两颗犬牙❶朝❷两边儿~着〔~宾〕~着耳朵听〔~补〕〈结〉两颗大牙~在外面〈趋〉牙都~出来了；一撮头发❸~起来了〔状~〕往外~；朝两边儿~

1. canine tooth 2. facing; towards 3. a few hairs

③ pay or draw (money)〔~宾〕〈名〉~点钱；到银行去~点款❶

〔～补〕〈结〉把这个月的工资❷全～走了〈趋〉把钱～出来吧；他昨天又～出去一百元〈程〉钱～得太多了〈可〉这个月～不出钱来了〈量〉～过好几次工资〔状～〕预❸～；先～；万一❹～不出来；从学校～；全部～出来了；三番五次地❺～；先后共～；从来不～；决不～

1. fund; a sum of money 2. wages; salary 3. in advance; beforehand 4. just in case; if by any chance 5. over and over again; repeatedly

④ send away; put sb. off 〔～补〕〈结〉爸爸跟李叔叔说重要的事呢，所以把我～走❶了〈趋〉快把她～出去吧；～到别处去吧〈程〉把她～得远远的〈可〉他不懂事❷，怎么支也～不走〈时〉～了半天他都不出去〈量〉～了好几次他也不走〔状～〕往外～；毫不客气地❸～；借口❹～把他～走；不好意思❺～；设法❻～

1. send away 2. thoughtless; not intelligent 3. bluntly; straightforwardly 4. use as an excuse 5. find it embarrassing (to do sth.) 6. try; do what one can

zhīchí 支持

① sustain; hold out; bear ≅ 支撑；坚持〔～补〕〈结〉～到什么时候？〈趋〉勉强❶～下来了；还能～下去吗？〈可〉累❷得～不住了；连续❸做两个手术❹，你～得了(liǎo)吗？头晕❺得～不下去了；他的身体～不下来～不下去？这种局面❻再也～不下去了〈时〉还可以再～一会儿；再～几天没问题〈量〉还能再～一下儿吗？〔状～〕勉强～；实在❼～不住了；简直❽～不住了；尽量❾～；很难～下去；勇敢地❿～

1. reluctantly 2. tired 3. in succession 4. operation 5. dizzy 6. aspect; phase; situation 7. indeed; really 8. simply; at all 9. to the best of one's ability 10. bravely

② support; back; stand by 〔～宾〕〈名〉～你的意见❶；～他们的主张❷；～这件事；～你们的合理❸建议❹〈代〉我～他这样做；～她去〔～补〕〈结〉～错了，不应该支持他〈趋〉他现在也～起我们的试验❺来了〈可〉这种意见可～不得啊！〔状～〕互相～；大力❻～；全力❼～；坚决❽～；尽量❾～；必须～；不得不～；公开❿～；暗中⓫～；千方百计地⓬～

1. idea; view; opinion 2. view; position 3. rational; reasonable 4. proposition; suggestion 5. experiment 6. energetically; vigorously 7. with all one's strength 8. firmly; resolutely 9. to the best of one's ability 10. openly; publicly 11. in secret; secretly 12. by every possible means; by hook or by crook

zhīpèi 支配

arrange; allocate; budget ≅ 安排〔～宾〕〈名〉她不会～时间，弄❶得自己很忙乱❷；不

知如何～这笔钱；～这笔遗产❸〔～补〕〈结〉应该把时间～好〈程〉时间～得很好〈可〉他家的钱他一点儿也～不了(liǎo)〔状～〕合理～；不好～；由谁～？受他～；如何～

1. do; manage; handle; get sb. or sth. into specified condition **2.** be in a rush and a muddle **3.** legacy

zhīdào 知道 know; realize; be aware of〔**～宾**〕〈名〉这件事他只～一个大概❶；我不～现在的情况怎么样了；他办起事来总不～深浅❷；我～你的意思；～内情❸；～详情❹；他们不～问题的严重性❺；～消息；～底细❻；～其中的❼奥妙❽；～他们的秘密❾；～他的想法；他～我的打算；～她的脾气❿〈代〉他那么有名⓫，谁不～他啊！关于这件事，他什么也不～〈动〉他～要开会；我～迟到了；我们～到哪儿去找他；他～怎么用洗衣机；不～应该怎么生活；孩子那么小就～应该帮助别人做事；现在有少数青年人不太～讲⓬礼貌⓭〈主－谓〉我只～他会俄语⓮，不～他还会法语〔**～补**〕〈结〉这件事我～晚了〈程〉～得很早；～得比较少；～得很详细⓯；～得真不少；这件事他～得比我清楚〈可〉老在家里待着⓰，外边有什么新闻⓱也～不了(liǎo)〈量〉有什么好消息，让我也～一下儿吧〔**状～**〕完全～；已经～了；还不～；一点也不～；终于⓲～了；到底被他～了；逐渐⓳～；不必～；不便⓴～；真～吗？

1. general idea; broad outline **2.** proper limits (for speech or action); sense of propriety **3.** inside information (或 story) **4.** detailed information **5.** the gravity of the question **6.** ins and outs; exact details **7.** among (which, them, etc.); in (whick, it) **8.** subtle; secret **9.** secret **10.** temperament; disposition **11.** well-known; famous **12.** stress; pay attention to **13.** courtesy; politeness **14.** Russian (language) **15.** detailed; minute **16.** stay **17.** news **18.** in the end; at last **19.** gradually; by degrees **20.** inconveniently

zhī 织 weave ≃ 纺；knit ≃ 编；编织〔**～宾**〕〈名〉～布；～地毯❶；～床单❷；～毛衣❸；～花样❹；蜘蛛❺又在～网❻了；～花边❼；～鱼网❽；～手套❾；～围巾❿〔**～补**〕〈结〉席子⓫～好了；花边～宽了；鱼网～密⓬了；毛衣～薄⓭了；～到什么时候才能织得⓮啊？〈趋〉这件背心⓯再～上来五行⓰就够了；把这两针一起～上去；这种花样很复杂⓱，你能～下来吗？一～起来就快了〈程〉布～得真粗糙；地毯～得真好看；～得快极了；～得不平；～得太紧⓲；～得不合适；样子～得过时⓳了〈可〉她～不好；～得合适吗？这种花⓴你～得上来吗？这个样本㉑上的图案㉒你～得出几种来？织错了以后，就有点～不下去了；这件毛衣一个月～得起来吗？〈时〉一个地毯得(děi)~几天啊；~了三个月才织完；刚~一会儿就累了〈量〉这种样子的，我~过好几次了；~了几针〔状~〕用机器~；手工❷~；一针一针地~；精心❷~；亲手❷~；偶尔❷~；赶紧~；慢慢~；不常~；成批地❷~；按图纸❷~；比着❷别人的毛衣~

1. carpet 2. sheet 3. woollen sweater 4. pattern; variety 5. spider 6. web 7. lace 8. fishnet 9. gloves 10. muffler; scarf 11. straw mat 12. close; dense 13. thin 14. be finished; be ready 15. a sleeveless garment 16. row; line 17. complicated; complex 18. tight; close 19. out-of-date 20. pattern; design 21. sample book 22. pattern; design 23. by hand 24. meticulously; elaborately 25. personally; with one's own hands 26. occasionally; once in a while 27. by batches 28. according to blueprint 29. model after; copy

zhíxíng 执行 carry out; execute; implement 〔~宾〕〈名〉~命令❶；~任务❷；~纪律❸；~政策❹；~计划❺〔~补〕〈结〉任务~完了；政策~错了〈趋〉今后还要继续❻~下去；开始~起来了〈程〉命令~得很好；~得不错〈可〉这个命令我~不了(liǎo)；这种政策已经~不下去了〈时〉这种法令❼~过一个时期；~了几年〈量〉象这样的艰巨❽任务，他~过好几次了〔状~〕认真~；灵活❾~；严肃❿~；严格⓫~；全面⓬~；忠实⓭~；坚决⓮~；尽快⓯~；从什么时候起~？一直~；仍旧~；正确~

1. order; command 2. assignment; mission; task 3. discipline 4. policy 5. plan 6. continue; go on 7. law and decree 8. arduous; formidable 9. flexibly; elastically 10. seriously; solemnly 11. strictly; rigorously 12. overall; comprehensively 13. faithfully 14. resolutely; firmly 15. as quickly as possible

zhí 值 ① be worth ≅ 值得〔主~〕〈动〉跑那么远路去买一个圆珠笔芯❶，真不~；为一点儿小事，伤❷了两家和气❸，太不~了〔~宾〕〈名〉你看看我这辆旧车~多少钱？那一幅画要是留到现在卖，可就~钱了〈动〉给你帮这么点小忙，不~一提❹；这个人真不~一理〔~补〕〈趋〉这种东西前几年都没人要，现在又~起钱来了〈可〉你那旧打字机❺~不了(liǎo)多少钱；为这点小事~不得吵架❻〔状~〕多~啊！一点儿也不~；根本❼不~；当然~了；太~了

1. refill (for a ball-point pen) 2. hurt 3. feelings 4. mention 5. typewriter 6. quarrel 7. at all; simply

② be on duty 〔~宾〕〈名〉~班；~勤〔~补〕〈结〉~完班❶就

回去；～到什么时候？〈程〉夜班～得累死❷人〈可〉他身体不好，～不了(liǎo)夜班；我～不惯❸夜班〈时〉～了三天早班❹；你先替❺我～一会儿班〈量〉从前～过好几次夜班，一个月～一次中班❻〔状～〕在场院里❼～；在仓库❽里～；隔两天❾一～；经常～；从来不～；连续❿～；轮流⓫～；认真～；替别人～；多～几个夜班；硬着头皮⓬～；三天两头儿地⓭～

1. shift; duty **2.** extremely tired **3.** not get used to **4.** morning shift **5.** replace **6.** middle shift **7.** threshing ground **8.** warehouse **9.** every two days **10.** in succession; in a row; running **11.** by turns **12.** force oneself to do sth. against one's will **13.** every other day; almost every day

③ happen to ≃ 正当〔～宾〕〈名〉正～外出❶期间，我孩子得了肝炎❷；正～校庆❸，同学们相聚在一起，真是非常高兴〔**状～**〕正～

1. go out **2.** contract (have) hepatitis **3.** anniversary of the founding of a school or college

zhíde 值得 be worth; merit; deserve ≃ 值〔**主～**〕〈动〉年轻的时候多学点东西很～，将来用处很多；出去旅行❶很～，可以增长知识❷；要买就买好的，多花点钱也～〔**～宾**〕〈动〉那本词典～买；那个电影～看；他的经验❸～推广❹；她那种刻苦❺精神❻～学习；小张的遭遇❼～同情❽；这个意见～重视❾；自然博物馆❿～参观；他们提⓫的方案⓬～研究；这点小事不～争吵⓭；这个生动⓮感人⓯的题材⓰，很～去写；他的作风⓱～赞许⓲；那个人的行为⓳～怀疑⓴；历史的经验～注意；他的建议㉑～考虑㉒；李叔叔的一番话㉓～深思㉔；这个问题～讨论；那个音乐会㉕真～去听一听〔**状～**〕确实～；特别～；非常～；相当㉖～；一点也不～；完全～；根本㉗不～

1. go out for travel (journey) **2.** broaden (enrich) one's knowledge **3.** experience **4.** spread **5.** assiduous; hard working; painstaking **6.** spirit **7.** misfortune; hard luck **8.** sympathy **9.** attach importance to; think highly of **10.** museum of natural history **11.** put forward **12.** scheme; plan; programme **13.** quarrel; wrangle **14.** lively; vivid **15.** moving; touching **16.** subject matter; theme **17.** style of work **18.** praise; commendation **19.** behaviour action; conduct **20.** doubt; suspect **21.** suggestions **22.** think over; consider **23.** talk; word **24.** ponder deeply over; think deeply about **25.** concert **26.** quite; fairly; considerably **27.** at all; simply

zhǐ 止 ① stop ≃ 停止〔**～宾**〕〈名〉～血❶；游人～步❷〈动〉～痛❸；～痒❹；～渴❺；～咳❻；

～泻❼〔～补〕〈结〉血～住了没有？〈程〉这种药❽止疼❾～得很快〈可〉咳嗽❿起来就～不住〔**状～**〕马上～；很快～；一下子就～

1. stop bleeding **2.** no visitors; out of bounds **3.** relieve pain; stop pain **4.** stop the itching **5.** quench one's thirst **6.** relieve a cough **7.** antidiarrheal **8.** medicine **9.** relieve pain **10.** cough

② to; till 〔**到…止**〕到下午五点～；到去年年底(为)～❶；到第10页～❷

1. up to the end of last year **2.** to page ten

zhǐ 指 ① indicate; point out; point at 〔**～宾**〕〈名〉～墙上的画儿；时针❶正～十二点；不要～东～西❷的；用手～人不礼貌❸〈代〉我～着他说；这话不是～你说❹的〔**～补**〕〈结〉时针正好～到十二点；～给我看；～向前方；他～出了我的毛病〈趋〉我有什么缺点❺请你给～出来〈程〉医生给他测❻视力❼的时候，他指方向～得都不对；～得很准❽；～得很慢〈可〉我～不出他的缺点；指南针❾有毛病，方向老～不准〈时〉这个字老师～了半天，我都没想起来念什么〈量〉她用教鞭❿～了一下儿黑板上的字〔**状～**〕往上～；向远处～；一一⓫～出；用教鞭～着；用手～着

1. hands of a clock or watch **2.** ... here ... there **3.** impolite **4.** not directed at you **5.** weakness **6.** test **7.** eyesight **8.** accurate **9.** compass **10.** (teacher's) pointer **11.** one by one

② depend on; count on ≌ 依靠，指望〔**～宾**〕〈代〉全❶～着你们帮忙了；这件事光❷～我一个人可不行；现在就～你出来说句公道话❸了〔**～补**〕〈可〉做饭❹可～不了(liǎo)她，她什么也不会〔**状～**〕一向❺～；一直❻～；从不～；总～别人；全～着大家呢；净～；单～一个人可不行

1. completely **2.** only; merely **3.** to be fair; in fairness to sb. **4.** do the cooking; prepare a meal **5.** consistently; all along **6.** all the time; always

zhǐdǎo 指导 guide; direct 〔**～宾**〕〈名〉～学生做实验❶；～中学生写作❷；～护士❸护理❹病人；导师❺～研究生❻写毕业论文❼；老艺人❽～青年工人雕刻❾〔**～补**〕〈结〉他都～错了〈趋〉他～起学生来很有办法❿〈程〉～得很细致⓫；～得很有经验⓬〈可〉他那两下子⓭～不了(liǎo)别人；她～不出什么名堂⓮来〈时〉～了三年，我总算⓯有了点儿进步〈量〉～了两次，她就全掌握⓰了；请你好好～一下儿〔**状～**〕耐心地⓱～；好好～～；热心⓲～；给他～；多多～；严格⓳～；认真⓴～；主动㉑～；积极㉒～；热情地㉓～；一遍一遍地㉔～；在这个问题上～

1. do an experiment; make a test 2. writing 3. nurse 4. tend and protect; nurse 5. tutor; teacher 6. post-graduate (student) 7. dissertation 8. actor or artist 9. carve; engrave 10. skill; ability; capability 11. meticulous; careful 12. experience 13. a few tricks of the trade 14. result; achievement 15. after all; finally 16. master; grasp; know well 17. with patience 18. warmly 19. strictly 20. seriously; conscientiously 21. on one's own initiative 22. actively 23. enthusiastically; ardently 24. one after another

zhǐdiǎn 指点 give directions

〔～宾〕〈名〉～着织女星❶给我看〈代〉这孩子什么都不懂，请您好好～～他〔补〕〈结〉他把织女星～给我看〈趋〉我有哪些毛病请您不客气地❷给我～出来〈程〉～得很清楚〈可〉～不出什么来；我～不了(liǎo)你〈量〉我写毛笔❸字,伯父❹给我～过好几次了；请您给～一下儿〔状～〕好好～～；不客气地～；细心地❺～；耐心地❻～；热情地❼～；已经～出来了；多次～；从头至尾地❽～；认真～

1. Vega (α Lyrae) 2. bluntly 3. writing brush 4. uncle 5. meticulously; carefully 6. patiently; with patience 7. warmly; enthusiastically 8. from beginning to end

zhǐdìng 指定 appoint; assign

〔～宾〕〈名〉你～一个人吧；你们～一个地方开会吧；由教授❶～时间〈代〉主任❷～他去；～她负责❸这项工作〔补〕〈结〉地点～在哪儿?〈量〉时间，地点，双方各～一次〔状～〕由谁～?早已～；无法～；单独❹～；共同～；给我们～

1. professor 2. director; head; chairman 3. be in charge of 4. alone; by oneself

zhǐhuī 指挥 command; direct; conduct

〔～宾〕〈名〉～军队❶；～交通❷；～乐队❸〔补〕〈结〉～错了〈趋〉～起来一点也不慌乱❹；～起来真紧张❺〈程〉～得秩序井然❻；～得很熟练❼〈可〉他～不了(liǎo)往来❽的车辆; 他只能指挥合唱队，～不了(liǎo)乐队; 他非常有经验❾，就是闭着眼睛也～不错〈时〉～了二十多年交通〈量〉～过一次军乐队❿〔状～〕盲目地⓫～；熟练地～；从来没～过；有条不紊地⓬～；从从容容地⓭～

1. armed forces; troops 2. traffic; communication 3. orchestra; band 4. not flurried 5. nervous 6. in perfect order; in good order 7. skilful 8. come and go 9. experience 10. military band 11. blindly 12. in an orderly way; systematically 13. calmly; unhurriedly; leisurely

zhǐmíng 指明 show clearly; point out 〔～宾〕〈名〉～出路❶；～原因〔状～〕给他～；已经～；必须～；立即～；再次～

1. way out; outlet

zhǐshǐ 指使 instigate; incite〔～宾〕〈名〉～孩子做坏事〈代〉～他打人；～他破坏团结❶〔～补〕〈量〉～过好多次了〔状～〕受人～；被人～；有意❷；故意❸～；屡次❹～

1. disrupt unity 2. 3. intentionally; purposely 4. over and over again; repeatedly

zhì 至 reach; be until ≅ 到〔～宾〕〈名〉时～今日❶；自始～终❷；早上八点～晚上十点〔状～〕直❸～

1. at this late hour 2. from start to finish; from beginning to end 3. to; till

zhì 治 ① treat (a disease); cure ≅ 医治〔～宾〕〈名〉～病；～伤❶〔～补〕〈结〉病～好了；差点儿❷(没)把人～死〈趋〉伤还没完全好，应该继续❸～下去〈程〉～得效果❹很显著❺；～得很及时❻；～得很彻底❼〈可〉这病哪儿也～不了(liǎo)；骨头❽摔❾折(shé)❿了用这个方法～得好吗；〈时〉皮肤病⓫～了好多年了也没好〈量〉用化学疗法⓬～过好几次了；～一下儿试试〔状～〕彻底⓭～；仔细⓮～；及时⓯～；慢慢～；用各种办法～；连续⓰～；马马虎虎地⓱～；不负责任地⓲～；敷衍了(liǎo)事地⓳～

1. wound 2. almost; nearly 3. continue; go on 4. effect 5. notable; marked 6. in time 7. thorough 8. bone 9. fall; tumble; lose one's balance 10. snapped 11. skin disease 12. chemotherapy 13. thoroughly 14. carefully; meticulously 15. in time 16. in succession; running 17. carelessly 18. irresponsibly 19. perfunctorily

② control; harness (a river); wipe out ≅ 消灭；治理〔～宾〕〈名〉～蝗虫❶；～水〔～补〕〈趋〉说治就～起来了〈程〉～得很及时❷；～得比较彻底❸；～得很有成效❹〈可〉不彻底治就～不好〈时〉了好几年，总算❺治好了〈量〉必须彻底～一下儿；隔两年❻～一次〔状～〕好好～；用杀虫药❼～；积极～；及时～；赶快～；必须～；尽快❽～；努力～

1. locust 2. in time 3. thorough 4. effect; result 5. at long last; finally 6. every third year 7. insecticide; pesticide 8. as soon as possible

zhì 制 make; manufacture ≅ 制造〔～宾〕〈名〉～版❶；～图❷；～糖❸；～药❹〔～补〕〈结〉这张图～坏了〈趋〉～出来的糖都是一个

味儿❺〈程〉这张图～得很好〈可〉～得了(liǎo)～不了(liǎo)〈时〉一张图要～几天?〈量〉～一下儿试试;～过几次〔**状～**〕精心地❻～;仿照别国❼～;用简便的办法❽～;少量❾～;成批地❿～;试着～一点儿

1. printing plate (plate making) **2.** picture (make a drawing or chart) **3.** refine sugar **4.** pharmacy **5.** same taste **6.** meticulously **7.** imitating other countries **8.** a simple and convenient method **9.** a small amount; a little **10.** by batches

zhìdìng 制定 lay down; draw up; formulate; draft

〔**～宾**〕〈名〉～规章❶;～政策❷;～法令❸;～法律❹;～宪法❺;～计划❻;～方案❼;～章程❽;～措施❾〔**～补**〕〈结〉～完了;～出了〈趋〉规章都～出来了〈程〉～得很详细❿〈可〉现在还～不了(liǎo);计划总～不好〈时〉～了不少时候了;～了三年多,才制定出来〈量〉以前～过一次〔**状～**〕认真⓫～;详细⓬～;逐条⓭～;共同～;按照⓮什么标准⓯～?立即⓰～;必须～;重新～

1. rules; regulations **2.** policy **3.** laws and decrees **4.** law; statute **5.** constitution; charter **6.** plan **7.** scheme; plan **8.** rules; regulations; constitution **9.** measure; step **10.** detail; minute **11.** seriously; conscientiously **12.** in detail **13.** article by article; one after another **14.** according to **15.** standard; norm; criterion **16.** at once; immediately

zhìzào 制造 make; manufacture

〔**～宾**〕〈名〉～大炮❶;～火箭❷;～飞船❸;～军舰❹;～货轮❺;～人造卫星❻;～各种设备❼;～各种产品❽;～矛盾❾;～分歧❿;～纠纷⓫;～紧张局势⓬;～惨案⓭;～谣言⓮;～假象⓯;～假现场⓰;～重重障碍⓱;～烟幕⓲;～内乱⓳;～舆论⓴;～借口㉑;～事端㉒〈动〉～分裂㉓〈形〉～混乱㉔〔**～补**〕〈结〉～成了;～出了〈趋〉火箭早就～出来了;他在群众中～出很多矛盾来〈程〉坦克㉕～得不错〈可〉现在很多东西,我们还～不了(liǎo);在我们之间他～不起纠纷来〈时〉一架飞机～了半年〈量〉她～过很多次谣言;先～一下儿舆论〔**状～**〕盲目地㉖～;根据㉗需要～;屡次㉘～;公开㉙～分裂;暗中㉚～内乱;净㉛～矛盾;一再㉜～障碍;别～紧张;竭力㉝～纠纷

1. artillery **2.** rocket **3.** airship; dirigible **4.** warship; navel vessel **5.** freighter; cargo ship **6.** man-made satellite **7.** equipment; installation **8.** product; produce **9.** contradiction **10.** difference; divergence **11.** dispute; issue **12.** a tense situation **13.** massacre; murder case **14.** rumour; groundless allegation **15.** false appearance (create a false impression) 16. false scene 17. one obstacle after another; numerous obstacles 18. smoke screen 19. civil strife; internal disorder 20. public opinion 21. pretext 22. incident; disturbance 23. fission 24. trouble; disturbance 25. tank 26. blindly 27. according to 28. over and over again; repeatedly 29. publicly; openly 30. secretly; in secret 31. only; merely 32. time and again 33. do one's utmost; with all one's might

zhìzhǐ 制止 curb; check; prevent; stop〔~宾〕〈名〉~通货膨胀❶〈代〉~他们这样做〈动〉~侵略❷；~这种事态的发展〔~补〕〈结〉~住了；~晚了〈程〉~得很及时〈可〉这种现象❸至今❹~不住〈量〉想一下儿这种行为❺，但是办不到，~过好几次了〔状~〕竭力❻~；幸亏❼~；赶快~；必须~；及时~

1. check (或 halt) inflation 2. invade; aggression 3. appearance; phenomenon 4. up to now; to this day 5. action; behaviour 6. do one's utmost; use every ounce of one's energy 7. fortunately; luckily

zhì 致 ① send; extend; deliver〔~宾〕〈名〉~函❶；~电❷；请来宾~向大会❹~辞❺〔状~〕向大会~辞

1. letter 2. telegram 3. guest; visitor 4. meeting 5. make a speech

② incur; result in; cause〔~宾〕〈名〉~病；~癌❶；~命的打击❷〈动〉~死的原因❸〔状~〕容易~

1. cancer 2. a deadly blow 3. cause of death

zhòng 中 be hit by; fall into; be affected by; suffer〔~宾〕〈名〉~了圈套儿❶；~了一颗子弹❷；~了奸计❸了；~暑❹了；食物~毒了❺；~了埋伏❻〔~补〕〈可〉空气流通❼就~不了煤气❽了〈量〉~过一次暑，真难受❾〔状~〕千万别~煤气；可别~暑；又~计了

1. fall into a trap 2. a bullet 3. be taken in 4. suffer heatstroke; be affected by the heat 5. food poisoning 6. fall into an ambush 7. circulation of air 8. gas 9. unbearable

zhòng 种 grow; plant; cultivate〔~宾〕〈名〉~树；~水稻❶；~菜；~庄稼❷；~豆子；~西瓜；~棉花❸；小孩都得(děi)~牛痘❹；~地❺〔~补〕〈结〉~晚了；~少了；已经~完了〈程〉~得真多，~得很快；~得不错〈可〉人手❻不够~不完；天太冷~不了(liǎo)〈量〉~过两次西瓜〔状~〕按时❼~；每年都~；按计

划❽～；按季节❾～；现在～〔习用〕～瓜得瓜，～豆得豆❿

1. rice 2. crop 3. cotton 4. give smallpox vaccination 5. field 6. manpower; hand 7. on time; on schedule 8. according to the plan 9. season 10. plant melons and you get melons, sow beans and you get beans — as you sow, so will you reap

zhòngshì 重视 attach importance to; pay attention to ↔ 轻视〔～宾〕〈名〉～这件事；～这个建议❶；～他的意见❷；～研究工作❸；～广告❹的作用〈动〉～医学科学的发展❺；非常～听取意见；～学习〔～补〕〈趋〉对卫生工作❻开始～起来了〈程〉～得不够；～极了〈可〉还～不起来〔状～〕对…～；非常；特别；相当❼；极端❽；一贯❾；不够～；从来不～

1. proposal; suggestion 2. opinion 3. research work 4. advertisement 5. development of medical sciences 6. work of hygiene 7. quite 8. extremely 9. consistently; all along

zhòu 皱 wrinkle; crease〔主～〕〈名〉衣服～了，裙子❶～了〔～宾〕〈名〉～眉(头)❷〔～补〕〈结〉～紧❸眉头〈趋〉又～起眉头来了〈程〉眉头～得很紧〈量〉～了一下儿眉头〔状～〕紧紧地～着眉；成天❹～着眉，不由得❺～起了眉；立刻❻～；忽然～；故意❼～；紧紧地～着

1. skirt 2. knit one's brows 3. tightly 4. all day long; all the time 5. can't help; involuntarily 6. at once 7. on purpose; intentionally

zhǔ 拄 lean on (a stick, etc.)〔～宾〕〈名〉～着棍儿❶；～着拐杖❷〔～补〕〈时〉他病刚好时～过几天拐杖〔状～〕一只手～着；两只手～着

1. stick; rod 2. walking stick

zhǔ 煮 boil; cook〔～宾〕〈名〉～饭；～饺子❶；～肉；～医疗器械❷；～针头❸；～病人用过的东西〔补～〕〈结〉饺子别～破❹了；鸡蛋～嫩❺点儿〈趋〉他～出来的花生米特别香〈程〉～得太烂❻了；～得不软不硬正合适❼；～得火候❽不够；～得过火❾了〈可〉～不熟，～得烂吗？一锅～不了(liǎo)那么多；米多～不下〈时〉还不熟再～一会儿吧〈量〉用这个小锅～过一次；病人用过的东西要好好～一下〔状～〕赶快～吧；容易～吗？一起～；尽量❿～；必须～；先别～；再～一～〔习用〕生米已经～成熟饭了⓫

1. *jiaozi* (dumpling) 2. medical apparatus and instruments 3. syringe needle 4. broken 5. 6.

tender **7.** just suitable **8.** duration and degree of heating, cooking, smelting, etc. **9.** excessive **10.** to the best of one's ability **11.** the rice is cooked — what's done can't be undone

zhǔfu 嘱咐 enjoin; tell; exhort ≃叮嘱〔**～宾**〕〈名〉大人～孩子别玩火；母亲～孩子放学早点回来；医生～病人好好休息；～孩子过马路要小心〈代〉他～我走时把门窗都关好；她～我替她保守秘密❶〔**～补**〕〈结〉什么事情都需要～到了，不然❷就要出事❸〈趋〉一件事情～来～去的总不放心〈时〉每天都需要～半天〈量〉～好几次了，他就是不听；一定要好好～一下儿他〔**状～**〕再三～；一再～；翻来覆去地❹～；刚～完你就忘了；已经～；好好～～；多～几句；临终❺～；一遍一遍地❻～

1. maintain secrecy; keep sth. secret **2.** otherwise **3.** meet with a mishap; have an accident **4.** again and again; repeatedly **5.** immediately before one's death; on one's deathbed **6.** one after another

zhù 住 ① live; reside; stay ≃居住；住宿〔**～宾**〕〈名〉～亲戚❶家；～旅馆❷；～宿舍❸；～公寓❹；～平房❺；～楼上；新房盖好❻还没～人呢；他又～院❼了；～监狱❽〔**～补**〕〈结〉在一个地方～久了，就觉得没意思❾了；旅馆里人都～满了；在这儿先～上几天再说❿；高楼我都～怕了；今天别走了，～下吧；～长了，大家都互相了解了〈趋〉今晚先～下来，明天再去找地方；你就在我这儿安心地⓫～下去吧；你是哪天～进来的，什么病啊？〈程〉房子～得很宽绰⓬；他家～得太挤⓭了；周围环境⓮不好，～得不太舒服⓯；邻居⓰在一起～得很和睦⓱〈可〉房租⓲太贵～不起；在别人家里总～不踏实⓳；突然来了这么多亲戚，我家可～不下；以前的旅馆总是～不满，现在总不够住；他名声不好⓴，在这个地方～不下去了；住在医院里老惦记㉑家，所以有点儿～不下去了〈时〉～了两个月医院；～了十年监狱；再～几天吧！〈量〉～过五次医院〔**状～**〕永久㉒～；长期～；经常㉓～；暂时㉔～；不能久～；临时㉕～；多～几天；再～些日子吧；不便㉖～；不宜㉗～；又～院了；千万别～；好容易～进去了；已经～；早就～；还没～呢

1. relative **2.** hotel **3.** dormitory **4.** apartment **5.** single-storey house; one storey house **6.** build up **7.** be in hospital; be hospitalized **8.** prison **9.** feel lonely **10.** put off until some time later **11.** feel at ease; set one's mind at rest **12.** spacious; commodious **13.** crowded; packed **14.** surroundings **15.** uncomfortable **16.** neighbours **17.** harmonious **18.** rent **19.** not feel relieved **20.** (have) an unsavoury reputation;

be notorious **21.** be anxious about; worry about; keep thinking about **22.** forever **23.** frequently; often **24.** temporarily; for a moment **25.** provisionally; for a short time **26.** **27.** unsuitably

② stop; cease ≌ 停止〔**主～**〕〈名〉风～了；雨还没～〔**～宾**〕〈名〉～手❶！不许❷打人；～口❸！你胡说❹些什么啊！～嘴❺！再骂❻人我打你；刚说到这儿，听见有人来了，就～了口；我上午没～脚地❼走了五个小时；我没～手地❽写，还写不完〔**～补**〕〈可〉这雨还～不了(liǎo)〈时〉～一会儿嘴吧〔**状～**〕赶快～手！一直没～；刚～

1. stop! **2.** not allow **3.** hold your tongue! shut up! **4.** talk nonsense **5.** hold your tongue; shut up! **6.** swear (at people) **7.** without a stop **8.** ceaselessly; incessantly

zhùyì 注意 pay attention to; take note of ↔ 忽略〔**～宾**〕〈名〉～身体；～饮食卫生❶；～营养❷；～这个问题；～礼节❸；～穿着❹；～谈吐❺；～仪表❻；～风度❼；～姿式❽；～长相❾；他一直～着我的行动〈动〉～休息；～保护；～保养❿；～打扮⓫；～遵守⓬交通规则⓭；～养成良好的习惯⓮；～别写错了；～锁车⓯；他说话我没～听〈形〉～安全⓰；～清洁⓱〈主－谓〉没～他长得什么样儿；没～她是什么时候走的；～他在干什么〔**～补**〕〈结〉那个人～上我的钱包了；警察⓲已经～上那个行迹可疑的人⓳了；我已经～到了这个问题〈趋〉直到最近才～起这件事来〈可〉事情太多，有时～不过来，请大家原谅⓴；有些事情我～不到，请你多提醒㉑〈时〉他注意我已经～了不少时候了〈量〉请大家～一下儿；你的身体可得好好儿～一下儿了〔**状～**〕非常～；特别～；一向㉒～；必须～；暗中㉓～；怪不得㉔～我呢！再不～，身体就垮㉕了；过分㉖～；从来不～；密切㉗～

1. dietetic hygiene **2.** nutrition; nourishment **3.** courtesy; etiquette **4.** dress; apparel **5.** style of conversation **6.** bearing; appearance **7.** demeanour; bearing **8.** posture; carriage **9.** looks; features **10.** keep in good repair; take good care of one's health **11.** dress up; make up **12.** observe; abide by **13.** traffic regulations **14.** cultivate good habits **15.** lock the bike **16.** safety **17.** clean **18.** police **19.** a suspicious character **20.** excuse **21.** remind; call attention to **22.** consistently; all along **23.** secretly **24.** no wonder **25.** break down; wear down **26.** excessively **27.** closely

zhù 祝 express good wishes; wish〔**～宾**〕〈名〉～酒❶〈代〉～你学习进步❷；～你万事如意❸；～你幸福❹；～你早日恢复健康❺；～您一路平安❻；～您一帆风顺❼；～你工作顺利❽；～你成功；

～你旅途愉快❾〔～补〕〈结〉～完酒才开始吃饭〈趋〉宴席上❿大家互相～起酒来了〈时〉大家互相～了半天酒〈量〉主人向客人～了一遍酒⓫〔状～〕在宴会上～；站着～酒，举杯⓬～酒，一次一次地～酒；互相～酒

1. drink a toast; toast 2. make progress in study 3. everything goes well 4. happiness 5. recover one's health 6. Bon voyage; pleasant trip 7. have a favourable wind throughout the voyage; plain sailing 8. smooth; without a hitch 9. Have a pleasant journey 10. at a banquet 11. round of drink 12. raise one's glass to toast

zhuā 抓

① grab; seize; clutch ≅ 拿〔～宾〕〈名〉～一点茶叶❶沏茶❷；～一把盐❸放在锅❹里了；她～了一把豆子坐在那里剥❺；他最会～机会❻了；他真会～权❼；～时间〔～补〕〈结〉茶叶～多了；把瓜子都～洒❽了；把桌子上的零钱❾都～走了；她～住我的胳膊❿不放，要～紧时机⓫；把权～在手里〈趋〉盘子里的花生米太多，容易洒，快～下点儿去吧；把这些吃的东西给孩子们～过去一些吧；下完了棋⓬把棋子⓭都～到盒子⓮里去了；她～起帽子来就跑出去了，从钱包里～出一把钱来〈程〉～得太多了；时间他～得真紧⓯；抓权～得很凶⓰〈可〉什么机会都～不着(zháo)；她总是～不住时机〈时〉～了半天也没抓满⓱一盘〔状～〕大把大把地⓲～；从茶叶筒⓳里～茶叶；紧紧地～着；牢牢⓴～着

1. tea; tea-leaves 2. infuse tea; make tea 3. salt 4. pot 5. shell; peel 6. chance; opportunity 7. grab power 8. scattered 9. change 10. arm 11. seize the opportunity 12. after playing chess 13. pieces (in a board game) 14. box 15. make the best use of one's time 16. fierce 17. full 18. one handful after another 19. caddy 20. firmly; safely

② scratch ≅ 挠〔～宾〕〈名〉脸上被指甲❶～了一个道子❷；她打架❸的时候，不是～人就是咬❹人〈动〉小猴子坐在地上～痒❺〔～补〕〈结〉把手～流血❻了；猫把孩子～哭了；别抓了，把手都～破❼了〈趋〉被猫～下一块皮去；小猴子又一起痒来了〈程〉得真疼❽；指甲印❾～得真深；他抓人～得可狠❿了〈可〉～不着(zháo)；～不破〈时〉小猴坐在假山⓫旁边～了半天痒〈量〉让猫～过一次；～一下儿可疼了〔状～〕被猫～了；别让它～着(zháo)；狠狠地～；用力～；拼命⓬～；往脸上～

1. nail; fingernail 2. mark 3. fight 4. bite 5. itch; tickle 6. bleed; shed blood 7. scratched 8. ache; pain 9. print; mark 10. ruthless; relentless 11. rockery 12. with all one's might

③ stress; pay special attention to 〔~宾〕〈名〉做任何事情❶都应该~重点❷；~工作；~大事；~出勤率❸；~学习；~纪律❹〔~补〕〈结〉~住重点,才能学好；~好纪律〈趋〉他~起工作来很有魄力❺；~出成绩❻来了；~出经验❼来了；~出麻烦❽来了〈程〉问题~得不彻底❾；~得很有成绩〈可〉这么多工作,我一个人~不过来；她学习总~不住要点；学习成绩还~不上去；短时间内还~不上来；能力❿太差⓫,什么工作都~不起来〈时〉~了一阵子⓬数学⓭又放下了⓮〈量〉纪律要好好~一下儿〔状~〕大胆(地)⓯~；适当地⓰~；有步骤地⓱~；有重点地~；认真~

1. anything 2. stress the essentials 3. rate of attendance 4. discipline 5. daring and resolution 6. achievement 7. experience 8. trouble 9. not thorough 10. ability 11. poor 12. a period of time 13. mathematics 14. put aside 15. boldly 16. suitably 17. systematically

④ arrest; catch; press-gang ≅ 捉拿；捉；逮〔~宾〕〈名〉~小偷；~流氓❶；~凶手❷；~逃犯❸；老鹰❹~小鸡〔~补〕〈结〉当场❺就把他~走了；看准❻了可别~错了人〈趋〉把逃犯又~回来了；老鹰把小鸡~起来了；~进监狱去了〈程〉~得真快,刚一天就把逃犯抓回来了〈可〉你一个人~得了(liǎo)小偷吗?我怕~不准,所以让你跟我一起去；~不着(zháo)我的任何把柄❼〈时〉~了三天就把逃犯抓回来了；~了一年才把凶手抓住〈量〉~过一次；需要好好~一下儿〈状~〉单独❽~；分头❾~；终于❿~到了；好容易⓫~住了；没费劲⓬就~住了；立即⓭~；赶快~；连夜⓮~；勇敢地⓯~；大胆地⓰~；积极地⓱~；专⓲~；赤手空拳地⓳~；〔习用〕~辫子⓴；~瞎㉑；眉毛胡子一把㉒~

1. rogue 2. murderer 3. escaped criminal 4. eagle; hawk 5. on the spot 6. accurate 7. handle 8. alone; by oneself 9. separately 10. at last; finally 11. with great difficulty 12. need no effort 13. at once; immediately 14. the same night; that very night 15. bravely 16. boldly 17. actively 18. specially 19. barehanded; unarmed 20. seize on sb.'s mistake or shortcoming; capitalize on sb's vulnerable point 21. find oneself at a loss; be in a rush and muddle; be thrown off balance 22. try to grasp the eyebrows and the beard all at once — try to attend to big and small matters all at once

zhuǎn 转 ① turn; shift; change

〔~宾〕〈名〉~身；~头；~弯儿❶〈形〉天气~暖了；天~晴❷了〔~补〕〈结〉~错方向❸了；转头都~晕❹了；转弯都~糊涂❺了〈趋〉~过身来；~过头去；~到

后边去了〈程〉头～得太猛❻了，有点晕; 汽车转弯～得太急❼了; 转身～得真快〈可〉脖子❽受风❾了, 连头都～不过来了〈时〉～了半天弯儿❿, 才说出来〈量〉头稍微⓫向左～一下儿〔**状～**〕由阴⓬～晴, 逐渐⓭～暖, 把头猛地一～; 突然⓮～; 马上～过头去了; 立刻～

1. turn a corner 2. clear up 3. direction 4. dizzy 5. muddled; confused 6. sudden; abrupt 7. quick; fast 8. neck 9. catch cold 10. speak in a roundabout way 11. a little; a bit 12. overcast 13. gradually 14. suddenly

② transfer; pass on 〔～**宾**〕〈名〉～学❶; ～系❷; ～业❸; ～帐❹; ～车; ～户口❺; ～一次手❻〔～**补**〕〈结〉请把这封信～给他; 这批货❼已经～到我们手里了; 我把那笔帐～错了; 户口已经～完了〈趋〉把帐都～过来了; 她～到历史系❽来了; 我的户口～回来了; ～到家里去了〈程〉转学～得很顺利❾; 转车～得很费劲儿❿; 这笔帐～得乱七八糟的⓫〈可〉他哥哥今年还～不了(liǎo)业〈时〉～了半天学也没转成〈量〉每天上下班要～好几次车; 请你给我～一下儿帐〔**状～**〕马上⓬～; 在哪儿～车? 帐全部～过去; 尽快⓭～

1. transfer to another school 2. department 3. (of an armyman) be transferred to civilian work 4. accounts 5. report to the local authorities for change of domicile 6. pass on 7. goods 8. department of history 9. (transfer to another school) smoothly; successfully; without a hitch 10. take a lot of trouble 11. in a mess; in a muddle 12. at once; immediately 13. as soon as possible

zhuǎnbiàn 转变 change; transform 〔**主～**〕〈名〉思想～了, 立场❶～了; 态度❷～了; 世界观❸～了; 风向❹～了〈代〉他～了〔～**宾**〕〈名〉要～立场〔～**补**〕〈结〉把一种能❺～为另一种能〈程〉～得很好, ～得很快〔**状～**〕彻底❻～; 突然❼～; 是怎么～的? 必须～; 已经～了; 终于～了; 慢慢～; 逐渐～

1. position 2. attitude 3. world outlook 4. wind direction 5. energy 6. thoroughly 7. suddenly

zhuǎnrù 转入 change over to; shift to; switch to 〔～**宾**〕〈名〉～敌后❶; ～地下❷; ～第二学期❸〈动〉～防御❹〈形〉～正常❺〔**状～**〕已经～; 正在～; 还没～; 就要～; 部分❻～; 全部～

1. enemy's rear area 2. underground 3. the second semester 4. defence 5. normal 6. partly

zhuǎnyí 转移 shift; transfer; divert 〔**主～**〕〈名〉部队❶～了;

工作重点❷～了〔～宾〕〈名〉～方向❸；～视线❹；～目标❺；～注意力❻；～阵地❼〔～补〕〈结〉～好了；～走了〈趋〉～到山洞❽里去了〈程〉～得非常迅速❾；～得太慢了〈可〉谁也～不了(liǎo)她的注意力〈时〉～了好几天才转移完〈量〉～一下儿；～了好几次〔状～〕必须～；赶快～；立即❿～；提前⓫～；偷偷地⓬～

1. troops; army **2.** focal point of the work **3.** direction **4.** line of vision; line of sight **5.** goal; aim; objective **6.** attention **7.** position **8.** cave; cavern **9.** quick **10.** at once **11.** ahead of time **12.** secretly; stealthily

zhuàn 转 turn; revolve; rotate

≃旋转；转动；转悠〔主～〕〈名〉地球绕着太阳～❶；狗围着❷主人～；老鹰❸在天上来回～；风车❹被风吹得直～；眼珠❺左右乱～；药房❻的药架子❼可以～；有一个形迹可疑的❽人在他家门口来回～〔～宾〕〈名〉他在那儿直～圈❾儿；那个人急得❿直～磨⓫〔～补〕〈结〉我都～晕⓬了；去了几个地方都～累了；所有的地方我都～到了，也没买着(zháo)〈趋〉你在这儿～过来～过去，要找谁啊？转了半天又～回原来的⓭地方来了〈程〉～得头晕眼花⓮；～得心里直难受⓯；～得真累；～得真猛；车轮～得很快〈可〉她太胖⓰，～不动了〈时〉～了半天，一个人也没找着(zháo)〈量〉～了那么多圈儿她都不晕；我～一下儿就恶心⓱了〔状～〕向左～；直～；猛⓲～；地球永远围着太阳～；飞快地⓳～；一个劲地⓴～；不停地～；日夜㉑～；一直㉒～；顺着一个方向㉓～；顺时针㉔（逆时针㉕）～

1. the earth revolves round the sun **2.** surround **3.** eagle **4.** wind mill **5.** eyeball **6.** drugstore **7.** shelf **8.** of suspicious appearance **9.** turn round **10.** be impatient; be anxious **11.** move from side to side **12.** dizzy; giddy **13.** original **14.** be dazzling **15.** feel unwell **16.** fat **17.** vomit **18.** vigorously; violently **19.** very fast **20.** continuously; persistently **21.** day and night **22.** all the time; always **23.** in the same direction as; with **24.** clockwise **25.** counter clockwise; anticlockwise

zhuàn 赚 make a profit; gain

↔赔〔～宾〕〈名〉做买卖❶～了一大笔钱；他做这么多年生意❷也没～多少钱；他给别人买东西～了人家很多钱〔～补〕〈程〉钱～得太多了〈量〉～过一次大钱〔状～〕经常～；容易～；好～；难～；多（少）～；又～；从来没～过

1. buying and selling; business; deal **2.** business; trade

zhuāng 装 load; pack; hold

≃放入↔卸〔～宾〕〈名〉这些产品❶今天～箱❷，明天就要运❸走了；这车全部～行李❹；这个仓库❺

能～多少粮食❻？～武器❼；～弹药❽；～军火❾；用饼干盒❿～饼干；书柜⓫～书；瓶子里可以～药⓬；往烟斗⓭里～烟丝⓮〔**～补**〕〈结〉这一盒～满了；枪膛⓯里已经～上子弹⓰了；奶粉⓱～在哪个瓶子里了？这瓶药～少了；别～错了；书都～乱⓲了；这一车行李要～到什么时候才完啊！〈趋〉把家具⓳先～上车来吧；天都黑了今天晚上车还要～下去吗？这一车～下来还得(děi)半个小时；把衣服都～进来了；先把东西～起来再说；把这些桌、椅都～到那辆车上去吧〈程〉～得很快；～得太慢了；口袋⓴～得鼓鼓的㉑；这一车人～得满满的〈可〉东西太多～不下；东西少～不满；一个小时～不完；人少～不过来；东西太大了～不进去；你一个人～得了(liǎo)吗？〈时〉这一车货～了好几个小时才装完；再～一会儿就休息〈量〉～过好几次车，没装过船；我装不进去了，快帮我～一下儿〔**状～**〕七手八脚地㉒～；匆匆忙忙地㉓～；勉强㉔～下了；实在㉕～不了(liǎo)了；马马虎虎地㉖～；仔细点儿㉗～；都白㉘～了；随便㉙～；装不下去别硬㉚～；重新㉛～；并排㉜～；这块地方不够～

1. products **2.** pack a box; put sth. in a crate **3.** transport **4.** luggage **5.** warehouse **6.** grain **7.** weapon; arms **8.** ammunition **9.** munitions; arms and ammunition **10.** use biscuit box **11.** bookcase **12.** medicine **13.** pipe **14.** tobacco **15.** bore (of a gun) **16.** bullet **17.** milk powder **18.** in disorder **19.** furniture **20.** pocket **21.** bulge; swell **22.** with everybody lending a hand **23.** in a hurry **24.** reluctantly **25.** really; truly **26.** carelessly **27.** carefully **28.** in vain **29.** casually; at random **30.** manage to do sth. with difficulty **31.** again **32.** side by side

② install; fit; assemble ≃ 安装；组装〔**～宾**〕〈名〉～电灯；～暖气❶；～煤气❷；～喇叭❸；～锁❹；～电话；～收音机〔**～补**〕〈结〉暖气～上了；锁～歪了❺；电灯再～高点就好了〈趋〉快把车铃❻～上去吧；自己～出来（～起来）的电视不行〈程〉～得真快；～得不错；～得太高了〈可〉自己～不了(liǎo)；～不起来〈时〉～了半天也没装上；这个电视机我们整整～了一年〈量〉电灯我自己～过好几次了；她让我帮她～一下儿〔**状～**〕在墙上～；往哪儿～？熟练地❼～；给别人～；赶快～；慢慢～；再～一个

1. central heating **2.** coal gas fittings **3.** loudspeaker **4.** lock **5.** askew; slanting **6.** bell of a bicycle **7.** skillfully

③ dress up; attire; play the part (role) of ≃ 扮；演；当〔**～宾**〕〈名〉～老头儿❶；～坏蛋；～哑吧❷；～聋子❸；～疯子❹；～仆人❺；～送信的❻；～法官❼〔**～补**〕〈结〉～成哑吧；～作盲人

❽〈趋〉又～起老太太来了〈程〉～得真象；～得一点儿也不象〈可〉他装谁也～不象〈量〉在那个剧❾里他～过一次军医❿〔状～〕总～不好；偶尔⓫～；经常～；初次～；在哪个戏⓬里～？

1. old man **2.** a dumb person; mute **3.** a deaf person **4.** lunatic; madman **5.** servant **6.** postman; mailman **7.** judge **8.** blind person **9.** play **10.** medical officer; military surgeon **11.** occasionally; once in a while **12.** play; drama

④ pretend; feign; make believe ≃装作；假装〔**～宾**〕〈名〉～样子❶；～好人〈动〉～疯❷；～聋❸；～哑❹；～病；～懂；～死；～不知道；～不认识〈形〉～穷；～傻；～糊涂❺〔**～补**〕〈结〉～成生气的样子；～作有学问❻的样子；～出一幅可怜相❼〈趋〉总～出恭恭敬敬的样子❽来；她又～起病来了〈程〉～得太利害了；～得不象〈可〉心里不高兴装笑也～不出来〈时〉～了半天样子〈量〉那个孩子想～一下儿病，结果❾让妈妈发现了〔**状～**〕净❿～穷；不懂可别～懂；又～病；故意⓫～；从来不～；假～〔**习用**〕～蒜⓬；～门面⓭

1. assume certain look **2.** feign madness **3.** pretend to be deaf **4.** pretend to be mute **5.** feign ignorance **6.** learned **7.** pitiable look **8.** respectful look **9.** as a result **10.** always; all the time **11.** intentionally; on purpose **12.** pretend not to know; feign ignorance **13.** maintain an outward show; keep up appearances

zhuàng 撞 bump against; run into; strike; collide ≃ 碰〔**～宾**〕〈名〉汽车～人了；今天又～车了；我往外跑❶，他往里跑❷，我们两个人～了一个满怀❸；他用头～墙❹，想自杀❺；头上～了一个大包❻〔**～补**〕〈结〉树被汽车～倒了；车把那个老奶奶❼～伤❽了；差点❾没～死；船～沉❿了；～翻⓫了；～疼⓬了吧？都～肿⓭了；走路看书，结果头～在电线杆子⓮上了；孩子摔了一交⓯，头～在桌子角上了〈趋〉他喝醉⓰了，一头～进来（～进去），就倒在床上了；人被汽车～出去好远；人真多，～来～去地没法儿买东西〈程〉～得真疼；～得利害不利害？～得鼻青脸肿⓱；～得头破血流⓲；～得晕头转向⓳；～得眼睛直冒金星⓴〈可〉离马路远点㉑儿就～不着(zháo)了〈量〉离汽车远远的，～一下儿可不得了(liǎo)㉒〔**状～**〕猛㉓～；不小心～；让谁～了？被什么～的；互相～；差一点儿～；几乎～；正好～；刚巧㉔～；眼看㉕就～上了

1. run out **2.** run in **3.** bump right into sb. **4.** bump against a wall **5.** commit suicide **6.** swelling **7.** granny **8.** wounded **9.** almost; nearly **10.** sunken **11.** turned turtle; capsized **12.** ache; pain; sore **13.** swollen **14.** (wire) pole **15.** tumble; trip and fall **16.** be drunk **17.** a bloody nose and a swollen face; badly battered **18.** run into bumps and bruises; break one's neck **19.** lose one's head (or bearings); muddledheaded **20.** see stars **21.** far away from the street **22.** desperately serious; disastrous **23.** violently; vigorously **24.** just right **25.** soon

zhuī 追 chase (run) after; pursue 〔**～宾**〕〈名〉～小偷；～流氓❶；～逃犯❷；～杀人凶手❸；～兔子；～被风刮跑❹的帽子〔**～补**〕〈结〉这孩子的个子❺长得真高，都快～上他爸爸了；看见小偷跑了，大家就～开了；坏人被～急了，从地上捡起❻一块砖头❼扔❽了过来；一直～到很远的地方才停下来〈趋〉5号运动员❾～上来了；他虽然缺了课❿，但非常用功，成绩一下子就～上来了；孩子们在院子里～来～去，玩得非常高兴；我忘了带房门钥匙⓫，妈妈从楼上～下来了；从五楼⓬一直～下去，也没追上他；他～进来跟我要钱；把小偷～进死胡同⓭里去了；一阵风似地⓮～出来了；我都走得很远了，她又～过来告诉了我一句话；8号运动员把所有的人都～过去了；大家一齐⓯～起那个坏蛋来了；我追他都～过桥去了；～到树林里去了〈程〉～得真快；～得很远；追他～得累死了⓰；～得上气不接下气⓱的；～得直喘⓲；～得腿都软了⓳〈可〉不知他跑到哪儿去了，看样子⓴～不着(zháo)了；他学得比我好，我怎么努力也～不上他；她已经走远了，你～不上了；老人看(kān)孩子不行，孩子在前边跑老人～不了(liǎo)〈时〉～了很长时间才把落下的功课补上㉑〈量〉～了一阵㉒也没追上〔**状～**〕赶快～；一直～；猛㉓～；拼命㉔～；骑车㉕～；别～；一齐～；从后边～；一阵风似地～

1. hoodlum; hooligan; rogue **2.** escaped criminal **3.** murderer **4.** blow away **5.** height; stature **6.** pick up **7.** a lump of brick **8.** throw **9.** sportsman No. 5 **10.** miss a class **11.** forget to bring the key to the door **12.** from the fifth floor **13.** blind alley; dead end **14.** like a gust of wind **15.** in unison **16.** tired to death **17.** gasp for breath; be out of breath **18.** breathe heavily; pant **19.** legs feel like jelly **20.** judging from appearance **21.** make up for the missed lessons **22.** a period of time **23.** fiercely; violently **24.** desperately **25.** by bike

zhuīqiú 追求 seek; pursue 〔**～宾**〕〈名〉～真理❶；～西方❷的生活方式❸；～名誉❹；～地位❺〈动〉～享受❻〈形〉～光明❼；～自由❽〔**～补**〕〈结〉没～上〈趋〉～起名利❾来了〈程〉～得太着急❿了；～得过分⓫了；～得过火⓬了〈可〉～不上；～不着(zháo)〈时〉～了很长时间；～了不少年〈量〉～过两次；～一下儿试试〔**状**

～〕不必～；一直⓭～；一心⓮～；一味⓯～；狂热地⓰～；再次～

1. seek truth; be in pursuit of truth 2. the West 3. way of life; life style 4. fame; reputation 5. status 6. enjoyment 7. bright 8. freedom 9. fame and gain 10. be impatient; be anxious 11. undue; excessive; over 12. go too far 13. all the time; always continuously 14. whole-heartedly; heart and soul 15. blindly 16. fanatically

zhǔnbèi 准备 ① prepare; get ready ≅ 预备〔**～宾**〕〈名〉明天的客人不是外人，用不着～太多东西；～点钱假期去旅行〔**～补**〕〈结〉发言稿❶已经～完了；功课～晚了；一定要把钱～充分❷；带走的东西都～齐了吗？路上喝的水一定要～充足❸；这么早就～上年货❹了〈趋〉饭菜都～出来了〈程〉功课～得很好；吃的东西～得太多了；～得真齐全；～得不算晚〈可〉时间太短～不完；演讲❺稿～不好；心里乱糟糟的❻，～不下去了〈时〉这几句外语～了半天没用上；多～一会儿吧〈量〉再好好～一下儿，明年再考〔**状～**〕认真❼～；及时❽～；随时❾～；尽量❿～；提前⓫～～；精心⓬～；全面⓭～；重点⓮～；从头到尾⓯～；好容易⓰～完了；白⓱～了；专心致志地⓲～；踏踏实实地⓳～；充分地⓴～；临时㉑～

1. the text of a statement of speech 2. abundant; full 3. adequate; sufficient 4. special purchases for the Spring Festival 5. lecture; speech 6. confused; perturbed (feel all hot and bothered) 7. seriously; conscientiously 8. in time 9. at any time; at all times 10. to the best of one's ability 11. ahead of time 12. meticulously; carefully 13. in an all-round way 14. emphatically 15. from beginning to end 16. with much difficulty 17. in vain 18. with single-hearted devotion 19. steadily and surely 20. fully 21. provisionally

② intend; plan ≅ 打算〔**～宾**〕〈动〉～坐飞机去；～毕了业❶再结婚❷；～买一辆轻便摩托车❸；～学画画儿❹；～请你给我刻一个图章❺；～照几张相❻寄❼给他；～写一篇文章❽；～反攻❾〔**状～**〕本来～乘❿飞机去；最近～

1. after graduation 2. get married 3. light motorbike 4. draw a picture 5. engrave a seal 6. take several pictures 7. send 8. article; essay 9. counter offensive 10. travel by

zhuō 捉 clutch; hold; grasp ≅ 抓；逮↔放〔**～宾**〕〈名〉～贼❶；～老鼠；～蝴蝶❷；～田鸡❸；～敌人❹；～逃犯❺；～活的❻〔**～补**〕〈结〉贼～着(zháo)了没有？把敌人～住了；看好了可别～错了人〈程〉他～得真多，一会就捉了十只〈可〉他一只麻雀❼也～不着

(zháo)〈时〉昨天～了一天知了❽〈量〉～过好多次青蛙❾〔状～〕好不好～?; 用网❿～; 在夜里～; 容易～

1. thief 2. butterfly 3. frog 4. enemy 5. escaped criminal 6. capture sb. alive 7. sparrow 8. cicada 9. frog 10. net

zhuōmō 捉摸 fathom; ascertain ≅ 揣摩〔～补〕〈可〉这个人的性格❶我有点儿～不透❷〔状～〕简直❸～不出来; 不可～; 怎么也～不透, 真难～; 难以❹～; 仔细～; 始终～不透

1. character 2. can't get to know 3. simply; at all 4. difficult to

zhuóxiǎng 着想 consider (the interests of sb. or sth.) ≅ 考虑〔状～〕应该多为别人～; 为今后❶的前途❷～; 你什么时候替我们～过?

1. from now on; in the days to come 2. future; prospect

zhuóyǎn 着眼 have sth. in mind: see (view) from the angle of 〔～补〕〈结〉不要只考虑眼前❶, 还要～于未来❷; 不能只～于一个方面❸, 忽略❹另一方面〔状～〕要从大处❺～; 从全局❻～, 应该从积极❼方面～

1. think of the present 2. future ... aspect 4. neglect 5. from

the general goal 6. in the interests of the whole 7. positive

zhuó 啄 peck〔～宾〕〈名〉鸟～食❶; 鸡～米; 啄木鸟❷～虫吃〔～补〕〈结〉把虫子都～死了〔状～〕专❸～虫子吃

1. feed 2. woodpecker 3. specially

zì 渍 be soiled (with grease, etc.) 〔～宾〕〈名〉机器❶上～了很多油泥❷〔～补〕〈结〉茶缸❸里面都～黄了❹; 炉灶❺上～满了油泥〈趋〉油泥都～到指甲❻里去了〈程〉～得很厚❼〈可〉做完饭就擦❽炉台❾, 一点油泥也～不上〈量〉～过好几次了〔状～〕厚厚地❿～了一层; 薄薄地⓫～了一层; 全部～上了

1. machine 2. greasy filth 3. mug 4. become brown 5. kitchen range; cooking range 6. finger nail 7. thick 8. wipe; clean 9. the top of a kitchen range 10. thickly 11. thinly

zǒu 走 ① walk; go ≅ 走路; 步行〔主～〕〈名〉车往前～; 船在大海里～; 马怎么突然❶不～了?孩子会～了, 病人能～了, 坐了一整天, 我们出去～～吧!〔～宾〕〈名〉～弯路❷; ～回头路❸; ～冤枉路❹; 别～绝路❺; 山里人❻最能～山路; 我最怕～夜路❼; 他们～水路❽还是～陆路❾; ～

平坦大道❿；～泥路⓫；你们是坐汽车去，还是～路去？学习不能～捷径⓬；那个杂技演员⓭会～钢丝⓮，也会～绳索〔 **～补** 〕〈结〉这段路～冤了；孩子～丢⓯了；大家的脚步要～齐⓰；我们大家一起出来的，现在都～散⓱了；我们两个人的路～岔⓲了，没遇上⓳；羊群里～失⓴了一只羊；～遍全国也找不到这么好的啊！〈趋〉～下山去了；她正从楼上～下来；用这个速度㉑～下去，走到半夜也到不了；从外边～进来了；刚～回来，又～回去了；～进死胡同㉒里去了〈程〉老年人走路～得真费劲㉓〈可〉走路谁也～不过他；累得我一点儿也～不动了；路那么远，一个小时～得到～不到？背那么多东西都～不进来了；桥那么窄㉔，汽车～得过来吗？〈时〉坐船～几天才能到〈量〉到全国各地～了一圈㉕；～了几个来回㉖〔**状～**〕昂首阔步地㉗～；大摇大摆地㉘～；独自㉙～；慢慢腾腾地㉚～；蹓蹓跶跶地㉛～；来回～；往前～；多～了三里；踉踉跄跄地㉜～；随便㉝～～；视而不见地㉞从我身边～过；拔腿就㉟～；迎面㊱～来；蹑着脚㊲～出病房㊳

1. suddenly **2.** take a roundabout route; make a detour **3.** turn back; retrace one's steps **4.** go the long way **5.** road to ruin; impasse; blind alley **6.** mountaineer **7.** night road **8.** water route **9.** land route **10.** smooth road **11.** muddy road **12.** take a shortcut **13.** acrobat **14.** walk the wire **15.** lost **16.** uniform; in step **17.** scattered; separated **18.** diverged **19.** meet; encounter **20.** lost **21.** speed **22.** impasse **23.** use or make great effort **24.** narrow **25.** go around **26.** back and forth; to and fro **27.** stride forward with one's chin up; stride proudly ahead **28.** strutting; swaggering **29.** alone; by oneself **30.** slowly **31.** stroll **32.** staggering **33.** casually; at random **34.** look but see not; turn a blind eye to **35.** start walking at once **36.** head-on; in one's face **37.** walk on tiptoe; lighten (one's step) **38.** ward

② depart from the original; lose the original shape , flavour, etc.

〔**～宾**〕〈名〉他唱歌爱～调儿❶；上课别～神儿❷；刚穿两天，这双鞋就～样儿❸了；这话传❹来传去就～样儿❺了；他一时不慎❻，把枪弄～火儿❼了；茶叶❽放在盒子里不盖❾盖儿❿就～味儿⓫了；大红纸晒⓬得都～色⓭(shǎi)了；这东西都～型⓮了；是不是电线⓯～火⓰了？你说话又～题⓱了；他这篇文章写得很好，就是～题了〔 **～补** 〕〈 程 〉走色(shǎi)～得太利害了， 刚一个星期，红纸都快变成白纸了〈可〉盖上盖儿茶叶就～不了(liǎo)味了〈时〉她～了半天神〈量〉上课的时候，我刚～了一下儿神，老师就叫我〔**状～**〕又～调了；净⓲～神儿；突然⓳～火了；别～题

1. out of tune 2. distract one's attention 3. lose shape; go out of form 4. spread 5. be distorted 6. not wary; cautious; or careful 7. discharge accidentally 8. tea 9. cover; put on 10. lid; cover 11. lose flavour 12. be exposed to the sun 13. lose colour; fade 14. lose shape; go out of form 15. electric wire 16. sparking 17. digress from the subject; stray from the point 18. always 19. suddenly

③ visit; call on ≅ 访问, 往来〔~宾〕〈名〉~娘家❶; ~亲戚❷〔~补〕〈结〉现在我们两家~远了〈趋〉以前他跟谁都没有来往❸, 现在也~起亲戚来了〈程〉他们两家~得很近; 我们和我姨❹家~得很远〔状~〕经常❺~; 不常~; 偶尔❻~

1. a married woman's parents' home 2. relative 3. dealings; contact 4. aunt 5. often; frequently 6. occasionally; once in a while

④ run; move ≅ 移动, 挪动〔主~〕〈名〉钟不~了; 表❶又~了〔~宾〕〈名〉~了一个棋子❷〔~补〕〈结〉这步棋~错了〈趋〉表擦完油泥❸又~起来了; 棋子~出去, 就不许拿回来了〈程〉这步棋~得真好; ~得很有策略❹; 表~得很准❺〈可〉钟坏了, ~不了(liǎo)了〈时〉~一个多小时还没走完一盘棋〈量〉这表刚~两下儿又停了〔状~〕连续❻~了两步

1. watch 2. piece (in a board game) 3. cleaning and oiling 4. tactful 5. keep good time 6. in succession

⑤ leave; go away ≅ 离去〔主~〕〈名〉卖东西的吆喝❶了几声就~了〈代〉时间不早了, 我们该~了; 他没带❷钱就~了〔~补〕〈结〉今天~晚了, 非迟到❸不可; 今天上班我~早了, 走的时候天还没亮呢? 〈程〉每天下班他都~得最晚〈可〉家里有病人, 我~不出去; 你可~不得, 你走了别人哄❹不好这个孩子〈时〉刚~一会儿, 就出事❺了〈量〉对不起, 请你~一下儿〔状~〕别~了, 早就~了, 还没~呢

1. cry one's wares 2. bring; carry 3. be late 4. handle; coax 5. meet with a mishap; have an accident

⑥ leak; let out; escape ≅ 漏出, 透漏〔~宾〕〈名〉本来想瞒❶着他, 可是一下子没注意❷说~嘴了❸〔~补〕〈结〉别~漏了风声❹; ~漏了消息❺〔状~〕千万别~〔习用〕三十六计, ~为上计❻; ~着瞧❼

1. hide the truth from 2. inadvertently 3. blurt out 4. divulge a secret 5. leak information 6. of the 36 stratagems, the best is running away — the best thing to do now is to quit 7. wait and see

zòu 奏 play (music); perform (on a musical instrument) 〔~宾〕〈名〉~乐; ~国歌❶〔~补〕〈结〉

~完了国歌，大家就坐下了；别~错了〈趋〉用钢琴❷~出来的曲子❸非常好听〈程〉~得真齐❹；~得不好〈可〉这个曲子他还~不好〈量〉这支曲子只~过一次；~了两遍〔状~〕已经~；正在~；远处在~

1. national anthem 2. piano 3. tune 4. uniform; neat; even

zòu 揍 beat; hit; strike ≅ 打〔~宾〕〈名〉别~孩子〔~补〕〈结〉差点没~死；把脸都~肿❶了；把腿❷~瘸❸了〈趋〉~下去可受不了❹(liǎo)；~上去可就不轻❺〈程〉~得太利害了；~得直叫❻；~得起不来床了〈可〉~不了(liǎo)；~不着(zháo)〈量〉~过几次；~了一顿；~了两个耳光❼；~了一拳❽〔状~〕狠狠地❾；一拳~下去就得吐血❿；用棍子⓫~；拼命地~；气呼呼地⓬~；眼看着~；揪⓭着头皮~；假装⓮~

1. be swollen 2. leg 3. be lame; limp 4. unbearable 5. serious 6. cry; yell 7. slap on the face; a box on the ear 8. give a punch 9. ruthlessly 10. spitting blood 11. stick 12. in a huff; panting with rage 13. pull; drag; tug 14. pretendedly

zū 租 rent; hire; charter 〔~宾〕〈名〉~房子；~汽车；~照相机❶；~书；~船；~剧场❷；~电影院❸；~家具❹〔~补〕〈结〉房子~着(zháo)了没有？汽车已经~好了；书~多了看不完〈趋〉把整幢楼❺都~下来了；把这几间房子都~过来了〈可〉去晚了就~不着(zháo)了，太贵~不起；一千块钱也~不下来；这房子地点❻不好，老~不出去；花❼多少钱也~不过来；这么多人租船，一上午也~不上〈时〉你们要~多长时间？这房子~了半年才租上〈量〉那个电影院我们~过一次；你再去~一下儿试试〔状~〕怎么~？经常~；千万别❽~；只好~；没~过

1. camera 2. theatre 3. cinema 4. furniture 5. whole building 6. place; site; locale 7. spend 8. be sure not to

zǔ'ài 阻碍 hinder; block; impede 〔~宾〕〈名〉~交通❶〔状~〕别~；一直❷~；的确❸~；必然❹~；竭力❺~

1. traffic 2. continuously; all along; always 3. indeed; really 4. inevitably; certainly 5. energetically; stubbornly

zǔzhǐ 阻止 prevent; stop; hold back 〔~宾〕〈动〉~车辆❶的前进；~事态的发展❷〔~补〕〈可〉~不了(liǎo)历史❸的前进〈时〉~了半天没人听〈量〉~过他好多次了〔状~〕一再~；拼命❹~；不必~；何必~；竟然❺~；居然❻~；毫不客气地~；偏偏我

1. vehicle 2. the development of events 3. history 4. desperately 5. 6. unexpectedly; to one's surprise 7. impolitely; bluntly

zǔzhī 组织 organize; form〔~宾〕〈名〉~一个小组❶；~一个登山队❷；~一个乐团❸；一个座谈会❹；~一次舞会〈动〉~参观，~访问，~旅游❺〔~补〕〈结〉访问团❻已经~好了〈趋〉乐队已经~起来了〈程〉这篇文章材料❼~得很好，那次舞会~得很好〈可〉我们这里青年人少，~不了(liǎo)舞会；乐队❽~不起来〈时〉~了半天也没组织起来〈量〉~过一次民乐队❾，后来又解散❿了，把大家好好~一下儿〔状~〕必须~；早点~；已经~了；正在~；还没~啊？公开⓫~；秘密⓬~；暗中⓭~

1. group 2. mountaineering party 3. philharmonic orchestra 4. forum 5. tour 6. group; society; delegation 7. material 8. orchestra 9. traditional instruments orchestra 10. dismiss 11. openly 12. 13. secretly

zuān 钻 ① drill; bore〔~宾〕〈名〉在铁板❶上~一个孔❷；在木头上~了几个眼儿❸〔~补〕〈结〉两个小孔都~好了；有一个眼儿没~透❹；~歪❺了；~坏了；两个孔~通❻了〈趋〉用电钻❼(zuàn)~起孔来可快了〈程〉眼儿~得太大了；~得浅❽了一点儿〈可〉木头太硬❾~不下去；~不动〈时〉四个眼~了十多分钟；~了半天也钻不过去〈量〉刚~几下儿，钻(zuàn)头❿就断⓫了〔状~〕用电钻~；使劲⓬~；比⓭好了再~

1. iron plate 2. hole; opening 3. small hole 4. through 5. in lined; askew 6. through 7. electric drill 8. shallow 9. hard 10. bit (of a drill) 11. break 12. exert all one's strength 13. model after; copy

② go through ≌ 穿过〔~宾〕〈名〉不许❶~铁丝网❷；火车~山洞❸；杂技演员❹会~圈儿❺〔~补〕〈结〉火车~进了山洞〈趋〉小船从桥下~过去了；月亮从云彩❻里~出来了；狗从栅栏里边~出去了；孩子们从水里~出头来了；夜里老鼠从洞里偷偷地❼~出来了；猎人❽~进密林❾里去了〈程〉~得真快；~得很费劲❿〈可〉~不了(liǎo)；~得过去吗？〈时〉~了半天也没钻过去〈量〉我坐火车~过好几次山洞了〔状~〕火车迅速地⓫~过了山洞；熟练地⓬~圈儿；老鼠偷偷地~；紧张地⓭~铁丝网，不要到处~

1. not allow 2. wire netting; wire meshes 3. cave; cavern 4. acrobat 5. jumping through hoops 6. cloud 7. stealthily 8. hunter 9. thick forest 10. need or use great effort 11. rapidly 12. skilfully 13. nervously

③ study intensively; dig into ≌ 钻研〔~宾〕〈名〉~业务❶〔~补〕

〈趋〉开始学有点枯燥❷，～进去就有兴趣❸了；他现在～起古文❹来了；好好～下去，总会有成绩❺的〈可〉她～不出兴趣来；怎么钻也～不进去〈时〉～了几年；～了一阵子❻〈量〉好好一下儿〔状～〕已经～；认真❼～；刻苦❽～；一点一点地～〔习用〕～牛角尖❾；～空子❿

1. dig into one's job or a subject 2. dull 3. be interested in 4. prose written in the classical literary style; ancient Chinese prose 5. result; achievement; success 6. a period of time 7. seriously; conscientiously 8. assiduously 9. take unnecessary pains to study an insignificant or insoluble problem; split hairs 10. avail oneself of loopholes (in a law; contract, etc.); exploit an advantage

zūnzhòng 尊重 respect; value; esteem〔～宾〕〈名〉～少数民族❶的风俗习惯❷；～别人的意见；～别人的人格❸；～他们的权利❹；～事实❺〈代〉要懂得～别人〔状～〕互相～；必须～；特别～；十分～；应该～；对人家～，人家才能对你～

1. national minority 2. habits and customs 3. human dignity; character 4. right 5. fact

zūnshǒu 遵守 observe; abide by; comply with ↔ 违反〔～宾〕

〈名〉～公共秩序❶；～交通规则❷；～时间；～法律❸；～协议❹；～学校的制度❺〔状～〕认真❻～；必须～；严格❼～

1. public order 2. traffic regulations 3. law 4. agreement 5. school regulations 6. seriously; attentively 7. strictly

zuómo 琢磨 ponder; turn sth over in one's mind ≅ 考虑；思索〔～宾〕〈名〉我一直❶～这句话；～这件事；～这个人〈主－谓〉～这句话是什么意思；～她说的有没有道理❷；～这个人怎么样〔～补〕〈结〉～到现在还不知道是什么意思〈趋〉这句话的意思我好容易❸才～上来❹；这句话我～过来～过去，也没琢磨出个结果❺来；她也开始～起那件事来了〈程〉～得头都疼❻了〈可〉～不出来〈时〉～了已经不是一天半天了，～了很长时间，再多～一会儿〈量〉～了好几遍；好好一下儿〔状～〕再～～；细心❼～；仔细❽～；多～～；什么情况都没掌握❾，无从❿～起；终于⓫～；经⓬他一～

1. always; all the time 2. reason 3. with great difficulty 4. figure out 5. result 6. headache 7. 8. carefully; attentively 9. grasp; master 10. have no way 11. finally; at last 12. after; through; as a result

zuò 坐 ① sit; take a seat〔～宾〕〈名〉～椅子不如～沙发❷舒服

❸；小孩子喜欢～小凳子❹；她喜欢～窗户那儿〔**～补**〕〈结〉抄❺了一天东西，我都～累了；他没～好；可别把椅子～翻❻了；让那个孩子～高点儿就看见了；坐的时候应该～直❼；～在河边钓鱼❽；他喜欢～在灯光❾照❿不到的角落⓫；请大家赶快⓬～好，电影⓭马上⓮就开演⓯了〈趋〉这儿有一个空⓰座位⓱，你～上来吧；大家赶快找地方～下来吧，就要开会了；外边太冷，里边有地方，～进来吧；屋里地方太小，人都～出来了；那边太挤⓲了，～过来点儿吧；他累得～下去就不想起来了〈程〉一个椅子两个人坐，～得太难受⓳了；～得太高了，把后边人的视线⓴都挡㉑住了〈可〉家里没人，我在这儿～不住；怎么坐也～不舒服；你怎么总～不直啊？这样会驼背㉒的；座位太高，孩子～不上去；他腿有毛病㉓，～不下去；一把椅子两个胖子可～不下〈时〉～了半天了，该回去了；忙什么再～一会儿吧〈量〉家里门没锁㉔，我待㉕不长，～一下儿就走〔**状～**〕规规矩矩地㉖～；重新～下；勉强㉗～；独自㉘～；安闲地㉙～在那里看书；安安稳稳地㉚～；安安静静地㉛～；跷着腿㉜～

1. not as good as **2.** sofa **3.** comfortable **4.** stool **5.** copy **6.** turn over **7.** straight **8.** angle; go fishing **9.** the light of a lamp **10.** light up **11.** corner **12.** at once; quickly **13.** film; movie **14.** at once; immediately **15.** (of a play, movie, etc.) begin **16.** empty **17.** seat **18.** crowd; cram **19.** feel unwell **20.** line of vision; line of sight **21.** block; get in the light **22.** hunchback **23.** have trouble **24.** lock **25.** stay **26.** (behave) correctly and cautiously **27.** reluctantly **28.** alone; by oneself **29.** leisurely **30.** smoothly; peacefully **31.** quietly **32.** with one's legs crossed

② go by; ride in (car, boat, plane, etc.) ≃乘，搭〔**～宾**〕〈名〉我没～过帆船❶；～直升飞机❷〔**～补**〕〈结〉今天上班的时候只顾❸了聊天❹儿，结果❺～过站❻了；～到哪儿？〈趋〉等了那么长时间，好容易❼～上去了；先～下来再买票；再～下去就过站了；车坐错了，所以～回来又～回去了〈可〉她晕车❽，所以～不了(liǎo)车；我也～不惯❾汽车；人太多，老弱病残❿都～不上去〈时〉每天上下班至少⓫要～三个小时车〈量〉～过很多次；～过两回〔**状～**〕人多车不好～；真难～；偶尔⓬～；来回⓭～

1. sailing boat **2.** helicopter **3.** be absorbed in **4.** chat **5.** as a result **6.** passed the bus stop due **7.** with great difficulty **8.** carsickness **9.** not be used to **10.** the old, weak, sick and disabled **11.** at (the) least **12.** occasionally **13.** back and forth; to and fro

③ put (a pan, pot, kettle, etc.) on a fire 〔**～宾**〕〈名〉在炉子❶

上~了一壶水❷;~了一锅饭❸〔~补〕〈结〉把水~开❹了;锅❺~歪❻了,把壶❼~好了;锅没~稳❽〈趋〉把大锅~到炉子上来吧〈时〉壶刚~了五分钟水就开了〈量〉一天要~好几次水

1. stove 2. a kettle of water 3. a pot of cooked rice 4. boil 5. pot 6. inclined 7. a kettle 8. steady

zuò 作 ① do; make〔~宾〕〈名〉~长期打算❶;~结论❷;~判断❸;~报告❹〔~补〕〈结〉结论~错了〈程〉报告~得非常精采❺〈时〉~了四个小时的报告〈量〉在他们学校~过一次报告〔~补〕认真❻~;给学生~报告

1. plan on a long-term basis 2. conclusion 3. judgement 4. report 5. wonderful 6. seriously; conscientiously

② write; compose ≅ 写作〔~宾〕〈名〉~曲❶;~诗❷;~文章❸〔~补〕〈结〉文章~好了〈趋〉她也~起诗来了;~出来的曲子非常好听〈程〉文章~得不错;他的诗~得很美〈可〉被你打断❹以后,她的曲子~不下去了;我可~不了诗〈时〉这篇文章~了三天都没作完〈量〉~过几次;~一下儿试试〔状~〕专心致志地❺~;埋头❻~;偶尔❼~;随便❽即兴❾~;特意❿~;为他~

1. (write) music 2. poem 3. essay; article 4. interrupt 5. wholly absorbed; with single-hearted devotion 6. immerse oneself in; be engrossed in 7. once in a while; occasionally 8. casually; at random 9. impromptu; without preparation 10. specially

zuò 做 ① produce; make; manufacture ≅ 制造;制作〔~宾〕〈名〉~鞋;~衣服;~菜;~点心❶;~家具❷;~工〔~补〕〈结〉鞋~大了,裤子❸~长了;书架❹~宽❺了;饭~多了〈趋〉饭菜都~出来了〈程〉~得真快,~得还不错〈可〉自己~不好,一天可能~不完〈时〉整整❻~了半个月;再~一会儿就休息吧〈量〉自己~过几次衣服〔状~〕精心地❼~;太难~了;在裁缝店❽~;经常~;亲手❾~;用缝纫机❿~;成批地⓫~;一件一件地~;正在~

1. cakes; pastry 2. furniture 3. trousers; pants 4. bookshelf 5. wide 6. whole; full 7. carefully; meticulously 8. tailor's 9. with one's own hands 10. sewing machine 11. in batches

② do; act; engage in ≅ 从事〔~宾〕〈名〉~生意❶;~买卖❷;~试验❸;~事情;~作业〔~补〕〈结〉工作~少了,生意~大了,试验~成功❹了〈趋〉说起来容易,~起来难❺;开始和外国商人❻~起生意来了〈程〉工作~得很细致❼;~得非常马虎❽;~得很有成绩❾;生意~得很兴隆

❿〈可〉~不好；~得到~不到？〈时〉~过三年；~过很长时间；~过一个时期〈量〉~过好几次了；~一下儿试试〔**状**~〕在市场~买卖；跟外商⓫~生意；一直⓬~；长期⓭~；连续⓮~试验

1. 2. (do) business; (make) a deal 3. experiment; test 4. succeeded 5. easier said than done 6. foreign businessman 7. careful; meticulous 8. careless; casual 9. result; achievement 10. prosperous; thriving; brisk 11. foreign businessman 12. always; all the time 13. over a long period of time 14. in succession; in a row; successively

③ be; become ≅ 充当；担任〔~宾〕〈名〉他已经~老师了；第一次~母亲；到他家去~客❶；给他~伴儿❷；~翻译❸；~售票员❹；~保姆❺〔~补〕〈结〉她终于❻~上演员了〈趋〉他~起教练❼来了〈可〉她有点儿紧张❽，怕~不好〈时〉一连❾~了十年住院医生〈量〉我以前没做过保姆，所以最好先~一下儿试试〔**状**~〕将要~；从来没~过；一直~；刚~；终于~了；初次~

1. guest (be a guest) 2. company (keep sb. company) 3. translator; interpreter 4. ticket seller; conductor 5. (children's) nurse 6. in the end; at last 7. coach; instructor; trainer 8. nervous 9. in a row; in succession

④ be used as ≅ 用作〔~宾〕〈名〉这间房子~教室，那间屋子~厨房❶；用这笔钱~安家费❷；树皮可以~纸；这篇文章❸可以~课外读物❹〔~补〕〈可〉这个地方太小，~不了(liǎo)足球场❺〈时〉这间教室~了三年仓库❻；~了半年厨房〈量〉这间房子~过一次仓库〔**状**~〕一直❼~；曾经~；原来❽~；现在~〔**习用**〕~一天和尚，撞一天钟❾

1. kitchen 2. allowance for setting up a home in a new place 3. essay; article 4. outside readings 5. football field 6. warehouse; storehouse 7. always; all the time 8. originally; formerly 9. go on tolling the bell as long as one is a monk — do the least that is expected of one; take a passive attitude towards one's work

⑤ write; compose ≅ 作 ②